Making Music in Montessori

Making Music in Montessori

Everything Teachers Need to Harness Their Inner Musician and Bring Music to Life in Their Classrooms

Michael Johnson

Published in cooperation with the
National Association for Music Education

ROWMAN & LITTLEFIELD
Lanham • Boulder • New York • London

Published in cooperation with the National Association for Music Education, 1806
Robert Fulton Drive, Reston, Virginia 20191; nafme.org

Published by Rowman & Littlefield
A wholly owned subsidiary of The Rowman & Littlefield Publishing Group, Inc.
4501 Forbes Boulevard, Suite 200, Lanham, Maryland 20706
www.rowman.com

6 Tinworth Street, London SE11 5AL, United Kingdom

British Library Cataloguing in Publication Information Available

Library of Congress Cataloging-in-Publication Data

Library of Congress Control Number: 2019955915

♾™ The paper used in this publication meets the minimum requirements of
American National Standard for Information Sciences—Permanence of Paper for
Printed Library Materials, ANSI/NISO Z39.48–1992.

For Bean

Contents

Preface

Threads unraveled from a dream saturate the pages of this book. In my dream, every Montessori child in every corner of the world has access to beautiful, authentic instruments that fit in their small hands and that they can play effortlessly. Children read and write original music, with teachers joining in and facilitating the children's efforts not with trepidation but with ease and confidence. Circles and lines of children sing, play, and dance together, smiling and joyfully sharing the reciprocal warmth and comfort that comes from groups of human beings enjoying each other's company in the spirit of unity and compassion.

Every child gains a deep understanding that music is not only a common human language but, like our very DNA, also contains *the* link that binds human beings together and makes us all the same.

Lest you think I'm spouting empty words, lest you think this dream of mine lacks substance, consider this tiny moment: you, the teacher, smiling, making eye contact with two children, who, hands touching, pretend to be trees. Smiling, they trap a fourth person, a child, a little "squirrel," in their branches.

All four of you sing in unison, fully committed to the rising and falling of the melody, fully invested in the images and dance cues in the words, united in anticipation of the moment when the melody will stop, the branches will go up, and all of the squirrels will scramble to find new trees to inhabit.

When this moment finally arrives, your intentions and the intentions of every child in the room become one. You and the children delight as the squirrels find their trees, the trees envelop their squirrels, and everyone's focus shifts to the squirrels that are left, laughter lighting up every face in the room.

In that moment your Montessori classroom has become a place where human beings feel united in intention and common purpose.

If you can make a moment like that happen in just *your* classroom, one among many classrooms in the world, then humanity will have taken that fraction of a step closer to peace. Now, imagine moments like that happening in all the Montessori classrooms throughout the world, for generation after generation, and you can see a clear, practical path to realizing world peace.

Because, let's face it, human beings don't learn to be peaceful by merely talking about or singing about peace. Human beings *become* peaceful in moments like these—moments, I dare say, unique to music-making.

Musical activity *manifests* peaceful action. Be it joining hands, harmonizing, communicating, following directions, waiting, responding to cues, turn-taking, and more, any peaceful action to which a flowery speech or a didactic song can give lip service comes into actual play when listening, singing, dancing, moving, or playing instruments. In making music, we *practice* peace.

Buoyed by the idea of a practical path to world peace through music, I developed and presented stories about famous composers and compositions to the children in my grade 6 to 9 classes at Sunstone Montessori School in Portland, Oregon. The result? Hearing about a man who composed music in a World War II prison-camp lavatory got the children fired up. The story whipped them into a frenzy of listening, researching, and composing.

Answering the children's call toward music, I did some further experimenting. I presented lessons from my Montessori music albums and combined them with some of the pedagogical techniques of Zoltan Kodály, filling the work cycles and gatherings with a steady stream of musical skill-building activities, performances, songs, dances, and singing games.

To my delight, as a result of my experiments, the children of the Trillium Room exploded into music. Candice, second-year, wrote piano music to accompany her lifecycle of salmon research. Oscar, Eric, Aiden, and Graciela composed and performed *Summer Forest,* a piece for percussion instruments accompanied by an original choreographed dance. Kevin wrote a short piano piece as a plaintive note of apology to a substitute whom he'd treated disrespectfully. The children improvised on a simple jazz tune for three forty-five-minute sessions in a row. Each day the children enriched our classroom with music.

Of course, I have a musical background, but I didn't do anything virtuosic or fancy. The children needed only the basic seven-note *do re mi* scale and rhythm patterns that anyone can understand to compose music.

Spurred further by the belief that every Montessori teacher can learn how to teach music, I poured all of my tricks and techniques into *Making Music in Montessori*.

Hand in hand with my goal of fostering world peace is the aim of helping both the children *and* the adults in the world's Montessori classrooms realize the potential for music-making that is inherent to their human nature. After all, the first step in inspiring the current generation to speak music as fluently as they speak their native language is to give you, the adult in their lives enough knowledge to project enthusiasm and passion for music and to guide their exploration.

For I believe that everyone is musical and anyone can teach music. With this book as a resource, I resolve to give you confidence in teaching music, so that when your children walk away from a lesson all fired up to compose their own piece for percussion instruments, tone bars, marimbas, and perhaps even piano, you will know exactly how to guide them.

This book aims to be your ultimate music guide, providing you all at once a snappy, practical handbook, a music theory mentor, a pedagogical manual, and a resource anthology. It features the following:

- A set of instructions and lists for optimizing the prepared environment for music.
- An easy-to-follow dissection of basic music theory in user-friendly vocabulary.
- A wealth of follow-up ideas to the Montessori lessons.
- A workable pedagogical method based on ideas gleaned from the Kodály approach.
- A cornucopia of Cosmic Stories about composers and compositions.
- A treasury of field-tested folk songs, dances, and games notated for the lay musician.
- A list of music education resources.

Before this book, you may have only dreamed of a classroom buzzing with children working, learning, and growing with music alongside all of the other subject areas in the Montessori curriculum. Now, you can make it a reality. This book will give you the following:

- knowledge of how to prepare your environment for music;
- mastery of "just enough" music theory and music notation;
- command of a pedagogical method for developing music literacy;
- concise, clear, and brief explanations catered toward novice musicians, but accessible to musicians of all levels of experience; and
- resources to implement in the classroom.

If, as Dr. Montessori says, children's minds are a fertile field, then *Making Music in Montessori* will stir you to don your overalls, roll up your sleeves, sow the musical seeds, and watch peace blossom under your children's flaming imagination.

I wish you all the best.

Michael Johnson
Paris, France, 2018

Foreword

When music and courtesy are better understood and appreciated,
There will be no more war. —Confucius

One rainy October day, not so many years ago, I stepped into Michael Johnson's elementary classroom and took a seat in the observer's chair. Everywhere my eye traveled, I saw evidence of great work in science, math, history, geometry, and literature, and (in equal measure) I saw art and music in many forms. Children were painting, drawing, sculpting, singing, and playing music right alongside the children who were computing, writing, researching, and experimenting.

Knowing that Michael is an accomplished musician, composer, artist, and polyglot, I was not surprised. However, on closer inspection, I observed that much of the science, math, history, geometry, and literature was being explored and represented in artistic forms. I reflected on the fact that little of this integrated art work required specialized training or knowledge, just a few supplies and a willingness to allow children the time to explore concepts using the activities they enjoy.

Yet the real genius became evident when Michael gathered a group of children and asked them to embellish a Halloween song with dramatic interpretation, creative lighting, and musical instruments to create mood and suspense. I watched as he turned group performance (so often fraught with anxiety and stress) into an improvisational, collaborative creation. He invited the children to listen, discuss, experiment, create, dramatize, and perform. He engaged them in truly joyful activity that was packed with experiential learning.

Educational research has demonstrated the impact of music on brain development. We've seen the remarkable videos of Alzheimer's patients brought back to coherent memory and conversation by listening to the music of their past. We've seen Parkinson's patients move from a stilted, struggling gait to fluid, unassisted walking by listening to the beat. We know that music and art have immense therapeutic properties for children who have experienced trauma. An enormous amount of research and anecdotal evidence has illustrated clearly that music is good for the brain.

Nevertheless, brain development is not the most important benefit music education holds for children. As an educator and advocate for children for almost thirty years, I can state with confidence that children have not changed. Yet childhood most certainly has. Perhaps every generation feels this urgency, but it seems now, more than ever, we need to look to our children, for they are truly the path to peace.

Teachers are not mere transmitters of information. We are guides to brain development and counselors for socioemotional growth. We are creators of the communities in which our children will practice living in society. These classroom communities are undeniably crucial to the development of human beings who can collaborate, negotiate, and delegate—in other words, people who can live and work with others.

Music educators (and by this, I mean anyone who brings music into the classroom) are uniquely poised to provide collaborative, goal-oriented, creative activity. Working with a group of singers or musicians to interpret and convey the feeling and meaning of a song is a perfect model for cooperating in society. Anyone who has had this experience can relate to the collective energy of group performance. Each individual voice is important, but the true beauty comes from the whole.

Thus, we are presented with two convincing arguments for enlivening our academic environments with art in its many forms: brain development and the creation of a peaceful society. All that remains is our hesitance or concern about our lack of "talent," and this is where we make a grave error. Children should be taught music and art not only by artistic and musical experts but also by people who can model the joys and challenges of trying new things and acquiring new skills. Teachers of art and music should demonstrate not only technique but also the value of the activity in and of itself, regardless of what it produces.

One need not be an expert or accomplished musician to bring music into the lives of children. Working with Michael taught me this. And now that we know how beneficial music and the arts are to brain development and socioemotional health, we can hardly let our own lack of experience in this area hold us back. Reading his book will inspire you with stories to share, games to play, ideas to uplift, and techniques with which to work. Bringing music into our classrooms will not only aid brain development and provide opportunities for creative collaboration. Perhaps even, one day, it will bring about a more peaceful society. But in the meantime, before any of these eventualities has had a chance to play out, you will be bringing joyful activity to your students and to yourself.

Annabeth Jensen, MEd

Acknowledgments

Every child who receives the gift of music as a result of this book owes a debt of gratitude to the following amazing people, and so do I.

I'm eternally grateful to my family. To my mother Judy Tandowsky, who brought me into the universe, sacrificed for me, loved me come what may, and nurtured my creative spark. To my stepfather Ross Tandowsky, who inspired me with his talents for acting, comedy, and writing, and who endured my piano practicing and band rehearsing over the years. To my brother James Johnson, who I have always looked up to and whose music and writing talents I emulated as a child. To my late uncle George Johnston, whose generous financial contribution made this book possible.

To my late father Darrell, who from his deathbed wore such a bright smile upon hearing my first attempts at guitar playing, that to this day it lights my path in the darkest times.

Huge love and thanks to my wife Stephanie Johnson, who provided unwavering support, including reading and editing chapters, hashing out ideas, giving me honest, wise advice, and providing love, feedback, and patience during the year-long hiatus I took from classroom work to write this book. To Lila Satori, my stepdaughter, for her love, support, and wisdom. I'm so grateful that Lila was a member of my class when I first experimented with the ideas in this book. To Dennis Clark, my father-in-law, for taking me seriously and for providing love and support.

Very special thanks to Katherine Clark, my mother-in-law, who not only provided me with love and encouragement, but who gave me invaluable writing advice. Thanks, Katherine, for lending me books about writing, for reading and editing chapters, and for helping me to shape and refine my book proposal.

I also want to thank Brad Hansen, who sat with me before the book was a book and brainstormed ideas, discussed formats, and offered me wonderful advice.

Special thanks to the team at Rowman & Littlefield, especially Caroline Arlington, who let me submit my manuscript a second time after it was rejected on the first try. To Ella Wilcox, who poured through the book with kindness and a fine-toothed comb. Ella was great fun to work with. She made me sound like a real writer. And to Carlie Wall, who expressed enthusiasm for the project, kept everything organized, fielded my silly questions, steered everyone along, and made me feel at home.

To my mentors and colleagues at Portland State University, especially Debbie Glaze, David Vinden, Susan Brumfield, and Carol J. Brown, whose training in the Kodàly method of music education changed my life. To my old friend Steve White, who ran a children's choir with me and who provided me a wealth of inspiration, laughter, and great folk songs. To all my other colleagues from the 2007–2008 cohort of music education students with whom I shared ideas.

Thanks also to Darrell Grant, head of the Portland State University jazz department, whom I worshipped like a rock star, and Brian, my piano teacher, whom I also greatly looked up to and admired.

I'm also grateful to my mentors and colleagues in the world of Montessori education. Thanks to Allyn Travis and Jay McKeever for their amazing training. To Mirela Duplancic, my first and dearest mentor, who taught me everything I know during my difficult first two years as a teacher. To Phyllis Pottish-Lewis, who provided priceless twinkle-in-the-eye feedback when consulting in my classroom.

Thanks to all my classmates and friends from the Montessori Institute of Milwaukee Elementary training class of 2010, with whom I still share ideas and benefit from mutual admiration and support.

Big thanks to Caroline D'Allo, who gave me friendship and encouragement, and who was instrumental in making the connections that set me on the path to working in France. To Aurelie Collin, Florence Rabier, Alexia and Tanguy Lieske, and Benoit Dubuc, who not only employed me, but who provided me with a venue and students on which to conduct my musical experiments. Thanks also to Rachel Esteve and the staff and trainees at CFMF, as well as to my friends and colleagues at Ellipse Montessori Academy in Paris, including Emmanuelle Gannat and my co-teacher Karima Bocquenet.

Mostly, I want to extend very special thanks to the staff and children at Sunstone Montessori School in Portland, Oregon, where I began my career in Montessori education and where the idea for this book first struck me.

Sincere thanks to Cathy Newman, not only for being the first person to introduce me to Montessori education but also for being a kind, generous, honest, and steadfast employer and mentor. Cathy's sense of humor, encouragement, expertise, and honesty have meant the world to me.

Thanks also to my friend and mentor Robert Salazar, who is not only responsible for the Music Grid Paper, but whose refined, effortless, funny, steel-hand-in-a-velvet-glove approach to teaching I have tried (in vain) to emulate throughout my career.

To Jenn Ryznar, who hooked me up with a marvelous opportunity to try out some of my ideas in front of 4,000 people at the 2013 International Montessori Congress.

Special thanks to Annabeth Jensen, who has been a good friend and mentor from the beginning of my Montessori career. Thank you, Annabeth, for your experience, your expert advice, for reading and editing chapters and Cosmic Stories, and for being such a cheerleader for this book from its very inception.

Thanks also to Sarah Werner-Andrews, a musical Montessorian whose modeling, mentorship, and moxie inspired me immensely when I was directing an after-school choir at Sunstone, back when I was first experimenting with these ideas.

Thanks also to Braden Pemberton, Sarah Miller, and Angelica Maduell, the wonderful people who worked side by side with me as assistants during my "mad scientist" years at Sunstone. You three provided incredible help and support while I test-drove the ideas and experiments that culminated in this book.

Finally, I want to extend extra special thanks to the children of the Trillium room at Sunstone Montessori School from 2012 to 2015, whose joyful singing, dancing, reading, composing, improvising, and playing brought the ideas that became this book to life. I'll never forget the joy of making music with all of you.

PART 1

YOUR MUSICAL MONTESSORI ENVIRONMENT

Chapter 1

Yes, You Are Musical—Five Music Myths Debunked

The children sit cross-legged on the stony carpet of their second-grade classroom listening to Mrs. Henley strum her guitar and warble "Skip to My Loo" in a voice like an opera diva. Suddenly the earth shakes. Lights pop on and off as the fluorescent fixtures creak and sway. An actual earthquake shakes the classroom while Mrs. Henley sings! As pieces of the ceiling smash onto the floor around them, the children scramble to find space under a desk or a sturdy plastic chair. When the trembling finally stops, the children shed tears of laughter, not fear, as they joke that the earthquake must have been caused by Mrs. Henley's singing.

Mrs. Henley's seismic voice has nothing on Miss McNeill's piano lessons. In preparation for the first exercise in a young boy's piano primer, Miss McNeill snatches the little seven-year-old's elbow, lifts his right arm above his head, yanks on his middle finger to stretch it out, and drops his arm onto the keyboard. After the boy's hand plows into the hard, cold keys, she pushes his arm across his body and lifts it up higher for a second plunge. All the while she barks, "Drop! Float! Lift!" When the boy struggles, Miss McNeil prods him off the bench and blazes through the passage, her arms flapping up and down at her sides like some infuriated duck.

If Miss McNeill's flapping arms strike you as funny, consider a less humorous musical misadventure that occurs during a middle-school choir rehearsal. Tall, lean, white-haired Mr. Driscoll slinks over and stands in front of the choir, directly across from a young girl standing with the other altos in the middle row. Without a word, he leans forward, stretches his arm over the heads of two rows of singers, places a thin, skeletal finger to the young girl's lips to stop her singing, and directs her to a chair across the room. "Sit over there," he oozes, "The choir sounds better without you."

Somehow, despite childhood musical experiences like these, a love for music flowers in some people. Others aren't so lucky. As adults, most people feel self-conscious about music. They proclaim, "I can't sing," at birthday parties, weddings, and places of worship. They protest, "I can't carry a tune." Or, if they already play an instrument, they insist that it's just a hobby: It's for them—they "don't really play for other people." In childhood, they inherited the anxiety of their household's adults who lamented that they themselves had no talent.

Sound familiar? If you believe you have no musical ability, this book gets you in touch with your inner musician. How? The first step is to challenge some of the mistaken beliefs about music that the Mrs. Henleys in your life warbled into you. In their book *How to Play the Piano despite Years of Lessons*, Ward Cannel and Fred Marx identify a handful of mainstream music myths. Here are five of them debunked.

MYTH 1: MUSIC IS FOR TALENTED PEOPLE; YOU EITHER HAVE IT OR YOU DON'T

You can thank a thriving entertainment industry for this common misconception. In today's world, music is a commodity that can only be recorded, sung, played, or written by an elite group of good-looking professionals whose music we exchange for money. How else would they sell records and tickets but by making us believe they are more talented than we are? Don't misunderstand, many of them indeed have talent. But even the most gifted musicians sounded terrible at one point.

Do you think Paul McCartney sounded good when as a child he practiced guitar in his bathtub? His secret to becoming Sir Paul McCartney: he kept practicing. He spent time with his instrument and honed his craft. It has nothing to do with magic. Almost anyone who spends enough time can learn to sing, play an instrument, or compose a song. And even "musical geniuses" like Paul McCartney have their shortcomings. Did you know Sir Paul can't read a note of music? Why's that? He never learned how.

So, you see, musical acumen comes not to the person born with a gift (assuming such a person exists); it comes to the person who spends his or her time wisely—a person like you, for instance. Right now, you are reading a book that will boost your confidence in your innate musical abilities.

MYTH 2: ONLY PEOPLE WITH SPECIAL GIFTS CAN COMPOSE MUSIC

Is that so? Do you think that early human beings who sat around a campfire making up songs about their universe received special gifts from on high? Quite the contrary, if you could go back in a time machine, you wouldn't see a single tribal gathering where one specially blessed musician steps onto a stage and sings a specially composed song while the rest of the group sits quietly and listens.

Instead, those early gatherings relied on participation from the entire group. The elders sang, the children sang, everyone sang. Certainly, a leader might have guided the group in a call-and-response song or chant, but for the most part, people sang together.

In fact, until about 800 years ago, people passed on music mostly through oral tradition. As songs were passed on, they changed a little bit, and then changed a little more, until, by the time an old song hits your ears today, you could say that it was composed by hundreds of people.

Some cultures still transmit their music through oral tradition. You can only imagine how their songs will have evolved one hundred years from now. And even then, whether you stand on a playground in urban Alabama, sit around a campfire in Lesotho, or stroll along the streets of Cairo, you will see people of all sizes, shapes, and gifts, making up music.

This is not to discount the hard work of those learned individuals who study how to perform or compose music after the Western or Eastern classical fashions. They certainly possess musical gifts. But for every one of those famous, gifted people, there are countless others with similar gifts who, for some reason, didn't make it into the history books.

Usually the reason you've never heard of them has nothing to do with their degree of talent. Look at the many talented women composers who happen to have been born in Europe before the year 1900. For every Felix Mendelssohn, there are dozens of women like Fanny Mendelssohn.

At any rate, a person can go to a conservatory and learn to play piano and compose like the Mendelssohn siblings. Many people have. Gifted people are a dime a dozen. The "gift" is merely knowledge and hard work. Believing

the basic tenet of this book, that, like those early human beings, you are a musician, is part of your work.

MYTH 3: THERE IS MUSIC, AND THEN THERE IS SOMETHING CALLED "MUSIC THEORY"

What if that heading read, "There is language, and then there is something called grammar." While it's true that languages have agreed-upon conventions that govern their use and give them structure so that everyone who speaks them can use them to express themselves, that needn't prevent a person from speaking. Even if you don't know what the subjunctive mood is, you probably unconsciously use it when describing cases of wishing or wanting. Knowing the guidelines or not knowing them doesn't preclude using them. You learn them, and then you forget them as you speak. The same is true of music.

But the grammar of music theory is even simpler than the grammar of rhetoric. The rich variety of patterns and colors for self-expression we find in music come from only twelve notes! And, thanks to composers of the twentieth century, unlike language, there are very few pitfalls to avoid in music. That specter we call "music theory" consists of nothing more than a structure that governs our culture's music.

Of course, you don't need to know what a secondary dominant is to make music, just like you don't need to know what a predicate nominative is to be able to say "Beethoven was a genius." Knowing the syntax of music, however, does prevent you from uttering the musical equivalent of "Genius a Beethoven was." So that you can avoid such gibberish when making music with your children, this book teaches you just enough music theory to enable you to forget about music theory.

MYTH 4: MUSIC IS ANOTHER LANGUAGE

This one is true, in a way. Of course, dance, theater, painting, architecture, and sculpture are languages too, but as Cannel and Marx put it: "If you think of them that way, you'll have a hard time speaking them" (Cannel and Marx, 1976).

Again, music is simpler than language. It only has twelve letters in its alphabet. Not only that, but music is a language that can be understood by everyone in the world. Fly to another country and try to speak to a native in your language. That person won't understand you. Play the native some sad music, however, and he or she will likely hear the same thing you hear and feel the same thing you feel. Music is the one language that everyone can understand. If you're able to make sounds, you can very likely speak music. Consider this book to be a Rosetta Stone.

MYTH 5: THERE ARE LOTS OF RULES AND REGULATIONS IN MAKING MUSIC

On the contrary, according to the old adage, there is only one rule of music: "If it sounds good, then it is good." "What sounds 'good' follows from us agreeing about what makes sense in a bunch of jumbled tones" (Channel and Marx, 1976). Our idea of what sounds good has evolved and changed over the past thousand years, and it continues to change and grow. What sounded good and made sense to powdered-wig-sporting aristocrats on the Esterhazy estate in the eighteenth century, sounded primitive and childlike to the Indian sitar players halfway around the world. People all over the world know how to assemble tones together and decide whether the result makes sense or whether it's hogwash.

Every culture and subculture, including that of your own classroom, has different criteria. When you and your children make your own music, these criteria are only options or guidelines. As you lead your classes through the lesson plans and follow up ideas this book offers, keep in mind that what is "good" is what sounds good to you and your young musicians.

The fact is people make music because they are people. Despite many of us having been ruined for music by the Miss McNeills of the world, nature hardwired our brains to make music. "Human beings [use] both music and language for spiritual and intellectual expression. No human civilization has ever existed that didn't have both music and language" (McKeever, 2009).

This means that you are musical. If you doubt this, just remember that your humanity endows you with a connection to "the [musical] heritage transmitted by all human groups all over the world" (Marchak, 1998). Early people who beat on sticks, stretched animal hides over hollow logs, danced rain dances, or performed stories to explain their existence have passed the baton of their musical acumen down to you. Whether you take hold of that baton or not depends only on how you spend your time and not on how talented you are.

You are human and therefore musical. It's as simple as that. Like the brilliant pianist and professor of jazz Darrell Grant once told his Jazz Improv students, "The only difference between you and me is that I've been practicing this eight hours a day for forty years, and you haven't yet." Isn't that the message you want to pass on to *your* students?

And make no mistake, you should be the one passing on the message, yet something prevents you. You want music to be a part of your classroom, but by and large, year after year, your Montessori bells gather dust, your tone bars remain uncovered, and your percussion instruments lie silent on the shelf.

And oh, how you avoid your album of Montessori music lessons. You flip through it occasionally because you know you ought to be doing more music lessons, but you don't venture very far because lesson titles like "The Order of Sharps," "The Degrees of the Scale," and "Pitch Dictation" bring back the Mr. Driscolls of your youth. You can't possibly give to your children what you feel you lack: knowledge, skills, and confidence in music, so you avoid it altogether.

Would it help you to know that you need to know very little about music to bring it to life in your environment? The Montessori materials contain everything you need. Moreover, you already have all the musical skills you need. You can already sing a tune, differentiate between high and low notes, play a steady beat on a drum or percussion instrument, clap, pat, or beat a pattern on your knees, and read symbols and translate them to sounds. If you're a professional Montessori teacher, odds are you can tell an engaging story.

If you have reservations about teaching music because, like many adults, you have the mathematical formula $i + c = n$ emblazoned in your brain (where i = a musical instrument, c = children, and n = noise), again, you are not alone. As Mario Montessori wrote in his 1956 article about his mother Maria Montessori's music program, many adults believe children "should be seen and not heard" (Montessori, 1956).

Who can blame them? After all, for children to work on music, they must make sound, and, theoretically, where else but in a Montessori classroom should the environment be sound-free, so the children can concentrate as they occupy themselves with their various work choices? Many teachers even balk at playing soft, recorded music in the background during the work period for fear the children won't be able to concentrate.

Their fears are not unfounded. A study conducted by musician and producer Mark Lemouse for HealthGuidance.org revealed that people were more productive in an atmosphere of silence than in an atmosphere in which music was playing (Lemouse, 2015). Music gets a bad rap in traditional classrooms for the same reason: Sound can be distracting.

But a Montessori classroom is seldom a completely silent place. According to longtime Montessori teacher, consultant, trainer, and author Phyllis Pottish-Lewis, "A perfectly functioning classroom should be noisy" (Pottish-Lewis, 2014). In the primary, the atmosphere buzzes with children moving, speaking, and going about their individual work. In the elementary, children's conversations, their debates, and their collaborations often generate background noise.

Plus, studies about the perils of music playing in the background while children work contradict each other. One study conducted in 2010 corroborated Lemouse's findings. Researchers gave three groups of college children a reading-comprehension test while music played in the background: One group listened to hip-hop, another group listened to classical, and the third group listened to no music. The study concluded that "the participants who scored the highest in the reading comprehension task were the control group who performed the reading task in silence" (Tze and Chou, 2010).

Another study published online in *Educational Studies,* however, found that when calming music played in the background during children's work, it "led to better performance . . . when compared with a no-music condition" (Hallman, Price, and Katsarou, 2010). With everyone on the fence about whether music affects or ruins children's concentration, should you or should you not have music in your classroom?

It probably comes as no surprise that this book advocates for the former. Distracting though music can be when played in the background while children work, distraction is a small price to pay for all the benefits that music offers your children. "Not only is music a luxury, it's a necessity" (Batipps, 2013). Among its many benefits, "music encourages creativity, promotes individual growth, develops sensitivity and a sense of well-being, and lifts the spirit. As a major form of communication, music is an aesthetic experience, a challenge, and a discipline" (Irwin and Nelson, 1986).

When you bring music into environment and share it with your children, you bring them:

- feelings of community;
- skills from other academic pursuits, such as math and language;
- opportunities to practice grace and courtesy;
- practice with emotional control and body regulation;
- behavior of the prosocial variety;
- components of the public-school curriculum; and
- joy.

But why belabor the point? You're reading this book because you already know the value of teaching music in the classroom. You seek a guidebook, a practical handbook that will broaden your skills, provide you resources, and show you how to teach music.

By the time you put this book down, you will have everything you need to begin singing, playing, dancing, composing, and improvising music with your children. Whether you are a trained musician or not, this book will give you the knowledge, confidence, skills, and resources you need to bring to your children the joy of music, so they can experience optimal development, *joie de vivre*, and a sense of profound solidarity in your environment.

This first part of the book explains how to prepare your environment and yourself for music-making. Part 2 enlightens you on some of the critical elements of music theory. Part 3 introduces a pedagogical program that shows you how to teach the children in your class to read and write music. Part 4 offers a wealth of resources ranging from musical activities to Cosmic Stories singing games, folk songs, and dances. In the appendices, you'll find tips for starting and leading songs and resource lists for further reading.

This book contains all the tools to help you make music in Montessori. Still hesitating? Join me on the next page, and we'll talk in more detail about how to prepare for music using the most important part of your children's environment—you.

Chapter 2

The Musician in You

Like all beautiful things, the Montessori bells carry an air of mystery. What to make of these two shiny rows of twelve umbrella-shaped bells, pitched from middle C to high C? Each bell in the front row perches atop a small brown pedestal, with its counterpart in the back row sitting atop either a black or a white pedestal, depending on its pitch. When gently struck with a mallet, the bell's chime shimmers seemingly forever until you extinguish it with a light touch of the velvet damper.

The staff of a small school in Portland, Oregon, had just gotten acquainted with the Montessori bells at a Making Music in Montessori workshop when a staff member named Karen quipped, "I can't carry a tune in a bucket!" Mind you, she said this after having just sung, in a voice like an angel, an ascending and descending major scale. Later, this same person shone in a performance of "Bow, Wow Wow" sung in five parts.

Perhaps you know of a scientific theory that explains why people tend to dismiss their sizable proclivities in music just moments after demonstrating them. Can you imagine if the same thing happened in the dental profession? After just having successfully extracted a wisdom tooth, the dentist grins sheepishly at her patient and says, "I couldn't pull a tooth if you *paid* me!"

Maria Montessori had little patience for people who thought themselves musically incompetent. Regarding her training of primary teachers in bell-matching exercises, she wrote, "Some individuals commenting on [the bells] have solemnly protested their native inability to understand music, insisting that music reveals its secrets only to a chosen few. We may point out in reply that, so far, our principal object is simply to distinguish notes so widely different from each other that the different number of vibrations can easily be measured with instruments. It is a question of a material difference which any normal ear can naturally detect without any miraculous aptitude of a musical character" (Marchak, 1996).

There you have it: distinguishing between distinct pitches is within the grasp of any normal ear.

If, like Karen, you doubt your musical acumen and therefore your ability to teach music, bear in mind also what Maria Montessori wrote in *The Advanced Montessori Method: Volume 1*. In a nutshell, she stated that before we even begin to think of ourselves as teachers, we must first think of ourselves as scientists. "In all things," she writes, "the scientist is humble" (Montessori, 1991a). He doesn't let his biases get in the way of his work. He "[renounces] all those cherished ideas of his own" (Montessori, 1991a).

At the time Nicolaus Copernicus was making his first observations of the solar system, everyone thought that the Earth was the center of the universe and all the stars and planets revolved around it, each star and planet affixed to glass sphere. In other words, the solar system was shaped like an onion, with layers of glass spheres moving outward from Earth, situated at the center. These glass spheres explained why the stars appeared to twinkle at night.

But Copernicus observed that the planet Mars appeared dim in the night sky at certain times of year and bright at other times. Had Copernicus been a staunch disciple of the "glass sphere" theory and not a keen, objective observer, he might never have concluded that Mars's brightness changed because its distance from the earth changed; the result of an *elliptical* orbit.

Church officials rejected Copernicus's idea of an elliptical orbit on the grounds that if Mars's orbit were elliptical, it would smash through all the other planets' glass spheres! Which of the two, Copernicus, or the Church, had knowledge, skills of observation, and humility?

These are the hallmarks of the teacher's preparation, according to Montessori. To become an effective teacher, a person must "be initiated into the ways of humility, or self-abnegation, of patience; and to destroy the pride which is built on the void of vanity" (Montessori 1991).

She writes that this humility precipitates the fundamental qualities for a well-prepared Guide: a capacity for observation, specialized training, and a heaping helping of patience.

Observation, training, and patience apply when working with your children in music, as well, but you will also need a little extra. You will need a basic knowledge of music, some basic musical skills, and a varied musical repertoire, the fruits of which bear the final necessity: confidence. This book will help you. In subsequent chapters we will go into specifics, but for the remainder of this chapter, let's elucidate the knowledge, skills, and repertoire you'll need to make music with children.

WHAT YOU ALREADY KNOW

To begin, consider what you already know. Remember that because you are human, you are musical. You already bring with you a wealth of musical experiences to draw from when approaching music with the children in your class. Odds are, whatever heritage you come from, you have absorbed your culture's music. If you're from the United States, for example, your musical memory is chock full of popular songs, Classical tunes, commercial jingles, show tunes, patriotic songs, Anglo-American folk songs, or blues and jazz standards.

So you know a lot of songs; do you know who wrote them? Sure you do. In fact, you can likely name at least five of the world's greatest composers, at least ten pop, hip-hop, rhythm and blues (R&B), or rock bands, and the names of at least five jazz performers. You probably already have a rich knowledge of the history of music. Can you imagine Mozart there in his powdered wig? What about Louis Armstrong's puffed out cheeks as he blows on his upward-curved trumpet? Close your eyes and feel the heat from Jimi Hendrix's flaming guitar.

And what about the musical history of your own family? Don't forget your grandpa who played the ukulele, or those times your family sat around grandma's organ singing holiday songs. Your family history effervesces with engaging musical moments you can pass on to your children. Somewhere inside the music history museum of your mind hides a treasure trove of stories.

Not only do you have stories to tell, but you are also familiar with lots of different musical instruments. You can tell a flute from a saxophone, a piano from a synthesizer. You probably know how many strings are on a violin. Your sensitivity to sounds and their cultural origins has been honed merely as a result of your walking the Earth. You can see the steaming jungles of Indonesia when you hear the soft, tinny droplets of a gamelan ensemble, or feel the sand under your feet when you hear the gentle plucks of the Persian oud. Do you blow into a harp to get a sound or pluck its strings?

Why don't you take five minutes to make a list of all the musical instruments you're familiar with and list everything you know about them? List what they're made of, how to get a sound out of them, and maybe even who is most famous for playing them. Once you're done, step back. Aren't you impressed with the size of your list? You have quite a wealth of knowledge about musical instruments!

WHAT YOU CAN ALREADY DO

If you take stock of all the things you already know about music, you'll be most impressed. You might be thinking, "Well, yes, I know a bunch of stuff about music, but I can't *do* music!" Is that really true?

Let's assume you know the song "Happy Birthday" by Mildred J. Hill. Can you remember the melody and words to that song? Congratulations—you have *musical memory*. If you can sing that song at someone's party, or anywhere for that matter, then you can *sing*. Not only can you produce musical sounds with your voice, but you can also *match pitch* and perceive *harmonic structure*. If you have ever sung "Happy Birthday" with lots of other people at a party, then you know how to *sing in a chorus*. You might protest that everyone at the party sang in unison, so it was no great feat. Consider the following:

- Your hearing is already developed to the point that your ears can perceive both *homophonic* texture—many voices harmonizing together—and *monophonic* texture—many voices singing one melody.
- You are familiar with the term *unison*, meaning many voices singing the same notes. During the Middle Ages, choirs of monks filled cathedrals with chants sung in unison. The result was some of the most beautiful music ever.
- Undoubtedly at one of those birthday parties some person sang a higher melody on top of your melody when everyone got to that last "Happy birthday to youuuu!" If that happened, and you kept singing your part, then you know how to hold onto your melody while another person harmonizes with you.
- You can *perceive the beat* of a song and sing the rhythm of your melody against it.

All things considered, you're pretty musical.

Don't stop there. Take a moment to sing "Happy Birthday" in your mind. Go ahead. Put this book down and try it. Did you get to the end? Now sing it again in your mind, only this time try to imagine that person from that birthday party throwing a harmony over the top of everyone else. Can you hear it? Imagine a guitar accompanying the song. Hear the guitar? If you can imagine all those sounds, you possess *inner hearing*. This is the very same skill that Richard Strauss used when he wrote "The Blue Danube" waltz.

WHAT YOU WILL NEED

So, you know a lot about music already. What's left? Here are some of the things you'll need to know to be effective in making music with children.

History

A well-prepared and effective Guide knows about music and musicians of the past so he or she can transmit the rich history of human beings and their music to children. Music and history share an intimate connection. By acquainting yourself with the music and musicians of the past, you can highlight for the child the breadth of human accomplishment. You also give the child context for listening and a foundation for exploration.

If a child, for instance, were to become curious about a busy sounding but beautiful piece of music in which some sassy, plucky-sounding instrument is accompanied by a small orchestra, you'll be able to tell him the story of the baroque orchestra, share a few facts about Europe during the years between 1600 and 1750. You might present a story about J. S. Bach: Bach had twenty children! He got into a knife fight when he was young when he called a fellow musician a "nanny-goat bassoonist" (Krull and Hewitt, 1993). Knowing little titbits like these will help you to captivate the child's imagination. Music history is full of rich, funny stories for young people. Part 4 of this book contains many to get you started.

Theory

A theoretical knowledge of music proves essential for a well-prepared Guide. Not only do the Montessori lessons assume that you know about scales, pitches, key signatures, and flats and sharps, they also assume you know how to read notes on a staff and how to notate and read simple rhythms. If you never thought you could read and write music, the Montessori green staff boards and the bells can help you learn to read and write music in just a couple of hours. The good news is that you only really

need to know twelve notes! Part 2 gives you all the theory you'll need.

The Montessori Music Curriculum

A grasp of music history and theory will help you to deliver the Montessori music lessons with confidence. Geniuses though Maria Montessori and her partner Anna Macherroni were, some of their lessons can be confusing to a musical novice. Once you are familiar with the concepts that they teach, you can successfully deliver those concepts to your children. Parts 2 and 3 acquaint you with musical theory and musical concepts and skills so you can feel confident delivering the Montessori music lessons.

Pedagogy

The most musically effective teachers have a few tricks up their sleeves that go beyond the Montessori music lessons. Familiarity with the key components of musical understanding, such as sound concepts, rhythm, melody, harmony, and form, and knowing how to craft lessons to deliver those concepts to the children becomes essential. Carrying off small lessons that build your students' musical literacy will help enrich their ideas for follow up and create opportunities for them to engage in spontaneous music-making.

A command of the techniques and practices of one of the famous methods of developing music literacy, the Kodály method, will expand your teaching repertoire. Part 3 discusses Kodály's pedagogical approach and shows you how to implement it in your classroom.

Recognizing children's developmental characteristics when it comes to music will help you to introduce to them appropriate activities and exercises. Did you know that children below age eight have trouble singing in parts? Use appendix B to acquaint yourself with children's musical development so you can make sense of performing music in a multiage Montessori environment.

Finally, you will want to acquaint yourself with the public-school curriculum for music in the country, state, or region where you're teaching. For Montessori teachers in the United States, a familiarity with the National Core Music Standards (NCMS) will prove immensely useful. On the Making Music in Montessori website (www.makingmusicinmontessori.com), you can download a document that spells out the NCMS for the United States. You can print it out and post it in the music area of your classroom. If you teach in another country, keep checking the website. Soon the core standards for music for most countries will be available for download.

Skills

It's important to be able to sing, but you don't have to sing like a professional pop star or an opera star. Your natural singing voice will do. All you have to remember is to "sing as beautifully as possible, phrasing the melodies carefully and paying attention to correct pronunciation in keeping with the character of the song. Beautiful singing on the part of the teacher is a valuable musical experience for the children and also a model for their own singing" (Forrai, 1998).

It's also valuable for the Guide to be able to play an instrument. But don't feel any pressure to be able to play piano or the guitar. As you'll discover in Part 3, both instruments can be useful, but neither instrument works well for accompanying children's singing. The piano, in particular, doesn't make for a good accompanying instrument.

Often people who play piano well play everything for the children: the melody, the bass, and the harmony all at the same time. This has the effect of covering up the children's singing and stunting the growth of their inner hearing skills. "Recent research suggests that instruction with harmonic accompaniment does not have an effect on singing accuracy. [Plus], piano accompaniment serves to distract children. [It is suggested] that teacher's not use the piano to accompany children's singing, especially in the primary grades" (Colwell and Webster, 2011).

Whenever the children sing, it's best for them to sing unaccompanied. If you must add instruments, add percussion instruments. They help to keep the beat and add color without obscuring the children's voices. Practice with each of the percussion instruments in your classroom so that you can model good technique. Learn to keep a steady beat while playing a rhythm and learn to play a variety of simple rhythm patterns.

If you do want to accompany the children with a harmonic or melodic instrument, learn to play the autoharp or a mallet instrument. Both are easy to play, and both lend gentle support to the children's singing. A key advantage of the autoharp and mallet instruments is that the children can easily play them to accompany themselves.

Music Library

In chapter 3, you'll find a comprehensive list of books to stock in your classroom library for your students' use. The books listed in table 2.1, however, should live on *your* personal bookshelf. They all have wonderful information about music and offer ways for you to develop your skills. They appear in no particular order.

Repertoire

Even if you were to reject all musical methodologies and clever teacher skullduggery, and simply sing with the children a rich variety of beautiful, inviting songs every day, you would stoke in them a passion for music. A vital part of your preparation, then, consists of gathering a collection of songs that stimulate the children's fantasy, open up endless possibilities, invite repetition, and delight and enliven them.

For reasons elucidated in chapter 10, avoid Broadway show tunes, current pop hits, and certain types of "children's music" that have didactic aims ("This is the way we brush our teeth/brush our teeth/brush our teeth . . ."). Try selecting songs instead from, among other places, the long tradition of children's songs that have been made up by children themselves. In part 4 awaits a rich variety of authentic folk songs and singing games from whose sounds, movements, and words, the children derive pure joy.

On Specialists

You may be wondering what learning to teach music yourself, in your own Montessori classroom, means for that literal "elephant in the room" at your school: the music specialist. After all, one aim of this book is to give you a "reasonable acquaintance" of music that will allow you to become the "enlightened generalist" that Dr. Montessori envisioned helming her classrooms; one who fulfills her responsibility "to learn and know enough to introduce and expose the children to all aspects of the universe" (Pottish-Lewis, 2014).

But once you master the music pedagogy on offer in these pages, does that mean your school shouldn't employ a specialist, or that your headmaster should pink-slip the one you have? Absolutely not.

Specialists are highly trained, professional, well-educated, gifted individuals who know their stuff and are good at what they do! So, you may be thinking, are sumo wrestlers. Whether you invite into your classroom a specialist or a sumo wrestler, you invite the same level of disruption. Then again, a person doesn't need to come stomping into your classroom wide-legged wearing a mawashi to cause disruption. The prepared Montessori environments are so delicate, so fragile, that even the quietest, most meek adult can slink in and still cause disruption.

Many Montessori teachers throughout the world express the sentiment that employing a specialist isn't only disruptive, but it also sends the wrong message—that only gifted people can make music. It also gives

Table 2.1. List of Books for the Guide's Library

Title	Author	ISBN
What to Listen for in Music	Aaron Copland	451531760
Hearing and Writing Music: Professional Training for Today's Musician	Ron Grow	962949639
Music in Childhood: From Preschool to the Elementary Grades	Patricia Shehan Campbell and Carol Scott-Walker	053458554X
Music in Preschool	Katalin Forrai	958629706
Classic Tunes and Tales: Ready-to-Use Music Listening Lessons for Grades K-8	Todd F. Kline	137626835
101 Music Games for Children	Jerry Storms	897931645
A History of Western Music	Donald Jay Grout and Claude V. Palisca	39397527
Norton Anthology of Western Music Vols. 1, 2, and 3	Donald Jay Grout and Claude V. Palisca	0393931269, 0393931277, 0393932400
150 American Folk Songs to Sing, Read, and Play	Peter Erdei	913932043
Sail Away: 155 American Folk Songs to Sing, Read and Play	Eleanor G. Locke	1423472969
150 Rounds for Singing and Teaching	Edward Bolkovac and Judith Johnson	1458411427
The King's Singers Book of Rounds, Canons and Partsongs (King's Singer's Choral)	The King's Singers	634046306
The Kodály Method	Lois Choksy	135167655
American Music: a Panorama	Daniel Kingman	534598323
Orff and Kodály Adapted for the Elementary School	Lawrence Wheeler and Lois Raebeck	697034720
The Lives of the Great Composers	Harold G. Shonberg	393038572
World Music: A Global Journey	Terry E. Miller	415808235

rise to inconsistency, problems in staff communication, and unnecessary transitions. Most of all, it flouts Cosmic Education.

In spite of all the contradictions and logistical challenges specialists present, however, they make a valuable contribution to your children's musical education, especially when it comes to areas that require learned musical expertise, such as refining the children's singing, giving private violin lessons, repairing and maintaining instruments, leading a choir, or rehearsing a band. Specialists have much to offer your children, whose development owes as much to your specialist's expertise as to any of your stories or materials.

Not only that, but specialists have a wealth of musical knowledge that you can tap to help deliver music to your children. Confused about some of the concepts in this book? Your specialist would probably delight in providing you the answers to all of these questions and more. Count yourself lucky to have a walking, breathing, living musical encyclopedia in your midst. You would do well to liaise with her.

You see, the problem isn't that Montessori schools hire music specialists, but that when specialists are on staff, Montessori teachers steer clear of music. Having a specialist doesn't mean you can't do music in your classroom; in fact, the fear that employing a specialist sends

the message that *only certain people are musical* is only a concern *when teachers defer all musical education to the specialist.*

When teachers at Montessori schools that employ specialists present music in their environments, on the other hand, children receive an altogether more nuanced message: that everyone is musical to varying degrees. Some people find joy in a casual, relaxed experience with music, and others prefer a cultivated, focused experience.

Teachers and specialists can and should work together. At the ideal school, musical cooperation and sharing happens between the Classroom Guide—an "enlightened generalist" who has just enough musical knowledge to fire the children up about music—and the music specialist, whose expertise in her field provides the children refined musical instruction. Classroom Guides can tell stories and give lessons that enthuse the children, encourage musical follow up, and spark musical research, while specialists fill in the important details. When both individuals share knowledge and ideas, children witness how music brings people together.

Teach music yourself. Don't defer music instruction to your specialist. Let none of what's written here, however, give you the impression that you need to know *everything* about music. Consistent to Dr. Montessori's principles of limitation, a little musical knowledge goes a long way.

Your aim is not to become John Williams or Rachel Portman but to give yourself enough background in music to set aside your ego and cultivate humility. The rest of this book will give you enough of a "reasonable acquaintance" (Pottish-Lewis, 2014) of music to assume the role of Maria Montessori's humble, objective scientist.

If you currently defer to your specialist for music instruction, take heart. It's common for a person feeling all thumbs when it comes to music. By the time you finish reading this book, however, the confidence you feel with your newfound knowledge and skills will give you a sense of excitement that I'm confident you will want to pass along yourself to the children in your classes.

Do you dream of your children smiling and singing in harmony while dancing in a circle with joined hands as you leisurely strum an autoharp or jingle out an accompaniment on a tambourine? Now is the time to make that dream a reality.

Now that you know what you know about music, consider that all that music-making occurs more readily in an environment that is specially prepared. This book, on the whole, prepares *you*, but now, turn your attention to the details of how to make *your environment* the perfect place for your children to sing, read, write, compose, dance, and play.

Chapter 3

Preparing Your Environment

Maria Montessori prescribes that your classroom environment be a beautiful "living room" for children (Travis, 2009). It should be as "homelike" as possible (Werner-Andrews, 2013). A music-rich "living room" for children provides a simple, enticing, beautiful, workspace that contains everything children need to spur them toward independent musical activity.

A musical environment motivates children to

* sing songs, move, and play musical games;
* play musical instruments;
* listen to music;
* read about music history, famous musicians, and famous pieces of music;
* learn about music and build musical skills; and
* compose and improvise music.

This chapter describes in detail how to configure your "living room" for your little musical artists.

SINGING, MOVING, AND PLAYING SONGS AND GAMES

The optimal environment for music includes lots of space for the children to sing, move, dance, perform, and play. In the primary classroom, where the children from ages three to six work and learn, the ellipse taped on the floor for "walking the line" creates a natural space for making music as a whole class. In the elementary classroom, home to the children from ages six to twelve, music occurs on the area rug where you hold gatherings and class meetings. Whichever level you work with, provide at least one large, open space in your classroom for circle games, line games, and games in scattered formations. Include little nooks in which the children can hide during activities in which they pretend to become mice or when they find each other by recognizing one another's singing voices.

Frame your open space so that when children want to perform for each other, they can position themselves as if on a "stage." If your rug is rectangular, for instance, place your musical instruments on a shelf near one end of the rectangle, so that when musical performances ensue, you or your children can easily reach and distribute the instruments. If you sit in a chair during gatherings, position your chair in a corner of the "stage" side of your rug, so that you can sit to the side and watch the children's performance without obstructing the other children's view, yet still maintain a strong position in the gathering.

Some circle games require lots of space outside of a circle of children with joined hands. Make sure to provide a rug large enough to allow the children space inside *and* outside such a circle. Avoid positioning furniture too close to the rug so no obstacles obstruct the children's movements as they play games that call for the entire circle to move clockwise or counterclockwise.

MUSICAL INSTRUMENTS

Musical instruments add color and dimension to classroom music. They provide accompaniment for songs, help children with musical concepts, and provide a means for composition and improvisation (Irwin and Nelson, 1986). Any musical instrument you put in your environment will remind the children of what human beings have achieved with their gifts of love and imagination as well as their hands. But not *any* musical instrument will do.

Moreover, not every musical instrument in the environment needs to be playable. Small instruments such as *mbiras,* little painted flutes, and other instruments from other cultures can function simply as beautiful, decorative objects. Items that make nice sounds but aren't necessarily instruments, such as little music boxes, or sets of chimes, are welcome in your environment; they cultivate an appreciation of music.

Since music is as natural to the child as finger painting, playing an instrument should be as natural as dipping a finger into paint and making marks on paper. In other words, when it comes to instruments that you and the children can *play*, you or a child must be able to walk up to the instrument and, with little to no experience, make pleasing sounds with it. Furthermore, the instruments in your classroom must be easy to combine with each other so that groups of children can effortlessly make music together. When instruments are easy to play alone and together, children are more likely to feel successful, competent, and capable.

What's more, instruments in your environment must be authentic and of the highest quality. The child doesn't want to struggle with a cheap wood or plastic instrument that doesn't make a lovely sound. Likewise, the children listening to the child in question don't want to be subjected to the buzzing of a kazoo or the piercing sounds of a whistle. Shy away, therefore, from toy tambourines, little plastic xylophones that roll, or any other objects that are marketed to children as "musical instruments."

The instruments you provide to the children must be more than mere toys. Anything less than a bona fide musical instrument will send the child the message that they are not important, and that music is not important. Worse, the children will grow bored with toy instruments, and, by extension, with music.

Finding authentic instruments that are easy to play, then, is your task. For guidance on what instruments to use, you can look to Maria Montessori. In *The Montessori Method*, she writes, "The stringed instruments together with the drum and the bells form the trio of the classical instruments of humanity" (Montessori, 2002).

You might be asking yourself, "What about woodwind instruments? Early human beings whittled flutes. Can't I have a flute in my classroom?" The answer is simply that, although flutes and other woodwind instruments make a beautiful sound, they require too much technique to make an *instant* sound. A child can't achieve a beautiful sound from a woodwind instrument without an intricate combination of finger positioning, embouchure, and breath control. To balance these three elements takes lots of practice.

Set children up for success. Don't make them fiddle with reeds, as they would if you offered them a clarinet or a saxophone. If you yourself play any of these instruments, by all means, play them for the children, but bear in mind author, educator, and advocate of "unschooling" John Holt's words about *competence models:* You want to inspire the children without coming off like a virtuoso and making them feel like they can't play music.

Also, limiting the instruments you offer the children falls in line with Maria Montessori's principle of limitation. That is to say, you don't want *every* musical instrument in your environment, you want just the *right* musical instruments.

If, after having been exposed to the ease and the joy of making music on classroom instruments, the children want to go outside of the classroom environments and take private lessons on, say, the flute or the saxophone, they can feel free to do so. Chances are they will take to their lessons much more enthusiastically after they have had some success with an instrument in the classroom than if they've had to struggle with one.

So, to find beautiful musical instruments that are effortless to play, let's look to the percussion and string families.

PERCUSSION INSTRUMENTS

A small basket of percussion instruments forms the staple of the classroom music diet. A word of caution, however: because the children are enthusiastic about percussion instruments, and because percussion instruments are easy to get a sound out of, you should take special care to establish orderly procedures for handling them. Include such guidelines as

- special routines for setting up and putting away the instruments;
- clear signals for starting and stopping together when playing;
- guidelines that enable all the children to play the instruments, along with consequences for those who demonstrate an inability to handle the instruments responsibly;
- designated times for when to play the instruments and when to keep them silent;
- skill-development lessons (something Maria Montessori calls "Grace and Courtesy") on how to politely ask someone to stop playing, how to invite someone to play with you, and so on; and
- procedures for care and maintenance of the instruments.

Percussion instruments can sound beautiful, or they can sound abrasive. The children will get the best sound out of percussion instruments if they hold them in a way that permits the instruments to vibrate freely. Hand drums have a lower opening that must be left open to create the best sound. Triangles must be dangled by their suspension loop and tapped lightly and quickly. Sticks and claves must be held lightly so their bodies can vibrate. Table 3.1 on the next page describes each percussion instrument and some general considerations concerning its use.

MALLET INSTRUMENTS

Mallet instruments are the most versatile and colorful instruments on your classroom menu. They consist of a

Table 3.1. Menu of Classroom Percussion Instruments

Name	Description	Considerations
Maracas	Maracas are hollow wooden instruments that are filled with rice or other sound-producing grains.	The child should always hold the maracas by the handle and never hit them against each other or any other object.
Güiro	The güiro is a solid, often football-shaped instrument with grooves carved into its dorsal section. It comes with a wooden stick that, when dragged across the grooves in a perpendicular stroke, makes a nice, scratchy sound.	Children should not hit the güiro. They should hold the güiro lightly and drag the stick quickly, but lightly across the grooves for the best sound.
Bongo drums	Bongo drums are a pair of attached hollow wooden cylinders each with a membrane stretched across one opening. Children can play them by slapping their hands upon the skin of the drum. By using different strokes, different parts of the hand, and different parts of the drum, the children can make a wide variety of nice percussive sounds.	The children should sit in a chair and hold the bongos between their knees. The open sides of the drum should be free so that the sound produced by the membrane vibrating the air inside the drum can resonate.
Finger cymbals	Finger cymbals are small cymbals attached to a loop. Each cymbal can either be held by the loop between the thumb and forefinger and gently struck together or worn on the middle finger and thumb of one hand and struck together by bringing the fingers together in a pinching motion.	The children should never use sticks or beaters to make a sound from the cymbals. To get a sound, they must clang the cymbals together quickly and then move them apart so that both cymbals can vibrate.
Tambourine	The tambourine is a small wooden hoop about as thick as a pie plate with a calfskin head and jingles on the sides. When the tambourine is struck, the cymbals vibrate to create a shimmering sound.	The child should hold the tambourine lightly by the part of the tambouring that is free of jingles. When playing the tambourine, the child may strike it with his or her fist or the fleshy part of his palm. Avoid allowing the child to strike the tambourine against his or her hip.
Triangle	The triangle is a bent metal rod shaped like a triangle with one corner. The child holds it by a cord suspended from the hand he or she is using to dampen it. The child strikes the triangle with a straight metal rod called a beater.	To get the best sound, the child should strike the triangle lightly and quickly, removing the beater right after impact so the triangle can vibrate. The child holds the triangle in front of him or her and strikes the beater on the bottom leg. The child should avoid doing "dinner rolls."
Claves	Claves are wooden dowels that the child can strike together to make a pleasing, wooden chirping sound.	To play the claves, the child makes a fist with one hand, with his or her thumb facing out. He or she then rests one clave gently in the space between his or her knuckles and the fleshy part of his or her thumb. He or she then brings the other clave, held gently, down to meet the clave in his or her fist. The claves should never be struck together like cymbals nor should they be used as beaters on another instrument.
Sand blocks	Sand blocks make a sound by holding them in each hand and rubbing them together.	The child rubs the sand blocks together in quick strokes to make the rhythmic "shh shh" sound.
Rhythm sticks	Rhythm sticks are narrow dowels slightly thicker than drumsticks. Usually they come in different colors so that the children can easily find a matched pair. They create a crisp, thick percussive sound.	Unlike claves, the child can hold one rhythm stick in each hand and bang them together. Like claves, the child should not use the rhythm sticks to bang on other percussion instruments.

frame of metal or wooden bars arrayed like a keyboard. The children play the instruments using light, soft-headed wooden or plastic mallets. The children can strike two bars simultaneously to provide harmonic accompaniments to melodies, or they can play one bar at a time to create lovely melodies. Certain bars of the mallet instruments can be removed to set the children up for success when the instruments are combined with other pitched instruments when making music—more about this in chapter 15.

Glockenspiel

A glockenspiel is usually a small instrument, often inside a portable case, with small metal bars arrayed like a keyboard. Often the bars have pitch names carved onto them.

Some words of caution: many "toy" instruments exist that pass themselves off as glockenspiels. A good rule is that if the instrument comes in a box and sits on the shelf at a toy store, it's not a suitable instrument. You will know right away, however, when you strike the small metal bars whether you have a quality glockenspiel. The sound will be bright and colorful. If the sound is clunky, like dropping a coin onto a metal desk, you are dealing with a toy.

Xylophone

"Xylophone" refers to several classroom instruments that have thick, removable wooden bars. An orchestral xylophone is a gigantic instrument with tube resonators below each bar. It is much too large to include in your classroom instrument collection. Xylophones that are suitable for classroom use are made up of a set of separate wooden bars suspended above rectangular wooden resonator boxes. One style of these instruments was created by composer and music educator Carl Orff for classroom use.

Metallophone

"Metallophone" is the name Orff gave to his classroom instruments that are similar to xylophones, but have removable metal bars. You can get both xylophones and metallophones at www.musicarts.com, among other sources. Not only are these instruments of high quality, but they also have a beautiful sound, and children can use them in different combinations to create delightful accompaniments, solos, and compositions.

STRINGED INSTRUMENTS

Stringed instruments are arguably the most beautiful, versatile, and flexible instruments human beings have devised. Listen to any orchestral piece, and you'll hear how the strings provide mood, melodies, and chordal accompaniment.

Solo instruments, like the violin, viola, and cello, while beautiful, are too difficult to master in a short time to make available in your classroom. Celtic harps have a lovely sound and are easy to play, but they often only come in one key, making them inconvenient for spontaneously making music.

The stringed instruments you want in your classroom are easy to play and can provide harmonic color and rhythmic accompaniment to the children's music-making.

Autoharp

Although nowadays it may seem like a relic, the autoharp is one of the simplest strumming musical instruments to play (Irwin Nelson 1986). Often shaped like a harp, but sometimes rectangular, an autoharp has a flat hollow wooden body with strings strung across the top.

A series of buttons on the right side of the instrument with the letter names of chords printed on them dampen certain strings when one button is depressed, resulting in the desired chord emanating from the remaining strings, which vibrate as the player strums.

An autoharp is as easy to play as pressing a button and strumming the strings. The player strums rhythmically, to a steady beat, with a large sweeping motion across all the strings. You can learn to play the autoharp easily and use it to accompany songs that you introduce to the children.

The autoharp adds color and beauty to the child's musical explorations. Young children thrill when given an opportunity to strum the autoharp while simply pressing a button. Two children can double up and play, one pressing the chord button as the other strums. Children can play the autoharp extremely softly by using a felt plectrum or by brushing the fleshy part of their thumb across the strings, making exploration on the instrument less distracting for the other children during the work period.

Guitar versus Ukulele

Children often find the guitar attractive. They associate the guitar's glamor with rock and pop music. It particularly appeals to older children. Engaging as it is, however, the guitar requires a lot of technique to be able to play. Its thick neck is too large for young fingers. Even adults beginning to play the guitar find it painful and difficult to get a good sound out of it.

If you play the guitar, bring it in occasionally to play a song with the children. If a child in your class takes private lessons and has already mastered the guitar basics, he or she can bring a guitar in once in a while. Watching a child play the guitar can be inspiring for other children. Nevertheless, having a guitar as a regular fixture in the classroom isn't advisable (unless as a decorative display object).

Instead of the guitar, I recommend stocking the guitar's little cousin: the ukulele. The ukulele's neck is the perfect size for young hands, and its widely spaced nylon strings are easy for the child's little fingers to depress. You can tune the strings of a ukulele to an open C major chord by tuning the strings, starting from the uppermost string to G, C, E, and G. This enables the child to accompany simple songs by simply holding the ukulele and strumming in rhythm. To change chords, the child can easily place an index finger firmly across all the strings and, by sliding this finger up and down the neck, produce different chords.

Older children who have moved past one-finger chords love the challenge of learning the fingerings for new chords. For upper elementary children aged nine to twelve, a baritone uke is a great alternative to the tiny, more common, soprano uke. Being larger and more resonant, the baritone uke is also more versatile and can serve as a scaffold for learning the guitar. It can be used effectively to accompany slow, lyrical songs, while the soprano uke is great for happier, more spirited songs.

This completes your collection of classroom instruments. Remember, consistent with Maria Montessori's principle of limitation, you should have only one of each instrument, with the exception of the xylophones, metallophones, and glockenspiels: To produce a rich variety of accompaniments and melodies during group performances, it's good to have more than one set of these. Larger, low-pitched bass bars are also good for repetitive bass patterns called ostinati.

PIANO

Even if you aren't a skilled pianist, the mere presence of a piano lends a musical ambiance to any environment. The piano can become the centerpiece of your class, be the highlight of your community gathering space, and truly turn your environment into a "living room."

Children can use the piano to practice pieces from their private lessons, or they can accompany the class with soft music during the work cycle. A high-quality electric piano with weighted, touch-sensitive keys, such as the Yamaha Clavinova, which also features volume control, speakers, and a headphone jack, makes for an excellent alternative to a wood-and-strings classroom piano.

Although you may find the idea of controlling the volume of the piano or asking the child to wear headphones appealing, however, nothing beats an acoustic piano. Not only does the mere presence of a bona fide wooden piano enrich the musical life of your classroom, but it alsoprovides a gateway to Cosmic Education,[1] it offers opportunities for Grace and Courtesy,[2] it fires up the children's imagination, and it enhances classroom musical experiences.

The story of the piano's rich history provides fertile ground for the children's explorations. The piano itself stands as a feat of engineering and craftsmanship. It boggles the mind that human beings managed to use wood, metal, and fabrics to create an object of such expressive power that can challenge us physically and intellectually while at the same time transmitting the depth of human emotion.

Leading your children to thinking about the piano in this way can open up their hearts to music history, physics, engineering, biology, geometry, and human interdependencies. Speaking of opening up, feel free once in a while to remove the panels from the piano and expose the children to its inner workings—its complex network of hammers, felt pieces, and tightly wound strings. Doing so gives children a direct connection to an amazing human achievement.

You might be fearing what many adults fear: the piano provides too easy an outlet for a precocious child. The child suffering from ennui can press lots of keys down at once, bang on the keys with her fists, elbows, or forearms, or play "Heart and Soul" until everyone in the room finds themselves driven to distraction. But with some established routines and rules of etiquette, the piano can become a valuable tool for the children's social development.

To develop the children's sense of social responsibility using the piano, for example, first help the children recognize the piano's inherent freedoms and responsibilities. Suppose any child has the freedom to play at the piano as a work choice. A responsibility balances that freedom: The child must actually work. Work at the piano might include bringing in literature from the child's lessons outside of school, practicing repertoire, or composing at the piano for follow up.

Work could also mean playing a duet with a friend. Maybe a child wants to play the right-hand part for "Heart and Soul" and teach another child the left-hand part. This also constitutes work. Playing random noises, mindlessly repeating the same song, or being silly at the piano with a partner, however, are not responsible uses of the children's freedom to play the piano. Children from ages six to twelve, with their sensitivity to fairness and justice (Travis, 1999), embrace this distinction. Once the children understand their freedoms and responsibilities, they can work to develop for the classroom some rules of piano etiquette.

Etiquette for the piano might begin with the question of when the piano can be played. Establish a rule that any of the most responsible children can play piano during the work cycle but only if their playing doesn't disturb anyone. As soon as the piano distracts another child, that child can walk up to the pianist and ask him or her politely to close the dust cover. If that happens, the child playing piano must stop, no matter what, and both children must find other work.

The children love opportunities to come up with new rules of etiquette. This should come as no surprise. After all, in Montessori environments "[The children] often establish their own rules, their own code of ethical behavior" (Travis, 1999). This is as true in music as it is in any other area of the classroom. Other rules of etiquette that children might come up with center around how loudly the piano should be played, how many people should sit at the piano at one time, and so on.

Other specific ideas for piano etiquette might be

- how to invite a friend to play the piano with you;
- how to accept or decline such an invitation;
- how to quietly raise and lower the dust cover;
- how to quietly position the bench;
- how to get help positioning the bench;
- how to ask someone to play more quietly or to stop playing;
- how to accept someone's request that you stop playing; and
- how to thank someone for playing piano for your community.

To deliver Grace and Courtesy lessons with the piano, try doing what Alan Travis recommends: "Role-play doing something incorrectly, and have the children show [you] how to do it properly" (Travis, 2009). At the piano, little skits can be quite funny.

To demonstrate how *not* to play the piano, for example, tease your hair into a wild, unruly mess of "composer hair." Then sit bolt upright on the bench; tuck in your upper lip; jut out your chin; make a face like sniffing manure; and bang out the most abrasive, outrageous, deafening chord you can manage. When the children's laughter dies down, they will articulate perfectly the drawbacks of such behavior.

Creating rules, developing social responsibility, and learning etiquette is useful, but bringing a piano into your classroom also sends a message to your children that you trust them. You trust they will care for the piano and use it responsibly. They will use it to beautify their classroom with wonderful, not distracting, sounds.

After all, every object that you add to your environment comes with freedoms and responsibilities. Why should a piano—or any other musical instrument for that matter—be any different? As Plato said, "The most effective kind of education is that the child should play among lovely things." That big glossy box with its pretty white and black keys, each of which rewards the child with the instant gratification of a beautiful sound, is one of humankind's most lovely things.

Use the piano to spark the children's imagination. Tell sound stories on the piano; accompany relaxation activities, like the ones in chapter 13, and have the children themselves provide the "soundtracks" for images and theatrical performances. The children can even write music for the piano in simple and creative ways. Part 4 outlines some creative uses for the piano that you can use even if you yourself aren't a pianist.

LISTENING TO MUSIC

Not only does listening to music benefit the brain, but, according to two research reviews using adult subjects, it also carries a wide range of health benefits. According to an article on the Los Angeles Philharmonic website by University of London professor Susan Hallman (2010), "There is every reason to suppose that these health benefits would also apply to children. The benefits include:

- physical relaxation and release of physical tension
- emotional release and reduction of feelings of stress
- a sense of happiness, positive mood, elation, and feeling high
- a sense of greater personal, emotional, and physical well-being
- an increased sense of alertness and energy
- a sense of purpose and motivation."

Having a quiet, calm place for children to sit and listen to music proves invaluable. Set up a comfortable, cozy "listening station" in your environment where the children can take an occasional break, cool off, and give their full attention to a piece of music. Locate your listening station in a quiet corner, or some other cozy nook in the room. Place a comfortable chair illuminated by the natural light from a window, or by a low-hanging lamp that casts soft light, such as a Chinese paper lantern, to invite a child to come and enjoy a calm moment.

A music-playing device, such as a CD player or iPod, can sit within the children's reach. Here it's worth mentioning that, at the time of this writing, technology has all but rendered CD players obsolete. What's more, Internet-based streaming services such as Pandora and Spotify have replaced the classic iPod as the preferred method for playing music.

Technology changes fast. Who knows what devices people will be using to listen to music even five years from now? (You can already imagine the recommendation in the fifth edition of this book: "Be sure to place your psycho-music brain implants in a pretty basket on the holo-shelf in your virtual environment.")

Whichever device you prefer, make sure the children can operate it on their own, with few distractions. Also be sure that it has as few "bells and whistles" as possible. A CD player with a radio or an iPod touch with tons of apps will distract your children. Instead, provide them a simple CD player with no radio or an old-school click-wheel iPod with no touch screen and no way to access social media or the Internet. Someone could write another book about the adverse effects of screens on children, but for now, be advised that the less time your children spend fiddling with the device, the more time they will spend listening to the music.

Along with your music-playing device, provide a solid pair of padded, noise-canceling headphones. Make sure the headphones are comfortable and of sufficient quality to allow the child listening to focus on the music while sparing the other children the loss of focus that results from also being able to hear it.

Whether your classroom music collection plays from a CD or an iPod, make sure it represents a wide variety of musical styles, genres, and cultures. The music in your listening library should be like an "ear-food buffet. You don't want [the children] eating only mac and cheese, or similarly, listening to the same [pieces] all the time. Your musical menu should consist of [music] from your culture and those around the world, as well as music that you love" (Lewis Brown, 2015).

To challenge the child intellectually, aim for music with a variety of rhythms and tonalities, with pieces in different keys. Stock "adult-quality music . . . that does not have strident tone quality, that is, music that changes its sound frequently. Orchestral music is best for this. By contrast, most thrash metal bands usually don't have much contrast from one song to the next, let alone within a song" (Lewis Brown, 2015).

If you're concerned that stocking your classroom music collection with orchestral music will only expose your children to the music of "old white men," take heart: composers of classical music represent an enormous variety of nationalities and ethnic backgrounds.

Clara Schumann (1819–1896), Lili Boulanger (1893–1918), Ellen Taffe Zwillich (b. 1939) are examples of wonderful women composers. Black composers such as William Grant Still (1895–1978), Nathaniel Dett (1892–1943), and Joseph Bologne (1745–1799) created unforgettable orchestral music. Toru Takemitsu (1930–1996) and Akira Ifukube (1914–2006) stand proud among the most prominent Japanese composers. Gay and lesbian composers include Franz Schubert (1797–1828), G. F. Handel (1685–1759), Aaron Copland (1900–1990), Francis Poulec (1899–1963), Pyotr Tchaikovsky (1840–1893), Ethel Smyth (1858–1944), and more.

Pretty much any place a person can be from has classical composers lurking among the populace. You don't believe it? Do a two-word Google search beginning with the nationality of your choice and the word "composers." Composers and musicians of all stripes await you and the children in your classrooms.

The composer's identity aside, when stocking your library with classical music, include pieces that tell a story or teach about instrumentation, such as *Carnival of the Animals* by Camille Saint-Säens, or *Peter and the Wolf* by Sergei Prokofiev. Although Eric Rasmussen, chair of early childhood music at the Peabody Institute in Baltimore, recommends avoiding very long orchestral music, you needn't. Large-scale works point to the breadth of human achievement, and children should experience them as a whole, as the composer intended.

Of course, the children don't have to listen to the whole piece in one sitting. Like reading a great thick book, they can listen to as much as they like and continue listening on another day. The children can choose for themselves which movements they like to listen to again and again. You should let children find their own way through the music. Making decisions for them about what to listen to deprives them of the opportunity to explore.

Worthy of consideration, however, is Mr. Rasmussen's assertion that "string quartets or other pieces that rely on only one class of instruments are not the best for young children because they may not demand as much of the child's attention" (Lewis Brown, 2015). The music in your collection should "shift in tonal color frequently" (Lewis Brown, 2015). Exceptions to this are solo piano music, solo guitar music, and the suites for solo cello by Bach. The piano and the guitar have the capacity to exude a large variety of tone colors and timbres, and Bach's cello suites are unique in that they portray different voices with a single instrument.

But don't just play Bach. Provide the children music from all eras of classical music, even from the more disjointed and atonal-sounding repertoire of the twentieth century. Children take as much pleasure from the screeching, dramatic violins of *Rite of Spring* as they do from the pleasant, lilting violins of *The Four Seasons*. Don't just limit yourself to dead composers, either. Check out Anna Clyne, Johnny Greenwood, David Lang, John Corigliano, Anna S. Thorvaldsdóttir (Icelandic!), or Max Richter. Supply children with music you love, but don't let your bias deprive them of rich musical experiences.

If you decide to stock your music library with classical CDs, avoid those that feature only single movements of large-scale works. Also steer clear of CDs that focus only on the artist playing the music, and not on the composer, as well as those of inferior production and performance quality.

As to popular music and jazz, having the originally released CD art in physical or digital form is ideal, especially with pop music, where the packaging and music go hand in hand in the total presentation of the artwork. The colorful, music on the Beatles album *Sgt. Pepper's Lonely Hearts Club Band,* for instance, can be experienced through the music as well as the album's artwork.

Additionally, the popular music you provide the children in your classes should be colorful and contain varied instrumentation and textures. The best pop albums reflect different influences from song to song. Again, avoid music that has all one sound or feel throughout an entire album.

While classical, pop, and jazz music contain lots of colorful dishes for your "ear-food buffet," don't forget to also include music from all around the world. Children delight in hearing combinations of instruments from different countries. The restful, colorful chime of Indonesian gamelan music; the rhythmic pulsations and silky vibrations of Indian classical music; and the haunting, sacred reverberations of Arabic music can entice children toward deep listening experiences.

The record label *Putumayo* (www.putumayo.com), has released a number of excellent collections of international music. Also check out the Smithsonian website (https://folkways.si.edu/), where you can listen to, download, or purchase folk music from all over the world.

Although there is no "bad" music, some music you should avoid. Many music educators caution against supplying your listening library with "children's music." Music marketed to children isn't necessarily appropriate for children. Recordings of such music often suffer from poor production, poor performances by children who are singing as if they were adults, and songs limited to major keys. "Follow this rule: If you think it's bad, it probably is" (Lewis Brown, 2015).

For young children, many music teachers prefer to avoid New Age music, which not only often appropriates and waters down music of other cultures, but which also "[lacks] tone and form" (Marchak, 1999). Formless, meandering music does nothing for a child's brain development. Always offer children music that challenges and stimulates their brains; if you want to play something relaxing for children, play a CD of nature sounds.

Refrain also from supplying children with music that contains inappropriate lyrics (Lewis Brown, 2015). Hip-hop can be a wonderful addition to your music library, but it can be difficult to find hip-hop songs with age-appropriate lyrics. Table 3.2 shows you a list from the website Sheknows.com of some hip-hop songs appropriate for young listeners.

Of course, to really reap the benefits of music, children should do more than just listen. "To get the most benefit from music, children need to sing, clap and dance along with the tunes. Singing and moving with music tells the brain to make meaning of it, a cognitive process called "audition" (Lewis Brown, 2015), sometimes defined as "critical hearing" (Merriam-Webster Online Dictionary, https://www.merriam-webster.com/dictionary/audition). While listening, children can sit in the listening chair and pat their knees, wave their arms in the air, or hum along to the music, provided that these activities don't disturb anyone.

Many children also enjoy drawing while listening to music. Provide a clipboard, a supply of blank paper, and some colored pencils for the children to draw lines and pictures while they listen. They can even interpret the music through the lines they make.

A basket of yarn nearby will encourage the children to knit. Some will enjoy to moving their needles rhythmically to the music.

The children can also follow along with listening maps that you or other children can create. (For more on listening maps, see chapter 11.) Really interested children can follow along with a paperback score.

Table 3.2.   Hip-Hop Songs for Kids

Artist	Song
Gym Class Heroes	"Stereo Hearts" (feat. Adam Levine)
Rhianna	"We Found Love" (feat. Calvin Harris)
Flo Rida	"Good Feeling"
Arrested Development	"Tennessee"
B.o.B.	"Magic" (feat. Rivers Cuomo)
D.J. Jazzy Jeff & The Fresh Prince	"Parents Just Don't Understand"
Kriss Kross	"Jump"
Macklemore & Ryan Lewis	"Same Love" (feat. Mary Lambert)
Vanilla Ice	"Ice, Ice, Baby"
Estelle	"1980"
Lupe Fiasco	"Kick Push"
Common	"Come Close" (feat. Mary J. Blige)
TLC	"What about Your Friends"
Estelle	"American Boy"
De La Soul	"Me Myself and I"
The Black Eyed Peas	"I Gotta Feeling"

Table 3.3.   Miniature Paperback Scores

Title	ISBN
Beethoven: Symphony No. 3 in Eb Major, Op. 55, "Eroica"	0-486-29796-9
Beethoven: Symphony No. 5 in C Minor, Op. 67	0-486-29850-0
Beethoven: Symphony No. 6 in F Major, Op. 68, "Pastorale"	0-486-40123-5
Beethoven: Symphony No. 7 in A Major, Op. 92	0-486-40418-8
Beethoven: Symphony No. 9 in D Minor, Op. 125 "Choral"	0-486-29924-4
Tchaikovsky: Symphony No. 6 in B Minor, Op. 74 "Pathetique"	0-486-29954-6
Tchaikovsky: Symphony No. 4 in F Major, Op. 36	0-486-40421-8
Tchaikovsky: Nutcracker Suite	0-486-43919-4
Richard Strauss: Till Eulenspiegel's Merry Pranks	0-486-40869-8
Dvořák: Symphony No. 9, Op. 95 "From the New World"	0-486-29892-2
Gustav Holst: The Planets, Op. 32	978-0486414027
Camille Saint-Saëns: Carnival of the Animals	978-0486404127
Igor Stravinsky: The Rite of Spring	0-486-41174-5
Bedrich Smetana: The Moldau and Other Works for Orchestra	0-486-49024-6
Claude Debussy: La Mer	0-486-29848-5
Claude Debussy: Nocturnes for Orchestra in Full Score	0-486-44545-3
Arnold Schoenberg: Five Orchestral Pieces, Op. 16	0-486-40642-3
Mozart: Symphony No. 40 in G Minor, K550, and Symphony No. 41 in C Minor, K551, "Jupiter"	0-486-29849-3
Bach: The Six Brandenburg Concertos, BWV 10146-1051	0-486-29795-0
Berlioz: Symphony Phantastique	0-486-298906

Following a score (or just merely looking at it) while listening can be an enriching experience for children. Supplement the classical music in your listening library with a rotating collection of miniature music scores. You can display these scores on a small bookstand in your music area. Many famous works of classical music have been published in miniature study score format by Dover Publications. These beloved scores with their brightly colored cover designs are not too expensive, and their simple cover designs each present a picture of the composer.

You might object that looking at a score is daunting, but finding one's way around a score is not as complicated as you might think. Plus, just having a score on display, whether children make sense of it or not, highlights the breadth of human accomplishment. Looking at all the little dots and sticks in a score can be an eye-opener for children. Table 3.3 on the preceding page suggests some miniature scores for your shelf.

READING ABOUT MUSIC

A well-prepared musical environment contains lots of books about famous musicians, composers, and musical instruments. Somewhere in or around your listening station, provide a shelf of music books about composers and famous compositions for research, books that tell stories about music, and books about music theory.

Also include books about multicultural music. You can find a full list of multicultural music books at the Multicultural Music Education website (http://multiculturalmusiceducation.weebly.com/books.html). Many of the best books come with a CD. Table 3.4 lists a number of music books for the classroom.

When choosing books for your library, coordinate with your CD collection. Having, for instance, a recording and a paperback score of Beethoven's Symphony no. 3, "Eroica" ("Heroic Symphony"), plus a copy of Anna Harwell Calenza's book *The Heroic Symphony*

Table 3.4. Menu of Classroom Books

Title	Author	ISBN
Clara Schumann: Piano Virtuoso	Susanna Reich	0-395-89119-1
The Kingfisher Young People's Book of Music	Nicky Barber, Mark Barratt, Alan Blackwood, Elinor Kelly, and Chris de Souza	0-7534-5250-2
Rock N' Roll	D. L. Gish	1-58340-677-8
The Elements of Music: Melody, Rhythm, and Harmony	Jason Martineau	0-8027-1682-2
Stories of Women Composers for Young Musicians	Catherine Wolff Kendall	0-96108-2-X
Getting to Know the World's Great Composers (Series)	Mike Venezia	Various
Beethoven Lives Upstairs	Barbara Nichol	0-15-314403-3
Strange Mr. Satie	M. T. Anderson	0-670-03637-4
Lives of the Musicians: Good Times, Bad Times (and What the Neighbors Thought)	Kathleen Krull & Kathryn Hewitt	978-0-15-216436-2
The Story of the Orchestra	Robert Levine	1-57912-148-9
American Negro Songs	John W. Work	0-486-40271-1
Pictures at an Exhibition	Anna Harwell Calenza	1-57091-492-3
Camille Saint-Säens's Danse Macabre	Anna Harwell Calenza	978-1-57091-348-8
The Farewell Symphony	Anna Harwell Calenza	1-57091-406-0
Music for the End of Time	Jen Bryant	0-8028-5229-7
Gershwin's Rhapsody in Blue	Anna Harwell Calenza	978-1-57091-556-7
The Heroic Symphony	Anna Harwell Calenza	1-57091-509-1
The Carnival of the Animals	Jack Prelutsky	978-0375864582
Sergey Prokofiev's Peter and the Wolf	Janet Schulman	978-0375824302
Zin! Zin! Zin! A Violin	Lloyd Moss	978-0689835247
In The Hall of the Mountain King	Alison Miller Flannery	978-1938633133
Vivaldi's Four Seasons	Anna Harwell Calenza	978-1570916373
Charlie Parker Played Be Bop	Christopher Raschka	978-0531070956
Follow The Drinking Gourd	Jeanette Winter	978-0679819974
Ella Fitzgerald: The Tale of a Vocal Virtuosa	Andrea Pinkney	978-0786805686
When the Beat Was Born: DJ Kool Herc and the Creation of Hip Hop	Laban Carrick Hill	978-1596435407
What Charlie Heard	Mordicai Gerstein	978-0374382926
The Extraordinary Music of Mr. Ives: The True Story of a Famous American Composer	Joanne Stanbridge	978-0547238661
Song of Middle C	Alison McGee	978-0763630133
Piano Starts Here: The Young Art Tatum	Robert A. Parker	978-0375839658
Duke Ellington's Nutcracker Suite	Anna Harwell Calenza	978-1570917004

(Continued)

Table 3.4. (Continued)

Title	Author	ISBN
The New Grove Dictionary of Music and Musicians	Stanley Sadie	978-1561591749
The New Grove Dictionary of Jazz	Berry Kernfield	978-0312113575
Music: 45 A.D. to 1995 A.D.	Mark Ammons	978-1580370530
Who Were The Beatles?	Geoff Edgers	978-0448439068
Young Mozart	Rachel Isadora	978-0670871209
Sebastian: A Book About Bach	Jeanette Winter	978-0152006297
Vivaldi and the Invisible Orchestra	Stephen Castanza	978-0805078015
The "Famous Children" Series: Mozart, Bach, Beethoven, Chopin, Tchaikovsky, etc.	Ann Rachlin	Various
This Jazz Man	Karen Ehrhardt	978-0544339224
The Encyclopedia of Popular Music	Colin Larkin	978-1561592371

gives children an in-depth experience with that particular work: They can hear it, look at it, and read about the story behind it.

BUILDING MUSICAL SKILLS

Once you provide space for singing and playing music games and outfit your environment with beautiful musical objects, musical instruments, CDs, and books, your environment will be almost complete. Next, children will need to learn about the "nuts and bolts" of music and gain musical skills. For that, equip your environment with the full complement of Montessori music materials. On the "Making Music in Montessori" website (www.makingmusicinmontessori.com), you'll find a list of Montessori music materials. Have these materials all in one place, preferably on or around your movable tone bar cabinet.

In addition to the Montessori materials, you'll want to have a few items for carrying off the Kodály lessons you'll read about in chapter 9. Table 3.5 lists these materials.

Table 3.5. Supplementary Music Materials

1. Four to eight small black bean bags
2. A ball of colored yarn
3. Manipulative icons of umbrellas, snails, and the like for Kodály *Presentation* lessons. (For details, see chapter 9.)
4. One-line staff paper
5. Three-line staff paper
6. Music Grid Paper (see appendix D)
7. Popsicle sticks
8. Large poster paper
9. Animal hand puppets, finger puppets, or a sock puppet
10. Oval-shaped paper note heads in different colors, with song lyrics on one side and *sol-fa* names on the other (for more information, refer to chapter 9)
11. Oval-shaped black paper note heads
12. Rhythm cards in various colors with stick notated rhythms on one side (see chapter 6), and umbrellas, snails, or other icons on the back (again, refer to chapter 9)

WESTERN MUSIC HISTORY AND WORLD MUSIC

Providing materials for children to read, listen to, play, and build their music skills is important, but in addition, you can have a variety of visual aids in the environment to help the children learn about the history of music.

For starters, place on your music shelves a small basket containing some composer picture cards. A company called Layton Music makes a set of forty-four picture cards that have composers' pictures on one side and an interesting fact about that composer on the other. You can cut them out and laminate them yourself. You'll find some good ones at this link: https://laytonmusic.files.wordpress.com/2008/10/composer-cards-facts.pdf.

Another place to find cards is on the Asmodee games website (https://www.asmodee.us/en/games/timeline/products/timeline-music-cinema/). They make a great game called *Timeline: Music and Cinema,* in which children place small cards that depict notable events in music history in order of occurrence. Remove all the cards that have to do with cinema and watch as the children build their own music history timeline.

Along with your composer cards, display a facsimile of a manuscript page from a famous piece of music written in a composer's own hand. You can find scans of handwritten composer manuscripts on the Internet at the International Music Score Library Project website at www.imslp.org. Scan one, print it out in color, frame it, and *voilá!*

Also check out the Dover Publications version of *Sports et Divertissements* by Erik Satie. Each little piece about a different pastime is handwritten in Satie's playful calligraphy and comes with an art deco illustration. They are charming to look at as well as to hear.

Last, you can display pages of musical notation through the ages. The Story of the Grand Staff (available for download from the Making Music in Montessori website) comes with examples of Greek, medieval, and classical notation. You can even display some pieces of graphic notation, such as the composer Ivan Wyschnegradsky's beautiful, circular, rainbow-colored "chromatic drawings," which are both beautiful designs *and* musical scores.

Instruments from around the world should grace your shelves as decorative objects or as instruments for the children to play. Carved flutes, a Japanese shamisen, some colorfully decorated Native American drums, tabla, a *mbira,* and other instruments from diverse cultures should complement your musical environment.

Speaking of decorative objects, a musical "living room" feels incomplete if its walls aren't decorated with authentic, framed, high-quality artworks. (Avoid didactic art, like posters that "teach" note values.) Displaying prints of authentic paintings that have music as their theme ties music to history and art. Some paintings that don't depict

musical instruments or musicians, nevertheless, capture the essence of a particular period in Western music. Hang at least one painting from each era of Western music— *ancient, medieval, Renaissance, baroque, classical, Romantic,* and *modern.* Table 3.6 offers some suggestions.

And don't limit yourself to just Western music! Hang colorful, beautiful images from other cultures as well. The African, Chinese, Japanese, or Arabic music traditions, just to name a few, are rich with imagery that represents that culture's music. The book *World Music: Traditions and Transformations* by Michael B. Bakan contains many wonderful illustrations depicting musicians and musical instruments from a wide variety of cultures.

COMPOSING MUSIC

With so many lovely musical objects to look at and to play with, so many books to read, so much music to listen to, and so many beautiful paintings to remind them of music, the children in your classrooms will want to make music of their own. Facilitate their creativity by stocking the room with all the supplies they will need. The Montessori music materials are essential for composition, but Table 3.7 lists some additional materials they will find useful.

Setting up a "living room" for the children testifies to the Montessori teacher's artistry. Alongside your Montessori materials in the mathematics, geography, and other areas of the classroom, pepper your classroom with everything the child needs to experience the joy of music, and you will have set up the optimal venue for delivering Cosmic Education. Your environment truly will have become a "place where the child may live in freedom"

Table 3.6. Paintings to Display in the Environment

Ancient (1500 BC/BCE to 475 AD/CE)

Any painting or sculpture that depicts Greeks, Romans, Etruscans, Egyptians, Native Americans, and so forth, preferably with musical instruments, will do. Paintings of early African, Chinese, or Arab peoples entice the children as well.

Medieval (400–1400)

This era is full of beautiful paintings that depict music-making. Do a Google search or check out Pinterest for lots of great images. Here's one of my favorites:

Muslim and Christian playing outs (thirteenthth century)

Renaissance (1400–1600)

The Lute Player (1596) by Caravaggio

Boy Playing the Lute (1665) by Vermeer

Baroque (1600–1750)

Although they don't depict music or musicians, framed pictures or sketches of baroque architecture highlight the complexities, decorations, and filagree that characterized music of this era. (You'll find out more about musical eras in chapter 4.)

If you prefer something more literal, try *An Elegant Couple with Musical Instruments* (1674) by Johannes Verkolje.

Classical (1750–1820)

A Concert of Frederick the Great (Eighteenth Century) by Adolf Friedrich Erdmann Menzel

Romantic (1820–1900)

The painting *Wanderer above the Sea of Fog* (1818) by Caspar David Friedrich, doesn't depict music or musicians, but it does sum up perfectly the mood of the Romantic Era, with its emphasis on stormy emotions, humanity's role in nature, and the yin-yang of peace and turmoil.

Modern (1900–Present)

Trio (1966) by Steve Magada

Black Man with a Mandolin (1930) André Derain

Table 3.7. Composing Materials

1. Music manuscript paper (print some free at www. blanksheetmusic.net):
   - Music Grid Paper (See appendix D)
   - Three-line staff
   - Five-line staff
   - Five-line staff with one or more lines for percussion
2. Large sheets of poster paper
3. Graph paper with dark lines (both large and small squares)
4. Measuring implements such as rulers of various lengths, triangles, T-squares
5. Graphite pencils (H- and B-sized)
6. Colored pencils
7. Colored markers
8. Scissors
9. Glue sticks
10. Popsicle sticks
11. Black bean bags
12. Rhythm cards with individual rhythmic elements written on them (see chapter 9)
13. Long strips of colored yarn

and experience the "spiritual liberty of internal growth" (Montessori, 1991).

Speaking of internal growth, with the preparation of your environment covered, it's time to prepare the most important aspect of the environment: you. Knowledge of the brass tacks of music will give you confidence in delivering Montessori lessons, fostering musical follow up, and crafting a solid pedagogical plan. The Montessori tone bars hold many secrets; unlock them with a mere turn of the page.

NOTES

1. "Cosmic Education" is the name Maria Montessori gave her pedagogical plan for children from ages six to twelve. The goal of Cosmic Education is to excite the children's imagination with stories and presentations that give them a broad picture of the whole universe, highlighting three important factors: that everything in the universe has a specific task, that human beings have a unique role and status in the universe, and that everything in the universe is interdependent. You will read more about Cosmic Education in chapter 15. For more information, see Mario Montessori's pamphlet *Cosmic Education* (1976).

2. "Grace and Courtesy" refers to the classroom management technique that Montessori teachers use to "teach" the children discipline, rather than boiling discipline down to a set of rules, though helping the children to articulate a set of classroom rules is often a part of the process. Grace and Courtesy begins when the children enter the Montessori program as toddlers and continues into adolescence. It takes the form of a series of short presentations, usually quick role-plays or skits. The Montessori teacher presents Grace and Courtesy lessons to sharpen the children's social skills and improve their behavior. Topics for Grace and Courtesy lessons vary widely depending on the needs of the particular group of children, but they include "how to speak in a soft voice," "how to ask someone politely for something," "how to invite someone to play or work with you," "how to interrupt an adult to ask a question," and more. For more on Grace and Courtesy, see the transcript of a Janet McDonell's lecture "Grace and Courtesy for the Primary Child: Theoretical Foundations" as printed in the 1999 *AMI Journal* entitled *Grace and Courtesy: A Human Responsibility. AMI/USA Conference (Oak Brook, Illinois, June 1998).*

PART 2

ALL THE MUSIC THEORY YOU'LL NEED TO KNOW

Chapter 4

What Is Music, Anyway?

Consider the petals of a daisy. When you look at those elegant tear-drop shapes sticking out of the flower's yellow head, your brain filters out their differences and focuses on their similarities, allowing you to think of them as the same object. Your brain groups them as "flower petals." A computer perceiving those same flower petals, however, would zero in on the differences between the petals. Even the slightest variation would cause the computer to consider each petal to be an entirely different object. This is one of the reasons that human beings were able to invent numbers. Human brains highlight similarities between objects so as to categorize them.

The point is, your brain makes sense of your surroundings using *organizing ideas*. You must have organizing ideas to conceptualize the universe and everything in it, including music. To distinguish certain tones from the other noises in your environment, you must have the organizing idea of *musical pitch*.

And there you have it: music is a form of organized sound. Its principles are so simple that infants can respond to and recognize songs long before they can make any sense of words and sentences. And since we all began our lives as infants, mostly everyone agrees on the same organizing ideas for making sense of tones. People hear tones coming at them, and their brains organize them and agree on their meaning.

Your brain does all the work. Even when you're listening to music, you're making music. When a certain combination of sounds hit your ears, your brain tells you that the sounds feel, for instance, "happy." What's more, people in many different parts of the world organize sounds in a similar way.

In the case of Western music, thanks to discoveries made by the ancient Greeks and refined by European composers and musicians over the centuries, everyone agrees on the idea to organize an octave—that's the measure of distance between the sound of the lowest and highest of the Montessori bells—into twelve distinct

tones. That's it, twelve. Our entire system of music is made up of combinations of twelve notes. Take a look at your Montessori bell setup: you'll see twelve tones.

Likewise, if you start at any tone bar on a Montessori tone bar setup and count to the right twelve tone bars, the next tone bar you come to will be an octave above the note you started with. As you play those tone bars moving to the right, the ruler in your mind measures out each note and tells you that the pitches are getting higher. Similarly, if you just play the notes at random, your brain's ruler tells you that some notes are higher or lower than others, or that some notes are a certain distance apart.

As a matter of fact, play those pitches in any organized way, and your brain organizes those sounds into a structure called a *melody*. We move letters into various positions to create words, and we choose various tones to make melodies. It's that simple. Unlike with language, however, your brain considers a few additional factors to make sense of music.

HIGH AND LOW

When a succession of pitches sounds increasingly higher, your brain tells you that the melody is going "up," and when a succession of pitches sounds sequentially lower, the brain labels the melody as going "down." To your brain, a melody seems to roll along like a wave moving up and down, eventually coming to a stop. Just as you don't need all the letters of an alphabet to make a word, you don't need all twelve pitches in the octave to make a melody. You can create a melody with just one note!

Find a note on the piano, and play it three times. The first two times, play the note short, and then, on the third time, play it long. Repeat that. Do you recognize that melody? If you grew up in the West, you will likely recognize the song "Jingle Bells."

If you can make such a catchy melody with just one note out of the twelve, think about how many catchy melodies you can make with two! Beethoven only used two for the opening motif of his Fifth Symphony. With *four* tones out of the possible twelve, you can make even more melodies. Using the notes C, D, E, and G, for instance, you can reproduce the beginning of *Begin the Beguine* by Cole Porter. Scramble those four notes, play them backward or play them in random order, and you can make melodies by Tchaikovsky or Jerome Kern.

What's more, you can make those same high and low patterns from any notes of the twelve, just as you can play the opening notes of "Jingle Bells" from any one note of the twelve. You could play "Mary Had a Little Lamb" using F#-E-D or E-D-C, and your brain would recognize the tune in either case. The ruler in your mind measures the same pitch relationship, regardless of what note you begin with. The distance between D and A is the same as the distance between C and G, just as the distance of an inch is the same whether you measure it from the ocean floor or from the top of Mt. Everest.

LONG AND SHORT

But hang on! If a melody comprises a succession of highs and lows, undulating like a wave, how come the first notes of "Jingle Bells" are considered a melody? After all, the note never goes up or down, it stays the same. The answer is that just because the notes don't go up and down doesn't mean the melody isn't shaped like a wave. You can think of a line, after all, as a wave without peaks.

More important, however, is the fact that a melody doesn't just organize itself by highs and lows; it also includes longs and shorts. Our brains organize notes by *duration* as well as by pitch. That means that you have a vertical ruler in your mind that measures distances in pitch and also a horizontal ruler in your mind that measures distances in duration, or time. Your brain understands that in every melody, some notes are wider than others in time, or "long," and some notes are narrower than others in time, or "short."

Furthermore, your brain must have a simple and well-organized idea of time to be able to organize oncoming tones by duration. It requires a regular, steady clock ticking in your mind in order to make and comprehend a pattern of tones by their widths. That regular tick-tock feeling, that built-in clock, is another organizing idea that people share about music. An inner clock makes it possible for us to recognize something called a *steady beat*. Human beings use this capacity to measure the duration of incoming sounds the moment they begin to hear music.

Using the idea of steady beat, your brain can organize and reorganize patterns of durations in recognizable melodies regardless of the highs and lows. Take, for example, the pitches G-C-E-E-D-C. Vary the widths of those notes in particular ways, and you'll get the opening of "Red River Valley," the Serenade in D and Concerto in A by Mozart, Beethoven's Sonata No. 2 in A, and the second movement of his Symphony No. 5. In each of those melodies the up and down pattern is the same. The difference is in the durations (wides and narrows).

You can see that as long as you and those around you are all using your internal "time-telling" system in the same way, then you can all organize oncoming single tones according to their height in space and their width in time to make meaning from music.

COMFORTABLE AND UNCOMFORTABLE

Suppose you arrive at school one morning, but everything has changed. Your neatly arranged shelves have been replaced by a giant round white-and-red-striped ring. In the middle of the ring lie scattered bits of bark chips and hay. Where your gathering rug used to be stands a lion. On the ground in front of the animal are a whip and some hoops. This would be an unusual setting for a Montessori teacher. Would you feel a little unsettled? Uncomfortable?

Well, it turns out that what makes a note feel restless and uncomfortable is the very same thing that makes a person feel unsettled or tense: *the setting*. A person who would be perfectly at ease in a ring with a whip and a lion might feel completely out of place in a classroom full of thirty independently working children. (Still a third person might feel quite at ease in both, considering that at times both settings feel quite similar.)

Likewise, certain notes feel uncomfortable when surrounded by certain other notes. Discomfort, however, doesn't prevent anyone from enjoying the entertainment. In fact, people eat up stories in which characters experience a degree of tension, restlessness, and discomfort—in a word *excitement*. Audiences take pleasure in the tension being resolved. People come back to those stories again and again even though they are familiar and even formulaic. For that very same reason, people love music that has uncomfortable, tense, unresolved tones followed by comfortable, resolved ones.

A formula for the comfort of a pitch, along with the high or low and width of a pitch, becomes another agreed-upon organizing factor in making music. The comfort formula doesn't have a fancy musical name. In general, the idea of comfort in music is called *harmony*, and a formula for creating harmony a *chord*.

A chord *in its most basic form* constitutes a formula consisting of three comfortable notes out of the possible twelve. These three notes when sounded together result in complete repose and restfulness. The moment a melody begins, your brain pulls together those three basic chord tones, and the mind's ear then scans the oncoming tones in the melody, categorizing them as comfortable and uncomfortable.

If you have an agreed-upon setting for what feels comfortable, then anything that belongs in that setting creates comfort, and anything that doesn't belong creates discomfort. Since a basic chord pulls together notes that sound comfortable together, that means that out of all the possible incoming tones, some will sound resolved, or settled, and others will sound unresolved, or tense. Put simply, in any given melody, some notes are *in the chord,* and some notes are *out of the chord.*

It's the same way with people. Suppose you leave work and instead of walking into the parking lot you find yourself walking into the middle of a wintry forest. At first, you might find it quite pretty there. After a short time wandering around, however, you'll start to get hungry and cold, and you'll long to be settled in the comfort of your warm, cozy home.

Notes feel the same way. A note that's out of place in a chord will want desperately to settle down into the harmony where it's most comfortable. This is called *resolution.* Music encompasses agreed-upon patterns of comfortable *chordal* tones and restless, *nonchordal* notes that long to come to rest—or *resolve*—on a chordal tone.

If you want to hear what this sounds like, get three other friends and head to your tone bar setup. Tell everyone you're going to start by playing a basic three-note chord. Starting with you, pick out any note you like and play it with your mallet. We'll designate this note to be the *root* of the chord.

Now have your first friend skip ahead four tone bars and play that note while you play the root note. Sound comfortable?

Let's add another note. Ask your second friend to skip three more tone bars and play the next note, adding it to your previous two notes. Play all three notes together simultaneously. Now you have a basic chord.

At this point, your fourth friend can play any of the other twelve notes one at a time. As he does so, decide which notes out of the other twelve sound comfortable against your basic three-note chord, and which ones sound unsettled, or restless.

You may discover that when you play a comfortable chord, any notes in the melody that are members of the chord will sound comfortable and at rest. If you play a C chord, for example, which consists of a cozy combination of C, E, and G, then any Cs, Es, or Gs in the melody will

sound at rest and resolved. Other notes, however, will not sound resolved and will want to immediately move to C, E, or G.

If you want to hear what this sounds like, play the first tone bar. That's C. Now have one friend skip up four tone bars to the tone bar called E, and have the other friend skip three more tone bars to the tone bar called G. Play those three notes simultaneously and you have a chord. Now, have your fourth friend play some melodies using the notes in between C and E, or E and G, occasionally including a C, E, or G. The notes in between the chord tones should sound like they want to go either up or down to one of the notes in your chord. How does it feel if your friend just lingers on a black note? Pretty unsettled, right?

As if by magic, you can move this pattern up and down the tone bars. From whatever note you choose, as long as you skip up four notes and then up three more and play all three notes, you'll get a nice, comfortable, three-note chord. Those comfortable notes make the other twelve notes feel unsettled and uncomfortable, no matter which notes you pick.

This interplay between discomfort and comfort, tension and resolution, restfulness and restlessness, creates *movement* in music. It tells us when a melody has begun, when it ends, and when it comes to a pause. It also tells us how simple or sophisticated a melody is. You might think of melodies that contain lots of notes of the chord as simple, because they sound comfortable, peaceful, and safe. On the other hand, you think of melodies that contain lots of notes that are out of the chord as more sophisticated. Sophisticated melodies feel more unsettled, more uncomfortable, more restless.

A BRIEF HISTORY OF WESTERN ORGANIZED SOUND

Again, music constitutes organized sound. In a nutshell, your brain considers three factors when organizing sounds into music: how high a tone is (pitch), how long it lasts (duration), and how comfortable it is (harmony)? (There are a few other factors, but they are beyond the scope of this book.) When your brain perceives an organizing idea of sound that seems to skillfully juggle pitch, duration, and harmony, you experience pleasure. The thing is, people from cultures in different parts of the world have different opinions about which organizing ideas they find most pleasurable.

In some cultures, for example, people love the sound of the notes in between the twelve notes in use in the Western part of the world. To Western ears, these *quarter tones,* as they have been called, sound out of tune and strange. To Eastern ears, without quarter tones, Western music can sound simplistic and childish.

How did this happen? How did different cultures come to agree among themselves what sounds are pleasing, and why do tastes between cultures differ? This topic is one of the things focused on by ethnomusicologists.

Maria Montessori based her music materials on the organized patterns of sound that people in the Western world agree on, and you can get the most use for the moment out of a more specific question: How did people in the Western part of the world come to agree on the organizing ideas of sounds *they* find most pleasing?

Obviously, it didn't happen overnight. In fact, it happened over thousands of years. You could say that the history of music in the West is the history of how people came to accept and enjoy increasingly unsettled, uncomfortable—in other words, sophisticated—patterns of organized sound.

PREHISTORIC AND ANCIENT MUSIC

Ug and his friend Grunt, a couple of Neanderthals, walk back to their camp. Fresh to Ug's mind comes the sound of the water rushing down the river where they were fishing. He notices a flat, slanted stone nearby. He scoops up a handful of small rocks and drops them onto the larger slanted stone. He likes how the rocks bouncing off the stone make a repeated sound like the water rushing in the river. On another day, Ug and Grunt seek shelter from a thunderstorm. After the storm passes, Ug stretches a dry animal skin over a hollow log and hits it to imitate the sound of thunder.

Of course, Ug and Grunt didn't exist, but their story rings true: historians believe that the earliest forms of music were probably drum-based, percussion instruments like rocks and sticks, which were likely readily available. Early humans may have used such instruments in religious ceremonies or to imitate the sounds of animals or nature. You know this because you can listen to the indigenous music of some Native American and African tribes, some of whom who still play music in the manner of their prehistoric ancestors.

But early humans also had voices. In addition to their drumming, they also probably used their voices to imitate animals and nature. It's hard to say whether they made up melodies, of course, since none of their music is written down. Perhaps Grunt made the sound of the rain with his voice, while Ug beat away on his drum. No one will ever know. But it's safe to guess that as early as human beings used their voices, they probably did some form of singing.

Regardless, Ug and Grunt were most likely limited by what was available to them: percussion instruments, simple wind instruments made from hollowed-out sticks and bones, and their voices. More complex musical instruments developed slowly over time. By 4000 BCE the Egyptians had created harps, and by 3500 BCE they had lyres and double-reed clarinets. One thousand years later, people in what is today's Denmark developed a valve-less trumpet in which pitch changes depended solely on the manipulation of the player's lips. Not long after that, around 1500 BCE, the Hittites came up with an early version of the guitar. Using frets to change the pitch of a string was quite an innovation.

By that time, human beings had all agreed that simply imitating the sounds of nature with their voices or on percussion instruments was not satisfying enough, and they began to organize sounds in more complex ways. They combined instruments with voices, for example. Songs dating from 700 BCE include voices accompanied by instruments.

THE GREEKS

At this point in the history of music everyone in the Western part of the world began to agree on which organized sounds make up "Western" music. In fact, when Pythagoras developed his theories about dividing up the octave into a scale around 500 BCE, he laid the first brick in that complex edifice known in the West as "music theory." Using Pythagoras's theories as a launching point, the early Greeks developed and gave fancy names to a variety of different scales—ordered series of tones—that they called *modes*. If you hum to yourself the song "Greensleeves," you'll hear a melody built from the Greek *Dorian mode*.

The Greeks thought their musical scales, or modes, had great power to influence human behavior. They were convinced, for example, that a certain king was roused to arms by hearing a flute play a melody in the Phrygian mode. Plato, the great Greek philosopher believed that hearing the Phrygian mode would make a man effeminate.

Because the Greeks had lots of leisure time, they were able to make great strides in music. Around 350 BCE, Aristotle brought about a form of musical notation that people still study today. But it was a Greek named Boethius who, in 521 CE brought musical notation to Western Europe. There, thanks to Boethius, the Europeans began to use the Greek's primitive form of notation to transcribe the folk songs of their lands. (Incidentally, Boethius was one of the first to write what we would now call an opera.)

THE MEDIEVAL PERIOD (*c.* 500–1400 CE)

After the Roman Empire fell in 476 CE, Europe dissolved into a smattering of small city-states. Nobody really had a collective organizing idea about music. Eventually, the Catholic Church rose to prominence and became the center of learning, culture, and the arts.

In 650 CE, Pope Gregory built the first music school in Europe, the Schola Cantorum. He arranged and collected a group of choral works in the form of chants. No one knows who wrote these Gregorian chants, but they were recorded as one unaccompanied melodic line, because the Church forbade the use of instruments and even prohibited singing in harmony. In fact, the Church was very strict about the character of the melodic lines people could sing. They only allowed certain comfortable notes. Notes with tension were considered sinful.

Originally, Gregorian church chants were passed on from generation to generation orally, but around 650, a new system of writing music using markings called *neumes* came about. Neumes were interesting little markings whose contours showed the high and low properties of a pitch. Unfortunately, neumes didn't tell a singer how high or how low to sing nor did they tell the singer what note to start from. So, the choir all had to agree on a starting note and basically find their way through the music together.

Over time, more and more people became interested in music as a vocation. The first music attributed to a particular composer came onto the scene. Notable composers of the time included Hildegard of Bingen (1098–1179), Perotin (1155–1377), and John Dunstable (1385–1453).

Music schools sprang up all over Europe. After Emperor Charlemagne had a collection of poems and psalms set to music, music became more fashionable within the Church. In 850 CE, Catholic musicians invented a series of Church modes, after the fashion of the Greeks. These modes gave rise to our present system of major and minor scales (which you'll read more about in the next chapter).

After a long period of singing unaccompanied, people began to experiment with new sounds. By 855 CE, the first *polyphonic*—two or more voices sung simultaneously—music was written. Over the next 200 years, polyphonic music overtook Gregorian chant as the fashion in the Catholic Mass. The Church eventually had to buckle under the pressure and lift its ban on singing in parts.

Then, along came Guido d'Arezzo (*c.* 990–1050), an Italian who made some marked improvements in music theory. He improved notation by adding staff lines and time signatures—ways to organize the vertical ruler of music in our brains. He was also the person who gave

pitches in a scale the names *do* (then called *ut*), *re, mi, fa, sol, la, ti,* and *do.* This was called *solfège*—an innovation that is still in use today.

Of course, although the Church was the center of learning about music, it wasn't the only place music was happening. Outside the cathedral walls, musicians sang in parts and played instruments, but their primitive "folk" music was frowned upon as pagan and deemed blasphemous. After 1400, however, as music spread outside the Church, people introduced more and more sophisticated organizing ideas for music.

THE RENAISSANCE PERIOD (*c.* 1400–1600)

Although it still remained the dominant influence in society, starting around 1400, the Church was beginning to lose influence in music. As people started to move toward more humanistic ways of thinking and look toward the literary and artistic heritage of ancient Greece and Rome, music became more secular. As a result, it became increasingly innovative and more sophisticated. Polyphonic music evolved to contain more and more voices singing together. People used instruments in new combinations, including *antiphonal* music where instruments seemed to "converse" with each other. Composers experimented with less comfortable sounds.

The Protestant Reformation in the 1500s saw the Church with its hands full, unable to regulate even the music under its own roof. New musical forms, such as motets, madrigals, and songs, were evolving alongside the old Catholic Mass, at the time the world's most prevalent large-scale composition. People were improving old musical instruments such as the violin, the lute, and keyboard instruments, and inventing new ones, such as the bassoon and trombone, giving rise to instrumental combinations that were previously forbidden.

The growth of commerce and the rise of the bourgeois class meant that the Church wasn't the only patron of music. Now, rich people hired composers to write music for important ceremonies such as christenings, weddings, and funerals. Nor were churches the only places people could go to listen to music. Thanks to Johann Gutenberg's printing press, people could write, print, and sell music. Theorists began to publish treatises on musical theory, and some of these perspectives encouraged the expansion of what the average person's ears deemed acceptable. It was during the Renaissance that printed notation started move toward what it looks like today.

As music became free of medieval constraints, composers were moved to write music solely for personal expression. They started to write music that reflected the texts they were setting. They wrote music not only for worship but also for entertainment. Remember Boethius? In 1490, his opera writings were published in Italian. Other notable composers of the Renaissance were Guillaume Du Fay (1397–1474), Josquin des Prez (*ca.* 1450–1521), and Pierluigi da Palestrina (1525/1526–1594). The music they wrote for its own sake blurred the lines between secular and sacred music as they sought out new sounds to satisfy their emotional needs.

Those comfortable sounds mentioned earlier, that basic three-note chord, began to become ingrained at this time. As more and more vocal lines were sung together, people decided which harmonies they liked best, and those harmonies were characterized by unsettled, unstable notes resolving into settled, stable notes. The church modes began to dissolve into a system of comfortable and uncomfortable sounds that is not unlike the system we're used to today. This system was called *functional tonality,* and after 1600, it really caught on.

THE BAROQUE PERIOD (*c.* 1600–1750)

For its time, the music of the baroque period was considered crazy and uninhibited. The name of the era comes from the Portuguese word *barroco,* which means *imperfect pearl.* It was actually a snide criticism of the flamboyantly decorated Pamphilj Palace in Rome, but it caught on as a description of the music of this era, which was also very busy and filled with frills and decorative flourishes.

The busyness and complexity of baroque music shocked and amazed its listeners with its quick chord changes and violent changes of volume and melody. Famous composers of the baroque period include Johann Pachelbel (1653–1706), Jean-Baptiste Lully (1632–1687), Antonio Vivaldi (1678–1741), and Johann Sebastian Bach (1685–1750).

During the baroque period, the centralized court had a great influence on music. (This was the point at which classical music began to gain its stuffy reputation.) The lifestyle of Louis XIV of France, with his gigantic palace and his court system of arts and manners, became a model for all of Europe. Wealthy noblemen began holding intimate salons or commissioning large-scale musical works for public performance.

The result was a demand for musical instruments and innovations in instrumentation. Small chamber music ensembles performed in wealthy people's courts, while huge ensembles played for public performances. Dance music became popular, and wealthy audiences enjoyed operas as well as oratorios (the latter being dramas sung by a choir accompanied by instruments rather than staged). The harpsichord became the favorite instrument for accompaniment.

As musical ensembles grew larger and more varied, so did musical forms. Composers featured individual instruments accompanied by a small orchestra in *concertos*—long multimovement pieces of music whose movements were marked by sharp contrasts of soft, loud, fast, and slow. Within each movement, composers pitted sections played by the whole ensemble and sections played by only a few instruments against each other.

During the baroque period, at around 1650, and established what we refer to today as *tonality.* Instead of simply combining independent lines, composers started to think in terms of moving patterns of harmonic tension and relaxation called *chord progressions.* Like individual tones, some chords sounded very restful, whereas others needed to resolve into the more restful chords. For baroque composers, chords, rather than single notes, created a sense of restlessness and closure.

Of course, baroque composers still combined independent melodic lines, a practice called *counterpoint,* but they made sure their lines fit comfortably into the quickly changing harmonies. In this way, they were similar to weavers creating a tapestry: they paid attention to how each individual thread (a melody line) fit into the pattern as a whole (the harmony.) In fact, chords and chord progressions became so ingrained during the baroque period that instead of writing out every note, composers wrote shorthand chord symbols at the bottom of the music for the keyboard player to interpret.

Musicians today still use many of the innovations of the baroque period, including changes in notation and in instrumental playing techniques.

THE CLASSICAL PERIOD (*c.* 1730–1820)

At around the middle of the eighteenth century, European art and architecture began to move toward a style that emphasized the ideals of classical antiquity, in particular those of classical Greece. Artists, architects, authors, and composers in general sought a "cleaner" style, with clearer divisions between parts, brighter contrasts and colors, and simplicity rather than complexity. Instead of being heavy, gallant, and full of grandeur, music became lighter and more elegant.

Thanks to the rising economy in European countries, the middle class grew. As people began making more money, they wanted luxuries that courtiers had, such as theater, literature, and music. Because the courts of the wealthy aristocrats were closed to the public, middle-class people held concerts. Many people, however, were not satisfied with having to go to concerts all the time.

Like their wealthy counterparts, middle-class people wanted to have music in their homes. They bought musical instruments and got their children lessons so their children could play as well as aristocratic children. The resulting demand for music drove many composers to write music for the public, music that amateur musicians could play. Notable composers of the classical period were C. P. E. Bach (1714–1788), Franz Joseph Haydn (1732–1809), Wolfgang Amadeus Mozart (1756–1791), and Ludwig van Beethoven (1770–1827).

Composers rejected the busy, decorated, complex music of the baroque in favor of structural clarity. Long, rambling baroque melodies gave way to small, digestible phrases that followed predictable patterns and had clear beginnings and endings. Music of this time was largely *homophonic*, meaning it was made up of a clear melody over a subordinate chordal accompaniment.

Chords became an even more prominent feature of music. Harmony gave melody structure, and the tonality of a piece of music became more obvious. Counterpoint wasn't abandoned completely, but, in general, the complex tapestry of independent melodies took a backseat to a simple, neatly phrased melody accompanied by a discernible harmony.

Themes—short melodic ideas—rather than whole movements, became the main vehicle for a composer's personal expression. Whereas in the baroque period, large, dramatic emotions were expressed in one entire lengthy section of a piece, in the classical period, emotions shifted within a single section of a piece.

The simplification of music into a melodic line with accompaniment meant that composers could emphasize details of dynamics and phrasing. As a result, contrasts became more pronounced. The invention of the piano fostered this enthusiasm for contrast. The piano could play loudly or softly, unlike the harpsichord. Eventually, the piano replaced the harpsichord as the favorite keyboard solo instrument.

Orchestras grew larger and increased in range. The harpsichord, the driving force of the baroque orchestra, fell out of use. The woodwinds got their own self-contained section. Instrumental music became more important as a result, with new, complex forms. An important form for instrumental music called *sonata form*, which is a kind of "hero's journey" of music, developed and became the most important form for the beginnings of large-scale works. (You'll read about sonata form in chapter 7.)

After about 1790, the classical style began to change dramatically. Ludwig van Beethoven (1770–1823) and others strove for even greater personal expression in music. Beethoven, in particular, expanded the classical style by writing more complex, emotionally expressive music, expanding the length and scope of the symphony, and giving more prominence to the harmonic accompaniment of the homophonic texture. Beethoven's innovations paved the way for more drama, more emotion, and more complexity in music.

THE ROMANTIC PERIOD (*c.* 1780–1910)

The drama, emotion, and complexity that Beethoven brought to music bubbled over during the Romantic period. In fact, elegance, lightness, and clarity of structure went out the window in favor of musical gestures that expressed the composer's emotional whims. This *romanticism,* as critics and scholars of the time called it, fueled in part by the Industrial Revolution, was a revolt of sorts by artists, authors, and musicians against Enlightenment thinking and the classical tendency to seek order and rationalization in nature.

Instead of writing music for its own sake, Romantic composers wrote music that explored or represented emotional, supernatural, exotic, natural, and spiritual themes. Many composers wrote pieces that conveyed a strong sense of nationalism (feelings of pride in one's homeland) and exoticism (feelings of fascination with a foreign land or culture). Exoticism was particularly reflective of the Romantic obsession with all things remote, picturesque, and mysterious.

Notable composers of this era were Johannes Brahms (1833–1897), Franz Schubert (1797–1828), Robert Schumann (1810–1856), Clara Schumann (1840–1856), Hector Berlioz (1803–1869), Antonin Dvôrak (1841–1904), Gustav Mahler (1860–1911), Franz Liszt (1811–1886), and Richard Wagner (1813–1883).

During earlier periods, composers had specific jobs, such as the music director of a church or court. In the Romantic period, composers freelanced. Beethoven was among the first musicians to freelance and to compose for his own pleasure. He inspired other composers to do the same.

Despite their independence, however, composers didn't make much money. This might have been because their biggest patrons were now members of the middle class, who also didn't have much money but who were continuing to grow and demand music in their homes. Giant orchestral works found themselves transcribed for the piano and played in people's homes. Many middle-class people in the Romantic era wanted to become musicians themselves. Public orchestras became more popular, and music conservatories sprang up all over Europe and in the United States.

Program music—music written to follow a story, poem, idea, or scene—became fashionable during the Romantic period. In a piece of program music, the instruments could represent characters, emotions, events, or the sounds and motion of nature. The earliest and most important piece of program music was the *Symphonie Fantastique* by Hector Berlioz, which tells the story of an artist whose longing for his beloved drives him to overdose on opium. The French composer Claude Debussy wrote much of his music in the "program" style. His piece *La Mer* is one of the finest examples of the genre.

An important form of program music was the *tone poem,* a single movement orchestral work that rendered an idea, a scene, or an emotion. In contrast with the structure of the symphony, the structure for tone poems came not from musical ideas, such as melodies and harmonies, but from their extramusical subject matter. Many Romantic composers wrote tone poems, but a master of the genre was Richard Strauss (1864–1949), whose *An Alpine Symphony* depicts in music the experiences of eleven hours (from daybreak until nightfall) climbing an Alpine mountain.

In general, the Romantics emphasized tone color over melody and structure. Romantic composers wanted the audience to feel a particular mood or atmosphere, so they sought new sounds and new harmonies. For the first time, they began to use all twelve of the notes in the octave so they could find new ways to create and resolve tension. They wrote extremely dissonant chords, releasing them into more stable consonant chords to create feelings of deep yearning, passion, tension, and mystery.

Composers during the Romantic period stretched the limits that had been established in the classical period. The nineteenth century was a time of considerable contrasts in size, technique, dynamics, and instrumentation. Composers wrote works of both staggering immensity and staggering brevity. Franz Liszt's sprawling, multivolume piano work, the *Années de pèlerinage (Years of Pilgrimage),* contrasts with Robert Schumann's collection of short piano pieces, *Kinderszenen (Scenes from Childhood).*

Music of the period contained sections of incredible virtuosity and childlike simplicity. Dynamics such as *fffff* (really loud) and *ppppp* (really soft) appeared in scores. Works written for hundreds of musicians existed alongside works written for a string quartet. Composers like Gustav Mahler, with his *Symphony of a Thousand,* and Richard Wagner, with his endless epic operas, pushed the limits in all directions.

IMPRESSIONISM AND MODERNISM
(*c.* 1875–1975)

The culmination of the Romantic tendency toward dissonant, uncomfortable harmonies resulted in tonality itself being tossed out the window. By the turn of the twentieth century, composers were experimenting with ways to dissolve feelings of comfort in music altogether by focusing solely on uncomfortable notes and harmonies. Some used non-Western scales as a basis for their music, while others invented their own scales and, indeed, entire systems of composition.

In France, Impressionist composers—inspired by the painting of artists such as Claude Monet and Pierre-Auguste Renoir—wrote music that rejected structure altogether in favor of rendering a mood or an impression of a subject rather than presenting a detailed tone picture. Claude Debussy (1862–1918) and Maurice Ravel (1875–1937) helped spearhead the Impressionist movement.

Composers during the last half of the Romantic era challenged and reinterpreted older trends in music and found new ways to organize and structure their musical ideas. Arnold Schoenberg (1874–1951), for instance, experimented with *atonal music*—a controversial term meaning music without a tonal center or home tone—eventually coming up with an entire system of composing music using all twelve tones of the octave in most uncomfortable combinations.

People associated atonality with Expressionism, a genre that explored subjective human experience and the darker side of human emotions, such as anger, fear, and anxiety. Along with Expressionism came all kinds of other-isms: Hyperrealism, Abstractionism, Neoclassicism, Neobarbarism, and Futurism, to name a few. The scope of all of these movements goes beyond the scope of this book. Suffice it to say, in the twentieth century, those twelve little notes in the octave got quite a workout as Western music spun in many new directions.

TWENTIETH CENTURY (*c.* 1900–2000)

In the short span of a hundred years, composers took the comfortable sounds that most people agreed were pleasant to the ear and threw them up in the air, scattered them about, and then put them back together again. No one style characterized the time, and composers explored every style imaginable. Tone color became more important than ever as composers added new, unconventional instruments such as xylophones (the big orchestral kind, not the classroom kind), magnetic tape machines, and computer sounds to the mix. Irregularity, atonality, and unpredictability became the only constant.

After World War I, Arnold Schoenberg's use of *atonality* blossomed into a technique he called *twelve-tone,* or *serial composition.* Schoenberg's system was an offshoot of Expressionism and featured the twelve tones of the chromatic scale arranged carefully so that all the tones could be experienced equally. The result was a disconcerting kind of music. Nevertheless, twelve-tone composition caught on, and the comfortable tonal system, for a while, was abandoned by many composers.

After a while, composers again started to look toward the past and started to build compositions based on traditional tonality again. These Neoclassicists included Igor Stravinsky (1882–1971) and Sergei Prokofiev (1891–1953).

This return to the past didn't last long, however, and soon composers were exploring the limits of tonality once again. Composers called Futurists incorporated everyday sounds, like those of machines and airplanes into their music. Microtonal composers even explored tones in between the twelve tones of the octave and wrote music in quarter tones! In the 1940s and 1950s, composers applied technology to music. Computers, magnetic tape, synthesizers, and other multimedia became the staple of a form of music called *musique concréte.*

In the 1950s, composers even stopped composing music and instead left everything up to chance. The American composer John Cage (1912–1992) was one of the first to start experimenting not so much with composing music as with setting up situations in which the resulting music was unpredictable, or determined by chance. Cage's experiments gave rise to *process music,* in which a composer explores a single compositional process which he or she lays bare in the work. Other forms of *chance music* arose, such as *minimalism,* in which composers combined the smallest, simplest rhythmic or melodic elements possible into unexpected or unintentional sounds.

Cultural trends also informed music of the twentieth century. In Russia, composers like Igor Stravinsky created a vision of early human cultures in his *Rite of Spring.* Dmitri Shostakovich (1906–1975) was forced to write music within the structures of the Soviet government's strict tenets of Socialist Realism. American composers created a unique sound and vocabulary of their own in music that featured an open, expansive sound reminiscent of the wide prairie. Composers from Spanish-speaking, Scandinavian, African, and Eastern European countries, as well as Japanese composers, infused their music with their cultural heritage.

Finally, the twentieth century gave rise to many diverse genres and styles of music, each with its own distinct organizing principles and musical vocabulary.

Beginning as early as the 1920s, a wedge drove itself in between "classical music"—Western art music—and "popular" music—almost everything else.

The United States, in particular, was the birthplace of many new genres such as the blues, jazz, rock 'n' roll, pop, folk, country, hip-hop, and more. Styles from other world cultures began to make their way into Western music as well. Indian music found its way into rock 'n' roll by the end of the 1960s, followed by African drumming, reggae, and Latin music by the 1980s and 1990s. The twentieth century offers a kaleidoscope of colorful sounds and patterns for our brains to decipher.

It's staggering to think that so many styles and varieties of Western music arose out of the endless variants of that original idea of how to organize sound: those twelve tones that were used to divide the octave. Centuries of music, primarily based on twelve notes! The concept is similar to the color combinations our eyes decode from the seven colors of the rainbow, or all of the words you can create from the twenty-six letters in the English alphabet.

Now it's time to look at these twelve notes in detail. You'll learn how those notes are organized into scales and how they're put together to make chords. You'll learn about the distances between notes and about which of those distances are generally accepted as sounding restful and comfortable, and which ones are generally accepted as sounding uncomfortable.

Speaking of uncomfortable, if you're feeling like putting this book down or throwing it into the recycling bin because you suspect it's about to launch into a conversation about the dreaded "music theory," please reconsider!

Remember that the name of this part of the book is "All the Music Theory You'll Need to Know," not "Everything There Is to Know about Music Theory." In other words, you're only going to examine those twelve notes you see laid out before you on your Montessori tone bars (twenty-four, when you consider that the notes repeat at the octave). That's all the music theory you'll need to be able to work wonders with the children you teach.

Not that you're going to just sit and teach your children music theory. You will be delivering exciting and fun Montessori music lessons. The information in this part of the book sheds light on the theory underpinning the concepts in those Montessori music lessons so you will have the knowledge and confidence to dust off your music album and get the children in your class organizing the sounds in their world into a beautiful tapestry of music.

Chapter 5

First Steps

The brilliant musician Bobby McFerrin often performs a wonderful routine involving his audience. To begin, McFerrin indicates a spot on the stage and gets the audience to sing a certain pitch when he jumps on that spot.

Each time he jumps on the spot, the audience sings the pitch.

Next, McFerrin indicates a space about a foot to his left and gives the audience a slightly higher pitch to sing when he leaps into that spot.

He leaps; they sing the new pitch.

McFerrin then hops back and forth between the two spots, with the audience singing each of the two pitches.

He then adds more pitches in the same way, until soon he's leaping around the stage, "playing" different melodies on an imaginary floor piano whose sound is generated by the audience's voices.

What a sophisticated display of abstract thinking on the part of the people in McFerrin's audience! As McFerrin jumps around, the audience makes a connection between the physical distance between the different spots on the stage and the difference in sound between the various pitches.

This rather fundamental concept forms the basis for the structure of the Montessori bells. Two bells adjacent to each other make sounds that are only *slightly* higher or lower, while two bells much farther apart make sounds that are *considerably* higher or lower. Likewise, on the tone bar setup, the farther apart two tone bars sit, the wider the musical interval between them.

Think of a ruler. Just as you measure distances in space using a ruler, you measure distances in sound with your ears. Distances in sound are called *intervals*. The smallest distance in sound between any two of the twelve Montessori bells is a *half step*.

Take a look at your full Montessori bell setup, black bells and all. Does the pattern of black and white bells look familiar? Maria Montessori and her colleague Anna Maccheroni fashioned the bells after a piano keyboard.

Each bell sits a half step apart. Play two adjacent bells. That's what a half step sounds like. Now play one bell, but skip a bell, and play the next one. You just played a *whole step*.

Half steps and whole steps play a crucial role in music.

SCALES AND MODES

Many of the musical concepts prevalent in Western culture were first described in classical Greece, but the Greeks borrowed their musical concepts from more Eastern parts of the world. Remember Pythagoras, who divided up a string into different pitches? Many of the basic concepts he systemized came from Persian music, the Persians being one of the cultures that uses not only half steps and whole steps but also quarter steps—tones that are *in between* half steps.

In other parts of the East, organized chains of pitches called *ragas* form a remarkable and central feature of Indian music. Ragas are musical frameworks comprising an array of at least five pitches arranged into small *motifs* that Indian musicians consider to "color the mind" or affect the emotions of the listener. The musician can improvise using specific notes within a raga. Other Eastern scales contain a distinct spacing of intervals that create rich, colorful sounds. All over the world, people use patterns of half steps and whole steps to derive musical color palettes called *scales and modes*.

Once Pythagoras found pitches he liked, he ordered them in various combinations all the way up or down up to the distance of an *octave*—the musical interval between any pitch and the higher or lower iteration of itself. (The Montessori tone bars span two octaves.) Pythagoras and other Greeks gave the resulting modes names like *Ionian, Dorian,* and *Phrygian,* based on the regions in which each supposedly originated.

But the Greek modes were complicated and full of patterns of disparate intervals. Imagine trying to measure distance with a ruler whose markings are first an inch apart, then a quarter-inch apart, then a centimeter apart. That's what Greek modes sound like to some people today.

And yet the ancient Greeks agreed among themselves that their modes were beautiful and, like the ragas of the Indian musicians, powerful enough to influence a person's behavior! During the Middle Ages, some leaders in the Catholic Church heard the Greek modes and thought, "Blasphemy!" They rejected all the Greek modes except for a few that they labeled the more "godly" ones, which they modestly designated as *Church modes*.

The upshot of all this? A scale constitutes an arbitrary selection of notes used to divide the octave. That definition has two important parts. First, the scale, any scale, divides the octave. Second, scales are *human-made*. People in the Western world share general agreement about some scales. Other scales are in use and agreed upon by people of other cultures, and still other scales are used only by a select group of composers and agreed upon by their devoted listeners (and few others).

Maria Montessori based her bells and tone bars on a scale that enjoys general agreement among people in the West. Composers of the baroque era used this scale about four centuries ago. These composers were tired of not being able to make sense of the Greek modes or the Church modes, so they divided the octave arbitrarily into a neat line of twelve tones, all exactly a half-step apart. Unfortunately, at the time, when they played the notes of this *chromatic scale* in an ascending or descending sequence, it didn't sound very nice. The sound didn't seem like it went anywhere. It was all tension and no release.

Today, we still learn and perform music with the most common scale used during the baroque period. Funnily enough, it's similar to the Greek mode called *Ionian*. It's a scale of only seven of the twelve notes (eight, if you count the one at the very top, which is essentially the same as the one at the bottom) arranged in a pattern of whole step, whole step, half step, whole step, whole step, whole step, half step. If you want to hear this scale on the Montessori bells, remove the black bells and play just the white bells from left to right starting from the first bell on the left.

THE MAJOR SCALE

This scale should sound familiar to you. It's our traditional, agreed-upon, basic, *do re mi* scale. It's our major scale. The white Montessori bells, taken together, comprise a major scale.

The pattern of half- and whole-steps is like the fingerprint of the major scale. To demonstrate this, again head over to your tone bar setup. Take out your major scale pattern strip, which should have numbers spaced like in figure 5.1.

Place the strip below the tone bars with 1 on any note you like. Now pull down the tone bars that correspond to the numbers and play the scale up and down. Doesn't that sound like a major scale? Try placing your scale strip with 1 on a different note. Play those tone bars. Same sound, right, just higher or lower? That's because the pattern of half- and whole-steps gives a scale its *identity*.

In other words, scales have structure. Just as the chromatic scale consists of twelve notes each separated by a half step, the structure of the major scale, no matter which note you start on, consists of eight notes separated by two whole steps, a half step, three more whole steps, and then another half step. As you move the scale strip up or down, you'll find that the scales only differ in that their pitches become higher or lower. The scale itself sounds the same because the pattern of half and whole steps remains unchanged. *Voilà:* the magic of *transposition*.

It's as if you projected a narrow rainbow-colored band of light onto a white wall with violet at the top and red at the bottom. Light is made of wavelengths, right? So is sound! Longer wavelengths of light produce redder colors, and longer wavelengths of sound produce lower notes. Shorter wavelengths of light produce increasingly violet light, and shorter wavelengths of sound produce increasingly higher notes.

Now imagine you're holding a white cue ball from a billiard set in front of your projected band of color. You're holding it in front of the yellow part, right in the middle, so that the cue ball takes on the yellow color of the light projected onto it. Move the cue ball up into the violet area. Does the cue ball change shape? Nope. But it does change color. The cue ball retains its spherical structure but takes on the violet color. It's the same cue ball in a new setting. Move the cue ball down into the red now, and again watch it change color but retain its shape.

1	2	3	4	5	6	7	8

Figure 5.1. Major Scale Strip

Essentially, this happens to a major scale when you move your scale strip up and down on the tone bars. Just as the cue ball retains its shape but takes on a different color as you move it up or down the projected rainbow spectrum, so the major scale retains its shape as you move it up and down the pitch spectrum.

THE COMFORT LEVEL OF TONES IN A MAJOR SCALE

True, scales have structure, but they alone don't make music. The masterful manipulation of tension and release on the part of a crafty composer is what makes music. Baroque composers used the twelve-tone chromatic scale to give music a sense of tension and release. Well, it turns out that in a major scale, certain tones are restful, comfortable tones, and certain other tones are tense and uncomfortable. A little story from the Montessori music albums illustrates this beautifully:

"Once there was a glorious kingdom ruled by a king and a queen. The boundaries of the kingdom were the two *tonics*. On each tonic sat two magnificent palaces, both of them sanctuaries of comfort and rest for the subjects of the kingdom. A king occupied the lower tonic, and a queen occupied the higher tonic, so that together they could rule over the entire kingdom.

One day the king decided he needed help ruling, so he appointed a High Chamberlain to occupy a beautiful castle a little more than halfway across the kingdom, at the fifth degree—an individual member of a scale is called a *degree*. He gave this High Chamberlain the name *dominant,* and appointed him to be his second-in-command. To communicate with his High Chamberlain, the king also appointed a messenger, the *mediant* and gave him a slightly smaller, but no less beautiful castle on the third degree. Now the king had an effective system for governing.

Together with his High Chamberlain the dominant and his messenger the mediant, the king had a strong structure.

Well, the queen saw what the king had done and decided she too needed help governing. So she appointed her own Lord High Chamberlain to sit in a lovely palace on the fourth degree. She called him the *subdominant*. The subdominant wasn't as powerful as the King's High Chamberlain, but he was a big help. Because the subdominant was more than halfway across the kingdom from the queen, she also had trouble communicating with him. So, she appointed a messenger as well, the *submediant,* and housed him in a grand palace at the sixth degree.

The court had two other important members. The king had a footman who rode above him on the coach. This footman resided in a domicile on the second degree and went by the name of *supertonic*.

The queen had a lady in waiting. She was called the *leading tone* and she lived in a little house near the queen's palace at the seventh degree. The leading tone was very shy and never went anywhere without her queen.

These are the names of all of the notes of the major scale that make up the court. Every member of the court, wherever they find themselves, long to be at peace in the magnificent palaces situated at each tonic. Sometimes foreign ambassadors enter the court in the form of black notes. They each add their own unique and exotic color to the kingdom's music" (McKeever, 2009).

As you can tell from the story, it so happens that the most important, most comfortable, most peaceful tones in a major scale are 1 and 8, the tonics. They have the distinction of being the namesake of the scale. To hear the relationships from the above story, place your major scale strip in front of your tone bars with 1 on the first tone bar. Play 1 and 8. Now play the other notes in whatever order you like and listen closely. Notice that wherever you go up or down the scale, every note wants to go back home to the beautiful palace of the tonic.

Now label your white tone bars with the white disks, placing the disk "C" on the first tone bar. The major scale starting from the note C is called a C-major scale, and its tonic, its home tone, the note corresponding to 1 on your major-scale strip is C. You'll find another C, an octave above, on 8. Those two Cs, the tonics, are the most comfortable tones in the C-major scale.

The next most comfortable tone is the dominant G, followed by the mediant E, the subdominant F, the submediant A, and the supertonic D. The least comfortable note is the leading tone, B. Wherever you move your major-scale strip up and down the tone bars, although the note names will be different, the hierarchy of tones will be the same. This hierarchy of tones is also pretty much the same in another kind of scale: the minor scale.

MINOR SCALES

Minor scales make up the next most common whole-step/half-step formula. With regard to intervals, the words *major* and *minor* just mean large and small, so a major third is a wider interval and a minor third a relatively narrower one. During the baroque era, those who studied music singled out three minor scales as the most useful. These three forms have been in use ever since.

A *melodic minor* scale looks just like a major scale, except it has a half step between 2 and 3 and whole step between 3 and 4. A scale strip for a *melodic minor* scale looks like figure 5.2.

The melodic minor scale, used frequently in jazz, sounds a little like the major scale's less cheerful cousin.

1		2	3		4		5		6		7	8

Figure 5.2.   Melodic Minor Scale

1		2	3		4		5	6		7		8

Figure 5.3.   Natural Minor Scale

1		2	3		4		5	6			7	8

Figure 5.4.   Harmonic Minor Scale

But the real downer in the family is the *natural minor* scale. It looks like figure 5.3.

Play that one and weep. By the way, you can make a natural minor scale by starting from the sixth degree of any major scale. Try it yourself: place your major scale strip with 1 on C, but start on 6 or A. Because these two scales are so closely related, the natural minor is known as the *relative minor*. (C major, likewise, is the *relative major* of A minor.)

Finally, in figure 5.4, you have the *harmonic minor* scale, which was a favorite among our baroque friends.

Notice that large interval between 6 and 7? It's rather exotic-sounding, isn't it? That interval is a step and a half, and it's used a lot in Middle Eastern music. It can be used to heighten the feeling of tension before melodies built from this scale came to rest. You get the feeling that a melody is coming to a rest when the notes move toward and finally arrive at the tonic.

Some scales in common use, however, have tones that never come to a rest. These scales are a bit more egalitarian than the major and minor scales. You already know about the chromatic scale, which is that original twelve-tone scale you've read about. That scale isn't ruled by a single tonic, but every member of the scale has equal weight. Sounds like a nice situation, doesn't it? See what you think of the sound of the following scales.

THE WHOLE-TONE SCALE

Think of the whole-tone scale as having resulted from a revolution in the kingdom of the major scale. A group of notes didn't like having to answer to the king and queen and their high chamberlains, so they revolted and created a kingdom in which all the tones had equal importance.

But unlike the chromatic scale, whose sound feels a little disconcerting, the whole-tone scale gives off a peaceful, floating sensation. Although no one tone has a feeling of being more restful or more comfortable than any other, still we never quite feel uncomfortable. It has a light, dreamy quality to it. In fact, you often hear a whole-tone scale when a character in a film or television show experiences a dream or flashback. The French composer Claude Debussy frequently used the whole-tone scale when he wanted to create a dreamy impression or mood.

While the chromatic scale is made up of half steps, the whole-tone scale consists entirely of whole steps. Figure 5.5 shows what the whole-tone scale strip looks like.

THE PENTATONIC SCALE

The tones of the *pentatonic* scale also have no hierarchy. Every note is as comfortable and pleasing as every other note. This five-note scale is a favorite of Eastern musicians and makers of wind chimes because, like the whole-tone scale, the pentatonic gives us a floating, peaceful feeling. Figure 5.6 shows a pentatonic scale strip.

The pentatonic scale comes in two varieties. Figure 5.6 shows the *major pentatonic*. It also comes in a minor flavor. Play the *minor pentatonic* scale from figure 5.7 on your tone bars. It's just as comfortable as the major pentatonic, albeit a little darker.

1		2		3		4		5		6		7

Figure 5.5.   The Whole-Tone Scale

1		2		3				4		5		

Figure 5.6.   The Pentatonic Scale

1			2		3		4			5		

Figure 5.7. The Minor Pentatonic Scale

Pentatonic scales are wonderful to use with the children because the notes played in any combination sound wonderful together. You can't play a wrong note!

MODES OF THE MAJOR SCALE

During the Middle Ages, educated Europeans rediscovered the writings of Plato and Aristotle, long lost after Rome fell. As a result, musicians developed a renewed interest in the Greek modes. It now appears that theorists of the day got the Greek modes all mixed up, but in their haste to free themselves of the restrictions of the Church modes, our medieval friends passed down seven modes to us, all named after Greek modes, and all derived from the major scale.

This means that if you play a major scale starting on the first note, as said before, you'll have played a scale that sounds similar to a Greek mode called the *Ionian mode*. That mode has a certain pattern of whole steps and half steps that give it a unique identity. Well, you can also play a scale starting on the second degree, and you'll get a different half-step and whole-step pattern, the result of which will sound much different, a little spookier.

The mode you hear is similar to a Greek mode called the *Dorian mode*. Starting on the third degree will give you the *Phrygian mode*, the one Plato thought had the power to make men effeminate.

Figure 5.8 shows all of the modes of the major scale.

Notice as you play the modes how the half-step and whole-step patterns result in a unique sound. Listen to how the comfortable and uncomfortable tones change and shift. To give a sense of how the choice of mode affects a piece of music, place your major scale strip in front of your tone bars with one on any note you like, and play a familiar song like "Mary Had a Little Lamb." You should have played: 3, 2, 1, 2, 3, 3, 3; 2, 2, 2; 3, 5, 5. Now change the scale strip, and play the song again. Hear how different it sounds in each mode?

Ionian (major scale starting on 1)

1		2		3	4		5		6		7	8

Dorian (major scale starting on 2)

1		2	3		4		5		6	7		8

Phrygian (major scale starting on 3)

1	2		3		4		5	6		7		8

Lydian (major scale starting on 4)

1		2		3		4	5		6		7	8

Mixolydian (major scale starting on 5)

1		2		3	4		5		6	7		8

Aeolian (major scale starting on 6)

1		2	3		4		5	6		7		8

Locrian (major scale starting on 7)

1	2		3		4	5		6		7		8

Figure 5.8. Modes of the Major Scale

You could also listen to, play, or sing the song "Greensleeves," which was written in something similar to the Dorian mode.

A word of caution: according to the ancient Greeks, if you play the Dorian mode too much, you might start to feel a little aggressive. Playing the plain old Ionian mode will lead you down the path to drunkenness and slothfulness. Nevertheless, it's worth it to have a scale strip for each mode in your bar cabinet. Children love to explore the sounds of the different modes.

MORE ABOUT INTERVALS

Look back at the pentatonic scale. Notice the wide distance between 3 and 4? That very special interval is called a *minor third*. It may come as no surprise to you that, just as distances have names like *inch* and *foot*, musical distances also have names. More than that, musical distances have particular sounds associated with them, as well as particular levels of comfort and discomfort.

Recall that the half-step is called a *minor second*. It's the least comfortable sounding of all the intervals. Play two notes a minor second apart simultaneously on your tone bars. Hear the sharp, almost cutting sound it produces? Now play them in succession. Spooky, eh? What is it that gives an interval its sound? Why, the number of half-steps!

Just as half-steps give scales structure and identity, half-steps also give intervals structure and identity. Table 5.9 shows you all of the intervals in an octave, the number of half steps they comprise, their level of comfort or discomfort, and a famous melody you can sing to hear what they sound like.

So clearly does the number of half-steps give an interval its identity that you can play the notes in an interval in succession—or *melodically*—or you can play them simultaneously—that is, *harmonically*—and you'll get the same feeling of comfort or discomfort. Likewise, you'll get the same sound and feel if you play them upwards melodically (*ascending*), or downwards (*descending*).

CHORDS

So far, you've looked at three different formulas. You began by looking at a formula that Johann Sebastian Bach used a few centuries ago. Bach's formula divided the octave neatly into twelve half steps. Then you saw another formula, also agreed upon by people in the West, that which selects seven notes from the complete twelve and orders them into a scale. The basic, *do, re, mi* scale

Table 5.9.　Intervals

Name	# of half-steps	Comfort Level	Song Reference
Minor second	1	Highly uncomfortable	*Jaws* theme
Major second	2	Uncomfortable	"Chopsticks"
Minor third	3	Somewhat comfortable	"Greensleeves"
Major third	4	Somewhat comfortable	"Michael Row the Boat Ashore"
Perfect fourth	5	Very comfortable	"Here Comes the Bride"
Tritone	6	Extremely uncomfortable	*The Simpsons* theme
Perfect fifth	7	Extremely comfortable	*Star Wars* theme
Minor sixth	8	Somewhat comfortable	"Johanna" from Sweeney Todd
Major sixth	9	Somewhat comfortable	"My Bonnie"
Minor seventh	10	Uncomfortable	*Star Trek* theme
Major seventh	11	Highly uncomfortable	"Take on Me" by A-Ha
Octave	12	Very comfortable	"Somewhere over the Rainbow"

beginning on C, for example, is C D E F G A B. You can get a major scale from any note by simply applying the same major-scale half-step, whole-step pattern.

A third recipe selects only three notes to give you a basic three-note chord. This is the three-note setting mentioned in chapter 4, the formula that identifies oncoming tones of a melody as being comfortable and in the chord, or uncomfortable and out of the chord. If you start the basic chord on the note C—the first note of a chord is called the *root*, by the way—the formula for a basic chord adds E and G.

This recipe of fixed intervals gives you what's called a *major chord*, and whether you start on C or on any other note, the ingredients are the same: to make a basic major chord you take a *root note*, add the note a *major third* above it, and then add the note a *minor third* above that. Root, major third, minor third: that's it.

Label your tone bars with white disks and get ready to play an F-major chord. Applying the formula you get a root note on F, a major third above the root gives you A, and a minor third above that gives you C. Play that. Now try it on G. The formula is G, B, and D. Hear that nice major sound?

You can use your major scale strip to quickly play major chords without worrying about note names, by the way. Place your major-scale strip 1 anywhere on the tone bars and play 1, 3, and 5, up and down. You should get a nice, strong, stable, comfortable major-chord sound. Now play 4, 6, and 8. You've discovered another major chord. Finally, play 5, 7, and 2. Once again, you found a major chord. As you'll discover below, a major scale contains three major chords.

Incidentally, you'll get those same stable major chords wherever you move the scale strip. Move it anywhere along the tone bar setup, pull down the corresponding tone bars, and play 1, 3, and 5, for example. You'll hear nothing but major chords. Now, if you want to, you can label your tone bars with the black and white disks to figure out what the note names are on every root. Or you can consult table F.2 in appendix F.

You'll find that once you apply the formula of root plus major third plus minor third, you'll be able to create a nice, solid, stable major chord starting anywhere you like. As long as you apply that simple recipe, no matter what your root note is, apart from being higher or lower, the chord you make will sound like the same stable, comfortable, major chord.

Of course, just as we have many scales, we have many varieties of chords. And, just like scales and intervals, every chord type has its own unique sound, identity, structure.

Another commonly used three-note chord is the *minor chord*. To make a minor chord, you just start with a root, add the note a *minor third* above it, and then add the note a *major third* above that. You could also just place your minor scale strip with 1 on C and play 1, 3, and 5. Now, play a minor chord on C and listen to what it sounds like. It turns out you're playing the notes C, E-flat, and G. Kind of tugs at your heartstrings doesn't it?

Again, you can dispense with letter names and quickly find minor chords using your minor scale strip. The minor chord on 1, 3, and 5 sounds nice, but so does the minor chord on 4, 6, and 8 and the minor chord on 5, 7, and 2. In a minor scale, there are three minor chords.

Any number of notes can be added to make a chord. Four-note chords in stacked thirds are called *seventh chords*. To make a basic seventh chord, we take a root, add the major third above it, then add two minor thirds above that. On C, a seventh chord would consist of C, E, G, and B-flat.

Lower the third and the fifth of that seventh chord by one half step. The unusual-sounding result is called a *diminished chord*. We will not go deep into these at this point, but since they pop up in major and minor scales, it helps to know they exist.

Table 5.10 shows you the formulas for the most common types of three-note chords (and the one four-note chord you've seen so far). Each chord has a name, a recipe, a spelling on the root C, and a shorthand symbol that identifies it.

Table 5.10. Common Chord Recipes

Chord type	Recipe	Symbol	Spelling on root C	Symbol on root C
Major	root, M3, m3	M	C E G	C
Minor	root, m3, M3	m	C E-flat G	C - or Cm
Diminished	root, m3, m3	dim, °	C E-flat G-flat	Cdim or C°
Augmented*	root, M3, M3	+	C E G#	Caug or C+
Seventh	root, M3, m3, m3	7	C E G B-flat	C7

* Although the augmented chord doesn't appear in the major or minor scales, it's still a useful chord. It goes nicely with the whole-tone scale that you discovered earlier. To see what I mean, go to your tone bars and place your whole-tone scale strip with 1 on C. Have your friends play C, E, and G# simultaneously while you play around with different melodies. You'll start to feel like you're floating away to Dreamland.

Earlier, I discussed how the comfort or discomfort of a tone depends on its setting. To hear how chords determine the setting for a melody, let's repeat our little experiment from before. Gather your three friends from earlier and tell them that together they're going to help you make a basic three-note major chord. Place your major scale strip in front of the tone bar setup and pull down the appropriate bars.

Play the root (the note on 1), have your friend play the third (the note on 3), and have your other friend play the fifth (the note on 5). Now, ask your third friend to play all the notes from the C-major scale, and see if together you can locate all the comfortable, settled notes that fit with the chord.

You should find that, although you have some comfortable and uncomfortable notes, some of the uncomfortable tones seem to melt into the comfortable notes, and, in general, all of the notes seem to give you more or less of a degree of general comfort. Now ask your friend to play the black notes as you play the basic C chord. Everyone should be feeling less comfortable.

Chords are built from scales. Every time you hear a chord, your brain knows which melody notes belong with that chord. It wants to hear a melody derived from the scale from which that chord is culled. The three notes from the chord will sound the most comfortable, true, but all the notes from the scale that the chord comes from will also sound more or less comfortable.

What's more, not only can chords provide a background that determines the comfort level of individual tones, but chords themselves also relate to each other within a scale in ways that make them sound comfortable or uncomfortable.

To understand how, think of that glorious kingdom of the major scale from earlier. Now imagine on each scale degree towers a magnificent dwelling in which lives each member of the court. Each courtier built his or her dwelling by stacking the notes in the major scale like bricks up on top of one another according to that basic, three-note pattern of root, third, and fifth. Each chord on each degree of the scale has a *quality*, or a major- or minor-ness. In the kingdom of C, the chords look like in Table 5.11.

Table 5.11. Basic, Three-Note Chords Built on a C Major Scale

5th	G	A	B	C	D	E	F
3rd	E	F	G	A	B	C	D
Root	C	D	E	F	G	A	B
	I	ii	iii	IV	V	vi	vii°

A capital Roman numeral denotes a major chord, a lowercase Roman numeral denotes a minor chord, and a lowercase with a little circle denotes a diminished chord.

Looking at those numerals, we see in the kingdom of C, the chords built on the tonic, subdominant, and dominant are all major. The courtiers on these scale degrees live in comfortable, stable, restful, formidable palaces. They are also bright, attractive, and cheerful.

Minor chords sit on the supertonic, mediant, and submediant degrees. These palaces enjoy a certain amount of stability, but they have a darker character. Finally, we see a diminished chord on the leading tone, which is not a stable chord at all.

The chords in a scale want to resolve in different ways. Some chords, like the diminished chord, are more restless than others and want desperately to resolve. Think of the diminished chord as a rickety old shack that feels at any moment like it will topple over into another chord. The other chords feel pretty stable and comfortable where they are, though everyone wants to eventually come to rest on the tonic.

Chords are identified by their root names. For example, a "C-major chord" refers to the root, third, and fifth of the basic seven-note major scale beginning on C. Similarly, an "A-minor chord" is a chord built on the 6th degree, and a "D-minor chord" is a chord built on the second degree. All of these chords could also be called by their courtly titles. In the kingdom of C, for example, C-major is the *tonic* chord, A-minor is the *submediant* chord, and D-minor is the *supertonic*.

Furthermore, the pattern of chord qualities is the same no matter what major kingdom you visit. If you go to the kingdom of A, the chord qualities will be the same, but the chord spellings will be different. The chord that sits on the tonic in A major is spelled A, C-sharp, E. The supertonic is a B minor chord, spelled B, D, F-sharp, and so on. Whatever major kingdom you're in, the courtiers stack up to form the same pattern of chord qualities.

Stacking the notes from a natural minor scale in thirds gives you a different pattern of chord qualities, an altogether different array of colorful palaces for the court members. Table 5.12 gives you a look at the chord spellings and qualities of the natural minor scale built on C.

Table 5.12. Basic, Three-Note Chords Built on a Natural Minor Scale

5th	G	Ab	Bb	C	D	Eb	F
3rd	Eb	F	G	Ab	Bb	C	D
Root	C	D	Eb	F	G	Ab	Bb
	i	ii°	III	iv	v	VI	VII

Here, the tonic is minor; the supertonic is diminished; the mediant, submediant, and leading tones are major, and the subdominant and dominant tones are also minor. Obviously, the levels of comfort we get from the chords in a minor scale differ considerably from those produced by a major scale.

Before moving on, take a look at tables 5.13 and 5.14, which show you the chord qualities in terms of numbers on the major and minor scale strips, respectively. Using these charts, you can set letter names aside and quickly find major and minor chords no matter where you place the scale strip.

Table 5.13. Three-Note Chords Using the Major Scale Strip

5th	5	6	7	1	2	3	4
3rd	3	4	5	6	7	1	2
Root	1	2	3	4	5	6	7
	I	ii	iii	IV	V	vi	vii°

Table 5.14. Three-Note Chords Using the Natural Minor Scale Strip

5th	5	6	7	1	2	3	4
3rd	3	4	5	6	7	1	2
Root	1	2	3	4	5	6	7
	i	ii°	III	iv	v	VI	VII

SOL-FA AND MOVEABLE *DO*

Out on her balcony, bathed in moonlight, while Romeo dreams from his hiding place in the bushes, Juliet says, "What's in a name? That which we call a rose by any other name would smell as sweet." Translation: the name of a thing does not reflect its true nature.

This goes for things as well as sounds. You have been, for instance, calling the notes of the major scale—that human-made, ordered series of seven notes arranged by whole-step, whole-step, half-step, whole-step, whole-step, whole-step, half-step—by their numbers on the scale strips and by their pitch names. Take a look at your tone bar setup after you've labeled the tone bars with white disks. Starting on C, the white bars are named C, D, E, F, G, A, and B.

But here's a little secret: in music, pitch is arbitrary. Selected tones have pitch names like C or A-flat for convenience, but the "standard" that defines those pitches has varied throughout history. If you were in a room with some other musicians and you used a tuning fork to pinpoint the exact frequency of the pitch A so you could all tune up, that would be easy enough. But who's to say that the tuning fork is "in tune?" Would it be productive to find the exact frequency of the pitch A, or can you all just agree on the best approximation of A, tune up, and start making beautiful music? The latter seems to be the way people have been making music throughout history.[1]

Intervals, on the other hand, are fixed ratios. They comprise a particular number of half-steps and, as such, they have an identifiable sound. The interval of a major sixth starting from A sounds just like a major sixth starting from E-flat, albeit at a different pitch level. And what is a scale, indeed, what is a melody, but a series of intervals? The intervals in a scale give it character, structure, and identity.

Since tones are arbitrary sounds in the air, and intervals are set structures, you can use a series of syllables to liberate yourself from the notion of pitch and let your ears measure the intervals when singing our scale. Herein lies the magic of *solemnization.* If you pick a pitch, any pitch, and call it *do* (pronounced "DOE"), then sing upward using the syllables *do re mi fa sol la ti do,* as long as you're singing the correct pattern of whole- and half-steps, your ear will recognize the major scale. You can sing it very high or very low, but the structure retains its identity.

The same is true of a melody, which is made up of a series of intervals. As such, just like a scale, a melody can be sung at any pitch and still be recognizable. Sing the melody *mi re do re mi mi mi.* Recognize the first line of "Mary Had a Little Lamb"? Now sing it much higher. You hear the same melody, right? Sing "Mary Had a Little Lamb" at any pitch using the syllables *do re mi,* and your ear recognizes it.

The concept that *do* can be assigned to any pitch and used as a starting point for singing was described in the eleventh century by the Italian Guido d'Arezzo, who took the beginning syllables from each line of a Latin hymn to St. John the Baptist, "Ut queant laxis" and used them to name the first six notes: *ut re mi fa sol la.*

Sometime in the 1600s, the Italian musicologist and humanist Giovanni Battista Doni changed the syllable *ut* to *do,* and added *si* as the seventh tone. It wasn't until the nineteenth century that English music teacher Sarah Glover changed *si* to *ti* so that every syllable would begin with a different letter.

This system of solemnization has come to be called *solfège* in French and English. It's also called *sol-fa.* The concept that *do* can start on any pitch is called *moveable do.* Moveable *do sol-fa* enables us to sing a melody or a scale at any pitch on *sol-fa* syllables and have that scale or melody retain its identity.

HAND SIGNS

Sarah Glover was responsible for simplifying the medieval *sol-fa* method and refining it for use in the English-speaking world. Her work inspired John Curwen, another English music educator and minister, to refine the system even further. He called his system, a system still in use today, *tonic sol-fa.*

Along with the syllables for each note in the scale, Curwen added a series of hand signs that foster a kinesthetic mind-body connection to make solemnization easier when singing. Zoltan Kodály, the composer and music educator whose method we'll delineate in chapter 7, adopted the Curwen hand signs for his method. You'll find them in figure 5.15.

Remarkably, the very shape of Curwen's hand signs actually helps the brain process the tones of the scale. *Do,* for example, is rendered as a fist. It's the strong, stable home tone. After *do,* the wrist naturally bends slightly as the voice steps up a whole step to *re.* Notice how *ti,* the uncomfortable leading tone that wants to resolve to its comfortable tonic, points upward to *do.*

To further support the mind-body connection, as you sing the scale, hold your hand out directly in front of your chest, elbow bent, forearm level with the floor at chest height. As you sing the scale upward, change your hand signs and raise your arm slightly, so that your hand moves upward as the pitches move higher.

Now do a little bit of practice singing melodies with hand signs. In figure 5.16, you'll find some melodies adapted from Zoltan Kodály's book *333 Reading Exercises.* To read them, pick a pitch, call it *do,* and form your hand signs as you slowly sing the pitches with tonic *sol-fa* names. Make sure to sing the correct pitch as you form the hand sign. Signing *re* while singing *mi* will confuse your brain. Remember also to raise and lower your hand as the pitch goes up and down. Don't worry about the rhythm for now. Just go very slowly, and concentrate on hearing, singing, and signing the pitches.

Those practice melodies were made of melodic steps. For an added challenge, sing some melodies that contain melodic leaps. If at first you have trouble hearing a melodic leap, softly sing the melodic steps in between. Then, when you have the leap in your ear, sing it louder. Figure 5.17 shows some melodies for you to read.

Now make up your own melodies using tonic *sol-fa* and hand signs.

Tonic *sol-fa* and its hand signs are not only useful for you in singing songs and getting acquainted with scales, but they are also extremely valuable for the children you teach. Since children are kinesthetic learners, using the hand signs will help them to sing more accurately, develop sight-reading and sight-singing skills, stay on

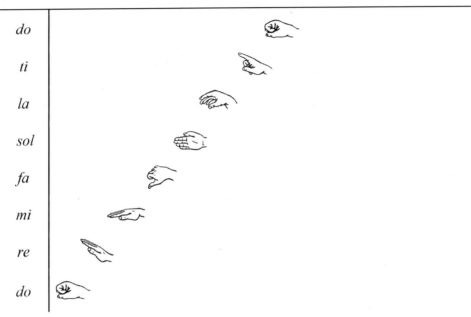

Figure 5.15. Curwen Hand Signs

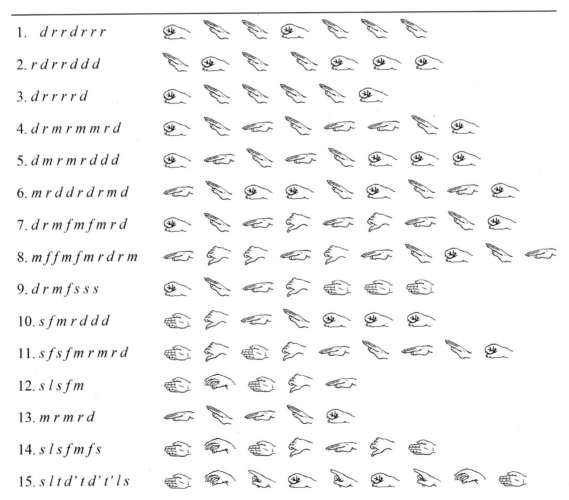

1. *d r r d r r r*
2. *r d r r d d d*
3. *d r r r r d*
4. *d r m r m m r d*
5. *d m r m r d d d*
6. *m r d d r d r m d*
7. *d r m f m f m r d*
8. *m f f m f m r d r m*
9. *d r m f s s*
10. *s f m r d d d*
11. *s f s f m r m r d*
12. *s l s f m*
13. *m r m r d*
14. *s l s f m f s*
15. *s l t d' t d' t' l s*

Figure 5.16. Tonic Sol-fa Reading Practice—Melodic Steps

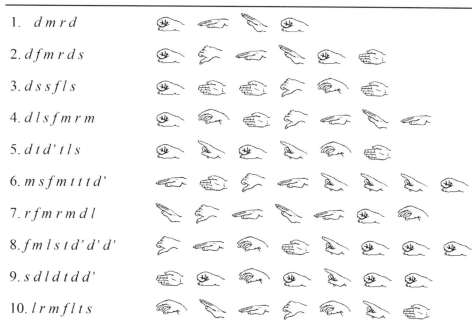

1. *d m r d*
2. *d f m r d s*
3. *d s s f l s*
4. *d l s f m r m*
5. *d t d' t l s*
6. *m s f m t t d'*
7. *r f m r m d l*
8. *f m l s t d' d' d'*
9. *s d l d t d d'*
10. *l r m f l t s*

Figure 5.17. Tonic Sol-fa Reading Practice—Melodic Leaps

Scale	Sol-fa syllables	Hand signs
Major	*d r m f s l t d'*	
Natural Minor	*l, t, d r m f s l*	
Major Pentatonic	*d r m s l d'*	
Minor Pentatonic	*l, d r m s l*	

Figure 5.18. More Tonic Sol-fa Reading Practice—Scales

their parts during part-singing, and develop fine motor skills. You'll learn more about how to use hand signs in the classroom in part 3.

For now, refer to figure 5.18, and sing some of the scales we introduced in the previous chapter using *sol-fa* syllables and hand signs. Remember to start with your hand at chest level and move it upward as you sing and change hand signs. As always, start on any pitch you like.

You'll explore pedagogical uses of the tonic *sol-fa* system in chapter 9. For the moment, keep practicing singing these scales with hand signs at different pitch levels. Sing "Mary Had a Little Lamb" or other folk songs you know using *sol-fa* syllables and hand signs. For an even greater challenge, try reading the melodies of the songs in chapter 14.

At this point in the book, you have enough information to make sense of the concepts in the Montessori music

lessons. Why stop there? Your success as a musical "enlightened generalist" depends not only on your ability to understand music, but to hear or see it, know what you're hearing or seeing, and communicate it through performance or music notation.

NOTE

1. Nevertheless, even though pitches are approximate, when you call the pitch you're singing A, you ought really to be singing an A. Here, Juliet's assertion doesn't hold water. With pitches, you can't call A by the name of E-flat any more than you can call a rose by the name of taxicab. A rose isn't a taxicab, and an A vibrates at a different frequency than an E-flat does (however approximate).

Chapter 6

Writing and Reading Music

When the noise from a jackhammer outside the classroom became too distracting to the class, Miss Katie gathered some children together for a nice, calm lesson on rhythm.

"Our hearts are like ticking clocks," she said. "We wouldn't be alive if it weren't for our hearts pumping blood with that steady, regular beat. Place your finger on your neck and feel your pulse. Take a moment to feel that steady tick-tick-tick-tick."

The children placed two fingers on their necks, while their eyes rolled up to the ceiling in quiet concentration.

But Charlotte couldn't feel anything. "I have no heartbeat!" she bellowed.

Startled, Andrew chimed in, "She's dead!"

An outburst of giggling. Chaos ensues.

You may be relieved to know Charlotte eventually found her heartbeat. Like Charlotte, music also has a heartbeat. Every piece of music has a fixed pulse that you can feel. You are conscious of this pulse, regardless of whether an instrument plays it. What's more, you feel that unwavering metronome tick-tock no matter how complex the pattern of longs and shorts is in the melody above it.

This heartbeat in music is called the *steady beat*. Listen to any music you like, and see if you can tap along with the steady beat. If your tapping is uneven, with lots of long and short durations, you aren't tapping the steady beat. Try again. Your tapping should be even and steady, like a heartbeat.

That steady beat forms the grid onto which you lay down durations of long and short tones. Very long tones can be stretched wide across a number of beats, while very short tones can be crammed into a single beat. The pattern of wide and narrow durations that gets laid across the steady beat is called the *rhythm*. Rhythms, like pitches and intervals, have names.

What follows are some of the simple rhythms that you can use to make music with the children in your classes.

RHYTHMIC ELEMENTS

First, recall the song "Rain, Rain, Go Away." Sing the song in your mind or aloud, and tap along with the steady beat. You're going to examine just the first line. Sing that line as you pat the beat on your knees. While singing the first phrase, "Rain, Rain, go a-way," you should have patted four times, as you see in figure 6.1.

This first line of your song has four underlying pulses, called *beats*, indicated by the horizontal lines. Turn your interest to the first beat, where you have only one sound. Likewise, the second and fourth beats have only one sound. This one-sound-on-a-beat rhythmic element is called a *quarter note* in Western musical language, but for your purposes, and for everyone's sanity, call this note by its *rhythmic sol-fa* name, *ta*. It's convenient to call the note *ta,* as *ta* is a nice one-syllable sound, as opposed to *quarter note,* which is a mouthful.

Now look at beat three. If you tap beat three and sing the melody, you should see that beat three has two sounds. The two-sounds-on-a-beat rhythmic element can be named *ti-ti* (TEE-TEE). Try tapping one beat and singing *ti-ti*. Make sure your *ti-ti*s are even so that you aren't sitting sipping one cup of "*ti*" longer than the other. Again, the musical term for *ti-ti* is a pair of *eighth notes,* but you'll find calling them *ti-ti* simpler and more useful.

If you sing the first line of "Rain, Rain, Go Away" using rhythmic *sol-fa* language, you get figure 6.2.

Rain,	Rain,	go a-	way.

Figure 6.1.

Figure 6.2.

Practice for a moment patting the steady beat and singing the first line of "Rain, Rain, Go Away" using *ta* and *ti-ti* names.

NOTATING RHYTHM

The symbol for *ta* is a short vertical line that looks like a stick, like in figure 6.3.

Figure 6.3.

We notate *ti-ti,* on the other hand, with two sticks joined at the top by a horizontal crossbar, like a hurdle (figure 6.4).

Figure 6.4.

Our song "Rain, Rain, Go Away," notated with rhythm sticks, looks like figure 6.5.

Figure 6.5.

You and your young musicians can make endless rhythm patterns using just *ta* and *ti-ti*. Try patting the beat and saying the rhythmic *sol-fa* names of the patterns in figure 6.6 (or invent your own). Then try clapping the rhythm patterns while *internalizing* the beat (feeling it or hearing it inside your mind). Now, get some percussion instruments, and play line 1 with your left hand, line 2 with your right hand, and lines 3 and 4 with your feet. Then go apologize to the neighbors.

When there are three sounds on a beat, you refer to the pattern as a *triplet*. To get the right sound out of a

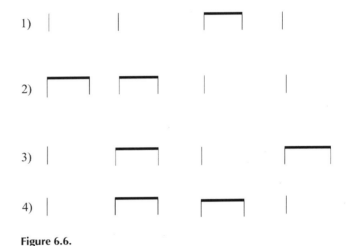

Figure 6.6.

triplet, pronounce it "trih-puh-let" while clapping the beat. A triplet looks like in figure 6.7.

Remember to make the three sounds even, so none of the three sounds is longer than the others. Try replacing one of the beats in the patterns in figure 6.6 with a triplet, and see what you get.

Four sounds on a beat go by the name *ti-ka-ti-ka* (TI KUH TI KUH). It looks like figure 6.8.

Figure 6.9 shows some patterns with *ta, ti-ti, tri-puh-let,* and *ti-ka-ti-ka,* all mixed up. Try patting the beat and saying the rhythmic *sol-fa* names for the patterns.

You can also practice clapping these patterns while internalizing the steady beat. Try that a few times.

So far, we've been slicing up a beat into one, two, three, and four sounds. But some rhythmic units encompass more than one beat. A sound stretched over two beats is called *ta-a* (figure 6.10), and it is notated with a stick that has a little white balloon on the bottom.

It's easy enough to say *ta-a* as you clap the steady beat, but to *clap* the rhythm *ta-a,* clap your hands together on beat one, hold them together, and then move them out slightly further in front of you on beat two.

Another useful rhythmic unit is a beat of silence, which is rendered by a *rest*. A rest of one beat is called *sh,* and it looks like in figure 6.11.

When "clapping" a *sh,* instead of bringing your hands together, pretend they're the pages of a floppy book, and open them apart. Try clapping the rhythm of the patterns in figure 6.12.

Obviously, many more complex rhythmic units and patterns exist. The goal here is to give you enough

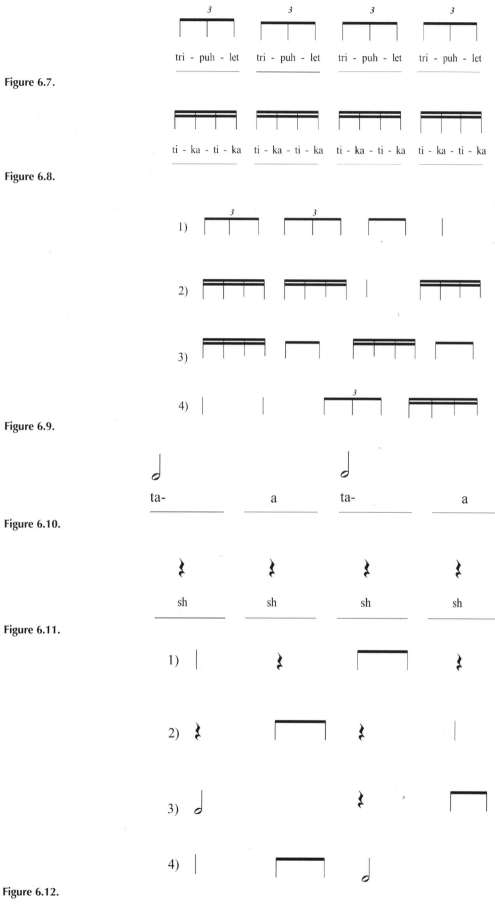

Figure 6.7.

Figure 6.8.

Figure 6.9.

Figure 6.10.

Figure 6.11.

Figure 6.12.

material to make music with the children you teach. You'll find that you can get a lot of mileage out of *ta, ti-ti, triplet, ti-ka-ti-ka, ta-a,* and *sh*.

Nevertheless, you ought to know a couple of other variations on these basic rhythmic units, since they crop up in some of the folk songs you'll use with your classes. Meet the first of these variations: dotted rhythms.

The two dotted rhythm elements in figures 6.13 and 6.14 are variations on a pattern of two *ti-ti*s. When you want to stretch out the first *ti* so that it encompasses all three of the first *ti*s, you remove the crossbeam and place a dot after the note. The fourth *ti* then gets a flag instead of a beam.

tai - ti

Figure 6.13.

You call this dotted rhythm *tai-ti* (TAH-EE-TI). When you read rhythms with *tai-ti,* you make sure that the *tai* sound encompasses three *ti* sounds. Figure 6.14 shows a comparison between *tai-ti* and *ti-ti, ti-ti*.

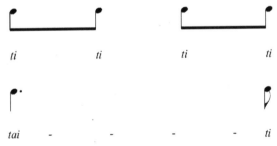

ti   ti   ti   ti

tai - - - - ti

Figure 6.14.

A dotted note becomes longer by half of its original value. Put simply, a dotted quarter note equals three eighth notes.

Let's move on to another variation of *ti-ti, ti-ti,* which occurs when you replace the *ti*s in the middle with a *ta*. The resulting rhythmic unit has the rhythmic *sol-fa* name *syncopa* (sin-COH-pah).[1] When you read it, stretch the "co" out long, as in "Syn-cooooh-pa." Figure 6.15 compares *syncopa* to two *ti-ti*s.

STICK NOTATION

You can easily write and read music by combining rhythm notation and melodic symbols, such as note

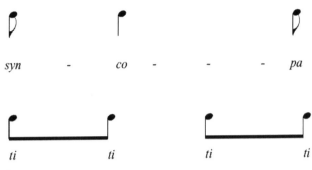

syn - co - - - pa

ti   ti   ti   ti

Figure 6.15.

names, numbers, or *sol-fa* syllables using a system known as *stick notation*. Here's how to write a melody in stick notation. Start by placing your major scale strip in front of your tone bars with 1 anywhere you like. Now, on a piece of paper, write a pattern in rhythm sticks using ta and ti ti. As in figure 6.16, below the rhythm sticks write numbers that correspond to the numbers on your scale strip. (You could also use note names if you've labeled the tone bars with black and white disks.)

Next, find a steady beat and play your melody on your tone bars. Do you recognize that melody? If you hear "Rain, Rain, Go Away," you just read some notated music! It's that easy. Now you have a simple way to compose music on the tone bars.

You can also use stick notation to *sight-sing* melodies. Using the same rhythm pattern as in figure 6.16, this time write below the rhythm sticks the first letter of a *sol-fa* syllable, as in figure 6.17.

Before you read this melody, sing up and down a major scale with *sol-fa* names starting from any pitch. Use your hand signs as you sing up and down the scale. Now, find your starting note *sol*. If you can just hear it and pluck it out of the air, well, that's one way to do it. You could also sing up the scale from *do*. However you find *sol*, give yourself a moment to feel the steady beat before using your hand signs and singing *sol-mi-sol-sol-mi*. Did you sing "Rain, Rain"?

Now try the melody in figure 6.18.

What melody do you hear? If you're singing the first four beats of "I've Been Working on the Railroad," try it again. You should be singing "Mary Had a Little Lamb."

Now that you have the concept of how to read stick notation, there are a few more elements to consider so your stick-notation system is complete. Take a look at the first line of the lovely song in figure 6.19 called "Bye, Bye, Baby".

Let's make sense of this together. You know the rhythmic elements *ta* and *ti-ti*. Direct your attention to those long vertical lines in between the groups of rhythm elements. Those aren't *ta*s. They're *bar lines*. The space in between two bar lines is called a *measure*—a grouping of beats.

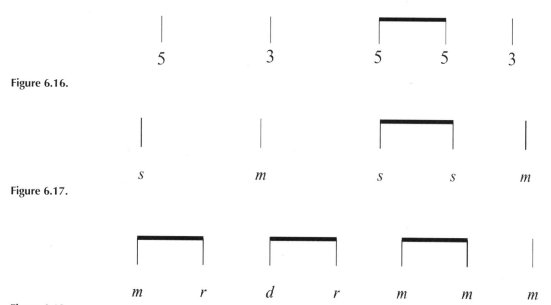

Figure 6.16.

Figure 6.17.

Figure 6.18.

Bye Bye Baby

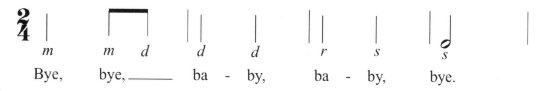

Figure 6.19.

Do you see two beats in each measure of this little tune? Do you see what looks like a fraction at the beginning of the melody? That number, called a *time signature,* tells you two pieces of information. The top number tells you how many beats are in each measure. You established already that each measure has two beats. The bottom number tells you which rhythm element gets one beat. A 4 stands for *ta,* an 8 stands for one *ti* of *ti-ti,* and a 2 stands for *ta-a.* Basically, this 2/4 symbol says there are two *tas* in each measure.

You read music from left to right. When you get to the end of a line of music, skip down to the next line and begin at the left again, like a cartoon bird eating corn on the cob. This first line of music consists of three rows of information. The rhythmic elements sit on top, the *sol-fa* syllables hang below them, and the lyrics take up the bottom. The second line of the music goes below, with rhythm, *sol-fa,* and lyrics in the same order. Take a look at the second line of "Bye, Bye, Baby" in figure 6.20.

Sing "Bye, Bye, Baby" using *sol-fa* and hand signs. If you accomplished that, congratulations! You can probably read the song in figure 6.21 on the next page, too, since you know all there is to know about stick notation. Be sure to sing the song and show the hand signs.

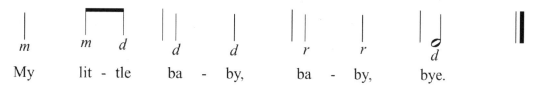

Figure 6.20.

Mystery Song

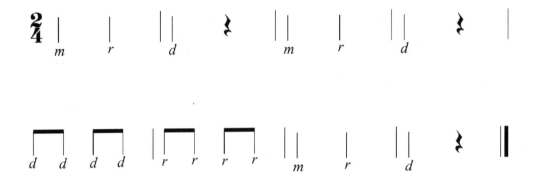

Figure 6.21.

Remember also that *do* can be any pitch. Find any comfortable *do,* and off you go.

Getting hungry? That might be because you just sang the song "Hot Cross Buns."

Stick notation is a versatile way to write music and to work on your sight-singing. It contains just about everything you need to write almost any form of music. If you want to move away from *sol-fa* syllables and tell people exactly what pitches you want them to play, just write pitch letter names instead of *sol-fa* syllables below the rhythm sticks. Writing "Hot Cross Buns" with note names looks like figure 6.22.

Again, you could also write "Hot Cross Buns" in stick notation using numbers, like figure 6.23 on next page.

Useful though it is, stick notation is still not as versatile as the notation system that Western musicians have developed over the past 800 years or so using the musical staff.

FROM STICK TO STAFF

Everybody loves a rainbow. All of the colors neatly stacked on top of one another in a striped pattern create a real visual treat. Most sighted people can distinguish each band of color from the other bands (though the colors fade into each other a bit). The red band on top can't be mistaken for the orange band nor can the yellow be mistaken for the purple. Each band of color in a rainbow gives your eye a distinct visual impression.

Remember that for the most part visual light is made up of waves. Longer waves of light strike your eye and

Hot Cross Buns

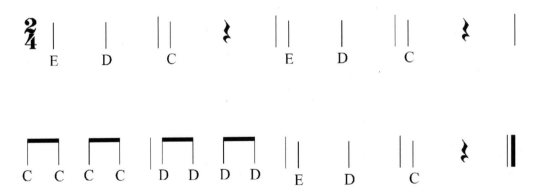

Figure 6.22.

Hot Cross Buns

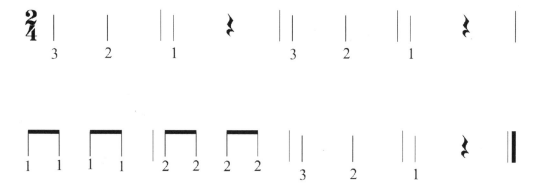

Figure 6.23.

appear red, while shorter waves appear purple. Sound is also made of waves. Short waves make higher sounds, and long waves make lower sounds.

Now you're going to think of a new kind of rainbow. To start, imagine a regular old rainbow, and stretch it straight like a ribbon. Place it in front of you, and instead of the red band on top as happens in nature, place the purple band—the color made of the shorter waves—on top. Instead of a rainbow made of stripes of visual color, you've made a rainbow of stripes of sound color. Because you can't see sound, your sound rainbow appears visually as a stack of alternating black lines and white spaces, as in figure 6.24.

Figure 6.24.

Don't be fooled by your rainbow's plain appearance. Just as each band in the visual rainbow houses a unique color, each line or space in your sound color rainbow houses a unique sound color, or *pitch*. The pitches on the upper part of the rainbow sound higher than the pitches on the lower part.

The pitch on the first line up from the bottom is called G (figure 6.25).

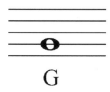

G

Figure 6.25.

That's not just any G, though—it's a very unique G. The wave that creates that G oscillates at a specific frequency range to create that G's particular sound. If you were to play that G on your tone bars, it would sound very different from any of the pitches on any of the other lines or spaces.

Unlike the visual rainbow, however, on which you can point to a band of color and immediately identify it as green or orange, the lines and spaces on your sound rainbow all look the same. At the moment, that line is only G because you've been told it is G. The way it's written now, anyone else could say that line was C, or D, or any other pitch. You need to use some kind of symbol so that everyone can agree that that line is G. Fortunately, such a symbol exists. It's called a *clef*. Clefs fix the lines and spaces of the sound rainbow in a certain pitch range. The little curly bit of this *treble clef* wraps around the line where you find G (figure 6.26).

(Still) G

Figure 6.26.

Your sound rainbow is starting to look almost as pretty as a visual rainbow. Lest the metaphor be milked to death, it's time to start calling your sound rainbow by its official name: *a staff*. This particular staff, with the G clef on it, is called the *treble staff*. Now that you know where

G is on your rainb . . . er . . . treble staff, you can easily identify every other pitch. The line below G—the bottom or first line—is an E (figure 6.27).

In between the E and G lines comes the space in which lives an F (figure 6.28).

Moving up from the bottom line, you have E, F, and then G as in figure 6.29. Do you see the pattern? The pitch names go in alphabetical order moving upward.

Figure 6.27.

Figure 6.28.

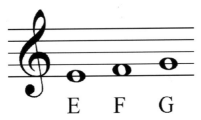

Figure 6.29.

Figure 6.30 shows all the pitch names on the treble staff from the bottom to the top.

You may be wondering why there are two Es and Fs. When musicians of old took seven notes out of the possible twelve to make scales, they gave each of the seven notes a name. Since the seven pitches repeat themselves every octave (only at a higher or lower frequency), for simplicity's sake the old musicians just gave the repeating pitches the same names. Consequently, the English musical alphabet only has seven letters, A, B, C, D, E, F, and G, which repeat in an infinite succession upward and downward.

Getting back to the staff, these lines and spaces can be easily memorized, which is useful. You can make all kinds of catchy acronyms for yourself. For now, it's *most* useful for you to know *these* staff lines and spaces, because they correspond to the pitches of the white Montessori bells, as shown in figure 6.31.

Notice that little line below the staff, on which the C is sitting. That *ledger line* is used to write notes that sit below or above the five lines of the staff. The first of the white Montessori bells sounds like this C.

The Montessori tone bars, however, encompass a much wider range. Figure 6.32 on the next page shows all the white tone bars from the lowest tone bar, the C below that ledger-line C, to the C in the middle of the treble staff.

You may not ever use that many notes at once when making music with the children you teach, but it's handy to identify every line and space on the staff so you can see where on the staff to find your tone bars. To help you, take out your white disks and label the white tone bars. Start by placing a C disk on the first tone bar, and proceed upward labeling all the white tone bars with the disks in alphabetical order.

Notice that little curly mark on the left? That's called a *bass clef*. It covers the low range of pitches. The little curly part of the clef wraps around the second-to-the-top line of the staff, marking that line as the home of F.

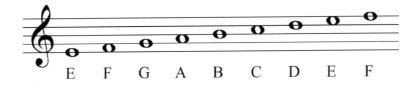

Figure 6.30.

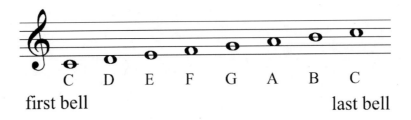

Figure 6.31.

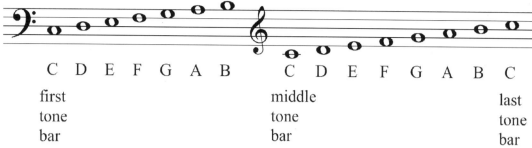

first
tone
bar

middle
tone
bar

last
tone
bar

Figure 6.32.

Using a bass clef prevents you from having to write too many ledger lines when you write notes below the treble staff. Of course, if you wanted to, you could draw ledger lines below the treble staff to write the notes going downward. Those low pitches could be written like in figure 6.33.

But it's much easier and more visually pleasing to write those low notes on the *bass staff* like in figure 6.34.

C   B   A   G

Figure 6.33.

C   B   A   G

Figure 6.34.

By the way, that C at the top ledger line of the bass clef is the same C found on the bottom ledger line of the treble clef. The treble and bass clefs are normally seen together in piano or keyboard music. When they are joined by a brace, they form the *grand staff*. Keyboard players usually read from a grand staff.

Figure 6.35 shows a grand staff with the pitch names on all the lines and spaces. The line that houses that special C, called *middle C* (because it's in the middle of a standard piano keyboard), isn't really that long. Of course, that line is imaginary. When you want to write a middle C, you use a ledger line.

Now you're going to read "Bye, Bye, Baby" from a staff and play it on the tone bars. You'll need your tone bar setup for this. Got it? Good. Did you label the white tone bars with the white note-name disks? Even better.

To begin, recall what the song looks like in stick notation as in figure 6.36 on next page.

For this example, place your major-scale strip so the 1 is in front of the middle tone bar. On the treble staff, that C is located on a ledger line below the staff. That C is called "middle C." Middle C = middle tone bar. Wasn't Maria Montessori a genius?

The first note of "Bye, Bye, Baby" is *mi*. When C is *do*, *mi* is E. In this case, you want the E on the first line of the staff. Figure 6.37 on next page shows "Bye, Bye, Baby" on a staff.

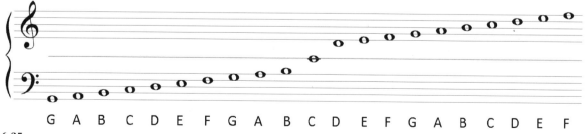

G   A   B   C   D   E   F   G   A   B   C   D   E   F   G   A   B   C   D   E   F

Figure 6.35.

Bye, Bye, Baby

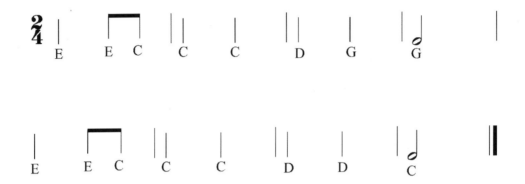

Figure 6.36.

Bye Bye Baby

Figure 6.37.

We've seen most of these symbols before. The treble clef sign indicates that we're in the high note range and that G is on the second line. The time signature tells us that each measure has two beats and that *ta* is worth one beat. You can even see vertical bar lines delineating the measures. Of course, you recognize the rhythm stems. This looks a lot like stick notation.

The only difference between this and stick notation, other than the staff lines, is how the notes look. Instead of a stick with a letter at the bottom, the notes take the shape of little black- or white-stemmed oval-shaped balloons. The oval rests either in a space, with its extremities touched by a line both above and below, or it rests on a line with the line slicing right through its center. On which staff line or space the balloon sits indicates which pitch to play or sing. The stem of the black notes tells us how long to play or sing the pitch—its rhythmic value.

Like in stick notation, a stem with no crossbeam or flag makes *ta*. Two stems joined by a crossbeam make *ti-ti*. A white note with a stem is *ta-a*.

So, to play the song on the tone bars, you may want to write the note names above the notes on the staff. Look at your white disks with the letter names. C should be above 1 on your scale strip, D above 2, E above 3, and so on. Write the names of the notes above the pitches on the staff, as shown in figure 6.38.

Now play the tune on the tone bars while reading from the staff. You did it!

If you want to *sing* this melody by sight-reading it from the staff, you can do that too. But because it's written on a staff, you ought to sing the exact pitches. (If it were just written in stick notation, you could pick any *do* you like.) No sweat, just plink out a C on the middle tone bar, match it with your voice, and call that *do*. If C is *do*, then E is *mi*, on the line above. The *sol-fa* syllables for this song are shown in figure 6.39.

As in chapter 5, sing the song slowly with hand signs. And, just like that, you can read music!

This version of "Bye, Bye, Baby" is easy to sing if you have a high voice. Give this melody to your grandfather, however, and he might have a hard time with it.

Bye Bye Baby

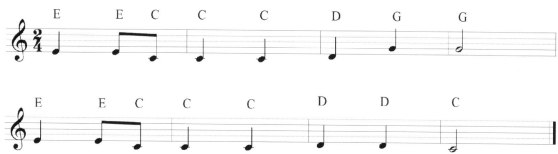

Figure 6.38.

Bye Bye Baby

Figure 6.39.

It would be much easier for him to sing at a lower pitch level.

Using the tone bars, you can easily *transpose*—move this melody to a higher or lower pitch level—so your grandfather can sing it. To transpose this melody, make sure your tone bars are all back where they started, and place your major scale strip on, say, E, the third white tone bar. Now, pull down the corresponding tone bars. Notice that you now have some black notes in your melody?

Before going any further, you'll want to know about those black notes.

SHARPS AND FLATS

The black notes in your tone bar or bell layout are called *accidentals*. They go by either of two names: *sharp* (a half-step higher or one tone bar to the right) or *flat* (a half-step lower, or one tone bar to the left).

Curiously, the musical staff accommodates only the white notes. To render a sharp or a flat note, you have to write a special symbol to the left of the note. The first black note you

come to when you place your major scale strip with 1 on E is *F-sharp*. On a treble staff *F-sharp* looks like (figure 6.40).

You can also call it *G-flat:* (figure 6.41).

But when your major scale strip starts on E, calling that note G-flat doesn't make sense. Here's why: in a musical scale, you must include *all of the letters in order without repeating a letter*. Put simply, you must spell your E scale with some kind of E, some kind of F, some

Figure 6.40.

Figure 6.41.

kind of G, and so on. Once you've exhausted all seven letters of the musical alphabet, you can repeat the letters starting where you began, in this case, E.

Saying the letters in alphabetical order starting on E, you get E, F, G, A, B, C, D, E. If you call that black note G-flat, you will have two problems. First, you will have left out F. Second, you will have two kinds of Gs. That will never do. So, in this context, call that first black note *F-sharp*.

The next black note you come to is *G-sharp* (not *A-flat*). The white note A is next, followed by B, then the black notes *C-sharp*, *D-sharp*, and, finally, the white note E. Figure 6.42 shows an E-major scale on the staff.

Now back to "Bye, Bye, Baby." In figure 6.43, you see it written on a staff when the major scale strip sits with 1 on E.

Two things stand out when you see this transposed melody. First, it has a lot of sharps in front of some of those notes. In the first, second, and seventh measures, each F and each G has a sharp in front of it. Musicians long ago thought that writing accidentals in front of every note looked too cluttered, so to eliminate the clutter they decided to *write the accidental only on the first accidental note in the measure*. Every accidental on that same line or space in that measure will also be sharp. After the bar line, however, the accidentals are discontinued and the measure is reset. Applying this rule gives you figure 6.44.

Well, that got rid of some clutter, but not much. Plus, the second G-sharp in measure 1 doesn't have an accidental in front of it. It kind of looks like it should be a regular G. You still want it to be a G-sharp, though. In

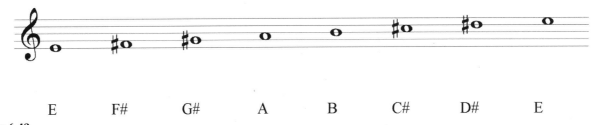

E   F#   G#   A   B   C#   D#   E

Figure 6.42.

Bye Bye Baby

Figure 6.43.

Bye Bye Baby

Figure 6.44.

Bye Bye Baby

Figure 6.45.

general, music looks too cluttered if you put a sharp sign in front of every note. Imagine transposing a melody into a key that has lots of sharps or flats. Writing an accidental sign in front of every sharp or flat note would cause things to get quite cluttered indeed.

Check out figure 6.45, which shows what "Bye, Bye, Baby" looks like when you place your scale strip with 1 on F#.

Here, almost every note has a sharp in front of it. To alleviate the confusion and clutter of having too many accidentals written in front of the notes on a staff, musicians came up with another important concept—the *key signature*.

KEY SIGNATURES

Imagine you're a medieval traveler on horseback approaching an unfamiliar kingdom. Before you towers a proud gate: the entrance to this new, mysterious land. Flapping on its ramparts, a colorful flag with a lavish design proclaims the ruler of this kingdom. A key signature is like that flag. It sits at the beginning of a piece of music and tells you, in essence, what notes sit on the court of that particular kingdom.

Remember the story of the court from chapter 5? When musicians use the word *key,* they're referring to all of the members of that court: the king and queen who sit at the *tonic* (1), the high chamberlains who sit at the *dominant* (5) and the *subdominant* (4), the messengers at the *mediant* (3) and *submediant* (6), and the little foot soldier and handmaiden sitting at the *supertonic* (2) and *leading tone* (7), respectively. All together these tones make up the kingdom of the major scale.

What's more, the tonic rules this kingdom like a despot. Every other note in the kingdom wants to come to rest on either 1 or 8, in the beautiful, comfortable palaces of the tonic. Whether the notes stand alone, as they might in a melody, or whether they're stacked together to form

chords, they always want to resolve to the tonic. The tonic rules over all.

Now, back to that flag flapping on the gate at the entrance to a musical kingdom: the key signature. Every key in music has its own unique key signature, whose design comes from the number of black notes in the scale. The kingdom of C, for instance, has no black notes, so its flag, or key signature, is just a clef on a blank staff. When you see a key signature of no sharps or flats at the beginning of a piece of music, between the clef and time signature, you know you're likely to be entering the kingdom of C. The tonic C resides in a glorious comfortable palace on the first degree. All the other tones in this kingdom bow to the tonic C.

The kingdom of the major scale starting on G (the key of G), has one black note: the leading tone F-sharp. When at the beginning of a piece of music you see a key signature with just one sharp perched on the F line—that's F-sharp (figure 6.46)—you'll know you're likely in the key of G, in which G, the powerful tonic, rules with an iron fist.

Figure 6.46.

Another kingdom worthy of mention is the kingdom of F, which also has only one black note, but it isn't a sharp, it's a flat. This flat note dwells on the subdominant in the key of F. Its name is B-flat, and it features prominently in F's key signature (figure 6.47).

Figure 6.47.

You have probably noticed that a key gets its name from its tonic note. Earlier, when you placed the scale strip with 1 on E in order to play "Bye, Bye, Baby," you declared yourself in the key of E. The key signature for the key of E has four sharps. Figure 6.48 shows "Bye, Bye, Baby" *in the key of* E.

Doesn't that look less cluttered? Check it out in figure 6.49 in the key of F#, whose key signature has six sharps.

Thanks to the key signature, you don't need to place sharps and flats on every note. The key signature tells us all the accidentals. Once again, it isn't necessary for you to memorize all the key signatures of the different kingdoms in music. Nevertheless, if you're curious, table 6.50 shows you the key signatures for the most commonly used major keys.

When working with your young musicians, you'll most often visit the keys of C, F, G, and possibly D (which has two sharps), because these keys contain notes that are situated right in the children's comfortable vocal range.

SIGHT-READING MAJOR KEYS

Now back to sight-reading. In a nutshell, all you have to do to sight-read a simple melody is to identify the key signature, which will tell you the tonic (in major keys: *do*). Then, once you've located the tonic on the staff, you can easily find the other scale degrees.

Take a look at the song in Figure 6.51 to see what I mean.

To read this song with the tone bars:

1. identify the key signature. One flat, B-flat, means that F is the tonic;
2. place your major scale strip so 1 is below F, and pull down the corresponding tone bars (if you forget where F is on the tone bars, you can label your tone bars with the white disks.);
3. find F on the staff. It's there, in the last measure. It's that *ta-a* on the first space;
4. now that you've found F, write a 1 below it. Then, label the other notes with their corresponding scale-strip numbers, as in figure 6.52.

Now, since you know the rhythms, you can play the tune. Recognize it? If you played "Ring around the Rosie," you have just sight-read music from a staff.

You can use a similar technique to *sight-sing* music from a staff. Sight-singing is a valuable skill. It can help you, for instance, to read notated melodies from folk-song

Bye Bye Baby

Figure 6.48.

Bye Bye Baby

Figure 6.49.

Table 6.50

Sharp Key Signatures			Flat Key Signatures		
Key Signature	Tonic (do)	Black Notes	Key Signature	Tonic (do)	Black Notes
	C	—		C	—
	G	F#		F	Bb
	D	F#,C#		Bb	Bb, Eb
	A	F#,C#,G#		Eb	Bb, Eb, Ab
	E	F#,C#,G#,D#		Ab	Bb, Eb, Ab, Db
	B	F#,C#,G#,D#,A#		Db	Bb, Eb, Ab, Db,Gb

Mystery Song

Figure 6.51

Mystery Song

Figure 6.52.

collections to collect song material to introduce to the children you teach. It certainly saves you the step of hunting for a recording of a particular song. Plus, it's fun. Once you recognize the key signature, it's easier than you think.

Try it with the little song in figure 6.53.

Okay, here are the steps to sight-singing this little tune:

1. Identify the key signature. One sharp, F-sharp, means G is the tonic. You'll call G *do*.
2. Find *do* on the staff. Do you see it there, on the second line of the staff? It's at the very beginning.
3. If G is *do*, then D is *sol*, E is *la*, and so on. Write the *sol-fa* syllables below the staff to guide you, as in figure 6.54.

Now that you have the *sol-fa* syllables written in, you're ready to sing. If you're away from your tone bars, you could pick any pitch you like and just call it G. If your tone bars are handy, you can play a G and match that pitch with your voice. Now find a steady beat, and sing the song slowly with *sol-fa* syllables and hand signs. Can you hear the melody? If you're singing "Twinkle, Twinkle, Little Star," congratulations: You can sight-sing music!

If you have difficulty, don't worry. Just keep practicing. Sight-singing is a skill that you can develop over time. If you need material for further practice, a hymnal from a church or a collection of simple children's folk songs will do nicely. You could even skip to the songs in part 4 of this book and read some of those.

SIGHT-READING MINOR KEYS

The kingdoms of minor[2] keys are slightly darker-sounding realms, but just as is the case with their major counterparts, a tonic rules over them. The difference is that in a

Mystery Song

Figure 6.53.

Mystery Song

Figure 6.54.

minor key, the tonic is *la*. An ascending tonic triad that begins on *la* makes a minor chord.

Don't worry that you might wander into a minor key by accident, though. Minor keys also have key signatures. Granted, their flags look just like major key signatures, which can be slightly confusing, but at least you'll get some warning before you pass through their mighty gates.

Why do minor key signatures look just like major key signatures? Because a minor scale shares a flag with its *relative major* counterpart. Do you recall reading in chapter 5 that a natural minor scale is built from the

sixth degree of a major scale? That's why you call the natural minor scale the *relative minor* of some particular major scale. The minor scale built on A, for example, shares a key signature with the major scale built on C. C is, therefore, the *relative major* of A minor.

This means a minor scale built on A has no sharps or flats. If you want to see for yourself, take out your natural minor scale strip, place it in front of your tone bars with 1 on A, and pull down the corresponding notes. You won't see any black notes.

Table 6.55 gives you the key signatures for the minor keys (the tonics appear in lowercase letters).

Sharp Minor Key Signatures

key signature	tonic (*la*)	black notes
	a	—
	e	F#
	b	F#,C#
	f#	F#,C#,G#
	c#	F#,C#,G#,D#
	g#	F#,C#,G#,D#,A#

Flat Minor Key Signatures

key signature	tonic (*la*)	black notes
	a	—
	d	Bb
	g	Bb, Eb
	c	Bb, Eb, Ab
	f	Bb, Eb, Ab, Db
	b-flat	Bb, Eb, Ab, Db,Gb

Table 6.55. Sharp and Flat Minor Key Signatures

Now that you can identify the minor key signatures, you can read music in minor keys. The trick is knowing whether a melody is in a minor or a major key, since the key signatures look the same. Here are a couple of ways to tell.

The first way: check out the first and last note, since most minor melodies usually begin or come to rest on the tonic, *la*.

Let's try reading the minor-key song in figure 6.56, called "Ah, Poor Bird.".

Before you read this song, take a closer look. The time signature tells you there are four beats in a measure. With that out of the way, you can identify the key signature. It has one flat, B-flat, which signifies the song as in either F major or D minor. Assume just for a moment that you don't already know the song is in a minor key. You can see that the melody begins and ends on D, which, in this case, is *la*, not *do*. Now that you know that the first and last notes

are *la*, label the other notes with their *sol-fa* names, as in figure 6.57.

By the way, notice the little comma next to *la* in figure 6.57? You also see one on the *ti*. You use that comma to show that this particular *la* and *ti* sit below *do*. You call *la* and *ti* below *do* "low la" and "low ti" and write them *l,* and *t,*.

Now you that you know how to identify a minor melody by recognizing the first and last notes as *la*, the second way to recognize a minor melody is simply to locate *do* and work out the notes from there. The key signature for "Ah, Poor Bird" has one flat, so the key is F. Searching "Ah, Poor Bird" you find F on the first space of the staff. There it is, the third note of the song, the *ta-a* in the first measure. Call that *do*. If that's *do*, then the other notes are easy enough to label and sing.

Want a third way to identify a key as minor? Notice that sharp in front of the C in measure three. Not only

Ah, Poor Bird

Figure 6.56.

Ah, Poor Bird

Figure 6.57.

Fly, Fly, Fly

Figure 6.58.

does that sharp sign not exist in the key signature, but it sits in front of *sol*. Remember from chapter 5 that there are three forms of the minor scale? The harmonic minor scale has a sharp seventh degree—the *leading tone*. If this melody is in D minor, then D is the tonic, and C-sharp is *ti*, the seventh degree.

Figure 6.58 presents a song called "Fly, Fly, Fly." Our three methods will help you read it.

Try it. First identify the key signature. Two sharps: the kingdom of D. And look: the first and last notes of the melody are both B, which in the kingdom of D is *la*. Method one checks out. Let's locate *do*. *Do*, D, is hiding down there below the staff in measure 3. Let's call that *do* and label all the other notes. As for your third method, looking for a sharp sign on *so*, well, this melody has no sharp signs outside of the key signature, so you don't have to worry about that.

So, "Fly, Fly, Fly" is in a minor key that you can easily read.

In sum, use these steps to sing any simple folk song, major or minor, written on a staff:

1. Identify the key signature.
2. Find *do* on the staff, regardless of whether the song is in major or minor. (Or, check the first and last notes; a minor melody will often start and end on *la*.)
3. Label the other notes with *sol-fa* syllables.
4. Tap the steady beat, and read the rhythm with rhythmic *sol-fa* syllables.
5. Sing up and down the major or minor scale a few times to get your bearings.
6. Sing the melody using *sol-fa* names and hand signs.

If you're looking at a stick-notated song, like the songs at the end of this book, your job is even easier.

Just find a comfortable pitch, call it *do*, and start from step 4.

If you find yourself struggling, again, remember that it only takes practice to improve at anything. Because you are human, you can read music. Start by practicing with the songs at the end of this book. Start with the two- and three-note songs, and gradually add pitches until you're comfortable.

For a good exercise book, check out Zoltan Kodály's little booklet *333 Reading Exercises* (Kodály, 1943). The book contains graded sight-reading exercises beginning with little two-note melodies containing *do* and *re* and ends up with melodies that encompass the entire major scale.

By now, you have a command of the major and minor scales, rhythmic *sol-fa*, tonic *sol-fa*, and stick and staff notation: the nuts and bolts of reading and writing music. But just as a pile of disparate parts means nothing until someone assembles the parts into a car or other machine, the nuts and bolts of music are meaningless without someone combining them to make musical ideas such as melodies, songs, and even symphonies. Musical structures go by the name of musical *forms* and an acquaintance with them will help you and the children you teach give shape to their musical follow-up work.

NOTES

1. This rhythm is technically called a "syncopation", which you'll encounter in the next chapter. It's more convenient when singing and playing, however, to give it the *sol-fa* name *syncopa*. Just as it's more convenient to call a quarter note *ta*.
2. From here to the end of the chapter, the word *minor* refers to the *natural minor* scale.

Chapter 7

The House That Music Built: Musical Forms

After a lesson using the Fundamental Needs chart to study the Pueblo people, Jackson and Chanté wanted to follow up by building an adobe-style house. Miss Amy asked them what materials they could use.

"Pudding!" Chanté smiled. "Mmmm."

Miss Amy held back a laugh. Jackson, on the other hand, screwed up his face into an expression of scorn. "Nobody has ever designed a house made of pudding."

Miss Amy acknowledged that Jackson had a point. No architect, Pueblo or otherwise, has ever designed a house out of actual pudding (although the Catalonian Antoni Gaudi used dripping, semiliquid concrete).

However, when architects design structures that display materials such as slabs of concrete and exposed girders, their buildings, in spite of the excitement that they initially generate among the architectural avant-garde, often end up looking boring and ugly. Yet both the unstructured blob and the painstakingly structured edifice have value in architecture. They both grapple in one way or another with the problem of order. Anyone who creates appreciates order in design, whether the person is an architect, a painter, a dancer, or a musician.

Lack of order couldn't be more antithetical to the concept of music. In nature, you already hear disorganized and random sounds. Only by putting sounds together, by assembling them into patterns, do you create music. What's more, music whose factors are chosen carefully and treated in close keeping with their relationship to each other and to the whole has *form*.

Since the ears appraise things by comparison and contrast, a sense of order in music depends on *uniformity*, which makes certain qualities perceptible and easy to grasp and enjoy, and *variety*, which counterbalances the monotony of predictable patterns. Put simply, people enjoy music that contains a skillful balance of unity and variety.

When you present musical forms to the children you teach, whenever they write, play, or compose their musical follow-up work, far from being limited by musical form, they will feel liberated knowing the breadth and scope of the playing field. When listening to music, they will better understand what they hear. When writing music, they will make informed choices about whether to work within or whether to exceed formal limits. To help them in this endeavor, you, too, should become aware of musical forms.

Now that you have some basic music theory under your belt, it's time to look at some common formal designs in music.[1] But first, you must ground yourself with a survey of the raw materials of music.

MUSIC'S RAW MATERIALS

The distribution of tones and chords into measures, the rhythm (long and short tone durations), and the accented and unaccented (heavy and light) pulses, function for composers of all cultures as timber, plaster, nails, and drywall function for carpenters of all cultures—they amount to the raw material used to knock together the finished product.

Just like you see an assemblage of wood, stone, and hardware and call it a house, so you might hear an assemblage of tones, chords, rhythms, and pulses and call it a melody, a pop song, or a symphony. And, just as a carpenter can't think about building his house without considering his materials, so you can't discuss musical forms without first considering yours.

Time

Most other art forms exist in two-dimensional or three-dimensional space, but music exists in time, making *time* music's most essential raw material. Time simply passes while someone sings, reads, or plays a piece of music. The carpenter erects a house on the area of the surface of a concrete foundation, the composer erects a musical edifice on the area of the surface of time. A composer divides this area into so many units of this or that to sketch out a musical design. Put simply, time is the canvas on which the composer draws musical gestures, the block of marble out of which she carves musical forms.

Tempo

A piece of music moves at a certain speed. Since, unlike a painting, photograph, or drawing, a musical picture unfolds panoramically, you perceive it as a procession of successive sounds. A musical scroll passes through your minds at a particular *tempo*, or rate of speed.

Beats

Beats amount to inches on your yardstick of time. They form the system of measurement, the particles of time, that you "count," or that a conductor marks with a baton, or that a drummer bangs out on a kit. The most fundamental beat unit equals about one second of regular time. Assigning a piece of music less or more than this means assigning it a faster or slower tempo.

Musicians often regard *ta,* the quarter note, as one beat, as in time signatures of 2/4, 3/4, and 4/4 (in which, as you recall from previous chapter, the top number specifies the number of beats and the bottom number specifies which note gets one beat). But when writing music, you can assign the beat to any note value you please (8th notes, 16th notes, and so on).

Measures

Musicians call a group of beats a *measure*. Compiling beats into groups of measures allows musicians to obtain a larger unit of time, because larger divisions make quantifying longer chunks of time more convenient, just as using astronomical units (one astronomical unit is the mean distance from the center of the Earth to the center of the Sun) makes expressing the distance between the Earth and other bodies in and beyond our solar system more convenient than using centimeters.

As in the previous chapter, you identify measures visually using vertical bar lines. Aurally, however, you identify measures by strong (accented) and weak (unaccented) beats. Whatever sound falls on the first and heaviest beat of a measure usually stands out as being louder than the measure's other sounds. As depicted in figure 7.1, a *simple* measure contains either divisions of two beats (heavy-light) or three beats (heavy-light-light).

Compound measures contain more than two or three beats, and they always appear as multiplications, or groups, of the units in a simple measure. For instance, think of a measure of four beats as two groups of two beats. The first beat gets the heaviest accent, and since the alternation of heavy and light beats remains constant, the third beat also gets an accent, only a slightly *lesser accent*. A measure of 6/8 time, by the way, consists of two divisions of three beats, with the accented beats on one and four (figure 7.2).

The sizes of measures can differ considerably. They can occupy so small a space as to encompass only the fundamental groups of two and three beats (as in measures of 2/4, 3/8, and 4/4) or they can span as large a space as to embrace as many as twelve beats or more (as in measures of 4/4, 6/4, or 12/8). Regardless of a measure's size, however, the size must be uniform throughout a particular section of music.

An odd distribution of accents results when a measure contains groups of five or seven beats. You can consider a measure of five beats, for instance, 5/4, to be 2+3 beats, in which case the accented beats fall on beats one

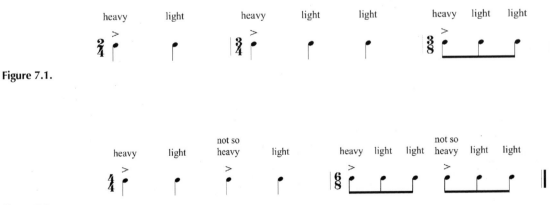

Figure 7.1.

Figure 7.2.

and four, or 3+2 beats, in which case the accented beats fall on beats one and three. For this reason, when you write music in 5/4, 7/4, and even 11/4, you can mix duple and triple groupings to create an irregular distribution of accents (figure 7.3).

Rhythm

The word *rhythm* refers to the arrangement of tones into patterns according to their various *time values* or *durations* (Goetschius, 1904). But the system of measurement given by the time signature as organized into measures alone does not give us the rhythm.

Rhythm refers to the differentiated note durations associated and opposed with each other into discernible patterns. In the first of the two measures in figure 7.4, for instance, the three *tas* constitute a rhythm, even though they merely outline the metric foundation stated in the time signature. Moving to the second measure, the pattern becomes more rhythmic, because it superimposes against the metric "ruler" three different time values.

(If you want to read this sample by the way, remember to identify the key signature as belonging to C, assign C as *do,* and sing *do do do ti, do re* with hand signs. The rhythm syllables are *ta ta ta, tai-ti ta.*)

Taken together, these two measures take on a particular significance and form a distinct pattern.

When you write music, you choose the rhythmic arrangement of tones arbitrarily, but your choices must adhere to certain natural rules. Every tone, for instance, has a rhythmic weight proportional to its duration, meaning that longer tones make heavier, and shorter tones make lighter, impressions.

We call a rhythmic pattern *regular* when longer tones occupy accented beats of the measure or group, and *irregular* when shorter tones occupy the accents, or when longer tones shift to lighter pulses of the measure or group. You identify the example in figure 7.4 as a regular rhythm, because the longest tone opens the beginning of the second measure, giving greater weight to the natural accent of the beat.

Check out the example in figure 7.5 of an irregular rhythm.

Here, a short note on beat one opens the rhythm pattern. The brevity of this opening note causes its weight to shift immediately to the longer *ta* that occurs on the next, weaker beat. Likewise, in the second measure, the succession of *tis* builds to the longer *ta,* which also sounds on a weak beat.

Having long notes on weak beats lends the weak beats a greater feeling of accent. When accents occur on weak beats, you call the resulting irregular rhythm *syncopation.*

Melody

If you and, say, five of your young musicians were to play a cluster of five adjacent tone bars so that all five tones sound simultaneously, you would produce a chord. Play each note in succession, however, and you have created a *melody*. Any succession of single tones constitutes a melody.

Melody, then, amounts to a *line of tones*. If you think of time as the canvas onto which you paint your musical ideas, then melodies make up the lines that trace the design or form of those images. Without those essential melodic lines, your music painting would be the

Figure 7.3.

Figure 7.4.

Figure 7.5.

equivalent of abstract daubs of formless color with no drawing, no evident form or shape. Lines outline shapes; melodies outline music.

In a good melody, all of the tones relate to each other in a way that makes sense harmonically. In other words, a good melody contains a satisfying balance of (comfortable) notes of the chord and (uncomfortable) notes out of the chord to give your ears the impression of tension and relaxation necessary to feel the line's shape, and sense its movement. Good melodies begin, move, rise and fall, and come to rest.

Whenever a number of instruments play successively, they describe a number of melody lines, as many, in fact, as there are instruments playing. In a four-part choir, for example, each voice, the soprano, alto, tenor, and bass, traces out a melody line as it sings, producing four simultaneously moving lines. In an unaccompanied duet, the singers only produce two melodic lines. As you add instruments to accompany the duet, so you add melodic lines. Then too, as multiple lines of melody make up a piece of music, so multiple lines of ink make up an architectural drawing. Very few drawings are made up of one unbroken line.

And, like a drawing, in which lighter lines sketch out broad shapes while darker, heavier, more prominent lines define the outlines of, say, a face, musical lines differ in their degree of importance and prominence. Very often in music one line overshadows all of the other lines and has the greatest prominence. Often you identify this strongest line as *the* melody. Furthermore, this predominant melody line becomes the most important component of the form. Your very recognition and definition of the form depends on it.

The principal melody must be conspicuous so as to attract the listener's attention. You often find it above the rest of the tone-lines, because higher tones tend to attract attention more than lower tones. Composers emphasize the main melody in other ways, too. They place it in the hands of an unusual-sounding instrument, for example, or give it to the low-sounding instruments and have the high-sounding instruments play softly, or drop out altogether. Musicians of all cultures use a variety of techniques to accentuate the chief melodic line.

UNITY AND VARIETY

Although opinions differ when it comes to enjoyment of art, everyone can agree on two important requirements for enjoyment: clarity and attractiveness. Opinions about the details may differ, but the artist's intentions must be intelligible and they must hold your interest. If the art is incomprehensible, or, worse, boring, the artist will have failed to make an impression, and we, the audience will walk away feeling numb.

Clarity and interest in music manifests in playing with the principles of unity and variety. In the area of unity,

the listener perceives the definitions of the form. This is where musicians pour all of their efforts into making their musical expressions clear, intelligible, and definite. In the sphere of variety, the musician generates interest. A soft chord at a moment when the dictates of the form set us up to hear a loud chord, for example, can lend excitement to a musical composition.

But unity and variety must be balanced. Too much unity and the music becomes stilted and predictable; too much variety and the distinctiveness of the form becomes obscured beyond recognition.

Composers express unity and variety in music by balancing the raw materials in the following specific ways (table 7.6):

Table 7.6.

Unity	Variety
Time	
Because music deals with time, divisions of time make up its metrical structure, the basis of which is the beat. Unity dictates that the beats associated with a musical form should be of equal duration. Musicians of all genres admit to the necessity of keeping "strict time," that is, marking the beat in regular pulses.	Although beats occur in uniform duration, they differ from each other by accent. Some beats feel stronger, or heavier, than others. Usually, the heaviest first beat in a group precedes weaker successive beats, giving rise to patterns of duple and triple rhythm patterns. In duple rhythm, the accented beat precedes one unaccented beat, and in triple, the accented beat comes before two unaccented beats. For familiar examples of duple rhythms, check out polkas, rock songs, and marches, for triple rhythms, listen to waltzes and mazurkas, African drumming, gamelan music, electro pop, Bollywood musicals, and so forth.
Measures	
Regular groups of beats occur in measures of uniform duration. The accent occurs on the first beat of each measure in uniform intervals of time.	Measures also contain accented and unaccented beats. The first of two successive accents always sounds a little heavier than the other. In 4/4 time, you accent the first and the third beats, the first being slightly heavier.
Melody	
We can usually find melodic ideas in the first measure of a piece immediately in the next measure and repeated throughout a piece of music. This gives the music a relatively uniform melodic impression that lends a piece of music its identity.	Although the melodic ideas in the first measure may appear again in the second measure, they will likely be varied or changed in the third measure. Doing so counteracts the principle of unity and avoids monotony. Or, the melodic contents may manifest rhythmically, with their pitch shifted higher or lower. Likewise, the pitches in the melody may repeat with a different rhythmic pattern.

Unity	Variety
A figure of accompaniment usually repeats itself from measure to measure throughout whole sections of a piece.	The accompaniment figures, although repeated in uniform rhythmic patterns and melodic directions, undergo many changes in pitch level and shape. They also change from section to section as needed to support the principal melodic idea of the moment.

Now that we've had an overview of the raw materials of music and explored their application in accordance with the principles of unity and variety, let's look at some specific musical forms. We'll begin with the smallest unit of musical construction, the *figure*, and then move through folk song and pop song forms, touch on blues and jazz forms, and, finally, finish up with the complex but logical *sonata-allegro* form.

FIGURES AND MOTIVES

Nowhere but in an examination of form do you see more clearly the resemblance between music and language. Just as expressions in speech grow from the smallest unit of language, the letter, expressions in music grow from the single tone. The smallest cluster of successive tones that has any meaning as a musical idea is called a *figure*. If single tones are the letters of the musical language, then figures are the little words made up of those letters. Extending the analogy, if a figure is a small word, then a small group of figures—called a *motive*—is equivalent to a small group of words (a subject with its article and

adjective, for example). Notice that neither a figure nor a motive constitutes a complete sentence. Two or three motives put together, on the other hand, make up a *phrase*—a complete musical sentence (a subject, predicate, and object), albeit a short one. Figure 7.7 shows the song "Bye, Bye, Baby" so you can see how melodic structure works.

Here, the tones bracketed *fig.* are the figures. Two of these figures make up a motive, and two of these motives make up a phrase.

Although you can compare figures to words, figures don't necessarily sound as concrete nor as distinctly separated as words on a written page. In written language, a convenient space separates every word. In music, figures often blur together, as you see in "Bye, Bye, Baby," where the figures are not separated by any moment of rest. In some melodies, the figures may be separated by a small interval of silence but, in general, figures so closely interlink that you can't distinguish them, so the whole musical sentence strikes us as one coherent tune.

Aside from brief moments of rest, often similarity of formation (rhythmic or melodic direction), and similar metric groupings help us to define the figures (as in the second and third measures of "Bye, Bye, Baby," where the figures are both made up of two *tas*).

Because identifying melodic divisions between figures, being the smallest particles of a musical sentence, can be vague, you can gloss over the details of their construction and move on to motives, as motives will be the little musical building blocks of your children's compositions.

Singing "Bye, Bye, Baby," your ears can clearly discern the motives. The motive in the first two measures is repeated in the beginning of the second phrase, making

Bye, Bye, Baby

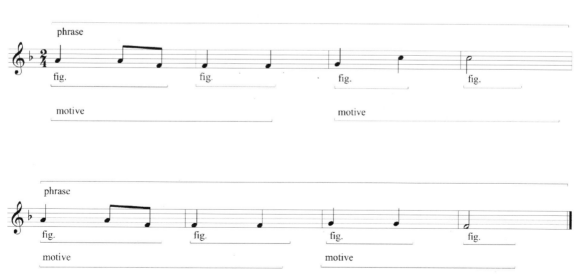

Figure 7.7

it unmistakable. You can also easily hear the second motive (taking up measures three and four), but you may have a harder time defining it as a motive; it has a similar rhythm but different pitches. When comparing these two motives, if you keep in mind the principles of unity and variety, you can see that their identical rhythm (unity) correlates them, yet their intervallic content distinguishes them (variety).

Also, because motives are longer than figures, often the "breaks," or spaces between them become more pronounced, making their extremities easier to define. Hearing no rest or pause, you can usually identify a motive by its length. Melodic motives can take up one measure or as many as four, but they usually only take up two measures. In "Bye, Bye, Baby," the motives extend exactly two measures in length. All in all, you can identify motives by short rests at their boundaries, similarity of melodic or rhythmic formation, and a regular (two-measure) length.

That should be enough information to give you an impression of the accumulative process of making meaning from music. The single tones of the main melody, which communicates the message of the music, unfold as a group of figures, which are organized into motives that combine into phrases, and so forth, until the musician delivers her message.

PHRASES

To express yourself in speech, you organize small groupings of letters, words, and phrases into complete sentences. The musical equivalent of the complete sentence is the *phrase,* except that, unlike a complete sentence, a musical phrase is hard to precisely define. Like so many aspects of music, defining a phrase demands a lot of leeway. Phrases don't conform to readymade technical conditions, such as length, number of measures, rhythmic makeup, or melodic contour.

Just consider the phrase to be the smallest musical unit that expresses a *complete* idea. The unit needn't necessarily be wholly complete nor completely independent of other phrases that surround it to be defined as a phrase, but it's meaning is complete *in and of itself,* much like a short sentence in grammar with its subject, predicate, and object.

To further refine your definition of a phrase, be aware that it has to be long enough to establish a sense of tonality, an awareness of beginning, moving forward, and ending, and it should have a certain amount of interesting, detectable melodic and harmonic material. For this reason the phrase, and nothing smaller, constitutes the *structural* basis of musical form.

Fortunately, you can identify one consistent feature of the phrase: its length. You can say with confidence that, thanks to formal landmarks that have been established over the past 400 years, in the great majority of cases a phrase encompasses exactly four measures in length. If we're dealing with small measures, on the other hand, the phrase may extend as long as eight. With few exceptions, however, phrases take up four measures.

Looking again at "Bye, Bye, Baby,"in figure 7.8, you see two phrases of four measures each.

Two things mark both ends of the phrase, first, an identical motive that signals the beginning of each phrase, and, second, a *ta-a* that gives the ends of each phrase a feeling of pause.

If phrases have a more or less fixed length, what about the content of a phrase? You might be asking yourself whether the harmony, the rhythm, or the melody gives the phrase its identity. The answer: all three.

Generally speaking, the harmony of a phrase regulates the choices of tones that sound simultaneously, like successive upright shafts of tone color that give the music

Bye, Bye, Baby

Figure 7.8

a *body*, or a framework, similar to posts on a fence. The melody of a phrase regulates the choices of single tones, selected from the successive fence posts of harmony, that form a connected strand of tones, like a string of colored lights affixed to each fence post. The melody describes the figure or the *outline* of the melodic image. The rhythm of a phrase gives it *life,* regulating the varying lengths and defining the steady tick-tock-ticking of the musical mechanism.

Although all three of these elements work together, and you can't get a satisfactory musical impression if one of the three is missing, in defining the boundaries of the phrase, the melody takes precedence over the harmony and the rhythm. In other words, when you listen for phrases in music, focus your attention on the melody. Listen for the repetition (with variety) of motives and for the moments of rest that set the phrases apart from each other.

CADENCES

When you speak, you bookend your sentences with natural pauses to catch your breath so that your meaning won't get lost in a jumble of run-on sentences. To indicate these pauses in written language, you use punctuation marks.

When you want a strong, final pause, rightly called a full stop, to bring your sentence to an end, you write a period. A less strong pause, one that doesn't signal the end of the sentence but puts space between the thought you just expressed and the thought coming next, you mark with a comma. When you want to ask a question, you end your sentence with a question mark, at which point the pitch of your voice raises slightly upward.

Phrases, the "sentences" of music, also have natural pauses. These moments of rest in a phrase go by the name *cadences*. Think of cadences as the "punctuation" of music. Strictly speaking, any slight pause in a phrase could be considered a cadence, but we're concerned with the cadences that occur at the ends of phrases in the fourth measure.

In Western art music, composers effect cadences in a variety of ways. A melody racing along might slow down

gradually until it comes to rest on the tonic note. Another melody might end with a loud, long crashing chord. Still another melody might leap upward or downward suddenly to mark the ending. Whichever device ends a piece of music, the cadential effect results generally from a progression of two or three chords, the last of which, the *cadential chord,* stands on the first beat of the composition's final measure.

Cadences, then, are built from chord progressions. It can sometimes take a string of four or five chords to effect a cadence, and textbooks and music dictionaries distinguish several varieties, but you can reduce all of the varieties of cadences down to two: the heavy, final, full-stop sort of cadence—which in rhetoric is equivalent to a period—and the lighter cadence—the equivalent of a comma. The former is called a *perfect cadence* and the latter a *semicadence*.

Perfect Cadence

The perfect cadence provides the ultimate "Ta-da!" at the end of a large-scale piece of music, the one method of concluding a melodic phrase with such a feeling of finality that it leaves no doubt that the entire piece of music, or a large section of it, has ended.

The final harmony in a perfect cadence is always the tonic harmony (I) of the key, with the tonic note, *do,* in the lowest and highest parts. The final note in a perfect cadence is generally a long note that lands on the accented beat of the final measure of the piece. In pieces made up of a single melody, the final tonic note *do* usually comes after *re* or *sol* both of those notes being members of the dominant harmony. In fact, for the perfect cadence to really have a feeling of finality, the tonic chord nearly always follows a dominant (V).

In "Bye, Bye, Baby," the last phrase of which is shown in figure 7.9, the melody lands on the accented beat of the fourth measure of the phrase on the note *do,* preceded by *re*. Our ears hear a dominant (V) to tonic (I) movement in the harmony, giving us a feeling that the song has ended.

Sing the endings of some other folk songs you know and see if they end with a perfect cadence. "Happy Birthday," for example, ends with a perfect cadence moving

Figure 7.9

Figure 7.10

from *re* to *do,* like "Bye, Bye, Baby." "Frère Jacques," on the other hand, ends with the penultimate note *sol* not *re.*

The ending of "London Bridge"shown in Figure 7.10 above, is slightly different. It ends with a perfect cadence, but on the last accented beat the melody lands on *mi* before moving to *do.* This would be unusual, except that *mi* and *do* are both members of the tonic chord. Sing the ending again and notice that *mi* occurs on the strong beat of the last measure of the song only to be succeeded directly by *do.* Sounding *mi* before *do* only serves to slightly delay the feeling of finality.

A cadence that ends on the tonic harmony but doesn't have *do* in the upper and lower parts is a weaker cadence and is therefore a *semicadence.*

Semicadence

You can think of *any deviation from the perfect cadence formula* as a semicadence. The most common deviation occurs when a phrase ends on a chord other than the tonic. The semicadence signals the ending of its phrase, but, like a comma in speech, it doesn't completely detach the phrase from what follows.

The semicadence rests most commonly on the chord of the *dominant,* the fifth step of the momentary key and the second most important harmony to the tonic. In a single melodic line, the notes that you can choose to effect a semicadence are *sol re,* and *ti.* Look at the first phrase of "Bye, Bye, Baby" in figure 7.11 to see the dominant harmony at the end of the phrase.

Singing this, you can't help but feel that the song wants to keep going. Other folk songs have the same effect. In "Happy Birthday," you can hear a semicadence on the words "*Happy Birthday, dear so and so. . .*" The semicadence in Frère Jacques occurs on the words "*dormez- vous?*"

On the third repetition of the words "falling down," you'll find the semicadence in "London Bridge," although it's a special case. In figure 7.12, you can see that although the tonic completes the cadence, you feel no feeling of finality for three reasons: the melody lands on a short note, *mi,* on the accented beat of the last measure; the long note occurs on a weaker beat; and the long note is *sol.* What an ingenious way to carry off a semicadence for such a simple folk song.

In the majority of cases, a phrase that ends in a semicadence, particularly one that begins a two-phrase structure, lands on the dominant.

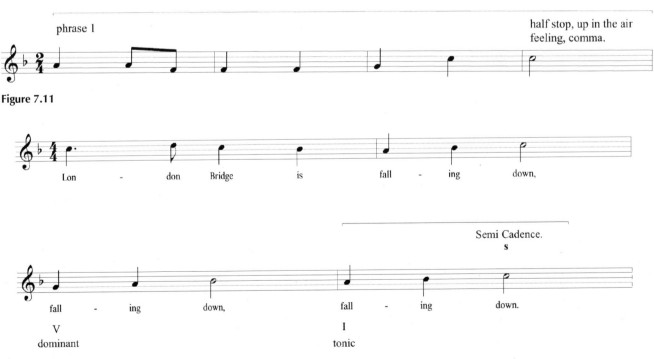

Figure 7.11

Figure 7.12

THE PERIOD

Imagine eavesdropping on your neighbors and hearing these two statements:

Neighbor A: The sky is blue.
Neighbor B: What a tasty cake.

Amusing as this conversation sounds, these two statements have nothing to do with one another. Rarely, in rhetoric, do two people converse in random sentences. More often, especially during an argument, one person makes an assertion, or a *thesis*, and the other makes a counter-assertion, or an *antithesis*, like this:

Neighbor A: The sky is blue.
Neighbor B: The sky *is* blue, except at sunset, when it's a bit pink.

Just as this thesis and antithesis structure forms the basis of conversation, so it forms the structural basis of music. Like sentences, phrases rarely exist alone. The phrase, after all, makes up only a unit, and because you require variety in music, you can't only assert one single phrase. You must add a phrase to a phrase, in order to strengthen and develop the meaning of the first phrase.

At the same time, thanks to the principle of unity, your second phrase can't be made of random material. It must be related to the first, so that the listener can detect a resemblance between the two phrases and hear them as a conversation. Furthermore, again because of variety, the additional phrase should be "new" in some way, so that it feels like it grows out of material from the first. Put simply, the phrases can't be separated. They are related, coherent components that balance each other.

A *period* results when you add a second phrase to the first, creating a double-phrase eight measures long, that is, double the length of a single phrase. Both phrases in a period consist of similar material, but they have their own individual cadence.

The first phrase—called the *antecedent*—brings about its cadence in the fourth measure, while the second phrase—the *consequent*—achieves its cadence in the eighth measure. The strong perfect cadence that ends the consequent phrase makes that phrase not only an addition to the antecedent, which concludes with a weaker semicadence, but also a complement, a "fulfillment." The period has an effect equivalent to the second conversation above: thesis and antithesis or question and answer. Figure 7.13 shows a simplified diagram of a regular period.

The form of "Bye, Bye, Baby," as you can see in figure 7.14, is a period. Sing it and notice the interrogative feeling of the first phrase, with its rising semicadence, and the answering quality of the consequent phrase (figure 7.14).

THREE-PART FORM

In a conversation like the one between your two neighbors earlier, a second speaker answers an assertion offered by a first speaker. A boring conversation might end right there. Interesting conversations, however, go on a bit longer. After answering the first idea, either speaker might offer a third related idea for the two speakers to chew on for a while, before perhaps returning to the original idea and giving it a new twist. In music, like in conversations, ideas must be introduced, developed, and then recapitulated for the conversation to be exciting and interesting, like the following conversation

Neighbor 1: *(assertion)* The sky is blue.
Neighbor 2: *(answer)* The sky *is* blue, except at sunset, when it's a bit pink.

Regular Period Form

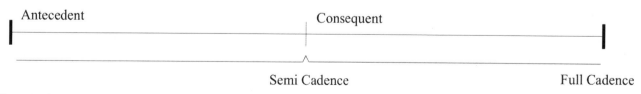

Figure 7.13

Bye, Bye, Baby

Figure 7.14

Neighbor 1: *(development)* Ah, pink, yes. Pink is the color of my beloved's rosy cheeks, or of the flowers surrounding us when you picnic under a summer afternoon sky.

Neighbor 2: *(further development)* An afternoon sky that melts into deep orange and rose hues as the sun begins to set.

Neighbor 1: *(return to main assertion, slightly changed)* Yes, but in the afternoon sky is still blue!

Neighbor 2: Well, It's more of a cobalt, with a little blush in it.

Okay, so maybe that conversation isn't so interesting, but it serves as a little experiment in illustrating the musical form in rhetoric.

From the time European musicians walked around stone cathedrals in brown robes to the time they sat around stone palaces in waistcoats and breeches, they have experimented with ways to combine periods together to make larger, more interesting musical conversations.

They experimented, for example, with putting two or more periods together to form sections of contrasting material and repeating those sections in innovative ways. Many of these groupings of periods have fallen out of fashion, but many stuck and are still with us today.

The strongest and most lasting of their experiments became known as the *three-part form*, which uses three periods consisting of:

PART I.—The statement of the main idea, the principal melody, in period form, closes with a decisive perfect cadence in the principal key. The melodies and rhythms in this first part contain all of the materials

from which the whole piece develops. Conventionally, the capital letter "A" is used as shorthand to refer to PART I. Often this first section repeats once before moving into PART II.

PART II.—A departure from the main idea or, more accurately, an evident continuation of the main idea. This section, referred to in shorthand as a capital "B," develops and builds upon the main idea in such a way that it simultaneously relates to it and furthers it. Also in period form, this section doesn't end as decisively as the first section. In fact, it avoids a decisive cadence in favor of a cadence that leads back to a restatement of the main idea.

PART III.—A restatement of Part I, the main idea. For this reason, convention dictates the use of a capital "A" to refer in shorthand to PART III. Sometimes you hear an exact and complete restatement, and sometimes you hear slight changes or striking variations, with only the first phrase of the main idea having enough material to prove that we've returned to the main idea. Musicians have a lot of latitude here, but in essence, this third section constitutes a return and a confirmation of the original material, with something extra to make us feel as though we've come to the end of a journey.

POPULAR SONG FORMS: AABA AND ABAC

Around the seventeenth century in Europe a very popular dance form emerged out of the three-part form called the *minuet and trio*, an ABA form that consisted of a two-part minuet (A), followed by a contrasting two-part trio (B), with the minuet repeated at the end (A).

The repetitions proved important. After all, they didn't have the capability of recording music then, so composers needed to repeat their ideas to stick them in people's heads.

This minuet form stuck with people, evolved a little bit, and gave Western music the classic song form known as AABA form. In this form, which encompasses thirty two measures—"bars" in more colloquial lingo—an 8-bar main theme (A) is stated, then repeated (A), before a new contrasting, but related, 8-bar secondary theme emerges (B) only to return to the original theme (A). Many classic songs from musicals use this three-part AABA form. Compare the songs "Can't Help Lovin' That Man" (*Show Boat*) and "Tomorrow" (*Annie*) and you'll see that although their themes and styles are completely different, they both follow the same *form*.

Another form, dubbed "Show Tune" form, came from American musical theater. This form feels somewhat stronger and more sophisticated than AABA, but it also spans 32 bars in length.

Its sections are similar to AABA in that each section is 8-bars long, but its sections unfold in a different order. The contrasting B section immediately follows the opening A section, *after* which the A section repeats. Then come the sophisticated bits. Instead of another B section, a C section made up of entirely new material follows. This C section can be climactic, bringing the song to a dramatic close. Good examples of ABAC form are "But Not for Me" (*Girl Crazy*) and "Getting to Know You" (*The King and I*). Literally thousands of songs, show tunes, pop songs, jazz and rock songs have been written using AABA and ABAC forms.

FOLK SONG FORMS

Classics though they are, the AABA form and the ABAC form are only two of a great many song forms. Folk songs, for instance, use a rich variety of structures. Furthermore, these simple forms exist in folk music all around the world. Many of them came to Western ears through the rich musical traditions of Africa.

Strophic Form

Having their origins in practical, useful situations such as, for example, telling a story, herding cattle, reporting news, or performing rituals around a campfire, many folk songs are in *strophic*, or AAA, form. They have different stanzas of lyrics sung to a repeated melody. A common example of a strophic song is "On Top of Old Smokey,"

originally an Appalachian love song. Sing both sets of the lyrics to the same familiar tune:

> *On top of Old Smokey*
> *All covered with snow,*
> *I lost my true lover*
> *from courtin' too slow.*

> *A thief will just rob you*
> *And take what you have,*
> *But a false-hearted lover*
> *Will lead you to your grave.*

AAA form lends itself well to long *ballads*—songs that tell a story—especially when the melody is beautiful and singable. Other examples of strophic folk songs include "Down in the Valley" and "Stewball."

Many Christmas carols, such as "O Little Town of Bethlehem" and "God Rest Ye Merry, Gentlemen" are in strophic form, as well as many beautiful, haunting Native American songs, like "Song of the Snowflakes" (see chapter 14).

Echo Songs

A strophic song that begins with a person singing a melody only to have the same melody repeated by the rest of the group is called an *Echo Song*. You have probably sung echo songs like "Purple Light" and "My Aunt Came Back" around a campfire. Introducing an echo song can get a whole group quickly involved in singing. Echo songs permeate the folk music of Africa.

Strophic with Refrain

Many strophic songs conclude each stanza with a repetition of some sort, called a *refrain*. During the westward expansion of Europeans across the United States, pioneers sang songs that utilized this structure. In "Sweet Betsy from Pike," the story of a pioneer couple enduring great hardships on their way to Nevada, some nonsense words punctuate each episode of the narrative:

> *Did you ever hear tell of sweet Betsy from Pike*
> *Who crossed the wide prairie with her lover Ike.*
> *With two yoke of cattle and one spotted hog,*
> *A tall Shanghai rooster and an old yaller dog.*

> *Singin' tu rali, ooh rali, ooh rali yay.*
> *Singin' tu rali, ooh rali, ooh rali yay*

> *One evening quite early they camped on the Platte,*
> *Made down their blankets on a green shady flat;*

Where Betsy, quite tired, lay down to repose,
While with wonder Ike gazed on his Pike County road.

Singin' tu rali, ooh rali, ooh rali yay.
Singin' tu rali, ooh rali, ooh rali yay

They swam the wide rivers and climbed the tall peaks
And camped on the prairies for weeks upon weeks.
They fought off the Indians with musket and ball
And they reached California spite of it all.

Singin' tu rali, ooh rali, ooh rali yay.
Singin' tu rali, ooh rali, ooh rali yay

As the pioneers settled into their new homes and began to herd cattle, cowboys invented strophic-with-refrain songs to ease their difficult work driving cattle. Look at the structure of the night-herding lullaby "Doney Gal":

We'll ride the range from sun to sun
For a cowboy's work is never done.
He's up and gone at the break of day,
A drivin' those doggies on their weary way.

Rain or shine,
Sleet or snow,
Me and my Doney Gal are bound to go.

A cowboy's life is a weary thing,
For it's rope and brand and ride and sing;
Day or night, in the rain or hail,
He'll stay with his dogies out along the trail.

Rain or shine,
Sleet or snow,
Me and my Doney Gal are bound to go.

Call and Response

The strophic with refrain structure likely found its way to the cowboy pioneers by way of African slaves. In the American South during the time of slavery, groups of African Americans sang and improvised songs together, giving rise to the *call-and-response* format. Like echo songs, in performing these *spirituals,* a leader sang a "call" and the rest of the group followed with a "response." Unlike echo songs, however, the response was often not a direct repetition of the call but rather a repeated word or phrase, an affirmation, an emphatic expression, or a repetition of some heartfelt plea, such as in the song "Mary Had a Baby":

LEADER: (call) *Mary had a baby!*
CHORUS: (response) *Oh, Lord!*
LEADER: *Mary had a baby!*

CHORUS: *Oh, my Lord!*
LEADER: *Mary had a baby!*
CHORUS: *Oh, Lord!*
ALL: (refrain) *The people keep a-comin' but the train*
done gone.

Often, as in the above, the whole group intones a *refrain* at the end of each stanza. You'll find the call-and-response structure in songs like "Amasee," "Just From The Kitchen," and "Mary Had a Baby."

Work songs lend themselves well to the call-and-response structure. Railroad work songs like "Hammer Ring" helped keep railroad workers in sync when slamming great hammers into railroad spikes. A leader sings the call and the entire group slams their hammers down at a particular moment during the response:

LEADER: *Oh, Black-a Betty Black-a Betty, let yo'*
GROUP: *hammer ring. (WHACK!)*

On sailing ships, sea men used *shanties* to pass the time during periods of very difficult work. California sailors used the song "John Kanaka," for example, to pace the hauling on the heavy halyard ropes when raising the sails. The midshipman begins with a call, and at key moments during the response, the crew sing in unison as they haul on the rope.

LEADER: *I heard, I heard, the old man say:*
GROUP: *John Kanaka-naka tu-lai-ay! (HAUL!)*

Sailors all around the world have worked to such call-and-response sea shanties as "Shallow Brown," "Cape Cod Girls" and "Blow, Boys, Blow."

Verse with Chorus (Pop Song Form)

When an especially catchy refrain is sufficiently long and stands alone as a stanza in itself, you call that stanza a *chorus* and the other sections of the song *verses.* This *pop-song* form, also known as ABAB (verse chorus verse chorus), is without a doubt the most common song form in use today.

Often, the verse will support the idea of the song, move the story along, or give further details or emphasis to the chorus, which carries the message of the song in a repetitious, often infectious, singable manner. Songwriters vary the format by adding a contrasting *bridge* section, singing more than one verse before the chorus, or padding the form with other sections, such as introductions or instrumental solos.

Perhaps this form became so popular because record companies discovered its effectiveness in selling songs: the repetition of the catchy chorus sticks the song in the listener's memory.

Round

Have you ever performed "Row, Row, Row Your Boat" by beginning the melody in different parts successively so that the imitations overlap harmoniously together? If so, you've sung a *round*.

Rounds have their origins in medieval England, where they gained popularity among street criers, who used them to grab the attention of potential customers passing by. The round "Chairs to Mend," for example, contains what would have been the cries made by a chair-mender, fishmonger and ragpicker as they plied their trades daily on the streets of Oxford in the 1700s and 1800s.

One of the earliest rounds, found in a manuscript dated from the twelfth century, happens to be "Three Blind Mice." This original version differs considerably from the modern version:

> *Three blinde mice,*
> *Three blinde mice,*
> *Dame Julian*
> *Dame Julian*
> *The Miller and his merry olde Wife,*
> *She scrapte her tripe licke thou the knife.*

Rounds make part-singing easy, since each part only has to learn one melody. You can sing the rounds "Frère Jacques" and "Dona Nobis Pacem" with your classes to produce beautiful harmonies.

Quodlibet

Simultaneously singing different folk melodies that harmonize well together gives you another form that lends itself easily to part-singing: the *quodlibet*.

In fifteenth- century Europe, the practice of combining folk melodies together gave rise to this very versatile form. Combining, for example, the songs "Seagull, Seagull" and "London Bridge" provides children a rich part-singing experience. Likewise, you can sing "Ah, Poor Bird," "Hey, Ho, Nobody Home," and "Rose, Rose" simultaneously for a sad, somber effect. You can find a lovely arrangement of "Turn the Glasses Over" combined with "London Bridge" in Celia Waterhouse's book *How Can I Keep from Singing*—a book published by the British Kodály Academy (see appendix E).

Combinations

Like all aspects of life, defining some song patterns and forms can be difficult. The sections in some songs flow in a "free form" manner, and other songs combine sections in innovative ways. "King Kong Kitchie" combines elements of strophic song with call-and-response and adds a chorus:

> LEADER: *Frog went a' courtin' and he did ride.*
> GROUP: *King Kong Kitchie, Kitchie kai me, oh!*
> LEADER: *A sword and a pistol by his side.*
> GROUP: *King Kong Kitchie, Kitchie kai me, oh!*
>
> ALL: *Kai-mo, Kee-mo, Kai-mo, Kee*
> *Away down yonder in the hollow tree,*
> *A bird and a bat and a bumble bee*
> *King Kong Kitchie, Kitchie kai me, oh!*
>
> LEADER: *Frog he rode an hour or more.*
> GROUP: *King Kong Kitchie, Kitchie kai me, oh!*
> LEADER: *Til' he came down to Miss Mousie's door.*
> GROUP: *King Kong Kitchie, Kitchie kai me, oh!*
>
> ALL: *Kai-mo, Kee-mo, Kai-mo, Kee*
> *Away down yonder in the hollow tree,*
> *A bird and a bat and a bumble bee*
> *King Kong Kitchie, Kitchie kai me, oh!*

THE 12-BAR OR VOCAL BLUES

After the American Civil War, many freed African Americans found themselves out of work and destitute. As a result, a handful of African Americans strapped guitars on their backs and wandered the country, playing and singing about their woes, busking for money. This phenomenon gave rise to a form of music called the blues. Of all the rich formats and variations of the Blues these travelers played, they favored the 12-bar or vocal blues.

The 12-bar blues uses AAB form, a variation of the period form comprising three phrases, the first phrase repeats and the last phrase provides some emphatic statement that closes the form.

> *I found my baby ambling down the road.*
> *I found my baby ambling down the road.*
> *My baby was a hitchin' to ditch her heavy load.*

The basic chord progression of the 12-bar blues unfolds over twelve measures. The chords progress as shown in table 7.15. (Each cell in the table represents one measure.)

Table 7.15 12-Bar Blues

I	I	I	I
IV	IV	I	I
V	IV	I	I

The Roman numerals, as you may remember from chapter 5, indicate the scale degree and quality of the chords to be played. All of the chords are dominant seventh chords. To hear a simple, clear example of the blues form, listen to "Good Morning Blues" by Leadbelly or "Prison Bound" by Memphis Slim. Both are available on the Smithsonian Folkways website.

RHYTHM CHANGES

Jazz musicians use the AABA and ABAC song forms and 12-bar blues extensively in their improvisations, along with one of the most common jazz song forms: *rhythm changes.*

When George Gershwin published the song "I've Got Rhythm" in 1930, people loved it so much that many musicians swiped the song's chord progression to use as a basis for their own songs. Don't worry, though, they weren't stealing. A musician can't copyright a chord progression any more than a painter can copyright a color palette.

The rhythm changes comprise thirty-two measures. The chords, in Roman numerals, progress as in table 7.16.

You might notice first of all the staggering amount of chord changes. Don't worry about memorizing all of those chords. Instead, notice something about the *organization* of the rhythm changes. Drawing your attention to the column to the right, recognize the AABA song form.

Other jazz songs, especially from the late 1930s and early 1940s, such as "Shoeshine Boy" by Lester Young and "Cotton Tail" by Duke Ellington use the rhythm changes form. Later, jazz musicians altered the chords a bit and used different harmonies as jazz became more complex. Even so, rhythm changes remains one of jazz musicians' favorite vehicles for improvisation.

Table 7.16   Rhythm Changes

I vi	ii V	I vi	ii V	**A Section**
I I7	IV vi	I V7	I	
I vi	ii V	I vi	ii V	**A Section**
I I7	IV vi	I V7	I	
III7	-	VI7	-	**B Section**
II7	-	V7	-	
I vi	ii V	I vi	ii V	**A Section**
I I7	IV vi	I V7	I	

JAZZ IMPROVISATION FORM

Yes, as wiggly and jumpy as it may sound, jazz actually follows a strict structure. When jazz musicians get together to improvise, they make things up as they go along, to be sure, but without a structural foundation, their solos would lack direction, shape, and scope.

Before looking at the jazz improvisation form as a whole, consider the history of jazz. Jazz is a uniquely American art form that originated in African American communities in New Orleans in the late nineteenth and early twentieth centuries. On the whole, jazz is a blend of European and African American musical heritages. Until around 1910, jazz was based solely in New Orleans, where brass bands combined marches, French musical forms, and polyphonic improvisation—that is, many voices improvising different melodies all at the same time.

By the 1930s, big dance bands formed, playing fast and hard swinging music with a more bluesy improvisational style. In the 1940s, a style called bebop emerged in which jazz departed the dance hall and became more cerebral "musician's music." Jazz musicians in the bebop era played at fast tempos and favored challenging music that required more chord-based improvisation. More prominent at this time were the soloists, always trying to one-up each other, stepping out in front and grabbing the spotlight. Later in the 1940s, cool jazz developed. Cool jazz musicians sought calmer tempos and smoother, longer melodic lines.

At some point during jazz's development, jazz musicians, perhaps out of pure cheek, started lifting repertoire from famous musicals to use as a vehicle for improvisation. These songs became known as "standards" as more and more jazz musicians learned their forms, chord progressions, and melodies. When playing together, jazz musicians were expected to have the melodies, chords, and structure of hundreds of songs memorized. To make things easier for everyone, a group of students from Berklee College of Music compiled hundreds of "standards" into a huge book called the *Real Book* so jazz musicians would have a reference to work from.

Now, it's time to talk about the brass tacks of improvisation. Essentially, when jazz musicians get together to improvise a song, each member of the group has a specific body of knowledge, that is, they all know the chords, the melody, and the form of the song they're playing.

What's more, each musician has a specific job. The job of the drummer, for example, is to keep the rhythm and mark moments in the song, such as the beginning of a new section. The bass player's job is to follow the drummer's rhythm while playing the roots of the chords so that everyone can hear the chord changes. The piano or guitar player plays the other notes in the chords and also keeps the rhythm going. Those four instruments make up the "rhythm section."

The foundation created by the rhythm section allows the soloist, the trumpet or the saxophone, for example, to step out and improvise his solo. As the soloist improvises, he makes up melodies that go with the chord changes played by the rhythm section.

You can see that even as the musicians make things up as they go along, they must do so in a way that everyone can keep the rhythm, the chord changes, and the form of the song together. When all the musicians are locked into the rhythm, when they're all playing the same chords, when the soloist is playing a melody that fits within the chords, and when everyone knows where they are in the song, beautiful music results.

To make this beautiful music, jazz musicians follow a three-part roadmap. In playing "But Not for Me," for example, the group begins with a short introduction, after which they merely play the song, with the solo instruments playing the main melody. As discussed earlier, "But Not for Me" is an ABAC song form, but it doesn't matter whether the song has an AABA structure, a 12-bar blues structure, or even a rhythm changes structure: In Part I of the improvising structure, everyone just plays the song.

When talking among themselves, jazz musicians refer to this as playing the "melody" (even though they're essentially also playing the chords and rhythm of the song). They call one pass through the song's form a "chorus." So, the first part of a jazz improvisation structure, as you see in table 7.17, is to play one "chorus" of the "melody."

After the group plays a chorus of the melody, they arrive at Part II: the solos (table 7.18). Whether the

musicians work out the soloing order beforehand, or whether they come up with the order spontaneously while playing, each person, including the drummer, plays a solo. When a soloist has improvised once through the song's form, he or she has played one "chorus."

A soloist can play over as many choruses as he wants. When he is finished playing his solo, the next soloist plays for as many choruses as he wants, and so on, until each player has played a solo. Depending on the size of the band, the number of choruses each soloist plays, and the attention span of the audience, this section can take a very long time.

Finally, after everyone in the band has played a solo, the group closes with another iteration of the melody (table 7.19). Usually they only play the melody once, but on this second pass, Part III, they add a little dramatic flourish at the end, such as slowing down the final few measures, or playing a "tag"—repeating the last little bit of the song's melody. Essentially, then, the group ends the three-part structure by repeating the melody again.

Table 7.19. Jazz Improvisation Structure

Part I: Everyone plays the "melody"	Part II: Solos	Part III: Everyone repeats the "melody"
Short introduction, then ABAC, AABA, 12-bar blues, ABAB, or rhythm changes.	Each member of the band plays a solo for an indeterminate number of "choruses"	ABAC, AABA, 12-bar blues, ABAB, or rhythm changes, then "tag" or dramatic ending.

If you thought that jazz musicians just made stuff up, well, you can see that they do and don't. To hear this structure in action, have a listen to Mile's Davis's album *Kind of Blue*. Most of the songs on *Kind of Blue* follow this format, especially "So What" and "All Blues." This improvisation structure occurs in much of jazz music.

Have you noticed a similarity, incidentally, between the jazz improvisation format and the three-part song format you looked at before? One is on large scale and one is small scale, but both essentially begin with an idea, spin that idea around and develop it, and then restate the idea. This tripartite pattern shows itself on the greatest scale in the first movement of most symphonies.

Table 7.17. Jazz Improvisation Structure

Part I: Everyone plays the "melody"
Short introduction, then ABAC, AABA, 12-bar blues, ABAB, or rhythm changes.

Table 7.18. Jazz Improvisation Structure

Part I: Everyone plays the "melody"	Part II: Solos
Short introduction, then ABAC, AABA, 12-bar blues, ABAB, or rhythm changes.	Each member of the band plays a solo for an indeterminate number of "choruses"

SONATA-ALLEGRO FORM

Thinking about that general three-part structure, you can see why it has withstood the test of time. The pattern shows up not only in music but also in painting, literature, history, and rhetoric. It exists in music on a small scale and on a grand scale. In fact, if three-part song form resembles a conversation, then *sonata-allegro form* corresponds to an epic hero's journey.

Picture it: the story begins with a short introduction, after which the heroine makes an appearance in the form of a principal theme. After a short transition, *Lo!*, a second theme appears, the subordinate theme—the word *subordinate* being a misnomer, for this second theme, this second hero, carries no less importance than his counterpart, though he contrasts with her considerably.

After introducing themselves, the heroine and hero depart on a little adventure. The adventure takes them through different kingdoms of the musical world, and in doing so, changes them a bit, though they don't lose their core identity. You recognize them in the twists and turns of their narrative. Finally, the two heroes return home. They have changed slightly after all they have been through, but their journey ends where it began.

From about the mid-1700s, European musicians used variations of this form, which grew out of smaller classical forms that cropped up as an antidote to the busy, formless music of the baroque era. Composers used sonata-allegro form in short, light pieces for harpsichord or piano called *sonatinas,* and for larger pieces for multiple instruments and one soloist called *concertos*. In no musical genre does the sonata-allegro form express itself more monumentally, however, than when hundreds of instruments assemble to play an epic, sweeping *symphony*.

Generally, sonata-allegro form has, again, three divisions: the exposition, the development, and the recapitulation. After a short introduction, the exposition begins, in which two themes take the stage and imprint themselves on the memory. The principal theme appears in the tonic key, or, the home key, and the subordinate theme appears in a different key, often the dominant. After you hear both themes, the exposition ends with some kind of final statement, a cadence, or a transition that will lead us into the middle section. You can diagram the exposition like you see in table 7.20.

The middle section, the development, spins the principal and subordinate themes in all different directions. You hear both themes and even parts of both themes scrambled up into a variety of rhythms and a variety of different keys before the music moves again into a transition that brings us into the third section (table 7.21)

Finally, in the recapitulation, you hear both themes return, only this time you hear both themes in the home key (table 7.22)

After the recapitulation comes some kind of ending. If, like me, you got your first taste of classical music from Bugs Bunny cartoons, you're familiar with the endless finales of grand symphonies that go something like: "Ta da! TA DAAA! TA DA DA DA DA DAAAA! DA! DAAA!" Those big endings have a way of wrapping the whole form up with a nice, fluffy, dramatic bow. For clear examples of the sonata-allegro form, listen to the first movements of Beethoven's 1st, 2nd, 3rd, and 7th symphonies, as well as any of the symphonies by Mozart or Haydn.

Table 7.21.   Sonata-Allegro Form

Exposition			Development
Principal theme	Subordinate theme	Cadence	Various keys, ending with a little transition back to the home key.
Tonic key	Second key		

Table 7.22.   Sonata-Allegro Form

Exposition			Development	Recapitulation		
Principal theme	Subordinate theme	Cadence	Various keys, ending with a little transition back to the home key.	Principal theme	Subordinate theme	Cadence
Tonic key	Second key			Tonic key		

So, there you have it. Music has form. Music has order. More to the point, music embodies *freedom and responsibility*. The saxophone player stepping out to take a solo has the freedom to play whatever he likes, but he's responsible to play within the bounds of the rhythms and harmonies played by the rhythm section.

On the other hand, musicians also have the freedom to subvert these structures. A symphony, for example, can begin in a key other than the home key. Listen to Beethoven's Symphony no. 9 to see how he deviated from the sonata-allegro structure. Still, such deviations must leave us with the impression that the template has been tweaked, not abandoned altogether. In music, as well as in many other aspects of your classrooms, freedom without limits is not freedom at all, but license (or sometimes chaos).

Your knowledge of musical form will help you to guide the children in your classes, to enrich and give shape to their independent musical explorations. Imagine

Table 7.20.   Sonata-Allegro Form

Exposition		
Principal theme	Subordinate theme	Cadence
Tonic key	Second key	

a scenario in which a child writes a melody called "Rain" on the tone bars. Maybe she starts with a sad tune to express her disappointment in seeing gray clouds in the sky and little raindrops plopping onto the pavement. But she stops there. She's stuck. You can spur her creativity by giving her a short lesson on AABA and ABAC song forms.

On another occasion, encourage her to write a second melody that contrasts with the first. Maybe the clouds have parted and a little sunshine slips through. She might make the connection and call her dour first melody the A section, and her slightly happier, more upbeat melody the B section. Now, she might naturally organize the sections of her little piece into AABA form. You can even show her how to organize her piece in different ways, encouraging her, perhaps, to add a splash of sophistication by writing a C section of different material to close her song.

You could help her explore many forms until she settles on one that suits her. As she pursues the formal templates, the child will likely want to write transitions, introductions, or endings. Maybe she will decide that her melody makes a good AAA folk ballad, and she'll pen some lyrics. These are the limits within which her creative expression will run free.

Speaking of structure, in this part of the book you have learned much of the music theory you will need to know to feel confident working with your young musicians. You learned how half-steps provide the building blocks for scales and chords, you learned how to read and write useful rhythms and notes, and you learned how to fit all those building blocks of music into formal structures.

Now that you know *what* to deliver, next, you'll learn *how* to deliver it. In the following chapters, you'll discover the musical concepts and skills that children in your classes will need to explore music independently. You'll discover the pedagogical principles of world-renowned music educator Zoltan Kodály, and you'll learn about a practical pedagogical method that you can implement parallel to your Montessori lessons to get help the children you teach with reading and writing music. Once you start introducing these concepts and activities in your classroom and using the pedagogical model to deliver them, you will notice a marked enhancement of your children's independent music-making.

NOTE

1. This is not to discount the rich variety of formal structures outside the confines of Western music. Iranian music, for example, proffers a complex musical form called a *radif* (meaning "order") which has six "movements": a rhythmic prelude for setting the mood, a rhythmic free-improvised motif, improvised free singing, an ode, some improvised rhythmic music without singing, and a closing dance tune. Since the Montessori music equipment is centered around Western scales, however, and in keeping with Maria Montessori's principle of limitation, we're going to explore just a few the musical forms of Western music. Like much of the world's music in the twenty-first century, Western music comprises diverse multicultural influences. Humanity has given the world a rich potpourri of music. You and your little ethnomusicologists can use the concepts in this chapter as a springboard for further exploration.

PART 3

GOING BEYOND THE BELLS TO BUILD
MUSIC LITERACY

Chapter 8

Musical Concepts and Skills

The children sat around a small table getting ready to have a lesson on composing music with colors (see chapter 12). Mr. Joseph was about to invite the children to choose a painting on which to base their compositions. But first, he opened the art history book and flipped to Botticelli's "The Birth of Venus," in order to help them to get over, as quickly as possible the "naked pictures."

After a quick conversation about the beauty of the human body and its interest for artists, Mr. Joseph invited the children to select a painting for their color compositions. As the children flipped through the art history book, their initial shock about the nudes proved mild (or at least it faded more quickly) compared to their outrage over one of Robert Rauchenberg's *White Paintings* (1951). Like the hostile crowd at the first public exhibit of Rauchenberg's "paintings," the children cried foul.

"Dude," bristled Finn, "A blank canvas is *not art*."

Mr. Joseph invited Finn to consider the artist's intention: to create a painting that looked untouched by human hands, as if it came into the world fully formed and absolutely pure.

"Pfff! Whatever," jeered Finn.

In further defense of Rauchenberg, Mr. Joseph pressed Finn and the others to ponder the conceptual framework of such paintings. In a white painting, the artist's intention is to provide a blank canvas for the lines, colors, and shapes made by the light and shadows playing about the room in which it is hanging.

What pleasure, Rauchenberg must have thought, for the viewer to watch the colors on the white surface change as the sun moves across the sky throughout the day, splashing on the canvas bluish-pink hues in the morning and golden-red hues in the late afternoon. What looks to the layman like a plain white painting is, to the more informed viewer, a dynamic work of art that *nature* creates. How wonderful that it's never the same painting at any given moment!

Rauchenberg understood that deep appreciation of a work of art depends just as much on what the work of art brings to you as what you bring to the work of art. Deep appreciation of a white painting, in other words, requires an understanding of the concepts advanced by the artist.

In music, as in art, part of the audience's enjoyment arises from having a command of a certain set of concepts and skills. The greater the development of those concepts and skills, the better an audience enjoys the music. Musical *concepts* form the material the brain needs to organize incoming sounds and comprehend them as music, while musical *skills* make music manifest for the enjoyment of performers and audiences alike.

In the case of the children you teach, the foundation for their independent music-making is a familiarity with the concepts of *sound,* sensations perceived aurally; *rhythm,* patterns of sound and silence occurring in time; *melody,* sequential strings of rising and falling musical tones; *harmony,* the simultaneous sounding of two or more tones; and *form,* the design or formal plan of musical thoughts and ideas.

Before going into detail about the musical concepts and skills that children need, however, take a look at this quick overview of the three stages of musical concept development, which are vitally important for building independent musical activity in children. These three stages give your musical exercises and activities shape and direction, and they help you identify the learning in every musical activity in which the children you teach are engaged.

MUSICAL CONCEPT DEVELOPMENT

Children acquire musical concepts via a three-stage process: *aural perception,* the processing of sounds though the ear; *accommodating,* the process of enlarging and interpreting aural information in the brain; and *transferring,* the application of previous learning to new situations (Irwin and Nelson, 1986).

Having these three stages of concept development in mind when using the short- and long-term planning strategies given in chapter 10, or when collecting, organizing, and designing songs and activities for the children you teach helps you enrich their musical experiences, turning an otherwise one-dimensional sing-along into a musical mini-lesson in which children perceive, accommodate, and transfer musical concepts.

You, the teacher, initiate the aural perception stage through directed activities such as singing, playing, moving, or creating. Accommodating happens inside the mind and body of the child. Transfer happens independently, when you initiate musical activities, present lessons from your Montessori music album, and make suggestions for follow up, all within an optimal environment for music-making (table 8.1).

Table 8.1.   Musical Concept Development

Aural Perception	Accommodating	Transferring
The teacher sets up an optimal environment and initiates musical activities such as singing, moving, playing, or creating. This includes visual cues, labeling, and manipulating.	The internal mental process of the child's brain makes sense of the musical concepts.	Encouraged by the teacher's lessons and activities and inspired by the environment, the child listens to music, sings, plays, moves, or creates independently.

Aural Perception

Musical learning begins with and centers around sounds received by the ear. In order for aural perception to happen, you must draw the children's attention to separate sounds. In a Montessori environment, children are surrounded by a rich variety of sounds every day. This can easily become white noise if you don't direct the children's attention to individual sounds in the environment.

Occasionally calling for everyone to listen to a specific sound during the work cycle or at times of transition throughout the day, or even playing the silence game, can help children develop their skills at hearing individual sounds. When you teach a new song or model singing a melody, the children must listen attentively. When you model a musical concept, you model it as genuinely and with as much reverence as you can, knowing that the children are listening.

For children, however, listening often isn't enough. Since children possess a variety of learning modalities,

you must facilitate and help aural perception through visual cues; acting and manipulating; and naming.

Drawing melodic contours in the air with your hand while you sing, placing black bean bags on a staff made of yarn stretched out on the floor, showing the children hand signs or *icons*—pictorial representations of musical sounds—and using musical notation are visual cues that reinforce aural perception. A picture of a bird *high* in a tree and a frog *low* on the ground, for example, gives children a visual perception of high and low sounds. For them to truly "hear" a musical concept, children must have aural experiences that go hand in hand with some visual cue.

Along with visual cues, children need many opportunities to manipulate and experiment with musical sounds and sound production. Stretching their bodies and reaching up high or crouching down low helps reinforce the concept of higher and lower pitches, as do standing up and sitting down, pointing to the ceiling, or pointing to the floor. Of course, they can also reproduce high and low sounds with their voices or on instruments.

While children are hearing, seeing, and manipulating musical concepts, they must *name* them, so they associate their aural experiences with symbols and terminology. Naming musical concepts helps ground and reinforce children's aural experiences. Learning the terms *high* and *low* to refer to higher and lower sounds, for example, provides children the vocabulary necessary to reflect on, share, and make sense of their aural experiences.

Accommodating

Once children have perceived a musical concept, such as a high versus low pitch, for example, seen it represented visually on a poster or as notation, acted it out with their bodies, and named it *high* and *low,* their brains file it away. Exactly what happens in each child's brain is a mystery, but somehow the newly acquired concept of *high* and *low* joins with previous information, changing and enlarging it in order to accept it and make use of it. The child *accommodates* the new understanding of high and low sounds along with the musical symbols and terminology associated with it and integrates it with previously learned concepts.

Transferring

The children *transfer* when they recognize, identify, or apply a previously learned musical concept to a new situation. In a Montessori classroom, where the children are free to move about and engage in independent activities, transfer often happens spontaneously. Two children might pair up to sing a learned song and have one child sing the "high" part and the other person sing the "low" part. They might move their bodies up and down spontaneously to the contour of a song they're singing. As they illustrate their dinosaur research with a pterodactyl up in the air and a brontosaurus down on the ground, they might make high squawks and low grunts.

You, the teacher, can facilitate transfer by asking the children to locate the highest sound in an unfamiliar song, or add high and low sound effects to a story, or select the lowest in a group of three new sounds. However transfer happens, the children identify previously-learned concepts and apply them to some new situation.

A full discussion of how and when to deliver the concepts and skills described in this chapter will follow in subsequent chapters. For now, familiarize yourself with the specific musical concepts and skills your children need to develop on the way to becoming musically literate human beings.

SOUND CONCEPTS

From writhing in the womb to writing at a desk, children who can hear are swaddled in a blanket of sound. Even in a "silent" classroom (a rare occurrence in Montessori), the sounds of birds outside, wind against the window, traffic on the street, and even the sounds of children's own heartbeats envelop them, reinforcing their sense of being alive and helping them make sense of the world.

Sound also forms the basis for language. We organize our thoughts, hopes, feelings, and dreams into recognizable patterns of sound and communicate them through speech. Musical sounds also help us communicate our feelings, enhancing our ability to express ourselves. Exploring the nuances in sound helps develop children's awareness and forms a solid foundation for further musical learning.

Kinds of Sound

The characteristics of sound fall into four categories: *pitch,* highness or lowness; *dynamic level,* loudness or softness; *timbre,* tone color or quality; and *duration,* length of sounds. In music, for example, a high note (pitch) can be played softly (dynamic), on a flute (timbre), and for four measures (duration). To grasp the components of sound, explore the following concepts with the children in your classes:

* Sounds surround us.
* Sounds can be described with words like high, low, soft, loud, short, and long.
* Sounds from different sources have distinct characteristics or tone colors.

Sounds and Mood

Besides the essence of sound, children should also gain an understanding of the expressive qualities of sound, the ways in which sound communicates feelings and mood. Develop children's understanding that

* sounds can tell us something. They can express thoughts and feelings; and
* sounds can enhance the mood of a poem, story, play, or film.

Timbre

Provide children experience with hearing and identifying the tone colors produced by various musical instruments. Through active listening activities, children learn that

* each kind of musical instrument produces a sound with a unique *timbre* or tone color.

Notation

* Like speech, you can represent musical sounds with symbols to be read by others.
* Many forms of musical notation exist, and composers and musicians continue to experiment with notation systems.
* The system in widest use today was developed by Western European musicians over the past 800 years.

Children need an awareness that sounds, the basis for speech, cradle us. Music consists of sounds with different pitches, dynamics, timbres, and durations. Music can set a mood or describe a feeling, and musical instruments have unique voices.

RHYTHM CONCEPTS

A child walking down the street hums to the beat of his   AuQ12
footsteps. He walks past a factory and hears the steady *clank-clank* of machines working at regular intervals. He rounds the corner and strolls along the beach, watching the waves crest and break with a certain regularity. That night, his father rocks him back and forth, back and forth, while reading him a story. Lying in the dark at bedtime, he hears the steady ticking of his alarm clock on the nightstand. All of these events occur in time. Each has its own rhythm.

Music also occurs in time and has its own rhythm. *Rhythm* pertains to *the progression of sounds and silences over time.* We respond most readily to the aspect of rhythm in music. We tap our toes, clap our hands, snap our fingers, and nod our heads because rhythm inspires us to move. Rhythm amounts to the life force of music.

The following rhythm concepts of *beat, meter, pattern,* and *syncopation* are essential to the child's understanding of rhythm.

Steady Beat and Tempo

The child's ability to perceive the presence or absence of a steady beat in music forms the basis of her understanding of the total rhythmic structure of a piece of music. Children should take part in activities that focus on steady beat as early as possible.

- Some music has a steady beat or pulse, other music has no steady beat or pulse.
- Beats move at different rates of speed, called the *tempo.*

Meter

An understanding of *beat groupings* is important for children to be able to make sense of music. They should understand that

- steady beats in music can be grouped in twos or threes;
- we refer to these groupings of steady beats as *meter*; and
- the first beat of each group gets an accent.

Pattern

Remember that steady beat and meter are the framework on which you hang arrangements of long and short sounds and silences. Children should understand that

- sounds can be long or short;
- rhythm *patterns* consist of groups of long and short sounds. Rhythm patterns also contain silences (or *rests*);
- our language, the words you use when you speak, forms rhythm patterns. When you move, work, or play, the sounds you make form rhythm patterns; and
- the element of *rhythm* in music results from a combination of beat, meter, and pattern.

Syncopation

When you feel accented pulses that occur off the beat, you get a special jolt or feeling of excitement and energy. Different styles of music have accents in different places in their rhythm pattern that produce unique effects. An understanding of this special kind of rhythm pattern encountered in folk, pop, jazz, and classical music begins with the concept that

- an accent or stress on a beat or a part of a beat not usually stressed creates a rhythmic effect called *syncopation.*

When children understand that rhythm pertains to the progression of sounds and silences in time, the components of which are steady beat, meter, and rhythm patterns, you've handed them another piece in the intricate puzzle of music.

MELODY CONCEPTS

Melody stands as the most elemental aspect of music. Long after you leave the theater, concert hall, or club, you may be humming one of the melodies, whose rising and falling and pleasing passage through time you remember with fondness. As you rake, sweep, haul, march, hammer, or walk, melodies lift your spirits and provide the antidote to tedium. Melodies can cause a person to instantly recall his or her fondest memories. The best gift you can give the children you teach is a rich repertoire of melodies that they can hum, sing, play, and pass on.

Melodies have *direction*—that is, they move by *steps* and *skips,* they are built from *scales,* and almost of them begin an end on a *home tone.* A classroom rich with music-making means that children have the opportunity to explore these melodic concepts.

Melodic Direction

Whether a melody is going "up" or "down" forms the most basic concept involved in the understanding of melody. Children learn that

- melodies can move up (to higher pitches);
- melodies can move down (to lower pitches); and
- melodies can stay on the same level.

Melodic Steps and Skips

A discerning ear can not only discern whether a melody traveled up or down but also discern by how much. Did the melody leap upward a large amount or by just a tiny step? Answering such questions provides another building block of melodic understanding. Children realize that

- melodies can move up and down by steps (tones that are close by) or by skips (tones that are far apart).

Scales

In chapter 6, you learned about chains of tones built on sequences of half steps and whole steps called *scales*. Melodies grow from scales, much like paintings grow from palettes of color (except for the white ones). Through scale exercises, children gain an understanding that

- pitches can be arranged into ordered sequences called *scales*;
- major and minor scales move by steps (whole and half), but pentatonic scales contain skips; and
- scales have a hierarchy of tones. The strongest tones feel very much at rest, while the weakest tones immediately give us a feeling of wanting to "resolve" to the more comfortable, peaceful tones.

Home Tone

Scales are the skeleton for the melodic structure of music. Many melodies move away from and return to the first tone of their parent scale, the *home tone*. The *tonic* has pride of place as the home tone in major and minor scales. Children should learn that

- in traditional music of many cultures, melodies generally move away from and return to a *home tone*;
- when the melody returns to its home tone, you feel a strong sense of completion and relaxation;
- the home tone is the first tone of some scales; and
- some scales, such as those that contain only half steps or only whole steps, have no home tone.

Sensitivity to melody helps children construct musical lines that have variety, pleasing shape, and solid endings that give listeners a feeling of satisfaction. Heightening your children's concept of melody increases their enjoyment of music and sharpens their composing and improvising skills.

HARMONY CONCEPTS

If you've ever been to camp and sat around a campfire singing, you likely have experienced the joy and pleasure that results from *harmony,* singing different pitches at the same time. Singing rounds and quodlibets, forms you explored in chapter 7, affords a quick and easy way to get children singing in harmony, as does simultaneously singing melodies made from pentatonic scales.

Children younger than seven often have a difficult time singing in harmony, but they can learn to perceive harmony, and they can create or perform accompaniments on instruments. Older children can sing or play repeated melodic motives—called *ostinati*—while younger children sing melodies in unison to create harmony.

Through listening, singing, playing, and creating music, children explore the harmonic dimension of music and come to an understanding of the nature of harmony. Your work with the children shows them that

- harmony results when two or more pitches sound at the same time;
- harmony has what you call *texture*;
- *homophonic* texture occurs when you sound a melody against a chordal accompaniment, such as when you strum an autoharp and sing; and
- *polyphonic* texture occurs when two or more independent melodies sound together.

Chords

Strumming on an autoharp can give children a sense of *chords*—three or more pitches sounding simultaneously. Children can study the following characteristics of chords:

- Some chords feel comfortable and stable: they provide relaxation or a release of tension.
- Some chords feel uncomfortable and restless: they create tension and need to move.
- Chords have *qualities:* they can be major or minor.
- Chords have *function:* their degree of comfort or discomfort gives shape and movement to a piece of music.

FORM CONCEPTS

With the skillful balance of similar and contrasting ideas, composers and songwriters make arrangements that appeal to people's imaginations, minds, and hearts. Like any great work of art, a piece of music carefully orders musical ideas and extends them into sections, juxtaposing the comfort of the familiar with the challenge of the unfamiliar to create a structure, a *form*.

Children can easily perceive the organizational plan of a piece of music. Young children understand repetition and contrast through movement, creative activities, and visual icons. Older children can create compositions that contain similar and different sections. A child's simple tone-bar melody, for example, can be added to other melodies he or she wrote to create a full-scale composition. Eventually, you can help children organize melodies into compositions with specific pre-established forms—unless, of course, they're inspired to create their own.

Unity and Variety

You read about the concepts of unity and variety in-depth in chapter 7. In a nutshell, songwriters and composers fill their music with enough repetition to create a sense of unity and enough contrast to create a sense of variety. Children can repeat or contrast everything from single melodic ideas to entire sections to learn that

- a piece of music may consist of sections or ideas that can be similar or different; and
- musical ideas can be repeated verbatim, or varied.

Motives

Musical compositions make use of very short melodic or rhythmic ideas called motives. If individual sounds are like letters, then motives are little words that result from combining different sounds. Motives may be repeated frequently within a piece. Guide children in their understanding that

- motives comprise short rhythmic or melodic ideas; and
- motives can be repeated and varied many times throughout a composition.

Phrase

Like words come together to make sentences, a group of motives come together to make a phrase. The phrase expresses a complete musical thought. You can show children that

- phrases have beginnings and endings;
- phrases can be short or long, but they should give us a sense of beginning, moving forward, and ending;
- some phrases end with a feeling of wanting to continue, like a comma in speech, while others end with a sense of finality, like a period; and
- we call these endings *cadences*.

Sections

One or more phrases linked together by their cadences make up the sections of a piece of music. Sections have beginnings and endings, plus transitions that link them together.

In pop songs, you identify sections by a single melody with chordal accompaniment, whereas in classical forms, sections can contain more than one melody in different keys, linked by a *transition* and brought to an end with a *coda*. Whichever style under discussion, you can show the children that

- we assign letters to whole sections of a piece of music;
- the first section and every section similar to it you call A;

- when a section contains material from a previous section, but is varied significantly, you use an apostrophe, as in: A'; and
- one type of a piece in which the first section is repeated is said to have ABA form.

Like our friend who bought that white painting, children who bring a grasp of musical concepts to a piece of music or a musical activity gain a deeper appreciation of the art form. Without a thorough grounding in these concepts, the children's independent musical activity tends to stagnate. On the other hand, practice with these concepts opens up possibilities and gives the children's musical explorations more depth. When a child with a grasp of musical form goes to the tone bars to compose, for instance, she might organize her music into similar and contrasting sections.

What's more, knowing these concepts helps you to pinpoint and direct the learning in the children's musical activities. You can be confident that a child with a grounding in these concepts who spends time sitting in your listening area wearing headphones is likely to be engaged in *active* listening.

MUSICAL SKILLS

Hand in hand with the concepts just described go musical skills, that is, the ability to *listen, sing, move, play instruments, compose,* and *improvise.* Just as a child who hasn't developed the ability to read and write will have a hard time embarking on independent research, so will a child who hasn't found his or her singing voice have a hard time engaging in singing. An awareness of these skills will guide you in bringing to your classroom those musical experiences that afford opportunities to practice the skills children need to become musically literate.

Listening

When a sound reaches the ears of a child who can hear, he or she may react to it, think about it, or just ignore it. It's easy for a hearing child to catch sounds, that is, merely to *hear* them. A child who *listens,* however, actively analyzes the characteristics of the sound. Knowing that sounds have characteristics, mood, and timbre, the child listens for those aspects. We develop children's listening skills when, in introducing a new song, you ask the children to listen to you sing, direct them to listen to music at the listening station, or call their attention to a specific sound in the environment.

When children reproduce sounds from the world in their minds, they practice *inner hearing,* a valuable skill for music-making. When a composer or songwriter writes music, he or she sometimes sings the melodies internally or imagines the soundscapes in his or her mind before committing them to paper. Likewise, a musician can imagine what a piece of written music will sound like before singing or playing it. Inner hearing is not a magic power; children can develop it with practice.

Singing

Every child whose vocal and auditory organs function properly can learn to sing. With frequent practice, children gain increased confidence in their ability to sing. Daily singing provides them with a repertoire of songs, builds community, and affords them deep enjoyment. When singing makes up a part of the daily routine, children's singing improves without special attention.

Merely introducing children to a wide variety of songs and singing games, incorporating singing into daily routines, such as transitions and dismissal, performing short tone-calls to signal the end of activities or time to come in from the playground, or accompanying singing with strummed or pitched mallet instruments are all ways to develop children's singing skills. (You'll find a number of these activities in chapter 13.)

Although children younger than age eight lack the ability to sing an independent melody part while others are singing a different part, older children have the ability to sing in parts. *Part-singing* makes for a rich experience, because it develops the child's singing skills and provides kinesthetic experiences with harmony concepts.

Moving

Children acquire musical concepts through movement (Campbell and Scott-Kassner, 2002). When they pat or hand jive a steady beat, snap rhythm patterns, clap or stomp to denote sections of a song, step to the tempo, or dance the melody, they experience musical concepts kinesthetically. They also experience deep enjoyment from the socialization and cooperation that arises from singing together, moving together, and performing together.

Movement is the means for leading children to more musical-singing and instrument-playing, to composing and improvising in a meaningful way, and to showing evidence of listening with a clear understanding of music's structures and sonic flow. Movement successfully merges children's energies, attitudes, and ideas (Campbell and Scott-Kassner, 2002). Whenever you engage the child in learning a new song, you also direct him or her to move in some way.

Playing Instruments

Children of all ages play musical instruments. Babies shake rattles or squeeze squeaky toys. Infants bang on cardboard boxes and tables or play toy pianos and xylophones. As children grow older, pitched instruments offer challenging and gratifying musical experiences. In our elementary classrooms, children enjoy instruments for playing melodies, such as xylophones and tone bars, and they explore the sounds of instruments for both melody and chordal accompaniment, such as autoharps or ukuleles.

Glockenspiels, xylophones, and metallophones provide both melodic and harmonic accompaniment. Furthermore, children can perform the music of diverse genres and cultures with aplomb, if given plenty of opportunities. Given enough experience, they can produce instrumental sounds by ear and read music that corresponds to sounds on a given instrument (Campbell and Scott-Kassner, 2002).

In fact, instruments are the cherry on top in the performance of classroom songs and singing games. You can enhance songs like "Skin and Bones" or "Hill and Gully Rider" by adding rhythm patterns on percussion instruments or accompaniments; countermelodies; and ostinati on marimbas, xylophones, or tone bars. Children can learn just enough on classroom instruments, including the piano, to provide soundscapes for storytelling or accompaniments for dramatic performances.

However you combine instruments together, facility on instruments comes only through numerous musical opportunities. Children can even use their bodies as percussion instruments, exploring the sounds they produce when clapping, patting, snapping, or stamping.

Composing

The child expresses herself creatively in music through deliberately crafting a melody or song. She organizes sounds to deliberately express a feeling, evoke a mood, or render elements of a story, such as the setting or characters. In doing so, she takes time to reflect and revise her work in a process called *composition*.

Also part of the composition process is notating her ideas so as to transmit them to others or to preserve them. The children needn't be fluent in traditional notation to write down their compositions. Children can progress from invented graphic notation to traditional notation.

You, the teacher, spur a single child or group of children into the composition process by telling stories that fire interest and imagination and by providing the limits of the composition, such as a topic to compose about, or a particular set of rhythms or tones. The compositional limits establish the boundaries of the canvas on which the children paint their musical ideas.

Improvising

Children *improvise* when they engage in spontaneous composition, that is, when they compose on the spot, in the moment. Improvisation lets children play with musical sounds and syntax. Children can experience improvisation on many levels, from improvising movements during a game of "That's a Mighty Pretty Motion" to improvising a jazz solo. At whatever level, the process of improvisation is essential to developing an ease and flexibility in manipulating the language of music (Campbell and Scott-Kassner, 2002).

Often, during a workshop, a teacher will express confusion as to why children in their classes don't independently take up music, even though the teacher sings songs to them on a daily basis. Simply singing to the children and asking them to listen only develops one skill: that of listening. The richest musical experience affords the children an opportunity to exercise as many musical skills as possible. In every musical experience, the children should utilize at least three musical skills, but as table 8.2 illustrates, you can exercise *all* the children's musical skills in any one musical experience.

Table 8.2.

	Activity	Musical Skills
1	Sing a folk song while the children listen.	Listening
2	Sing a folk song while children pat the steady beat.	Listening, moving (gross motor movements)
3	Sing a folk song while children pat, clap, and snap a hand jive pattern.	Listening, moving (fine and gross motor movements)
4	Sing a folk song and have the children sing along in unison while they pat, clap, and snap a hand jive pattern.	Listening, moving, singing
5	Sing a folk song together with the children while they pat, clap, and snap, with one small group of children singing a repetitive pentatonic ostinato.	Listening, moving, singing in parts
6	Sing a folk song together with the children while they pat, clap, and snap, with one small group of children singing a repetitive pentatonic ostinato. Hand another group of children a marimba (making sure to remove the bars that clash) and give them an ostinato to play.	Listening, moving, singing in parts, playing instruments
7	Sing a folk song together with the children while they pat, clap and snap, with one small group of children singing a repetitive pentatonic ostinato. Hand another group of children a marimba and have them play an ostinato they composed.	Listening, moving with fine and gross motor movement, singing in parts, playing instruments, composing
8	Sing a folk song together with the children while they pat, clap, and snap, with one small group of children singing a repetitive pentatonic ostinato. Hand another group of children a marimba and have them play an ostinato they composed. Hand another child or group of children a glockenspiel (with the clashing bars removed) and have them improvise an accompaniment.	Listening, moving with fine and gross motor movement, singing in parts, playing instruments, composing, improvising

Listing these experiences in order doesn't imply that either of them have greater or lesser value. After all, sitting and listening to a song engages children's listening skills and fosters a sense of community. If you only sat and sang to your children, they would at least have some musical experience. The children are less likely to engage in further independent musical activity, however, if they only practice one skill. What they need to spur them on to musical activity is a comprehensive music program to give them an understanding of musical concepts and give them practice with musical skills.

Take heed: in a Montessori environment, full of children of mixed ages, you must pay particular attention to the developmental characteristics of children with regard to music. Children younger than eight, as stated earlier, frequently have difficulty singing in parts. Younger children also lack the motor skills necessary to perform complex movements. Appendices A and B cover children's musical capabilities at various ages and offer advice on how to put together a performance for groups of mixed-age children.

Also, a word to the wise: when performing music activities with your children, start from the beginning. Depending on your children's sense of community and level of obedience, you may need to begin by having them sit and listen to a folk song while patting the steady beat. Gradually, as the children show greater responsibility, you can move them toward performing multiple parts with movement and instruments. It's best to be cautious. Start simple and see what your particular group can handle before moving them up to the next level of complexity.

In September, for example, you might be singing to the children while they listen and pat a steady beat. They might not be singing, moving, or playing musical instruments until May. It all depends on your group. Trying to get a class of children that hasn't cohered into a group with a sense of community spirit to sing in parts, move, and play instruments will only frustrate all involved (check out appendices A and B for more on teaching and leading songs).

THE MONTESSORI MUSIC ALBUM

Having outlined the musical concepts and skills you'll be developing in the children in your classroom, you'll find that the next chapters are dedicated to crafting your music program.

Fortunately, you already have a great start; Maria Montessori and her colleague Anna Maccheroni crafted lessons that develop many of the concepts and skills listed here. These Montessori lessons constitute your foundation. With your newfound command of music theory, it's time to dust off your music album and present those lessons.

You may ask, "What *are* the actual Montessori music lessons?" It seems that every Montessori training center presents a different set of music lessons. My music album from the Montessori Institute of Milwaukee looks very different from that of my colleagues who trained in Portland, Oregon, or San Diego, California.

Fortunately, I and others have been compiling lists of Montessori music lessons, culled from the various training centers. Visit the Making Music in Montessori website (www.makingmusicinmontessori.com) to download my list, which, although for copyright reasons doesn't contain the full lesson scripts, does come complete with lesson summaries and clarification of the musical concepts and skills each lesson addresses. A website called Montessori Commons (www.montessoricommons.cc) has a complete list that includes scripts and all.

After you get the lessons, proceed with caution. Remember that, in a Montessori classroom, the teacher's lesson is only 10 percent of the learning. The rest comes from the child's own repetition, exploration, and practice with the lessons presented. (If you're an elementary teacher, you can inspire the children to work with the follow-up ideas in chapter 11.)

With the lessons alone, the children refine their sense of hearing and gain an intellectual understanding of music theory and notation. Without a grounding in reading, writing, singing, playing, and performing music, however, the children will still only take music so far. Comprehensive as the music lessons may be, by presenting them you only just begin to fulfill the promise of music literacy.

You see, when children can converse in music the same way they converse in their native language, you say they are musically *literate*. A musically literate child, a child who can "read, write, and think music" has the freedom not only to engage in endless varieties of musical follow up but also to express himself or herself in music. No matter what lesson you've shared, such a child will breathe music into your classroom environment.

If you want to get the children in your classrooms *listening*, *singing*, *moving*, *playing instruments*, *composing*, and *improvising*, and if you want them to come in contact with all of the *sound, rhythm, melody, harmony,* and *form* concepts, they need to be musically literate. As you'll see in the following chapters, you can supplement the Montessori lessons with concrete musical experiences that pave the way for children to absorb musical concepts and master musical skills.

Now that you know *what* concepts the children must understand and *what* skills they must develop, this section will outline *a complete pedagogical model* for delivering these concepts and skills.

The model proposed in this book, which you'll see in detail in chapter 10, borrows ideas and techniques from acclaimed composer and music educator Zoltan Kodály. As you'll see, presenting Maria Montessori's lessons and introducing to the children in your classrooms the components of the Kodály method constitutes an *optimal* music literacy program.

Chapter 9

The Kodály Approach

Imagine you're on a road trip that winds through the cities along the Danube River. Heading eastward into Budapest, Hungary, you marvel at the enclaves of pink and yellowish buildings nestled among the grassy hills and rocky rises as you drift by along the highway. Seemingly every billboard that springs up advertises a musical performance of some sort, be it a pop concert, or a performance by a dance troupe, or symphony.

It's no wonder: music has woven itself into the fabric of Hungarian life. Almost everyone in Hungary plays an instrument; almost everyone sings, reads, and writes music. This small country of only ten million people boasts four orchestras in its capital city, several orchestras in every country town, and countless amateur orchestras. Here, the locals consider a person without music education to be illiterate.

This wasn't always the case. Hungary's journey toward musical literacy began in the early 1900s, when Zoltan Kodály (pronounced koh-DIE), a noted Hungarian composer and educator, found himself shocked by the level of musical illiteracy among students entering his academy. His students couldn't read or write a note, and they lacked the slightest familiarity with their musical heritage. At the time, Hungary was still part of the Austro-Hungarian Empire, and only German and Viennese music was considered "good." Kodály's students had little exposure to the richness and depth of Hungarian folk music.

Kodály took upon himself the mission to give the people of Hungary their own musical heritage and to raise the level of musical literacy among not just his students, but among the population as a whole (Choksy, 1974).

BACKGROUND

Kodály was born in Kecskemet, Hungary, on December 16, 1882. His father worked on the railroads and played the violin, and his mother played the piano and sang. As a child, Kodály took piano and violin lessons. Evenings found the whole Kodály household playing chamber music as a family. With the help of his parents, young Zoltan developed a high degree of musical literacy.

As a young man, Kodály developed a fascination with the music of the Hungarian peasants. In 1905, he amassed a collection of over 150 folk melodies. This initial collection, which he considered to be "small masterpieces," formed the basis for his intense study and eventual doctoral dissertation on the structure of Hungarian folk song.

In 1907, Kodály earned his teaching diploma and began giving lectures at the Academy of Music in Budapest. Over time, as he toured the country and observed in schools, he became increasingly aware of the poor condition of music education in Hungary. Though many of the rural peasants could sing Hungarian folk songs, few of them could read or write music. Kodály became distressed at this lack of musical literacy among his people.

As a result, Kodály campaigned to create a musically literate Hungarian society. He worked vigorously on an approach and a method that would improve the music education of future teachers. He pressed for the use of tonic *sol-fa* (a method for using syllables to read music described earlier in this book), gave public addresses, published essays, and actively advocated the establishment of Hungarian folk music as the basis for Hungarian music education. He insisted that this education be approached through the instrument most accessible to everyone—the human voice.

Kodály lived long enough to see many of his ideas put into practice. Between 1950 and 1960, more than a hundred musical primary schools, where music is taught daily, opened in Hungary. As the children in these schools began to learn to think, read, and write music, the population of Hungary gained the musical literacy that Kodály had envisioned (Irwin and Nelson, 1986).

Even today, Kodály's methods thrive in Hungary. In her book *The Kodály Method: Comprehensive Music Education from Infant to Adulthood*, Lois Choksy described going to a summer course at the Danube Bend Summer University at Esztergom, where she "saw and heard group after group of Hungarian school children singing, reading, and writing music." She recalls observing "music permeating the life of the Hungarian people, in both the villages and the cities" (Choksy 1974). Today, Kodály's doctrine has spread far beyond the borders of Hungary.

You're about to get an overview of Kodály's successful system for teaching music: a sequential system that leads to an understanding of musical notation. The basic aim of Kodály's method is to teach children to read and write music through singing, moving, and playing music games. This broad-brush survey of his method will introduce you to Kodály's

- philosophy;
- advocacy of the use of folk songs;
- tonic *sol-fa*;
- rhythm syllables;
- teaching sequence; and
- teaching strategy.

Using Kodály's method parallel with your Montessori lessons, you will give the children you teach the gift of the ability to think, read, and write music.

KODÁLY'S PHILOSOPHY

Kodály believed fundamentally in *music for everyone*. Every person can learn to read and write music as naturally as learning to read and write his or her own language. His mission to create a musically literate population began with the child. He wanted children to learn to love music as *human* sound and as an experience that enriches life.

Kodály maintained that the child's own voice is the most natural instrument, since all children carry their voices with them. Singing is the most direct, powerful means of musical expression, and, because we learn best what we produce by ourselves, singing provides children a strong feeling of success and accomplishment. For this reason, singing should precede instrumental training, as it's in the child's best interest to learn to read and interpret musical notation *before* taking up the study of an instrument.

By having children sing and perform folk songs from their own heritage, and through the use of relative solemnization, Kodály's method aims to aid in the well-balanced social and artistic development of the child and to produce a musically literate adult—"literate in the fullest sense of being able to look at a musical score and think sound, to read and write music as easily as words. Kodály wanted to create a people to whom music was not just a way of making a living, but a way of life" (Choksy, 1974).

USE OF FOLK SONG

The quality of the songs, rhymes, and games you introduce to children has a profound effect on their musical sensitivity. What constitutes an appropriate song, then, becomes your most important concern. The determination of the *beauty* of a song should be made from a child's point of view. A song that seems clever or humorous to you might be puzzling to a child, and a song you might consider boring and repetitive might seem joyful to a six-year-old.

Questions to consider when choosing songs are: Does it stimulate fantasy? Does it open up endless possibilities and invite repetition? Does it delight and enliven? Or does it simply serve a useful pedagogical purpose? (Forrai, 1998)

The determination, however, of the *appropriateness* of a song is up to you. Teachers often fall prey to the Froebelian approach to the "education" of young children, when it comes to selecting songs for music instruction.

One principle Froebel advanced was that songs can be "used" to teach skills and concepts adults considered important for children: how to behave, how to say the alphabet and count, how to brush one's teeth, even how to work and play together. In our own Montessori schools, children learn songs that contain the names of all the continents or all the times tables. Teachers even go so far as to write songs (to existing melodies) that, they hope, will help children remember facts and concepts in a playful and easy-to-recall form.

You have good reason to avoid this approach. For one, children tune out a song's lyrics in favor of the musical characteristics. A child who memorizes a song about the multiples of two, for example, won't necessarily remember specific multiples of two asked to recall them outside the context of the song (though if you ask him to sing the song, he will remember everything about it).

For example, if asked what 2 times 7 is, the child will sing through the song until he arrives at the answer. He will have the same difficulty with songs about continents, manners, or whatever song you use to feed him facts. Not only that, but such songs are limited in scope.

Their purpose is purely didactic, not artistic. The *music* is incidental to the academic, health, or social message the lyrics promote.

Kodály regarded these kinds of songs as poison. Rather than didactic songs, "the young child's nearly infinite capacity to absorb everything in the environment and to incorporate it into his developing sensitivity and values cries out for the rich nourishment of real art. Artistry is not a function of the complexity of the melody or of a pedagogical point made by the text, but of the sheer joy and delight of the sounds, movements, and words. True art does not 'do' anything; it simply is, and by its very existence, it enhances our own" (Forrai, 1998).

A delightful song never gets old. It delights over and over again and never goes out of fashion. The imagery and poetry of a song make a song art, not its didactic or objective accuracy. A song in which a child imagines himself or herself a bluebird or a farmer is of greater artistic value than one that describes the way to brush one's teeth.

Furthermore, the lyrics to a good song needn't be current. The lyrics to the song "Cobbler, Cobbler" are way out of date, but performing the song is just as much fun for a Nike-wearing child of today who runs rubber-soled past the Foot Locker store as it was to the child of the eighteenth century who ran wooden-soled past the cobbler shop. After all, "just as in great poetry, images in songs of nature or of the past are more likely to transport the child beyond his concrete, everyday existence into the realm of ideas and dreams, where art rules" (Forrai, 1998).

Folk songs embody music made by the people and for the people. They form the musical heritage and tradition of human communities. Unlike music that has been composed by an individual for profit, or by a teacher for instruction, folk songs are the product of many people who have written, sung, changed, edited, and passed them along to subsequent generations.

Folk songs are authentic. They arise from useful situations in real life. Pioneers sat around a campfire singing stories for entertainment (e.g., "Sweet Betsy from Pike"). Native Americans sang their children to sleep ("The Owl Sings") or glorified the beauty of the natural world ("Song of the Snowflakes"). To the sailor and the railroad worker, folk songs provided a means of easing the tribulation of back-breaking work ("John Kanaka," "I've Been Working on the Railroad"). To African American slaves, songs made intolerable living conditions more bearable ("Go Tell It on the Mountain") and sometimes provided an aid to escape ("Follow the Drinking Gourd").

Because children learn folk songs from their own heritage as easily as they learn their mother tongue, artful, authentic folk songs from the child's own musical heritage form the basic repertoire of the Kodály method of music education. Also, the melodies of their own folk music, with words in their own language, form the most suitable foundation for the children's singing and improvisation (Forrai, 1998). As the children develop facility with musical literacy, we can expand their musical repertoire to include music of other cultures, nationalities, and languages (Irwin and Nelson, 1986).

Folk songs are often accompanied by *singing games*, which play a vital role in Kodály's vision. As a vehicle for the development of musical skills—listening, singing, moving, and so on—singing games remain unparalleled. When you regularly introduce singing games to the children you teach, it becomes unnecessary to give them technical musical exercises in abstract settings, separated from their games. Skill-building develops easily during singing and performing. Clapping the rhythm of a song or representing higher and lower pitches with hands in the air, for example, are experiences cultivated in the natural, playful performance of a singing game.

Not only musical skills but also the entire personality of the child develops through singing games. A game offers the child a free, pleasant, voluntary activity in which to participate free of judgment. Singing games are cooperative in nature, rather than competitive, and because children can play without pressure or fear, they are less likely to engage in aggressive behavior. The singing game has rules for the order and sequence of its actions. Because the children sing and move together in real time, the singing game carries its own discipline. The children know the rules of the game and accept them.

The imaginary situations engendered by the singing game foster a close relationship between the child and the teacher, since both are "acting" as though they believe the child is a "doggie," for example, or a "grizzly bear." When the child takes on the role of an animal, or a symbolic object such as a little boat or a tree, he or she naturally emphasizes the most important characteristics of the animal or object, coming closer to real artistic expression as arms become sails or tree branches. Finally, the dramatic structure of singing games develops the child's understanding of musical forms. Usually, the activity opens with an image or movement, proceeds through rising tension and comes to a satisfactory conclusion. In a simple game of "Snail, Snail," for example, the game opens with a child at the head of the line leading the other children into a coiled, squished up (often giggling) ball, which he or she then unwinds until, at the end, this leader chooses a new partner to stand at the head of the line. When the child chooses another partner, the tension of the wound-up line dissipates, constituting a kind of "punch line."

This is exactly what happens in a novel, a stage work, or a musical composition, but on a much smaller, faster scale. Through singing games children become sensitive to the essential artistic elements of tension and release.

Singing games generate positive feelings within a group of children as they experience the joy of giving and taking turns. The more they experience the increasing tension and eventual release of the game, the more they enjoy themselves and feel satisfied. The teacher, too, enjoys the game, takes full part in the imaginary situation, plays roles, and manifests relaxation and happiness (Forrai, 1998). When the entire group is singing, moving, and dancing together, they mirror and reinforce the good feelings generated by the entire group buzzing about during the afternoon or morning work cycle.

One final consideration: You will get the most mileage out of song materials whose melodies are based on pentatonic (5-note) scales. For one, unless the child has had many lessons on whole and half steps, which is unlikely, he or she will not have the ability to perceive half steps nor are his or her vocal chords developed enough to distinctly sing half steps in tune (see appendix A, for the musical developmental characteristics of children).

Once children can sing the comfortable, stable, pillar tones of the pentatonic, they'll find it easy to fill in the half steps in between. In fact, children's ability to find pitch, especially in melodies with skips and leaps, benefits more from singing the pentatonic than does singing the major or minor scales. Very young children, from about ages three to six, find the most success in singing pentatonic melodies within the range of a sixth. As they enter the elementary level, you can gradually increase the range of their singing, but only if they have had lots of singing experience at the primary level.

Another value in using pentatonic scales, particularly for the young children, lies in the scales' versatility. The pentatonic scale lacks clashing half steps. As a result, when stacked together in any harmonic combination, the tones of the pentatonic sound beautiful and blend well together. For that reason, you can enrich and enliven a pentatonic folk song with as many countermelodies, ostinati, and instrumental accompaniments as you like. You can also easily add pentatonic countermelodies to folk songs in major or minor keys (check out appendix B, for specific ways to add vocal and instrumental parts to folk song and singing game performances).

TONIC *SOL-FA*

Songs and singing games from the child's cultural heritage lie side by side with tonic *sol-fa* in the child's music literacy toolbox. With practice, children can use tonic *sol-fa* to perceive, identify, and label sound relationships.

Tonic *sol-fa,* also known as movable or relative *do,* has the obvious advantage that the basic pattern *sol-mi,* for example, is the same at any pitch level. When children know the relative sounds of these two tones, they can read them however they are notated.

As children's sight-singing vocabulary increases to the five tones *do, re, mi, sol,* and *la,* they can read and write melodies that can be combined in innumerable creative ways, with beautiful results. Tonic *sol-fa* endures as an invaluable aid in Kodály's method for developing children's ability to think, read, and write music.

Recall from chapter 5 that in tonic *sol-fa,* each step of the major scale has a syllable name: *do, re, mi, fa, sol,* and *ti. Do,* as we said earlier, can be any pitch. Once again, try picking a pitch, calling it *do,* and singing the following:

do re mi fa sol la ti do

Figure 9.1 shows the C-major scale on a staff in tonic *sol-fa.*

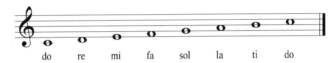

Figure 9.1.

Unlike the above, normally we only use the first letter of the syllable in notation, as in figure 9.2.

Figure 9.2

All major scales come to rest on the *home tone of* do. Kodály found it most convenient to place the home tone, or tonal center, for minor scales on *la.* Try starting on the *la* below *do* (sing down from *do* to find it), and sing figure 9.3, which is in A minor:

Figure 9.3.

Also in notation, whether we're looking at a major or minor scale, we place a subscript comma after the syllables below *do*. We call the tonic of the minor scale on *la* "low la" and we write it *l,*. Likewise, we call the *sol* below *do,* "low sol" and write it as s,. The *do* an octave above the *do* we establish as the tonic gets a superscript apostrophe, as in: d'. Every pitch above that *do* also gets an apostrophe: *d r m f s l t* become *d' r' m' f'*, and so on.

Flipping back again to chapter 5, you'll recall the John Curwen hand sings for the tonic *sol-fa* syllables. Kodály adopted Curwen's hand signs for his method. Sing any of the above examples using the hand signs, and you may find the scales easier to sing. Remember to hold your hand out in front of you and as the scale rises upward, raise your hand accordingly. As the scale falls, lower your hand.

The hand signs function as a visual and kinesthetic link between the sounds and their symbols. Each symbol serves as a visual representation of the sound relationships—the comfort and discomfort—of the tones in the scale.

To render *do,* the most stable, strongest tone, we make a fist. *Re* steps up a little bit, so we make a ramp down which the tone wants to slide back to *do* (*re* is a slightly uncomfortable feeling tone that wants to resolve—come to rest—at *do*). Next comes *mi,* another stable, comfortable tone, which we represent by placing our hand flat, like a platform for the tone to stand on. *Fa* wants to resolve downward to *mi,* so we make a fist pointing our thumb downward.

Next comes *so,* another comfortable tone. We represent *so* by holding our hand out perpendicular to the ground like a wall. *La* is a comfortable tone, but not as comfortable as *do, mi,* or *so,* and it wants to drift upward toward *do,* so we hold our hands limp, with fingers hanging downward, like a jellyfish, or a parachute being pulled upward. Because *ti* wants so badly to resolve upward to *do,* we point our index finger upward. To resolve *ti,* we raise our hand up and fold our index finger back into our fist, landing back on our strong, stable home tone.

Not only do the hand signs help the development of aural perception and in-tune singing by reinforcing sound

relationships with a visual cue, but they also get children physically participating in sound production (Irwin and Nelson, 1986).

Rhythm Syllables

For working with rhythms, Kodály chose syllables close to those in use in the French system. He gave the quarter note, which takes up one sound on a beat, the syllable *ta* and the eighth note—two sounds on a beat—*ti-ti*. The syllables don't constitute names, rather they allow the child to *verbalize the duration of the sounds*.

Using duration syllables, the child can chant a rhythm pattern using the correct rhythm, which would be impossible if he or she used the names of the rhythms. "Quarter note," for example, contains three syllables, that is, three separate sounds, even though the quarter note itself only expresses one sound on a beat. This isn't to say that children shouldn't know the names "quarter note" and "eighth note." The Montessori lessons help the child to understand these terms and their meanings, but for the purposes of *rhythm reading* and performance, the child needs rhythm syllables.

Of course, Kodály came up with rhythm syllables for every possible pattern and combination, but thanks to Montessori's principle of limitation, the most useful rhythm syllables you'll need to get your children going are shown in figure 9.4.

In the beginning, you introduce rhythms without note heads (stick notation) and off the staff. Stick notation facilitates ease of reading and writing while children learn to read notes on a staff. We can also write rhythm patterns using a kind of hybrid of stick notation and standard percussion notation, which features note heads but is disconnected from any kind of staff. You often see this type of notation used for Montessori rhythm card material. Try reading the rhythm pattern from figure 9.5 as you pat or clap the steady beat.

Figure 9.4.

Figure 9.5.

Now try writing some of your own rhythm patterns. Add *sol-fa* syllables to your rhythm sticks, and you'll have composed some melodies.

SEQUENCE OF THE METHOD

When deciding upon an order for teaching musical elements, Kodály rejected the subject-logic approach in favor of a child-centered, child-developmental approach. In a subject-logic approach, the teacher might introduce rhythms according to their note values, starting with the whole note, which encompasses four beats, and then moving down in multiples of two: half notes, quarter notes, and so forth. This sequence makes logical sense intellectually but proves useless to children in practice.

Rather than the subject-logic approach, Kodály's system sequences the material based on the normal child's general abilities at certain stages of growth. Since children experience moving rhythms more readily than sustained ones, Kodály introduces quarter notes and eighth notes first, with quarter notes being the child's walking pace and eighth notes being the child's running pace. These two *elements* form the rhythms of the child's day-to-day life.

The *melodic* elements Kodály introduces come from some of the first tone calls of the playground. When first experimenting with inventing melodies, children in many cultures throughout the world use the tones in figure 9.6.

Figure 9.7 shows the *sol-fa* syllables that make up these early tone calls.

Just as children around the world begin with these first utterances, so Kodály's sequence begins with the *sol-fa* syllables *so, mi, la,* and the rhythm syllables *ta* and *ti-ti.*

We Montessori teachers have a challenge in implementing the Kodály method, in that Kodály designed his sequence for single-aged groups of children. Introduction of the elements encompasses one school year, beginning with a kindergarten sequence and moving year by year

until sixth grade. During each year, Kodály introduces a new developmentally appropriate element that builds on the previous learning. This book adapts the sequence for mixed-age classrooms.

In the primary, children first need to develop a foundation for music-making by using the Montessori materials to refine their senses and gain musical vocabulary. The lower elementary sequence then builds on that foundation by introducing specific melodic and rhythmic elements.

Table 9.8 shows Kodály's sequence adapted for the levels of development as Montessori envisioned them.

TEACHING STRATEGY: "UNFOLDING ELEMENTS"

Overall, Kodály's long-term teaching strategy enables children to (1) recognize the above elements aurally and visually and (2) perform and notate the elements accurately. He introduces *sol-fa* and rhythm syllables in the above order through a detailed long-range teaching plan that resembles a drawn out Montessori Three-Period Lesson. His approach "unfolds" each musical element gradually, in three distinct stages: *the preparation stage, the presentation stage,* and *the practice stage,* so that over a number of experiences, the children attain musical literacy. As you can see from table 9.8, the process can unfold over a long time.

To clarify the Kodály approach's long-range plan, take as an example the unfolding of the melodic elements *sol* and *mi,* an interval pattern that occurs often in folk songs. Since *sol* and *mi* are the first two elements you will introduce to your elementary child, let's assume the children have come into the elementary with a command of the musical concepts and skills introduced in the primary. Here is how the *sol* and *mi* sequence unfolds.

Figure 9.6.

Figure 9.7.

Table 9.8.   Overview of Kodály Sequence Adapted for Montessori Developmental Planes

First Plane	Elements of General Readiness	
	In-tune Singing	
	Free Movement in Space	
	Motions With Songs	
	Stepping/Skipping	
	Comparisons:	
	Same/Different	
Toddler & Primary	*Fast/Slow*	
	Loud/Soft	
	Short/Long	
	High/Low	
	Steady Beat	
	Rhythm	
	Beat vs. Rhythm	
Second Plane	Melodic Elements	Rhythmic Elements
	1. *s* and *m*	1. *ta and ti-ti*
	2. *l*	2. *sh*
	3. *d*	3. *ti-ka-ti-ka*
	4. *r*	4. *4-meter*
Lower Elementary:	5. *l,*	*barlines*
6 to 9	6. *s,*	*measures*
	7. *do-pentatonic*	5. *too*
	(see chapter 6)	6. *dotted half-notes*
		7. *half and whole*
		rests
	8. *so-pentatonic*	8. *sync-o-pa*
	(s l d' r' m' s')	9. *tri-pa-let*
	9. *re-pentatonic*	10. *ti ti-ka*
	(r m s l d' r')	11. *ti-ka ti*
Upper Elementary:	10. *la-pentatonic*	12. *tai ti*
9 to 12	*(l, d r m s l)*	13. *ti tum*
	11. *fa*	14. *3 meter*
	12. *ti*	15. *6/8, 9/8*
	13. *Major Scale*	
	14. *Minor Scale*	

Table 9.9.   Songs Containing *so* and *mi*

S M S M	S M SS M	Mixed Patterns
Bluebird, Bluebird	Hey, Hey, Look	Shoo Rah
Snail, Snail	At Me	Wall Flowers
Starlight, Star Bright	Rain, Rain	Great Big House
Witch, Witch	See Saw	Amasee
Lucy Locket		Shake Them
Pizza Pizza		'Simmons Down
Frog in the Meadow		Just from the Kitchen
Que Llueva		Hill and Gully
		Rider
		Lead through That
		Sugar and Tea

Stage 1: Preparation

In the second phase of a Montessori Three-Period Lesson, the teacher and the child play simple games with the target concept in order to provide the child fun play and repetition. Kodály's Preparation Stage relates to Montessori's Second Period, except that it happens first and takes a lot longer.

Your first task is simply to select four to six songs, dances, and singing games that feature *sol* and *mi* in a prominent place. Table 9.9 shows a partial list of folk songs that contain *sol* and *mi* in clear, obvious contexts.

Once you select a handful of suitable songs that contain *sol* and *mi*, simply sing and perform them over a long period of time to give the children experience with *sol* and *mi* in a variety of contexts. These songs also, incidentally, provide fun opportunities to develop the children's skills of listening, singing, moving, playing on instruments, composing, and improvising.

Initially during the early Preparation Stage, play and sing as naturally as possible, without drawing attention to *sol* and *mi*, the target element. This is what Kodály practitioners refer to as the "happy chaos" stage of learning. During this stage, allow the children to learn the songs very well. Depending on the difficulty of the concept and the developmental stage of your children, this stage can take many days to many years (Brumfield and Glaze, 2006).

Kodály himself recommends that, if you sing, dance, and play with your class every day, this first stage should take about four weeks. Use this as a guideline, but don't rush. Allow plenty of time for exploration and immersion.

Remember that children in the elementary love repetition with variety. Although many of the songs and dances listed above come with established choreography, once the children learn those movements, feel free to use your creativity to invent new movements, combine the songs with instruments, develop the songs into small plays or dramatic performances, or sing the songs as rounds or quodlibets.

Allow children to experience the new elements in a variety of contexts. You can add ostinati to the songs to get the children singing in parts. When you vary the songs and provide the children a variety of ways to experience them, the songs become old friends that children love to revisit over and over again.

Above all, teach the songs by rote.[1] In the early part of the Preparation Stage, refrain from discussing *sol* and *mi* with the children, but feel free to use your hands to shape the rise and fall of the melody or call their attention to the words that occur on *sol* and *mi*. As the children experience *sol* and *mi* in a variety of contexts, gradually draw their attention to and lead them to recognize and identify *sol* and *mi*.

As you enter the middle and late parts of the Preparation stage, begin to focus on *sol* and *mi* (again, without identifying them), by asking children to *compare sol* and *mi*. Lead them to recognize *sol* and *mi* through a variety of aural and physical activities. Ask them to describe the characteristics, or critical attributes, of *sol* and *mi* by making observations such as, "Which sound is higher? Which is lower?"

Finally, as you enter the late part of the Preparation Stage, narrow your song performances to those songs that show *sol* and *mi* in the most obvious context. Use visual cues to get the children reading *sol* and *mi*. At this point, for example, you can have the children read and write *sol* and *mi* physically using hand signs or visually with icons.

Alongside songs and singing games, introduce a series of quick skill-building activities to help children internalize the target elements. To develop their aural skills, children can echo clap or echo sing a song containing *sol* and *mi*, tap the rhythm of the words to a song while singing internally, or perform an ostinato containing *sol* and *mi* while singing.

Physical skill development activities include placing manipulatives on the floor or a felt board, keeping a steady beat while singing, or showing the melodic contour with body signs. Children can also develop their reading skills by reading *sol* and *mi* motives from icons and manipulatives. You'll find a host of these activities in chapter 12.

Table 9.10 summarizes the Preparation Stage.

Table 9.10.   Stage 1: Preparation

Early	Middle	Late
Children sing and perform folk songs and singing games, as well as take part in activities that develop:	As the class performs singing games and songs and take part in skill-building activities, the teacher asks leading questions that direct children to:	Teacher leads previous songs and games and introduces new ones, all the while calling attention to the elements (without naming them) and giving opportunities for the children to:
Listening		
Singing		
Moving		
Playing instruments		
Observation	*Analyze*	*Read and write*
Imitation	*Compare*	*physically and*
Exploration	*Describe*	*with icons*

Stage 2: Presentation

Renowned Kodály educator Susan Brumfield calls the Presentation Lesson the "Presentation Nanosecond." Compared to the Preparation Stage, which can take anywhere from two weeks to a month, the Presentation Lesson constitutes just a fleeting moment. Much like the first stage of the Montessori Three-Period lesson, in which the teacher points to and simply identifies the target element, the Presentation Lesson of the Kodály method sees the teacher (1) isolating the element, (2) naming it, and (3) introducing its notation. All of this happens in less than ten minutes.

Give the Presentation lesson after the children can perform the songs and singing games *accurately*. In the case of *sol* and *mi,* simply gather a small group of children, or

gather the entire group into a gathering and perform the lesson plan (figure 9.11).

After introducing *sol* and *mi*, Kodály teachers present each new melodic element by comparing it to previously learned elements. To demonstrate how the subsequent melodic elements unfold, take a look at figure 9.13 on page 108, where you'll find the Presentation Lesson for the next melodic element, *la*.

The Presentation Lesson for every melodic element you introduce after *la* follows the same format:

- Introduce a mystery song.
- Place the words below the staff.
- Have the children derive the known motives and place them on the staff.
- Ask the children to sing in *sol-fa* syllables and hand signs the previous elements while you "hum" the new melodic element.
- Ask questions that focus on the characteristics of the new element, comparing it to the known elements. ("Is it higher or lower?" "Does it leap away, or is it closer?")
- Place the new notes on the staff.
- Identify the new notes, show the hand sign, and sing the entire motive.
- Have the children sing with *sol-fa* syllables and hand signs.

Setting aside the *so* and *mi* discussion just for a moment, the Presentation Lesson for rhythmic elements has its own script. Let's skip over to figure 9.14 and look at the Presentation Lesson for the first rhythmic elements you'll introduce, *ta* and *ti-ti*, before coming back here and continuing our discussion of Kodály's year-long strategy.

Getting back to our discussion of Kodály's strategy for teaching *sol* and *mi*, so far you have prepared the children for learning *sol* and *mi* by performing and singing many songs and singing games containing *sol* and *mi*, along with some skill-building activities, over a period of weeks. After that, you gave either a small group of children or the entire class a quick, ten-minute Presentation Lesson, where you identified *sol* and *mi*, gave the symbol, showed the staff placement, and gave the hand sign.

Table 9.12 summarizes the first two stages of Kodály's program. Imagine a big fat "You are here" sign after Stage 2.

Stage 3: Practice

Now that the children you're teaching know *sol* and *mi*, their hand signs, and where they are placed on a staff, they can begin the *transfer*—identifying *sol* and *mi* in other contexts. Your next endeavor, in other words, will

Procedure: 1. Sit facing the children.
2. Place a strip of yarn in a straight line out on the floor, between you and the children. (This becomes a 1-line staff.)
3. Invite the children to listen to a "mystery song."
4. Sing "Rain, Rain" on "loo" and ask the children to:
   a. identify the song
   b. draw the melodic contour in the air
5. Say something like "I'm interested in the part that goes…" and place oval icons on the floor, lyrics facing up, pink ones above the line, blue ones below.

6. Children read from the icons showing the melodic contour in relation to the 1-line staff:
   1. sing in parts (half sing the pink, half sing the blue)
   2. sing only the high sound aloud, then only the low (inner hearing)
7. Place two more lines on the staff. Ask children which icons are in the *high space,* and which are in the *low space.*
8. Children sing again, using "high" and "low" names and showing the melodic contour on their bodies (head and shoulders).

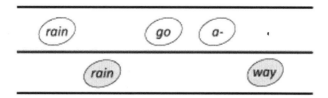

9. Children discover that there is a high sound and a low sound.
10. Give the pitch name of the high sound as *so,* flip over the pink icons, and show the hand sign ☝.
11. Give the pitch name of the low sound as *mi,* flip over the blue icons, and show the hand sign ↳.

12. Sing the staff placement rules. ("When *so* is in a space, *mi* is in the space below it.")
13. Point to the line above *so.* "When *so* is on a line, *mi* is on the line below it."
14. Sing "Rain, Rain" using Sol-fa syllables and hand signs.
15. Children read and sing "Rain, Rain" from the staff using syllables and hand signs.
   Replace icons with black icons or bean bags.
16. Rearrange the black icons or bean bags to make new melodies and have the children read them using syllables and hand signs.

Figure 9.11. Presentation Lesson for so and mi

108 *Making Music in Montessori*

Table 9.12.

Stage 1: Preparation	Stage 2: Presentation
Over a number of weeks, children have daily opportunities to sing, perform, and play folk songs and singing games featuring *so* and *mi*.	A ten-minute presentation during which you, the teacher: • name *so* and *mi* • give the symbol • give the staff placement • show the hand sign

be to give the children *practice* with *sol* and *mi* in new situations.

In the Practice Stage, revisit the songs from the Preparation Stage, this time locating the phrases containing *sol* and *mi*, and singing these phrases with *sol-fa* and hand signs.

This stage, which is equivalent to the third period in a Three-Period Lesson, takes about as long as the Presentation. Children need many opportunities to identify

Procedure:
1. Sit facing the children.
2. Place 5 evenly spaced strips of yarn in straight lines on the floor between you and the children, drawing a 5-line staff.
3. Invite the children to listen to a "mystery song."
4. Sing "Snail, Snail" on "loo" and ask the children to:
   a. guess the song
   e. Say something like, "I'm interested in the part that goes…" and place word cards below the staff and ask the children to:
   a. sing the song while showing the melodic contour.
   b. derive the known Sol-fa syllables (s,m) and place them on the staff.
   c. sing the known pitches in Sol-fa with hand signs, while the teacher "hums" the "new notes"

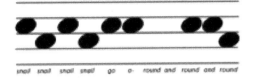

6. Children identify the words on which the "new sound" occurs. ("round" "and")
7. Ask:
   1. "Is the new sound higher or lower than *so?*" (It is higher.)
   2. "Does the new sound skip away from *so* or is it closer?" (It is closer.)
8. Place the new notes on the staff line directly above *so*.

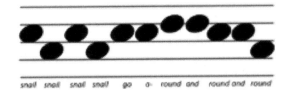

9. Identify the higher sound as *la,* show the hand sign, and sing and sign **s l s m.**
10. Give the staff placement rules, "When *so* is on a space, *la* is on the line above it."
11. Sing "Snail, Snail" using Sol-fa syllables and hand signs.
12. Children read and sing "Snail, Snail" from the staff using Sol-fa syllables and hand signs.
13. Replace the icons with bean bags.
14. Compose a new melody with *so, la,* and *mi* for the children to read using Sol-fa and hand signs.

Figure 9.13. Presentation Lesson for la

Procedure: 1. Sit facing the children and place four pieces of yarn on the floor in front of you, between you and the children.

———   ———   ———   ———

2. Clap a mystery song ("Rain, Rain").
3. The Children identify the song.
4. While you point to the blank space on each beat, the children:
    a. sing while patting the beat
    b. sing while clapping the rhythm.
5. Identify places that have one sound on the beat, then places with two sounds on a beat.
6. Arrange colored umbrella icons showing the rhythm of the target motive: | | ⊓ |

7. Show the symbol for one sound on a beat as | , replace the icons with rhythm cards and name it "ta," then repeat the process with ⊓ , naming it "ti-ti."

| | ⊓ |

8. Read the target motive using rhythm names, children echo.
9. Children speak and sing, reading rhythmic notation.

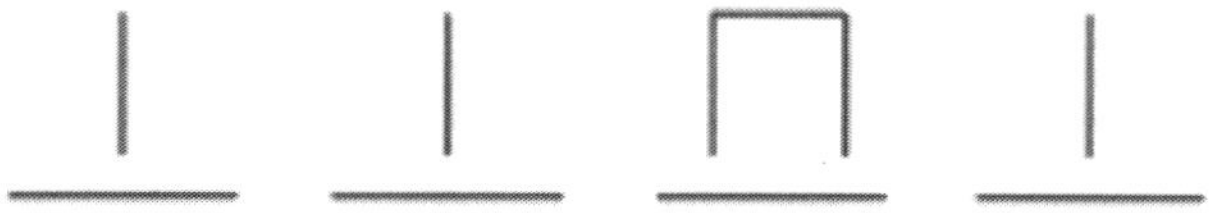

| | ⊓ |
(ta)   (ta)   (ti-ti)   (ta)

10. For early practice, mix up the rhythm syllables and ask the children to read the new rhythms.

Figure 9.14   Presentation lesson for ta, ti-ti

sol and *mi* in new songs and to play motives containing *sol* and *mi* on instruments. By the end of this third stage, the children can use manipulatives or pencil and paper to write melodies containing *sol* and *mi*. (Children delight in composing two-note melodies on a three-line staff.) The children can also improvise ostinati on instruments or with their voices using *sol* and *mi*, having gained proficiency with the two elements.

Of course, in addition to reviewing previous songs and games, lead small groups of children or the entire class in skill-building activities that allow them practice with *sol* and *mi*. Examples include:

- reading four-beat motives with *sol* and *mi* from cards or from a whiteboard;
- reading new songs that contain *sol* and *mi;*
- composing two-note *sol* and *mi* melodies for other children to read;
- identifying new songs from your hand signs;
- singing known songs as partner songs, quodlibets, and rounds; and
- improvising four-beat *sol* and *mi* motives on a mallet instrument while singing.

This book provides many examples of Practice Activities in chapter 12. For now, table 9.15 shows you a breakdown of the Practice Stage.

Table 9.15.   Stage 3: Practice

Early	Middle	Late
Revisit songs from the Preparation Stage, drawing the children's attention to *so* and *mi*. Lead practice activities that reinforce *so* and *mi*. Children, for example, can read and write melodies with *so* and *mi:*	Children continue to do practice activities and experience familiar and new songs with *so* and *mi:*	Children use *so* and *mi* in different ways:
		Part-singing *Dictation* *Creating* *Composing* *Improvising*
	Listening *Singing* *Moving* *Playing*	
Physically (with hand signs) *with icons* *with traditional notation*		

Zooming the camera out gives you a broad perspective of Kodály's three-stage "Unfolding Elements" teaching strategy (table 9.16) for any musical element.

Again, the Kodály strategy unfolds over a long time, depending on your children's developmental level and

Table 9.16.   "Unfolding Elements" Teaching Strategy

Preparation	Presentation	Practice
Select and introduce to the entire class plenty of folk songs, singing games, and skill-building activities that contain the target element. Perform the songs, activities, and games frequently to give the children multiple chances to experience the elements through: • *Listening* • *Singing* • *Moving* • *Playing Instruments* • *Exploring* • *Analyzing* • *Describing* • *Comparing* • *Reading and writing (with icons)* Also present small-group and whole-group skill-development activities. At this stage, we don't name the element.	Give a quick, small-group or whole-group presentation during which you: • *name the element* • *give the symbol* • *give the staff placement* • *show the hand sign*	Revisit the known songs and introduce new ones, drawing the children's attention to the target element. Lead skill-building activities that allow the children to practice the element by first: *Reading and writing:* • *physically (with hand signs)* • *with icons* • *with notation* And then by: • *Listening* • *Singing Moving* • *Playing* • *Part-singing* • *Diction* • *Composing* • *Improvising*

experience. To give an idea of how the process plays out over the course of one school year, let's take the case of a hypothetical Montessori teacher named Miss Nancy. Miss Nancy is a lower elementary teacher who wants to start the year with four elements. She could introduce more, depending on her children, but we'll stop at four for the purposes of this illustration.

Taking care to introduce both melodic *and* rhythmic elements, and proceeding with the elements in Kodály's prescribed sequence, Miss Nancy starts with *sol* and *mi*, then *ta* and *ti-ti*, then *la*, and finally *sh*. Introducing just these four elements, incidentally, will give Miss Nancy's children a lot to go on in terms of generating musical follow-up.

Table 9.17 shows her year-long plan.

Each box in table 9.17 represents one week. Looking at the table, you can see that Miss Nancy starts the year by

Table 9.17. Year-Long Plan for Unfolding Elements

	Sept	Oct	Nov	Dec	Jan	Feb	Mar	Apr	May	June
1	> > > @ < < <									
2		> > > @ < < <								
3			> > > @ < < <							
4				> > @ < <						

1 = *so & mi*   >>>>>> = *Prepare*
2 = *ta & ti-ti*   @ = *Present*
3 = *la*   <<<<<< = *Practice*
4 = *sh*

introducing the elements *so* and *mi*. She chooses the songs "John Kanaka," "Bluebird," "Dinah," "Great Big House," "Snail, Snail," and "Shoo Rah" to prepare *sol* and *mi*.

During the first two weeks of September, in gatherings and during transition times, or even at times when the class is feeling squirmy, Miss Nancy and the children play and perform these songs in a variety of ways. Miss Nancy combines the songs with instruments, sings them with the children in parts, creates spontaneous role-play performances with the songs, and, in small group lessons, she has the children read some of the songs using manipulatives. All the while, during these first two weeks, Miss Nancy gradually calls the children's attention to that *sol* and *mi* motive that all of the songs have in common.

As the class nears the third week, Miss Nancy begins focusing on the song "Snail, Snail," because in that song the motive *sol* and *mi* is clearly defined.

Now Miss Nancy's class has reached the fourth week of September. She observes that the children can sing songs in tune and read the *sol mi* motive accurately. The children seem ready for the Presentation Lesson for *sol* and *mi*. She gathers a small group of children together during the work cycle and gives them the Presentation Lesson. The children follow up the lesson by writing two-note melodies with *sol* and *mi* on the floor with black bean bags on a three-line staff made of yarn. Later, Miss Nancy repeats the *sol mi* Presentation Lesson for the entire class. The next day, some children choose the work of composing melodies with *sol* and *mi* on paper.

So far, Miss Nancy is on track with the elements *sol* and *mi*. She's moved her class through the Preparation Stage and given her children the Presentation Lesson. Looking at her plan, she sees that the fourth week of September is also the time she had planned to start the Preparation Stage for the rhythm elements *ta* and *ti-ti*. During that fourth week, then, Miss Nancy is simultaneously in the Presentation Stage for *sol* and *mi*, and in the Preparation Stage for *ta* and *ti-ti*.

On Wednesday of that week, Miss Nancy introduces some new songs that contain *ta* and *ti-ti*. "Great Big House," which the children already know, contains *ta* and *ti-ti*, so that's one down, Miss Nancy thinks. She adds to

the children's repertoire "Rocky Mountain" and "Wall Flowers."

Consistent with Miss Nancy's plan, the class enters October simultaneously preparing *ta* and *ti-ti* and practicing *sol* and *mi*. An observer in Miss Nancy's class in the first two weeks of October would therefore see the children dancing, singing, and playing instruments to songs with *ta* and *ti-ti*, as well as composing melodies with *sol* and *mi*, accompanying the songs with *sol* and *mi* ostinati and more. By the third week of October, Miss Nancy gives the presentation lesson for *ta* and *ti-ti* as she both finishes practicing *sol* and *mi* and introduces new songs that contain *la*, and so on.

Miss Nancy gave herself three weeks for her Preparation and Practice stages, based on the development and skill level of her children. You may opt to give your children more or less time, depending on their developmental level and experience. Also, some elements may be more difficult than others and may take longer for your children to absorb. The length of the first and third stages of Kodály's program is up to you. Try to block out an approximate length of time for each stage, but remember that observing carefully and assessing your children's facility with an element takes precedence over sticking to an arbitrary time constraint.

Kodály, like Montessori, valued the indirect route, preferring to set up a situation in which children make natural "discoveries" about the critical attributes of musical elements, rather than force-feeding children musical elements with a subject-logic spoon. Chapters 12 and 14 will give you more activities and songs so you can implement Kodály's "Unfolding Elements" program in your Montessori classroom.

Song Collecting

Before closing the topic of Kodály's method, here are a few tips on collecting song material.

Since the invention of portable recording technology, collectors of folk music have gone into communities to gather song material for archival purposes. These archivists have made intimate, personal recordings of elderly people singing their community's ballads and ritual music, have gone to playgrounds in rural communities and recorded the children's games and songs, and they've attended performances of play party dances and square dances. The efforts of these individuals resulted in a wealth of American folk music, from cowboy songs, to work songs, to children's playground songs and rhymes, to ballads.

Kodály practitioners carefully collect and catalog songs. They spend lots of time building and maintaining binders of songs so that all of the songs are organized, for example, by subject or by melodic range. You don't need to become a song archivist, but it's worth it to pay particular attention to what elements the songs in your collection contain.

The song collections cited in Appendix E not only contain some of the best American folk music ever collected, but they also make finding songs with your desired element easy. Each volume organizes songs by melodic and rhythmic elements, so that, if you're looking for songs that contain *la*, a flip to the index will show you all of the songs in the collection containing *la*. These collections also clearly walk you through any movements or dance steps that might go with a particular song.

Also check out *120 Singing Games and Dances for Elementary Schools* by Lois Choksy and David Brummitt (ISBN 136350380), but be warned that although the book has clear, excellent diagrams of the dances and movements for the songs, it lacks an index indicating the melodic elements in each song. Thankfully, the authors organized the songs roughly according to Kodály's sequence, so that simpler songs containing *sol* and *mi* appear at the beginning and the songs get progressively more complex as you near the end of the book.

The Kodály Center for Music Education at Holy Names University has an excellent index of songs online at http://kodaly.hnu.edu/song.cfm?id=592#analysis. Each song contains an analysis of its featured elements.

For the best song collections, contact Kodály organizations, such as the Organization of American Kodály Educators, or the International Kodály Society. Again, Appendix E lists a wealth of resources.

You will find the Kodály approach to be a comprehensive, successful approach to music literacy. In the primary, the method provides the children a scaffold for success. In the elementary, it provides the children the knowledge, skills, and confidence to embark on deeply satisfying follow up. Imagine elementary children writing music to accompany their research or creating musical interpretations of natural phenomena using instruments, voices, and even dance movements. Applying and pairing Kodály's concepts with Montessori music lessons will make this a reality.

NOTE

1. Appendix B gives detailed procedures on the "rote" and "note" methods of teaching a song.

Chapter 10

Putting It All Together

You sit down to observe a primary classroom one morning. The classroom's calm, tranquil atmosphere envelops you. A child washes a table over by the windows. Another child labels the one-thousand chain with numbered tickets.

To your delight, over at the bell cabinet, a child seeming to accompany these activities plinks out a gentle song on the bells. The pleasant chiming tones infuse the room with calm as the other children go about their business. This is the ideal effect of music in the primary: tranquility, concentration, and peace.

You bask in the stillness for a little while before returning to your elementary classroom. A couple of children perform multiplication on the large bead frame. Next to them, another group works with the logical analysis material. Still another group assembles their own leaf-shaped booklets. Yet the atmosphere is far from calm. Who's making all that noise?

The culprits are off in the corner, kneeling in front of a large poster and writing out percussion parts for their music composition, which they titled "Winter Forest." Another group across the room rearranges popsicle sticks on the floor into rhythm patterns and claps the patterns they created. Still another group rehearses the follow up they had devised from a lesson on US history: Some of them sing, dance, and play instruments, while others act out the scenes from the American pioneer ballad "Sweet Betsy from Pike." Debates and conversations ensue. The noise is a small price to pay for the amazing work going on.

In the elementary, music serves a different purpose than in the primary: it provides a context for stimulating debate and urgent, creative energy. What a difference between the two environments: one calm, one buzzing. Both reap the benefits of music in their own unique way.

At this point, you have all the tools you need to create an environment in which musically literate children work in harmony with all of the other academic pursuits. With your understanding of the concepts and skills necessary for musical literacy, your treasure trove of Montessori music lessons, and your grasp of the Kodály method, along with the wealth of activities, lesson plans, and Cosmic Stories coming up in part 4, you have a rich, colorful palette of pigments with which to paint the pictures just described in your classroom.

Now you need a process—a workable method for delivering an almost overwhelming wealth of ideas into a single, manageable, pedagogical plan.

One challenge you face in creating such a plan comes from the fact that Zoltan Kodály designed his approach for traditional classrooms, where two significant conditions prevail. One, the teacher engages the entire group of children in a single activity. Two, the children are all the same age. In your Montessori classroom, where children of different ages engage in diverse activities in small groups, how can you plan multilevel sequenced instruction?

Another challenge you face arises from the question of what musical activities to do and when. With two open, three-hour work cycles per day, it might seem that there isn't much time to implement whole-group music lessons, especially when our method strives to limit teacher-directed experiences as much as possible. Not only that, but within such a structure, how can small groups of children work on music without distracting the others? When is the best time for music?

Yet another question: What damage, if any, does the teacher-led focus of Kodály do to the children's independence? If the teacher apportions musical elements into a sequenced program of instruction, as in Kodály's "unfolding elements" model, isn't that antithetical to the more holistic Montessori approach?

These specific questions can be answered by a comprehensive pedagogical model that

- offers a music teaching plan for a group of multiage children,
- integrates musical activities seamlessly into the fabric of the Montessori work cycle,

- gives children tools for independent exploration to inspire further work,
- provides the children big-picture experiences to spark their interest, and
- balances direct teaching with the children's independent learning.

The pedagogical model on offer here lays those concerns to rest. Juggling Montessori and Kodály ideas into a concise, field-tested method for igniting the fire of music in your classroom without sacrificing the goals of Montessori's vision of independent human development turns out to be easier than it might seem.

Fortunately, the Montessori model, with its uninterrupted work periods and its diversity of children's spontaneous activity, offers us the flexibility to implement a rich, multilevel approach to music pedagogy. Assuming your environment has become a "musical living room" stocked with all the materials, books, recordings, musical instruments, and visual art that stimulates children's interest in music; and assuming you are feeling knowledgeable and confident about both music theory and the concepts and skills children need to make music independently, you're ready to implement this four-level model (table 10.1).

Table 10.1. Making Music in Montessori

LEVEL 1:
Deliver your Montessori music lessons.
LEVEL 2:
Introduce folk songs, singing games, dances, and concept- and
  skill-development activities.
LEVEL 3:
Prepare, present, and practice a sequence of musical elements *a
  la* Kodály's "unfolding elements" model.
LEVEL 4:
Tell Cosmic Stories.

Think of this model as a sandwich, a hamburger, a building—whatever metaphor you like. Whichever way you want to think of it, know that each level of this model is vital. To truly get music off the ground in your elementary classroom, you must be operating all four levels simultaneously.[1]

If you leave out a level, however, you haven't failed. Your children will still have music in their classroom, but, as occurs in classrooms around the world, leaving out any one level will deprive the children's musical explorations of deeper significance, and music will tend to fizzle out. Conversely, if you only implement one level, such as only delivering the Montessori music lessons, your classroom will have music, to be sure, but without a command of the concepts and skills necessary

for follow up, your efforts will be in vain. Music-making among the children will stagnate.

Many Montessori teachers, for instance, accomplish only the most basic requirement for introducing music to their children: that of stocking the classroom with books, recordings, and musical instruments. The children may have an interest in these materials, they might explore in the books and listen to the recordings, but without musical experiences that refine their grasp of musical concepts and hone their skills, their explorations will lack depth, and they will quickly become bored with the classroom music collection.

To truly engender musical independence in your children, deliver all four levels.[2] This chapter explains how to implement each level of the model in depth. By the end of this chapter, you will have a sound picture of how each level works in tandem with the others to foster optimal, independent musical development in your children.

In this chapter, you'll explore each level of the model, become acquainted with a year-long planning overview, and, finally, see the model in action via a narrative picture of a typical day in a musical primary and elementary class.

LEVEL 1: DELIVER YOUR MONTESSORI MUSIC LESSONS

This first level (table 10.2) proves crucial to the flowering of your musical Montessori classroom. Needless to say, these lessons are the cornerstone of our pedagogy. Sprinkle the lessons into your weekly plans alongside your lessons in other areas. Follow the planning model that works for you, but, in general, start at the beginning of your music album and proceed forward, presenting at least one or two music lessons per week, depending on how you do your planning.

Table 10.2. Making Music in Montessori

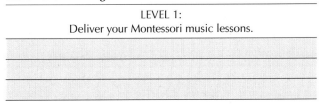

| LEVEL 1: |
| Deliver your Montessori music lessons. |

Deliver each lesson as you do all the lessons in your albums:

1. Gather together a small group of mixed-age children.
2. Tell them a quick story to provide context and to spark interest.
3. Give the lesson in ten minutes or less.

4. Brainstorm or assign follow-up work and facilitate it as necessary.

Although lessons look a little bit different in the primary (you only invite one child, for example), as a primary teacher, you have an imperative to present your music lessons. The work you do lays the groundwork for the children's musical experiences in the elementary. I implore you to bring out your music album and fold in with your other lessons as many music lessons as you can.

If you only deliver your Montessori lessons, you will have already brought your children a long way toward developing music in your classroom, especially if you insist on follow up. Elementary children have a wealth of nonmusical follow-up options. They can research composers or famous pieces of music, for example, build three-dimensional models, such as a mobile of note values; or make a puppet show and act out the "Degrees of the Scale" story. The children may likely want to follow up by composing their own music. (Chapter 11 contains many follow-up ideas.)

Enrich your Montessori classroom with real musical experiences so that the children you teach can practice and develop musical concepts and skills *in context*. They'll gain the skills they'll need to play, improvise, and compose their own music while expanding their follow-up repertoire, taking your classroom music-making to the next level.

LEVEL 2: INTRODUCE FOLK SONGS, SINGING GAMES, AND SKILL-BUILDING ACTIVITIES

Parallel to presenting Montessori presentations, introduce to your children a repertoire of songs, dances, and singing games, as well as concept development and skill-building activities (table 10.3). Ah, yes, you're thinking, but when?

Table 10.3. Making Music in Montessori

LEVEL 1:
Deliver your Montessori music lessons.
LEVEL 2:
Introduce folk songs, singing games, dances, and concept- and skill-development activities

True, the structure of the day in a Montessori classroom calls for two uninterrupted three-hour work periods. Many teachers make room within that structure, however, to bring the whole class together into gatherings. These usually occur in the morning, just before lunch, and in the afternoon at the end of the day.

If each gathering takes, at most, fifteen minutes, that gives you forty-five minutes a day of potential time for music-making. Since each activity takes about five to ten minutes, you could easily start the morning with a song or game, do a quick skill-building or concept-development activity before lunch, and end the day with a song. This is not to suggest that you make music three times a day with your entire class, only that you have that much time to play with.

Concept- and skill-building activities really work well when integrated into the work cycle. Gather a small group of children together and teach a chant, work on steady beat, do some echo-clapping, read rhythms from cards, compose rhythms using popsicle sticks to accompany songs, or compose melodies on the tone bars to accompany chants. Present these mini-lessons in the same manner as you would a Montessori lesson, including follow up.

If you only present your Montessori lessons and introduce songs, dances, games, and concept- and skill-building activities to the children in your class, you will have gone even farther toward optimizing the children's musical experience. The singing, dancing, and playing provided by the songs will hone the children's skills and reinforce the concepts they learn during their Montessori presentations, not to mention expanding their possibilities for follow up.

But you can take music-making to the next level by giving the children the gift of being able to think, write, and read music fluently. Developing music literacy takes children to a much higher level than simply being music consumers—they can become creators as well.

LEVEL 3: PREPARE, PRESENT, AND PRACTICE "UNFOLDING" MUSICAL ELEMENTS

By carefully selecting songs and games that contain particular musical elements, isolating those elements, and then giving children practice with the elements in context, you will give the children in your classroom the gift of being able to read and write music (table 10.4). This means they won't just learn, for example, that quarter notes take one beat; they will be able to hear quarter notes in their heads, play them, sing them, write them down, and read them as if they were words in their own language.

Unfolding elements requires a bit of long-range planning. Start the year by deciding on the set of elements you want to teach. Follow the sequence of elements laid out in chapter 9. Map out the three stages for each element on a yearly calendar, allowing at least seven weeks

Table 10.4. Making Music in Montessori

LEVEL 1:
Deliver your Montessori music lessons.

LEVEL 2:
Introduce folk songs, singing games, dances, and concept- and skill-development activities

LEVEL 3:
Prepare, present, and practice a sequence of musical elements *a la* Kodály's "unfolding elements" model.

per element. Kodály recommends that the children have at minimum seventeen experiences with each element to truly master it, but mastery depends on the skills and musical development of your particular children. Don't rush. Seven weeks is simply a good general guideline.

Suppose, as a lower elementary teacher, you want to introduce the first six melodic elements and the first four rhythmic elements of Kodály's sequence. Table 10.5 shows your year-long plan:

Table 10.5. Year-Long Plan for Unfolding Elements

```
    Sept  Oct  Nov  Dec  Jan  Feb  Mar  Apr  May  June

1 >>>@<<<
2    > >>@<<<
3       > >>@<<<
4          > >>@<<<
5             >>>@<<<
6                >>>@<<<
7                   >>>@<<<
8                      > >>@<<<
9                         > >>@<<<
10                           > >>@<<<
```

1 = *so & mi*	>>>>>> = *Prepare*
2 = *ta & ti-ti*	@ = *Present*
3 = *la*	<<<<<< = *Practice*
4 = *sh*	
5 = *do*	
6 = *re*	
7 = *la,*	
8 = *so,*	
9 = *ti-ka-ti-ka*	
10 = *too*	

Now select a group of songs that contain motives that clearly showcase the elements you want to teach. To make it easy for you to select appropriate songs for each element, the index in appendix E organizes the songs in part 4 by the elements they showcase.

Perform your selected songs, dances, and singing games with the whole class during gatherings. With 3 gatherings per day at most, assuming you only perform music during gatherings, you can treat your children to three musical experiences per day, 21 experiences per week, and 147 over the seven weeks. In total, within seven weeks, you have approximately forty-five

preparation experiences, one short presentation lesson, and forty-five practice experiences. That's a lot of music.

Another opportunity for music-making arises when the children have trouble finding focus during the work cycle. Playing "The Old Gray Cat" with the children when the work cycle gets off-track, for example, can be somehow calming for the children. They get to pretend to be little mice, crouching behind shelves or under tables before creeping carefully toward the sleeping kitty in the middle of the room, who then wakes up and tries to tag the little mice as they flee back to their hiding places. Five minutes of that game, and the children will have let off enough steam to refocus on their work.

During the course of the Preparation and Practice stages, in addition to performing with your children songs, dances, and games, you can lead the children in concept-development and skill-building activities that focus on particular elements.

In the Preparation stage, for example, invite a group of children together to tap the rhythm of the words to a known song while singing internally, identify words on which a new element occurs, or read known motives from manipulatives on a rug.

In the Practice Stage, echo-clap, read known motives from flash cards, combine rhythmic patterns to create rhythms from known songs, or write some melodies using known melodic elements. These activities can take the form of whole-class lessons during gatherings, or small-group lessons during the work cycle (flip to chapter 12 for a full list of such activities).

Moreover, work these concept-development and skill-building activities into the daily routines of the classroom. Dismiss children by clapping or playing the rhythm of their name, or by showing a card with the rhythm of their name written on it. During the work cycle, instead of ringing a bell for attention, sing a soft "Hello!" using a *sol mi* motive. Echo-clap to get children's attention, and make sure you have it when they clap the pattern back.

Look for opportunities to gather children together for a quick musical game or activity, perhaps to refocus them during a chaotic work period. Beat a steady beat on a drum as a signal that it's time for the gathering. Make your drum beats faster and softer as the children complete the circle. While waiting in line, sing signals on short melodic motives, or clap signals on short rhythmic motives. If you look, you'll find plenty of opportunities for working the children's musical muscles.

Recall that the presentation lesson is also a short, ten-minute lesson, much like your Montessori lessons. The children can follow up or not, depending on your plan for their musical development. The children could, for example, follow up a presentation on *sol* and *mi,* by composing two-note melodies. Use their melodies as accompaniments for song performances.

In fact, at any time, accompany songs that you introduce with body percussion or composed and improvised instrumental accompaniments. You could, for instance, compose an accompaniment to the sea chantey "John Kanaka" using a full complement of non-pitched percussion instruments; fold in child-composed and child-improvised parts for metallophones and xylophones; have actors play out some drama to the song while other children sing; and end up with a rich, multifaceted musical experience that builds skills, reinforces concepts, *and* prepares the children for learning musical elements.

Giving your Montessori lessons; introducing songs, dances, and singing games; and using that repertoire to prepare, present, and practice musical elements to foster music literacy will certainly be enough to enrich music-making in your classroom. When you take the children to the final level, however, you accomplish what Maria Montessori set out to accomplish when she and her son Mario developed their concept of Cosmic Education.

LEVEL 4: STORYTELLING

Elementary children need a broad context for everything they do in the classroom. Every year, you tell the first Great Lesson, the "Story of God Who Has No Hands," a broad-brush picture of the creation of the cosmos that contains connections to every area of the curriculum. In your capacity as a "storyteller of the truth," you inundate the children with stories that inspire them and cause them to make connections to the material universe around them, and, in turn, to the greater universe (table 10.6). Moreover, your stories excite the children because they appeal to them at their particular plane of development.

Table 10.6.   Making Music in Montessori

LEVEL 1:
Deliver your Montessori music lessons.
LEVEL 2:
Introduce folk songs, singing games, dances, and concept- and skill-development activities
LEVEL 3:
Prepare, present, and practice a sequence of musical elements *a la* Kodály's "unfolding elements" model.
LEVEL 4:
Tell Cosmic Stories.

When you tell the children stories about the history of music, the development of notation, the development of musical instruments, famous composers, and famous pieces of music, you not only provide the children a big-picture perspective through which they can experience enthusiasm and find a deep sense of connection, but you also highlight the two most important aspects of Cosmic Education: that music is a human achievement, and that music shares a deep connection with every other aspect of the universe.

Deliver Cosmic Stories like you would any other music lesson. During the work cycle, invite a small group of children to a rug or a table and simply tell them a story. Make your story short, but dramatic and compelling. Supplement your story with photographs, music, or artwork.

When telling longer stories, like the "Story of the Grand Staff," which you can download from the Making Music in Montessori website (www.makingmusicinmontessori.com), gather the whole class together, turn off the lights, and captivate them. Chapter 15 offers you a wealth of Cosmic Stories about music and musicians that you can tweak as you see fit and use at your discretion. You can write your own Cosmic Stories as well.

By the time you have implemented all four of the levels of this pedagogical model, the children's options for follow up to your Cosmic Stories will be limitless. Their excitement will lead them to compose music, complete with a written score; to listen with deep intention to pieces of music; or to research famous musicians with the fine-toothed comb of an amateur music scholar.

Moreover, as music becomes part of the culture of the classroom, children will bring music into their other work as well. They will compose music to include in their animal research, set their history puppet shows and dramas to music, compose chants and rhymes about the parts and shapes of leaves and flowers, explore the relationships between geometric shapes and musical scales, and more.

In sum, the structure of the Montessori classroom provides us with plenty of flexibility to deliver the lessons in our other albums, while at the same time delivering Montessori music lessons; introducing a repertoire of songs, dances, games, and enrichment activities; preparing, presenting, and practicing musical elements; and telling Cosmic Stories. All these levels can run parallel, and all of them work together to achieve the ultimate aim: to make music an integral part of a musical classroom in which a small society of musically literate children flourishes.

To give you an idea of the model in practice, take a look at this narrative about a typical week in a primary and an elementary class.

A TYPICAL DAY IN A MUSICAL PRIMARY CLASS

On a warm, April Monday morning in Miss Lucy's primary classroom, the children gather in a circle on the rug where Miss Lucy leads them in the chant "Bumble Bee, Bumble Bee" (see figure 10.7).

Bumble Bee, Bumble Bee,
    Stung a boy upon his knee,
Stung so hard he had to shout.
    I declare that you are out.

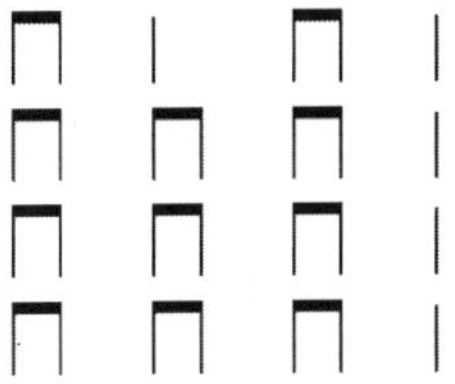

Figure 10.7.

Since they are in the Preparation Stage for the element *steady beat* (see chapter 9 for the primary elements), Miss Lucy simply tells them to do as she does, and they all pat the steady beat while chanting. After a couple of times through the chant, Miss Lucy says, "Let's clap how the words go," and claps the rhythm of the words while the children clap along with her. Then, with a quick "Repeat after me," Miss Lucy claps just one rhythm pattern from the song and asks the children to echo her pattern.

After some classroom business, the children go off and find their work. Miss Lucy's assistant, Caroline, straightens materials and dusts as Miss Lucy gives a lesson on washing a table to Marcus, who's feeling squirrelly this morning. Marcus gets through the lesson and sets about doing the work on his own. Other children focus on their individual work. Nancy polishes a mirror. Ramon works at the painting station. Tyrell gets lost in a pin map. Miss Lucy gives Autumn a presentation.

For her next lesson, Miss Lucy invites Alejandro to the bell cabinet. Alejandro has been through many of the music lessons, and he's ready to start writing melodies on the green staff boards. Miss Lucy places black disks on the green staff board and plays her melody on the bells, inviting Alejandro to place black disks on the board to finish the melody. After doing this a couple of times, Miss Lucy leaves Alejandro free to compose his own melodies. He records his melodies in a little booklet that has pride of place near the bell setup.

As the hands of the clock near lunchtime, the children start feeling unfocused. Miss Lucy gathers everyone together for a quick game of "Paige's Train." (An appropriate game, since the children haven't finished the Practice Stage for *comparing fast and slow tempos*.) Everyone sits in a circle and Miss Lucy begins the song, substituting the word *allegro* for "fast" and *andante* for "slow." The children delight in the game. They set up for lunch and head out to recess.

In the afternoon, Miss Lucy gives a lesson on the movable alphabet to Charlotte, who's practicing her reading, and plays the "Bring Me Game" with leaf shapes with

Shantise. She notices Bea and Samuel seem keen to walk on the line. So, Miss Lucy takes out her hand drum and plays a soft, steady *ta ta ta ta* rhythm for Bea and Samuel, who know that is the cue to *walk* on the line. Other children hear the drum and want to join, so Miss Lucy allows it, only this time, she takes out her rhythm movement cards.

She holds up the quarter note card and the children walk around the room slowly and carefully. She holds up the eighth note card and they walk a little faster, almost at a run. The children smile and laugh as they move around the room. Then, Miss Lucy shows the dotted quarter eighth card and the children skip around the room.

After a few rounds of this, the children grow tired. They settle back into their individual work. Miss Lucy gives Jenny a lesson on addition with the small bead frame. She then gives Quinn a lesson on matching the bells before the children clean up and gather at the rug. After reading to the children, Miss Lucy dismisses them by clapping the rhythm of their names. Genevieve and Anthony become confused. Each of their names contains three claps! They decide to leave together.

In this narrative, Miss Lucy worked the first three levels of our model into the fabric of the children's day. She presented lessons from her music album and performed chants and songs with the children during gatherings or times of transition. She selected the chants and songs carefully, as "Bumble Bee, Bumble Bee" and "Paige's Train" contain musical elements from the "unfolding elements" primary track.

Not only that, but Miss Lucy used musical activities during transitions and at times when the children were restless. Notice that Miss Lucy played a drum, rather than a CD of recorded music, for the "walking on the line" activity. If Miss Lucy weren't available to play for the children, the classroom assistant or even an older child could play the drum. Either way, playing a live instrument sends a particular message: Everyone can make music.

A TYPICAL DAY IN A MUSICAL ELEMENTARY CLASS

The last week of October has descended on Mr. George's upper elementary class. Just outside the classroom's tall windows, the leaves on the trees reveal bright red, orange, and yellow hues under the light gray morning sky. The children sit in a circle around the gathering rug.

Mr. George stands up and motions for all the children to do the same. Smiling, he announces that he's thinking of a song they know. He tells them to do as he does. Mr. George claps and pats his knees to a rhythm pattern from the song "Skin and Bones." As the children echo his movements, he watches carefully to see who is imitating the motions accurately.

Since Crystal displays exemplary clapping technique, Mr. George hands her a tambourine and quickly teaches her the pattern. He then asks the class if they can guess, judging by the rhythm pattern they played using body percussion, what song he was thinking of. Ryan raises his hand and guesses "Skin and Bones." Mr. George tells the class to do as he does. He leads the class in singing "Skin and Bones." As they sing, they pat their knees to a different rhythm pattern derived from the song, all except Crystal, who plays the previous pattern on the tambourine.

Mr. George sees that Genevieve is patting her knees accurately and invites her to play a xylophone with the C and F# bars removed. (Since "Skin and Bones" is in the key of E minor, he prepared the xylophone player by only using the bars from the E-minor pentatonic scale. See appendix F.) He tells Genevieve to play the second rhythm pattern they just patted using whatever pitches she likes. Since the class is in the Practice Stage for the element *la-pentatonic*, Mr. George asks if anyone knows what scale the melody comes from. He helps Archer, who volunteered an answer, to name the scale.

Mr. George invites the class to sit in a circle now, except for Genevieve, who sits behind the xylophone. He wonders aloud: "If you were to act out the song, what characters would you need?" The children call out the names of different characters. "An old woman!" "Ghosts!" "Zombies!" "Dead bodies!" Mr. George selects Giselle to play the old woman. Giselle steps into the middle of the circle. He then selects a few children to play ghosts, a couple of children to play zombies, and still a few more to play dead bodies.

The children and Mr. George decide that whenever they sing "Oooo," various creatures will pop out quickly into the center of the circle, acting like their characters, and rejoin the circle by the end of the phrase. They decide on the order in which creatures will pop out: during the second verse, the ghosts; the third verse, the zombies; and the fourth verse, the dead bodies.

They begin the song. Mr. George sings, "There was an old woman all skin and bones," while playing the steady beat on rhythm sticks to keep everyone together, and the children answer "Oooo." All the while, Crystal plays her rhythm on tambourine, Genevieve plays her rhythm on the marimba, and Giselle acts out the words to the song while walking around the center of the circle.

In the second verse, on "Oooo," the children playing ghosts emerge from the circle and move around in the center making scary faces and body movements. The ghosts rejoin the circle by the time everyone finishes

singing "Oooo." On the third verse, out come the zombies, mouths open, tongues lolling out, and arms stretched straight out in front of them. On the fourth verse, children playing dead bodies fling themselves into the center of the circle, lying with their bodies limp. Sophie, in particular, gives herself to the role and lies on her back, holding her arms and legs straight up in the air and flopping her tongue out.

Tyrone chides her, "You aren't supposed to be a dead *dog!*" Everyone laughs.

Mr. George helps the children regain their focus for the final verse. On the climactic "BOO!" Giselle pretends to faint, and the song ends in laughter and a feeling of camaraderie.

The children giggle and talk as Mr. George sets the instruments aside close by the gathering. The whole performance took about ten minutes, so the class has time for an announcement or two before Mr. George dismisses them from the gathering by hearing their work choices.

The children go off to work. A pair of children gets out the pegboard and square a binomial. Another small group glues sugar cubes into the shape of a castle for their medieval castle research. After some redirection by Robert, the classroom assistant, a trio of girls sits down to work on their Wright Brothers research. Still another group works on the geometric solid book they're creating. Mr. George starts his morning giving a lesson on long division to a small group of children.

After getting out some graph paper and helping the children devise some division equations to work on, Mr. George invites another group to a rug to hear a story about the composer Erik Satie. After the story, David wants to compose some music at the tone bars. He goes to the tone bars and takes out some Music Grid Paper, while Allison and Chelsea get out a CD of Satie's music and camp out in the listening area. Kristof goes off to do research about the city of Paris. Sarah wants to finish her fraction work, however, so Mr. George allows it, hoping she'll at least be thinking about Satie while she works.

As the morning moves along to the pleasant sound of David's tone-bar composing, Mr. George presents a few more lessons. He gives a lesson on the Composition of the Earth, he tells a story about the Aztecs, and he goes out into the garden with Felicity and Jesus to supervise their leaf collecting.

When he returns to the room, Mr. George notices that the class is losing focus. The children speak in loud voices and move disruptively about the room. He observes this for a few moments to see if the children will settle down on their own. When they don't, he claps a rhythm pattern featuring the element *syncopa* (since the children are in the Practice Stage for that element) to get everyone's attention. He claps more rhythm patterns with *syncopa,* and the children echo-clap his patterns until everyone is quiet. Mr. George makes a calm appeal for order and redirects the children to work.

As lunchtime approaches, the children pack away their work and come to the gathering. Mr. George leads a quick, ten-minute class discussion. He then smiles and makes up a chant. (the rhythm of his chant contains the element *syncopa*) (figure 10.8).

"Halloween's coming! You'd Better be prepared. Vampires and witches! Who Wouldn't be scared?"

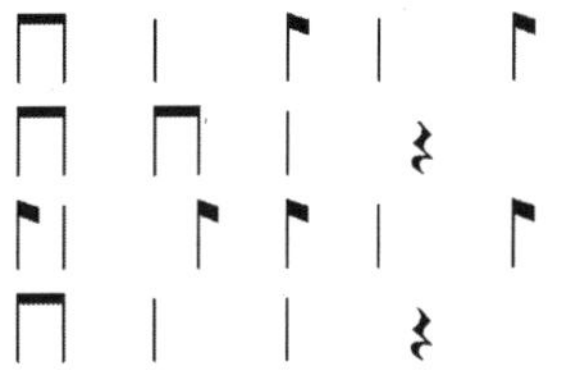

Figure 10.8.

Mr. George tells the children to do as he does. As the children repeat the chant with Mr. George, they copy his movements as he stamps, pats, and claps various body percussion patterns to a rhythm derived from the chant. After five minutes, the children set up the classroom for lunch, eat, and head out to recess.

The afternoon work period finds the children again busy with their various projects. Mr. George gives a lesson on the use of pattern in art. He discusses the Mickey Mouse painting by Andy Warhol with Evelyn and Simon. As he does so, he glances up and with satisfaction notices Sarah, reclining in the listening chair wearing headphones, her nose in a book called *Strange Mr. Satie.*

After the art lesson, when Evelyn and Simon have gone off to draw Zentangle patterns as follow-up, Mr. George helps different groups of children with their various projects. He reads with Chloé, who's struggling with reading. He pulls Andy and Damir aside to help them resolve a conflict. A few minutes later, Mr. George rounds off his afternoon work cycle with a lesson from his Montessori music album on intervals.

By the end of the afternoon, rain spatters the windows. Mr. George signals the end of the work cycle by playing a familiar melody on a little glockenspiel. The children clean up, but they lack focus. Mr. George plays a regular beat on a single note on the glockenspiel as the children tidy the room, giving them a certain number of beats to get the room tidied and gather in the circle. They manage to make it, some children sliding into place just as the last beat of the note sounds.

In the gathering, Mr. George hums the melody of a familiar mystery song while playing the steady beat on the D and F# tone bars. Jasper correctly identifies it as "Great Big House," a song Mr. George taught them earlier in the year. Since Halloween is near, Mr. George proposes that they change the words to "Haunted House in New Orleans, forty stories high. Every room that I've been in, filled with pumpkin pie!" The children wince and playfully call Mr. George a nerd.

Mr. George suggests a further revision. He asks the children to listen as he sings the song again. Without naming what he's doing, he sings the song, this time accompanying himself with a steady beat on F# and A, so that now the song is in *la-pentatonic.* Mr. George asks the children to describe how the song sounds now. The children describe it as sounding "darker," more "serious," even "scary."

Mr. George tells the children that he changed the melody from *do-pentatonic* to *la-pentatonic* the moment he started playing F# and A. (The class is in the Practice Stage for *la-pentatonic,* so Mr. George has named the element.) He elicits from the children comparisons between the two scales. *Do-pentatonic,* they all agree, sounds brighter and more cheerful than *la-pentatonic.*

Mr. George plays the beat on tone bars as the children sing and go through the dance movements of the song. As they sing, they stand up in a circle, join hands, and step clockwise during the first line. On the second line, the girls move forward into the circle and join hands. On the third line, the boys then move toward the center and reach both arms across between two girls and then down toward the floor, as if to pick up a pail of water, which the children agree should be a pail of "blood."

As they sing the next lines, the boys join hands and swing their arms up over the heads of the girls, making a circle behind their backs at waist level. Then, all the children sing the last verse as they slide-step around the circle clockwise. Finally, the girls raise their arms back over the boy's heads, freeing everyone, after which the boys step one position counterclockwise to start the next round with a new partner. Of course, since the song sounds darker and scarier now, they effect all these motions as if they were zombies.

Performing this song takes about ten minutes, and now the children are ready to go home. Mr. George dismisses them, echo-singing short melodies built from *la-pentatonic.* The day ends, on a high note.

Notice that during this school day Mr. George implemented all four levels of the pedagogical model. Along with lessons in art, geography, science, math, and biology, he presented the "Intervals" lesson from his Montessori music album, he told a Cosmic Story about Eric Satie, and he facilitated three musical activities during the gatherings, all three of which developed musical concepts and skills within the "unfolding elements" model.

The first musical experience occurred during the morning gathering, when children practiced *la-pentatonic* by singing, acting out, and playing instruments to "Skin and Bones." In the midday gathering, they performed body percussion to accompany Mr. George's chant, the rhythmic patterns of which prepared them for the rhythmic element *syncopa*. Finally, at the end of the day, Mr. George again practiced *la-pentatonic* with the children by creating a new spin on a familiar song.

Mr. George even integrated music into the routines of the classroom. When the children lost focus, he saw them through an echo-clapping exercise (featuring *syncopa*) to regain their attention. To help the transition from clean-up to the gathering, Mr. George played a repeated note on the glockenspiel.

As a result of Mr. George's careful attention to even the most rudimentary aspects of music, these upper elementary children enjoyed a rich day of music-making along with all their other work. When you implement all four levels of this model in the elementary, the environment becomes saturated with deeply meaningful music experiences.

Nothing Mr. George or Miss Lucy did was overly complicated or virtuosic. They worked within a very limited range of rhythmic and melodic elements. They, like you, are not experts, not specialists, but better: they're truly enlightened generalists. If you take anything away from these past ten chapters of this book, it's that you— yes, you—have the power to make music.

Now it's time to take stock of just how far you've come. In part 1 of this book, you learned how to set up your "musical living room," complete with all the best books, recordings, musical instruments, and paintings to stock on the shelves, display in a basket, and hang on the walls. Then, in part 2, you learned all the music theory you need to know to read, write, and play simple melodies yourself. Plus, you learned about musical forms. Finally, in part 3, you learned a pedagogical model for delivering musical concepts and skills that seamlessly combines your Montessori practice with techniques from composer and music educator Zoltan Kodály.

All in all, you've come a long way. And yet, your journey is just beginning.

With this last chapter, this book sets you squarely on the path toward realizing Maria Montessori's vision of Cosmic Education. You are ready to harness the power of music to

- build community;
- sharpen academic skills;
- strengthen Grace and Courtesy;
- promote emotional and body regulation;
- advance prosocial behavior;
- realize the public school curriculum; and
- create and maintain a joyful atmosphere.

So, congratulations: You've arrived. You're ready for part 4, which lays out at your disposal an abundance of follow-up ideas; concept- and skill-building activities; lesson plans; songs, games, and dances; as well as Cosmic Stories. Searching for an idea to follow up your "Tetrachord" lesson? Flip to chapter 11. Looking for an activity to introduce during a gathering to practice a musical element? Head on over to chapter 12. Looking for songs to perform with the children to prepare *so, mi,* or *la*? Check out the songs in chapter 14. Looking for a story about Beethoven's *Eroica* Symphony? You get the idea.

In short, the fourth and final part of this book is your box of tools, your tin of crayons, your set of watercolors. So, take up your brush, friend, and with it, get ready to make music in Montessori.

NOTES

1. Primary teachers, of course, can leave the fourth level, since Cosmic Education is part of the elementary program.
2. Again, unless you're a primary teacher, although you can leave out Level 4, you must implement all three of the other levels: deliver your Montessori lessons; introduce folk songs and singing games; and prepare, practice, and present musical elements. This is the best way to lay a solid foundation for the children's musical experiences in the elementary.

PART 4

MAKING MUSIC IN MONTESSORI

Chapter 11

Follow-Up Ideas

Genevieve and Arthur wanted to follow up a music lesson by "listening to music." Too swamped to police the two children, Miss Anna let them go off into the music listening station without any direction, vowing to check on them later. Naturally, she forgot.

By the time it had occurred to Miss Anna to check on them, Genevieve was already by her side, clamoring to show her what she and Arthur had made. She held up a CD of Arnold Schoenberg's music housed in a clear plastic jewel case. On the front of the jewel case she and Arthur had affixed multiple pieces of torn paper in myriad bright colors, with Arnold Schoenberg's name scrawled in bold letters across the front. They had designed their own album cover. "We thought this is what this crazy music sounded like!" cried a bouncing Genevieve.

Needless to say, their Schoenberg album earned pride of place on the classroom music shelf.

This chapter offers you Genevieve and Arthur's follow-up idea, plus a wealth of others (table 11.1).

Table 11.1.   List of Follow-Up Ideas

DESIGNING ALBUM COVERS

In chapter 3, you read about how changing technology has made CD players all but obsolete. While the term "album" these days still refers to a cohesive collection of songs or pieces of music, the physical form the album takes has changed and may change again by the time this book goes to print. Historically, albums have been commercially available on wax cylinders, black vinyl disks, eight-track tapes, cassette tapes, CDs, and as collections of MP3 files. Who knows how artists will release music in the future?

All the media just mentioned have one thing in common: a cover, which takes the form of a graphic image that contains some kind of artwork and usually includes the name of the artist and the title of the album.

You can have children design original album covers for the albums in your classroom listening collection. After a lesson, invite those children who are interested in this follow-up to imagine that they work as graphic designers for a record company. They must design a cover for a particular album. (You could even inspire them by telling them a story about the history of recorded music, from wax cylinders to MP3s.)

Of course, the "album cover" the children create needn't adorn an actual album. It can simply be a piece of artwork that interprets the piece of music the child is listening to. If the children do want to use their album designs on actual, physical albums, however, here's how you can make that happen.

Skills: *Listening*
Materials: *A CD in a clear jewel case, card stock paper cut to fit the CD jewel case, various art supplies*

1. Gather the materials with the children.
2. From the classroom library, take out a CD that you've burned (e.g., *Orchestral Variations* by Arnold Schoenberg).
3. Listen to all or part of the CD with the children. As you listen, have the children do creative movements or make gestures in the air.
4. Ask the children how they might design an album cover based on what the music sounded like. Tell them the only rule for the design is that it must have the composer's name on the front cover and CD spine so that others can find it when they want to listen to it.
5. Take out the card stock pieces and work with the children in designing a cover. Suppose, for example, they believed the music was colorful but disjointed. As such, they might decide to tear up pieces of colored paper and glue them at random on the card stock paper to make a colorful, ripped-paper design.
6. After you complete the design, admire the work, and place the CD on the shelf where everyone can admire it.
7. Invite the children to design more CD album covers.

Note: You can also do this activity by simply removing all the paper packaging material in the jewel case of a CD you've bought from a music store (i.e., until music stores also become a relic of the past).

If your children listen to music on an iPod rather than on CDs, you can still do this activity.

1. Have the children create their designs on a square piece of paper or canvas.
2. Scan the children's album cover artwork and save it as a JPEG file.
3. In iTunes, select the collection of songs you want to compile into an album.
4. Copy and paste the JPEG file of the children's artwork into iTune's "Artwork" dialog box.
5. Drag the songs onto your iPod.

Now, when the children listen to the album, their artwork will pop up on the iPod's screen. Depending on the computer you use, the procedure for steps 3 and 4 may vary. For a detailed tutorial, check out the support section of the iTunes website.

You can have the children design album-cover graphics for all the classical music in your listening library. Go ahead and display pop and jazz albums, however, or CD compilations of world music, such as the Putamayo series, with their original covers. Often, the art design for pop albums works together with the music, and established pop album art can inspire the children when coming up with their own designs.

CONTOUR DRAWING

If, after a lesson about a composer or piece of music, the children want to follow up by simply listening to the music, ask them to draw what they hear as a good way to focus their attention on what they're hearing.

Skills: *Listening*
Materials*: Colored pencils, paper, clipboard, a CD of music*

1. Gather the children in the listening area.
2. Tell them you're going to listen to, for example, the first movement of Beethoven's Symphony no. 5 and draw what you hear. The only rule: you must draw your line without lifting your pencil or crossing your line over itself.
3. As you listen to the music, move your pencil on the paper in one continuous line. When the music gets soft, peaceful, and graceful, make your line smooth and curved. When the music becomes loud and violent, allow your line to become spiky, quickly drawn, and jagged.
4. Listen to the piece again, and follow your line to see how you interpreted the piece.
5. Now you have created an abstract drawing from a piece of music. Title your art work with the name of the piece, and mount it onto colored paper or put it in a frame.
6. Invite the children to do some contour drawing of their own.

CREATING A LISTENING MAP

Let's assume you've told the children a Cosmic Story about the French composer Camille Saint-Saëns and his composition "Danse macabre." To follow up, some children want to listen to the music. You can enrich their listening experience by showing them how to make a listening map. A listening map is a visual guide through a piece of music that can focus a child's attention on events as the music unfolds.

Skills: Listening

Materials: *Blank paper, graphite pencil, colored pencils or watercolors*

1. Gather the materials with the children.
2. Tell the children that today you're going to do something special while you listen to the Camille Saint-Saëns composition "Danse macabre." Listen to the music, and discuss with the children how Saint-Saëns illustrates the different characters in the story using musical themes. Listen for skeletons, ghosts, and other spooky characters. Get to know the piece very well.
3. With your pencil, draw a thick, snaking road on your paper, much like a path you might find on the board game Candyland™ or Life™.
4. Divide your snaking path into segments to create spaces, again, similar to a game board.
5. Label the first space START.
6. Listen to the piece again, pausing at key moments to decide which icons or images to draw in the spaces that represent each unfolding event in the piece (indicated by musical themes). For example, the piece begins with the sound of a clock ticking twelve strokes of midnight accompanied by strings. Draw a spooky clock in the first space.
7. Next, the sound of basses plods along like ominous footsteps. You can draw footsteps in the second space.
8. A screeching violin melody comes next. That's Death playing his fiddle. In the third space, draw a violin, or draw Death playing his violin to represent that melody.
9. Now, we hear the woodwinds playing a jumpy, staccato kind of melody. Those could be skeletons popping out of their graves and dancing. Draw some skulls or skeletons next.
10. The strings copy the woodwinds before the violin returns with a mournful theme in long notes. These are ghosts coming out to fly around the graveyard. Draw some ghosts in the fourth space.
11. The skeleton theme comes back in the brass and strings. Draw the skeletons again.
12. Now we hear the ghost melody in the entire string section. Draw those ghosts!
13. Then, we hear the skeleton theme again, this time accompanied by a xylophone. Draw a xylophone in the next space.
14. Continue on through the piece, drawing icons for each musical theme in the subsequent spaces.
15. When you finish, write the title of the piece at the top, then decorate, color, and laminate your listening map.

Extensions: You can also create your listening map on a giant poster. Once you and the children have listened through the piece and agreed on the different characters and events, make little laminated icons for each character and event. You can then affix the icons to the poster using Velcro, for example, in the order they appear in the music to create a great big listening map.

Children can create listening maps for every piece of music in your listening library. The easiest pieces for making listening maps are tone poems—also known as symphonic poems—that tell a story or describe a series of vignettes thorough music. Here is a list of some:

- *An Alpine Symphony* by Richard Strauss
- *Till Eulenspiegel's Merry Pranks* by Richard Strauss
- *Carnival of the Animals* by Camille Saint-Saëns
- *Prélude à l'après-midi d'un faune* by Claude Debussy
- *Scheherezade* by Nikolai Rimsky-Korsakov
- *My Homeland* by Bedrich Smetana
- *Night on Bald Mountain* by Modest Mussorgsky
- *The Sorcerer's Apprentice* by Paul Dukas
- *Les Preludes* by Franz Liszt
- *Pictures at an Exhibition* by Modest Mussorgsky

The children's contour drawings (see earlier) can also be used as listening maps. They can use colored pencils or watercolors to depict different moments in even a purely abstract piece of music. Cool splashes of color could represent moments of calm and grace, while warm, bright colors could represent energetic, loud moments. They could even identify different themes and draw them with the same colored, expressive line. A child could draw the opening statement of Beethoven's Symphony no. 5, for example, as a large, spiky red squiggle. Each time he hears that theme, he draws the spiky red squiggle again.

Display the children's listening maps on the shelf for all the children to follow along as they listen to a particular piece of music.

PROSE COMPOSITION

Some composers' scores, like those of Pauline Oliveros, contain written instructions to the performers rather than traditional notation. Oliveros's piece "Mirror-rim," which she wrote for two instrumentalists, instructs the players to start on concert E-flat. From there, the score is made up entirely of written instructions: "If he goes up she goes down. If he goes down she goes up. Try to do this more or less simultaneously without knowing what the other is going to do . . . PLAY. If you get confused it's part of the piece" (Hickey, 2012).

Children can follow up a music lesson with a prose composition.

Skills: *Listening, playing instruments*
Materials: *Any classroom instruments, pencil, lined paper*

1. Gather a group of children together and collect the materials.
2. Tell the children that you're going to compose some music, but instead of using musical symbols, your score is going to consist of written instructions for the players.
3. Play some sounds on, say, a tambourine. Lead the children to describe what it is you're doing. Guide them in thinking about different verbs for the various sounds you make, such as "shake," "tap," "jiggle." Help them describe the sounds as high or low, soft or loud, long or short. Work with them on coming up with adverbs such as quickly, softly, or descriptive phrases such as "like a swan," or "like an explosion."
4. Divide the children up into groups of three. For each group, give two children, the players, an instrument. The third member of each group is the composer, who will write instructions for the players.
5. Remind the children to think about the sounds they'd like to hear, and use resources like the classroom dictionary or thesaurus to help them think of the best ways to write the instructions.
6. After some time working on the compositions, the children can write out their prose scores in their best handwriting, decorate them, and perform them for the class.[1]

COMPOSING WITHOUT INSTRUMENTS: TWO-NOTE MELODIES

After a presentation lesson of the elements *sol* and *mi* (see chapter 9), the children delight in following up by composing two-note melodies on three-line staff paper.

Skills: *Singing, composing, reading and writing*
Materials: *Pencil, three-line staff paper, colored pencils or watercolors*

1. Tell the children you're going to compose a two-note melody using the elements *sol* and *mi*. Give them some guidelines: The notes must be spaced horizontally about a pinky's width apart and they can't be stacked on top of each other.

2. Remind the children quickly of the staff placement rules by singing and pointing on the staff to the areas indicated: (singing *sol*) "When *sol* is in a space, (singing *mi*) *mi* is in the space below it." (Singing *mi*) "When *mi* is in a space, (singing *sol*) *sol* is in the space above it." (Singing *sol*) "When *sol* is on a line, (singing *mi*) *mi* is on the line below it." (Singing *mi*) "When *mi* is on a line, (singing *sol*) *sol* is on the line above it."
3. Make a show of taking a moment to think of a melody. Sing and show the *sol-fa* hand signs as you compose your melody out loud.
4. Make a point to sing the notes as you write black oval-shaped note heads in the two spaces (or on the two lines) on the three-line staff paper. Write only note heads; no rhythm stems.
5. When you are finished, hold up your melody and sing it aloud while showing the hand signs.
6. Invite the children to show the hand signs as they sing your melody.
7. Give your melody a title and decorate the page.

Note: when a child brings you his or her finished melody, always sing it out loud and give the hand signs before commenting on it. When you read their melodies, the children get into the habit of sight-reading their melodies. You want the children to sing as they write, as well as read what they wrote.

By "two-note" melody, I don't mean a melody using only two notes: one *sol* and one *mi*. You can write any number of notes in your melody, as long as each note is either a *sol* or a *mi*.

As the children learn more melodic elements in the Kodály sequence, they can write melodies with more notes and expand from three-line staff to a five-line staff. In fact, if you keep up Kodály's "unfolding elements" curriculum, your children could be reading and writing pentatonic melodies by third grade, and diatonic melodies by sixth grade.

The children can also play their two-note melodies on the tone bars. Have them place a Major Scale Strip with 1 on any note they like. *Sol* and *mi* will be at 5 and 3, respectively.

CREATING PIANO COMMAND CARDS

A nice way to get children exploring at the piano is to devise a set of "Piano Command Cards" on which are printed commands such as "Play two low notes" or "Play four low notes and one note in the middle." Make some of the commands fun, such as,

"Rake your finger across the keys from low to high." These commands make touching and making sounds at the piano a friendly rather than an intimidating experience.

1. Gather some children at the piano.
2. Draw a card from the basket of piano command cards.
3. Perform the command on the card, being careful to model proper technique, as well as care and respect for the instrument.
4. Allow the children to have a turn.

Extension: You could make command cards for all of the classroom instruments.

COMPOSING FROM AN IMAGE

You can show the children a photo of, for example, a nebula from a book of astronomy photographs. Have the children examine the image and think about what sounds they might use to paint a picture of it.

Invite one child at a time to come to the piano and, since space makes one think of the color black, make sounds *only on the black keys.* Hold up the picture for the other children to look at as the child at the piano plays. Invite them to almost feel the nebula swirling slowly in space as they gaze at it, listening to the other child's music.

Skills: *Playing Instruments, improvisation*
Materials: *The black bells or tone bars, a piano, a book of photographs of scenes from space.*

Gather the children.

5. Hold up an image of a galaxy, planet, star scape, or any beautiful photograph from the cosmos.
6. Invite the children to look at the photograph and imagine what music they might use to paint a picture of the image.
7. Tell the children that since black reminds us of space, they may use only the black tone bars or the black keys on the piano.
8. Invite a child up to play his interpretation of the image. Elicit positive feedback from the others about the child's interpretation.
9. Listen again and look at the image as the child plays his or her musical painting.
10. Tell the children to notate their music in whatever way will help them remember it.

Extension: The children can use photographs depicting animals, geographic locations, planets, or virtually anything as prompts for musical composition.

TONE-BAR COMPOSING: WORDS, POEMS, LYRICS

After a lesson on the tone bars, Elementary children who don't know conventional notation can begin composing right away. They can take any group of words, such as a catchy phrase, a short poem, or a song or rhyme, and set it to music. Primary children can do this activity on the bells.

Skills: *Composing, playing instruments, reading and writing*
Materials: *The tone bars, a scale strip, mallets, graphite pencil, colored pencils or watercolors*

1. Accompany a child to the tone-bar cabinet.
2. Place the scale strip below the tone-bar setup, slide down the tone bars corresponding to the numbers on the strip.
3. Tell the child you're thinking of some words, such as someone's name, a catchy phrase, or a poem. For this example, we'll use a short poem by the ancient Japanese poet Issa:

A few flies
And I
Keep house together
In this humble home.

4. In pencil, write the poem on the blank paper, taking care that the lines of text are straight. Leave a significant amount of space between each line.
5. Tell the child you're going to clap the rhythm of the words and count the number of syllables the poem has. This poem has fifteen syllables.
6. Now compose a melody that has fifteen notes. One for each syllable. Don't worry about the rhythm at this point.
7. Write the numbers for your melody in red above each syllable in the poem, like so:

1 2   3
A few flies
1   6,
And I
6   6   5 5 3
Keep house together
1 2   3 5, 6,
In this humble home.[2]

8. Play your composition on the tone bars. When you and the children are acquainted with the melody and words, sing the song together.
9. Decorate your song.

Extensions: The children can also use note names instead of numbers. First, they can label the tone bars with the black and white disks. Then, they can either use a scale strip or pull down random tone bars.

They can also write *sol-fa* syllables above the words so others can sight-sing their composition.

Children can use this idea to set their research to music. They can make musical compositions out of the names of leaf shapes, geometric shapes, or any of the nomenclature in the classroom. They can write musical thank you notes or set their fictional stories to music.

After writing many songs, the children can compile a collection of their compositions into a hand-bound book.

If children want to add a chordal instrument like ukulele or autoharp to their song, they can simply write the letter name of the chord or draw a fretboard diagram above the line of numbers to indicate which chord should be played (figure 11.2).

C

1 2 3

A few flies

Figure 11.2.

Appendix F offers you some guidelines for helping children find chords to accompany their melodies.

When the children are familiar with the rhythm elements *ta, ti-ti, tri-pa-let,* and *ti-ka-ti-ka,* they can add rhythm to their compositions using stick notation. See composing chants below.

TONE-BAR COMPOSING: NUMBERS (WITHOUT WORDS)

The children can compose songs at the tone bars using the numbered scale strips. To facilitate their composition activities, place the tone bars below a window, so the children can look out at the world and get inspiration for their compositions.

Skills: Composing, playing instruments, reading and writing
Materials: The tone bars, mallets, a scale strip, Music Grid Paper, pencil, colored pencils or watercolors

1. Bring a child to the tone-bar cabinet.
2. Make a show of looking out the window, in a book, or around the classroom for a painting or object for inspiration.
3. Give your composition a title. Write the title at the top of the Music Grid Paper.
4. Select a scale strip to use for composing your melody.
5. Place the scale strip below the tone-bar setup AND slide down the tone bars corresponding to the numbers on the strip.
6. Play some melodies on the tone bars. When you settle on a melody you like, write the numbers you played on the Music Grid Paper, being careful to use only one number per box.
7. When you finish, play your melody, reading from the Music Grid Paper.
8. Write down the name of the scale strip you used at the bottom of the paper.
9. Decorate your composition.

Extension: The children could also use note names instead of numbers.

The children could compose a collection of pentatonic ostinati. You can then compile their ostinati into a library that you can draw from to accompany classroom songs, dances, and games.

INVENTING SCALES

After the lesson about naming scales, the children can use blank scale strips to invent their own scales to use as a basis for their compositions. This is also good follow up for stories about composers such as Olivier Messiaen, who developed his own scales that he called "Modes of Limited Transposition."

Skills: Composing, reading and writing, playing instruments
Materials: The tone bars, a blank scale strip, pencil, Music Grid Paper

Bring the children over to the tone bars.

1. Tell them that today they're going to invent their own scales to use in their compositions.

2. Place a blank scale strip in front of the tone bars with the first box in front of C.
3. Choose eight random notes to use in your scale and slide them down. Give each note a number from 1 to 8. (You can make a scale that contains five to ten notes.)
4. Play the scale up and down, singing with it.
5. Give your scale a name. Write the name of your invented scale on the back of the scale strip.
6. Bring out the Music Grid Paper, and compose a melody using your original scale, writing the numbers for each scale degree in the boxes.
7. Give your melody a title and decorate it.
8. Store your new scale along with the other scale strips for other children to use.

Extension: The children can do any of the tone bar composing activities in this chapter using their invented scales.

By sliding their original scale strip up and down the tone bars, the children can transpose their scales, possibly even coming up with their own system of key signatures.

TONE-BAR COMPOSING: COLORS

A classroom painting can provide the children with inspiration for composing music. After a lesson about an artist or a famous work of art, the children can create a musical composition based on the colors in the artwork.

Skills: *Composing, playing instruments, reading and writing*
Materials: *Colored pencils or watercolors; the tone bars; a tone bar scale strip; a graphite pencil; an art history book, a book of paintings by a particular artist, or a classroom painting; Music Grid Paper*

1. Gather the materials with the children.
2. Tell the children you're going to create a musical composition based on the colors in, say, Van Gogh's *Starry Night.*
3. Ask the children to examine the painting and write down all of the colors they see.
4. Now, place the tone bar scale strip of your choosing anywhere you'd like on the tone bars. For this example, suppose you're using the natural minor scale strip. Pull down the corresponding tone bars.
5. Assign each number in the scale a color from the list and color in the numbers on the scale strip. So, if you want 1 to be dark blue, color in that box on the scale strip dark blue.

6. Now, using the Music Grid Paper, compose a melody by coloring in the boxes. (It helps to write the numbers in the boxes as well, in case the children forget which color they assigned which note. Then again, they can keep their colored scale strip handy as a reference.)
7. Play the resulting melody.
8. Give your piece the title of the painting. Decorate and display your composition.

Extension: The children can also use a blank scale strip to compose with colors. To do this, invite them to

1. place their blank scale strip wherever they like in front of the tone bars;
2. select certain tone bars to slide down; and
3. assign each note a color by coloring in the boxes on the scale strip.

Color composing works with any image. The children can look at pictures of the planets, for example, list the colors they see in each planet and create a suite of music for each planet. They could write music for each season, listing the colors in a picture of summer, spring, winter, and fall, assigning those colors to notes, and then composing a piece for each season.

TONE-BAR COMPOSING: GRAMMAR BOX SYMBOLS

Coming up with follow-up ideas for the Grammar Boxes can be a struggle. Thanks to music, the children can assign each grammar symbol a note and compose music from their phrases and sentences.

Skills: *Composing, playing instruments, reading and writing*
Materials: *Grammar Box, symbols and cards, pencil, Music Grid Paper, tone bar scale strip*

1. After the children have worked through all of the Grammar Boxes, they know enough symbols for every note in an eight-note scale. Tell the children to lay out a group of symbolized sentences on a rug.
2. Place the tone bar scale strip in front of the tone bars. For this example, let's use the major scale strip. Pull down the appropriate tone bars.
3. Assign each note in the scale a Grammar Box symbol by placing the symbol on the numbered square on the scale strip. For example, the child assigns the red

circle to 1, the black triangle 2, the small dark blue triangle 3, and so on.

4. To make melodies, look at the children's symbolized sentences and write their corresponding numbers on the Music Grid Paper. Table 11.3 shows an example.

Table 11.3.

Major Scale Tone #	Grammar Box Symbol
1	Red circle–verb
2	Black triangle–noun
3	Light blue triangle–article
4	Tall purple triangle–pronoun
5	Orange circle–adverb
6	Pink dash–conjunction
7	Dark blue triangle–adjective
8	Gold key–interjection
9	Green bridge–preposition*

* While 9 is not on the major scale strip, 9 is the number we assign to the tone one step above 8. It is the tone an octave above the *supertonic*. If we place our major scale strip on C, for example, 9 would be D above the next C.

A melody built from the sentence "Wow! He sure is strong," from the interjection grammar box, for instance, would contain the notes 8, 4, 5, 1, and 7. The children could make melodies from more sentences until they fill up a piece of Music Grid Paper.

5. Give your composition a title and decorate it.

Extension: The children could use this method to create larger compositions by making melodies from logical analysis sentences, poems, and research.

TONE-BAR COMPOSING: STICK NOTATION

Each box on the Music Grid Paper represents one beat. Once the children know some rhythmic elements, they can add rhythm to the songs they've composed. Or, they can compose new songs using rhythm.

Skills: *Composing, playing instruments, reading and writing*
Materials: *The tone bars, mallets, a scale strip, Music Grid Paper, pencil, colored pencils or watercolors*

1. Bring a child to the tone-bar cabinet.
2. Make a show of looking out the window, in a book, or around the classroom for a painting or object for inspiration.
3. Give your composition a title. Write the title at the top of the Music Grid Paper.

4. Select a scale strip to use for composing your melody.
5. Place the scale strip below the tone-bar setup, slide down the tone bars corresponding to the numbers on the strip.
6. Play some melodies on the tone bars. Pay attention this time to rhythm patterns. Play rhythms that have one (ta), two (ti-ti), three (tri-pa-let), or four (ti-ka-ti-ka) sounds on a beat, including the quarter rest (sh.) When you settle on a melody you like, write the melody in stick notation on the Music Grid Paper. Use the tone bar numbers or note names for note heads, like in figure 11.4.

Figure 11.4.

Take care to use only one rhythm element per box.
7. When you finish, play your melody, reading from the Music Grid Paper.
8. Write down the name of the scale strip you used at the bottom of the paper.
9. Decorate your composition.

Extension: The children can add lyrics to their compositions by writing the words below the sticks. Make sure they use one syllable per stick. The convention in lyric writing is to break up multisyllable words with a hyphen, as in figure 11.5.

Flow - ers

Figure 11.5.

Once the children can write in stick notation, they can set aside the Music Grid Paper and repeat any of the composition activities above, such as composing with words, numbers, colors, or Grammar Box symbols, on blank paper. Show them how to organize their rhythms into patterns of two, four, or three beats using bar lines with a time signature at the beginning, as in figure 11.6.

COMPOSING WITH POPSICLE STICKS

When the children have a grasp of stick notation, they can compose music using popsicle sticks on the floor.

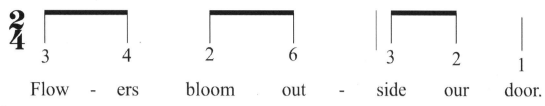

Figure 11.6.

Skills: Composing, playing instruments, reading and writing
Materials: Popsicle sticks, white and black disks for naming tone bars, five tone bars that form a pentatonic scale, drum, tambourine, maracas

1. Gather a small group of children and seat them in a circle.
2. Tell the children to do as you do as you clap a four-beat rhythm pattern. Observe to see which child is clapping appropriately and accurately.
3. Hand that child an instrument, and write the rhythm pattern in popsicle sticks on the floor in front of the individual. This child plays throughout the following.
4. Repeat steps 2 and 3 with the other instruments.
5. Tell the children to do as you do, and pat another rhythm pattern on your knees. Observe to see if the remaining child can pat appropriately and accurately.
6. Label the five tone bars with the white and black disks and place them in front of the child. Place the rhythm pattern in popsicle sticks above the tone bars so he can see the pattern.
7. Tell the child to improvise the tone-bar notes he will play, but stick to this rhythm pattern. If the child wants to record what notes he or she's playing, labeling disks can be placed below the popsicle sticks to create stick notation.
8. Conduct as the children play their parts together.

Extensions: The children can write all of their parts down on paper and create a score from their combined parts (see the "Creating a Score" activities below).

MUSICAL CRYPTOGRAMS

Children can compose melodies using musical cryptograms derived from their own names or from the names of friends or loved ones.

Skills: Playing instruments, composing, reading and writing
Materials: The tone bars, mallets, the white and black disks for naming the tone bars, a table of note names

in different note-naming systems (see below), pencil, Music Grid Paper or blank paper

1. Bring some children to the tone bars.
2. Label the white tone bars using the white disks with the note names printed on them.
3. Tell the children that you're going to write a melody for your friend Jane Doe by deriving a melody from the letters in her name. To do this, you're going to use as your "alphabet"—the seven letters of the white tone bars: C, D, E, F, G, A, and B.
4. Now that you know what letters are available, tell the children that the convention for making musical cryptograms in the English system is to use only the letters that correspond to the note names available and ignore the other letters. A child named Jane Doe, for example, could use the English note-naming system to make a melody using the notes A, E, D, and E.
5. Continue by telling the children that you can also look to the note-naming systems of other cultures to get more letters. In the German note-naming system, for example, the note E-flat is called S. (Bring down the E-flat tone bar and label it.) You can even use the first letter of the *sol-fa* system to get the letters D, R, M, F, S, L, and T. Table 11.7 shows note names in several different systems.

Table 11.7.

English	C	D	E	F	G	A	B
Solfage or Neo-Latin	Do	Re	Mi	Fa	Sol	La	Ti (Si in French)
German	C	D	E (Eb= S)	F	G	A	H
Byzantine	Ni	Pa	Vu	Ga	Di	Ke	Zu
Japanese	Ha	Ni	Ho	He	To	I	Ro
Indian	Sa	Re	Ga	Ma	Pa	Dha	Ni

6. So, to make a melody from Jane Doe's name, you could add the letter N from the Japanese system. You could even add the O from the Japanese note "Ho" if you wanted to play with the convention a little.

7. Next, write a melody consisting of the letters A, N, E, D, O, and E. (The actual notes will be A, D, E, D, E, E. When selecting notes for your melody, you can use any octave.)
8. Use the Music Grid Paper to write down your melody, being careful to use only one letter per box, or, if you want to include rhythm, write out your melody in stick notation.
9. Give your melody a title and decorate it.

Extension: This activity has broad application. Children can

- compose melodies for their friends and family to give as gifts;
- create musical portraits of friends and loved ones;
- investigate to find more note-naming systems;
- make new black and white disks with note names from other systems;
- come up with their own note-naming system;
- use the musical cryptograms as a kind of musical "code" to write messages; and
- create melodies from their sentence analysis or Grammar Box work.

In fact, they can create melodies from virtually any text they find in the environment, such as the names of historical figures, elements from the periodic table, planets, trees, or animals.

SERIAL OR TWELVE-TONE COMPOSING

This activity is a nice follow up to the lesson on naming tone bars or naming scales or a Cosmic Story about Arnold Schoenberg. It could also be used after the Degrees of the Scale lesson.

Skills: *Composing, playing instruments, reading and writing*
Materials: *The tone bars, the black and white disks for naming notes, mallets, a scale strip, Music Grid Paper, pencil, colored pencils or watercolors*

1. On a rug, bring out the first twelve tone bars.
2. Tell the children you're going to compose music using the method invented by Arnold Schoenberg in the early twentieth century. Say something like, "Arnold Schoenberg wanted to destroy the hierarchy of traditional tonality that we heard about in the Degrees of the Scale lesson. His method is known as *serial* composition. In serial composition, all the tones in the scale are equal. There is no tonal center, or tonic. Mr. Schoenberg's method is also known as *twelve-Tone Composition.*" If the children haven't heard about Arnold Schoenberg, write and tell them a story about him or invite them to hear the story on another day.
3. Label all of the tone bars with the black and white disks. For the best effect during this activity, feel free to mix up the sharp and flat note names. You could label the tone bars, for instance, C, D-flat, E, F, F#, G, A-flat, and so on.
4. Tell the children you're going to compose what Arnold Schoenberg called a "tone row" by mixing up the tone bars.
5. Mix up the tone bars in any random order you like.
6. Tell the children that this "tone row" is the basis for your composition. To give the children the sound of the "tone row," play the tone bars in order from left to right, playing one note per beat.
7. Tell the children that for the rhythm of your melody, you're going to compose patterns made from a menu of the rhythm elements *ta, ti-ti, trip-a-let,* or *ti-ka-ti-ka.* (The menu, of course, depends on which rhythms the children know.)
8. Before you compose your melody, tell the children that Arnold Schoenberg had some rules for playing the tone row: (1) you must first play the *entire* tone row forward, all the way through from beginning to end; (2) you can't repeat a note; and (3) after you play the tone row forward, you may play the notes in the row again in any order you like, but you *may not repeat a note* until you've played all the notes in the row.
9. Compose a melody using different rhythm patterns.
10. Write your melody on the Music Grid Paper. Use only one rhythmic element per beat. For note heads, use the note names,
11. Play through the composition. Elicit a title from the children based on the sound.
12. Decorate your composition.

SHORT SOUND COMPOSITION

Skills: *Listening, playing instruments, reading and writing*
Materials: *Any found object or percussion instrument*

1. Guide the children in coming up with graphic symbols for four different kinds of sounds, such as ⟨symbol⟩ for a ringing sound, ⟨symbol⟩ for a tapping sound, ⟨symbol⟩ for a short loud sound, and ⟨symbol⟩ for a scratchy sound.

2. Work with the children to figure out how to produce these four sounds on one or more classroom objects or instruments.
3. Create a composition using those four sounds and notate it using the four symbols. The finished score might look like figure 11.8.

CREATING A SCORE 1: GRAPHIC NOTATION—SQUIGGLES AND SHAPES

Even before they know how to compose music using conventional notation the children can compose a score for any number of instruments. Graphic notation gives children a beautiful way to compose for a variety of instruments.

Skills: Listening, playing instruments, moving, composing, improvising, reading and writing

Materials: Poster paper, colored markers or pencils, black Sharpie, yard or meter sticks, drum, güiro, tambourine, maracas, black tone bars

1. Help children gather the materials.
2. Tell the children that the composition is going to be sixteen beats long. Have them pat a steady beat and count to sixteen to get an idea of how long the composition will take.
3. Tell the children you'd like to compose a drum part. Tell them to pat a beat and count to sixteen as you make a sound on the drum (it could be a rhythm pattern, a scraping sound, or anything you like.) When you settle on something to play, tell the children you've got your part. Repeat the part a few times. Tell them you've memorized your part.
4. Ask the children to describe qualities of the sound as high/low, long/short, loud/soft. Ask

Score:

Key:

	snap
	clap
	sigh
	scratch
	bang on a drum
	make a droplet noise with your lips
	yelp
	go "moo"
	say, "Swish!"

Figure 11.8.

them whether the sound can be played faster or slower.

5. Decide with the children what color and symbol you will use to write down your part. You could use spirals, star shapes, triangles, circles, squiggly lines, or patches of color, for example. You could use bigger shapes for loud sounds or small shapes for soft sounds. You could use different colors to indicate a high sound or a low sound. Write the symbol down on the paper.

6. Hand the drum to the child who clapped best, and invite that individual to play the drum part. Practice the part a little with the drummer while the others pat the steady beat and count to 16. Have them repeat the beat count as necessary until the child playing the drum has mastered his part. This child should play throughout.

7. Repeat steps 6 through 9 with the other instruments. Encourage the children to be creative with the musical symbols. Think about using different kinds of lines and shapes. Use contrasting colors, but be sure to use only one color per part, so each part stands out distinctly.

8. When you finish writing the parts, admire your cool-looking score.

9. Tell the children to play as you pat your knees and count. Listen to each part, check the child's accuracy, and make positive corrections.

10. Write a title on your score and decorate it.

11. Invite the children to write another score on their own.

Extensions: This kind of activity lends itself well to dance and movement. The children can come up with choreography that matches each sound. In doing so, they could devise a full-scale dance performance, with a "conductor" counting out the beats, the "orchestra" playing from the score, and behind them, the dancers performing their choreography to the music.

COMPOSING FROM AN ABSTRACT PAINTING

You can stimulate the children to make a composition for follow up after studying an abstract piece of art. The lines, shapes, and gestures in the painting itself can be "read" as a graphic notation score.

A good example of this kind of work is Earl Brown's *December 1952*, which is one of the first pieces of music written in graphic notation (Hickey, 2012).

Skills: Listening, playing instruments, composing, improvising

Materials: An abstract painting, any combination of classroom instruments or found objects, pencil, paper

1. After a lesson on either a painter such as Juan Miró or Paul Klee or one of their works, gather the children together and collect the materials.

2. Place an abstract painting in front of them.

3. On a small piece of paper, list the colors, lines, and shapes in the painting by describing them or recreating them on a piece of blank white paper.

4. Assign each line, color, or shape a sound. Aim for a variety of sounds. Lines might have long, flowing percussive sounds; splashes of color might have notes or melodies associated with them. The sounds can come from musical instruments or found objects in the environment. Help the children to use as many of the possible sound categories as they can, for example, high/low, soft/loud, long/short.

5. When the children have matched the gestures in the painting with a sound, have them decide how long the piece will take, for example, sixteen to thirty-two beats.

6. Start the children off and count out, say, thirty-two even beats. While counting, trace your finger from left to right across the bottom edge of the painting to guide the children as they "read" the paining like a musical score.

7. If possible, record your interpretation of the painting, and add the recording to your classroom library. You can also create a "score" of your painting by affixing a color copy of the painting to a piece of paper along with your break down of the symbols and their corresponding sounds.[3]

Extension: The children could create their own abstract drawings and paintings to use as material for musical compositions.

CREATING A SCORE 2: GRAPHIC NOTATION—COLORED DOTS

Skills: Listening, playing instruments, moving, composing, improvising, reading and writing

Materials: Poster paper, black Sharpie, colored markers or pencils, yard or meter sticks, drum, güiro, tambourine, maracas, tone bars that form a pentatonic scale (1, 2, 3, 5, 6), ukulele

1. Aid the children in gathering the materials.

2. With your ruler, draw an L shape in black Sharpie or in pencil on the left side of the poster paper. Leave about an inch and a half of space between the axes of your L shape and the edge of the paper. Tell the

children that the left axis represents "what to play," and that the bottom line represents "when."

3. Below the bottom line, number from 1 to 8, evenly spacing the numbers about a two-finger-length apart.

4. In pencil, draw a line not far from the top of the left axis. Begin the line on the left axis and extend it across the paper, but not all the way. To the left of this line, draw a little drum or simply write "drum." This is the drum part!

5. Below the drum line, repeat step 3, drawing one light, straight pencil line for each of the other instruments, leaving plenty of space in between each line.

6. Tell the children you'd like to compose a drum part. Play a rhythmic pattern that only includes one sound or two sounds on a beat. Repeat the pattern and tell the children you've got your part.

7. Tell the children to clap and count from one to eight as you play the pattern. Have them listen for which beats the sounds occur on. Once they identify which beats, ask them how many sounds they hear on each beat.

8. Select one color for the drum part. On the line for the drum part, aligned with the beat numbers on the bottom axis, draw a single-colored dot for one sound on a beat, and two small dots side by side for two sounds on a beat. Play the drum part again while the children pat their knees, read, and count.

9. Hand the drum to a child to play the part. Tell him to play through the part while the other children pat and count. From here on, the child playing the drum plays throughout.

10. Repeat steps 6 through 10 with the other percussion instruments.

11. Place a pentatonic scale strip in front of your tone bars with 1 on C. Compose a simple pentatonic melody (remember to play only one or two notes on a beat). Repeat your melody and tell the children you have written your part. Tell the children to pat and count while you play your part. When you finish, ask them which notes you played on what beats.

12. Choose a color, and write out your tone-bar melody on the corresponding line using scale strip numbers. You can write them above the line, below the line, or on the line. Write one letter to show one sound on a beat and two small letters to show two sounds on a beat. Hand a child the tone bars.

13. Repeat for the ukulele part. Write the letters of the chords or draw the chord diagrams above the ukulele line. You can render the strum pattern in arrows: down arrows for down strokes and up arrows for upstrokes. (To find the best ukulele chords to play, select from those chords built on the *major scale* of the *tonic* (1) of the pentatonic scale you selected for

the tone bars. So, in this case, C major, D minor, E minor, F major, G7, A-minor, and B diminished will all sound good.)

14. When you finish writing the parts, admire your cool-looking score.

15. Tell the children to play as you pat your knees and count. Listen to each part, check the child's accuracy and make positive corrections.

16. Write a title on your score and decorate it. See figure 11.9 to see what your finished score might look like.

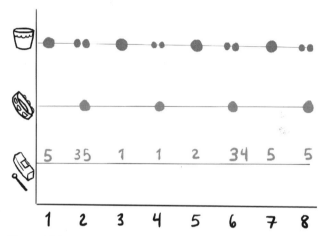

Figure 11.9.

CREATING A SCORE 3: STICK NOTATION

The children can compose a score using stick notation as soon as they've had lessons on *ta* and *ti-ti*.

Skills: *Listening, playing instruments, moving, composing, improvising, reading and writing*
Materials: *Poster paper, black Sharpie, pencils, yard or meter sticks, drum, güiro, tambourine, maracas, tone bars that form a pentatonic scale (1, 2, 3, 5, 6), ukulele*

1. Help the children gather the materials.

2. With your ruler, draw an "L" shape in black Sharpie or in pencil on the right side of the poster paper. Tell the children that the left axis represents "what to play," and that the bottom axis represents "when."

3. Below the bottom line, number from 1 to 8, evenly spacing the numbers about a two-finger-length apart.

4. In pencil, draw a line not far from the top of the left axis. Extend the line across the paper, but not all the way. To the left of this line, draw a little drum or simply write "drum." This is the drum part!

5. Below the drum line, repeat step 3, drawing one light, straight pencil line for each of the other instruments, leaving plenty of space in between each line.
6. Tell the children you'd like to compose a drum part. Play a rhythmic pattern that only includes *ta* and *ti-ti*. Repeat the pattern and tell the children you've got your part.
7. Tell the children to pat their knees and count from one to eight as you play the pattern. Have them listen for which beats the sounds occur on. Once they identify which beats, ask them how many sounds they hear on each beat.
8. In pencil, write out the drum part using stick notation, one stick for *ta*, and two sticks joined by a cross bar for *ti-ti* (see chapter 6). For note heads, draw an "x" on the line. Make sure your note heads and stems align with the beat numbers on the bottom axis of the score. Erase the line.
9. Play the drum part again while the children pat their knees, read, and count.
10. Hand the drum to a child to play the part. Tell him to play through the part while the other children pat and count. From now on, this child plays throughout.
11. Repeat steps 6 through 10 with the other percussion instruments.
12. Compose a simple melody on the tone bars (remember to play only one or two notes on a beat). Repeat your melody and tell the children you have written your part. Tell the children to pat and count while you play your part. When you finish, ask them which notes you played on what beats.
13. Write out your tone bar melody on the corresponding line in stick notation using note names or numbers as you please for note heads.
14. Repeat for the ukulele part. Write the letters of the chords or draw the chord diagrams above the ukulele line. You can write the strum patterns in stick notation with arrows for note heads: down arrows for down strokes and up arrows for upstrokes.
15. When you finish writing the parts, admire your cool-looking score.
16. Tell the children to play as you pat your knees and count. Listen to each part, check the child's accuracy and make positive corrections.
17. Write a title on your score and decorate it. Figure 11.10 shows what the finished score might look like.

Extensions: As the children gain facility notating music in this way, you can drop the numbers at the bottom axis and write a time signature at the beginning of each instrument's line. The children can use this method to compose original scores to accompany classroom songs.

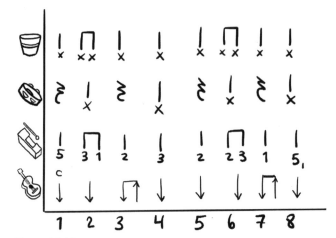

Figure 11.10.

The children can add dance choreography to their scores as well.

Note: Appendix F contains advice that will help you make the right note and chord choices when the children want to enrich their music with chordal instruments, such as ukulele or autoharp.

CREATING A SCORE 4: STANDARD PERCUSSION NOTATION

Before too long, children will be able to follow all the steps above to create a score in standard percussion notation. You will detect only a few differences between stick notation and standard percussion notation. Figure 11.11 shows the top line of an accompaniment written for a drum in standard percussion notation.

Figure 11.11.

Notice that each stem now has a note head and that the notes sit on a one-line staff. Take a look at the accompaniment in figure 11.12, written for drum, sticks, and triangle.

COMPOSING "FILMSTRIP" OR "SLIDE SHOW" SOUNDTRACKS

Graciela, a third-year in Miss Anna's class, made a "filmstrip" of the lifecycle of a salmon. She used a black shoebox with slits on either side and a rectangular "window"

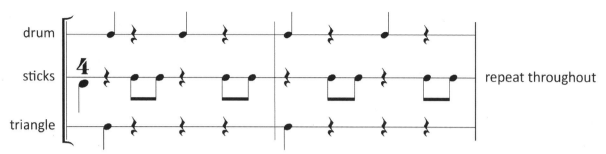

Figure 11.12.

carved out of the bottom. She then rigged up some ribbon paper so that she could pull the paper through the slits and create a kind of filmstrip or slide show. Finally, she wrote out some piano music to accompany her filmstrip, which she played whenever other children wanted to look at it.

Skills: *Composing, playing instruments, reading and writing*
Materials: *A box, a roll of ribbon paper, graphite and colored pencils, scissors, musical instruments*

1. Gather the children and see them through the construction of a filmstrip box.
2. Tell the children to watch as you pull the ribbon paper through to create the slide show. As they watch, invite them to think about some music that might accompany each image in the slide show.
3. Tell them to use the tone bars, classroom mallet instruments, or percussion instruments to compose a short piece of music for each slide or "scene." Guide the children through the above process for creating a score using graphic or stick notation.
4. When the music is finished, invite one child to pull the filmstrip, while the others play the various accompaniments.

WHO ARE YOU?
MUSICAL SELF-PORTRAITS

Many composers have created musical portraits of friends and loved ones. Edward Elgar's *Enigma Variations* contains musical sketches of his friends. As follow up, children can compose short musical compositions that reflect their identity.

Skills: *Playing instruments, singing, improvising, composing*
Materials: *Instruments, writing materials*

1. Gather the children together and collect the materials.

2. Give the children musical instruments and let them explore for about five minutes. After the time is up, take the instruments back and ask them, *Who are you today?* They may give a variety of answers.
3. Now tell them that, rather than use words to tell you who they are, they can compose a short piece of music, around thirty-two beats long, using any of the instruments in front of them that they feel best describes who they are today. They may also use their voice.
4. Tell the children they may write down their composition in any way so that they can remember it.

Extension: The children can repeat this follow up over the course of a week or so and compile their compositions into a hand-bound book to create a musical photo album.[4]

MUSIC INSPIRED BY AN EVENT

Many composers have created instrumental compositions that depict either an important event either in their lives or in history. Charles Ives's "The Fourth of July," from his *Holidays Symphony* depicts his boyhood recollections of Fourth of July celebrations. In his music, you can almost hear the crowds gathering and the fireworks exploding.

You can tell the children a story about that work or other works that depict historical events, including:

• Beethoven's *1812 Overture, or Wellington's Victory;*
• John Adams's *On the Transfiguration of Souls;*
• Steve Reich's *Come Out;* and
• Krzysztof Penderecki's *Threnody to the Victims of Hiroshima.*

After a story about any of these pieces, or about an epic historical event, the children can compose music inspired by events in history or events in their lives.

Skills: *Composing, playing instruments, reading and writing*
Materials: *Musical instruments, writing materials*

1. Gather the children and work with them to collect the materials.
2. Remind the children of the lesson they had about a piece of music that depicts an event. Ask questions such as: *How did the composer use the events to compose his or her music? How did the moments in the event inspire the music? What musical devices did the composer use to depict the moments in the event? Which sounds directly represent moments in the event and which sounds are more abstract? How did the composer maintain the listener's interest?*
3. Tell the children you're going to choose an event and compose a piece of music that depicts the event. Suppose you pick Halloween.
4. Start off by listing moments, people, or feelings that come to mind when you think of Halloween.
5. When you have a good-sized list, pick up your instruments and make musical gestures that depict each item on the list. You might depict walking up to the front porch with a spooky melody on the tone bars and a knock on the door with a short rhythm on the claves.
6. Write down your musical gestures using graphic notation or stick notation.
7. Perform your piece.
8. Invite the children to compose their own music to an event in their lives or a historical event.[5]

Extension: The entire class can compose music for a school event or celebration such as an anniversary of the school's founding or a staff member's birthday.

In addition to holding the Sandpaper Globe and walking around a candle, a child could enhance the birthday ritual by composing music for each event on his or her personal timeline.

THEME AND VARIATIONS

A "Theme and Variations" piece begins with a simple theme followed by a series of variations in which one or two aspects of the theme have been changed. Children can undertake a "Theme and Variation" composition activity. Proceed as follows:

1. After a story about a "Theme and Variations" composition (suggestions below), gather a small group at the tone bars.

2. Tell the children you're going to work with them to compose a "Theme and Variations."
3. Have the children first come up with a musical idea that they can all play together. Have them write down their idea in graphic or stick notation. That's their theme.
4. Then, tell them to come up with three or more different variations of the idea, altering a note of the melody, changing the rhythm, transposing it, or even using a different scale strip. Have them write down these ideas.
5. Tell them to finish the piece with their original idea.
6. Tell the children to give their piece a title that incorporates the words "Theme and Variations" and decorate it. If they like, they can perform it for the class.

Note: Notable "Theme and Variation" compositions are

- Mozart, *12 Variations on "Ah vous dirai-je maman"*; K.265 ("Twinkle, Twinkle, Little Star");
- Beethoven, *Diabelli Variations;*
- Felix Mendelssohn, *Variations sérieusses;*
- Dvorak, *Symphonic Variations;*
- Edward Elgar, *Enigma Variations;*
- Anton Arensky, *Variations on a Theme by Tchaikovsky; and*
- Charles Ives, *Variations on "America."*

MUSIC INSPIRED BY OTHER ARTS

Children can follow up virtually any art lesson by composing a piece of music inspired by a work of art. Many interesting pieces of music have been written about works of art. The composer Cindy McTee, for example, wrote "California Counterpoint" after seeing the painting "Twittering Machine" by Paul Klee.

You could give a lesson on both works and then guide the children in following up with this activity.

Skills: *Playing instruments, composing, reading and writing*
Materials: *An image of a piece of art or an original piece of art, musical instruments, writing materials*

1. Gather the children and collect the materials.
2. Select an image of a famous painting, sculpture, or piece of architecture from an art history book, or select an art object or painting from the classroom.
3. Tell the children you're going to compose a short piece of music inspired by that piece of art.
4. Make a list of as many adjectives as possible to describe the painting.
5. Create musical gestures on the instruments for each of the adjectives on your list.

6. Assemble your musical gestures on paper, notating them in whatever way you wish.
7. Place a title on your finished piece and decorate it. Invite the children to compose music inspired by a work of art.

Note: Other musical works inspired by paintings include:

- *Isle of the Dead* by Rachmaninoff, inspired by the painting *Isle of the Dead* by Arnold Böcklin;
- "Rothko Chapel" by Morton Feldman, inspired by the paintings of Mark Rothko;
- *Pictures at an Exhibition* by Modest Mussorgsky, inspired by various paintings and architectural drawings by Viktor Hartmann.

COMPOSING CHANTS

Children can follow-up lessons in all areas of the curriculum by composing chants. They can turn poems, nursery rhymes, and classroom stories into chants, or they can write their own chants from everyday experiences in the classroom, vocabulary from their studies—virtually anything.

Through composing chants about animals, leaf shapes, historical figures, and so on, the children make connections to all areas of the curriculum.

Skills: *Moving, singing, composing*
Materials: *None*

1. Sit with the children and tell them you'd like to compose a chant. A chant is a song that's spoken, not sung, to a particular rhythm.
2. Look around the room and find something to compose a chant about. Tell the children to pat a steady beat while you chant something like

Adjective, preposition,
Adverb, noun;
Grammar Boxes are more
Fun with sounds.[6]

3. Clap out the rhythm of the words and, as in figure 11.13, write the rhythms on paper in stick notation or on the floor with popsicle sticks.[7]
4. Invite the children to compose their own chants and notate the rhythm in rhythm-stick notation.

CREATING A SCORE 5: COMPOSING INSTRUMENTAL ACCOMPANIMENTS TO CHANTS AND SONGS

The children can compose body percussion movements or instrumental accompaniments to their chants. They can

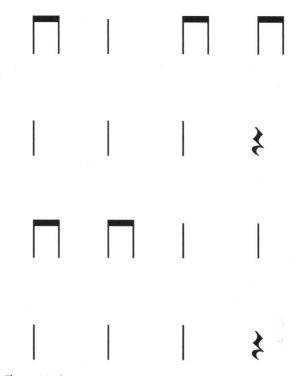

Figure 11.13.

write out their accompaniments in stick notation, standard percussion notation, or a combination of both. This example creates an accompaniment that combines all three so you can see the different notation samples together.

Skills: *Moving, singing, composing, reading and writing*
Materials: *Drum, maraca, tambourine, C, D, E, G, A, tone bars, pencil, rulers, paper*

1. Gather the children and together collect the materials.
2. Tell the children you'd like to compose an accompaniment to a chant using percussion instruments, body percussion, and tone bars.
3. Tell the children to do as you do as you clap the rhythm of the first line of the chant. (This is preparation for playing the hand drum.)
4. Select a child who can move his hands properly to play the hand drum accompaniment from figure 11.14:[8]
5. Tell the children to join you as you do the body percussion pattern depicted in figure 11.15.
6. When they can perform the above easily, tell the children you'd like them to echo you as you chant a chant you composed. Have them begin the accompaniment with you. When they play with rhythmic stability, bring in the hand drum. When both the hand drum and the body percussion accompaniment feel stable, have everyone continue as, without stopping, you begin the chant. For this example, figure 11.16 shows a chant about polygons.

Figure 11.14.

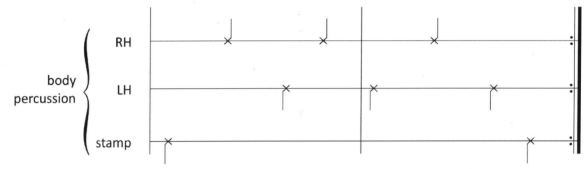

Figure 11.15.

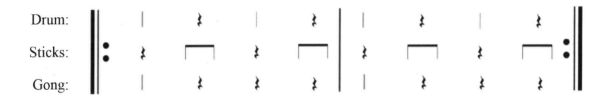

Figure 11.16.

7. Have the hand drum continue for a couple of measures after the chant ends.

8. Now, tell the children you'd like to see if they can do the chant all the way through *without echoing*. Have them begin the accompaniment. When they can play it accurately, bring in the hand drum. After a few moments, have the class chant together with you.

9. Now it's time to fold in the tone bars and the maraca.

10. To bring in the tone bars, tell the children you're interested in the line that goes "Parallelograms and." Have the children do as you do and pat the rhythm of the third line on your knees, alternating hands. Observe carefully to see which child does the hand motions accurately. Place the tone bars in front of that child, asking that individual to play the accompaniment from figure 11.17.

11. Repeat step 10 with the maraca (patting the rhythm below). Have the child who pats most accurately play the accompaniment in figure 11.18.

12. Now that all of the instruments know their parts, perform the chant. Start the children on the body percussion accompaniment. When they are stable, bring in the hand drum, tone bars, and maracas. On cue, have everyone else perform the chant. Repeat until everyone feels satisfied.

13. Invite the children to write their own accompaniments to classroom chants.

Note: When children write their accompaniments all together on a score, it will look something like the score in figure 11.19, albeit with colorful decorations.[9]

In addition to creating accompaniments for their chants, the children can create accompaniments for classroom songs. Follow the steps in *Creating a Score: Stick Notation* to create accompaniments for a song in duple meter, such as in figure 11.20.

An accompaniment for a song in triple meter looks like figure 11.21.

Figure 11.17.

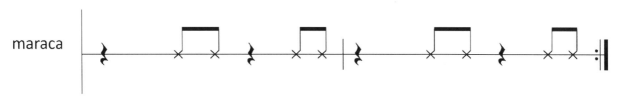

Figure 11.18.

Triangle, Rhombus

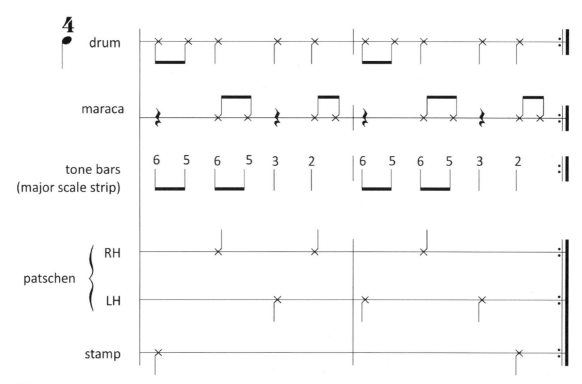

Figure 11.19.

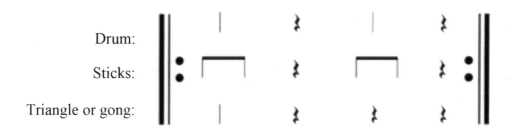

Figure 11.20.

Figure 11.21.

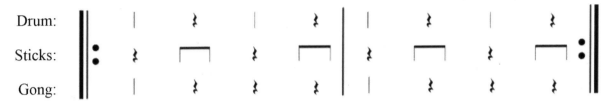

Figure 11.22.

Rhythmic accompaniments written by the children can enrich classroom songs. Check out figure 11.22 for an accompaniment to the song "Turn the Glasses Over," which you'll find in chapter 14.

NOTES

1. Adapted from Hickey (2012).
2. Like *sol-fa* syllables, the convention when notating with numbers is to use a comma to indicate the tones below 1 (*do*), as in "7."

3. Adapted from Hickey (2012).
4. Ibid.
5. Ibid.
6. Make sure to use known rhythms in your chant. This chant assumes the children know *ta* and *ti-ti*.
7. Adapted from Wheeler and Raebeck (1977).
8. The child plays this ostinato throughout.
9. Adapted from Wheeler and Raebeck (1977).

Chapter 12

Activities for Growth

One afternoon before dismissal, just before the gathering, Katy brought Mr. Chris a piece of paper she'd folded into a piano.

Mr. Chris brought the tiny paper piano into the middle of the gathering.

"Katy doesn't know this, but her little paper piano really makes a sound!" he proclaimed.

"When I touch the little keyboard on the right here, like this," he told the children, "it makes a high sound," and while touching the keyboard, he made a high-pitched "Ooo" sound in his head voice. The children followed suit, making high-pitched "Ooo" sounds in their head voices whenever Mr. Chris touched the little paper piano on the indicated spot.

"When I touch the little keyboard on the left part, it makes a low sound," and Mr. Chris touched the piano again, making a low grunting sound in his chest voice. Again the children followed suit.

Next, Mr. Chris directed the children to hold the sound when he held his finger on the keyboard and stop the sound when he lifted it, and then to make a loud sound when he quickly brought his finger down onto the keyboard, but to make a soft sound when he touched it slowly.

Finally, Mr. Chris tousled his hair into its "composer hair" configuration, made a big show of cracking his knuckles, wriggled his fingers, and set about touching the keyboard in different ways, the children making the corresponding sounds before everyone collapsed into giggles.

With this simple activity, Mr. Chris gave the children practice finding their singing voices and exploring the concepts of soft/loud and high/low. The entire enterprise took less than ten minutes.

This chapter provides you with a wealth of the same kind of short, fun, activities. If you have any concern that these activities are too teacher-led for a Montessori environment, allow the following to allay your fears: remember that before children can work independently, they usually need an adult to present and model the concepts.

These exercises reinforce musical concepts and give the children in your classes musical skills so they can embark on independent musical exploration. Perform these activities with frequency. You can unobtrusively pepper them into your classroom routines to give the children practice with the concepts and skills outlined in chapter 8. Perform these activities during gatherings, or gather small groups of children to do a quick lesson during the work period. Limit each performance to five to ten minutes.

These activities differ from "follow up" in that they don't necessarily yield a finished product. Their value lies solely in the experience. Reading rhythms from a grid of squares, for example, effectively develops children's music-reading and instrument-playing skills, among other things, without requiring the children to hand anything in to your inbox.

The activities are presented here in no particular order in terms of difficulty or skill level, and you needn't feel any pressure to present all of them.[1] Choosing any one of them from any particular category suffices to develop a particular concept or skill. Any of the activities given in section I.C., for instance, will develop the children's sense of steady beat.

On a typical day you might use more than one activity on the menu. You might, for example, look to section IV.E to find a *la* practice activity for the morning gathering; flip to section III.A for a quick afternoon listening activity; and find in section II.B a rhythm concept activity for the whole class at the end of the day.

Table 12.1.   List of Activities for Growth

I. ACTIVITIES FOR DEVELOPING READINESS SKILLS (PRIMARY)[2]

Before children are ready to consciously learn symbolic representation for sounds, they must have had aural, kinesthetic, and oral experiences with music. In the primary, you can help children learn to sing beautifully; step the beat accurately; clap rhythms; differentiate between "high and low," "fast and slow," "loud and soft," and "long and short"; and develop a repertoire of good songs. These *readiness skills* form the core elements we must develop in the children of the primary in order to give them a solid foundation for musical exploration in the elementary.

The lessons in your Montessori primary album address some of these skills. Present them parallel with the activities listed below.

I.A ABeautiful Singing

Whenever you sing with children, encourage them to sing in light, energetic voices with a simple, natural voice quality. Teach them to breathe at the ends of phrases rather than in the middle and model good enunciation.

Sing short songs within a limited range, that is, a range in which children can sing comfortably in their head voice. Most children find the range from D to A or B-flat on the treble staff most comfortable.

A word of advice to male teachers: model good singing but be aware that the child's voice is an octave higher than yours. Singing in your natural range, especially if you have a deep voice, may cause the child to imitate you in your octave, producing a froggy, growly sound. Discourage children from attempting this very low range.

Instead, use your falsetto (head voice) to match their range, and contrast the two sounds, encouraging children to match the higher of the two. If this doesn't help, ask another child or a woman to model the pitch. By all means, *do not* feel that you have to sing in falsetto with the children all the time. Use it as an aid. Most children adapt quickly to the male voice.

Some very young children who haven't yet distinguished between the singing voice and the speaking voice will sing with speech-pitched or drone-like singing. To help the child, sing and have the child echo you.

If the child continues to sing inaccurately, simply ask him or her, "Was that your singing voice or your speaking voice?" If he's unsure, say, "That was your speaking voice." You can even allow the child to place his or her fingers on your throat when speaking or singing to hear the difference in the vibrations.

To help a child having trouble differentiating melodic pitches, try singing in his or her right ear. As funny as that sounds, A. A. Tomatis, a French hearing specialist, found the right ear to be the ear that identifies intervals (Brumfield, 2006).

I.A.1 Lost in the Forest

1. Have the children move about the room as if they're in a forest, imitating the motions of different animals.
2. Pretend that you are a lost baby animal of a particular type. Call your "mother" by making the sound of a particular animal and having the child impersonating that animal echo you.
3. Switch and allow a child to be the baby animal.

I.A.2 Yoo-Hoo!

1. Stand behind "an old dead tree," and call particular children to you with a high "Yoo-hoo!"
2. Tell the children to echo as they come join you behind the tree.

I.A.3 "Paige's Train" or "Engine, Engine"

1. Have the children echo you as you imitate a train whistle.
2. Play "Paige's Train" or "Engine, Engine," letting children take turns being the conductor.

I.A.4 Puppets

1. Use various puppets to make sounds that the children can imitate, such as a cow ("Moo!") or a scary ghost ("Ooo!")

Variation:

1. Show two puppets: a bear and a parrot.
2. Say, "The bear sings it too low. The parrot can help him sing it higher," as you pantomime the action.

I.B Steady Beat

I.B.1 Heartbeats

1. As everyone sings a known song or game, have the children pat the steady beat by touching heart icons on the board or on a rug.
2. Start with a pattern of just four heart icons, then elongate the pattern with eight, and then sixteen. Later, the children can progress to other icons and even pictures (of snails or seesaws).

I.B.2 Step to It

1. After the children demonstrate an ability to pat the beat while sitting or standing stationary, have them step the beat in place while singing a known song.
2. Challenge them by having them march while the teacher plays a drum or bells.
3. Eventually, move the children toward walking on the ellipse-shaped line of tape on the floor to the teacher's music.

I.B.3 Radio Game

1. The children sing a known song while patting the beat.
2. When you give a signal, such as pantomiming turning a knob, the children sing in their heads while still keeping the beat going. Turn the knob again to indicate the children should sing out loud again as they maintain the beat. Use the signal to bring their voices in and out, like tuning a radio.

After lots of repetition with these preparation activities, you can use this activity to present or name the steady beat.

I.B.4 Tick Tock

1. Bring in a metronome. Let the metronome play for a bit.
2. Talk with the children about things that tick, like clocks.
3. Chat the rhyme "Hickory Dickory Dock" while the metronome plays.
4. Talk about a steady heartbeat.
5. Name the "steady beat."

I.C Comparisons

Start with the most important comparison in music: "same/different." Beginning with sounds from the children's environment, compare the sound-specific percussion instruments, speaking voice versus singing voice, echo songs versus question and answer songs, and more. Develop this essential comparison often as the children experience music in the classroom.

I.C.1 Fast/Slow

1. Sing known songs fast and slowly, and then have the children echo you.
2. Prompt the children by asking them to hold up one finger if you're singing fast and two fingers if you're singing slowly.
3. When singing or performing, use icons such as a picture of a hare and a tortoise.
4. Name the concepts *fast* and *slow*.
5. Play the children art music, pop, or jazz music that has fast and slow tempos. A good example is Modest Mussorgsky's "Ballet of the Unhatched Chicks" from *Pictures at an Exhibition.*
6. Good songs for fast and slow are

   - "Paige's Train,"
   - "Goin' on a Bear Hunt,"
   - "Bee, Bee,"and
   - "Burney Bee."

I.C.2 Loud/Soft

1. Perform known songs loud and softly, with the children echoing you. Ask the children to sing like "Linus" or like "Lucy."
2. Have the children hold up one finger if you're singing softly and two fingers if you're singing loudly.
3. Examples of art music for loud and soft:

   - Vaughn Williams: *"March Past the Kitchen Utensils,"*
   - Debussy: *"Clair de lune,"* and
   - Haydn: Symphony no. 94 ("Surprise").

3. The following songs prepare loud and soft especially well:

   - "Engine, Engine,"
   - "El Mar Estaba Serena," and
   - "Grizzly Bear."

I.C.3 Short/Long

1. Using known songs that contain *ta* and *ti-ti*, have a puppet that "taps" a child's hand to the rhythm of the words.
2. Have the children move their hands like puppets to the rhythm of the words.
3. Echo-clap the rhythm of the words to songs while first saying the words aloud, and then inner hearing the words.
4. While singing the phrases, point to picture cards representing the four-beat patterns.

5. After a lot of this kind of preparation, describe the sounds as "short" or "long."
6. Examples of art music to get a sense of short and long include:

   • Haydn: Symphony No. 2 ("Surprise"),
   • Mozart: *Variations on "Ah! vous dirai-je, Maman,"* and
   • Beethoven: Symphony No. 7, Movement 2.

I.C.4 High/Low

1. Beginning with a wide range, produce high and low sounds with your voice and with instruments, and have the children echo you, then gradually decrease the range to octave, fifth, minor third (very young children have difficulty differentiating the tones in major and minor seconds).
2. Have the children point upward if the sound is high and downward if the sound is low. They could also stand up when hearing high sounds and crouch down when hearing low sounds.
3. Perform rhymes and chants in a high or low voice, switching back and forth on some visual cue, such as frog and bird cards.
5. The following art songs showcase high and low:

   • Aaron Copland: "Circus Music" from *The Red Pony and*
   • Modest Mussorgsky: "Ballet of the Unhatched Chicks" from *Pictures at an Exhibition.*

II. ACTIVITIES FOR DEVELOPING MUSICAL CONCEPTS (ELEMENTARY)

II.A Sound Concepts

II.A.1 Body Sounds

Concept: Types of sounds, characteristics of sounds
Skills: Listening, improvising
Materials: The children's own bodies

1. Guide the children in experimenting with how many body sounds they can make (hand claps, tongue clicks, finger snaps, and so forth). The children don't have to make the sounds in rhythm.

II.A.2 Found Sounds

Concept: Types of sounds, characteristics of sounds
Skills: Listening, improvising
Materials: Any objects in the environment

1. Gather some objects from the classroom (such as books, papers, pencils, and the like) and have the children make different sounds with them by scraping, rattling, striking them, and so on. *How many sounds can you make?*
2. Try this with surfaces and furniture around the room. *How many sounds can we find in our classroom?*
3. Try striking objects with different strikers such as rubber mallets, drumsticks, pencils. *How does it sound different when you strike it with that?*

Extension: Do this activity with classroom percussion instruments. Try to find ways to produce specific sounds described as long, short, high, low, soft, loud, smooth, scratchy, twangy, and so forth.

II.A.3 Vocal Range

Concept: Types of sounds, characteristics of sounds
Skills: Listening, singing
Materials: Tone bars, mallet instrument, or piano

1. Have the child approach the tone bars, a mallet instrument, or the piano and check the range of his or her singing voice. *What is the highest pitch you can sing? What is the lowest pitch you can sing? Notice that as you go right on the instrument the pitches get higher, and as you go left, the pitches get lower.* (This is good follow-up to the "Establishing Up and Down" lesson in the Montessori albums.)

II.A.4 Sound Classification

Concept: Types of sounds, characteristics of sounds
Skills: Listening
Materials: Various sets of percussion instruments and classroom objects

1. Lay out three rugs, one for each category: timbre, dynamics, and pitch.
2. The children go around the room, making sounds on objects and instruments and classifying them based on their timbre, dynamics, or pitch. For example, the children might place the C bell and the C tone bar on the "pitch" rug along with the classroom attention chime (if it also produces a C). They might place a pair of cymbals and finger cymbals on the "timbre" rug because they have a similar splashy, bright sound.

Note: instruments and objects with similar sound quality go on the "timbre" rug, with soft or loud sounds go on the "dynamics" rug, and with high or low sounds go on the "pitch" rug. You could even have two designated spaces on each rug for comparisons. The timbre rug could have spaces designated for woody sounds, tinny sounds, and the like.

II.A.5 Sound Hunt

Concept: Types of sounds, characteristics of sounds
Skills: Listening
Materials: None

1. Have the children close their eyes and listen to the sounds they hear in the environment.
2. Add a few sounds by shuffling your feet, rustling a paper, jiggling a pencil in a pencil holder, and so on.
3. Compile a list of all the sounds the children heard.

Extension: Have the children listen for a sound you designate, such as the "ping" of a fork on a glass. Tell them to raise a hand when they hear the sound.

Children can compile a "Listening Journal" in which they log all of the sounds they hear during the day, including descriptions of the sounds.

II.A.6 Descriptive Music

Concept: Sound and mood
Skills: Listening, moving
Materials: Recordings of famous music

1. Sing with the children "El Mar Estaba Serena." Discuss the way the song makes them feel. *How does the sound of the music evoke such a mood?*
2. Make a chart on a whiteboard, or lay out different rugs that represent different moods. Play the children select pieces from the Western and world music repertoire and have them classify the moods.
3. Represent each piece of music with an icon that the children can place in the particular category.
4. Good pieces from the Western tradition for this activity include:

   • Debussy: *"Clair de lune,"*
   • Rimsky-Korsakov: "Flight of the Bumblebee," and
   • Stravinsky: *The Rite of Spring.*

II.A.7 Unique Voices

Concept: Sound: timbre
Skills: Listening
Materials: Various pitched percussion instruments, tone bars, bells

1. Gather the children around the instruments.
2. Play the same pitch on a tone bar, a bell, and a marimba.
3. Discuss the tone quality of each instrument. Give the children vocabulary to describe the sound of the instrument.

II.A.8 Great Big Mystery

Concept: Sound: timbre
Skills: Listening
Materials: Various pitched and nonpitched percussion instruments, tone bars, bells

1. Gather the children together and sing the song "Great Big House."
2. Invite the children to hide their eyes and sing the song again, this time, not singing but just listening on the words "pumpkin pie."
3. When that moment in the song arrives you play the rhythm of the words "pumpkin pie" (*ti-ti ta*) on an instrument. Have the children identify the instrument while their eyes are still covered.

II.A. 9 Track It Down[3]

Concept: Sound: timbre
Skills: Listening, playing instruments, improvising
Materials: Various pitched and nonpitched percussion instruments, tone bars, bells

1. Seat children in a circle and give each an instrument.
2. Blindfold a child in the middle.
3. Name an instrument, such as a bongo drum and have all of the children improvise on their instruments at the same time as the blindfolded child listens carefully for the named instrument and locates it among the children seated in the circle.

Extension: Before the game begins, name all of the instruments and give the children a chance to hear the sound of each. Make sure the child in the middle knows all of the instruments are in the circle. Start the children playing, but signal one instrument not to play. The blindfolded child can guess which instrument didn't join in.

II.B Rhythm Concepts

II.B.1 Things That Go Tick-Tock

Concept: Rhythm: beat and tempo
Skills: Listening
Materials: Writing materials, various recordings of famous works

1. Gather the children and tell them you're thinking of something that makes sound that recurs at regular intervals. The children will make many guesses (heart, clock, turn signal). Pick one.
2. Make a list of such objects. Make another list of physical activities (rowing) and children's games (jumping rope, patty cake) that follow a steady beat.

3. Listen to pieces of music like the following compositions:

- Vivaldi: "Spring" from *The Four Seasons,*
- Joplin: "The Entertainer," and
- Haydn: Symphony No. 101 ("The Clock"), Movement 2.

II.B.2 Follow the Leader

Concept: Rhythm: beat and tempo
Skills: Listening
Materials: Percussion instruments

1. Have children *follow the leader,* imitating you as you make steady movements or body sounds while reciting a rhyme or chant.
2. Begin with patting the knees and gradually increase the intricacy and difficulty of the movements.

II.B.3 You're the Conductor

Concept: Rhythm: meter
Skills: Listening
Materials: A conductor's baton (optional)

1. Introduce the children to the conducting patterns for duple meter. (Refer to figure 12.2 for the duple meter conducting pattern.) To conduct in duple meter, raise your right hand (palm flat facing the ground if you're not using a baton), or raise the tip of the baton to chin level in front of your body; then let it drop on the first beat until your arm is parallel to the floor. Let the hand and forearm bounce slightly curving upward to the right; then bring them back up to their original position. Reverse the bounce for the left hand.

Figure 12.2.

To conduct in triple meter, repeat the hand drop, but swing your hand and forearm right for a second bounce; lift it slightly upward and make a third higher, smaller bounce, as in figure 12.3.

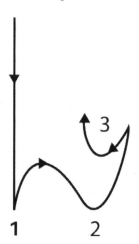

Figure 12.3.

Notice that in both conducting patterns, we indicate the first beat with a downward, accented gesture from the same starting position.

2. Practice with the children conducting in twos and threes while performing songs and dances in duple and triple meters.

Extension: The children can conduct along with pieces in your CD library as they listen.

When the children compose a piece for multiple instruments, have them appoint a "conductor" when performing the piece.

II.B.4 Echo Clapping

Concept: Rhythm: patterns
Skills: Listening, moving
Materials: Percussion instruments

1. Clap a rhythm pattern and tell the children to clap *with* you, doing exactly as you do. (The most effective clap technique is to extend the left hand at waist level and clap the palm of the right hand into the palm of the left hand with a free wrist movement.)
2. Practice *dynamics* by making broad, heavy movements for *forte* (loud), and smaller movements for *piano* (soft.) Likewise, practice *tempo* by clapping faster or slower.
3. After some practice with this, when the children can clap along with you easily, select one child to play a nonpitched percussion instrument such as a tambourine instead of clapping.

4. Eventually, on another day, lead the children in some echo-clapping exercises. Clap short rhythmic patterns for the children to repeat and gradually increase the length and complexity of the patterns.

5. Lead the children in some question-and-answer clapping activities. Clap a short pattern to one child and tell him to improvise a pattern of the same length. Then invite all of the children to repeat the child's improvised pattern. To fold instruments into this exercise, play a pattern on an instrument, hand the instrument to a child to play an answer, and let that child keep that instrument as you play a new pattern on a different instrument for a new child.

II.B.5 Hand Jive

Concept: Rhythm: meter
Skills: Listening, moving, singing
Materials: None

1. Invent a simple body percussion sequence in twos, such as pat clap, pat clap, pat clap.

2. Have the children perform the pattern in figure 12.4 as they chant.

P   c P   c
One potato two potato

P   c P   c
Three potato four,

P   c P   c
Five potato six potato

P   c P   c
Seven potato more.

Figure 12.4.

3. Set up a simple body percussion sequence in threes, such as pat, pat, clap, pat, pat, clap.

4. Have children perform the pattern as they chant something like:

Jeremy, Jennifer,
Harvey and Jo,
Walked down the street but had
Nowhere to go.

5. Perform your patterns with other classroom songs and chants in duple and triple meters.

II.B.6 Body Percussion

Concept: Rhythm: patterns
Skills: Listening, moving
Materials: None

1. Tell the children you're going to pat your knees, stamp, clap, and stamp fingers in rhythm. Tell them to do exactly as you do, then perform a pattern like figure 12.5.

2. Repeat each lettered pattern above as many times as necessary until the children can follow easily.

3. Challenge the children with increasingly complex patterns.

4. Try having the children echo your body percussion patterns.

5. Sing a known classroom song while performing a body percussion pattern as an *ostinato*.

Extension: The previous notation is for your reference. The children can notate their body percussion exercises by coming up with a symbol for various body percussion sounds, such as a cat for patting their knees, a car for clapping, an umbrella for snapping, and a star for stamping one foot. They can use the Music Grid Paper to write out a little score-like in figure 12.6 on page 154.

II.B.7 Category Chants

Concept: Rhythm: patterns
Skills: Listening, moving
Materials: Percussion instruments

1. Gather the children and come up with a list of words in a category, such as foods, fruits, colors, flowers, or birds.

2. Chant the words in a category until they form simple rhythm patterns (that needn't rhyme). For example:

Blackbird, robin, sparrow, jay
Chickadee, mockingbird, bluebird, owl

3. Verbalize the patterns using the words *short* and *long* or using rhythmic sol-fa.

4. Notate the patterns using icons or stick notation.

5. Perform the patterns on percussion instruments or body percussion.

II.B.8 Clap or Dance Your Name

Concept: Rhythm: patterns
Skills: Listening, moving
Materials: Percussion instruments

1. Help children discover and clap the rhythm of their own names.

2. Chant each name several times, then ask the children to *clap the way their names sound*. For example:

Speak: Mary Mary Mary
clap: X x X x X x

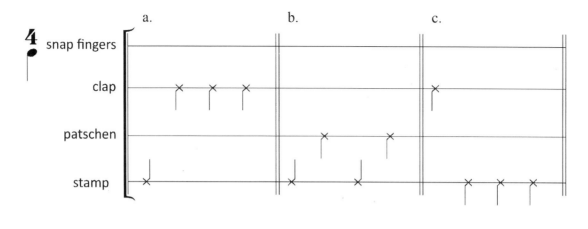

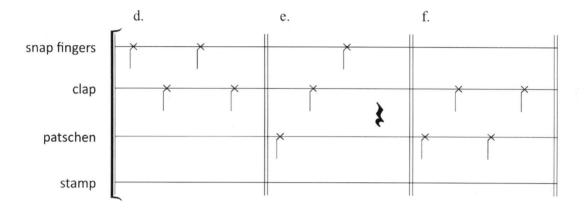

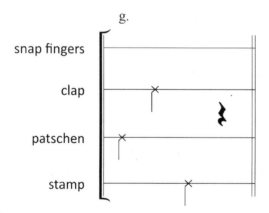

Figure 12.5.

3. Perform body percussion to the children's names. Perform Mary's name with *stamp, clap, stamp, clap,* for instance.
4. Combine the children's names to form a chant and perform the chant with body percussion or percussion instruments.

Extension: This works as a lovely name-learning exercise for the beginning of the year. Go around the circle and have each child perform a body percussion accompaniment to their name. The other children repeat the child's movements as they repeat her name.

The children could compose *Rhythm Cryptogram* pieces for their friends and loved ones using rhythm patterns derived from their names.

II.B.9 Syncopation

Concept: Rhythm: syncopation
Skills: Listening, moving, singing, playing instruments

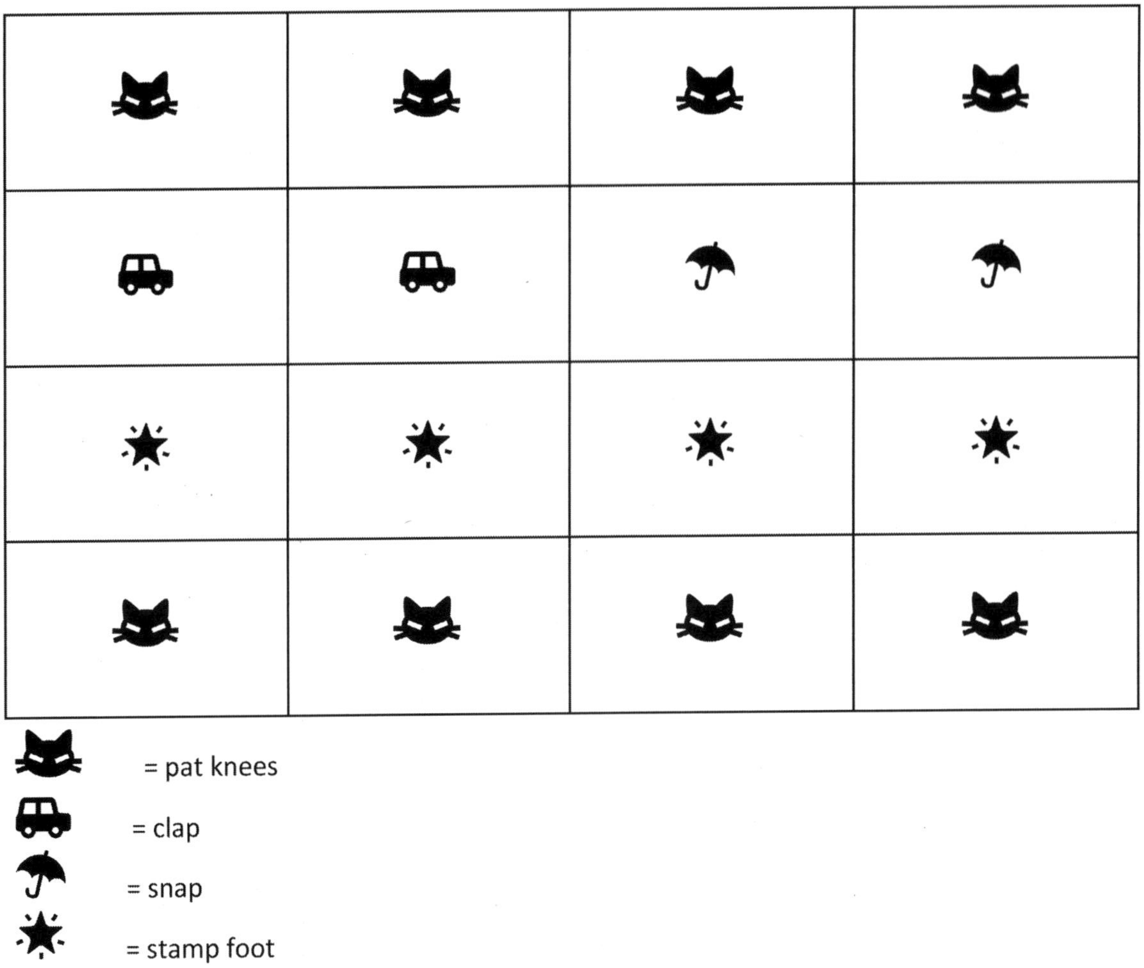

| = pat knees |
| = clap |
| = snap |
| = stamp foot |

Figure 12.6.

Materials: Percussion instruments, dry-erase markers of various colors, whiteboard

1. In black, write a line of numbers 1 to 8 across the whiteboard.
2. Circle in red beats 1, 3, 5, and 7. Have the children clap, stamp, or pat on the circled beats as you count the steady beat.
3. Write another line of black numbers from 1 to 8 and circle in red beats 2, 4, 6, and 8. Have the children clap, stamp, or pat on the steady beat. Discuss how the two lines feel different.
4. Draw a third line of numbers and circle beats 1, 4, and 7. Perform it and discuss how this line feels different. *The accents on 4 and 7 occur on weak beats. Feel that uneven, but nice forward-moving feeling?*
5. Draw a fourth line with the red circles on 2, 5, and 9. Perform and discuss.

Extension: Many classroom songs, such as "John Henry," "Hill and Gully Rider," and "My Momma's Calling Me"

have syncopation. These songs provide good preparation for the rhythm pattern *syn-co-pa.*

II.C Melody Concepts

II.C.1 Stair Stepping

Concept: Melodic direction
Skills: Listening, moving
Materials: Tone bars, bells, or mallet instrument

1. Play an ascending melody on a pitched instrument one note at a time.
2. Separate each note so that as you play, the children pretend to walk up a staircase step by step, making their bodies tall or crouching down.
3. This is especially fun to do if the child's body is obscured by an overturned table or a low bookshelf.

II.C.2 Leaps and Bounds

Concept: Melodic steps and skips
Skills: Listening, moving
Materials: Tone bars, bells, or mallet instrument

1. Play examples of short melodies that move by steps and by skips.
2. Improvise some melodies and have the children move around the room. If the melody moves by a step, the children walk, if it moves by a skip, they leap. The higher the melodic skip, the higher the children leap.

II.C.3 Joy to the World

Concept: Melodies are built from scales
Skills: Singing, playing
Materials: Tone bars

1. Play the song "Joy to the World" as a mystery song. See if the children can guess it.
2. Sing the song with the children. Notice that the song is made up of a descending major scale.
3. Play the notes in different orders to make other known songs from the major scale. Sing the other songs.
4. Place the minor scale strip in front of the tone bars and play "Joy to the World" again. Have the children sing and describe what's different.
5. Play and sing "Joy to the World" in as many different scales as you like.

II.4.C Cliffhanger

Concept: Melodies come to rest on their "home tone"
Skills: Singing
Materials: None

1. Sing "Happy Birthday," pausing at the end of each phrase and emphasizing the last note of the phrase. Ask the children does the song feel finished yet?
2. Sing songs that end on *do* and stop just before the last note. Ask the children how that feels. *Does it feel restless, like it isn't finished yet?* Then sing the last note, *do,* and notice the feeling of relief and of finality.

Extension: Sing "Michael, Row the Boat Ashore," with *sol* as the final note and then again with *do* as the final note. Discuss with the children the difference in feeling between the two.

II.C.5 Sing Backs

Concept: Melodies are made from scales
Skill: Singing
Materials: None

1. Sing a short pentatonic motive, speaking the sol-fa syllables.
2. Have the children echo what you sang showing the hand signs.

3. Reverse this: you sing a motive using hand signs, the children echo singing the syllable names.

II.D Harmony Concepts

II.D.1 Canoe Song

Children above the age of seven can experience harmony in a variety of fun ways. They can accompany classroom songs with ostinati that can be sung or played on pitched percussion instruments. They can sing canons, rounds, quodlibets, and part songs. Finally, they can use a ukulele or autoharp to strum chords to classroom songs.[4]

When several independent melodies come together to create harmony, we call that texture *polyphonic* ("poly" meaning "many" and "phonic" meaning voices). When one or two melodies move together in harmony with chordal accompaniment, we call that texture *homophonic.*

Concept: Harmony: monophonic and polyphonic texture
Skills: Singing, listening, playing instruments
Materials: Ukulele or autoharp, pitched percussion instruments

1. Teach the song "Canoe Song" by rote. Have the children pat their knees to keep the steady beat as they learn the song.
2. Visit activity IV.E.1 and appendix B to learn how to teach the children to sing with multiple vocal parts.

II.D.2 How Many Pitches?

Concept: Chords
Skills: Listening, playing instruments
Materials: Autoharp or ukulele

1. Strum a chord on the autoharp or ukulele.
2. Ask the children how many notes they hear.
3. Give a C, E, and G tone bar to three children and ask them to play individually and then simultaneously. Discuss with the children the words *chord* and *harmony.*

II.D.3 Making Chords

Concept: Chords
Skills: Listening, playing instruments, improvising, composing
Materials: Tone bars or bells

1. Gather a group of three children together in front of the tone bar cabinet and label the tone bars.
2. Child 1 picks any tone bar and plays it very lightly, with a repeated, steady beat.
3. Child 2 plays the other tone bars and selects one that doesn't clash with the first tone bar. When he or she

finds one, he or she taps it repeatedly coordinating rhythm with the first child.

4. Child 3 plays the other tone bars until he or she finds one that doesn't clash with the first two. When he or she finds one, he or she joins the other two children.
5. The three children can make a note of what three tones they selected.

II.E Form Concepts

II.E.1 Same, Change, Different

Songwriters, composers, and musicians love to play with the concepts of same and different in their compositions. This "theme and variations" activity is a fun way for children to become sensitive to this basic concept of musical form.

Concept: Same and different, unity and variety
Skills: Listening, playing instruments, improvising, composing
Materials: Tone bars, writing materials

1. Seat the children in a circle, with a set of tone bars in the center.
2. Go up to the tone bars, set up the tone bars with a scale strip, and play a simple motive of three or four notes.
3. Invite a child to come up and play what you played (same). Then, tell him or her to alter one note in the motive or alter the rhythm (change).
4. Invite another child to approach the tone bars, play the previous child's motive (different), and then alter one note or the rhythm of the motive.
5. Continue at your discretion.

II.E.2 Motive Magic

Concept: Motives
Skills: Listening, moving, improvising, composing
Materials: Tone bars, bells, mallet instruments

1. Gather the children together to sing a known folk song, such as "London Bridge."
2. Without singing the words, clap a short recurring motive from the song, such as the rhythm on the words "falling down" (*ti-ti, ta*).
3. Perform the song and have the children identify on which words the motive occurs.

II.E.3 "Classical" Structure

In chapter 7, you read about the details of Sonata Allegro form, a form that features prominently in classical music, especially in the first movements of major symphonies. This lesson is a simple and effective way to begin to understand form and how form unfolds in music.

Concepts: Motives, phrases, unity and variety, sections

Skills: Playing instruments, composing
Materials: A set of label cards and picture cards as pictured in figure 12.7 on next page:

- two *primary theme* cards colored pink,
- one *secondary theme* card colored blue,
- one *secondary theme* card colored pink,
- one bridge card colored lavender,
- one bridge card colored pink,
- white label cards: primary theme (2), secondary theme (2), bridge (2), EXPOSITION, DEVELOPMENT, RECAPITULATION,
- a recording of the first movement of Mozart's *Eine kleine Nachtmusik*.

Tell the children a story: *Once there lived a distinguished court gentleman and a graceful court lady. The two were in love. They both lived quite far from each other on opposite sides of a great river. Fortunately for both of them, a stone bridge stretched across the river and made it possible for the two to meet. One evening they met at a ball. They danced, talked about their lives, and generally had a nice time together. Eventually, the gentleman asked the lady to marry him. She agreed, and the two walked across the bridge and spent the rest of their days living in happiness.*

4. Play Mozart's *Eine kleine Nachtmusik* and lay down the cards as the music progresses. When the piece finishes, the cards should look something like figure 12.8 (Note: In *Eine Kleine Nachtmusik*, unlike in most sonata allegro forms, the exposition doesn't repeat and the development is quite short.
5. Invite the children to write their own composition in sonata allegro form. Guide the child through the framework as follows:

- Create and write down two short musical ideas (exposition).
- Next, write at least three short variations on these two ideas (development).
- Repeat the two original ideas (recapitulation).
- Add an ending to the music.
- If you like, you can go back to the beginning and write an introduction.

Note: The children can listen to other first movements and make their own cards for analysis. Other good examples of sonata allegro form include:

- First movements of symphonies by Haydn
- *Barber of Seville Overture*, by Rossini
- *Symphony No. 40* and *Piano Sonata KV 283*, by Mozart. With this symphony, you can use pirate

primary theme (2 pink):	secondary theme (1 blue):	secondary theme (1 pink):	bridge (1 lavender, 1 pink)

EXPOSITION	DEVELOPMENT	RECAPITULATION	CODA

Figure 12.7.

Sonata Allegro Card Layout:

exposition				recapitulation			
primary theme (pink)	bridge (lavender)	secondary theme (blue)		primary theme (pink)	bridge (pink)	secondary theme (pink)	
			coda	dev.			coda

Figure 12.8.

cards and a ship instead of a bridge to tell the story of a couple of swashbuckling pirates. During the development section, the two pirates can have a sword fight, and in the recapitulation, we see that the second pirate has been captured. (The second theme appears in the recapitulation in the minor key.)

- *Symphony No. 5* and *Piano Sonata Op. 10* No. 2, by Beethoven.[5]

II.E.4 Song Forms

By studying the formal plan of blues, folk, pop, and jazz songs, children develop an ability to recognize formal sections in music and find direction in their own song-writing and composing. Each of these mini-lessons leads to a refined sense of the formal plan of music. Break them up and present them at different times rather than presenting them all in one sitting or all in one day. The songs listed are just suggestions. Feel free to listen to other songs that follow these forms.

Concepts: Sections
Skills: Listening
Materials: Different colored index cards (the colors are arbitrary) as in table 12.9.

Table 12.9.

Quantity	Color	Front	Back
6	pink	A	verse
3	blue	B	chorus
2	yellow	C	bridge
4	white	D	pre-chorus
1	green	A'	verse
1	lavender	intro	
1	orange	ending	
2	red	link	
2	pink	A	"melody" or "head"
1	blue	B	solos

The following recordings:

"Good Morning Blues" by Leadbelly from *Leadbelly Sings for Children* [Smithsonian Folkways SFW45047_114]
"The Times They Are a-Changin'" by Bob Dylan from *Bob Dylan's Greatest Hits, Vol. 1*
"Ol' Man River" by Paul Robeson
"But Not for Me" by Chet Baker from *Chet Baker Sings!*
"Yesterday" by the Beatles from *Help!*
"Candle in the Wind" by Elton John from *Goodbye, Yellow Brick Road*
"Fix You" by Coldplay from *X&Y*
"Don't Look Back in Anger" by Oasis from *(What's the Story) Morning Glory?*

"Imagine" by John Lennon from *Imagine*
"So What?" by Miles Davis from *Kind of Blue*

1. Gather the children at a rug or table.
2. Sing "Happy Birthday," drawing the melody in the air. Pause after each phrase to ask the children if the song feels finished yet. When the song is over, heave a deep sigh, as though you've finally gotten to the end. Say something like: *"Happy Birthday" has four phrases: The first three end with a feeling of wanting more, while the last phrase ends with a definite feeling of finality.*
3. *Musicians organize melodies and harmonies into larger sections. One or more of these sections strung together makes up a composition, be it a song or a symphony. The sections often contrast with one another and can be distinguished by their melody, their harmony, and their mood. The sections have definite beginnings and endings, but they usually flow together seamlessly.*
4. *We're going to listen to a selection of musical pieces and attempt to analyze the way their sections are organized.*
5. *When we refer to sections of a musical piece, we use big capital letters, starting with A (hold up an "A" card). If a section of a piece repeats, but is slightly different, we place a little apostrophe after the letter, like this (hold up the "A" card).*
6. *Let's analyze the form of various songs.*

12-BAR BLUES

1. Tell a story similar to this: *In the United States before the 1860s, many black Americans worked as slaves. They had no freedom, no pay, and no rights. They were bought and sold and mistreated. Some Americans thought slavery was wrong, others depended on slavery for their livelihood. The country fought the Civil War whether some of the states could break away from the United States, in part over the question of whether people could own slaves. The side against slavery, the North, won the war, and black people were at last given their freedom. The trouble was, some of their fellow countrymen were angry about having to give up their slaves, so many former slaves found it extremely difficult to find employment. Many of them entered into contracts without pay, just like when they were slaves! Others, however, took to wandering the country, playing their guitars and harmonicas on street corners for money. These lone wanderers wrote and played a sad, mournful kind of music that reflected the suffering in their lives. Because of its sad quality, their music became known as "the Blues." Let's listen to some blues and see if we can't figure out how it's structured.*

2. As the music progresses, place cards on the table indicating each section. *This is A, this is B, and so on.* At the end of the song, you should have cards laid out in front of you in the pattern AAB.

3. The children can write their own blues songs by first coming up with two lines of lyrics. The first line will repeat and the third line will be some kind of refrain.

4. Once the children have finished their lyrics, they can come up with a melody and accompany it with ukulele or autoharp. The children can write original songs for every song form that follows.

STROPHIC FORM—AAAA

1. Tell a story something like the following: *The Blues had a huge influence on American music. In fact, much of the folk, rock, pop, and jazz music you hear today was inspired by the blues. Let's talk right now about folk music. In the mid-twentieth century, many white folk singers strapped on harmonica holders and strummed acoustic guitars just like those old bluesmen. Woody Guthrie is a well-known folk balladeer. The form of these balladeers' songs, however, was much simpler than the blues. Bob Dylan was a famous songwriter who wrote in the folk style. Let's listen to the form of this song "The Times They Are a-Changin'"*

2. Repeat steps 2 and 3 above. You should have laid out AAAA . . . when the song is finished.

POPULAR SONG FORM—AABA

1. Tell a story like this: *In New Orleans, in the early 1900s, music from Africa, France, the British Isles, and many other places all got swirled together. Military brass bands played a loose mix of European classical instruments and harmony together with the African musical qualities of complex rhythm and improvisation. This new form of music became known as jazz. Jazz became so popular that composers started to use it in classical music and in the theater. Before long, musical theater became a vehicle for hit popular songs. One song form that grew out of musical theater and stuck consisted of a strong statement (A), repetition (A), a contrasting new statement (B), and a return to the original statement. Let's listen to "Ol' Man River" from a play called* Showboat *to hear what I'm talking about.*

2. Play the song and repeat steps 2 and 3. You should have cards laid out in the pattern AABA.

SHOW TUNE FORM—ABAC

1. *Here is another form that grew out of musical theater. It's a little bit more sophisticated than AABA because the last section can be pretty dramatic. Let's listen to a song and you'll hear what I mean.*

2. Play "But Not for Me" as performed by Chet Baker. As you listen, place the cards in the pattern ABAC.

ROCK AND POP—AABABA

1. This story goes something like this: *By the 1960s, rock and pop music became influenced by many other musical genres: the blues, musical theater, folk, and jazz. In fact, rock music was born when African American musicians started playing a kind of sped-up version of the blues with a driving backbeat. The Beatles, a quartet from England who became one of the most famous and influential rock and pop bands in the world, were really huge fans of African American rock music. This song, "Yesterday," however, doesn't sound at all like a rock song. It sounds more like a folk song accompanied by string quartet. That's because when the Beatles wrote it they were just starting to experiment with incorporating classical instruments as well. I'll tell you a story about the Beatles another day, for now, let's listen to the form of the Beatles song "Yesterday."*

2. Listen to "Yesterday." Lay out the cards as you listen. You should have AABABA laid out.

ROCK AND POP—VERSE, CHORUS

1. Tell a story similar to this: *Some pop and rock songs are made up of an A section called a "verse," which contains musical material that states an idea or sets up a mood. The verse largely serves as build up to the B section, called the "chorus," which is much fuller and which contains the songs catchiest material. Often the chorus carries the main point of the song. Sometimes, a musical introduction is tacked on to the front of the song to establish the mood and preview some of the musical ideas. The form can even be filled out by little instrumental "links" in between the sections. Let's listen to "Candle in the Wind" by Elton John to hear what I mean.*

2. Listen to the song. Lay out the cards for the different sections: intro, AB, link, AB, link, AB, B

3. Flip over the A and B cards to show the words "verse" and "chorus."

Verse, Chorus, Bridge

1. Some pop and rock songs add a little variety to the "verse, chorus" structure by adding a C section, called a "bridge." The bridge sometimes also goes by the name of "middle eight" or "breakdown." This third section usually occurs only once in the song. It forms

a contrast to the A and B sections and, in some cases, develops some of the musical ideas. A recent example of this structure was recorded by the band Coldplay on their album *X&Y*.

2. Play "Fix You" by Coldplay. The structure is: intro, AAB, link, A, B, link, C, B.

Verse, Prechorus, Chorus

1. The story: *Sometimes the chorus is so catchy that it requires a section of music, called a "prechorus" (D) to build up to it. The prechorus is a transitional section that prepares us for the rousing chorus to come. Prechoruses vary in length. Let's listen to a couple of songs with prechoruses to give you an idea of what they sound like. This song, "Don't Look Back in Anger" is by an English rock band called Oasis. The prechorus here is six lines long! It begins with the words "So I start a revolution from my bed" and takes a long time to build up. Then again, that chorus on "So Sally can wait" is pretty powerful and catchy.*

2. Play "Don't Look Back in Anger." The cards should be laid out: intro, ADB, link, ADBD (instrumental), B, B.

3. *Another song, called "Imagine," by John Lennon, has a very short prechorus of only one line! Let's listen to it.*

4. Listen to "Imagine." The structure: intro, ADADBADB.

JAZZ IMPROV STRUCTURE

1. *Remember when we talked about jazz music? Well, improvisation plays a big role in jazz music. Jazz musicians call it "jamming." Often, when jazz musicians get together, they jam to a combination of composed music and improvised music. By that I mean, jazz musicians will start a jam session by playing either a popular song or a song they composed. This is the A section, which jazz musicians call the "melody," or "head." After they've played the melody, they will then trade-off improvising solos over the chords in the song. This is the B section. The jam session finishes with everyone playing the melody again. Sometimes the musicians play an introduction at the beginning or an ending at the end. Jam sessions are really fun to listen to. Let's hear a song that Miles Davis wrote called "So What." The funny thing about this song is that the bass plays the melody. Let's listen!*

2. Listen to "So What" and lay out the cards. When the song finishes, you should have laid out: intro, ABA.

3. It's interesting to point out that, beginning with the entrance of the trumpet, the musicians are improvising. See if you can help the children to hear the order of the solos: trumpet, tenor saxophone, and alto saxophone playing a kind of "dialog" with the piano.

Notes:
Place the cards in a basket on the listening shelf, so that children can use them to analyze other song forms when they listen to music. They can also use the cards to plan out the structure of their own compositions.

II.E.5 Songs Have Sections

Concepts: Sections, unity and variety
Skills: Listening, playing instruments, moving
Materials: Pitched and nonpitched percussion instruments, ukulele or autoharp, icons

1. Sing "Rock-a My Soul" with the children. Discuss with them how many sections the song has. *Are the sections the same or different? How are they similar? How are they different?*

2. Come up with a hand jive or a motion for both sections.

3. Sing the song again, performing the physical motions.

4. Divide the class into two groups and sing the song as a canon.

Arrange icons on a rug or whiteboard to highlight similar or different phrases or sections in a song that has multiple sections. Icons representing "Twinkle, Twinkle, Little Star" might look like figure 12.10.[6]

Figure 12.10.

II.E.6 A Multimovement Composition

This lesson brings together many of the earlier ideas about musical form for children to compose their first multimovement composition. With the children, you can call it their first symphony. Remember, the word "symphony" refers to the *structure* of a multimovement work and not the *instrumentation*. The children can use any instruments they like in any combination to write a symphony (i.e., tone bars and ukulele, triangle and marimba, singers and tambourine, and the like).

This is a high level of musical thinking, as the children not only have to consider the form for a single piece, but they have to think about how multiple movements can be linked together. This exercise works for older children, but a child of any age who has had even limited experience with composition can do it. It works best as a culminating activity for children with long attention spans who have tried many other types of composition activities.

Concepts: Motives, phrases, unity and variety, sections
Skills: Playing instruments, composing
Materials: Instruments, writing materials

1. Listen to a variety of classical multimovement symphonies and share with the children a sense of how each movement is structured, as well as how the movements fit together.
2. Present the lessons in musical form above.
3. Gather some children and tell them you're going to write a four-movement symphony that follows the movement descriptions in figure 12.11. Say: *We can choose any combination of instruments. As we write our music, we're going to think of a unifying idea that will tie all the movements together. This could be a little rhythm, a melodic motif, or a story. Whatever we use, we want to make sure it helps our symphony to sound as though the four movements belong together. (As an example, you could use a musical cryptogram derived from the name of a notable songwriter, say, John Lennon. Looking at the musical cryptogram table in chapter 15, we would build a theme from the notes E, B, C, A, E, D, C, E, and C.)*
4. Work through the composition process with the children roughly as follows:

   - Begin by composing two short contrasting themes.
   - Compose up to five variations of those two themes. From those building blocks, write the first movement as in the "Classical" structure lesson above. Use three of your five variations in the development section.
   - From there, use the remaining variations, or new ideas developed from those first two themes to compose the other three movements.
   - Next, write a big, grand ending.

   - Go back to the beginning of your first movement and write an introduction.

Note: The children can notate their symphonies in whatever notation they feel comfortable.[7]

III. ACTIVITIES FOR DEVELOPING MUSICAL SKILLS

III.A Listening

III.A.1 Active Listening

When children go off into the listening area of your environment, provide them with some activity to do rather than sitting and passively listening. Use these fun active listening activities to engage more than just the ears and the mind.[8]

Skills: Listening, singing, moving, playing instruments, reading
Materials: Various

1. While listening to a piece of music, have the child do one of the following:

   - raise her hand when she hears a particular instrument, such as the first trumpet or violin;
   - clap to the pattern played by the bass;
   - pantomime a violin whenever she hears it;
   - sing along with the pattern of the timpani;
   - sing with the female voice, listen only to the male voice;
   - select a percussion instrument and improvise a rhythm to accompany the recording;
   - holding a sheet with pictures of instruments, circle the pictures of the instruments she hears in the piece;
   - number the pictures in order of the entrance of the instruments she hears;
   - follow a sample score and cue the instruments as they enter;
   - tap or pat the beat, off beat, or rhythm on her knees;

Movement I: follows a "Classical", sonata allegro structure.
Movement II: slow and soft (i.e., a pretty melody with chords, or slow mysterious sounds). This movement can be in any song form you like, AAA, ABA, AABA, etc.
Movement III: quick and light, dance-like. Again, use any song form you like.
Movement IV: follows "Classical", sonata allegro structure but features a big, grand ending.

Figure 12.11.

- identify a repeated pattern in the music and pat along with it, or play along with it on a percussion instrument whenever it occurs;
- draw the contours of the melody in the air;
- show the highest and lowest notes of the piece by making some body gesture;
- follow a listening map of the piece, pointing to the various sections and moving her finger as the music progresses;
- make a repetitive motion and change it each time a chord changes;
- sing along with the melodic line on "loo";
- make a contour drawing, outlining the shape of the melody (see chapter 15);
- make a contour drawing using different colors, outlining the shape of all of the melodies in a polyphonic piece;
- hum or sing on "loo" a countermelody or harmony to the main melody;
- trace the line of a melody on a score as she listens;
- show changes in dynamics using arm or hand gestures;
- lay out cards with characters, shapes, or icons to show the sections of a piece;
- label each section as it occurs on a score;
- assign each theme a motion and make the motion whenever the theme appears;
- develop a creative story that conveys the "events" or mood of the piece; or
- use puppets to improvise or play out a drama to the piece as she listens.

III.B Singing

You can find specific information about techniques to help the children improve their singing in appendix A. Here, you'll find activities designed to run parallel with the daily singing of folk songs.

III.B.1 Singing, Speaking, Shouting Voice

This activity can help your children find their singing voice.

Skills: Singing
Materials: None

1. Tell the action story of Mr. Black and Mr. Brown:

   PART 1: *Once upon a time there lived two fine fellows, Mr. Black* (with bent elbow, hold up your closed left fist out at your side, with fingers curled around your thumb) *and Mr. Brown* (hold up your right fist, same). *One day, Mr. Brown decided to go and visit Mr. Black.* (Move your right fist up and down and across your body to meet your left fist during the following.) *So, he opened his door* (open the fingers of your right fist), *walked outside,* (stick out your thumb), *closed the door* (fold your fingers down into your palm, thumb sticking out), *and he went* (deep singing voice) *down the hill* (falsetto singing voice) *and up the hill, and* (deep singing voice) *down the hill* (falsetto singing voice) *and up the hill and* (deep singing voice) *down the hill* (falsetto singing voice) *and up the hill* (repeat this as many times as you like), *until at last he came to Mr. Black's door. So, he knocked on Mr. Black's door* (knock fists together). *No answer. He knocked again* (knock fists together). *No answer. He shouted: "Hey, Mr. Black!" No answer. "Nobody's home," thought Mr. Brown. So, he went . . .* (repeat the journey back to your fist's original position). *When he got home, he opened his door* (unfold your fingers), *went inside the house* (curl your thumb into your palm), *and he closed the door* (fold your fingers down over your thumb), *and went to sleep.*

   PART 2: *The next day, Mr. Black decided to go and visit Mr. Brown. So, he went . . .* (repeat PART 1 from Mr. Black's point of view).

   PART 3: *The next day, both Mr. Brown and Mr. Black decided to go and visit each other. So, they went . . .* (repeat the journey, bringing both fists to meet in the middle) *. . . and had a nice conversation* (pantomime a little conversation between the two fellows). *When at last night fell and it was time to go home, Mr. Brown and Mr. Black decided they'd better head home. So they . . .* (repeat the journey back home, ending with . . .) *and they both opened their doors* (uncurl the fingers of both hands), *stepped inside,* (tuck in your thumbs), *closed the door* (curl your fingers back over your thumbs), *and went to sleep.*

2. Ask the children when in the story you used your speaking voice, your singing voice, and your shouting voice. Demonstrate your speaking voice by speaking "This is my speaking voice." in a calm tone. Demonstrate your singing voice by singing "This is my singing voice" in your best falsetto (improvise the melody, or use the melody *s m l s m*).

III.B.2 *Tone Calls*

Improve the children's singing by sprinkling tone calls into their daily routine.

Skills: Singing
Materials: None

1. Teach the children a tone call for when you want to get their attention during the work cycle: softly sing, "Hello!" on *sol, mi* to get the children's attention.
2. When calling a child from across the playground, use a call and response tone call, such as singing "Shantay!" on *sol, mi,* and having them sing "Coming!" on the same pitches.
3. Use tone calls in situations when you need to do a headcount. Sing "Shantay," on *sol, mi* and have the child answer "I'm here" on the same pitches.
4. Vary the length and complexity of tone calls as the children learn more melodic and rhythmic elements.

III.C Moving

III.C.1 *Exploring Movement*

From the Command Cards to the rhythm cards, your Montessori albums contain some wonderful lessons about movement. Present them parallel with some of these quick activities to help your children improve, among other things, coordination, synchronized rhythmic movement, body awareness, as well as nonlocomotor and locomotor movements.[9]

Skills: Listening, moving
Materials: bell or tone bar

Gather the children, and challenge them to

• discover how many different ways they can move their fingers, hands, arms, elbows, shoulders, feet, legs, head, and hips;
• walk their own path without touching anyone;
• walk around every chair, block, or hoop placed on the floor;
• lightly touch two fingers of their neighbor as they pass;
• after the teacher has completed a movement, follow the teacher in exactly the same way;
• move a body part: fast, faster, slow, slower, gradually faster or slower;
• walk forward, backward, sideways, toward the door or windows;
• walk in high space (standing tall) and low space (crouching down). Walk, alternating between high and low space;

• make themselves heavy (like a boulder), light (as a feather), strong (as a tree root), or limp (like a scarecrow).
• walk without stopping;
• walk and stop suddenly or gradually (at some cue, like the clapping of a pattern or a tone call);
• draw with their hands, elbows, head, or feet a straight line, a curved line, a zigzag, or a loo;
• shape their body into a box, a triangle, a T, or a V;
• move from one shape to the next within four or eight beats; and
• walk, leap, lunge run, jump, hop, gallop, skip, strut, slide to a beat.

III.C.2 *"Hi, My Name's Joe"*

Skills: Listening, moving
Materials: None

1. Gather the children around a chair where you're sitting. Tell them the following story: *Hi! My name's Joe. I work in a button factory. I got a wife and two kids. One day, my boss comes up to me and he says, "Hey, Joe, are you busy?" I say, "No." So he says, "Then push this button with your right hand"* (push an imaginary button with your right hand). *Hi! My name's Joe. I work in a button factory. One day, my boss comes up to me and he says, "Hey, Joe, are you busy? I say, "No." So he says, "Then push this button with your left hand"* (push imaginary buttons with your right and left hands).
2. From here, introduce every button-pushing motion with the same story. As you initiate a new movement, be sure to keep all of the previous movements going. Gradually, as the children listen to the story, they will imitate your movements.
3. The movements proceed as follows:

    • push buttons with your right and left elbows;
    • push buttons with your right and left knees;
    • push buttons with your right and left feet;
    • push a button with your head; and
    • push a button with your tongue.

4. The final line of the story goes *Hi! My name's Joe. I work in a button factory. I got a wife and two kids. One day, my boss comes up to me and he says, "Hey, Joe, are you busy?" I said, "YES!"*

III.C.3 *Experiments in Creative Movement*

Creative movement involves more than just dancing. With their bodies, the children portray certain ideas, feelings, or pieces of musical expression. They can be inspired to move by a word, an image, a picture, a poem, a story, the melody of a song, a rhythmic pattern, or a symphonic work. Creative movement can be used to better the children's social skills, provide a break from work, reinstate a sense of calm, and cultivate the children's ability to express feelings on a deeper level.[10] All of the following movement activities can be accompanied by instruments.

Skills: Listening, moving
Materials: In some cases, percussion or mallet instruments

- Children can portray words in movement and sound. Present children with words to be turned into movement and sound pieces. Invite children to move silently when they hear words such as yawn, tramp, spin, shuffle, ooze, flutter, drip, crackle, or slither, then invite them to play those words on instruments.
- As they learn musical vocabulary, the children can act out musical terms such as legato, staccato, forte, and lento in creative movement. Later, they can compose melodies that express the terms.
- The children can depict a piece of music in movement. The movements in Camille Saint-Saëns's *Carnival of the Animals* each depict a different animal in music. The movement titled "The Lion" even features a musical roar. After a few listens, the children can listen to the music and move like a lion, stopping to "Roar!" at just the right moment. The movement can also be used to elicit words associated with a lion—such as large, strong, forceful, or proud—which the children can use as prompts for creative movement.
- Movement can arise from a visual image. Show children a copy of a painting or a photograph and encourage them to use silent movement to make the visual image come to life.
- Bring children together to create a collaborative movement piece. In a group of four to eight children, each child invents a movement to be included in a "movement collection." Their movements can flow one into the next or take place simultaneously to create a kind of "moving statue." They can allow each movement a certain number of beats or repeat some or all of the movements. They can even express the movements with a certain mood or energy, such as tired, angry, happy, or gentle.
- Children can express the events in a story through creative movement. Action stories, such as those found in *Best-Loved Folktales of the World* by Joanna Cole, provide wonderful tales for dramatization.
- Children move to gentle music played by the teacher, with a partner mirroring their movements.

III.D Reading

III.D.1 Magic Piano

Skills: Reading, singing
Materials: None, found objects, musical instruments

1. In the gathering or with a small group play the following game.
2. Tell the children when you touch your left knee to make a low pitched sound, such as a grunt or a growl. Touch your left knee a few times to make sure they have it.
3. Have the children make a high-pitched sound, such as a sigh or chirp, when you touch your right knee.
4. Compose by patting your knees in different patterns as the children make the sounds.
5. Experiment with dynamics and duration (*when I bring my hand slowly to my knee, sing softly, when I bring my hand quickly to my knee, sing loud. When I hold my hand on my knee, keep the sound going. When I just tap my knee, make a short sound*).

III.D.2 Zilch or the Magic Sampler

A sampler, sometimes called a "looper," is a device that records short sound snippets and plays them back at the touch of a button. When a button is pressed, the sound "loops" repeatedly until it's lifted. Some loopers have more than one channel, so sounds can be layered together to create complex combinations. Qualities of the sound, such as its pitch, can be modified to create variety. Pop musicians and hip-hop musicians make wide use of sampling and looping.

Skills: Reading, improvising
Materials: None

1. Gather the children around an everyday object or a mallet instrument.
2. Tell the children you're going to turn the object into a sampler and loop different sounds to make interesting patterns.
3. Touch one bar with your finger and tell a child to say, "Zilch" every time you press that bar. When you hold your finger on the bar, tell the child to repeat the word until your finger is lifted.
4. Touch your finger to another bar and tell another child to say, "Mr. Doubelina, Mr. Bob Doubelina."
5. Repeat by assigning the phrases: "Never mind the furthermore, the plea is self-defense" and "China people calling on the meter" to a bar.
6. Having assigned the four phrases to a bar, play a piece of music by touching the bars and having the children say their phrases. Switch and have a child come up and play the magic sampler.

Extension: Experiment by assigning one word or phrase to the middle bar on the instrument. As you touch each bar to the left, the children say the phrase in an increasingly lower voice, and as you touch each bar to the right, the children say the phrase in an increasingly higher voice. Try it with exact pitches, so that if you touch a C bar, the children sing the word or phrase on C.

Pretend that each bar has a little "knobs" that can adjust the speed or the pitch of the phrases. Pantomime turning different knobs to adjust the child's pitch or speed.

Play the game with a "sampler" made out of cardboard or a shoebox or an old electronic device with lots of knobs and switches on it.

The children can loop any noises, phrases, or random sounds they like.

III.E Playing Instruments

III.E.1 Experiments with Nonpitched Percussion Instruments

Much like the earlier creative movement exercises, the children can use poems, stories, or word prompts to generate creative sound making on instruments.

Skills: Playing instruments, improvising
Materials: Various nonpitched percussion instruments

- Read a poem together and ask the children to choose instruments that can help in expressing an interpretation of the poem.
- Ask the children to select a scene, such as a seashore, a forest, a busy downtown street, or a construction yard. Have them create an aural image of the scene by making a sound piece performed on nonpitched percussion instruments. Encourage free rhythms as well as repeated rhythmic patterns.

III.F Composing

Children who haven't had much experience with composing can use these short activities as a starting point or as a supplement to their more focused composition work.

III.F.1 Musical Scribbling

Skills: Playing instruments, composing, improvising
Materials: A variety of mallet and percussion instruments

1. Collect some classroom instruments with the children.
2. Give them an instrument and tell them to "scribble" with their instrument as you count to, say, twenty-four.

In other words, like scribbling on paper, just come up with sounds. Tell them not to edit their playing but to just let their ideas flow quickly and freely.

3. At the end of your twenty-four count, ask them to scribble once more, but to listen to themselves and listen for a musical idea, such as a melody or a rhythm pattern, that they like. This time, give them only an eight count.
4. Once they find a phrase, ask them to repeat it several times until they can remember it and replicate it. If it helps, they can teach their phrase to another child.

Extension: The children can notate their phrases in graphic notation or stick notation, whichever they're comfortable with.[11]

III.F.2 A Trip to the Zoo

Skills: Playing instruments, composing, moving
Materials: A variety of mallet and percussion instruments

1. Ask children to think about the qualities of movements of various animals one might find in a zoo. Observe the children carefully as they make movements such as smooth or jerky, fast or slow, continuous or random.
2. Review with the children what they noticed about the movement qualities of the animals.
3. Give children musical instruments and have them develop a short composition, say, sixteen to thirty-two beats, that conveys the sense of movement of an animal. Practice and refine it.

III.F.3 Motivations for Composition

When presenting children an opportunity to compose, it's best to set up limits. Creativity is best channeled through specific limitations. Often just a word will provide the children a creative spark. Here is a list of compositional prompts and frameworks to focus children's creative activity.[12]

Skills: Composing, playing instruments, singing
Materials: A variety of mallet and percussion instruments

- Titles such as "Life and Death of a Mosquito," "Clouds," "The Earth from Space."
- Emotions or moods: angry, happy, sad, excited, proud.
- Pictures or images: photographs, paintings, designs, maps.
- Stories: wordless books, children's own stories, fairy tales.
- Poetry: a sound setting or melodic setting of other's or the children's own poetry.
- Sounds: families of sounds, individual sounds, contrasting sounds.

- Patterns or cycles: "The Seasons," "My Day," "The Butterfly," "A Storm."
- Musical elements: a rhythm pattern, a limited number of notes, a melody, a scale, tone color, tempo, dynamics.
- Aesthetic principles: density, texture, tension and release, repetition and contrast.
- Musical structures: ostinato, phrase, motive, ABA, ABAC, blues, sonata allegro.
- Instrument choices: *Compose a piece for hand drum and maracas.*

III.G Improvising

III.G.1 Improvisation Starts

Try these quick activities as frameworks for improvisation.

Skills: Playing instruments, improvising
Materials: A variety of mallet and percussion instrument

1. To improvise with rhythm, have children:

   - improvise over a steady beat using body or mouth sounds;
   - improvise over a rhythmic pattern or ostinato;
   - improvise to a recording, fitting rhythms into the musical ideas; and
   - improvise over a metric pattern.

2. To improvise with melody, have children:

   - improvise singing a melody on "loo" over a drone or ostinato;
   - improvise a melody over the top of a sequence of chords played on ukulele or autoharp;
   - improvise a melody using scat syllables such as do-be-do, or shoo-bop-dwee-bop;
   - improvise using only a few pitches or pitches from a known scale; and
   - improvise based on a melodic theme or motive.

III.G.2 Musical Conversation[13]

Skills: Listening, playing instruments, improvising
Materials: Various nonpitched percussion instruments

1. Have two groups of children sit facing each other in two lines and give everyone instruments.
2. One pair at a time, the child in line A plays something on his instrument to the child opposite him in line B. The child in line B then echoes what child A played as closely as she can. Work down to the end of the line and switch.
3. Now have the children in line A play something for the children in line B to *respond to,* as if answering a question.

4. Finally, join two pairs of children together into a group of four. Have one child in the group start a musical conversation by playing a short improvisation. Any of the other three children react to that statement by *answering* with a reply, to which another child then replies, just as one might in a normal conversation.
5. Stop the "conversation" after a few minutes and check in with the children. *Were you really listening to each other? Who spoke a lot and who spoke a little? What did this way of playing express?*

IV. PREPARATION AND PRACTICE ACTIVITIES FOR UNFOLDING MUSICAL ELEMENTS[14]

In general, the Preparation Stage of Kodály's "unfolding elements" curriculum involves preparing rhythmic or melodic elements by simply performing songs containing the target elements. In addition, however, you can enhance the child's preparation using the following quick and fun activities.

In a Montessori context, you can perform these activities during gatherings, with small groups of children during the work cycle or at times when the work cycle gets a bit off track. You can even take individual children aside to perform the activities.

IV.A Activities for Preparation of Rhythmic or Melodic Elements

IV.A.1 Echo Clap, Echo Sing

Skills: Listening, moving, singing, preparation for playing instruments

Clap a rhythm pattern or sing a short melody and tell them to echo your pattern or melody.

1. Gradually increase the complexity and length of the patterns.
2. When the children can echo proficiently, divide them into groups. Echo clap or sing with one group, while they're clapping or singing your pattern, echo clap or sing a different pattern with the next group, so the patterns overlap. Do this with four groups to make rounds.
3. This can also be done with other motions too, such as patting knees, snapping, stamping, or playing a pattern on an instrument.

IV.A.2 Tap and Inner Hear

Skills: Listening, moving, singing, inner hearing

Tell the children you're going to tap the rhythm of the words of a known song while you sing the melody in your head. Have them do what you do.

1. Repeat the activity, gradually adding words. For example, using the song "Here Comes Sally:" *Let's tap the rhythm of the words and sing all the words in our head, except for the word "Sally," which we'll sing aloud: (tap "Sally," tap tap tap tap, tap tap "Sally" tap tap tap tap and so on).*

IV.A.3 Ostinato with a Known Song

Skills: Listening, playing instruments, singing, composing, improvising

Gather the children around some mallet instruments.

1. Think of a pentatonic ostinato that contains the known element.
2. Tell the children to pat the rhythm of the ostinato as you play it on the mallet instrument or tone bars.
3. Hand the instrument to the child who plays most accurately and appropriately.
4. Start the ostinato and after a couple of measures, start everyone singing a known song.
5. Invite the children to compose or improvise an ostinato to play while everyone sings.

IV.A.4 Identify the Element

Skills: Listening, singing

1. With the children all together, sing a known song that contains the target element.
2. Have children sing with you, listening for the target element and identifying on which words the element occurs.

IV.A.5 Inner Hearing Games

Skills: Listening, singing

1. Sing a known song that contains the element.
2. Isolate the element by having the children sing the words on which the element occurs in their heads and all the other words aloud.
3. Switch and have the children sing the words on the element aloud and the other words in their heads.

IV.A.6 Element Hunt

Skills: Listening, singing

1. Sing a known song and ask the children to listen and decide whether it contains the new element.

IV.A.7 Don't Say It!

Skills: Moving, playing instruments, singing

Sing a known song using *sol-fa* or rhythm syllables.

1. Tell the children to tap or hum the unknown melodic or rhythmic element. They can even play the rhythmic element on a percussion instrument.

IV.A.8 Reading from Icons

Skills: Singing, playing instruments, reading

1. Gather around a whiteboard or a rug.
2. Place visual icons, such as umbrellas, fruits, etc. on the whiteboard or rug in the configuration that they'll appear in a known song, such as "Rain, Rain." Icons showing the rhythm of the song might look like figure 12.12.

Figure 12.12.

Figure 12.13 shows what icons showing the melody might look like.

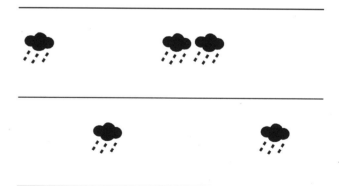

Figure 12.13.

3. Invite the children to sing the song. Point to the icons as they sing.
4. Scramble the icons to make new rhythms and melodies for the children to read.
5. Instead of icons, you can also use words.

IV.A.9 Form Game

Skills: Reading, memory

1. Show icons to represent short rhythmic or melodic motives or phrases that are the same or different. Icons can be anything from shapes, to colors, to fruits, as in figure 12.14.

IV.B Activities for Preparation of a Rhythmic Element[15]

IV.B.1 Steady as She Goes

Skills: Moving, singing

1. The children sing a known song that contains the target element and keep a steady beat while singing by patting their knees, clapping, doing a complex hand jive, performing body percussion, or playing instruments.

IV.B.2 Mystery Rhythm

Skills: Moving, singing, inner hearing, playing instruments

1. The children sing a known song in their heads, only singing and clapping on the words of the unknown rhythm.
2. Try this activity with percussion instruments.

IV.B.3 Voices in Your Head

Skills: Moving, singing, inner hearing, playing instrument

1. The children sing the words to known songs in their heads while tapping the rhythm of the words using body percussion or instruments.

IV.B.4 Rhythm Remix

Skills: Moving, singing, inner hearing, playing instruments

1. Have the children sing a known song while clapping the rhythm pattern from another song. Switch.

IV.B.5 Ostinati

Skills: Moving, singing, inner hearing, playing instrument

1. The children clap or perform a rhythm ostinato on instruments or body percussion while singing a known song (see section IV.D.16 for ideas).

IV.B.6 How Many Sounds?

Skills: Listening, writing

1. Clap a rhythm pattern and have the children identify how many sounds they heard on a beat.
2. The children can identify the number of sounds by holding up a number of fingers, placing icons or popsicle sticks on blank spaces on a whiteboard or on a rug, or by clapping.

IV.C Activities for Preparation of a Melodic Element[16]

IV.C.1 Drawing in the Air

Skills: Moving, singing

1. Tell the children to do as you do and sing a known song that contains the target element while drawing the melodic contour in the air with their arms.
2. Now, have them draw the melodic contour with their bodies, getting into low space when the melody goes low and high space when the melody goes high.

"Paw, Paw Patch"

"Where, oh, where is pretty little Suzie?"

"Where, oh, where is pretty little Suzie?"

"Where, oh, where is pretty little Suzie?"

"Way down yonder in the paw paw patch!"

Figure 12.14.

IV.C.2 Reading Magic

Skills: Reading, singing

1. For this example, the motive we want to work on is *sol, mi.* Hold up an everyday object, such as your left shoe, and tell the children when they see that object to sing *sol.*
2. Hold up your right shoe and tell the children to sing *mi.*
3. Improvise melodies by holding up your shoes in random order to make two-note melodies.

Extension: The children can read from

- icons or words placed spatially to show the melodic contour;
- a tone ladder which has the *sol-fa* letters stacked vertically with *do* at the bottom;
- your body signs. Tap your head for *la,* your hips for *sol,* and your knees for *mi,* for example; and
- your hand signs.

IV.C.3 Invisible Piano

Skills: Reading, singing

1. You can use any object for this activity. For now, we're going to use spaces on the floor. Let's use *do-pentatonic* as an example.
2. Stand in a spot and tell the children when you step in that spot they are to sing *mi.* Bounce up and down in that spot a few times to get them singing *mi* together.
3. Step one pace to the left and tell children when you step in that spot to sing *re.* Practice *re* and *mi* a few times. For each of the following steps, practice a few times before moving on to the next note.
4. Step one more pace to the left. When you step there, have the children sing *do.*
5. Step back and forth between the three spaces as the children sing the notes to make melodies with *mi, re,* and *do.*
6. Step two paces to the right of the spot where you assigned *mi.* Tell the children to sing *so* when you step there.
7. Step one more space to the right of *so,* and tell the children to sing *la.*
8. Now, you can have fun making melodies by jumping around the five spaces as the children sing.
9. You can also do this activity by touching spaces on the edge of a table, on your arm, or anywhere in the classroom.

IV.C.4 Which One's Higher?

Skills: Reading, singing

1. The children identify the high and low sounds in melodic motives.
2. They can identify the sounds orally or using body movements, such as pointing upward or standing tall for the high sounds and pointing down or crouching down for the low sounds.

IV.D Activities for Practice of a Rhythmic Element[17]

IV.D.1 Rhythm Reading

Skills: Reading, moving, playing instruments

1. Place known four-beat motives on a whiteboard, on big cards on a rug, or on flash cards and have children clap, stamp, or perform them on instruments.
2. Gradually increase the length of motives to eight beats and sixteen beats.

Extension: When using rhythm pattern flash cards, challenge the children with this sight-reading game:

1. Hold up the stack of cards and have children memorize the rhythm on top.
2. Flip the card on top to the back of the stack to reveal a new card.
3. Have the children clap the rhythm of the previous card while clapping the card on top.
4. Repeat.

IV.D.2 Mystery Songs

Skills: Reading, moving

1. On a whiteboard or rug, place rhythm patterns that create known songs.
2. Have the children clap the patterns and guess the song.

IV.D.3 Makin' Progress

Skills: Reading, moving

1. Begin by placing just one rhythm element on a whiteboard or rug, and have the children clap it or perform it with body percussion while counting.
2. Adding one element at a time, increase the number of elements to create a rhythm pattern.

IV.D.4 Messy Rhythms

Skills: Memory, reading, moving

1. Place a rhythmic pattern on the whiteboard or on a rug. Have the children examine it.
2. You, the teacher, clap the rhythm, but change one beat.
3. Have the children identify the changed beat and correct the rhythm.

Extension: You can use this activity to transition to teaching a new song.

1. Place the rhythm of a known song on the whiteboard or on a rug. Have the children examine it.
2. Now, tell the children to hide their eyes while you change one beat in the rhythm.
3. When the children open their eyes, have them identify the changed beat and read the new rhythm.
4. Repeat until your rhythm pattern becomes the new song.

IV.D.5 Rhythm Squares

Skills: Reading, moving, playing instruments

1. On a 4 × 4 grid of squares on a whiteboard, rug, or a worksheet, write rhythm elements in each square.
2. The children clap, say, or play each rhythm element on instruments as you point to the squares in any order (up, across, diagonal, down, and so on).

Extensions: Number the squares so that the children end up clapping a known song. Have them guess the song.

Clap a square and ask the children to identify which square you clapped.

IV.D.6 Rhythm Relay

Skills: Reading, moving

1. With the children seated in a circle, clap a four-beat motive to the child to your right.
2. The child to your right claps that four-beat motive to the child to his or her right, while you clap a new motive to the child on your right. The child then claps the new motive to the child to his or her right, while that child claps the original motive to the next child.
3. Continue this until every child in the circle has clapped each rhythm.

IV.D.7 Rhythm Race

Skills: Writing, reading, memory

1. Two pairs of children sit with a small whiteboard or before a rug. Each has a little bell or chime.

2. Clap a known rhythmic motive.
3. The children write down the motive using markers on the whiteboard or popsicle sticks on the rug and ring the bell or chime when they're finished.
4. The first pair to write down the rhythm correctly wins!

IV.D.8 Quick Change

Skills: Writing

1. Write a four-beat rhythm motive in popsicle sticks on a rug.
2. Have the children clap the motive.
3. A child copies the motive in popsicle sticks below, changing one beat.
4. Everyone reads the new rhythm.
5. Continue until everyone has had a chance to change the rhythm.

IV.D.9 Rhythm Dictation

A word of caution: writing down rhythm patterns that the children hear requires a combination of skills: listening, memory, and writing. Take the time to develop these skills individually before attempting this exercise.

Skills: Memory, listening, writing

1. The children listen as you clap a four-beat rhythmic motive.
2. Clap the motive again as the children listen a second time, tapping and saying the rhythm names.
3. After the third time, the children tap the rhythm but say the sol-fa rhythm names in their heads.
4. The children write the rhythm down on paper or a whiteboard, or show the rhythm using popsicle sticks on the floor.
5. Gradually increase the length of motives from four to eight to sixteen beats.

IV.D.10 Name That Song

Skills: Reading, memory, inner hearing

1. Write a rhythm motive on a whiteboard or on a rug in popsicle sticks.
2. The children list all of the known songs that begin with that motive, using picture icons to represent each song.

IV.D.11 Rhythm Match

Skills: Reading, memory, inner hearing

1. Write three rhythm patterns on a whiteboard or on a rug in popsicle sticks and number them.

2. Clap one of the rhythm patterns.
3. Have the children show which pattern you clapped by holding up one, two, or three fingers.

Extension: You can also write motives in different colors and have children hold up a color card to show which motive you clapped.

You can also play this game with melodic elements.

IV.D.12 Post Office

Skills: Reading, memory, inner hearing

1. Give each child an envelope containing cards with four-beat motives.
2. Clap a rhythm from one of the cards and have the children find the card with that rhythm in their envelopes and hold it up.

Extension: You can also play this game with melodic elements.

IV.D.13 Slippery Syllables

Skills: Reading, memory, inner hearing

1. Place the rhythm for a known song on a whiteboard or on a rug.
2. Have the children clap or say the entire rhythm out loud.
3. Clap or say the rhythm again, but tell the children to say or clap *ta* out loud, while saying *ti-ti* in their head.
4. Switch. Have the children say or clap *ti-ti* while putting *ta* in their head.

Extensions: Try this game without having a rhythm written out.

Assign groups of children or individual children a rhythm element. Have the children clap or play an instrument on *only* their element when it occurs in a known song.

IV.D.14 Rhythmic Partwork

You can practice rhythmic elements while singing classroom games, rhymes, and songs in a variety of ways. These quick little exercises also add variety, repetition, and challenge to singing classroom repertoire. Each exercise is numbered separately.

Skills: Listening, singing, moving, playing instruments

1. Have the children sing a known song while:

- patting the beat,
- tapping the rhythm, and
- performing body percussion.

2. While singing a known song, perform the beat or a rhythm from the song and ask the children to identify which you performed, the rhythm, or the beat.
3. On signal, the children switch between patting the beat or patting the rhythm while singing a known song. Try this while singing out loud and "in your head."
4. While singing a known song, perform the rhythm and the beat simultaneously in the following ways:

- Have the class perform the beat while you perform the rhythm and then switch.
- Have the class perform the beat while you and a few children perform the rhythm and then switch.
- Divide the class in two groups. One group performs the beat while the other performs the rhythm. Switch.
- Have two small groups or have two individuals alternate between performing the beat and the rhythm.
- Have the class alternate between performing the beat and the rhythm.
- Have the class step to the beat while clapping the rhythm.

5. Sing a known song while all of the children, a small group of children, or an individual child plays one or more short rhythmic ostinati:

- The ostinati can be two beats in length, then four beats in length.
- Divide the class in two groups: group 1 plays one ostinato, group 2 plays another. Switch.
- Divide the class into three or more groups depending on how many ostinati you have.
- Children perform the ostinati by clapping, performing body percussion, or playing instruments.

6. Clap the rhythm from a different song while singing a known song. (Children between the ages of nine and twelve have the most success with this activity.)

- The children can read the rhythm from a whiteboard or the rug.
- They can clap the rhythm from memory.

7. Sing a known song while clapping the rhythm backward from the board or from memory. (This is also for children ages nine to twelve.)
8. Sing a known song while clapping from rhythm flash cards.

- One at a time.
- At four-beat intervals.
- At two-beat intervals.
- Consecutively.

9. Write a two-part rhythm exercise on the white-board or on the rug. A two-part exercise has two rhythm lines stacked on top of each other. Assign each part to a group of children and have the groups clap *only their part* while everyone sings the song.
10. Clap the rhythm of a known song in canon.

   • The children can read the song or clap it from memory.
   • Start after two beats.
   • Start after four beats.
   • Perform the rhythm canon in body percussion.
   • Clap the canon while singing.

IV.D.15 Rhythm Chain

Skills: listening, moving, improvisation

1. With the children in a circle, clap four beats using known rhythm elements to the child on your right.
2. The child on your right turns the child on his or her right and claps the last two beats from your pattern, and adds two of his or her own.
3. Repeat until everyone has clapped a rhythm.

IV.E Activities for Practice of a Melodic Element[18]

IV.E.1 Part Singing

Each activity in this section is numbered separately.

Skills: Listening, singing, moving, playing instruments

1. Sing and perform many dialog and call-and-response songs.

2. Combine known songs as partner songs[19]:

   "Bee, Bee" with "Burnie Bee"
   "See Saw" or "Rain, Rain" with "Lucy Locket"
   "Rain, Rain" with "Little Sally Walker"
   "Seagull" with "London Bridge"
   "Rocky Mountain" or "Turn the Glasses Over" with "Lil' Liza Jane"

3. Sing known songs while listening to a melodic osti-nato containing the known elements. Pentatonic melodies and ostinati work best. You or the children can play the ostinato on tone bars or mallet instruments. You can also sing the ostinato or give it to part of the class to sing. Try splitting up the class into four groups, three groups singing different ostinati and one group singing the song.
4. Sing known songs in canon. Again, pentatonic songs work best for this. Divide up the parts in several ways:

   • Class/teacher
   • Class/teacher and a few children
   • The class in two groups
   • The class divided into a number of small groups

IV.E.2 Reading Four-Beat Motives

Skills: reading, singing

1. Sing a known song on "loo" and have the children guess which song it is. *That's right, I sang "Rain, Rain."*
2. Say, "I'm interested in the part that goes . . .," and iso-late for the children the part of the song where the target element figures prominently. *I'm interested in the part that goes (singing) "Come again another day."*
3. Reading from icons on a whiteboard, big cards on the floor, or flash cards, have the children read the known element, as in figure 12.15.

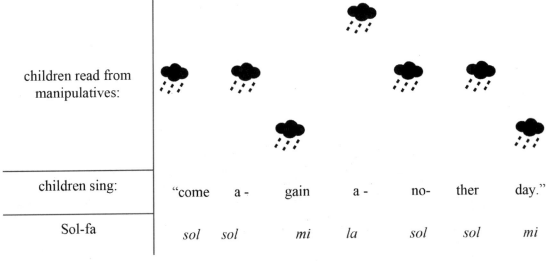

Figure 12.15.

5. Vary the activity by reading from icons, *sol-fa* letters, hand signs, stick notation, and staff notation.

IV.E.3 Combining Patterns

Skills: reading, composing, improvising

1. Tell the children to read from your hand signs as you make melodic patterns from known elements to create known songs. *I'm thinking of a song that goes (figure 12.16):*
2. Children guess the song "Little Sally Walker."
3. Scramble the elements to create new known songs.
4. In addition to hand signs, the children can read from icons, stick, or staff notation on a two-line, three-line, or five-line staff, note heads, or everyday objects.

IV.E.4 Transition to New Songs

Skills: reading, singing

1. Place *sol-fa* letters on the board or on the floor on a rug (without rhythm sticks) to create a motive from a known song.
2. Have the children read the *sol-fa* letters as you point to them and then guess the song.
3. Now, scramble the letters to form the new song.

IV.E.5 Reading Exercises from a Book

Zoltan Kodály wrote a series of progressive exercises that Boosey and Hawkes published as a small book called *333 Reading Exercises*. The exercises are notated in stick and staff notation. The children could practice reading melodies from that book, much like they would practice reading in their language from a Bob Book or reading primer.

Children can also read simple melodies from church hymnals. Additionally, check out the book *A New Approach to Sight Singing* by Berkowitz and Kraft (1960).

IV.E.6 Write with Icons

Skills: writing, composing, reading

1. Collect manipulatives such as bean bags, differently colored umbrella icons, rainy cloud icons, and the like.
2. Place yarn on the floor to make two-line, three-line, or five-line staff.
3. Have a child compose a melody using known melodic elements by placing icons on appropriate staff lines or spaces.
4. Everyone reads the child's melody, saying sol-fa syllables and showing hand signs.

IV.E.7 Adding Rhythm

Skills: writing, reading

1. Place yarn staff lines on a rug in front of you.
2. Using black bean bags for note heads, write a melody on the staff.
3. Invite children to come up and place popsicle sticks on your bean bag note heads to make various rhythm patterns from your melody.
4. While patting a steady beat, read the melody with the new rhythms.

IV.E.8 Melody Match

Skills: Listening, reading, memory

1. Place cards with melodic patterns (notated in sol-fa letters, stick notation, or staff notation) in a grid on a rug.
2. Sing a melodic pattern and have the children find the pattern among the various cards.

Variation:

1. Split up the children into two groups.
2. Give each child in group A a card with a notated melody.

hand signs:

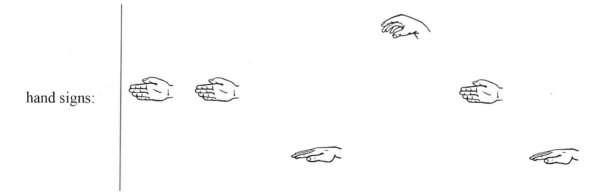

Figure 12.16.

3. Teach each child in group B a short motive to memorize.
4. Bring the two groups together, the children in group A search for a child whose memorized melody matches the melody on their card, and the children in group B search for a child whose card matches the melody in their head.

IV.E.9 Radio Game

Skills: Inner hearing

1. The children sing a known song, switching from singing aloud to inner hearing on signal.
2. The children can do this exercise:

   • with words,
   • singing in *sol-fa* with hand signs, and
   • while stepping the beat, clapping, or performing body percussion.

IV.E.10 Messy Melody

Skills: Inner hearing, reading

1. Write a motive containing known elements on the board using *sol-fa* letters, staff notation, or stick notation.
2. Bring out a puppet, who sings the motive incorrectly.
3. Tell the children to identify and correct the puppet's mistake.

IV.E.11 Mystery Song

Skills: inner hearing

1. Using hand signs, sol-fa letters, staff notation, or stick notation show the children the melody from a known song (without singing it).
2. The children identify the song.
3. If the children have difficulty, have everyone sing the melody one note at a time (i.e., *Let's sing every so in the melody. Now let's sing every* so *and every* mi *in the melody . . .*).
4. See how few notes it takes before the children can identify the song.

IV.E.12 Substitution Games

Skills: Improvising, singing, moving

1. Sing a song like the ones below and have the children substitute colors, names, motions, and the like.

   "Hey, Hey, Look At Me"
   "We Are Dancing"

"Down Came a Lady"
"Ida Red"
"Wallflowers"

IV.E.13 Question-and-Answer Games

Skills: Improvising, singing

1. Sing a short motive containing known elements and have the children improvise a melody containing known elements in response.

IV.E.14 Pin the Tail on the Melody

Skills: Improvising, reading, singing

1. Write a melodic motive on the board or on a rug using icons.
2. Next to it, write three endings.
3. Sing the melody at left for a child and have him or her sing the ending of choice.
4. Take away the three endings and have the children improvise their own endings.

IV.E.15 Melody Baseball

Skills: Reading, moving, singing

1. Place four bases in a baseball diamond out on the playground or, if you have room, in the classroom.
2. Team A is at bat. Their batter stands at home plate.
3. One member from team B stands on each base.
4. You, the teacher, play the role of pitcher. With a dramatic wind up, throw a pitch by showing the batter the hand signs for a motive that contains known elements.
5. The batter at home plate sings the motive. If the batter reads it correctly, he or she runs the bases.
6. While the batter is advancing around the bases, the teacher signs the melodic motive to the baseman of the base the batter is headed to. If the baseman sings it correctly, the batter is out. If the baseman doesn't sing it correctly, the batter can keep going or stay where she is.
7. If the batter doesn't sing the motive correctly, he or she gets a strike.
8. After three outs, the teams switch places.
9. One point is scored whenever a batter crosses home plate.
10. Modify the rules as you like.

NOTES

1. Keep in mind, when presenting these activities, however, the developmental characteristics of your children (refer to appendix A, for details). Remember that children younger than age seven have difficulty singing in parts and have not developed the motor skills to perform some of the more physically intricate activities, such as section II.B.6, Body Percussion.
2. Adapted from Brumfield and Glaze (2006).
3. Adapted from Storms (1981).
4. For guidance in matching chords to classroom songs, see appendix F.
5. Adapted from Hickey (2012)
6. Adapted from Irwin and Nelson (1986).
7. Adapted from Hickey (2012).
8. Adapted from Campbell and Scott-Kassner (2002).
9. Ibid.
10. Ibid.
11. Adapted from Hickey (2012).
12. Adapted from Campbell and Scott-Kassner (2002).
13. Adapted from Storms (1981).
14. Adapted from Brumfield and Glaze (2006).
15. Ibid.
16. All exercises except "Invisible Piano" adapted from Brumfield and Glaze (2006).
17. Adapted from Brumfield and Glaze (2006).
18. Ibid.
19. Introduce partner songs with a little story to give the pairing context and to create drama and excitement. A little story about Lucy Locket, who was playing the rain when she dropped her pocket, for instance.

Chapter 13

Spontaneous Performances

Remember Mr. George's class performing "Skin and Bones" back in chapter 10? Mr. George did a similar performance with a song called "Sweet Betsy from Pike" (see chapter 14). With the children seated in a circle, Mr. George read and sang the song. When a certain character was mentioned, the children jumped out into the middle and acted out their roles.

Violet positively immersed herself in the role of the tough pioneer woman. She strutted around in the middle of the circle of children, skipping and swinging her arms. One half of the circle, the "orchestra" played instruments as the other children sang "Too rali, ooh rali, ooh rali yay!"

On the words "The Indians came down in a wild yelling horde," a group of boys and girls jumped out of the circle and pantomimed tomahawks, rifles, and bows and arrows. Sweet Betsy and Ike shot pretend rifles at them. Such commitment! Andrew even pretended to get shot and hobbled behind Violet, his hands gripping his stomach and his tongue lolling out.

With each verse, a new group of children embodying different characters jumped out of the circle and joined "Sweet Betsy." Even the hog and the dog were into their parts. Everyone laughed when the cows died, for the children playing cows flopped onto on their backs with their legs and arms stuck straight up in the air.

At the end of the song, on the words, "Sweet Betsy, you're an angel, but where are your wings?" Ian, playing Ike, put his arms around Violet, and a few children were visibly moved by the gesture.

All of this occurred with minimal planning and no rehearsal whatsoever.

Spontaneous performances promote teamwork, build community, provide the children opportunities for theater and drama, and create an atmosphere of joy in the classroom. With only simple props, a few instruments, and nothing else, you too can turn any ballad or folk song, such as "Sweet Betsy from Pike," into a theatrical performance.

Spontaneous performances can be complex, like the one described earlier, or they can be quite simple. A simpler form of spontaneous performance is the "sound story," in

which you or the children punctuate a known or improvised story with sounds that add atmosphere and drama or stand for the actions in the story. You and the children can use any combination of instruments to tell a sound story, even just your voices or bodies. However you perform them, sound stories benefit children's memory, provide activities for community-building, and motivate children's spontaneous music-making.

Jazz can be another venue for the children's spontaneous performance. Using rudimentary piano skills, you can "walk" a bass line and play the chords for simplified modal jazz tunes such as Miles Davis's "So What?" If no piano is available, use a drum or scat-sing to provide a foundation for the children's improvising. With the right combination of percussion and mallet instruments, the entire class can then participate in a jazz improvisation session. This chapter shows you how to make it happen (table 13.1).

Table 13.1.   List of Spontaneous Performances

I. Bringing Stories to Life
  I.A. Sound Story 1
  I.B. Sound Story 2
  I.C. Found Sound Story
  I.D. Weather Report
II. Multi-part Performances
  II.A. Adding Singing Parts to Songs Using Hand Signals
  II.B. Using Body Movement to Accompany a Rhyme or Song
  II.C. Rhythmic Canons with Body Movement
  II.C.1. Clap Your Hands, Stamp Your Feet
  II.C.2. Pat, Stamp, Clap, Snap
  II.C.3. Ali Baba and the Forty Thieves
  II.C.4. Black Cats
  II.D. Adding Melodic and Rhythmic Ostinati to a Song
  II.E. Adding Chordal Accompaniment to a Song
III. Musical Dramatization of Classroom Songs and Ballads
  III.A. "Skin & Bones"
  III.B. "Sweet Betsy from Pike"
  III.C. "Purple Light"
  III.D. Goldilocks and the Three Bears
  III.E. Work at the Rock
IV. Jazz Improvisation
  IV.A. So What?

I. BRINGING STORIES TO LIFE

I.A. Sound Story 1

You don't have to be a virtuoso pianist to tell a sound story at the piano. Play any combination of notes on the black keys and you'll sound great. For this performance, you'll tell a story and accompany your story with piano sounds. All that is required is that you remember and be able to recreate the sounds you play.

Concepts and Skills: Sounds and mood, listening
Ages: All

1. Gather the children in front of the piano and make up a story: *This weekend, I was walking along the beach. The waves lapped the shore.* (Make the sound of waves on the black keys of the piano.) *Seagulls chirped overhead.* (Play quick two-note trills on the higher black keys.) *Suddenly, I saw a bottle bobbing up and down in the waves, washing up onto the shore.* (Play a soft, slow, up-and-down melody on the low black notes.) *Inside the bottle, I found a note. I opened the note and do you know what it said? It said, "Whosoever finds this note shall be granted three wishes."* (Make a bright, happy "ta-da" kind of sound in the middle of the black keys.) *Hm . . . I thought and thought about three things I could wish for, but I was so happy and content just walking there on the beach, that I honestly couldn't think of anything I could possibly want. So, I slid the note back in the bottle, corked the top, and threw it back into the water.* (Make a "plunk" sound on the low black keys.) *"Maybe someone less fortunate than I will find the bottle and get three wishes," I thought as I went on my way. The End.*
2. Play one of the sounds from the story and ask the children to raise their hands and tell you what happened in the story when they heard that sound. Repeat with all of the sounds you played.

Extension: You can tell a story at the piano with only sounds and have the children decide what events the sounds represent. For example, give the children the title of a story, such as "My Walk on the Beach." Tell the story but don't give away what the sounds stand for, as in: *This weekend I was walking along the beach. I saw this* (sound), *and this* (sound). *Then, suddenly, this happened* (sound)!

When the story is finished, ask the children to fill in the events represented by the sounds you played.

I.B. Sound Story 2

In this activity, the children perform the sounds that represent events in a story. When performing the sounds, they listen rather than relying on a visual cue. At first, you will model the sounds for the children and have them play the sounds you came up with. Eventually, you can ask the children to come up with their own sounds.

The story in this example is a fanciful story about your day. You might want to perform a musical retelling of any of the Great Lessons or tell any other story you like.

Concepts and Skills: Sounds and mood, playing instruments, listening, composing, improvising
Ages: All

1. Gather the children together and collect the musical instruments.
2. Place the musical instruments in front of you, and tell the children you would like to tell them a story about your day.
3. Your story might go something like this: "This morning, I was sleeping very soundly . . ." (Play an even rhythm on the güiro to give an impression of the sound of snoring.)
4. "Suddenly, my alarm went off!" (Vigorously jiggle the tambourine.)
5. "I shot up out of bed, but instead of being in my bedroom, I found myself in a hot air balloon!" (Play a slow, floating pentatonic melody on the marimba.)
6. "Panicking because I thought I might be late for work, I rode the balloon, dressing in my work clothes as I drifted helplessly toward our school." (Repeat the floating melody.)
7. "Luckily, right over the school, a little bird alighted on the balloon and started pecking at it!" (Play a fast rhythm on the claves.)
8. "Much to my dismay, the balloon popped!" (Clap a fast beat on the hand drum.)
9. "I fell down down, down, . . ." (Play a rapid, falling sound on the marimba.)
10. ". . . and landed right in front of the school just in time for work." (Crash two cymbals together.)
11. Repeat the sounds from the story and ask the children if they remember what happened. Say something like, "Raise your hand if you know what happened in the story when you heard this sound?" (Jiggle the tambourine.)
12. Now, tell the children you'd like to tell the story again, only this time, tell them that you'd like them to improvise different sounds to accompany your story.
13. Hand out the instruments and tell the story again, cueing each child when it's his or her turn to play.
14. Invite the children to come up with their own stories or to create sound stories from classroom books.

Extension: Children can write out their stories on a score using graphic or stick notation.

Children can include their written music in their research. First, they can devise musical sounds to accompany ideas or events in their research, then they can write their musical ideas down on paper and bind their handwritten pages together. They could perform their research by reading it aloud and having a small group of children play the sounds.

Should the children decide to use the piano for this activity, they can place colored dot stickers on the keys and draw colored dots underneath note heads in the score to indicate which notes to play.

I.C. Found Sound Story[1]

Concepts and skills: Sound and mood, listening, playing
   instruments, composing
Ages: All

1. Tell the children a brief story about a person or an event.
2. Work with the children to plan a background of sounds to help enhance the story.
3. Perform the story. It might go like this:

This is the story of Ziryab the Slave. Ziryab (789–857 AD) was a Persian polymath: a poet, musician, singer, cosmetologist, fashion designer, celebrity, trendsetter, strategist, astronomer, botanist, geographer, and former slave. Most people have never heard of Ziryab, yet at least two of his innovations remain to this day: he introduced the idea of the three-course meal (soup, main course, dessert) [the sounds of a bowl, a dish, and a cup being plunked onto a table], *and he introduced the use of crystal for drinking glasses (previously metal was the primary material)* [gently tinkle glasses]. *He introduced asparagus and other vegetables into society,* [the sounds of vegetables being cut on a cutting board], *and he made significant changes and additions to the music world* [gentle notes on the tone bars or bells]. *He had numerous children* [the sounds of babies crying], *all of whom became musicians* [plink one string at a time on the ukulele]. *His ideas were spread throughout Europe.*
The list of societal changes Ziryab made is immense—he popularized short hair [make snipping sounds with scissors] *and shaving for men* [scraping sounds]. *He wore different clothes based on the seasons* [rustle some fabric.] *He created a pleasant-tasting toothpaste* [children smack their lips and go "Mmm!" followed by the swishing sound of sand

blocks] *which helped personal hygiene (and longevity) in the region, and also invented an underarm deodorant* [children make sniffing sounds]. *He also promoted bathing twice daily* [sound of water splashing in a bowl].

Extension: Children can make sound backgrounds for just about any poem or story. They can develop their own notation or use graphic, stick, or conventional notation to write their sounds on a score (see chapter 15 for details on developing a score).

The children can invent a story and accompany it with sounds.

I.D. Weather Report

The children can use instruments to render the sounds of various weather patterns in a pretend weather report.

Concepts and skills: Sound and mood, playing instruments, listening reading, improvisation
Ages: All

1. Gather the children together and collect the materials.
2. Tell the children you're going to make weather map of the country for a weather report.
3. On the map, represent regions of icy-cold weather with, for instance, variously shaped triangles, regions of rain with little diagonal lines and some umbrellas, sunny areas with little suns, and snowy zones with lots of little round snowflakes.
4. Make a sound on one of the instruments and elicit from the children which weather pattern that sound might represent. Alternatively, depending on the children's level of responsibility and experience, you could hand a child an instrument first and ask him to make the sound of, say, rainfall.
5. Repeat with the other instruments until you have a sound for each weather pattern.
6. Tell the children that you will play the weather announcer. As you point to different regions on the map, tell the children make the sound of that weather pattern on their instruments.
7. After one time through, let a child be the weather announcer.

Extension: You could also interview a child about a fictional road trip he took across the country. You could move a little car around the map as you and the child improvise details of his road trip. When the child talks about certain regions he drove through, the children play the sounds of the weather in that region.

II. MULTIPART PERFORMANCES[2]

II.A. Adding Singing Parts to Songs Using Hand Signs

Perform this activity using known melodic elements. Depending on the children's experience, keep the tempo slow and the rhythm simple. Increase the tempo and the rhythmic complexity as the children's skills improve. This activity works best with children older than second grade.

Concepts and Skills: Listening, singing, reading
Ages: Eight and twelve

1. Tell the class you are going to sing in parts. Explain that they will sing the *sol-fa* syllables as indicated by your hand signals.
2. Divide the class into two groups. The group on your left will follow the signals of your left hand and the group on your right will follow the signals of your right hand (figure 13.2).
3. On both hands, make the hand sign for *sol* and give the pitch to both groups. As shown in Figure 13.2, hold *sol* in your left hand for group one and proceed slowly, giving group two the hand signals *mi, sol la, sol*. At that point, hold *sol* on your right hand for group two and give group one the hand signals *mi, sol la, sol*. Give the signals slowly enough so that the children can sing with good intonation. Sing along with them if they have trouble. End the exercise on *sol* and *do* or *do* and *mi*.

GROUP 1 (left hand):   *s ——— s m s s*
GROUP 2 (right hand): *s m s l s ——- d*

Figure 13.2.

4. Give the children plenty of these experiences.

Extension: When the children have had lots of practice with this, use it to create a spontaneous choral performance. Have everyone sing a known pentatonic song. Divide the class into three groups. One group sings the song; the other two read melodic ostinati from your hand signals.

You can add the ostinato parts spontaneously or one at a time. For example:

1. Gather the class, and sing "Cotton-Eye Joe."
2. Split the class into two groups. Have one group sing "Cotton-Eye Joe," while the other group reads a melodic ostinato from your hand signals. When the second group is comfortable and all are coordinated, drop the hand signals.

3. Divide the class into three groups. Group one sings "Cotton-Eye Joe," group two sings the previous ostinato, and group three reads another ostinato from your hand signals. Again, when the third group is comfortable and everyone is coordinated, drop the hand signals.
4. Repeat with as many parts as you like.

This exercise can also be useful for teaching choral parts in the upper grades. Instead of an ostinato, you can have the second group read a harmony part from your hand signals as the first group sings the melody. Figure 13.3 provides you an example.

You can find nice two-part American folk songs in the book *46 Two-Part American Folk Songs for Elementary Grades* by Denise Bacon. Figure 13.4 shows an example of the first four measures of Denise Bacon's arrangement of "Cotton-Eye Joe."[3]

Group 1: (melody)

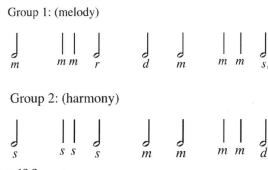

Group 2: (harmony)

Figure 13.3.

Group 1: (melody)

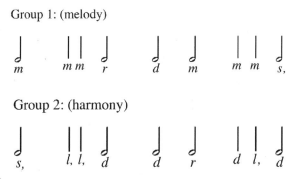

Group 2: (harmony)

Figure 13.4.

Keep in mind that children younger than second grade have difficulty singing harmony parts (see appendix A for details). Because of this, group your first and second years together and give them a short, repetitive ostinato to sing. Children as old as third grade can sing harmony parts.

You can combine ostinati with harmony parts by splitting up your class into four groups: two groups of first-years singing an ostinato, a mixed group of older children singing the main melody, and a fourth group of mixed-age children singing a harmony part. For more about part-singing, see appendix A.

II.B. Using Body Movement to Accompany a Rhyme or Song

For this example, you're going to use body movements to create a performance from the simple rhyme "Jack and Jill." You can use this procedure to accompany any rhyme or song with movement.

This simple example is for primary grades, but you can create more complex body percussion accompaniments for the upper grades.

Concepts and Skills: Listening, singing, playing instruments, moving, improvising
Ages: Eight to twelve, but six and seven year olds can step or clap the steady beat

1. Have the children form a circle. Tell them to step in rhythm to your claps as you clap figure 13.5

Figure 13.5.

2. When the children can step the beat, tell them to continue to step that rhythm as you clap a different rhythm. Clap the ostinato from figure 13.6.

Figure 13.6.

3. Tell the children to clap the ostinato with you as they continue to step the beat. When they can step the beat and clap the rhythmic ostinato accurately without becoming confused, begin chanting the rhyme, as in figure 13.7.
4. When the children can step the beat, clap the ostinato, and listen to you chant the rhyme, have them join you in chanting the rhyme.

5. Turn this rhyme into a song by inventing a melody using tones from the pentatonic scale. When the children are comfortable stepping the beat, clapping the ostinato, and chanting the rhyme, have them join you in the song.
6. Expand the experience by adding instruments. As the children continue to step, clap, and sing, teach a child to play the stepping part on a hand drum. Teach another child to play the clapping pattern with a tambourine.
7. Teach still more children to play pentatonic accompaniments on mallet instruments. Add as many parts as the children can manage.
8. Continue until the room is full of music.

II.C Rhythmic Canons with Body Movement

II.C.1. Clap Your Hands, Stamp Your Feet

Concepts and Skills: Listening, singing, moving
Ages: All

1. Have the children form a circle.
2. Tell the children to watch and listen, then do exactly as you do. Echo-chant figure 13.8 on the next page, clapping hands, stamping feet, and turning around as the text dictates. On the last line, "Isn't that sweet?" clap hands on each syllable.
3. When children can echo the chant comfortably, ask them to do it straight through *with* you, then once alone using the actions. Repeat until they have it.
4. Tell the children you'd like to perform the chant as a round. Have them begin the chant, and you begin as they say the word "Stamp." Repeat until they can do it easily.
5. Gradually add a few children to your part, until the class is equally divided between the two parts.

Extension: Use this procedure to perform rounds, such as "Are You Sleeping?" "Dona Nobis Pacem," and "Chairs to Mend." You can also use this procedure to sing regular folk songs in canon, such as "Bow, Wow, Wow."

When singing quodlibets or songs with two sections that combine easily together, such as "Rock-a My Soul,"

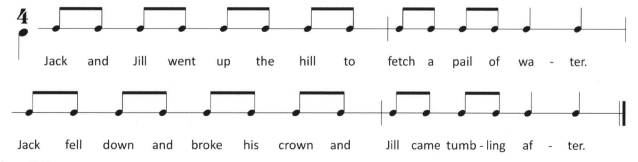

Figure 13.7.

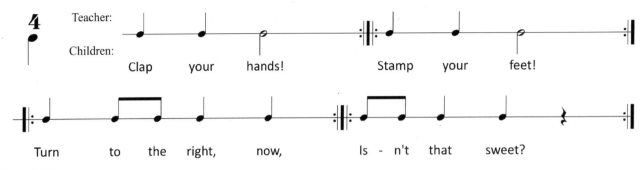

Figure 13.8.

assigning movements to each part is a great way to keep the children on their part and reinforce the concept of form.

II.C.2 Pat, Stamp, Clap, Snap

Concepts and Skills: Listening, singing, moving, playing instruments

Ages: All, but six and seven year olds may not have developed the fine motor skills to snap fingers. You can use another gesture for them.

1. Teach the pattern from figure 13.9 in the following manner:

a. Have the children echo each measure.
b. Have the children echo the first two measures.
c. Have the class echo the third measure, then the fourth measure.
d. Have the class echo the third and fourth measures.
e. Have the class perform the entire pattern with you.

2. When the children know the pattern well, divide them into four groups. Perform the pattern as a four-part round, with each new group beginning a measure apart.

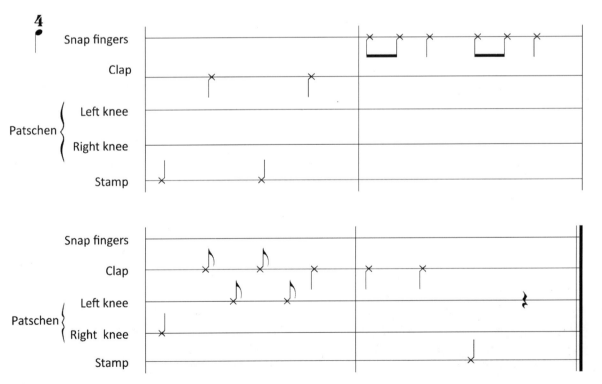

Figure 13.9.

II.C.3. Ali Baba and the Forty Thieves

Concepts and Skills: Listening, singing, moving
Ages: All, but group the six and seven year olds together, and give them simple movements. Older children can be in mixed-age groups.

1. Have the children stand in a circle and clap the steady beat as they chant figure 13.10.
2. Tell the children you want to play a game with this chant. Explain that the first child in the circle will watch you and on your signal will make the exact motions that *she saw you do*. The child to his or her right will watch the first child and do the motions he or she just saw the first child do. The third child will watch the second child and do the motions he or she just saw the second child do, and so on around the circle. The children must understand that they will *not* be doing the motion you are doing as they watch you—they will do the motion they just saw you do as they watch you doing a new motion, which they will then do, and so on.
3. Begin chanting the rhyme, using some movement, such as clapping. Repeat, changing your motion and signaling the first child to begin changing as he does the first motion. Repeat the rhyme over and over again changing the motion for each repetition. Motions to perform include:

   - clapping hands,
   - patting head,
   - hopping,
   - moving your arms,
   - jumping in place,
   - crossing legs, and
   - bending knees.
   - snapping fingers
   - tapping shoulders

4. On other days, individual children can be the leaders, creating their own movements.

II.C.4. Black Cats

Use the same procedure from section II.C.3 to create a speech canon with bodily movement and instrumental interludes.

Concepts and Skills: Listening, singing, moving, playing instruments
Ages: All, but group the six and seven year olds together and give them simple movements. Older children can be in mixed-age groups.

1. Teach the lines from figure 13.11 on next page by rote or write them on a whiteboard or lay them out in cards on a rug.
2. Ask for volunteers to clap and chant each line individually. Have the entire class clap and chant the entire rhyme. Encourage them to change their voices to express the feelings appropriate to each line. Repeat until they can chant the rhyme from memory with accurate rhythm.
3. Elicit from the children which instruments go with which lines. The black cats could be finger cymbals, the jack-o'-lanterns could be claves, and so on.
4. Divide the class into four groups. Group one begins, group two begins when group one reaches the first word of the second line. Group three begins when group one reaches the first word in the third line, and so on. Practice until the class can do this effortlessly.
5. Hand instruments to children selected to play each part without chanting the rhyme. For guidance, suggest that the children with instruments chant the rhyme in their heads while playing.
6. Ask for ideas for bodily movement to be used as the rhyme is chanted. The children might come up with the following:

   Black cats: Stamp feet on half notes.
   Pumpkin lanterns: Pat knees with both hands.
   Bats and goblins: Stand and clap hands.
   Eeeek!: Stand and make circles in the air with the dominant arm.

6. Have the class chant the rhyme as they perform the bodily movements; have the children playing instruments play their lines.
7. The children could structure the performance like the following:

   a. The instruments play the rhyme straight through.

A - li   Ba - ba   and   the   for - ty   thieves.

Figure 13.10.

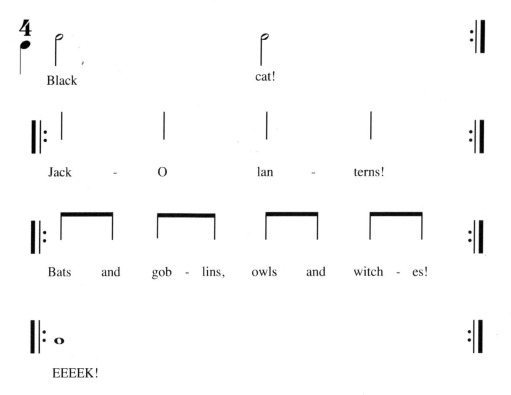

Black   cat!

Jack   -   O   lan   -   terns!

Bats   and   gob - lins,   owls   and   witch - es!

EEEEK!

Figure 13.11.

b. All the children join the instruments in performing the speech chant all the way through with body movements.

c. The instruments stop as the children perform the speech canon in four parts with body movements.

d. The instruments play again one time through.

8. Create new performances by experimenting with other structures for the performance.

II.D. Adding Melodic and Rhythmic Ostinati to a Song

Use this procedure to add rhythmic ostinati to any classroom song. For this example, we'll use the song "Camptown Races."

Concepts and Skills: Listening, singing, playing instruments, moving, composing

Ages: All, but give first and second years a simple part that outlines the steady beat

1. Begin the rhythmic accompaniment from figure 13.12 in a medium tempo, signaling that children should follow you.

2. Continue doing the pattern as you chant a spoken ostinato on the words "Oh, doo dah day" as in figure 13.13 on next page.

3. When the children can securely perform the ostinato above, tell them to continue to do as they're doing while you sing. Continue the pattern as you sing "Camptown Races" in the key of D.

4. Having sung through the song once, select a small group to sing with you as the other children chant the ostinato. Start the entire class on performing the rhythmic accompaniment. When they are stable, have a small group begin singing the song.

5. Add a few more children singing and repeat step 4

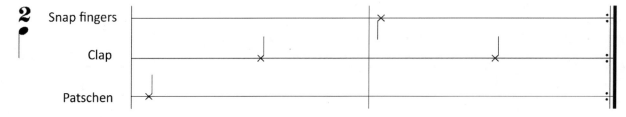

Snap fingers

Clap

Patschen

Figure 13.12.

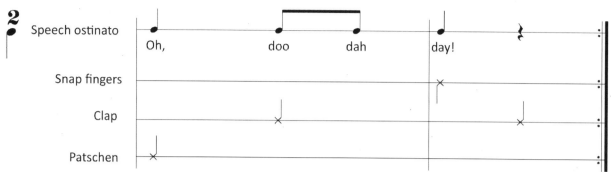

Figure 13.13.

until you have a good balance between the singing and the ostinato.

6. Now prepare the first ostinato accompaniment. Tell children to do as you do, then perform figure 13.14.

7. Select a child to play the ostinato on the xylophone. Remove the bars next to the ones to be played (see appendix F, for a guide), and teach the child the part in figure 13.15.

8. Practice chanting the vocal ostinato with the xylophone part until the children can perform both securely.

9. Tell the entire class to begin the rhythmic accompaniment. At intervals of two measures (four beats),

signal the chanting ostinato, then the xylophone part, and then the group of children singing "Camptown Races."

10. Prepare the second instrument ostinato by performing figure 13.16 and telling the children to do as you do.

11. Select a child to play the glockenspiel. Remove the bars next to the ones to be played, and teach him or her how to play the ostinato from figure 13.17 on next page.

12. Begin again by having the entire class perform the rhythmic accompaniment. Bring in the spoken

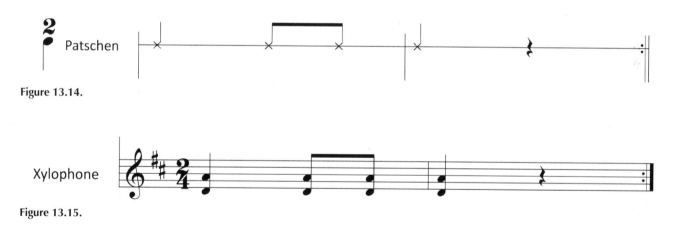

Figure 13.14.

Figure 13.15.

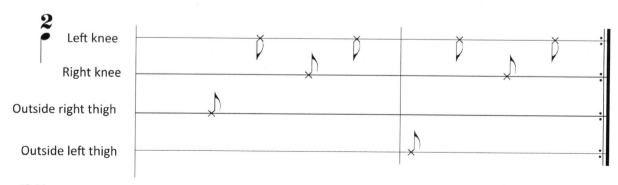

Figure 13.16.

Glockenspiel

Figure 13.17.

ostinato, the xylophone, and the glockenspiel, and finally the group of children singing "Camptown Races."

13. Extend the experience by teaching more ostinati, adding rhythm instruments, and encouraging the children to invent new body movement.

II.E. Adding Chordal Accompaniment to a Song

Concepts and Skills: Listening, singing, playing instruments, moving, composing

Ages: All, but give the ukulele to eight and twelve year olds. Six and seven year olds can play the autoharp.

1. Gather the children in a circle, and sing a known song or teach a new song by rote. For this example, we'll use the song "Simple Gifts" in the key of F.

2. Tell the class that the melody for this song comes from the major scale and that we can harmonize the melody with I and V chords. *Let's listen to determine where each chord fits in the song.*

3. Select a child to play an F (the root of the I chord in this case) on the tone bars, low keys of the piano, or bass marimba in a regular half-note rhythm.

4. Ask the class to sing and pat their knees as the tone bar accompanies them. When they hear clashing notes, they are to raise their hands. Repeat until everyone detects the first off note, which should occur on the third appearance of the word "gift."

5. Have another child play a C on a tone bar (the root of the V chord in this instance).

6. Work out the chord changes in this way until you arrive at the chord progression, as in figure 13.18.

7. Once the chord progression is established, sing the song all the way through as you accompany the class by strumming an autoharp or ukulele. Hand a child the ukulele or autoharp as you sing the song one more time.

8. On another day, teach the children a dance to the song and add further instrumental accompaniment. Assign two children to each instrument, one playing a pentatonic ostinato on the I chord, and another playing a pentatonic ostinato on the V chord. (For a guide to which pentatonic scales to use, see appendix F.) Sample accompaniments might include those in figure 13.19 on next page.

I
'Tis a gift to be simple, 'tis a gift to be free,

        V
'Tis the gift to come down where we ought to be,

    I
And when we find ourselves in the place just right

V   I
It will be in the valley of love and delight.

I
When true simplicity is gained,

                V
To bow and to bend we will not be ashamed.

  I
To turn and to turn will be our delight,

     V   I
'Till by turning, turning we come 'round right.

Figure 13.18.

The children could also improvise the instrumental accompaniments.

Try not removing any bars from the mallet instruments and telling the children when they hear the I chord to play a melody in F pentatonic (F, G, A, C, D), and when they hear the V chord, to play C pentatonic (C, D, E, G, A).

III. MUSICAL DRAMATIZATIONS

III.A. "Skin and Bones"

Use the following steps to model for the children how to create a dramatization of a well-known classroom song or folk ballad.

Concepts and Skills: Listening, singing, playing instruments, moving, improvising

Ages: All, but give simple, straight quarter-note parts to six and seven year olds

1. Aid the children in gathering the percussion instruments and sit together in a circle.

Figure 13.19.

2. Tell children you're going to sing a mystery song and that you'd like them to listen and guess the name of the song. Sing the song "Skin and Bones" on "loo."

3. When the children have identified the song, sing through it once all together.

4. Tell the children you'd like to create a musical dramatization of "Skin and Bones" with musical instruments and actors.

5. Improvise a rhythm on the drum and elicit from the children what sound that might be in the song's setting. They might say, for example, that it sounds like footsteps in a graveyard.

6. Sing the first verse of the song again, this time tell the children to clap the steady beat while you play the drum.

7. Hand the drum to a child who is clapping most appropriately and tell that individual to improvise a drum part, like you did. The child playing the drum should play throughout the following steps.

8. Repeat steps 5 through 7 with each percussion instrument, singing each subsequent verse as you add an instrument. Designate the instrument players as the "orchestra."

9. Elicit from the children what characters might appear if we were to act out the story. Obviously, for example, you'll need an old woman. Cast a child to be the old woman. Give her a head scarf to wear

as a prop, and instruct her to pantomime the actions from the song in the center of the circle as everybody sings. Sing the first verse.

10. Now, solicit some more characters. The children might want to have some spooky ghosts. Cast one or two children to be spooky ghosts, and instruct them to come out of the circle into the center and act like ghosts during the second verse but to return to their place in the circle by the end of the verse.

11. Add new characters to come out of the circle and act out their characters for each subsequent verse. You might have some skeletons dance around, some dead bodies, or some zombies. Each character should disappear back into the circle by the end of the verse that describes the character.

12. For the final verse of the song, a child could play a black cat that pops out of the cupboard and frightens the old woman.

13. Now, perform the entire song with all of the instruments playing while the actors act out their parts.

14. Repeat and enjoy!

Extensions: The children could write out their instrumental parts on a score using graphic or stick notation.

Instead of acting the song out in a circle, they could perform it on a stage with sets and costumes. During a performance, the old woman could wander the stage as the various other characters pop in from the wings. The orchestra could be placed in front of the stage, as in a traditional musical, or off to the side.

This format for dramatizing musical classroom songs also works well with puppets.

III.B. "Sweet Betsy from Pike"

You can sing folk ballads such as "Sweet Betsy from Pike" during read-aloud. The procedure is the same as for "Skin and Bones" except that you hold the song book out in front of you and sing the song alone, unless the song has a refrain, in which case the children can join you for the refrain. Something about reading a song from a book just like you would a story from a book normalizes music and reinforces for the children music's link to language and storytelling.

Concepts and Skills: Listening, singing, playing instruments, moving, improvising
Ages: All, but give simple, straight quarter-note parts to six and seven year olds

1. While children are seated around the gathering in a circle, take out a book with the song "Sweet Betsy from Pike" and tell the children you'd like to read a story, but this story is a special kind of singing story called a "ballad." Give a quick introduction to give children an impression of the historical context for the narrative in the song.
2. Before singing the story, tell the children you're going to teach *your part*. Have them echo sing the refrain.
3. Reading from your book as you might during read-aloud. Sing the story all the way through, signaling the children to join you on the refrain.
4. Now that the children have heard the story, ask them what characters would be necessary if we wanted to act out the story.
5. Cast the characters of Sweet Betsy, Ike, the spotted hog, the Shanghai rooster, the Indians, and so on.
6. Once everyone is cast, have the "actors" sit back in the circle. As you sing each stanza, the actors are to come out into the middle of the circle and play out the scene, dipping back into the circle when the scene is over as the song dictates.
7. Sing the song again, one verse at a time, with the children acting out the scenes. Refine their movements and allow them to come up with ideas about how to play out each scene.
8. With everything set, sing the song all the way through, with the children acting out the scenes.

9. On another day, add singing parts and instrumental parts to the performance using the techniques from sections II.A, II.D, and II.E described earlier.

Note: *The Ballad Book of John Jacob Niles* by Niles (2000) contains many interesting folk ballads.

III.C. "Purple Light"

Musical instruments can create a kind of "sound portrait" to accompany classroom songs. The song "Purple Light" is set in a desert canyon in the Southwestern United States. Instruments can become crickets, rustling tumbleweeds, mule hooves, or even render the color of the sunset.

Concepts and Skills: Listening, singing, playing instruments, moving, improvising
Ages: All

Figure 13.20 on next page shows the song so you can get acquainted with it.

To begin, gather a group of nonpitched percussion instruments as well as mallet instruments. This example uses

- güiro,
- claves,
- tambourine,
- sand blocks,
- xylophone (with B-flat and E bars removed),
- metallophone (with B-flat and E bars removed), and
- the Montessori D, F, G, A, and C bells.

This arrangement begins with teacher-composed ostinati for nonpitched percussion instruments, then combines them with the children's composed or improvised melodies for mallet instruments. Here goes:

1. After the children have learned the song "Purple Light" by rote and can sing it very well, gather them together and tell them that today you are going to create a musical performance of the song. Tell a story about riding through a beautiful painted desert canyon on a donkey. Explain that you're going to use musical instruments and voices to paint that beautiful picture in your minds as you sing and perform the song. Perform the song once while the children sing and pat the steady beat.
2. Bring out the güiro. Ask the children to listen as you play a few measures of the precomposed rhythm in figure 13.21 on next page.[4]

    Ask the children to imagine the setting and tell you what that sound might be. Suppose they liken it to the sound of crickets chirping under the sunset.

Purple Light

2. Whippoorwill in the willa.
   Sings a song, a melody,
   For my three good companions:
   My knapsack, my pony, and me.

3. Gonna hang my sombrera
   On the limb of a tree.
   Over my three good companions:
   refrain

4. Yellow stars in the heavens
   Shine their light down on me
   And my three good companions:
   refrain

Figure 13.20.

giro

Figure 13.21.

3. Prepare the children for playing the güiro. Tell them to do as you do as you sing the first verse, mimicking the motion of playing the güiro by pretending to hold a stick in your right hand and gently sweeping it across the palm of your open left hand. Do this motion to the rhythm in figure 13.21. Model the motion as everyone imitates you and sings. Observe carefully to find children who can make the motion and sing accurately.

4. Select one child who performs most accurately, and hand that individual the güiro. Tell the child to play that rhythm throughout the following steps. (To facilitate music reading, place a large card in front of the child with the notated part and tell him or her to read from the card. You could also write the pattern in popsicle sticks.)

5. Next, bring out the claves. Play your composed rhythm for a short while on the claves, and elicit from the children what the sound might be. Suppose they hear the hooves of the donkey clopping on the rock.

6. Prepare the children for playing the claves. Give the güiro player a four count in the steady beat and direct him or her to begin. After a few measures, start everyone else singing the second verse while mimicking the motion of playing the claves to your precomposed pattern. Figure 13.22 offers a suggestion.

   Select a child who performs the movements accurately, hand that individual the claves, and instruct him or her to play that rhythm part throughout the next steps.

7. Repeat steps 5 and 6 with the tambourine, eliciting a sound from the children (the pots and pans jingling in a knapsack), then preparing them by clapping the rhythm from figure 13.23 and singing the third verse. Again, give the instrument to the child who can best sing and perform the motions.

8. Repeat steps 5 and 6 again with the sand blocks. Elicit a sound (a tumbleweed moving slowly across the sand) and prepare the children by rubbing palms together to the rhythm in figure 13.24 while singing the fourth verse, and then hand the sand blocks to the child who performs most accurately.

9. Now sing and play the song all the way through, with the orchestra playing as the other children sing and pat the steady beat on their knees.

10. End this musical experience as soon as the children have had success performing the song all the way through at least once. This way, they leave the experience with a good feeling—a feeling of wanting more.

11. On another day, gather the children together once again. Tell them they're going to add more instruments to your musical dramatization of "Purple Light." Produce the rhythm cards you used before and give them to the children who previously played in the orchestra, or select a new group of children if you're confident that they can read and play the rhythms. Alternatively, quickly go through the above steps, selecting a new child to play each instrument.

12. Start the orchestra playing, and after a few measures, once they are playing accurately together, tell the

Figure 13.22.

Figure 13.23.

Figure 13.24.

children to do as you do as the orchestra plays and everyone sings the first verse of the song while those not playing instruments pat the steady beat.[5] Observe carefully which children can sing and pat the steady beat most accurately.

13. Bring out the marimba (with B-flat and E bars removed) and invite a child to go off to the side and compose a simple melody for the marimba using stick notation. Provide the child with a menu of notated rhythms, or ask him or her to use only *ta, ti-ti,* and *sh.*

14. While that child is working on his or her melody, again start the orchestra, and tell the children to sing the second verse with you and do as you do. This time, while singing, pat the steady beat, as in figure 13.25, alternating hands.

15. Bring out a xylophone (with the B-flat and F bars removed) and hand it to the child whose movements best mirror yours. Tell that child to improvise a part, playing whatever pitches he or she likes. If you feel this child can play rhythm patterns in time to the steady beat, allow him or her to play a rhythm of choice as well.

16. Invite the child who is off composing a marimba part back into the group as a member of the orchestra. Ask that individual to lay the stick-notated part down in front of him or her, making quick corrections to the notation if necessary.

17. Now, the children can sing the third verse along with you and do as you do. Start up the orchestra, and, while singing, mimic the motion of striking and dampening a bell to the steady beat. Choose a child to go off to the side and compose a part for the Montessori Bells.

18. While the last child is composing, play through the fourth verse with the orchestra performers playing their parts and singing while everyone else simply pats the steady beat.

19. Finally, invite the last child back to the group. Play and sing through the entire song, with everyone singing to the orchestra's accompaniment,[6] creating a beautiful musical performance.

To give you an idea of how all the parts come together, figure 13.26 shows the first two measures of the above performance in full score with the marimba, xylophone, and Montessori Bell parts written in stick notation:

To simplify this process, you could also have the children improvise or compose their own accompaniment pattern to the song. To simplify the performance even further, especially if you're working with younger children, have each instrument play the quarter-note motive in figure 13.21.

III.D. Goldilocks and the Three Bears[7]

The children might want to follow up by creating a musical theater performance, complete with actors and orchestra. Fairy tales and children's stories make great fodder for staging musical dramatic performances. You can use this performance of Goldilocks and the Three Bears as a template.

Concepts and Skills: Listening, composing, playing instruments
Ages: All

1. Tell the children that today they are going to act out the story of Goldilocks and the Three Bears. Explain that the characters in the story, when mentioned, will be accompanied by musical instruments. Tell them that first of all you're going to teach individual children to play the accompaniments assigned to each instrument. (You can compose these accompaniments beforehand or invite the children to compose them.) Parse out the accompaniments as above: before teaching each accompaniment, prepare the entire class by having them mirror the actions you suggest. Select a child from the group who accurately performs the preparatory motions.

2. Help the children as a group to explore ways of moving like each of the characters. Observe carefully to find individuals who move responsibly.

3. Select individual children to play the part of each character, and let them practice with the children playing instruments until they perform easily together.

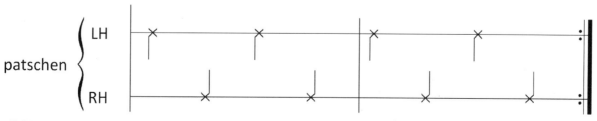

Figure 13.25.

Purple Light

Figure 13.26.

Explain that during the telling of the story, when you signal an individual character and the corresponding accompaniment to move or play, the child on the instrument should play the accompaniment twice, unless the character is moving to another spot, in which case the child should repeat the accompaniment until the character reaches his or her destination.

4. With the help of all the children, decide where in the room should be the woods, the home of the three bears, the dining room table with the porridge bowls, the fireplace with the three chairs, and the bedroom. Set up the instruments in a place close to the bear house, but not so close that they interfere with the action. Before the story starts, have the children playing the three bears take their places in the room at the table with the porridge. Stand Goldilocks in a place in the woods where the three bears won't see her when they exit the house.

Remind all the actors and the members of the orchestra to be prepared to move or play exactly as practiced whenever you signal them. Tell the actors that at all other times they should improvise actions that are indicated in the story. Make sure the children understand what to do.

5. Tell the story (figures 13.27–13.31) as follows: "Once upon a time there were three bears living all together in a yellow house in the middle of a big forest."

"One of them was a papa bear." (Signal using figure 13.27.)

"One of them was a mama bear." (Signal using figure 13.28.)

"And one of them was a wee baby bear." (Signal using figure 13.29.)

"One day, Mother Bear prepared a big pot of delicious hot porridge for breakfast."

"There was a big bowl for Papa Bear." (Signal.)

"There was a medium-size bowl for Mama Bear." (Signal.)

"There was a wee tiny bowl for Baby Bear." (Signal.)

"Each bear had a chair by the fireplace."

"There was a big chair for Papa Bear." (Signal.)

"There was a medium-sized chair for Mama Bear." (Signal.)

"There was a wee tiny chair for Baby Bear." (Signal.)

"The porridge was too hot to eat, so the bears decided to go for a walk while waiting for the porridge to cool."

"Near the forest lived a little girl named Goldilocks." (Signal using figure 13.30.)

"Goldilocks was not a well-behaved little girl. That morning she was playing in the forest throwing stones at squirrels when she smelled the smell of the delicious porridge that Mother Bear had made."

" 'Oh, I'm so hungry!' thought Goldilocks. 'I wonder if they will share their porridge with me.' "

"She knocked on the door of the house. No one answered. She then peeked into the window. She saw three bowls of porridge on the kitchen table, but it seemed that nobody was home. So Goldilocks entered the house."

"First, Goldilocks tasted the porridge in Father Bear's bowl. (Signal 'Ow! This porridge is too hot!' she said."

"Then, Goldilocks tasted the porridge in the bowl of Mother Bear. (Signal 'Ooo! This porridge is too cold!' she said."

"Finally Goldilocks tasted the porridge in Little Bear's bowl. (Signal 'Mmm, this porridge is just perfect!' she said, and she ate the whole bowl of porridge!"

"Stomach full and satisfied, Goldilocks looked for a place to sit down. She saw three chairs beside the fireplace."

"First, she sat on Father Bear's chair. (Signal) 'This chair is too hard!' she complained."

"Then, she sat on Mother Bear's chair. (Signal) 'This chair is too soft!' she fussed."

"Finally, she sat on Little Bear's chair. 'Ahh, this chair is just perfect,' she sighed. But just then the chair broke!" (Signal the sound of Goldilocks falling through the chair-from figure 13.31.)

" 'I must have eaten too much porridge.' Goldilocks thought to herself."

"She was still tired, so she went up the stairs to go to the bedroom, where there were three beds."

"First, Goldilocks tried the bed of Father Bear, but she did not like it. (Signal) 'This bed is too hard!' she said."

"Then she tried Mother Bear's bed, but she did not like it either. (Signal) 'This bed is too soft!' she said."

"Finally, she tried Baby Bear's bed. (Signal) 'This bed is just perfect!' she said happily, and fell into a deep sleep, dreaming of cookies and kittens.

"Shortly after this, the bears returned from walk, ready to have breakfast. But they were surprised to see that the spoons were already in their bowls of porridge."

"Someone has eaten my porridge!' exclaimed Father Bear." (Signal.)

'Someone has eaten my porridge, too!' exclaimed Mother Bear." (Signal.)

"'Someone has eaten my porridge . . . and it's all gone!' (Signal instrument.) sobbed Baby Bear. He loved porridge."

"Then, the three bears saw that their chairs had been used. 'Who has been sitting on my chair?' asked Father Bear." (Signal.)

Papa bear:

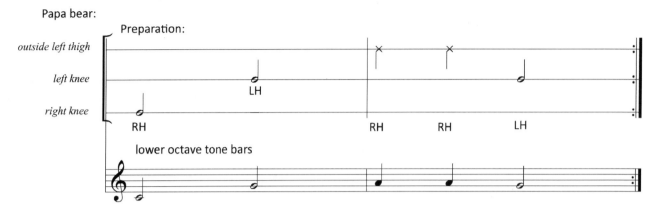

Figure 13.27.

Mama bear:

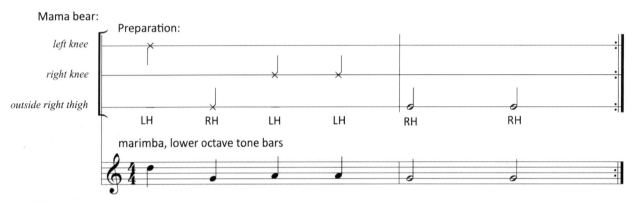

Figure 13.28.

Baby bear:

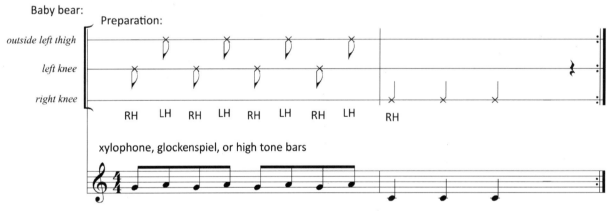

Figure 13.29.

Goldilocks:

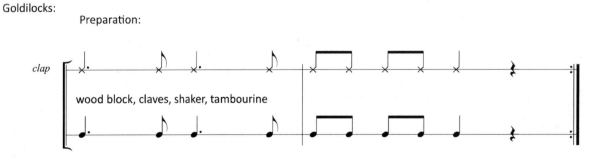

Figure 13.30.

Falling through the chair:

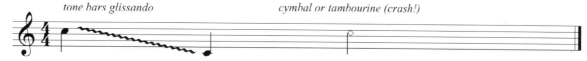

Figure 13.31.

"'Who has been sitting on my chair?' asked Mother Bear." (Signal.)

"'Who has been sitting on my chair . . . and broken it?!' asked Baby Bear, and he began to cry." (Signal.)

"The three bears went up the stairs running to check the bedroom. 'Someone has been sleeping in my bed!' growled Father Bear." (Signal.)

"'And someone has been sleeping in my bed,' growled Mother Bear." (Signal.)

"'Someone has been sleeping in my bed!' whined Baby Bear." (Signal.)

"And she's still there!' continued Baby Bear so loudly that Goldilocks woke up."

"When she saw the three angry bears, Goldilocks was very frightened. She jumped out of bed, ran down the stairs, ran out the door, and didn't stop running until she reached her own house."

"Inside she found her own bowl and her own chair. And that night, just before she went to sleep in her own bed, she promised herself: 'I will never take things that aren't mine without being invited.'"

III.E. Work at the Rock[8]

Skills: Listening, composing, moving, playing instruments
Materials: Percussion instruments, mallet instruments

1. With the children standing in a circle, tell them to join you as you perform the body percussion ostinato from figure 13.32.
2. Continuing to perform the ostinato, tell the class first to listen, and then to echo you. Chant figure 13.33 on

next page, varying the tone color, pitch, and volume of your voice, encouraging the children to do the same.

3. When the class can echo-chant the poem easily, have them chant it all the way through while performing the body movements and varying the tone color, pitch, and volume of their voices.
4. Discuss the voice colors that the children have used. Help them to decide which ones best interpret the text. Let them experiment to figure out which sounds best. The children might decide:

Chorus: The entire group of boys and girls chant at full volume, using a comfortable pitch.
Verse 1: The boys chant only, starting at a low pitch, and raising it at the end of the line.
Verse 2: One boy only, starting high and loud, and lowering in pitch and volume and singing the second line softly.
Verse 3: Girls' voices only, starting high and excited and moving to a medium pitch, dipping low on "Break that ground!"

5. Discuss the possibilities for a rhythmic dramatization for the chorus and for each verse. *What characters might feature in the poem if we wanted to act it out? How would they move?* The class might come up with:

Chorus: A small group of boys steps out and pantomimes chopping at the rock with a pickaxe.
Verse 1: One girl (the boss), struts up to the group, scowling, and points upward toward the sky.
Verse 2: A boy moves like an eagle swooping down from the sky and back up again.

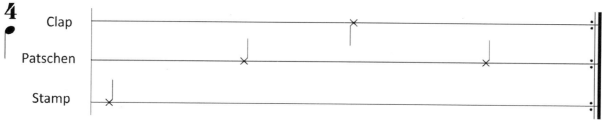

Figure 13.32.

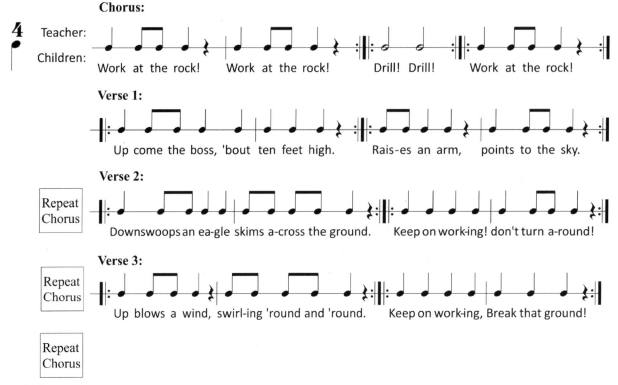

Figure 13.33.

Verse 3: A group of children steps out, swirling around and around like gusts of wind.

6. Select children to act out each of the choruses and the verses and have them step aside. Help the children decide where in the room the action will take place.

7. To begin the performance, have the rest of the children begin the body percussion accompaniment. After two measures, signal the boys enacting the chorus to enter as the rest of the children chant the chorus. Proceed through the poem without missing a beat, signaling children acting the verses to enter at the proper times and encouraging the chanters to use the agreed-on pitch and dynamics. On the last chorus, let the body percussion and the boys working with pickaxes continue for two measures after the end of the poem.

8. Discuss the dramatization with the class. Practice any parts that need improving, and make changes. Let the same group of children perform the refined version of the dramatization as in step 7.

9. Choose new children to act out the parts and repeat until everyone has had a chance. Guide the class in making their chanting, moving, and acting more expressive.

10. On another day, add instruments by preparing the parts with body percussion and selecting children to play the instruments, or by handing the children instruments and having them improvise parts.

Figure 13.34 on next page suggests some ideas for instrumental parts.

Extension: Use this template to create musical dramatizations of other poems and rhymes.

IV. JAZZ IMPROVISATION

IV.A. So What?

Much of the raw material for improvisation in jazz music up until the 1940s and 1950s consisted of songs from musicals. These songs contained many complex chord changes that jazz musicians found exciting and challenging to improvise over.

Sometime in the late 1960s, however, especially on the West Coast of the United States, jazz musicians started to experiment with a more mellow, relaxed, and "cool" sound. Instead of basing their improvisations on incredibly difficult chord changes, "cool jazz" musicians stuck to one single harmony for long stretches of time, allowing them to create longer melodic lines and to experiment with harmony in innovative ways. Sometimes this kind of jazz goes by the name "modal jazz" because improvisers explored just one or two single modes, or scales, for entire sections of a piece.

Miles Davis wrote a few songs in the modal style. An easy song to perform with children is "So What"

Figure 13.34.

from his album *Kind of Blue*. The song contains no chord changes, but instead adheres to two main modes: D Dorian and E-flat Dorian. These two scales are quite easy to comprehend, as D Dorian has all the same notes as the C-major scale, that is, all the white keys on the piano. E-flat Dorian contains all the black keys plus C and F.

The song is in AABA form, each section being eight measures each. The A sections are in D Dorian, and the B section is in E-flat Dorian. To simplify the song even further for the children, however, just drop the E-flat-Dorian section and loop the D-Dorian sections.

Follow these steps to create a "jam session" based on Miles Davis's "So What."

Concepts and Skills: Listening, singing, moving, playing instruments, improvising
Ages: All

1. Set up a number of contrasting classroom instruments, including tone bars and bells. For this example, we're going to use glockenspiel, tone bars, marimba, bells, and hand drum. On the glockenspiel and the marimba, remove the B and F bars to make a C major or A minor pentatonic scale. Bring out the D, F, G, A, and C tone bars and bells to make the D-minor or F-major pentatonic scale.
2. Have the children sit in a circle around the instruments, with the instruments free in the center.
3. Begin with a brief story about Miles Davis. *Miles Davis, a trumpet player, is considered to be one of the greatest jazz musicians ever. He was born Miles Dewey Davis III in a suburban, middle-class home in Illinois. As a young boy, he took trumpet lessons from a friend of his father who ran the local music school. At age eighteen, Miles traveled to New York City to pursue music. He enrolled at T Julliard school, a very prestigious institution. While studying at Julliard, Miles began playing trumpet in Harlem nightclubs with a friend of his, another jazz musician who would become famous named Charlie Parker. The ultrafast, complex music that Miles played with Charlie Parker and other musicians became known as bebop, a style of playing that had the greatest influence on modern jazz music. In 1945, Miles dropped out of Julliard and devoted himself full time to performing and recording music. Miles and his friends innovated jazz music. At that time, a jazz combo normally consisted of drums, saxophones, a trumpet, and maybe a guitar, but by 1949, Miles was playing jazz with a slower tempo and using uncommon instrumental combinations such as French horn, trombone, and tuba. In 1959, Miles recorded a jazz album that was the biggest seller in history:* Kind of Blue. *His song "So What" that we're about to play is on that album. Miles went on to have a long, successful career. He died in 1991. We can be glad that Miles Davis brought the world such wonderful music.*
4. Tell the class a little bit about the structure of jazz improvisation. First, everyone sings or plays the

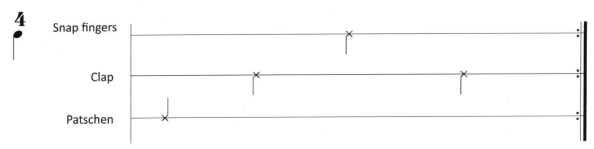

Figure 13.35.

melody, then the soloists, one at a time, sing or play solos. Then, everyone sings or plays the melody again.

5. Teach the children the melody. Begin by telling the children to do as you do. Perform the rhythmic body percussion ostinato from figure 13.35.

6. While continuing the body percussion pattern, have the children echo you as you sing the melody from figure 13.36 (with a slight swing feel to the eighth notes).

7. Once the children feel comfortable singing the melody along with the body percussion pattern, tell them to only sing on the "Bah dap!" parts, while you sing the rest. Sing the melody once more through in a call and response manner, like in figure 13.37 on next page.

8. Now select children to be the soloists. Have each child sit in front of his or her instrument ready to

play, but tell them not to play during the melody. They should instead sing the melody with the whole group.

9. Explain that after everyone sings the melody twice, the first soloist will begin his solo. (Everyone continues the body percussion ostinato during the solos.) Each soloist can solo for as long as he likes. When a soloist feels he's finished, he must look the next soloist right in the eye and signal that it's her turn. When the last soloist finishes playing a solo, everyone sings the melody twice again.

10. When the structure is clear, begin the body percussion pattern. After about two measures, or when everyone feels secure, signal everyone to begin the melody. Have everybody sing the melody twice.

11. While the soloists are playing, you can "walk" the bassline from figure 13.38, also on next page. In

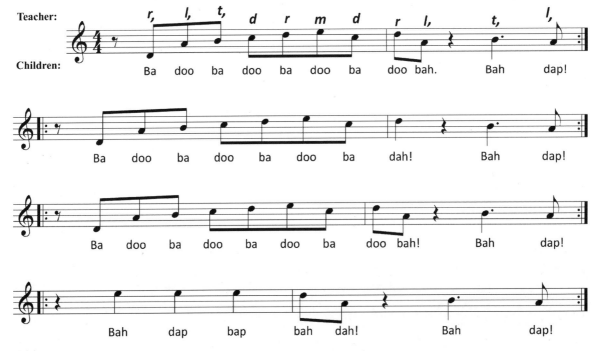

Figure 13.36.

Figure 13.37.

Figure 13.38.

jazz, to "walk" simply means to play the part with a steady quarter-note pulse. Play the line on whichever instrument you feel comfortable. Options include:

- on the piano with your left hand, playing any chords you like with your right hand using any of the white keys (they will all sound good);
- only with your left hand, with a child improvising chords above you on the white keys; or
- on a bass marimba, with a child improvising chords on the white keys of the piano or on a mallet instrument with the F and B bars removed.

12. When the soloists have all finished, have everyone sing the melody twice again. End the song by holding the syllable "Bah!" on whatever note you like as you play the chord from figure 13.39.[9]

13. Switch soloists and play the song through again. Repeat the performance for as many times as the children feel enjoyment.

14. Add tone colors by giving a few children in the circle percussion instruments to play throughout.

Figure 13.40 on the next page shows a good ostinato for percussion instruments.

Extension: Other modal jazz songs for improvising include "Impressions" by John Coltrane, which follows the same form as "So What," and "Milestones," also by Miles Davis, for which you can use a G-Dorian scale.

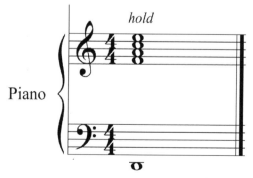

Figure 13.39.

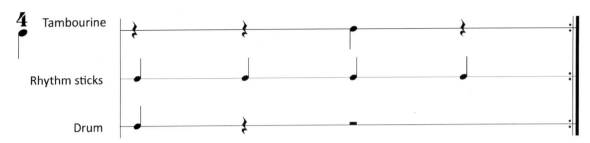

Figure 13.40.

NOTES

1. Adapted from Irwin and Nelson (1986).
2. Sections II.A. to II.F. Adapted from Wheeler and Raebeck (1977).
3. Refer to the resources section in appendix E to see where you can acquire this excellent book.
4. Notice that this is simply the rhythm of the steady beat. It's a good idea to compose at least one straight quarter note rhythm and introduce it first in order to mark the steady beat. This helps the children stay together as you add more instruments. Eventually, as you see that the children have internalized the steady beat, you can drop this part or change it.
5. This time, you aren't asking the children to play a particular rhythm, since you want them to improvise a melodic accompaniment. In this case, it suffices to prepare just the motion required to play the instrument.
6. Throughout this experience, the children playing instruments also sing.
7. Adapted from Wheeler and Raebeck (1972).
8. Ibid.
9. Again, you can play this in various combinations: (1) play with both hands on a piano; (2) play the bass note, and have a child play the top chord; or (3) play the bass note on a bass marimba with a child playing the top chord on the white keys of the piano or a xylophone with the F and B bars removed.

Chapter 14

Fifty-five Songs to Sing, Read, Dance, and Play

Graciela made a fuss one afternoon when faced with the prospect of playing "Hold My Mule." She defiantly marched to the fence and sulked while the other children joined hands and formed a double circle.

Graciela eyeballed Miss Carrie with a scornful expression as Miss Carrie sent two children, the "racers", behind the fence to hide. When Miss Carrie selected one pair of children in each circle to form the "arches," Graciela grumbled audibly. As Miss Carrie placed a little plush toy in the center of the configuration, she spied Graciela muttering to herself and kicking the fence.

When the children started singing, however, and walking in two circles with hands joined in opposite directions, Graciela's face softened. She clapped her hands together as the two "racers" paced outside of the circle waiting for the singing to stop. Finally the song ended, the class stopped, the children designated as arches raised their arms up, and the racers dashed into the circle, vying to be the first to grab the plush toy in the middle. As the children laughed and egged the racers on, Graciela stood on tip toes, calling out, "Go! Go!"

Jaqueline with triumph held up the plush toy, having reached the center before Oliver. The class cheered and clapped. Miss Carrie asked Jaqueline and Oliver to pick one person each to be the racers for the next round. To everyone's astonishment, Graciela appeared among the throng of children, stretching out her hand and clamoring for Oliver to pick her.

Even the grumbliest child loves to sing and dance. Simultaneous singing and movement forms a vital and natural part of the child's musical experience. You can harness this natural instinct for movement to develop the children's musical potential. Through games and dances, children experience, directly and with joy, the musical elements of rhythm, melody, and form, as well as the social and emotional elements of turn taking, risk taking, individual acceptance, partner switching, and community building.

Because the formations of these songs are so rich and variable, children who sing and play them become all at once singers, dancers, improvisers, and composers. What's more, each of these songs showcases a particular rhythmic or melodic element that you can isolate, name, and practice with the children so as to develop their musical literacy.

The 55 songs listed here feature:

- Infectious, easy-to-sing melodies
- Memorable, repetitive, descriptive, or narrative lyrics
- Clearly defined forms
- Simple scales and modes whose notes can be easily combined
- Authentic origins arising from human spiritual needs
- Clear directions for action
- The song's source

Appendix G contains an index of the songs organized in various ways, by rhythmic and melodic elements, for example.

To free you from the constraints of any particular key, I have notated the songs in stick notation. This way, you can sing the songs using Sol-fa syllables at a pitch that you and your children find most comfortable. The tone set for each song appears at the top right, with the starting tone circled.

To make it easy for you to add mallet instruments, tone bars, and pitched percussion instruments to the songs, refer to Appendix F to find out which pentatonic notes work best for setting up mallet instruments, tone bars, and bells, and which chords to use when adding ukulele or autoharp.

Action Songs
  1.1 My Aunt Came Back
  1.2 Paige's Train
  1.3 Rain, Rain
  1.4 Snail, Snail

Songs
  2.1 Bye, Bye Baby
  2.2 Come Let Us Gather
  2.3 Cotton Eye Joe
  2.4 Hello, My Friends
  2.5 Hill And Gully Rider
  2.6 King Kong Kitchie
  2.7 El Mar Estaba Serena
  2.8 Lil' Liza Jane
  2.9 The Owl Sings
  2.10 Purple Light
  2.11 Rock My Soul
  2.12 Rocky Mountain
  2.13 Seagull, Seagull
  2.14 Skin & Bones
  2.15 Sweet Betsy From Pike

Rounds and part songs
  3.1 Banuwa
  3.2 Dona Nobis Pacem
  3.3 My Paddle (The Canoe Song)
  3.4 Senua De Dende
  3.5 Si Si Si

Singing and Movement Games
  4.1 Bluebird
  4.2 Bow Wow Wow

  4.3 Charlie Over The Ocean
  4.4 Follow The Drinking Gourd
  4.5 The Farmer In The Dell
  4.6 The Farmer's Dairy Key
  4.7 Green Grows The Willow Tree
  4.8 Grizzly Bear
  4.9 Hold My Mule
  4.10 John Kanaka
  4.11 Just From The Kitchen
  4.12 Let Us Chase The Squirrel
  4.13 Little Johnny Brown
  4.14 My Mama's Calling Me
  4.15 Oats And Beans And Barley
  4.16 The Old Gray Cat
  4.17 Pizza, Pizza, Daddy-O
  4.18 Riding On The Railway
  4.19 Sailor, Sailor
  4.20 Shoorah
  4.21 Song Of The Snowflakes
  4.22 That's A Mighty Pretty Motion
  4.23 Turn The Glasses Over

Dances
  5.1 Amasee
  5.2 Great Big House In New Orleans
  5.3 Here Comes Sally
  5.4 Lead Through That Sugar And Tea
  5.5 Paw Paw Patch
  5.6 Shake Them 'Simmons Down
  5.7 Shoo Roun'
  5.8 Tideo

My Aunt Came Back

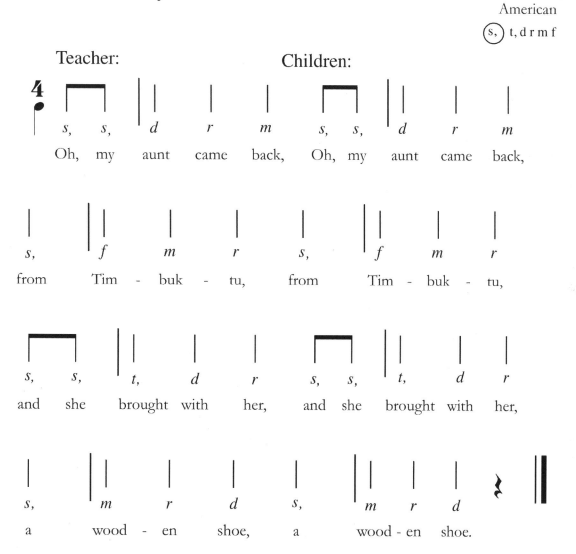

Source: Becca Barlow, Bridlemile Elementary School, 2008.

2. Oh, my aunt came back from old Japan,
   And she brought with her a paper fan.

3. Oh, my aunt came back from Guadelupe,
   And she brought with her a hula hoop.

4. Oh, my aunt came back from _____,
   And she brought with her a _____.

Action: Children stand in a circle, pantomiming motions as the lyrics suggest. On "wooden shoe" they tap one foot in the center. On "paper fan," they imitate fanning themselves. On "hula hoop," they make hula motions. Repeat, eliciting 3-syllable place names, objects that rhyme, and motions to perform.

Paige's Train

North Carolina

d r (m) s l

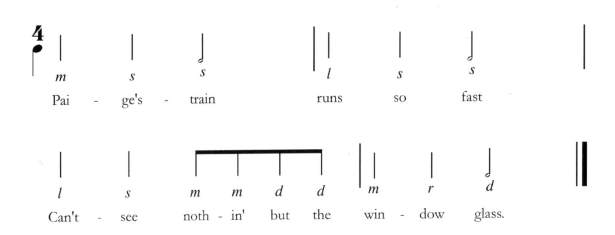

	m	s	s	l	s	s
	Pai	- ge's -	train	runs	so	fast

	l	s	m	m	d	d	m	r	d
	Can't	- see	noth	- in'	but	the	win	- dow	glass.

2. Paige's train runs so slow
    Takes so long to get to Buffalo.

Action: Children sit in a circle. Everyone pats their knees to the steady beat. The song proceeds at a medium tempo the first time through both verses. On the third time, the teacher asks a child *Which do you like best, fast or slow?* If the child answers *fast*, everyone sings the first verse at a breakneck tempo. If the child answers *slow*, everyone sings the second verse at a painstakingly slow tempo. Repeat as many times as the children enjoy it.

Source: Peter Erdei (1974). 150 American Folk Songs to Sing Read and Play. Boosey & Hawkes.

Rain, Rain

American
m (s) l

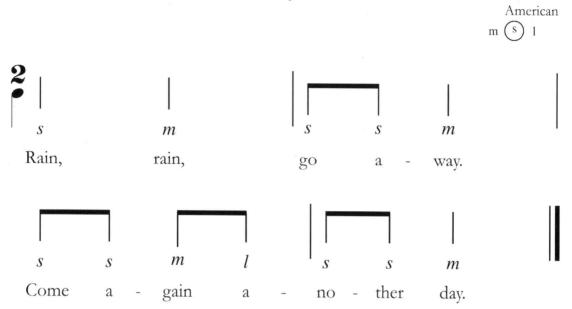

Actions: The children stand in a circle. The teacher walks around the inside of the circle and taps the children in time to the steady beat. She hands an umbrella to a child when the song ends. That child walks around the outside of the circle holding the umbrella and goes back to her place.

Alternatively, a child could walk around the outside of the circle holding the umbrella as everyone sings the song. By the end of the song, the child walking around the circle hands the umbrella to a new child, who then goes around the circle, and so on.

Source: Peter Erdei (1974). 150 American Folk Songs to Sing Read and Play. Boosey & Hawkes.

Snail, Snail

American

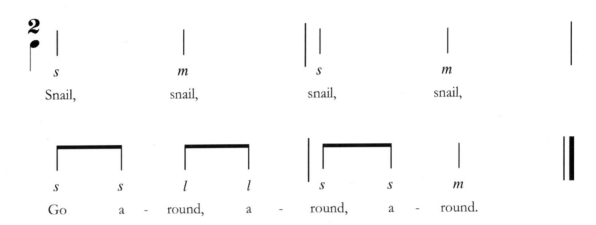

Action: Children form a line. One end player stands still, and the child at the other end moves in a wide circle, slowly winding the line up tight around the stationary person. After all are wound up tight, the outer coil wheels sharply in a contrary direction and all follow, retracing their steps.

Source: Locke, E. G. (1981). Sail Away: 155 American Folk Songs to Sing Read and Play. Boosey & Hawkes. pg. 4

Bye, Bye, Baby

American
d r (m) s

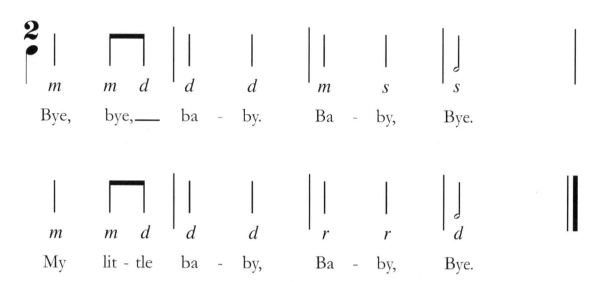

m m d d d m s s
Bye, bye,— ba - by. Ba - by, Bye.

m m d d d r r d
My lit - tle ba - by, Ba - by, Bye.

Action: Children rock a little doll back and forth to the steady beat of the song. This song can be paired with a second melody line. Try the following:

d s, l, s, d s, l, s, d s, l, d m r s, d

Source: Bacon, D. (1973). *46 Two-part American Folk Songs*. Olympia, WA: Kodály Center of America.

Come, Let Us Gather

Traditional round
New text by Judy Bond

s, l, t, (d) r m f s

4

d   d r m d   r   s,   d   m   m   f   s   m   f   r   m

Come let us ga-ther now to sing.   Sing from your heart great joy to bring.

s   f   m   r   d   t,   l,   s,   l,   t,   d

Bo - dy,   mind___ spi - rit   voice___   come   let's   sing!

Ostinato 1:

°d   s,   s,   d

Sing!   Come   let's   sing!

Ostinato 2:

s   m   r   s   s

Sing!   Sing!   Come   let's   sing!

Action: You can use this song as a signal for children to come to the gathering. Pair it with the two suggested ostinati, sing it as a round, or accompany it with any instruments you like.

Source: Kelly Foster Griffin, Southern Washington and Oregon Kodály Educator's workshop, October, 2007

Cotton Eye Joe

Afro-American

s, l, d r (m)

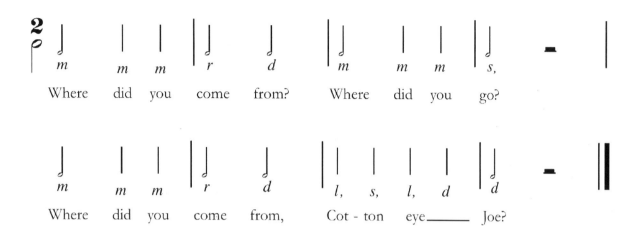

2. Come for to see you. Come for to sing.
    Come for to show you my diamond ring.

Action: This song works great with many vocal parts. Experiment with ostinati and pentatonic countermelodies.

Source: Bacon, D. (1973). *46 Two-part American Folk Songs*. Olympia, WA: Kodály Center of America.

Hello, My Friends

American

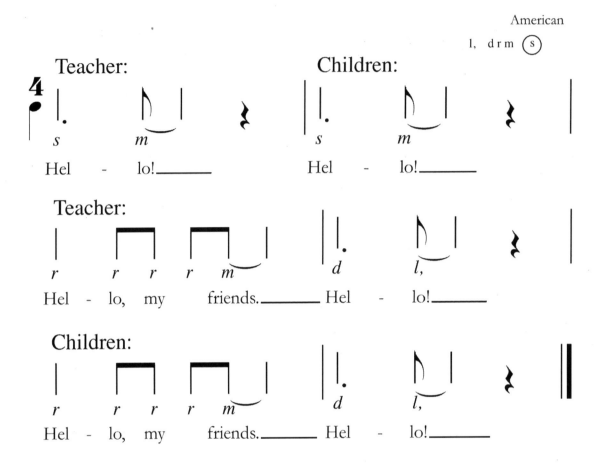

1. Bonjour! Bonjour, mes amis, bonjour!
2. Hola! Hola, mis amigos, hola!
3. Guten Tag! Guten Tag, mein Fruende, guten Tag!
4. Privyet! Privyet, druzya, privyet!
   (Привет! Привет, друзья, привет!)
5. etc.

Action: Ask the children what languages they heard when you sang the song. Elicit from the children some other languages. Sing "Hello, my friends!" in as many languages as you like.

Source: Becca Barlow, Bridlemile Elementary School, 2007

Hill And Gully Rider

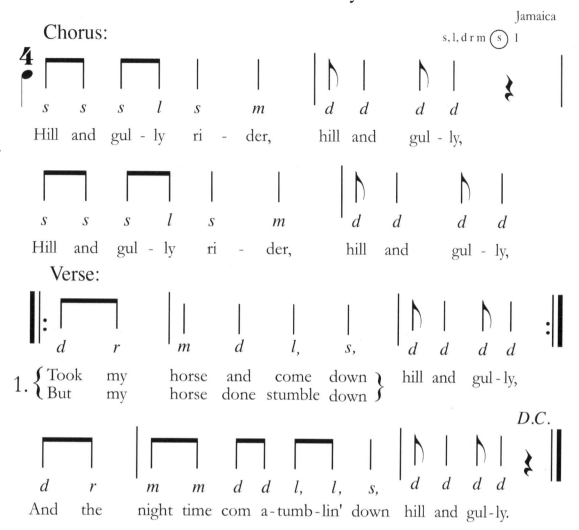

2. Oh the moon shines bright down, hill and gully,
Ain't no place to hide 'em down, hill and gully,
An' a zombie come a-ridin' down, hill and gully. *Chorus*

3. Oh, my knees they shake down, hill and gully,
An' my heart strings start quakin' down, hill and gully
Ain' nobody goin' to get me down, hill and gully. *Chorus*

4. That's the last I sit down, hill and gully,
Pray the Lord don' let me down, hill and gully,
Ain' nobody goin' to get me down, hill and gully. *Chorus*

Source: Locke, E. G. (1981). *Sail Away: 155 American Folk Songs to Sing Read and Play.*
Boosey & Hawkes. pg. 3

King Kong Kitchie

American

s, l, (d) r m s

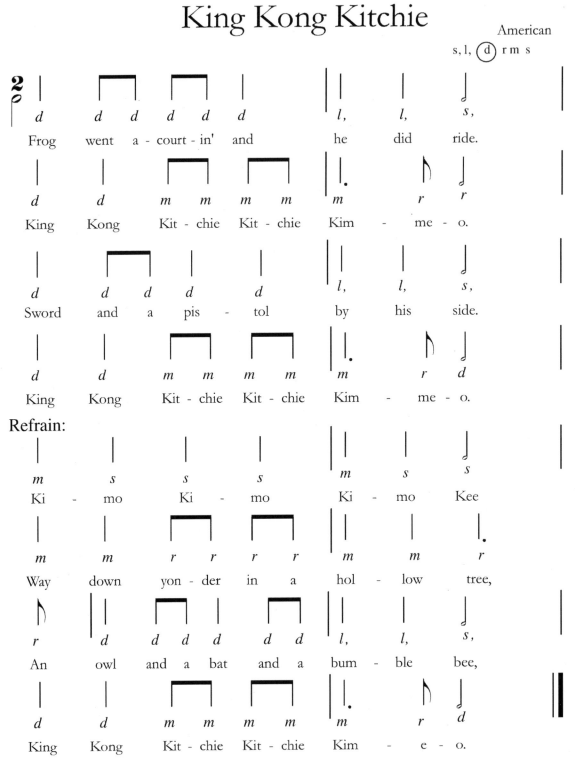

| d | d d d d | d | | l, | l, | s, | |

Frog went a - court - in' and he did ride.

d | d | m m m m | m | r | r

King Kong Kit - chie Kit - chie Kim - me - o.

d | d d d | d | l, | l, | s, |

Sword and a pis - tol by his side.

d | d | m m m m | m | r | d

King Kong Kit - chie Kit - chie Kim - me - o.

Refrain:

m | s | s | s | m | s | s |

Ki - mo Ki - mo Ki - mo Kee

m | m | r r r r | m | m | r

Way down yon - der in a hol - low tree,

r | d | d d d | d d | l, | l, | s, |

An owl and a bat and a bum - ble bee,

d | d | m m m m | m | r | d

King Kong Kit - chie Kit - chie Kim - e - o.

2. Frog he rode for a month or more,
   King Kong Kitchie Kitchie Kimeo
   Rode 'til he came to Miss Mousie's door
   King Kong Kitchie Kitchie Kimeo

   Refrain

3. Frog got down on bended knee,
   Said, "Miss Mouse, will you marry me?"

4. "Sir, I cannot answer that,"
   "You'll have to ask my Uncle Rat."

5. Rat came home the very next day,
   Said, "Whose been here while I've been away?"

6. "Well, a very nice frog has been here."
   "And he wants for me to be his dear!"

7. So, Uncle Rat he went to town,
   And he bought his niece a beautiful gown.

8. What will the wedding supper be?
   Three green beans and a black-eyed pea.

9. Where, oh, where will the wedding be?
   Way down yonder in the hollow tree.

10. And all my girls are a sittin' there.
    Wearing pretty ribbons in their hair.

11. Well in attendance are all my boys.
    Sittin' in the back makin' lots of noise.

12. So they all took a boat out on the lake.
    And they got swallowed up by a big black snake.

Action: This song works well as a call-and-response tune, with the teacher singing the first and third lines and the children singing *King Kong Kitchie Kitchie Kimeo*. All sing the lines beginning *Kimo Kimo Kimo Kee...* as a refrain.

Source: Susan Brumfield, Portland State University Summer Kodály workshop, August, 2007.

El Mar Estaba Serena

Chile

(m,) l, t, d r m f

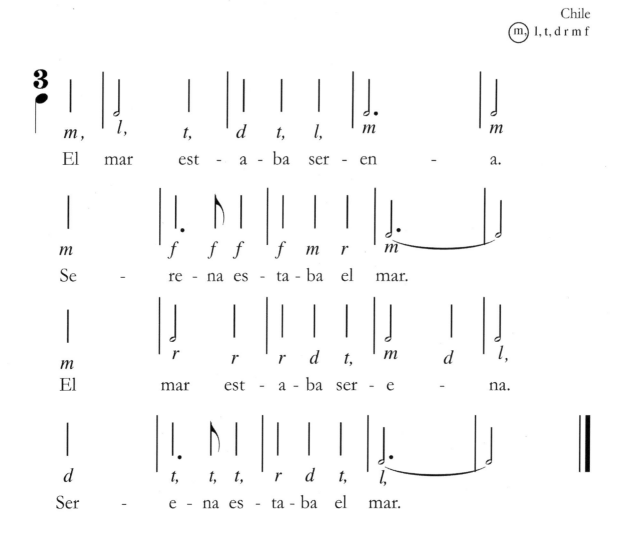

m,   l,   t,   d   t,   l,   m   m
El   mar   est - a - ba ser - en - a.

m   f   f   f   f   m   r   m
Se   -   re - na es - ta - ba el   mar.

m   r   r   r   d   t,   m   d   l,
El   mar est - a - ba ser - e - na.

d   t,   t,   t,   r   d   t,   l,
Ser   -   e - na es - ta - ba el   mar.

"The sea is calm."

Source: Barb Harvey, S. C. *Young Voices, World Songs*. Seward Montessori School. Recorded by Russell Packard while on a small boat during an ocean storm in the Straights of Magellan off the coast of Chile. "The people gathered the frightened children together as the waves crashed around them and sang this melody, which soothed the frightened youngsters." The song is frequently used to teach Spanish vowels and articulation to Spanish-speaking children in Latin America.

Li'l Liza Jane

American

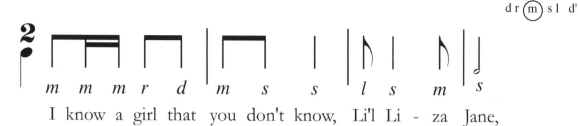

I know a girl that you don't know, Li'l Li - za Jane,

Way down south in Bal - ti-more, Li'l Li - za Jane.

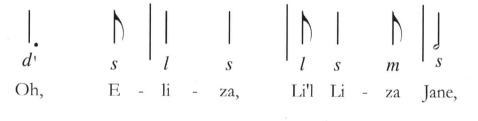

Oh, E - li - za, Li'l Li - za Jane,

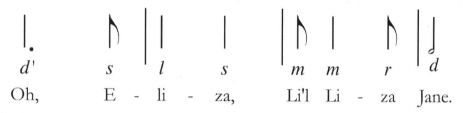

Oh, E - li - za, Li'l Li - za Jane.

1. Liza Jane looks good to me
   Sweetest one I ever did see.

2. Where she lives the posies grow
   Chickens round the kitchen go.

3. What do I care how far we roam?
   Where she's at is home sweet home.

Source: Waterhouse, Celia, Lucy Allen, Elspeth Compton, Nandita Hollins. *How Can I Keep From Singing!: Songs and Musical Activities From Around the World for 8-13 Year Olds.* London, UK: British Kodály Academy, 2007. Pg. 60

The Owl Sings

Yuma Indian Lullaby

l, d r m (s) l

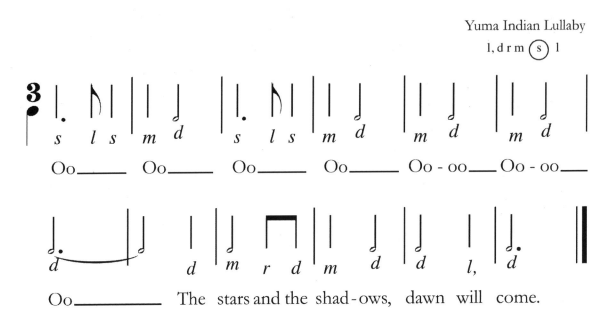

Source: Locke, E. G. (1981). Sail Away: 155 American Folk Songs to Sing Read and Play. Boosey & Hawkes. pg. 18

Purple Light

American

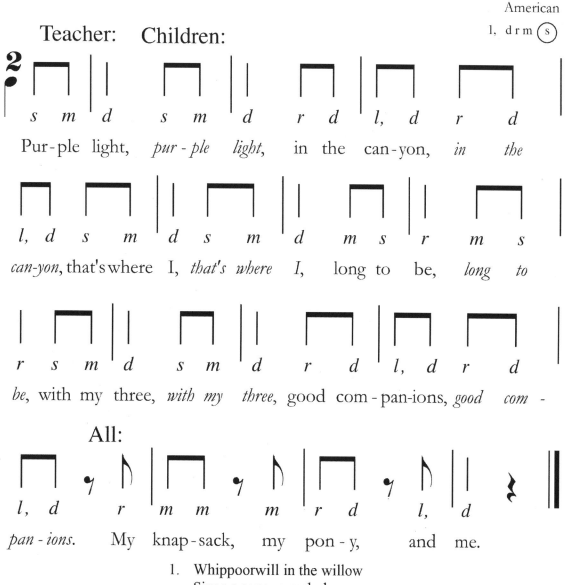

Teacher: Children:

s	m	d	s	m	d	r	d	l,	d	r	d

Pur-ple light, *pur-ple light,* in the can-yon, *in the*

| l, | d | s | m | d | s | m | d | m | s | r | m | s |

can-yon, that's where I, *that's where I,* long to be, *long to*

| r | s | m | d | s | m | d | r | d | l, | d | r | d |

be, with my three, *with my three,* good com-pan-ions, *good com -*

All:

| l, | d | r | m | m | m | r | d | l, | d |

pan-ions. My knap-sack, my pon-y, and me.

1. Whippoorwill in the willow
   Sings a song, a melody
   For my three good companions:
   My knapsack, my pony, and me.

2. Gonna hang my sombrero
   On the limb of a tree,
   Over my three good companions:
   Refrain

3. Yellow stars in the heavens
   Shine their light down on me
   And my three good companions:
   Refrain

Source: Becca Barlow, Bridlemile Elementary School, 2007

Rock My Soul

African-American Spiritual

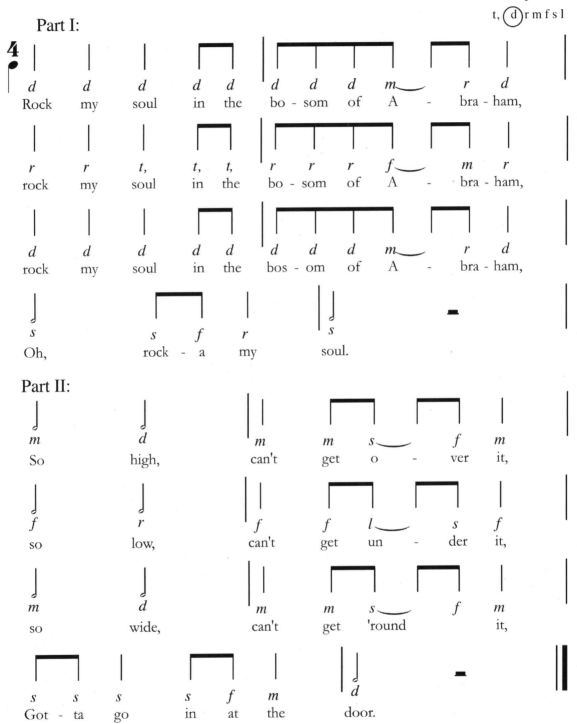

Source: Stuart Young, the Rhein-Main International Montessori School, Friedrichsdorf, Germany, 2010

Rocky Mountain

American
(d) r m s l

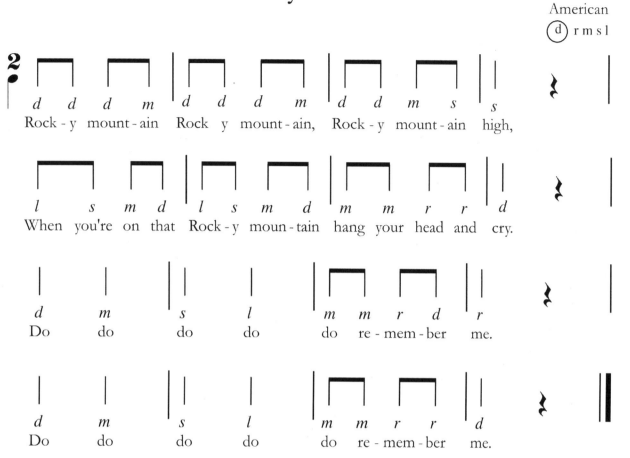

2. Sunny valley, sunny valley, sunny valley low,
   When you're in that sunny valley sing it soft and slow.
   Do do do do do remember me.
   Do do do do do remember me.

3. Stormy ocean, stormy ocean, stormy ocean wide,
   When you're on that stormy ocean, there's no place you can hide.
   Do do do do do remember me.
   Do do do do do remember me.

Source: Peter Erdei (1974). 150 American Folk Songs to Sing Read and Play. Boosey &
Hawkes. pg. 19

Seagull Seagull

American
s, (d) r m f s l

	d	s,	d	r	m	m	f	m	r	r	m	r	d	d	r	d
1.	Sea-gull,	sea-gull,	sit	on	the	shore,			sit	on	the	shore,	sit	on	the	shore,
2.	Cap-tain,	cap-tain,	hoist	up	the	sails,			hoist	up	the	sails,	hoist	up	the	sails,

d	s,	d	r	m	m	f	m	m	r	r	f	m	r	d	d
Sea - gull,	sea - gull,	sit	on	the	shore,	and	sail	on	my	San - ty	An	-	na.		
Cap - tain,	cap - tain,	hoist	up	the	sails,	and	sail	on	my	San - ty	An	-	na.		

s	l	s	f	m	f	s	r	m	f	m	f	s
For	my	love	is	far	a - way,		far	a - way,		far	a	way,
'Cross	the	waves	and	back	a - gain,		back	a - gain,		back	a - gain,

s	l	s	f	m	f	s	r	s	m	d
For	my	love	is	far	a - way,		San -	ty	An - na.	
'Cross	the	waves	and	back	a - gain,		San -	ty	An - na.	

3.   Blue horizon, heading for home, heading for home, heading for home
       Blue horizon, heading for home, sail on my Santy Anna.
       'Cross the waves and back again, back again, back again,
       'Cross the waves and back again, Santy Anna.

Action: The two melodies in this song can be combined in a variety of interesting ways. A successful arrangement is Section A ("seagull"), Section A ("captain"), Section B ("for my love"), Section A ("blue horizon") and Section B ("'cross the waves") together, with everyone repeating the last two measures to end the song.

Source: Brumfield, D. S. (2008). Making Music!: Musicianship in the Children's Chorus. Lubbock, TX: Texas Tech University. pg. 17

Skin & Bones

American

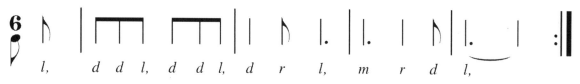

1.There was an old wom-an all skin and bones. Oo - oo - oo - oo!

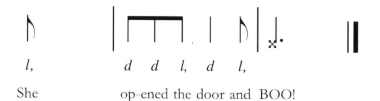

She   op-ened the door and BOO!

2. She lived down by the old graveyard, Oo…

3. One night she thought she'd take a walk, Oo…

4. She saw the bones a'lyin' 'round, Oo…

5. She went to the cupboard to get a broom, Oo…

Source: Locke, E. (1981). Sail Away: 155 American Folk Songs to Sing Read and Play. Boosey & Hawkes. pg. 52

Sweet Betsy From Pike

American

d r m f s l t d'

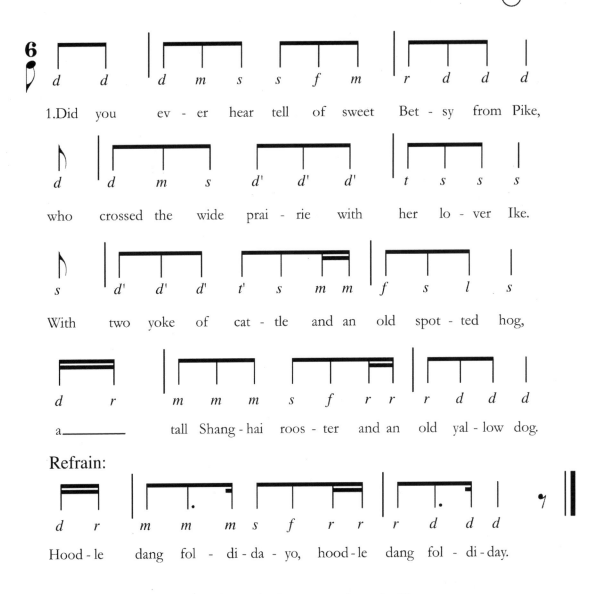

6

d   d   d m   s s f m   r d d d

1.Did you ev - er hear tell of sweet Bet - sy from Pike,

d   d m s   d' d' d'   t s s s

who crossed the wide prai - rie with her lo - ver Ike.

s   d' d' d'   t' s m m   f s l s

With two yoke of cat - tle and an old spot - ted hog,

d r   m m m s f r r   r d d d

a_____ tall Shang - hai roos - ter and an old yal - low dog.

Refrain:

d r   m m m s f r r   r d d d

Hood - le dang fol - di - da - yo, hood - le dang fol - di - day.

2. One evening quite early they camped on the Platte,
   Made down their blankets on a green shady flat;
   Where Betsy, quite tired, lay down to repose,
   While with wonder Ike gazed on his Pike County road.
   Refrain

3. They swam the wide rivers and crossed the tall peaks,
   And camped on the prairie for weeks upon weeks.
   Starvation and cholera and hard work and slaughter,
   They reached California spite of hell and high water.
   Refrain

4. Out on the prairie one bright starry night,
   They broke out the whisky and Betsy got tight;
   She sang and she shouted and danced o'er the plain;
   And made a great show for the whole wagon train.
   Refrain

5. The Indians came down in a wild yelling horde,
   And Betsy was steered they would scalp her adored;
   Behind the front wagon wheel Betsy did crawl;
   And fought off the Indians with musket and ball.
   Refrain

6. They soon reached the desert, where Betsy gave out,
   And down in the sand she lay rolling about;
   While Ike in great terror looked on in surprise,
   Saying, "Get up, now, Betsy, you'll get sand in your eyes."
   Refrain

7. The wagon tipped over with a terrible crash,
   And out on the prairie rolled all sort of trash.
   A few little baby clothes done up with care
   Looked rather suspicious - though 'twas all on the square.
   Refrain

8. The Shanghai ran off and the cattle all died,
   The last piece of bacon that morning was fried;
   Poor Ike got discouraged, and Betsy got mad,
   The dog wagged his tail and looked wonderfully sad.
   Refrain

9. One morning they climbed up a very high hill,
   And with wonder looked down into old Placerville;
   Ike shouted and said, as he cast his eyes down,
   "Sweet Betsy, my darling, we've got to Hangtown."
   Refrain

10. Long Ike and sweet Betsy attended a dance,
    Where Ike wore a pair of his Pike County pants;
    Sweet Betsy was covered with ribbons and rings.
    Said Ike, "You're an angel, but where are your wings?"
    Refrain

Source: Peter Erdei (1974). 150 American Folk Songs to Sing Read and Play. Boosey & Hawkes. pg. 93

Banuwa

Liberia

d, f, s,   d r Ⓜ f s l t d' r' m' s'

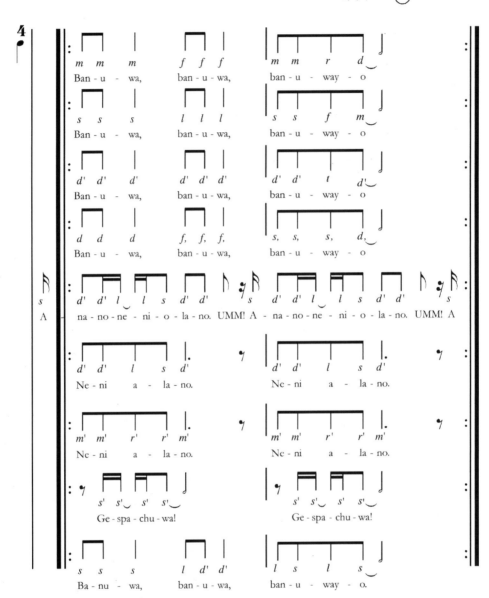

Actions: Divide the group into nine sections. Each group sings one line. Group 1 sings the first line twice before adding the other groups in turn. Each group continues to sing only one line until the song builds to a crescendo of sound. Children can improvise or compose other parts. When the song reaches a climax, each group falls silent, starting with the last group.

Source: Celia Waterhouse, ed. (2007). How Can I Keep From Singing!: Songs and Musical Activities From Around the World for 8-13 Year Olds. London, UK: British Kodály Academy. pg. 71

Dona Nobis Pacem

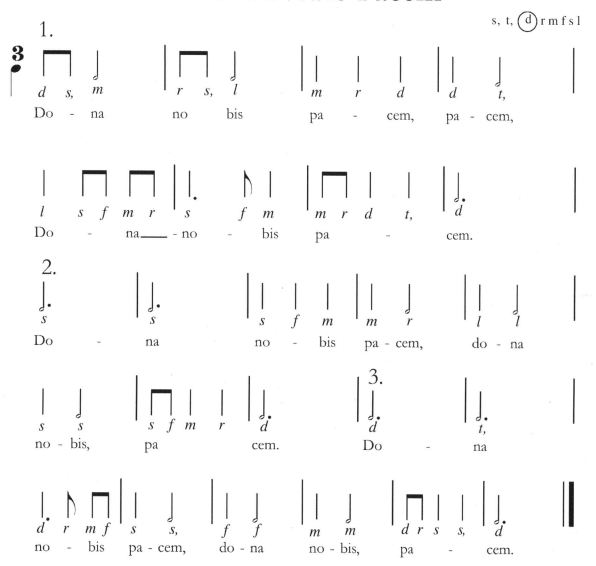

"Give us peace."

Source: Johnston (1996). 150 Rounds for Singing and Teaching. Milwaukee, WI: Boosey & Hawkes. pg. 14

My Paddle (The Canoe Song)

Words and music by Margaret McGee, 1918

m, l, d r (m) l

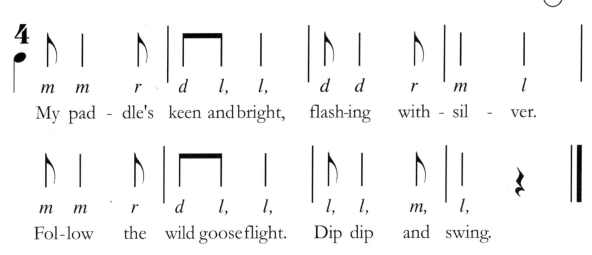

m m r d l, l, | *d d r m l*

My pad - dle's keen and bright, flash-ing with - sil - ver.

m m r d l, l, | *l, l, m, l,*

Fol-low the wild goose flight. Dip dip and swing.

Source: Johnston (1996). 150 Rounds for Singing and Teaching. Milwaukee, WI: Boosey & Hawkes. pg. 38

Senua de Dende

Ghanian folk song

d r m f (s) l t d'

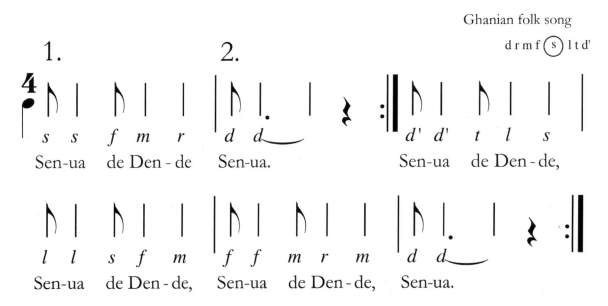

1. 2.

s s f m r d d | *d' d' t l s*

Sen-ua de Den - de Sen-ua. Sen-ua de Den - de,

l l s f m f f m r m d d

Sen-ua de Den - de, Sen-ua de Den - de, Sen-ua.

Source: Celia Waterhouse, ed. (2007). How Can I Keep From Singing!: Songs and Musical Activities From Around the World for 8-13 Year Olds. London, UK: British Kodály Academy. pg. 17

Si Si Si

Congalese folk song

d r m f (s) l t d'

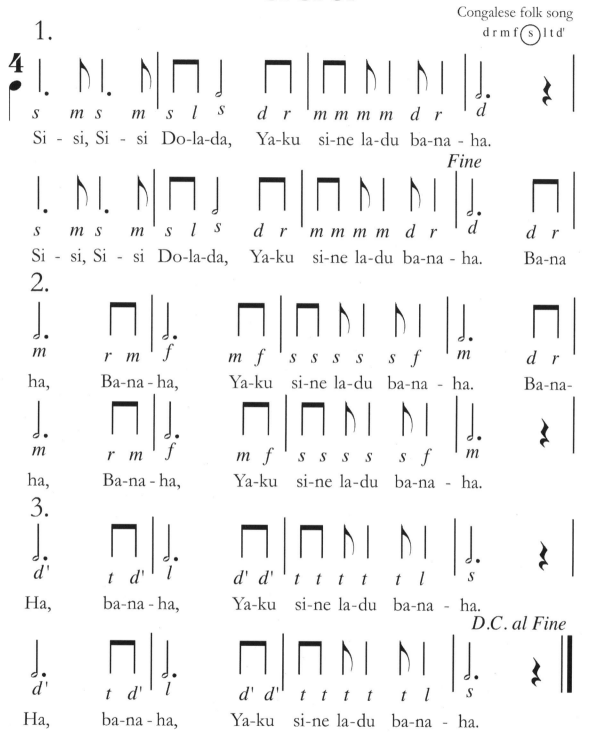

1.

s m s m s l s d r m m m m d r d

Si - si, Si - si Do-la-da, Ya-ku si-ne la-du ba-na - ha.

Fine

s m s m s l s d r m m m m d r d d r

Si - si, Si - si Do-la-da, Ya-ku si-ne la-du ba-na - ha. Ba-na

2.

m r m f m f s s s s f m d r

ha, Ba-na - ha, Ya-ku si-ne la-du ba-na - ha. Ba-na-

m r m f m f s s s s f m

ha, Ba-na - ha, Ya-ku si-ne la-du ba-na - ha.

3.

d' t d' l d' d' t t t t l s

Ha, ba-na - ha, Ya-ku si-ne la-du ba-na - ha.

D.C. al Fine

d' t d' l d' d' t t t t l s

Ha, ba-na - ha, Ya-ku si-ne la-du ba-na - ha.

Action: Divide the class into three groups and perform the song as follows: 1) Part 1, Part 2, Part 3, 2) Parts 1, 2, and 3 together, 4) Part 1.

Source: Celia Waterhouse, ed. (2007). How Can I Keep From Singing!: Songs and Musical Activities From Around the World for 8-13 Year Olds. London, UK: British Kodály Academy. pg. 69

Bluebird

American

d r m (s) l

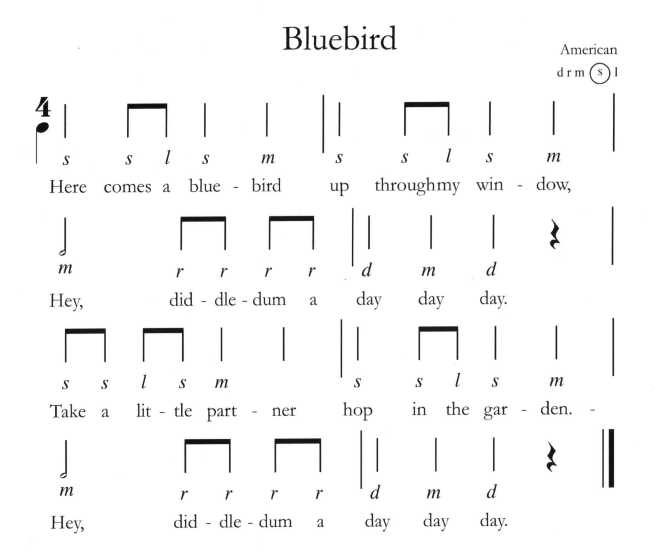

s   s   l   s   m   s   s   l   s   m

Here comes a blue - bird   up through my win - dow,

m   r   r   r   r   d   m   d

Hey,   did - dle - dum a day day day.

s   s   l   s   m   s   s   l   s   m

Take a lit - tle part - ner   hop in the gar - den. -

m   r   r   r   r   d   m   d

Hey,   did - dle - dum a day day day.

Action: Children stand with hands joined in a circle, facing the center, raising their arms up to make arches. One child walks in and under the arches. On "take a little partner" this child takes a partner and does one of the following:

1. With two hands joined, the partners face each other and gallop out though the opening where the child was taken from the ring and back again, the new child becoming the bluebird and the previous bluebird taking her place in the circle, or
2. The two partners gallop in the same way inside the circle, ending as in 1.
3. The two partners join one hand and weave in and out of the arches in the circle. At the end of the song, end as in 1.
4. The two partners join one hand and weave in and out of the arches in the circle. When the song ends, a third child is added and the three weave in and out of the arches and so on, until only two children remain to form an arch. On the last repetition, one of those two remaining children are chosen and the child who remains becomes the new bluebird.

Source: Peter Erdei (1974). 150 American Folk Songs to Sing Read and Play. Boosey & Hawkes. pg. 18

Bow Wow Wow

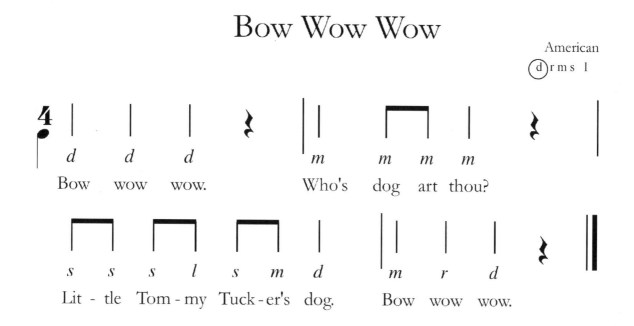

Action: Children stand in a circle facing partners and perform the following actions:

1. On the first line, stamp four times.
2. Second line, hit fist in palm once and point thumb back over shoulder three times.
3. Third line, take partner's hands and exchange places.
4. Fourth line, stamp four times while turning around to face a new partner.

Source: Forrai, K. (1998). *Music In Preschool* (J. Sinor, Trans. Second Revised and Expanded Edition ed.). Fitzgibbon, Australia: Clayfield School of Music. pg. 163

Charlie Over The Ocean

American
s, l, (d) r m

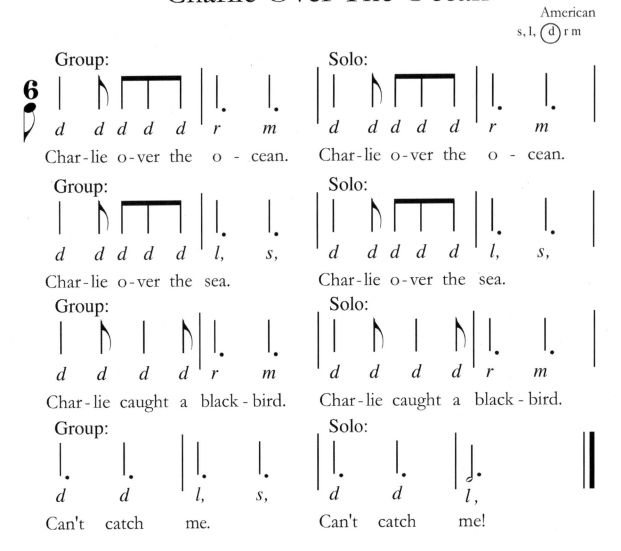

Action: One child, "Charlie," skips around the outside of the circle and echoes each phrase sung by the group. On the last word, "me," "Charlie" lightly touches a child in the circle, who then chases "Charlie" around the circle. The one who reaches the vacated spot becomes "safe," the other becomes "Charlie," and the game continues.

Source: Lois Choksy, D. B. (1987). 120 Singing Games and Dances for Elementary Schools. Englewood Cliffs, NJ: Prentice-Hall, Inc. pg. 60

Follow The Drinking Gourd

Afro-American

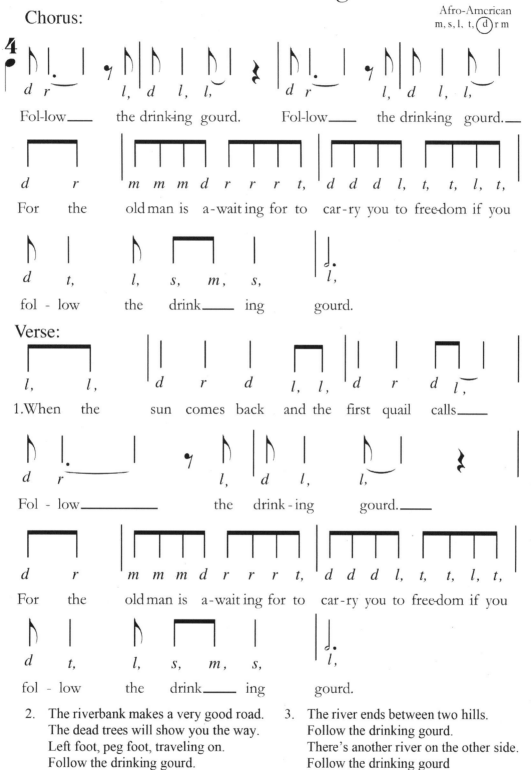

Chorus:

d r l, d l, l, d r l, d l, l,

Fol-low___ the drink-ing gourd. Fol-low___ the drink-ing gourd.___

d r m m m d r r r t, d d d l, t, t, l, t,

For the old man is a-wait-ing for to car-ry you to free-dom if you

d t, l, s, m, s, l,

fol - low the drink___ ing gourd.

Verse:

l, l, d r d l, l, d r d l,

1. When the sun comes back and the first quail calls___

d r l, d l, l,

Fol - low_____ the drink - ing gourd.___

d r m m m d r r r t, d d d l, t, t, l, t,

For the old man is a-wait-ing for to car-ry you to free-dom if you

d t, l, s, m, s, l,

fol - low the drink___ ing gourd.

2. The riverbank makes a very good road.
   The dead trees will show you the way.
   Left foot, peg foot, traveling on.
   Follow the drinking gourd.

3. The river ends between two hills.
   Follow the drinking gourd.
   There's another river on the other side.
   Follow the drinking gourd

4. When the great big river meets the little river.
   Follow the drinking gourd.
   For the old man is a-waiting for to carry you to freedom.
   Follow the drinking gourd.

Source: Becca Barlow, Bridlemile Elementary School, 2008

The Farmer In The Dell

American Game Song

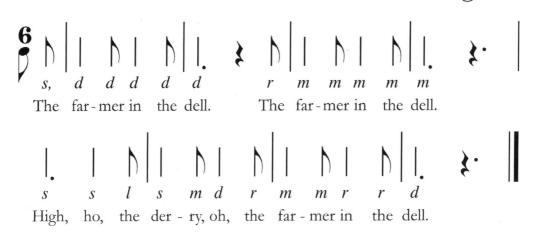

s, d d d d — r m m m m

The far-mer in the dell. The far-mer in the dell.

s s l s m d r m m r r d

High, ho, the der - ry, oh, the far-mer in the dell.

1. The farmer takes a spouse,
   The farmer takes a spouse,
   High, ho, the Derry O,
   The farmer takes a spouse.

2. The spouse takes the child, *etc.*

3. The child takes the nurse, etc.

4. The nurse takes the dog, etc.

5. The dog takes the cat, etc.

6. The cat takes the rat, etc.

7. The rat takes the cheese, etc.

8. The cheese stands alone, etc.

Action: The farmer stands in the center of the circle of children, who sing with hands joined and revolve around him. He slowly walks in the opposite direction of the revolving circle. When the song stops, all stop. The child in the circle next to whom the farmer is standing becomes the "spouse." That child joins the farmer in the center, standing behind him with hands resting gently on his shoulders.

On the second verse, the two walk around the center of the circle in the opposite direction of the moving circle. When the verse ends, the person in the circle standing opposite the spouse becomes the "child," etc. This continues until the "cheese" is chosen. At that point, the other children leave the cheese alone in the center and return to the circle. The "cheese" then becomes the next "farmer."

Alternatively, at the end of each verse each child could choose the next person to go in the center in turn. The farmer chooses a spouse, the spouse a child, and so on. With each verse, the chosen children walk slowly around the center of the circle as above.

Source: Peter Erdei (1974). 150 American Folk Songs to Sing Read and Play. Boosey & Hawkes. pg. 49

The Farmer's Dairy Key

Afro-American Game Song

(d) r m s l d'

2 (time signature)

d m s s l | s m d r | m s s l | s m

I lost the farm-er's dair-y key I'm in this la-dy's gar - den.

d' d' | s m d r | m s r m | d d

Do do let me out I'm in this la-dy's gar - den.

Action: GAME 1: Children form a circle with one child in the center. They walk around with joined hands singing until "Do, do, let me out," at which point, while still walking, they all clap or pat their knees just after the word "do" and on the words "me" and "I'm," joining hands immediately after clapping or patting. They keep hands joined again on "in this lady's garden." When the hands aren't joined, the child in the center takes the opportunity to escape the circle. If he succeeds, another child goes in the center. If he fails, the song begins again with him in the center until he succeeds.

GAME 2: Children stand in two concentric circles, each with joined hands. Two children holding old-fashioned keys stand in the center of the inner circle. The two children in the center close their eyes as the teacher secretly selects a pair of children in both circles to raise their joined hands up to form an arch when the song ends.

When the arches are established, the song begins. Both circles walk around the center children in opposite directions. When the song ends, the arches go up, and the two children in the center race, passing through the arches to get out of the formation. After they break out, the two racers hand their keys to two different children, who switch places with them as play begins again.

Source: Peter Erdei (1974). 150 American Folk Songs to Sing Read and Play. Boosey & Hawkes. pg. 42 and Susan Brumfield, Portland State University, 2007.

Green Grows The Willow Tree

Anglo-American singing game North Carolina, 1950s

s, d r m f s

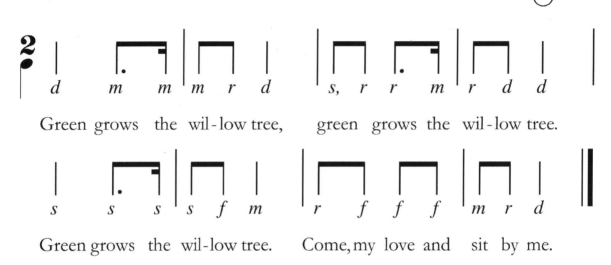

d m m m r d s, r r m r d d

Green grows the wil-low tree, green grows the wil-low tree.

s s s s f m r f f f m r d

Green grows the wil-low tree. Come, my love and sit by me.

2. On the banks the rushes grow (3 times)
   Kiss your love and let her (him) go.
   (Or: Shake his/her hand and let him/her go)

Action: The children stand scattered about the room with arms swaying like trees in a forest. A bench stands in the center of the room. One child wanders among the other children. At the end of verse 1, the child gently touches a "tree" and the two children walk to the bench and sit together for verse 2. At the end of verse 2, the pair on the bench kiss cheeks or shake hands and the first child leaves the bench to become a tree while the chosen partner wanders among the children and the game repeats.

You can tell an original story to go with the game that runs something like: *Once upon a time a very sad and lonely little child wandered in a dark forest of willow trees. One day, the child came upon an old woman, who said, "My child, you look sad and lonely. I will grant you a magic power. All you have to do is touch one of these trees and it will turn into a child. Then you will have a companion!" The child thanked the old woman, who went away laughing mischievously.*

To test out her new magic gift, the child went up and gently touched a tree. To her astonishment, the tree became a child! So, the two happy companions sat on a bench by the river and watched the water. What the old woman didn't tell the child was that with her new power came a curse. After touching a tree, the child herself would eventually become a tree! Sure enough, the child's skin grew hard, her arms turned into branches, and her hair sprouted leaves. She became a tree and joined the other trees of the forest. Without her, the new companion became sad and lonely. One day, while she wandered the forest, she also came upon an old woman…

Source: Locke, E. G. (1981). Sail Away: 155 American Folk Songs to Sing Read and Play. Boosey & Hawkes. pg. 81

Grizzly Bear

American
t, d r m f s

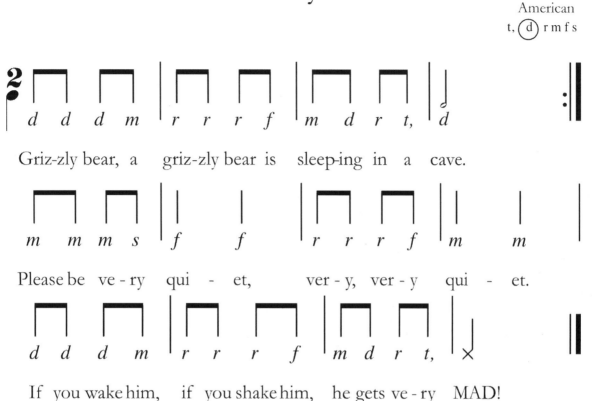

Griz-zly bear, a   griz-zly bear is   sleep-ing in   a   cave.

Please be ve - ry   qui – et,   ver - y, ver - y   qui – et.

If you wake him,   if you shake him,   he gets ve - ry   MAD!

Action: The children stand in a circle with joined hands facing the center, where there lies a child: the sleeping, ferocious "grizzly bear." The children sing the first line and its repetition very softly, creeping slowly around the grizzly bear, trying not to wake him. On the line "please be very quiet," the children sing even more quietly and sneak ever closer the grizzly bear, being careful not to touch him. Finally, the children sing the line "If you wake him…" gradually louder until the end of the song, when they shout, "Mad!" and run away from the grizzly bear, who wakes up snarling and tries to tag one of them. The tagged child becomes the new grizzly bear.

Source: Becca Barlow, Bridlemile Elementary School, 2008

Hold My Mule

Afro-American

(s,)l, d r m s l

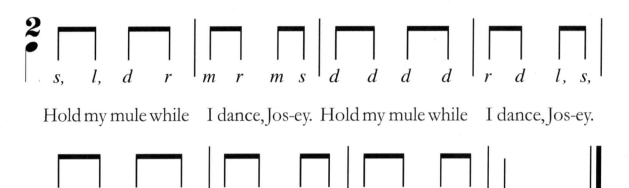

s,   l,   d   r | m   r   m   s | d   d   d   d | r   d   l,   s,

Hold my mule while   I dance, Jos-ey. Hold my mule while   I dance, Jos-ey.

d   d   d   r | m   r   m   s | l   s   m   r | d

Hold my mule while   I dance, Jos-ey. Oh, Miss Sus-an Brown.

2. Wouldn't give a nickel if I could dance, Josey. (3 times)
    Oh, Miss Susan Brown.

3. Had a glass of buttermilk and I danced, Josey. (3 times)
    Oh, Miss Susan Brown.

Action: Children stand in two concentric circles facing the center with hands joined. In the middle of the inner circle lies a fun object, such as a mule plush toy. Two children selected to be "racers" leave the room or hide their eyes. The teacher secretly designates one pair of children from each circle to raise their joined hands up to form an arch when the song ends. When the "racers" come back in the room, the song begins. While singing, the circles walk in opposite directions. When the song ends, the children stop and the arches go up. The two racers enter the formation through the arch in the outer circle and race to be the first to get the plush toy in the middle. The winner is congratulated and the two racers pick new children to be the racers.

Source: Song: Peter Erdei (1974). 150 American Folk Songs to Sing Read and Play. Boosey & Hawkes. pg. 52. Game: Susan Brumfield, Portland State University, 2007

John Kanaka

Clipper ship shantey

s,   d r (m) s l d'

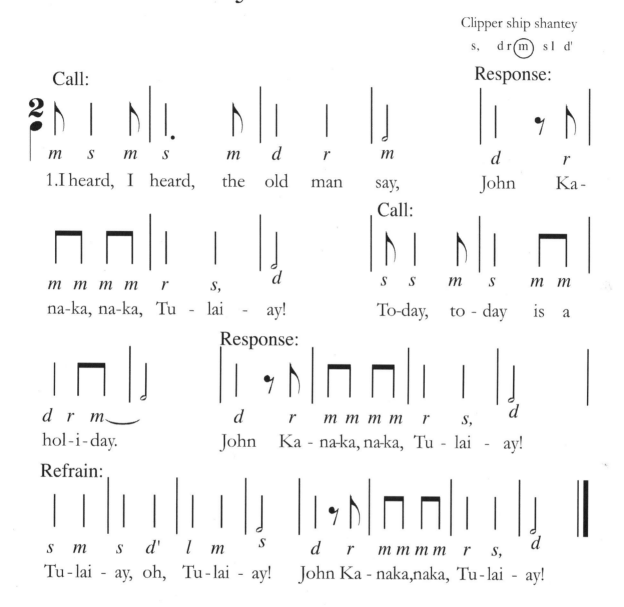

Call:

m   s   m   s   m   d   r   m

1. I heard, I heard,   the   old   man   say,   John   Ka-

Response:

d   r

m   m   m   m   r   s,   d

na-ka, na-ka, Tu - lai - ay!

Call:

s   s   m   s   m   m

To-day,   to - day   is   a

d   r   m

hol-i-day.

Response:

d   r   m m m m   r   s,   d

John   Ka - na-ka, na-ka, Tu - lai - ay!

Refrain:

s   m   s   d'   l   m   s   d   r   m m m m   r   s,   d

Tu-lai - ay, oh, Tu-lai - ay!   John Ka - naka, naka, Tu-lai - ay!

2.   We'll work tomorrer, but no work today,
     John Kanaka, naka, Tulai-ay!
     We'll work tomorrer, but no work today,
     John Kanaka, naka, Tulai-ay!
     Refrain

3.   We're bound away for 'Frisco Bay, etc.
     We're bound away at the break of day.

4.   We're bound away around Cape Horn,
     We wish to Christ we'd never been born.

5. A Yankee ship with a Yankee crew,
   Oh, we're the bucks for to push 'er through.

6. Oh, haul away, oh, haul away!
   Oh, haul away, an' make your pay.

Action: The children stand in two concentric circles facing each other, inner circle partnered with outer circle. During each response section, the children make the following movements:
1. On the word "John" the children stamp one foot.
2. On "Kanakanaka" they pat one hand on each knee, as in: *Ka* (right), *na* (left), *ka* (right), *na* (left), *ka* (right).
3. On "Tulaiay" they clap hands across with their partner, as in: *Tu* (clap partner's hands), *lai* (clap own hands), *ay* (clap partner's hands).

On the final verse, each child in the inner circle takes one step to the left and each child in the outer circle takes one step to the right with the result that each child gets a new partner for the next round.

Source: Locke, E. G. (1981). Sail Away: 155 American Folk Songs to Sing Read and Play. Boosey & Hawkes. pg. 39 Game: Susan Brumfield, Portland State University, 2008

Just From The Kitchen

American
s, l, ⓓ r m

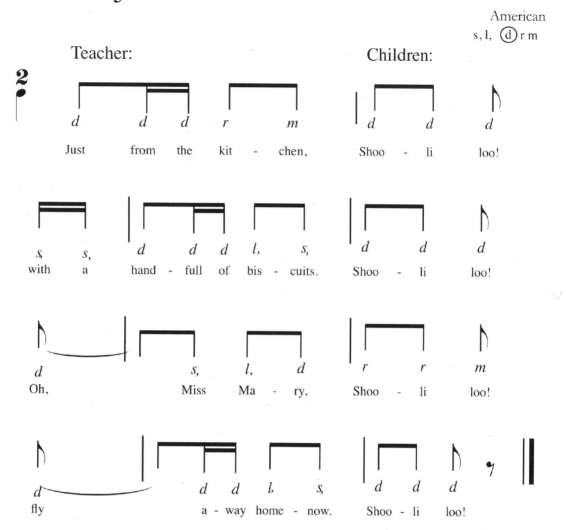

Action: The children sit on the floor in a circle, leaving one empty place. On "Oh, Miss ____,"
the named player "flies over" to the empty place. Play repeats without pause.

Source: Georgia Sea Island variant of a traditional African-American children's singing game.
Locke, E. G. (1981). *Sail Away: 155 American Folk Songs to Sing Read and Play*. Boosey &
Hawkes. pg. 26

Let Us Chase The Squirrel

American

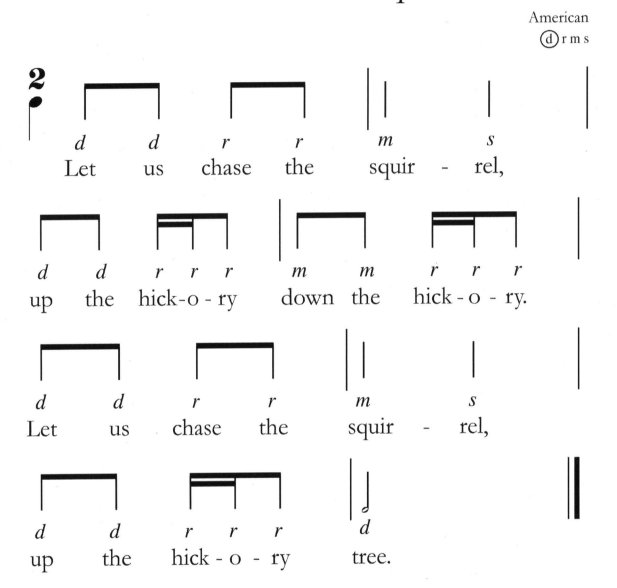

d   d   r   r   m   s
Let us chase the squir - rel,

d   d   r r r   m   m   r   r   r
up   the hick-o - ry down the hick - o - ry.

d   d   r   r   m   s
Let   us   chase   the   squir - rel,

d   d   r r r   d
up   the hick - o - ry   tree.

Action: GAME 1: The children stand in a scattered formation of "trees" (two children standing facing each other with hands joined in front of them) with a "squirrel" inside each tree. One leftover squirrel stands outside of the trees. Everyone sings the song. When the song is over, the "trees" raise their joined hands and the squirrels switch trees, the extra squirrel also trying to find a tree. When everyone has found a tree, one squirrel will be standing without a tree.

GAME 2: A circle of "trees" and "squirrels" with some left over squirrels in the center. At the beginning of the song, all of the squirrels leave their trees and move around the outside of the circle while the squirrels in the middle stay still. At the end of the song, all squirrels, even those in the middle, find safety in a tree. Those left without trees go into the center of the circle.

Source: Kelly Foster Griffin, SWOKE Workshop, October 2007

Little Johnny Brown

Afro-American

s, l, (d) r m f s

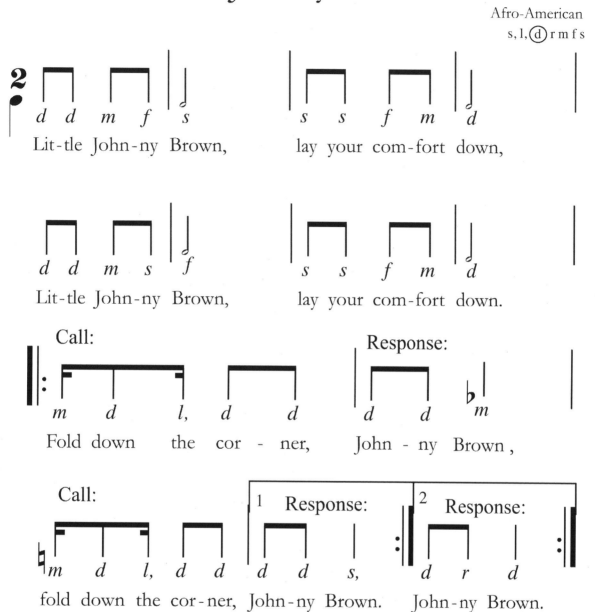

Action: Players stand in a circle facing the center, clapping: with one player in the center.

Group and Lead Voices Sing, slowly:
Little Johnny Brown, Lay your comfort down, etc.

Action:
Center player dances in the middle of the ring holding a small blanket, spreads the blanket in the center by the end of the second phrase.

Lead Voice (faster tempo):	Group :	Action:
1. Fold down the corner	Johnny Brown	Johnny Brown in the center follows the
2. Fold another corner	Johnny Brown	directions of the text.
3. Fold another corner	Johnny Brown	
4. Fold another corner	Johnny Brown	
5. Take it to your lover (2x)	Johnny Brown	Johnny Brown dances over to a partner.
6. Show her/him your motion (2x)	Johnny Brown	Johnny Brown improvises a motion.
7. We can do the motion (2x)	Johnny Brown	All imitate Johnny Brown's motion.
8. Lope like a buzzard (2x)	Johnny Brown	All imitate as J.B. lopes like a buzzard.
9. Give it to your lover (2x)	Johnny Brown	Johnny Brown hands blanket to partner.

Play continues without pause, with chosen partner becoming Johnny Brown in the center.

Variations:

Substitute the name of the player in the center for Johnny Brown, i.e., "Little Julie Brown", "Little Manuel Brown", etc.

Source: Bessie Jones, et al. (1972). Step it Down: Games, Plays, Songs, and Stories from the Afro-American Heritage. Harper & Rowe. pp. 92-94

My Mama's Calling Me

American
d r m s l (d')

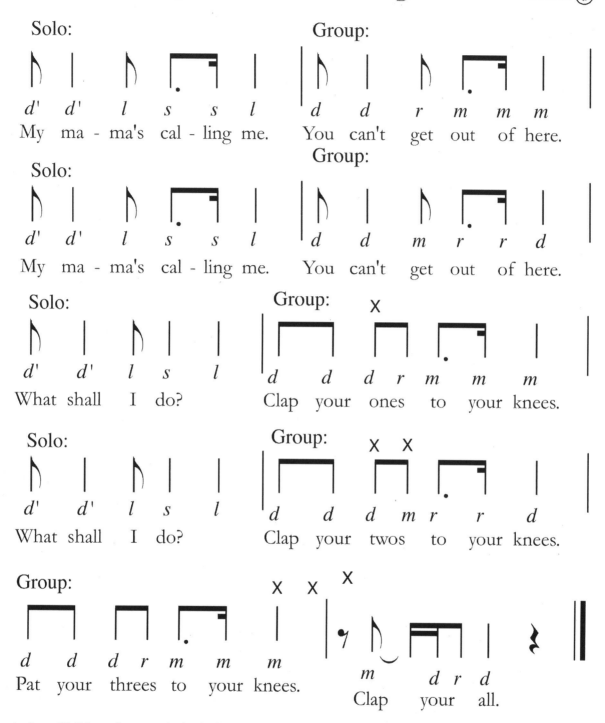

Action: Children form a circle facing center with joined hands. One child in the middle tries to break out of the circle when the other children let go of hands briefly. The only possible moments to break out are when the children pat their knees once, twice, and finally three times (indicated in the music by an X).

Source: Kelly Foster Griffin, SWOKE Workshop, 2007

Oats and Beans and Barley

American
d r ⓜ f s

Oats and beans and bar - ley grow. Oats and beans and

bar - ley grow. Do you or I or

any-one know how oats and beas and bar - ley grow?

2. First the farmer sows his (her) seed
   Then he (she) stands and takes his (her) ease
   Stamps his (her) foot and claps his (her) hands
   And turns around to view the land.

3. Waiting for a partner
   Waiting for a partner
   Break the ring and choose on in
   While all the others dance and sing.

4. Tra la la la la la la,
   etc.

Action: A standing circle of children facing center with joined hands walks to the left while singing the first stanza. On the second stanza, the farmer acts out the motions indicated by the words, with the circle standing and imitating his movements. On the third stanza, the circle moves left again while the farmer chooses a partner. On the fourth stanza, while the circle moves to the left, the farmer and his partner promenade to the right inside the circle. The farmer joins the circle and the partner becomes the farmer as the game is repeated.

Source: Peter Erdei, K. K. (1974). 150 American Folk Songs to Sing Read and Play. Boosey & Hawkes. pg. 68

The Old Gray Cat

American
(s,) l, t, d m

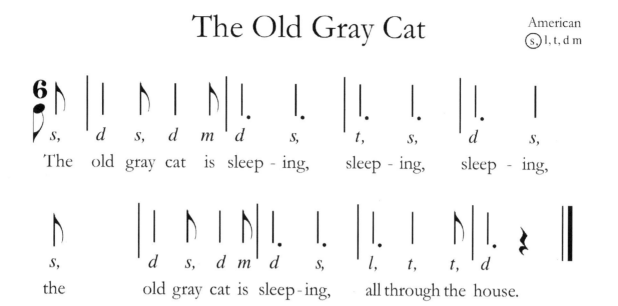

s,   d   s,   d   m   d   s,   t,   s,   d   s,

The old gray cat is sleep-ing,   sleep-ing,   sleep-ing,

s,   d   s,   d   m   d   s,   l,   t,   t,   d

the   old gray cat is sleep-ing,   all through the house.

The little mice are creeping
Creeping, creeping,
The little mice are creeping
All through the house.

Action: One child, "the old gray cat," lies sleeping in the middle of the play area. The other children, pretending to be little mice, find hiding spots. On the first stanza, all the mice sing softly as the cat sleeps. On the second stanza, the mice slowly and quietly creep out of their hiding places toward the sleeping cat without touching or disturbing her. When the second stanza ends, the cat wakes up and tries to tag a mouse as the mice scamper back to their hiding spots. The mouse who gets tagged becomes the new cat.

Source: Susan Brumfield, Portland State University, 2007

Pizza Pizza, Daddy-O

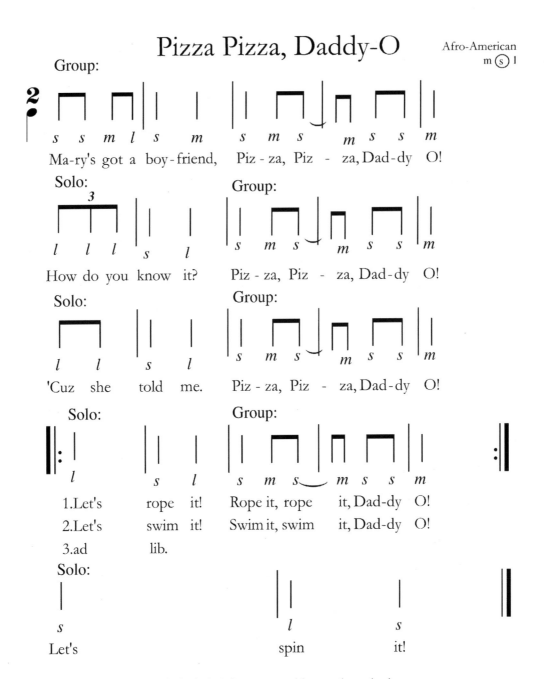

Group:

s s m l s m | s m s m s s m

Ma-ry's got a boy-friend, Piz-za, Piz-za, Dad-dy O!

Solo:

l l l s l

How do you know it?

Group:

s m s m s s m

Piz-za, Piz-za, Dad-dy O!

Solo:

l l s l

'Cuz she told me.

Group:

s m s m s s m

Piz-za, Piz-za, Dad-dy O!

Solo:

l s l

1. Let's rope it!
2. Let's swim it!
3. ad lib.

Group:

s m s m s s m

Rope it, rope it, Dad-dy O!
Swim it, swim it, Dad-dy O!

Solo:

s l s

Let's spin it!

Action: Children stand in a circle facing the center, with one player in the center.
All begin song, substituting "Mary" for the name of player in center. On "piz-za, piz-za" all players do the following foot pattern:

On "piz" jump, landing with feet apart
On "za" jump, landing with right foot crossed over left
On "piz" jump, landing with feet apart
On "za" jump, landing with left foot crossed over right
On "daddy" jump, landing with feet apart
On "o" land, with feet together.

The center player then initiates as many actions as he or she is willing or able to invent, deciding when to stop by singing "Let's spin it;" closing his or her eyes and turning in a circle, pointing with index finger and extended arm, choosing the next player. Play continues without pause.

Source: Locke, E. G. (1981). *Sail Away: 155 American Folk Songs to Sing Read and Play*. Boosey & Hawkes. pg. 6

Riding On The Railway

American

d r (m) s l

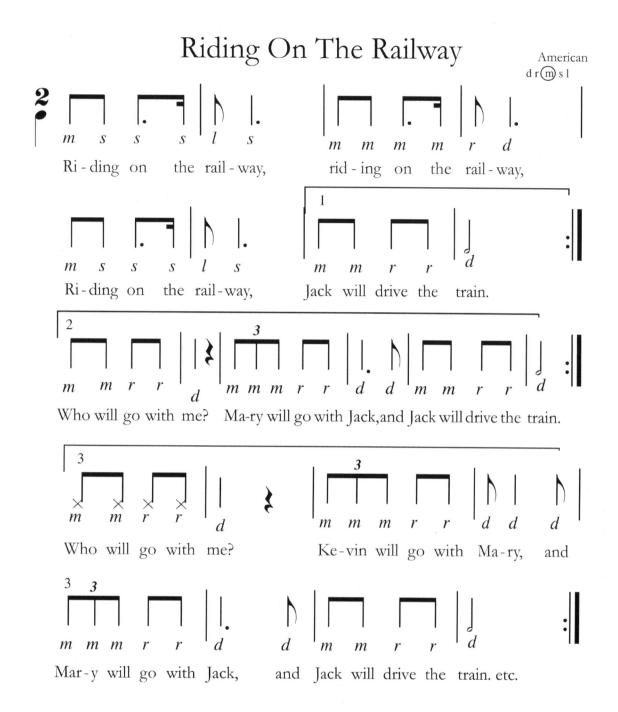

Ri-ding on the rail-way, rid-ing on the rail-way,

Ri-ding on the rail-way, Jack will drive the train.

Who will go with me? Ma-ry will go with Jack, and Jack will drive the train.

Who will go with me? Ke-vin will go with Ma-ry, and

Mar-y will go with Jack, and Jack will drive the train. etc.

Action: The children sit in a circle with one child in the center, for this example, his name is Jack. As the children sing and clap a steady beat, Jack walks around the inside of the circle, stopping at "Jack will drive the train." The child in front of whom Jack ends up standing, Mary in this example, steps behind Jack, placing her hands gently on his waist or shoulders. The two stand together as the children sing "Mary will go with Jack and Jack will drive the train." On, "Riding on the railway," the two children walk around the inside of the circle until "Who will go with me?" at which point they stop. The child in front of whom Mary is standing, in this case Kevin, stands behind Mary and the three children stand through the next line until "Jack will drive the train." The game repeats, adding one child at a time until all the children are in a big line moving through the play area.

Source: Susan Brumfield, Portland State University, 2007

Sailor, Sailor

American
d r Ⓜ f

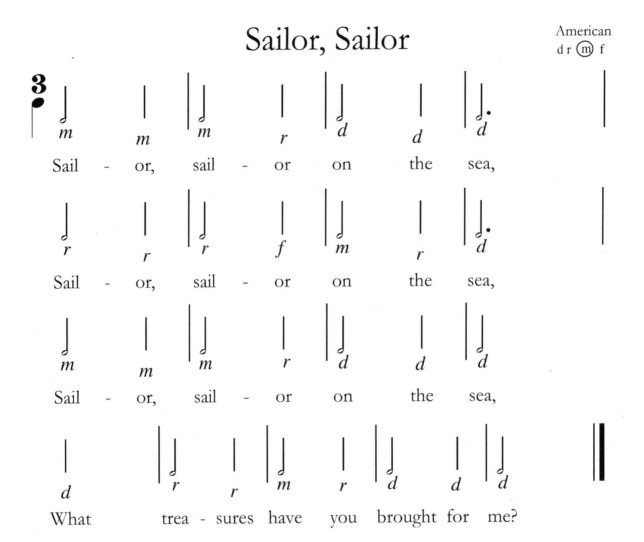

3

m   m   m   r   d   d   d.

Sail - or, sail - or on the sea,

r   r   r   f   m   r   d.

Sail - or, sail - or on the sea,

m   m   m   r   d   d   d

Sail - or, sail - or on the sea,

d   r   r   m   r   d   d   d

What trea - sures have you brought for me?

Farmer, farmer on the land, etc.
I've gold and jewels in my hand.

Action: Children pretending to be islands sit cross-legged in separate places all around the play area. One child, the "sailing ship," has a mystery number of coins, jewels, or other treasure enclosed in his hands. While everyone sings the first stanza in a soft, slow tempo, the ship drifts slowly around the play area, coming to a stop in front of an island as the stanza ends. The sailing ship sings stanza two alone to the child on the island, who then guesses how many of the objects are in the sailor's hand. If the island guesses incorrectly, the song begins again and the sailing ship moves on. If the island guesses correctly, the two switch places and the island becomes the new sailing ship.

Source: Ida Erdei, et al. (2002). *My Singing Bird: 150 Folk Songs from the Anglo-American, African-American, English, Scottish, and Irish Traditions.* The Kodály Center of America, Inc. pg. 2 Game by Susan Brumfield, Portland State University, 2007

Shoorah

Afro-American

d r (m) s

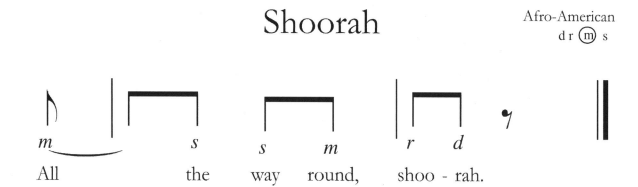

m _____ s   s   m   r   d

All   the   way round, shoo - rah.

2. Pick your lover, shoorah.

3. Face to face, shoorah.

4. Back to back, shoorah.

5. Side to side, shoorah.

6. Now pat your lover, shoorah.

Action: Children stand in a circle with one child in the center. The action follows the text. The center player walks around the inside of the circle on verse one. On verse two, she stands before her chosen partner. On verse three, she greets her partner with a bow or a handshake. On verse four, the two partners bump backsides. On verse five, they turn side to side and bump hips. On verse six, the child in the middle taps her partner gently on the shoulders with both hands. At the end of the song, both children walk around the middle of the circle choosing partners, and so on, until everyone has had a turn.

Source: Locke, E. G. (1981). Sail Away: 155 American Folk Songs to Sing Read and Play. Boosey & Hawkes. pg. 13

Song Of The Snowflakes

Mono Tribe
North Fork, CA

l, d r m (s)

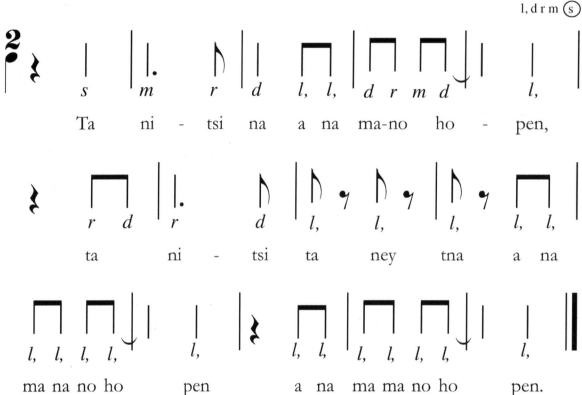

Actions: The children walk in a circle. A small group of them sing the last three measures as an ostinato. During the first line, the children raise their arms up. During the second line they gently lower their arms, mimicking the motion of falling snow.

Source: Locke, E. G. (1981). Sail Away: 155 American Folk Songs to Sing Read and Play. Boosey & Hawkes. From Molly Pomona, a basket weaver of the Mono Tribe, North Fork, CA, recorded by Albert Pietroforte on July 7, 1959. Movements by Kelly Foster Griffin, SWOKE Workshop, 2008.

That's A Mighty Pretty Motion

Afro-American

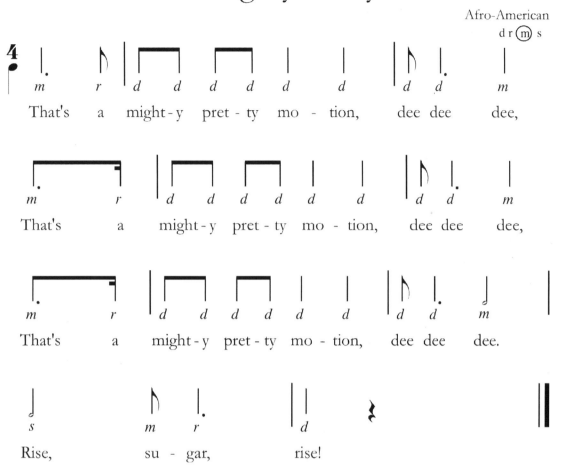

That's a might-y pret-ty mo - tion, dee dee dee,

That's a might-y pret-ty mo - tion, dee dee dee,

That's a might-y pret-ty mo - tion, dee dee dee.

Rise, su - gar, rise!

Action: The children stand in a large circle facing one child in the center. At the beginning of the song, the child in the center makes any motion she likes, usually some kind of dance step in rhythm to the music, while the other children clap vociferously on the first and third beats. On "rise, sugar, rise," the child in the center selects another child from the circle to trade places with her, and that new child goes into the center to make a motion, etc.

Source: Peter Erdei, K. K. (1974). 150 American Folk Songs to Sing Read and Play. Boosey & Hawkes. pg. 9

Turn The Glasses Over

Anglo-American
s, l, (d) r m s l

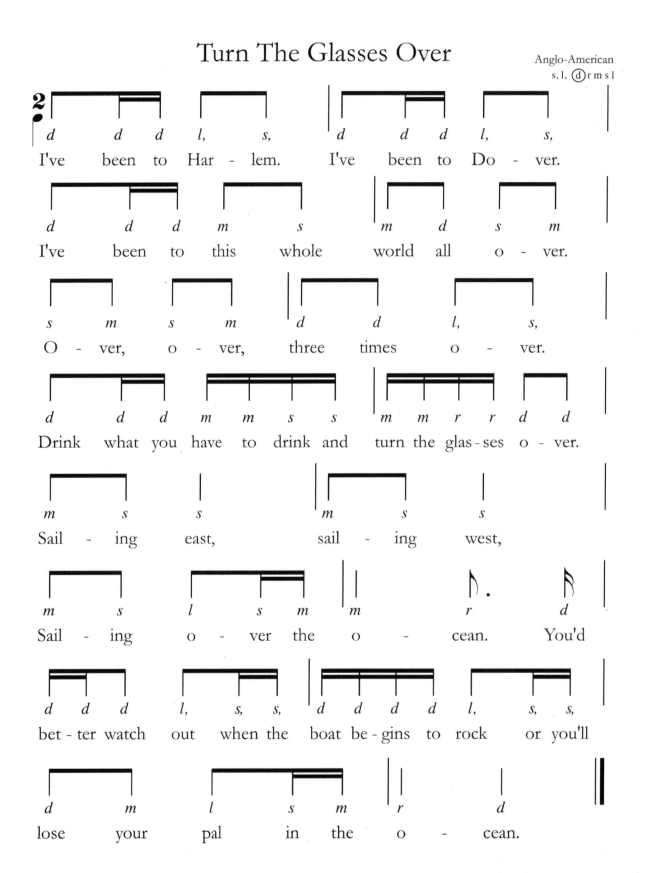

d d d l, s,
I've been to Har - lem.

d d d l, s,
I've been to Do - ver.

d d d m s
I've been to this whole

m d s m
world all o - ver.

s m s m
O - ver, o - ver,

d d l, s,
three times o - ver.

d d d m m s s
Drink what you have to drink and

m m r r d d
turn the glas - ses o - ver.

m s s
Sail - ing east,

m s s
sail - ing west,

m s
Sail - ing

l s m m
o - ver the o -

r d
cean. You'd

d d d l, s, s,
bet - ter watch out when the

d d d d l, s, s,
boat be - gins to rock or you'll

d m
lose your

l s m
pal in the

r d
o - cean.

Action: GAME 1: The children form a circle holding cross-hands facing clockwise in promenade position. On the first and second lines, the children promenade in a clockwise direction for eight beats. On the third line, the children face their partner holding hands and swing their arms right round overhead. On the fourth line they mime drinking from a glass and turning the glass over. On the fifth through the eighth lines, each child turns to the right and walks (in the opposite direction of their partner, passing by the left shoulder) around the edge of their own circle, to find a new partner ready to start the song again.

GAME 2: This song can also be played as an object passing game. Players sit in a circle. Each player has a pencil, stick, rock, or any small object they might find that can be passed. With the strong beats of the song, each player places his object in front of the player to his right and lets go. On the weak beats, he picks up the object that has been placed in front of him by his neighbor to the left.

Source: Celia Waterhouse (2007). How Can I Keep From Singing!: Songs and Musical Activities From Around the World for 8-13 Year Olds. London, UK: British Kodály Academy. pg. 61

Amasee

Afro-American

s, l, d r ⓜ

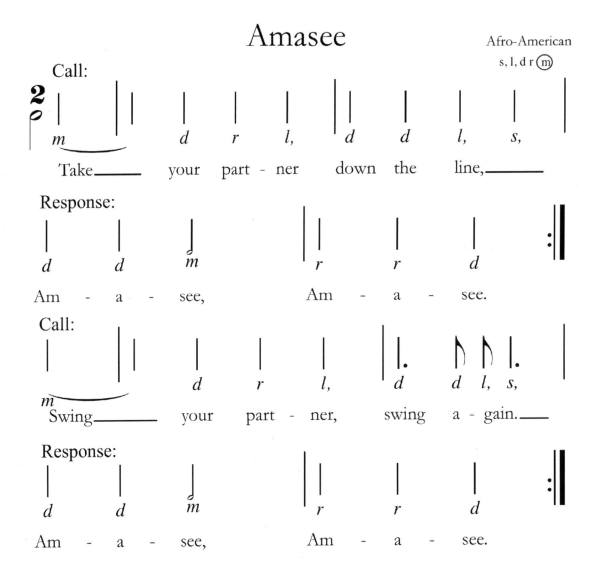

Call:

m ___   d   r   l,   d   d   l,   s,

Take ___ your part - ner down the line, ___

Response:

d   d   m   r   r   d

Am - a - see,   Am - a - see.

Call:

d   r   l,   d   d l, s,

m ___ Swing ___ your part - ner, swing a - gain. ___

Response:

d   d   m   r   r   d

Am - a - see,   Am - a - see.

Action: The children form two parallel lines, called a "set," with an alley in between and partners facing each other. A leader may be chosen to sing the call, with the group coming in on the words "Amasee." The two children at the front of the set are the "head couple."

On verse one, the head couple takes hands and sashays down the set between the lines. On verse two, this couple swings right elbows and takes their place at the bottom of the set. The dance begins again with the new head couple. Each time the set shifts a little as the head couple repeats the above dance steps and joins the bottom of the set. All the children keep a steady hand-clap throughout.

Source: Locke, E. G. (1981). Sail Away: 155 American Folk Songs to Sing Read and Play. Boosey & Hawkes. pg. 23

Great Big House In New Orleans

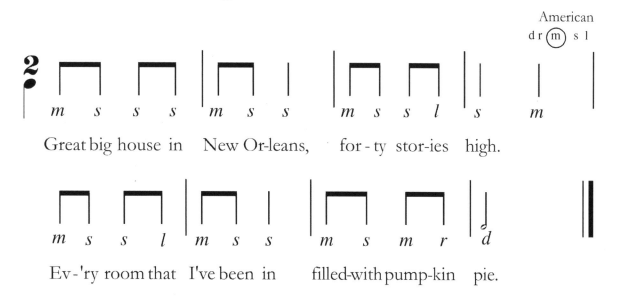

American

d r (m) s l

Great big house in New Or-leans, for-ty stor-ies high.

Ev-'ry room that I've been in filled-with pump-kin pie.

Action: Children form a circle of partners, girls on the right. You may separate the children by "boy" and "girl," "ones" and "twos," or "*As*" and "*Bs*." For this example, we'll use As and Bs. The dance steps proceed as follows:

1. With a strutting step and swinging arms, the children sing and move in a clockwise direction.
2. On "went down to the old mill stream," *Bs* take four small steps toward the center of the circle and join hands.
3. On "fetch a pail of water," *As* move toward the center and reach both arms across between two *Bs*, and down toward the floor as if to pick up a pail of water, then,
4. *As* join hands in the center at the end of the "picking up" gesture and swing arms (on "put one arm") over the heads of the *Bs*, making a circle behind their backs at waist level.
5. On "the other round my daughter" *Bs* raise their joined hands back over the *As* heads and make a circle behind their waists.
6. All the children sing verse three in this position while gently slide-stepping around in a circle clockwise. On the third "fair thee well" *Bs* raise their ams back over the heads of the *As*, freeing all the dancers, and on the fourth phrase "with the golden slippers" the *As* move along one position to be ready to start the next round with a new partner.

Source: Locke, E. G. (1981). Sail Away: 155 American Folk Songs to Sing Read and Play. Boosey & Hawkes. pg. 17

Here Comes Sally

American
s, t, ⓓ r m f s

d d d d | m s m d | r r r r | t, r t, s,

Hands on shoul-ders prom-en-ade,   hands on shoul-ders prom-en-ade,

d d d d | m s m d | s f m r | d d

Hands on shoul-ders prom-en-ade,   down in North Car' - lin - a.

1. Here comes Sally down the alley
    Here comes Sally down the alley,
    Here comes Sally down the alley,
    Down in North Car'lina.

Action: The children form a double circle of partners with an extra child in the middle. On the first verse, the pairs promenade in a circle either in promenade position or by putting their arms around each other's shoulders. On "Car'lina," the partners separate and face each other, raising their joined hands above their heads to create an "alley" covered by arches. The player in the middle moves through the arches. Substitute the name "Sally" for the name of the child in the middle. You can also play with multiple children in the middle to allow for more turns and less repetition.

Source: Kelly Foster Griffin SWOKE Workshop 10/12/07

Lead Through That Sugar And Tea

American
s, l, d r (m) s

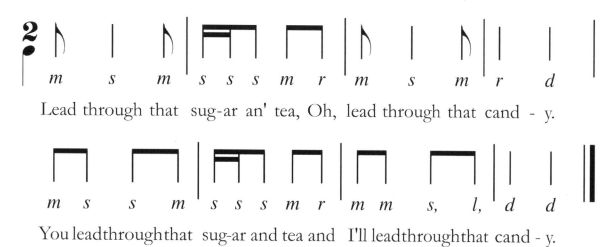

m   s   m   s   s   s   m   r   m   s   m   r   d

Lead through that sug-ar an' tea, Oh, lead through that cand - y.

m   s   s   m   s   s   s   m   r   m   m   s,   l,   d   d

You leadthroughthat sug-ar and tea and I'll leadthroughthat cand - y.

You swing that sugar an' tea, Oh, you swing that candy.
We'll all swing our sugar an' tea, an' we'll all swing that candy.

Action: The children form a lengthwise set (two straight lines) of partners facing each other with an alley in the middle. For this example, we'll partner boys and girls, but this isn't necessary. Regardless, we call the pair at the bottom of the set the "head couple." On phrase one of the first verse, the head couple walks up between the lines and on phrase two the boy swings the head girl, the girl swings the head boy, and they end up at the top of the set. On phrase one of the second verse the new head couple swing first right, then left elbows. On phrase two of the second verse all of the couples swing right, then left elbows. The dance repeats until each couple at the bottom of the set has had a chance to be the head couple.

Source: Locke, E. G. (1981). Sail Away: 155 American Folk Songs to Sing Read and Play. Boosey & Hawkes. pg. 32

Paw Paw Patch

American

s, t, (d) r m f s l

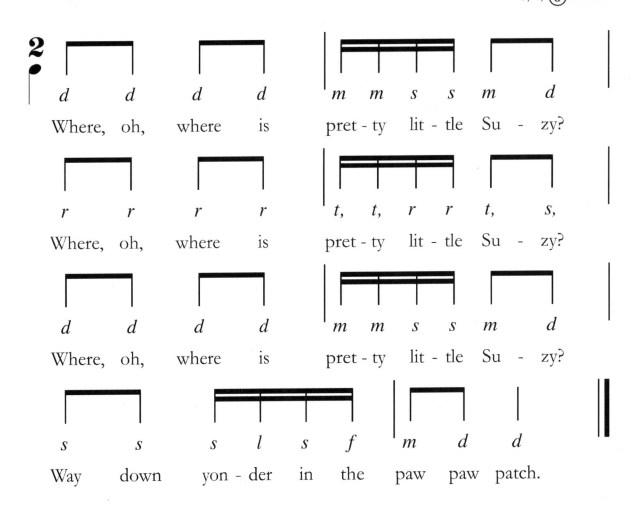

2. Come on boys, let's go find her, etc.
3. Pickin' up paw paws, puttin' 'em in your pockets, etc.

Action: The children from a set of two straight lines of partners with an alley in the middle. The "head girl" is at the bottom of the leftmost line of girls. On the first verse, the head girl walks alone counter-clockwise around the set and ends up back at her place. On the second verse, she walks counter-clockwise around the set again, the boys walking behind her in a single-file line, the head girl and the line of boys ending up back in their places. On the third verse, the head girl and head boy sashay up and down the set, ending up at the top of the set, leaving a new head girl. This continues for as long as everyone enjoys themselves.

Source: Peter Erdei, K. K. (1974). 150 American Folk Songs to Sing Read and Play. Boosey & Hawkes. pg. 102

Shake Them 'Simmons Down

Texas
(s.)l,   d r m

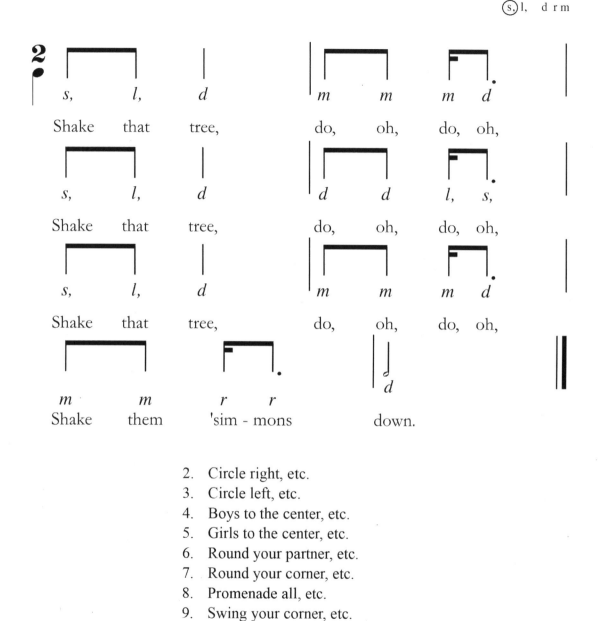

2. Circle right, etc.
3. Circle left, etc.
4. Boys to the center, etc.
5. Girls to the center, etc.
6. Round your partner, etc.
7. Round your corner, etc.
8. Promenade all, etc.
9. Swing your corner, etc.
10. Left foot in, etc.
11. Right foot in, etc.

Actions: The children form a circle. The child to each child's right is his "partner" and the child to each child's left is his "corner." Children clap and sing as they follow the words of the text. On each occurrence of "Shake them 'simmons down", the children all stand facing the center and mime shaking a tree (on "shake them 'simmons") and then lift their hands above their heads and bend forward at the waist, making a falling motion (on "down").

Source: Locke, E. G. (1981). Sail Away: 155 American Folk Songs to Sing Read and Play. Boosey & Hawkes. pg. 25

Shoo Roun'

Afro-American

s, l, d (m) f

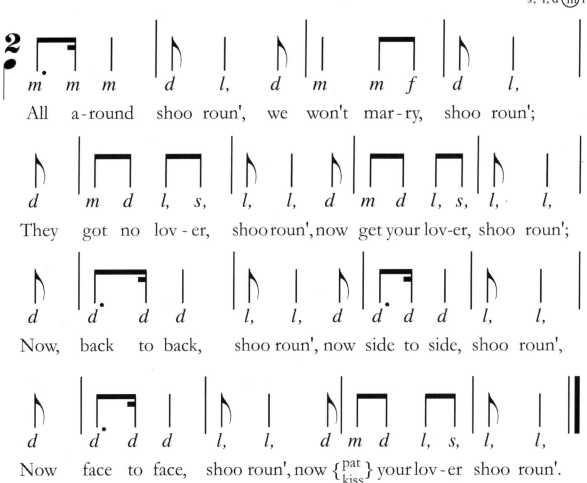

All a-round shoo roun', we won't mar-ry, shoo roun';

They got no lov-er, shoo roun', now get your lov-er, shoo roun';

Now, back to back, shoo roun', now side to side, shoo roun',

Now face to face, shoo roun', now { pat / kiss } your lov-er shoo roun'.

Action: A circle of children facing the center, with one child in the middle. As the song begins, the child in the center walks around the inside of the circle. On "now get your lover," she selects a partner by standing in front of him or her. On "back to back" the two partners bump backsides. On "side to side" they bump hips. On "face to face" they stand and shake hands. On "pat/kiss your lover" they tap each other's shoulders, kiss cheeks in the manner of the French greeting, or simply hug before swapping places, the child in the center taking her partner's place and the partner becoming the new child in the center.

Source: Locke, E. G. (1981). Sail Away: 155 American Folk Songs to Sing Read and Play. Boosey & Hawkes. pg. 54

Tideo

American
d r (m) s l d'

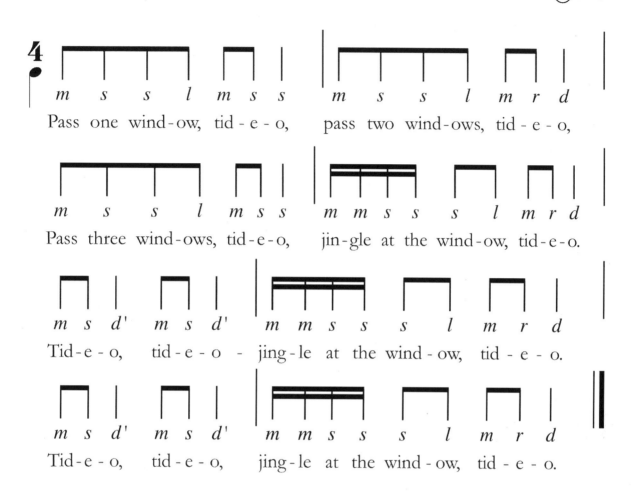

m   s   s   l   m   s   s   m   s   s   l   m   r   d

Pass one wind-ow, tid-e-o,   pass two wind-ows, tid-e-o,

m   s   s   l   m   s   s   m   m   s   s   s   l   m   r   d

Pass three wind-ows, tid-e-o,   jin-gle at the wind-ow, tid-e-o.

m   s   d'   m   s   d'   m   m   s   s   s   l   m   r   d

Tid-e-o,   tid-e-o - jing-le at the wind-ow, tid-e-o.

m   s   d'   m   s   d'   m   m   s   s   s   l   m   r   d

Tid-e-o,   tid-e-o,   jing-le at the wind-ow, tid-e-o.

Action: Children form a double circle with partners (children in the inside circle partnered with children in the outside circle). On the words "pass," each child moves to their right for a new partner. On the words "tideo," the children pat legs, clap hands, and then pat their partner's hands. On the first "jingle at the window," each pair "rings the dishrag." (Partners join hands high to make an arch, then turn themselves around in place, lowering their arms as necessary while still holding hands.) On the second and third "jingle at the window," partners join hands and trade places.

Source: Kelly Foster Griffin, SWOKE Workshop, 2007

Chapter 15

Cosmic Stories

After Miss Elisabeth's story about John Cage's famous piece *4'33"*, in which any number of musicians sit for four minutes and thirty-three seconds in total silence, the children wanted to follow up by performing the piece. It should be emphasized that a performance of *4'33"* requires the children to sit with their instruments for a little over four minutes *not making a sound*.

Miss Elisabeth and the children selected some percussion instruments from the classroom instrument basket. It struck Miss Elisabeth as funny to watch Jacob and Constantine argue over who got to "play" the sleigh bells.

Once each child finally settled on an instrument and became still, Miss Elisabeth started a timer. Expressions of deep concentration fogged over the children's faces as they focused all of their willpower on the task of not making any sound.

They found it enormously difficult. They giggled and wriggled. Miss Elisabeth had to restart the timer three times. In the end, the children carried off a successful performance. The other children in the class gave them high-fives and begged to be able to perform the piece themselves. ("How lovely the silence felt while it lasted," mused Miss Elisabeth.)

Think of Miss Elisabeth and her children whenever you consider the power of storytelling on the children's learning and motivation. Good stories excite and inspire. Not only that, but stories about music and musicians also form an important component of Maria Montessori's plan of Cosmic Education.

In a lecture given in 1976, Mario Montessori sums up his mother's plan. He said, "We believe that in the cosmos there is harmony; that everything there is in it, both the animate and inanimate, have collaborated in the creation of our globe, correlating in doing this, their single tasks. But we think that among the innumerable agents which participated in this creation man has had and has a very important task" (Montessori, 1976).

From this statement we can glean two important things. First, that everything that exists, from the tiniest molecule to the most complex organism, contributes to the universe's subsistence and is, therefore, interconnected. Second, that within that interconnectedness, human beings have a very special place. Perhaps, even, human beings have an even higher place than any other agent of creation in the universe. Mario says, "[Man] has detached himself from nature to create—with his work—something above it, a *supranatura*" (Montessori, 1976).

In sum, as a Montessori Guide, you further Maria Montessori's plan of Cosmic Education by telling Cosmic Stories, which are specially designed to make the child aware of the interconnectedness of all things and of the human being's special role in the shaping of not only the makeup of the universe but also its fate. I can think of no better subject than music for accomplishing these aims.

You can tell Cosmic Stories about:

- musical instruments;
- musical eras;
- music ensembles;
- musicians, such as composers, instrumentalists, conductors, rock and pop stars, jazz and blues musicians;
- pieces of music;
- the development of musical notation;
- musical theater; and
- the list goes on.

What's more, to highlight the point that music, in particular, constitutes a uniquely human achievement, a sublime result of human beings making use of their three gifts of the mind, the hand, and love, when you tell Cosmic Stories about musicians, you must select from the widest possible variety of ethnicities, nationalities, and cultural backgrounds. Human beings of all genders, from all times in history, too, should feature in your stories.

An attempt has been made in collecting these stories to get you started with a sample of some of the most interesting stories from Western music. You'll find represented here composers from many eras. They represent various nationalities, ethnicities, religions, and cultural backgrounds. I encourage you, when you go and research your own Cosmic Stories, to cast your net wide in search of composers and pieces of music from every tradition and from every corner of the Earth.

The stories collected here have been adapted specially to align with Maria Montessori's views on child development. The story about Olivier Messiaen in any other collection—say, Krull and Hewitt's excellent *Lives of the Musicians: Good Time, Bad Times, and What the Neighbors Thought* (New York: Houghton Mifflin, 1993)—contains lots of facts and funny anecdotes about the composer's life, but it lacks appeal to the child's developmental characteristics at the Second Plane, such as hero worship, love of cryptic languages, and a heightened sense of justice and compassion, to name a few. The story about Messiaen in this book aligns with the Montessori philosophy in that it contains:

- anecdotes about his heroism;
- incidents that showcase his fallibility, and therefore, his humanity;
- moments when he exhibited compassion or fought for justice;
- digressions about how music is a language, like his native French;
- episodes that connect to other subjects, such as biology, geometry, or mathematics;
- evidence of the breadth of human achievement;
- encouragement that the child, too, can become a "Messiaen"; and
- appeals to the child's imagination and reasoning mind.

But these stories fulfill another important purpose besides the lofty aims of Cosmic Education: They spur children, like the ones in Miss Elisabeth's class, to action. Feel free to use and adapt the stories in this book to "enthuse your children to their innermost core," generating the busy, productive, joyous work so prevalent in Montessori environments.

Table 15.1. List of Cosmic Stories

I. Famous Western Composers and Musicians
  A. Aaron Copland (1909–1990)
  B. Antonio Vivaldi (1678–1741)
  C. Charles Ives (1874–1954)
  D. Clara Wieck Schumann (1819–1896)
  E. Dmitri Shostakovich (1906–1975)
  F. Duke Ellington (1899–1974)
  G. Erik Satie (1866–1925)
  H. George Frederick Handel (1685–1759)
  I. Hildegard von Bingen (1098–1179)
  J. Igor Stravinsky (1882–1971)
  K. Ludwig van Beethoven (1770–1827)
  L. Nadia (1887–1979) and Lili Boulanger (1893–1918)
  M. Olivier Messiaen (1908–1992)
  N. The Beatles (1962–1970)
II. Famous Compositions
  A. *4'33"*
  B. *Carnival of the Animals*
  C. *Farewell Symphony*
  D. *Heroic Symphony*
  E. *Pictures at an Exhibition*
  F. *Rhapsody in Blue*
  G. *The Danse Macabre*
  H. *The Four Seasons*
III. Musical Instruments and Ensembles
  A. The Western Symphony Orchestra, Part I: Sections and Instruments
  B. The Western Symphony Orchestra, Part II: History and Development

I. FAMOUS WESTERN COMPOSERS AND MUSICIANS

A. Aaron Copland (1909–1990)

Welcome! I want to tell you the story of a composer named Aaron Copland. When people hear Aaron Copland's music, they get the feeling of being out West in a wide-open space or in a peaceful meadow on the prairie. Have any of you ever been out in the Midwestern part of the United States and seen those wide prairies? Listening to Aaron Copland's music feels like being there. Often Copland's music depicts rodeos, country dances, or Mexican festivals. Funny that his music should sound like that, since he lived most of his life in busy, noisy Brooklyn, New York. Copland didn't think he needed to actually be in those places to write about them, though. He used his imagination to take him and his music wherever he wanted to go. Let me tell you some more about him.

Copland was born in 1900, right at the beginning of modern times. When Copland was a child, many new inventions were cropping up—inventions that made huge changes in people's daily lives, such as the automobile, the telephone, and electric lights. It seemed that the world was changing from the old to the new. As a child, one of Aaron's favorite new inventions was the phonograph, a machine that played music by dragging a needle across the tracks in a round, spinning disk. Aaron loved to sit and listen to records on the family phonograph.

As a boy, Aaron pestered his sister Laurine into giving him piano lessons. Right away, he started to write his own songs. Later, his parents agreed to pay for Aaron's piano lessons from a professional teacher. Aaron's parents wanted him to have all the best opportunities. They came from Lithuania at a time when many people in that country had no money and no homes. Once they came to the United States, the Coplands owned a large department store and could afford a better life.

At the beginning of the twentieth century when Aaron was growing up, it seemed that everyone was after a better life. Not only were new inventions cropping up, as mentioned earlier, but artists and writers were trying out new ideas as well. In Europe, musicians and composers were rejecting old traditions and experimenting with new techniques and new conceptions.

In America, however, classical music lovers cared only about music that had been written years before by the famous European composers like Mozart, Beethoven, and Chopin. I have stories about those people for later! Aaron Copland respected those composers, but he wanted to learn about modern composers, too.

At the age of twenty, Copland auditioned and won a spot at the Summer School of Music for American Students at Fountainebleau, France. At that time France was the modern-music center of the world. His teacher was Nadia Boulanger, one of the best music composition teachers of the twentieth century. Many composers who studied with her went on to become famous. I can tell you a story about her on another day. For now, let me tell you that Copland was very excited to learn about

modern European composers like Stravinsky, whose *Rite of Spring* caused a riot, and Ravel, who shocked people with new sounds.

While in France, Copland had many opportunities to travel throughout Europe, and while there, he heard many people playing jazz. Although jazz was invented in America, it really caught on first in Europe. Copland decided to incorporate jazz sounds into the modern European music he was learning to write in France.

Copland experimented so much that his early compositions didn't sound much like the music he'd been studying. Though his teacher Nadia Boulanger liked them, the general public did not. When one of his first works, the *Symphony for Organ and Orchestra*, was played in public, it was actually booed! Copland didn't let that stop him, however. He was still experimenting.

Eventually, musicians performing his music complained that some of his pieces were too hard to learn and play. Even performers didn't care for Copland's modern-sounding music, in particular the jazzy parts. But Copland didn't give up. He knew it might take a while for people to get used to the music he was writing.

Once, Copland went to Mexico. Wherever he went he saw people playing guitars, singing, and dancing. Music in Mexico was not just for concert halls and auditoriums. It was a part of people's everyday daily lives. He was so inspired by some of the fast-moving, joyful music he heard being played in dance halls and at festivals that he was moved to write a piece of music about Mexico.

He blended bits and pieces of Mexican folk tunes with his own music in what became one of his best-loved early pieces: *El Salon Mexico*. Listening to it, you immediately get an impression of the Mexican countryside. *El Salon Mexico* became very popular in the 1930s.

In 1938, Copland had the opportunity to write music for a ballet based on the life of the legendary Wild West outlaw Billy the Kid. (You might want to do some research about him.) Copland loved Wild West stories, and he thought it would be good to use the same technique he'd used in writing *El Salon Mexico*, only, instead of incorporating parts of Mexican folk songs, he used American folk songs. You can hear lots of American folk melodies in *Billy the Kid*. When people heard it, they liked being able to pick out melodies that they had heard when they were younger. Copland had scored another hit.

At around this time, Americans were disheartened by something called the Great Depression. Many Americans lost their jobs, lost their savings, and became very poor. Many people lost their homes. Not only that, but it looked as though the United States was going to become involved in a terrible war that had already started in Europe. Many artists, writers, and composers started looking around for images, stories, and sounds that were uniquely American in order to give people feelings of comfort, happiness, and hope and to help them to feel proud of their country.

Copland's contributions were some of his most famous pieces like "*Unitalicze Fanfare for the Common Man,*" the ballet *Rodeo,* and his most beloved work, the ballet *Appalachian Spring.* In all these works, Copland again combined familiar American folk melodies with his own musical ideas to create a unique, all-American sound.

Eventually, Copland moved to Hollywood, California, where he wrote music for films. He even won an Academy Award for his score for the film *The Heiress* (1949). In his old age, he spent less time composing and more time conducting and teaching. Even though he was famous, he wasn't snooty; he wanted to work with students. He told his students to strive to be original, to always experiment, and to make music that was part of modern times.

Copland encouraged young musicians in their work and even composed pieces especially for high-school bands and orchestras. Because of his accomplishments in music education, Aaron Copland has a school of music named after him—the Aaron Copland School of Music at Queens College, New York.

Speaking of young musicians, I'd like to show you some of Copland's music. I wonder if, as you listen to it, you'll picture the wide-open prairies, the arid deserts, the high mountains, and the sweeping plains of the United States. Shall we give it a try?

LISTENING:

Orchestra:
El Salon Mexico
"Fanfare for the Common Man" (from Symphony no. 3)
Appalachian Spring
Rodeo
Billy the Kid
Piano:
"Down a Country Lane"
"In Evening Air"
"Midday Thoughts"
"The Cat and the Mouse"

B. Antonio Vivaldi (1678–1741)

Picture a city floating in a sea, built on top of long stilts that go way down into the ocean floor. It's a magnificent city, with canals of jade-colored water and buildings with ornately decorated facades. Here in this city, great towering cathedrals cozy up next to quaint restaurants in

a maze of twisting cobblestone alleyways and peacefully rippling canals. The sun warms the city most of the year as gondolas drift along the water and seagulls fly around in the town square.

Do you think I'm imagining such a place? Well, I'm happy to tell you that this city really exists. It's in Italy, on the Adriatic sea. It's called Venice, and it's one of the most beautiful cities on earth. Venice has no cars. When people want to get somewhere they go by foot, by water taxi, or by gondola. Have you ever heard of a gondola? It's a long, narrow boat poled through the water by a someone called a gondolier.

In addition to its awe-inspiring art and architecture, Venice is full of music. Gondoliers sing up and down the canals, vendors whistle, and birds sing from morning to night. Festivals, theaters, parties, church bells, and religious services provide a constant supply of music. Well, in 1678, into this world of music, the composer Antonio Vivaldi was born. I'd like to tell you about him.

Antonio's father was a church man. He was quite an ambitious man who had big plans for his son. He not only taught Antonio violin, but he also got him a job as a violinist and sent him off to the priesthood, all by the time Antonio was fifteen years old. Imagine how proud Antonio's father was when Antonio, as a young man of twenty-five, got a job teaching violin at the Pietá orphanage for girls, earning nearly four times as much as his father.

Antonio Vivaldi spent most of his life at the Pietá, where, next to the big, iron gate in a little nook in the wall, the porter checked daily to see if anyone had dropped off a new baby. In Vivaldi's time, many people were poor. Those who could not afford to take care of their babies left them at Pietá. For here, abandoned and orphaned girl babies were given a home and taught music. The girls often gave concerts that were a fixture of musical life in Venice.

These orphan girls sang like angels and played in the most disciplined orchestra in Italy at the time. Yet these girls were mysterious, because no one ever saw them. When they performed a concert, they sat hidden behind an iron gate. Because they performed in a church, the audience wasn't allowed to applaud. Instead, they coughed or shuffled their feet to express their appreciation. Sometimes they even blew their noses.

Vivaldi was in charge of making sure everything ran smoothly. The girls at the Pietá were fond of him. He was a kindly man, with thick, curly red hair and long flowing red robes. This earned him the nickname "the Red Priest." And while Vivaldi was indeed a real priest, people said he wasn't very priest-like. He was always missing church services because of his asthma, and often in the middle of a mass he would disappear from the altar altogether to go jot down some musical idea.

Although he was a sickly man, Vivaldi worked very hard. He wrote music for the girls to play, conducted concerts, maintained the instruments, taught lessons, and even played violin for the audience during intermissions. When he wasn't working at the Pietá, he was touring Europe performing his own compositions. Vivaldi wrote so much music during his lifetime that he is known as one of the world's most prolific composers.

Vivaldi had a great sense of humor. He liked to write little jokes into his music. He also had a rather high opinion of himself and enjoyed boasting about his fame, his wealthy patrons, and about how much music he'd written. Some people think he exaggerated, saying he wrote forty-nine operas when only forty-five have been found.

Vivaldi was also a great lover of money. He charged the highest prices possible for his music and spent his money faster than he earned it. He loved to buy lavish clothes and would only play the best musical instruments. Just as in modern times, the fame and popularity of musicians waxes and wanes.

When Vivaldi died at age sixty-three, he died poor—his music no longer in fashion. His music was largely forgotten until, more than a century years after his death, someone rediscovered the music of Vivaldi's era, and the music of the Red Priest became popular and fashionable once again. Antonio Vivaldi enjoys lasting fame. His is some of the world's best-loved music.

One of his best-known large works is called *The Four Seasons*. Vivaldi wrote parts of the music to create sound effects such as turtledoves, goldfinches, flashes of lightning, barking dogs, howling winds, and even chattering teeth. In this, he was ahead of his time. Although *The Four Seasons* is one of Vivaldi's most popular pieces of music, it was voted "Most Boring Composition" by a New York radio audience in 1984. How could a piece of music that captured the feeling of the changing seasons be considered boring? Let's listen to it, and you can tell me your opinion.

LISTENING:

The Four Seasons
Concerto a la Rustica in G Major
Six Violin Concertos

C. Charles Ives (1874–1954)

Have you ever wondered what your teacher, your mail carrier, or your bus driver does when they finish work? Do you think they go home and only think about teaching, delivering mail, or driving buses? Do you ever wonder whether, as soon as they get home, they jump right into doing what they love most?

Imagine your teacher coming home from work and toiling over his or her paintings, your mail carrier throwing off a uniform, putting on a writing jacket, and sitting down to write a novel, or your bus driver composing a symphony during lunch breaks. I bet many of the teachers at this school are painters, dancers, novelists, and artists outside of work. I want to tell you about a composer who made his living as an insurance salesman but spent his free time composing music. His name was Charles Ives.

Ives was born in Danbury, Connecticut, in 1874, into a musical household. His father, whom he worshipped, played trumpet, piano, and organ, taught music, and led the town's brass band. Young Charles loved to hear his father play music. When his father practiced all day in the barn, Charles loved to sit with him and listen. At an early age, Charles began learning to play the organ and writing his own music. By the time he was thirteen, he was not only an excellent organist, but he also played a fun, plinky-sounding type of music called ragtime piano in bars.

Charles's early experiences with his father influenced the music he composed. Once, as a boy, Charles got to ride on a float during a Fourth of July parade while his father's band was playing. Charles loved to hear the bright blaring of the brass instruments and the pounding of the drums.

Another time, a church bell rang during a thunderstorm and his father dashed out of the house into the rain, only to stand outside for a moment listening, dash back in again, bang out chords on the piano, and say, "No, no that's not quite it!" This he repeated over and over again until finally, he was satisfied that he had recreated the sound of a church bell in a thunderstorm.

Charles's father encouraged his son to plunk around on the low notes on the piano to try to make the sound of a big brass drum. When he began taking drum lessons with the town barber, who was also a talented drummer, his father recruited him to play drums in his all-girl cornet band.

You might think being in an all-girl band would be embarrassing to a boy, right? But not for Charles; he relished every opportunity to make music. Charles's father regularly took him to the town church's tent meetings, where Charles would revel in the sound of the singing of hymns, even though the voices weren't perfect.

There was even an occasion when Charles's father had two brass bands march around the town square in opposite directions playing different songs while he and Charles stood in the middle just so he could hear what it would sound like. Ives thought it was a wonderful noise. He tried to replicate the effect in one of his own symphonies later on.

In addition to music, Charles also loved sports. Throughout his school years, he participated in football, baseball, track, and tennis, and he was quite good at all of them. He was even the star pitcher on his school baseball team.

Charles composed music all through high school and went on to study music at Yale University, which is a very prestigious school, but, oddly enough, he didn't pursue music as a career. Instead he started a successful insurance business. In fact, Ives never made a living at music. He would go to the office, work a busy day, and then head home to do his musical work, sometimes even composing on the train. His colleagues had no idea of his musical work outside of work.

Charles Ives didn't pursue music because he didn't want to compromise his music by making a living at it.

You see, Ives's music was innovative and strange. It didn't follow any rules. His music borrowed from lots of other music. In his music you can hear cowboy songs, old hymns, Christmas carols, African American melodies, even "Ode to Joy" theme from Beethoven's Symphony no. 9—all used in new ways. He tried to recreate the sounds of brass bands, drums, sunsets, car horns, crickets, and all sorts of things in his music. This was not the kind of music people were used to enjoying.

Still, Ives sent his music to musicians and orchestras everywhere, but no one would play it. He tried with little success to get his music performed. His musical ideas were met with rejection, even rage. No one understood it, so no one performed it. On his off-hours, he wrote four symphonies and hundreds of other pieces. He became exhausted and ill by the time he reached his fifties and could no longer compose music. Instead, he revised his earlier music and continued to send it out to people. Still, no one wanted it.

Eventually, little by little, people began to record and perform some of Charles's music. The Boston Symphony once played one of his compositions, then a famous violinist. Finally, in 1947, his 3rd Symphony won a Pulitzer Prize. He gave away the prize money, saying, "Prizes are for boys. I'm a grown-up!"

At last, in 1951, when Ives was seventy-seven years old, a very famous conductor named Leonard Bernstein broadcast his Second Symphony from Carnegie Hall in New York City, and his music was heard all across the United States, and eventually the world. This sparked a great enthusiasm for his music and, finally, people began to listen. Three years after that, in 1954, Charles Ives died. In the years since that famous broadcast people all over the world have grown to love Ives's music. His Fourth Symphony is considered a masterpiece.

You know, Ives's big ambition in life was to put all the sounds in the world into a colossal Universe Symphony. He meant for it to be performed outdoors, by orchestras sitting on the tops of several hills. He made sketches of it, but he never finished it. I wonder whether *you* would like to try to compose your own Universe Symphony. We've been learning about the universe. What would you include in a "Universe Symphony?" How could you create the sounds of a solar system, a meteor, or a black hole? Maybe when you get home from school you can get started on it. We could even start on it right now!

LISTENING:

Three Places in New England
The Unanswered Question
The Holidays Symphony
Symphony no. 2, 3, and 4
The Universe Symphony (Unfinished)

D. Clara Wieck Schumann (1819–1896)

Gather around! I want to share a story with you about a talented pianist and composer named Clara Wieck Schumann, who is considered to be one of the greatest pianists of all time. From the time she was just a child, her playing was renowned all over Europe. She earned the nickname "Queen of the Piano."

Clara was born in Leipzig, Germany, in 1819. She had a difficult childhood. As a little girl, she couldn't talk. Everyone thought she was a deaf-mute. Her father Friedrich, an accomplished piano teacher, gave her piano lessons just to see if she could hear. Clara worked hard at the piano from an early age. Her father made her practice every day. She played so beautifully that he took her out on concert tours, despite the fact that she was so young. By the time Clara began speaking at the age of eight, she was already a world-famous pianist.

Clara performed all over Europe. Her concerts were so popular that police had to be there in order to control the crowds. She loved touring, but she always got nervous before a performance. Clara considered performing to be such a special occasion that to every performance she wore a different white dress.

In between concert tours, Clara learned to sing, to play the violin, and to write her own music. She wrote a piano concerto when she was only fifteen and performed it with a full orchestra. The critics loved it, but Clara got upset when they included in their review the phrase "considering the composer is a lady."

You see, at the time Clara was growing up in Germany, it was not considered acceptable for a woman to be a professional musician or perform in public. Nevertheless, Clara wrote twenty-three piano works, all of which she performed. At the age of twenty, however, she gave up composing because society had convinced her that "a woman must not desire to be a composer."

One day, when Clara came home from a tour at the age of eleven, a young musician twelve years older named Robert Schumann came to live with the Wieck family. Hearing Clara play inspired him to become a composer. He took up piano lessons with her father. Robert and Clara were close friends. Eventually they fell in love. When Clara was eighteen, Robert sought permission from Clara's father to marry her, but her father objected and became angry. He wanted Clara to focus on her music career.

Clara and Robert fought hard to win the right to marry. In 1840, when Clara was twenty-one, they took Clara's father to court and won. The two married and lived happily in Leipzig, teaching music at the Leipzig Conservatory.

Clara and Robert's marriage was a remarkable business partnership. Like Clara, Robert was a gifted composer. He also wanted to be a concert pianist, but due to a lifelong illness, two of his fingers were paralyzed, so he devoted himself instead to composition. He wrote all of his music for Clara to play. Some of Robert's best music, such as his *Album for the Young* and his *Scenes from Childhood*, were all inspired by his friendship with Clara when she was young. He used some of her melodies in his music, and she played his music at her concerts.

Clara Schumann worked hard. She continued to perform concert tours throughout her marriage. In fact, she was more successful as a concert pianist than her husband was as a composer. She earned more in three weeks than he could earn in a year. She was a consummate businesswoman. She organized, booked, and tended to all the details of her concert tours. She managed all of this while supervising a household of three servants, spending several hours each day writing letters, taking care of her sickly husband Robert, and looking after their eight children. She maintained her sanity by taking long walks each day.

Clara was friends with many of the prominent European composers of her day. The Schumanns often had popular composers and musicians over to dinner. Her best friend was a highly esteemed composer named Johannes Brahms; you might know his famous lullaby. As with Robert, Brahms's career was inspired by Clara's playing. Brahms once wrote that all of his music should contain an epigram: "Really by Clara Schumann."

By the time Clara's husband Robert reached middle age, he was insane. He suffered from a lifelong mental disorder that caused him to have severe recurring episodes in which he alternated between manic exaltation and profound depression. Sometimes he would have delusional ideas that he was being poisoned or threatened with metallic items like knives, screws, or even frying pans.

One day Clara's husband wrote in a letter that he was being driven mad by the persistent sound of voices, angels, and the note A in his head. After trying to commit suicide, he had himself committed to a mental asylum. He died in the asylum at the age of forty-four, making Clara a widow at age thirty-seven.

Clara loved her husband's music and devoted herself to the performance and interpretation of his works. Soon after Robert's death, Clara published a complete edition of his compositions. Later, at seventy-seven, she published a volume of his letters. The only reason the world knows Robert's music is because of Clara Schumann.

After her husband's death, Clara continued to perform well into old age. She died at seventy-seven, having enjoyed a sixty-year career as a concert pianist, longer than any man at the time.

LISTENING:

"Geheimes Flüstern hier und dort"
Piano Trio in G Minor, op. 17

E. Dmitri Shostakovich (1906–1975)

Dimitri Shostakovich was born in St. Petersburg, Russia, in 1906. His mother started teaching him piano when he was nine. As a child, Shostakovich was so good at the piano and had such a good musical memory that his mother sometimes caught him "pretending to read" his music. That is to say, Shostakovich would look at the music his mother put in front of him and play note-for-note the music he had heard her play during a previous lesson! When he was only thirteen, Shostakovich got accepted to a very prestigious music school in Russia, the Petrograd Conservatory. Can you imagine moving away from home and going to college at thirteen?

By the time Shostakovich started writing music (he wrote his First Symphony at the age of nineteen), the Russian government was very different than it is today. In fact, in 1917, when Shostakovich was only eleven, Russia experienced a revolution that resulted in a change of governments and a unification with some of the nations on her border. The country even adopted a new name, the Union of Soviet Socialist Republics, or USSR.

The government of the Soviet Union was communist, meaning all material goods and means of production were not owned by private individuals but by the entire country as a whole. This included the means of producing art and music.

To elevate the ideals of communism, the Soviet government felt that music had to be worthy of the average working people; that is, accessible, tuneful, traditional stylistically, and folk-inspired. A musician who wrote something that was too complicated, or too new in style, was accused of "formalism" and could be fired from his or her job, forbidden to write or play music, put in jail, or even put to death. Imagine being put to death for writing the music you love!

Under such conditions, you can imagine how hard it was for Shostakovich to write the music that he wanted to write. Because he was the Soviet Union's most prized composer, the government scrutinized his music very carefully. The leader of the Soviet Union, Joseph Stalin, attended Shostakovich's first opera and hated it so much that he denounced it in the national newspaper. Other denouncements followed and, as a result, Shostakovich had trouble getting people to pay him for his work.

Well, Shostakovich was a very clever man. He managed, in his music, both to please and to protest against the Soviet government by weaving covert messages into his music, such as quoting melodies from anticommunist songs or from his own works that the government had previously denounced. Sometimes he wrote music that conformed so blatantly to the government's demands that the music was almost comical. Other times, he would deliberately try to make the music sound bad, knowing the government censors weren't clever enough to notice. During the entire closing movement of his Fifth Symphony, for example, while the other instruments are playing a rousing march theme from one of Shostakovich's previous compositions about an artist being criticized, the piccolos, flutes, and violins loudly repeat a constant barrage of shrill A notes. Of course, no one from the government noticed. In fact, the opposite happened; the government praised the Fifth Symphony, and Shostakovich regained their favor. In this way, Shostakovich had his little joke.

Of course, he wasn't always joking. Sometimes Shostakovich wanted to say serious, important things in his music and these were things that the government didn't want to hear. Well, this music he just tucked in his desk drawer so nobody could see or hear it. In fact, Shostakovich wrote a lot of music, such as his fifteen string quartets, that were never published because he feared being persecuted by the government. You could say that Shostakovich wrote two kinds of music: his "true" music for himself, in private, and a number of pieces of "false" music for the public.

Another way that Shostakovich worked under the radar was to put himself, literally, into his music. He often wove in a special melody that he made from the letters of his own initials. Would you like to see how he did it?

Well, if you label all the tone bars, you'll see that the second white one is called D. So, he let that note stand for the first letter of his first name. The first letter of his last name is a Russian letter that makes the sound "SCH." For the S and the H, Shostakovich used E-flat, which, in the German naming system, is called E-es, or S, and B-natural, which is called H. So, by playing the notes D-S-C-H (D—E-flat—C—B), Shostakovich was able to fashion a nice little melody. Let's pull down the D, E-flat, C, and B tone bars and hear what that sounds like.

In spite of what the Soviet government thought, people loved Shostakovich's music. His music is still performed today, some fifty years after his death. Once, a very prestigious organization in Russia called the Union of Soviet Composers spent an entire three-day conference praising his Tenth Symphony. Can you imagine yourself writing music that inspires people so much? I bet you could. Why don't you try it?

LISTENING:

Symphony no. 5, op. 47
String Quartet no. 8, op. 110
Children's Notebook, op. 69
Symphony no. 10

F. Duke Ellington (1899–1974)

Gather 'round, my friends. I'd like to share a story about a famous composer named Duke Ellington. Duke was born in Washington, D.C., in 1899, when, only thirty years after the abolition of slavery in the United States, many African American people were living in poverty and suffering from the effects of segregation. Duke is famous for being a piano player, a bandleader, and a great composer of jazz music. He's considered to be one of America's greatest composers.

African Americans in the city of New Orleans in the state of Louisiana invented jazz right around the time Duke was born. At that time, jazz had a big, loud, brass sound that was inspired by marching bands. Jazz has exciting rhythms and feelings that come from two other kinds of music: ragtime and blues. We can hear a story about those styles of music on another day. People loved to dance to jazz.

Duke's birth name was Edward Kennedy Ellington, and he was born to a loving family. He was particularly close to his mother, who encouraged him and made sure he was brought up properly. Duke's father taught him manners, good grammar, and a stylish way of talking. Papa Ellington worked as a butler. He worked at the White House when Teddy Roosevelt was the president of the United States.

As a child, Duke was passionate about baseball and art, but when he was accidentally hit in the head with a baseball bat, his mother started him on piano lessons, thinking it a much safer activity. Young Duke didn't like his piano lessons, however, and his mother eventually gave up on him ever learning to play.

Duke didn't touch the piano again until he was a teenager. One day he heard a piano player called Harvey Brooks, also a teenager, and was so impressed that he gave the piano another chance. And do you know what? He learned to play the piano without lessons! Duke learned the piano all on his own, although he did get advice from local piano players and other pianists who were passing through town. The first song Duke wrote and performed was for a high-school dance. Everyone loved it! He began writing as many songs as he could. Instead of going to art school as planned, Duke decided to make music his career.

Around this time, most popular jazz musicians had a catchy nickname, like Willie "The Lion" Smith, Jelly Roll Morton, or Dizzy Gillespie. Ellington gave himself the name "Duke" because of his stylish and gentlemanly ways.

To kick-start his career in music, Duke and some friends formed a small band called the Washingtonians. The band consisted of piano, drums, bass, some trumpets and saxophones, and a banjo. They played at parties, dances, and clubs all over Washington D.C. Although they were doing well, Duke knew that in order to really make it as a jazz musician, he and his friends would have to move to New York City, where all the great jazz bands of the day were playing.

Duke loved New York, but for he and his friends, the most glamorous and exciting part of New York was Harlem. Harlem was a place where African Americans could live without being looked down on or treated badly, as they were in many other American cities at that time. Harlem was full of black doctors, lawyers, writers, artists, and musicians. Together, they created an exciting period that is known as the Harlem Renaissance. (Perhaps describe this in context of what had come before.)

At first, it was almost impossible for the Washingtonians to find work, because so many other bands from all over the United States were moving to Harlem. Bands from Chicago, St. Louis, and far away New Orleans flooded Harlem, having heard about the money they could make in the dance halls and nightclubs of New York. Eventually the luck of the Washingtonians changed and they were hired to play in a popular nightclub called Barron's Exclusive Club.

Another problem for the Washingtonians was that they played quiet, moody music that wasn't very good for people to dance to. Things improved for them considerably when a trumpeter called Bubber Miley joined the band. He played his trumpet using a mute, which was basically a toilet plunger placed over the bell of the trumpet, and often made all kinds of growling sounds when he played. Bubber Miley gave the Washingtonians a wild, lively, hot-jazz sound that differed greatly from many other bands. Soon, the Washingtonians were getting gigs in nightclubs all over New York.

By 1927, the Washingtonians changed their name to the Duke Ellington Orchestra. They were playing at the Cotton Club, which was the most famous nightclub in New York. Duke recruited many new members and was writing hit song after hit song. Even white people loved to listen to his music. Musicians loved to play in Duke's band because he wrote his music especially for them.

Duke surrounded himself with the best musicians he could find—musicians with a one-of-a-kind sound—and he wrote his music to accommodate their individual talents. Duke thought of his whole band as an instrument, giving each player a chance to do his or her special thing. This gave Duke's music a unique jazz sound and made his band members feel good about being an important part of the ensemble.

Duke also loved to mix different instrumental sounds in his band. He liked to mix sounds like he was mixing colors. Sometimes sounds remind us of colors. A cool clarinet sound might remind us of the color blue or a hot trumpet sound might call to mind the color red. Having been an artist, Duke was very interested in colors. The names of his famous songs often contained colors, such as "Mood Indigo," "Black and Tan Fantasy," or "Magenta Haze."

Duke always had a picture or a story in mind when he composed or played music with his band. In a piece called "Harlem Airshaft," Duke and his band depicted in sound all the daily-life activities happening around them on the busy Harlem streets. Tuba blasts might depict the horns of cars, clarinet melodies might represent people bustling back and forth. Duke filled his music with the energy and life of the city.

Duke Ellington's band was so popular that they regularly toured all over the United States. Unfortunately, they lived in a time when many people in the United States were extremely prejudiced against African Americans. Often Duke and the band had a hard time finding hotel rooms or getting service in a restaurant.

Duke decided to solve this problem by traveling with his band by train. This eliminated the need to find accommodation, as each musician had his own private train car. They could eat, sleep, and live comfortably whenever they rolled into a new town. Duke loved to travel by train.

The sounds of the wheels rolling along and the sight of the beautiful scenery rolling by gave Duke many new ideas for compositions.

Duke's band was very popular until around the 1950s, when people started listening to rock and roll. By then, the jazz band sound had become old-fashioned. Duke didn't give up. In 1956, Duke got invited to play at a famous jazz festival in Newport, Rhode Island. It was very late before Duke's orchestra went on to play. Many people in the audience were tired and wanted to go home.

But then, Duke did something special.

He gave his saxophone player permission to do his very best solo. Not only did the saxophone player play his best solo, but he also played the most legendary solo in the history of jazz. People in the audience went crazy and started to come back into the arena to cheer and dance. So, Duke and his band found popularity once again.

For the rest of his life, Duke wrote and composed music. He died in 1974, having shown the world that jazz music could be more than just dance music, but that it could be as sophisticated, beautiful, and important as classical music.

And that's my story. Let's listen to some of Duke Ellington's music. Maybe you'll see some colors or a busy Harlem street!

LISTENING:

"Mood Indigo"
"It Don't Mean a Thing If It Ain't Got That Swing"
"Black and Tan Fantasy"
"Red Hot Band"
"Sophisticated Lady"

G. Erik Satie (1866–1925)

I want to tell you a story about a very funny, very peculiar man who also happened to be a brilliant composer. His name is Erik Satie. He was born in 1866, in the little coastal town of Honfleur in France.

From a very young age, Satie loved to play music. As a young man he went to a special school for musicians to learn to play and compose. All his life he imagined a new, special kind of music, but when the stiff, formal, starchy-collared academics at his school heard the music he was inventing, they didn't like it at all. They were interested in music that followed rules, and Satie's music had rules all its own. Well, everyone at the school thought Satie was crazy and that his music was strange, even bad. So Satie dropped out and struck out on his own.

Soon Satie found himself in Paris, where a painter friend introduced him to a popular café called Le Chat Noir. It was a big, majestic building, with gilded fixtures, mahogany decor, gilded ceiling fans, and a grand sweeping staircase. It even had its own little black cat named Maigriou. Inside the back of the cafe was a theater where people put on shadow puppet plays. The club was busy and always crowded with poets, artists, clowns, dancers, painters, and puppeteers.

Satie got to play piano at Le Chat Noir.

One day when Satie was twenty-two years old, he wrote a series of pieces of piano music called *Gymnopedies* and performed them for the first time at the café. As soon as everyone heard the first gentle, floating chords, they stopped talking and gave their full attention to the music as if it had come to them from a dream. Even Maigriou sat calmly on top of the piano, purring. It seemed Satie had found a home for his strange new music.

Eventually, Satie composed music for puppet shows and ballets to be performed at the café. He gave his pieces names like "The Dreamy Fish," "Real Flabby Preludes (for a Dog)," or "Unappetizing Chorale." In his scores he included playing instructions for the pianist such as "from the end of the eyes," "in the throat," "on yellowing velvet," "surly and peevish," or "in the morning before eating."

Did I mention that Satie was peculiar? Well, I hate to tell you this, but as lovely as his music was, and as funny and strange a person as he was, Satie had a terrible temper. He often lost friends just as soon as he had made them. Once, he and the woman he loved had a fight. Satie was so angry with her that he threw her out of his apartment window! Thankfully, she was an acrobat and simply landed on her feet and walked out of his life.

Not only did Satie have a temper, but he also had idiosyncrasies. For one, he never took baths. To clean himself he scraped himself with a stone. He had seven of the same identical suit, which he wore exclusively, and he lived for thirty years in a tiny room. He was very poor because a lot of important people didn't like his music.

Thinking perhaps he'd made a mistake in dropping out of school, Satie went back to school at the age of thirty-nine. This time he did what he was told, followed the rules, and didn't complain. Despite being in classes with musicians half his age, Satie had a wonderful time at school. After graduating, he was so pleased with himself that from then on he dressed like an elegant businessman, complete with bowler hat, umbrella, and pocket watch.

Music historians agree that when Satie was older, he wrote some of his greatest music. In 1914, he wrote *Sports & Divertissiments*, a book of short piano pieces about leisure activities, such as golfing, yachting, fishing, being on a swing, fireworks, and swimming. Satie composed the pieces to accompany colorful illustrations by his artist friend Charles Martin, a well-known illustrator of the day. The collection wasn't published until 1925, and then only in a limited edition of 900 copies. *Sports & Divertissiments* is one of Satie's most celebrated works.

Another celebrated work of Satie's was *Parade*, an opera for which Pablo Picasso did the set and costumes. The music for *Parade* sounded like jazz and included xylophones, typewriters, and sirens. For costumes, some of the actors had to wear tall buildings on their heads. At the opera's premier, the audience hated it so much that they started a fight. A music critic gave the opera a bad review, and Satie sent him a very angry, insulting letter.

Remember I told you Satie had a temper? Well, his letter to the critic read: "Sir, not only are you an ass, you are ass without music." The reviewer, in turn, was so insulted that he sued Satie. In court, Satie's friends started a fight with the police, and Satie almost went to jail.

Also notable among Satie's works was a ballet called *Cancelled*, which he wrote with another painter friend. The ballet included a film of the Satie and his friend shooting at the audience with a cannon. It even had a funeral scene being led by a camel. For Satie, the hardest part about working on the ballet was finding a place to put the camel.

Shortly before the opening of the ballet, the lead actor, fearing the audience would hate the ballet and that his career would be ruined, got such performance anxiety that he got sick and couldn't perform. So the premier of the ballet was cancelled. Luckily, the flyers already read "Cancelled." The ballet eventually did get performed, and this time, audiences loved it. For the curtain call, Satie and his painter friend drove up onto the stage in a little car.

Shortly after this, Satie became very sick. He died on the first of July 1925. His last words were "Ah! The cows . . ." Many artists, poets, and musicians attended his funeral but, thankfully, no camel.

Although Satie's musical output was small, and although he was poor and obscure, his music influenced many musicians that followed him, including Debussy, Stravinsky, John Cage, and many jazz musicians. His piano piece *Vexations* is meant to be repeated 840 times, can take more than eighteen hours to perform, and is in the Guinness book of world records. Many composers after Satie were impressed by his innovative harmonies, his freedom of form, and his mastery of understatement. Let's listen to some of his music.

LISTENING:

Gymnopiedes
Gnossiennes
Sonatine bureaucratique
Sports et Divertissements

H. George Frederick Handel (1685–1759)

George Frederick Handel was born in 1685 in Halle, Germany. Although even as a young child Handel was talented at the keyboard, his father hated music and didn't want him to become a musician. In fact, he was so adamant that Handel not become a musician that he didn't allow him to practice, and even forbade him to go to school for fear he would learn to read notes. Instead, Handel's father wanted him to be a famous lawyer.

Handel's mother, on the other hand, recognized her son's talent. The attic in the Handel home was rather small, with thick wooden floors and thick paned windows that had a way of dampening any sound. So, Handel's mother put a harpsichord up in the attic so that Handel could practice any time he wanted without disturbing anyone or alerting his father. Handel would disappear for hours up in that dark attic, practicing by candlelight on his little harpsichord.

I should pause here a moment and tell you about the harpsichord. You see, when Handel was alive, the piano hadn't been invented yet. The harpsichord is a predecessor to the piano. It has a keyboard and strings, like a piano, only, instead of having hammers that strike the strings when the player presses a key, the harpsichord has little plectra (a part resembling small picks) that pluck the strings. Because of the way the instrument is built,

players can't control how loudly or softly they play. In general, harpsichords have a tinny, thin sound. They are a lot quieter than pianos. Can you imagine now why no one could hear young Handel practicing?

Well, one day, when Handel was about seven, his father went on a trip to see his other son, who was employed by the Duke of Saxe-Weissenfels. The Duke lived in a big castle. Handel wanted to go on the trip, but his father insisted he was too young and made him stay at home.

Well, Handel was determined to go, and when his father's coach left for the trip, against his father's wishes, Handel simply followed behind the coach on foot, keeping pace. Everyone in the coach thought Handel would get tired and give up, but he kept right on walking, such was his determination. Finally, his father gave in, stopped the coach, and let little Handel ride with him to see the Duke.

At the castle, Handel immediately made friends with the court musicians. The Duke himself heard the boy play and was astonished by his talent. The Duke immediately demanded that Handel's father let him study music. So, when Handel and his father returned to Halle, Handel got to take lessons from the church organist. This organist taught Handel not only harpsichord but also violin, oboe, harmony, and composition. Handel learned so quickly that eventually he surpassed his teacher, who proclaimed, "The boy knows more than I do!"

When Handel was only twelve years old, his father died. Though he was saddened by this, he took the opportunity to travel a bit. He spent some time in Berlin studying with some other teachers, and then went to Hamburg, which at the time was quite famous for musicians. In Hamburg, he wrote some operas that became very popular. He even spent some time in Italy. But although Handel traveled to many beautiful places, he dreamed most of all of going to England. Well, he got his chance.

You see, when Handel got back from Italy, he became friends with the Elector of Hanover, who offered him a job as Kapellmeister of the cathedral there. A Kapellmeister is a person who is in charge of all of the music in a cathedral. He rehearses the choirs, directs the orchestras, plays the organs, and even composes music for services. It was a dream job for Handel. But he wanted so badly to go to England that he accepted the job only if the Elector would allow him to take a trip to England first. Luckily, the Elector agreed.

At last, Handel went to England. When he arrived, he found that he was already famous. People especially loved his operas. Handel was so enchanted by England and so happy about how his music was received there, he forgot all about his Kapellmeister job back in Germany and stayed.

Well, wouldn't you know it, while Handel was living in London, the Elector of Hanover was crowned the king of England: King George I. Handel was worried that the king was angry with him for skipping out on his previous job. Luckily, a friend got Handel a job composing the music for the king's coronation ceremony.

The ceremony took place on two barges that floated down the Thames River, right through the heart of London. On one barge sat the king and his entourage, and on the second barge sat an entire orchestra playing Handel's music. The piece, appropriately named Water Music, is one of Handel's most celebrated. The king loved it! When he found out Handel wrote it, he immediately forgave him and the two men became friends. Handel even got to ride on the king's barge during the ceremony.

Handel fell in love with England and made one last trip to Germany before became a naturalized English citizen. His great ambition was to write operas, but operas weren't in fashion at the time. The English preferred oratorios, which are basically operas sung by a choir with no actors or sets or costumes. The most famous of Handel's oratorios was *Messiah*. You've probably heard the part that goes "Haaaa-lelujah! Haaaa-lelujah! Hallelujah! Hallelujah! Hal-le-ay-lu-jah!" Does that ring a bell?

Handel spent his last days caring for children at a children's hospital in London. He loved the children there so much that he donated lots of money to the hospital and even staged *Messiah,* complete with full choir and orchestra, there at the hospital just for the children. He died on April 13, 1759. The English people loved Handel so much that they buried him in Westminster Abbey, the cathedral where they crown their royalty and hold royal weddings.

LISTENING:

Water Music
Messiah
Music for the Royal Fireworks
Organ Concerto no. 1 in G minor

I. Hildegard von Bingen (1098–1179)

I want to tell you today about a very special woman named Hildegard von Bingen. She was the first woman composer whose work survives to this day. During her lifetime, she wrote not only beautiful music, but she also wrote handwritten books about nature and medicine that she illustrated herself. Do you want to know more about her?

Hildegard was born the youngest of ten children in Bemersheim, Germany. When she was very young, she used to have powerful visions of angels that revealed religious truth and inspiration to her. Her parents took these visions very seriously and sent her off to be educated as a nun. At that time, nuns were educated in religion, languages, the arts, and music. Little did Hildegard's parents know their daughter would become a celebrated poet and composer.

At the Benedictine monastery where she got her start, Hildegard enjoyed her quiet life of study. She shared a small living area with eighteen other nuns, and loved to walk in the quiet cloister and contemplate her visions. Eventually, the abbess of the monastery died, and Hildegard was given the post of abbess, or the head of the monastery.

Her first move as abbess was to relocate her congregation to Bingen, near Mainz on the Rhein River, where her visions were most intense. Once, she saw tongues of flame lash out from heaven and envelop her. From then on, she devoted herself to a life of creativity. It took her ten years to write down the stories of her visions, with beautiful paintings and illuminated letters. In addition to her visions, she wrote two books on natural history and medicine.

Because of the availability of her books, Hildegard became well-known all over Europe by people from all ranks and classes. Something you must understand about Hildegard's time is that rank and class were very important to people. People who were wealthy and owned land enjoyed high status and an easy life, whereas people who were poor had had extremely difficult lives. Emperors, popes, abbots and abbesses, lower church officials, peasants, and ordinary people all came to visit Hildegard, to listen to her visions, and to seek her counsel and advice. Even King Henry II of England regularly corresponded with her.

Also, at the time she was writing music, in the twelfth century, the Church had very strict rules about liturgical music, that is, music that was meant to be sung for worship. For one, the lyrics had to come from the Scriptures. Hildegard was the first woman to write her own lyrics. Sometimes she even invented her own language for her lyrics. Mostly, she set her melodies to her own poetry. Hildegard wrote beautiful poems; they were rich and full of images from her colorful visions.

This richness and beauty came through in her melodies. Here is one of her poems about love:

> *Love overflows*
> *In all things,*

From the planetary depths
To her highest dwelling place
Beyond the stars,
And love is surpassing herself
In all things,
Because she has given the kiss of peace
To the highest King.

What's more, the leaders of the early Church insisted that music be written as one unaccompanied melody without harmony, a tradition that comes from the Divine Service, prayers that monks and nuns in monasteries had to sing nine times a day at particular hours. We call music like this monophonic. *Mono* comes from the Greek word *monos,* meaning " one" or "alone," and *phonic* comes from the Greek word *phonos,* meaning "voice." Hildegard's melodies stretched the vocal range of singers at the time and adhered closely to the sentiments and feelings expressed in her poems.

Hildegard even wrote a musical morality play called the *Ordo Virtutum,* Latin for "The Order of the Virtues," which is one of the first examples of a musical play. The play included monophonic voices for the human soul (Anima) and the sixteen Virtues. She even wrote a speaking part for the Devil.

Hildegard von Bingen was the most celebrated woman of her age: she was a visionary, naturalist, playwright, poet, and composer. In 2012, Pope Benedict declared her a saint—St. Hildegard. She even has a minor planet named after her, too—868 Hildegard. Let's listen to some of her music!

LISTENING:

Note: Excellent recordings of Hildegard von Bingen's complete works have been released by a group called Sequentia that performs and records medieval music. Among the best are:

> *Ordo Virtutum*
> *Celestial Hierarchy*
> *Symphony*

J. Igor Stravinsky (1882–1971)

Have you ever experienced a time when you had something important to say, but other people weren't ready to hear it? Maybe others didn't get your meaning and they got angry. Well, the same thing happened to Igor Stravinsky, a Russian composer whose *Rite of Spring* caused a riot when it was first performed in Paris in 1913. I'd like to tell you about him.

To begin, Igor Stravinsky was born in the small coastal town of Lomonosov in northern Russia. As a child, Stravinsky loved fairy tales and folk music. His father was a famous opera singer, but he was an angry man with an uncontrollable temper, and Igor was frightened of him. He didn't get along with his mother, who was a famous pianist. Even in later life she used to scold him for not writing the kind of music that she liked.

When Igor was just a boy, his family moved to the exciting and beautiful city of St. Petersburg. There, he was captivated by the great variety of lovely sounds. Once, at a carnival, he saw a folk musician sitting on a stump clicking his tongue, slapping his knees, and making armpit noises. At home Igor loved to make those noises himself.

Even the everyday sounds of the city enthralled him. The echo of horse hooves, the clacking of wagon wheels, the chiming of bells, and the rhythmic hammering from the machine shops all gave him ideas that he used in his later music. Young Igor loved playing piano more than anything. Early on he started making up his own music.

When Igor was ready to go to college, he wanted to study music, but his parents were against it. They wanted him to be a lawyer. So, he went to the University of St. Petersburg to study law. He found it awfully boring and spent all his time thinking about music. At school he became friends with another soon-to-be famous composer, Nikolai Rimsky-Korsakov, who belonged to a group of Russian composers nicknamed "The Mighty Five." They wrote music based on Russian history, Russian folk legends, and Russian folk music. Before those composers came along, popular music in Russia was written by people from other countries, like Germany and France.

After Igor's father died, he quit law school and devoted himself to composing. When he was twenty-six years old, one of his first compositions, *Fireworks,* was performed in St. Petersburg. It was a huge hit. In the audience was the leader of an excellent new ballet company, Sergey Diaghilev. Mr. Diaghilev was hiring all of Russia's best dancers and musicians for his new company, which he planned to take to Paris, France, so as to show the rest of the world how wonderful Russian ballet could be.

Igor Stravinsky's ballets for Diaghilev's company were wonderful and innovative. His ballet *The Firebird* featured striking music, beautiful costumes, creative dancing, and wonderful sets. Stravinsky's music, particularly at the moment when the actress playing the Firebird leaps across the stage, was dazzling. He created sounds no one had ever heard before. *The Firebird* turned Stravinsky into a star overnight.

His next ballet, *Petruschka,* was about three puppets—a ballerina, a soldier, and Petruschka the clown—being controlled by an evil musician. It also created a sensation. Many people felt that this ballet did a wonderful job of telling a story with music.

His next ballet, *The Rite of Spring,* on the other hand, caused outrage. The story is about a prehistoric tribal human sacrifice ritual. The music is full of powerful energy and strong rhythms. It even seemed violent in parts. People weren't used to the unexpected new sounds and the explosive dancing. They started to riot, right there in the theater. People across the aisles were yelling at each other and fights broke out. No one could hear the music. The police had to come and keep the peace. To top it off, all of this happened during the performance!

Stravinsky fled the theater and spent the next two weeks sick in bed. Despite its riotous premiere, *Rite of Spring* is considered one of the greatest pieces of music of the twentieth century.

Soon after, World War I hit Europe, and Stravinsky found it difficult to find work. By this time he had a wife and four children. Always in search of a quiet place to write his music, he moved his family to Switzerland. But quiet still eluded him, as the Stravinsky family lived together in a tiny, crowded apartment. Eventually, a family friend who was a piano dealer set Stravinsky up with a piano, but it was beat up and out of tune. Not only that, but Igor had to play and compose where the piano was kept: in a combination lumber storage shed and chicken coop.

To make money, Stravinsky started conducting and playing piano in public. He was extremely nervous when performing. He once got so nervous that he froze up during a performance of one of his own pieces when he saw the reflection of his fingers in the polished wood of the piano.

After World War I, Stravinsky dramatically changed the style of his writing. Instead of writing modern sounding music based on Russian folk tunes, he wrote music that was more like music written centuries earlier by people like Mozart, Haydn, and Bach. Of course, he added his own touches and created a brand new style of classical music.

Although Stravinsky's new music was based on past traditions, he continued to try new things, experimenting with jazz and writing music for movies. He even wrote circus music for dancing elephants wearing tutus. Eventually he moved to Los Angeles, California, where he continued to conduct and compose until he was eighty-five.

Stravinsky lived to be eighty-nine years old. He's considered one of the best composers of the twentieth century. Would you like to hear some of his music? Let's listen to *The Rite of Spring.* But be careful now—we don't want to have to call in the police!

LISTENING:

> *The Rite of Spring*
> *The Firebird*
> Symphony in C
> *Circus Polka*

K. Ludwig van Beethoven (1770–1827)

I'm thinking of a famous melody that you probably know. It was written about 200 years ago and has endured to such an extent that even today it is considered a treasure by much of humanity. The melody is so beloved that when the countries of Europe got together to form the European Union, they adopted it as their national anthem. When the Berlin Wall that divided East and West Germany fell in 1989, the song was played to symbolize the reunification of the country.

Can you imagine writing a melody that stirs people's hearts even 200 years after you wrote it? The melody I'm thinking of is the "Ode to Joy" by Ludwig van Beethoven. Can you sing it with me? What do you think Beethoven would think if he were alive today and knew we were singing his little melody? After you hear my story, you'll probably agree that Beethoven would not be surprised that his melody is still so popular. He thought he was pretty impressive. But then, history has proved he was right.

Ludwig van Beethoven was born in 1770 in a little yellow house in Bonn, Germany. His father wanted him to become a child prodigy so badly that he told people young Ludwig was two years younger than his actual age to make him seem even more talented than he was. And though Beethoven was talented even without having to lie about his age, he didn't owe his piano skills to talent alone: he worked very hard at the piano. His father gave him lessons when Beethoven was still so small he had to stand on a stool to reach the keys.

As a piano teacher Beethoven's father was a cruel taskmaster who used to hit Beethoven's knuckles whenever he made a mistake. When Beethoven was a little older, but still a boy, his father sometimes woke him up in the middle of the night to have him play piano for friends he had brought home from the tavern. Difficult as his boyhood was, by the time Beethoven was twelve, he could play so well that he supported his family by playing the organ at a church.

Beethoven had a challenging childhood not only because he worked so hard at the piano but also because he was a dirty boy. He didn't bathe, he didn't wash his hands, and his clothes were often unclean. He carried these bad habits on into adulthood. Once a policemen, mistaking Beethoven for a vagabond, arrested him and was astonished to learn that this dirty man with his thick, wild unkempt hair and dirty, smelly clothes was the great Beethoven.

Indeed, during his lifetime, Beethoven was famous. He played the piano so beautifully that his listeners would weep. Yet he would laugh at them, saying, "Composers do not cry. Composers are made of fire!" Well, this man of fire certainly had a hot temper. If people talked while he played, he would storm out of the room in a huff. If he didn't like his audience, he would refuse to play. He was stubborn and preferred to blaze his own trail rather than learn anything from anybody else.

Beethoven was famous for his piano playing and composition, he was also known for being eccentric. He was notorious for being a terrible cook and someone who behaved badly in restaurants. Once he was so dissatisfied with a meal that he poured gravy on the waiter's head.

Sometimes he would leave restaurants without paying or just write music on the bill. Beethoven was also difficult to live with. He mistreated his servants and had to move all the time because he didn't get along with his landlords. His neighbors often complained because he composed late into the night, banging on the floor, marching around, stamping his feet and making howling noises. To keep himself awake he splashed water over his head, which often leaked through the floorboards onto the heads of his neighbors below.

No, Beethoven didn't care much for the manners and niceties of his day. You see, when Beethoven was alive, people in Europe paid great attention to class distinctions. Wealthy people considered themselves to be better than people of the "lower classes." The nobility had all the power because they owned much of the land. They gave themselves titles like "Duke" and "Prince" and generally thought that everyone else was beneath them.

Beethoven, however, considered himself to be equal to, even better than, the aristocracy. He once insulted a wealthy prince by telling him, "There are, and there always will be thousands of princes. There is only one Beethoven."

Beethoven probably lived this way because he was too preoccupied with his music to care what others thought of him. His daily routine was to wake up at dawn and write music, have macaroni and cheese with strong coffee for lunch, and then wander around Vienna in the afternoons muttering to himself and scribbling in his little notebook, which he pulled out of a satchel overstuffed with manuscript paper. His handwriting was so messy that no one but he himself could read it.

Strange though this behavior was, we can be grateful Beethoven lived this way. He wrote such exquisite music. In fact, he wrote such deeply emotional, heroic, and nature-loving music that he ushered in a whole new era of music: the Romantic era.

The biggest tragedy of Beethoven's life was that from the time he was twenty his hearing began to deteriorate, until, at fifty he was completely deaf. Imagine not being able to hear with your ears the music you imagine in your head. Although his deafness disheartened him, it didn't stop him from writing his beautiful music. Undeterred by being unable to hear himself play, he continued to write music. He even cut the legs off of his pianos so he could feel the vibrations of the strings on the floor.

Beethoven insisted on conducting his symphonies, though he couldn't hear what the orchestra was playing. During a rehearsal for his Symphony no. 9, the conductor had to instruct the orchestra to ignore Beethoven, who used to "conduct" by standing in front of them waving his arms around while they were playing.

When the world premiere performance of his 9th Symphony was over, the first violin player had to spin Beethoven around so he could see the audience's standing ovation. So enthusiastic was the audience's reaction to his symphony that, even though Beethoven couldn't hear them cheering, the sight of them on their feet with their happy faces and enthusiastic applauding made him cry.

Beethoven died in 1827 during a violent thunderstorm. It is said that his last gesture was to thrust a defiant fist into the air. He was so beloved in the city of Vienna that one out of every ten citizens came to his funeral. Throughout his life Beethoven suffered and worked so hard because he believed his music could change the world. You know what? It did!

LISTENING:

Symphony nos 9, 7, 5, 3, 6
Bagatelle in A Minor WoO 59, "Für Elise"
Sonata No. 14 in C-sharp minor, Op. 27, no. 2, "Moonlight"
(Sonata quasi una fantasia)

L. Nadia (1887–1979) and Lili Boulanger (1893–1918)

The story I have for you today is about a pair of musical sisters who became famous all over the world for their contributions to music. Nadia Boulanger was an accomplished musician and composer, whose skills as a teacher earned her greater reputation and influence than her work playing and composing. Her younger sister Lili was the first woman ever to win the highest award for music in France: the Prix de Rome. Sit back and listen as I tell you the tale of these two remarkable sisters.

When Nadia Boulanger was a little girl growing up in Paris, she was terrified of music. She screamed and cried and threw terrible fits whenever she heard it. Both her father and mother were singers, and when they would give lessons, or when their famous musician friends would come over to play music with them, Nadia would scream and cry and even hide under the piano. Even in public, if she and her mother heard music on the street, Nadia would hide behind her mother in fright.

Nadia's mother, however, was a very strict, stern woman, who demanded much from young Nadia. So, in an effort to please her mother, Nadia made a change. Instead of throwing a fit whenever she heard music, she made an extra effort to listen and learn. When her father had a student over for a singing lesson, Nadia listened intently. She even sat in on her parents' weekly "open house musicals" attended by many of the Boulangers' famous musician friends. There she would sit, looking like a little boy in her little velvet suit, listening to the adults play and discuss music.

Finally, at six, having got over her fear completely, Nadia devoted herself seriously to the study of music. All the while she was studying and writing her own compositions, however, she never felt like she met her mother's high expectations.

When Nadia was six, her little sister Lili was born. Madame Boulanger held Nadia responsible for Lili's care, a task which was no small responsibility, since Lili was born in poor health. Nadia promised to always care for her sister, a promise she took very seriously all of Lili's life. Nadia even took it upon herself to teach her younger sister music. Lili was a talented musician even as a small girl. She was a quick learner.

When Lili was two years old, a famous French composer named Gabriel Fauré, who was a friend of the Boulanger family, discovered that she had perfect pitch, meaning that she could identify any note by name just by hearing it without referencing an instrument. Can you imagine? At two, Lili could sing any song you played for her. When, at age seven Nadia began working extra hard at studying music with the intent to apply to the Paris Conservatory when she turned nine, Lili listened in on her lessons and imitated everything she did.

As it turned out, Nadia was accepted to the Paris Conservatory. Her mother, ever the taskmaster, attended classes with her and made sure she kept up with her studies. Madame Boulanger would even stand next to Nadia during performances and brush her bangs out of her hair so she could better see the music! During Nadia's fourth year at the Conservatory, when she was thirteen, her father died. At that time, it was difficult even for grown women in France to make a living, yet Nadia became the family's breadwinner. She worked extra hard at the Conservatory in order to someday get a job and support her mother and sister.

One way she earned a bit of money was by winning first prize in harmony. She even earned a little bit of money when, after she had taken organ lessons and played a recital, Gabriel Fauré asked her to fill in for him at the church where he was a regular organist. But, would you believe it, even after Nadia won a prize and played a professional gig for a famous composer, her mother still wasn't satisfied, asking her, "Are you certain that you are doing all that you can?"

Nadia was an accomplished musician, but, as I said before, her real contribution to the world of music was as a teacher. Her teaching career began at seventeen, when she won triple honors at the Conservatory: She won first prize in organ, piano accompaniment, and composition. This qualified her to teach music, and she became one of the finest teachers in France and later in America for people who wanted to learn musical composition—this despite wanting to be known as a composer.

Nadia loved teaching because it gave her the means to support her mother and sister. You can imagine how hard it was for her. Women in France were paid only half as much as men for the same work. Nadia worked long days teaching, composing, and caring for her family.

Alongside caring for her mother and sister, Nadia's big ambition was to win the Prix de Rome, France's most prestigious prize in musical composition. Her first attempt at the Prix de Rome failed, but on her next try, she won the Second Grand Prize. This was a big victory for not only for Nadia herself, because it cemented her reputation as a fine musician and composer, but also for all women composers, as many of the members of the all-male jury didn't want to give the prize to a woman. Still, victory though it was, Nadia told herself that someday she would win first prize.

But it wasn't to be. Instead Nadia focused on teaching her talented sister Lili, whose natural talents were blossoming, and who, by this time, in spite of her poor health, was becoming well known for her musical compositions. When Lili was eighteen, her mother threw a big party for her and invited many of France's most renown musicians to come and hear Lili's work. The composers and musicians who attended were as astounded by Lili's talent as they were charmed by her fashionable dress and her sparkling, bubbly personality. They welcomed her into the music world as a promising new composer.

That evening, excited by the accolades her music received at the party, Lili announced that she was going to try for the Prix de Rome. Her mother and sister discouraged her, saying that with her poor health, such a competition would be too strenuous. (Indeed, on Lili's first attempt to compete for the Prix de Rome, her illness caused her to collapse during her performance!) Nevertheless, Lili persisted, and, at the age of nineteen, she became the first woman to win the Prix de Rome. Unfortunately, she died from illness six years later at the young age of twenty-four.

Meanwhile, Nadia continued to branch out and challenge established expectations of what women could achieve in music. She explored conducting. At first she had a hard time making headway in conducting, it being an unusual profession for a woman. Plus, Nadia supported "new music" that audiences didn't understand. When the audience rioted in reaction to the premiere of Igor Stravinsky's extremely difficult ballet *Rite of Spring,* Nadia spoke out in defense of the music and was sad that others mocked it.

Though she did manage some small achievements in conducting, Nadia became famous worldwide for her work as a teacher. The women who studied with her loved her so much they formed the Nadia Boulanger Society to encourage women to take their own emotional, intellectual, and musical development seriously.

In addition to her teaching and conducting, Nadia established a reputation as a doer of good works. At the outbreak of World War I, the French people were suffering great hardship. People were starving; orphans were living homeless on the street. To ease the suffering of her people, Nadia organized the French American Committee to raise money to aid people in need. After American troops entered the war, the situation in France improved, and the French people were eager to show the Americans their appreciation. So Nadia organized a concert for US soldiers and Red Cross nurses stationed in France.

The concert was a huge success. At the end, Nadia played the French and American national anthems on the organ. Can you imagine? Nadia Boulanger organized the first Live Aid concert!

Nadia earned a special place in the hearts of the French and American people for her musical talents and for her good deeds, but perhaps her most notable deed was in helping her friend Walter Damrosch realize his dream of establishing a music school in Fontainbleau for Americans wanting to study music in France. During her long association with the Conservatoire Americain, Nadia, gave lecture-recitals and taught many composers from all over the world.

Many famous American composers of the twentieth century studied with Nadia. Her influence can be heard in much American music of that time. Eventually, Nadia became the director of the American Conservatory. Nadia's students revered her as a teacher because she helped students to develop their own individual gifts. She didn't push her ideas onto them. Maybe you'd like to do a research on Nadia and Lili Boulanger. I wonder what new things you'll discover!

LISTENING:

> Lili Boulanger:
> "Nocturne"
> *Theme & Variations for the Piano*
> "Cortege"
> "D'un Jardin Clair"

M. Olivier Messiaen (1908–1992)

I'm glad you're here, because I want to tell you a story about a very special composer named Olivier Messiaen (o-LIV-ee-yay MAY-see-an). Messiaen was born on December 10, 1908, in Avignon, France. As a young child, he taught himself to play the piano, and when he was only eleven, he was enrolled at the Paris Conservatoire. Can you imagine going to college when you're eleven?

Like most of us, Messiaen had another passion besides music. He was an avid bird watcher and ornithologist. Birdsong fascinated him. He spent a great deal of his life writing down bird songs, and by the time he was a young man he'd amassed quite a catalog of bird melodies, many of which he used in his music.

Messiaen did very well in school and earned himself many prizes, but his education was put on hold in 1940, when World War II came to France. Messiaen was drafted into the French army. Because his eyesight was so poor, he became a medic. Eventually the German army defeated France. They captured Messiaen and sent him to a prison camp in Gorlitz, in what is now Poland.

Life in the prison camp was hard. The Germans gave the prisoners very little to eat. Messiaen had to wear a threadbare prison uniform even in the cold weather. At night he slept in a wooden bunk in a drafty wooden barracks building with thousands of other prisoners, all packed together like sardines. He had no pillow or blanket. He used to lay awake, dreaming of home and of his piano, listening to the birds sing just beyond the electrified fences. In spite of the harsh conditions in the camp, Messiaen managed to compose his most celebrated composition: *The Quartet for the End of Time*. Imagine finding the inspiration to do the work you love even under such poor conditions!

The story goes that one night Messiaen snuck out of his barracks and went for a walk. A guard in a tower spotted him, but Messiaen didn't care about getting shot. Thankfully, the guard didn't shoot him, and Messiaen made it all the way to the prison's electrified fence. On the other side of the fence, just beyond a wide patch of grass, sitting on a branch at the edge of the wood, there sang a nightingale. The nightingale's song was so beautiful that Messiaen was compelled to write it down. Fortunately, he had brought some of his music paper with him to the prison. By some miracle the Germans had let him keep it.

Speaking of Germans, the guard who had spotted Messiaen approached him and turned out to be a very kind young German officer. When he found out that Messiaen was a composer, he showed him to a small private room in the camp bathroom and allowed him to compose there. For three hours every day, Messiaen shut himself in that small bathroom and wrote his music.

Eventually, the German guard arranged for him to have an old, beat-up piano. Another prisoner at the camp was a cellist, and the Germans managed to get him a beat-up old cello. Messiaen was very happy when two more musicians arrived at the camp: a violinist and a clarinetist. These two newcomers brought their instruments with them, and the four musicians formed a quartet.

Finally, Messiaen finished his *Quartet for the End of Time*. He and his three musician friends spent much time rehearsing in the camp bathroom. On January, 15, 1941, an audience of 500 prisoners and guards gathered in the camp mess hall to hear the piece performed.

The German guards even carried wounded and sick prisoners on stretchers up to the makeshift stage to listen to the beautiful music. Messiaen's quartet was about a passage in the Bible in which an angel descends from the sky and announces, "There will be no more time." Can you imagine all those prisoners from all walks of life, gathered together with the German soldiers, all peacefully listening to Messiaen's music? It must have been a timeless moment indeed. When asked later about the performance, Messiaen said, "Never has my music been heard with such attention and understanding."

You'll be happy to know Messiaen survived the camp. After the war, he continued to compose and to teach at the Paris Conservatory until his death on April 27, 1992.

Messiaen led a very colorful life, don't you agree? In fact, he claimed to have a condition called *synesthesia*, which means he could literally see colors when he heard certain chords. He often said that there are no scales, notes, chords, or melodies in music, only color. Let's listen to the *Quartet for the End of Time* and see if we can see some of the colors that Messiaen saw.

LISTENING:

> *Quartet for the End of Time*
> *Catalogue d'Oiseaux*
> *Chronochromie*
> *Des canyons aux étoiles*

N. The Beatles (1962–1970)

Gather 'round! I have a story for you about four rock musicians who at one time formed the most popular and influential band in the entire world. From about 1964 to 1970, these four musicians from Liverpool,

England made music that changed popular music forever. They were John Lennon, Paul McCartney, George Harrison, and Ringo Starr. What you must remember about these four musicians is that neither of them had any musical training or formal music lessons. They basically learned music as they went along. They even had a pretty silly name for themselves: the Beatles.

When John, Paul, George, and Ringo were growing up in the 1950s, Liverpool was a grimy, poor, industrial seaport city. Despite its poverty, it was an exciting place for new music, because sailors returning home to Britain from overseas brought back records from the United States. The favorite records among young people in Liverpool were rock 'n' roll records.

At that time, rock 'n' roll was just beginning. It grew out of many different musical styles, such as country and Western and African AmericanR&B. Rock 'n' roll had an out-of-control, energetic sound with its use of drums, pianos, guitars, and even saxophones. Before the Beatles ever met, each of them was passionate about rock 'n' roll music. They coveted records by singers like Buddy Holly, Bill Haley, Little Richard, the Everly Brothers, and especially Elvis Presley. It might be interesting to do some research on some of those musicians.

But let's get back to the Beatles. John Lennon started the group. He was born in 1940 when German planes were dropping bombs on England during World War II. His father left when he was only five, leaving his mother to raise him. But John's mother, Julia, was too much of a free spirit and left John in the care of his aunt and uncle. Julia visited often, though, and she and John were very close. John's mother helped him get his first guitar. Since she could play banjo, she taught him a few things. John was a real troublemaker at school. He was very smart, but he was always getting into fights, playing the class clown, and getting bad grades.

Later, John went to art college. He was good at drawing and writing, but his main interests were in playing guitar and singing. John formed a band in art school called the Quarrymen. They practiced their music in empty classrooms at lunchtime and after school.

Paul McCartney joined the Quarrymen after he heard them playing at a church picnic. Paul thought John Lennon was cool. When John forgot the lyrics to a song, he just made up his own words. Paul played guitar for John later that day, doing a perfect imitation of some famous rock 'n' roll musicians of the time. John thought Paul was cool and asked him to join the band.

Paul grew up in a musical household. His father directed a small dance band and played the piano. But Paul didn't get interested in music until he heard rock 'n' roll music as a teenager. At age fourteen, Paul became very good at picking out his favorite songs on the piano.

Once he got a guitar, he practiced all the time, even in the bathroom.

So, John and Paul played together in the Quarrymen, when along came George. George was the youngest of the four Beatles. George's parents encouraged him to play guitar. He taught himself to play and often got discouraged, but his mother always told him to keep trying. George could play really well by the time he was fourteen. He went to the same school as Paul, and the two became good friends.

Paul introduced George to John, but John thought George was too young to play in the group. So, George went off on his own for a while, but he kept hanging around with the Quarrymen until one day he played a rock 'n' roll song that happened to be one of John's favorites. John let George into the band right away. And, just like that, John, Paul, and George were in a group together. But they weren't the Beatles yet.

The last member to join the group was Richard Starkey, better known as Ringo Starr. He changed his name because he thought it sounded good for show business. Plus, he loved to wear lots of rings. Ringo had a difficult childhood. He was the same age as John, but he came from one of the roughest parts of Liverpool. He had lots of illnesses that kept him in and out of the hospital until he was at least fifteen. Ringo developed an interest in the drums, and by the time he met John, Paul, and George, who by now were calling themselves the Beatles, the band Ringo started was playing in the same clubs as John's band.

You see, the Beatles already had a drummer, and they were playing regularly at some clubs in Hamburg, Germany. These clubs were not very nice. They were dark and dank and situated in the seediest part of town. The Beatles had to sing for hours, often playing all night. They often had to have their meals right on the stage. They loved to goof around and insult each other and the audience. Their audiences loved them.

But John, George, and Paul liked Ringo's drumming better than their current drummer, so they asked him to become their regular drummer instead. Now they had everything they needed to become a great rock 'n' roll band. John played rhythm guitar, Paul played bass, George played lead guitar, and Ringo played the drums.

Before long, the Beatles were becoming very popular in their hometown of Liverpool, with regular gigs at a popular club called the Cavern. What they really wanted, however, was to become popular outside of their hometown. One day, a record store owner named Brian Epstein heard the Beatles and was blown away. He met with the four guys and told them he could get their songs recorded by a big record company, set up concerts, and get them on the radio and on television shows. But to work with Brian, the Beatles had to agree to stop goofing around on stage and wear matching suits.

With Brian's help, the Beatles were soon playing all over England. They even got to play for the Queen. Their fans went crazy when the Beatles would shake their floppy hair around and sing "Oooo!" Fans would scream and yell at the stage during their shows and even faint. Eventually, the Beatles made their first million-selling record with a song called "She Loves You," which features their trademark "Yeah, yeah, yeah!" By this time the Beatles were the most popular group in England and the rest of Europe.

But the Beatles wanted to become popular in the United States, where all of their favorite rock 'n' roll idols lived. America was the place where rock 'n' roll began. So, Brian contacted the most famous talk show host in the United States at the time, and the Beatles got to make an appearance on his show. In 1964, on the night the Beatles appeared on *The Ed Sullivan Show,* just about everyone in America tuned in. People in the studio audience were screaming so loud that the TV audience could hardly hear the Beatles' music. After that appearance, the Beatles were the most popular rock band ever. They toured all over the world.

Indeed, the Beatles became so popular that it was difficult for them to travel. During shows, fans screamed so much that the Beatles could hardly hear themselves sing and play. They had to rush from their hotel to the venue and back again because fans would mob their cars, thumping on the windows and yelling. Everywhere the Beatles went, a crowd of screaming fans followed them. Also, their tour schedule coupled with their recording schedule meant they rarely had any time off. The Beatles were starting to get fed up.

Finally, the Beatles decided to stop traveling so they could devote their time to recording albums. As soon as they made that decision, their music started to change in a very important way. In the recording studio, the Beatles had the freedom to experiment with all kinds of new sounds, sounds that no one had ever heard on a record before. They used the recording studio like a musical instrument, layering sounds upon sounds until they were satisfied with the results.

In the studio, the Beatles tried different things, like putting echos on their voices, playing back their guitar solos backward, using sound effects and loops, experimenting with noisy feedback, and even recording their voices at different speeds. They tried out different instruments, too. They brought in musicians and instruments from India, as well as symphony orchestra musicians. In fact, the Beatles became the first rock group to use orchestral instruments on their records. They inspired rock musicians with their eclectic sound. One of their greatest albums, *Sgt. Pepper's Lonely Hearts Club Band,* contains many of their most colorful, wonderful sounds.

By the time the Beatles broke up in 1970, they had done what no other group had done before. They elevated rock 'n' roll music to the same level of importance as classical and symphonic music worldwide. Many people who listened to rock started listening to symphonies and vice versa. The Beatles music caused many rock 'n' roll fans to become curious about Indian classical music, reggae music, and even symphonic music. The Beatles' catchy melodies, deep lyrics, and sophisticated structures had a huge influence on rock musicians who followed them.

After they broke up, each of the four Beatles went on to have successful solo careers. Sadly, John Lennon was killed in 1980, and George Harrison died of cancer in 2001. But you can still go to a concert and see Paul McCartney or Ringo Starr play. For now, why don't we just listen to some of the Beatles records?

LISTENING:

> *Sgt. Pepper's Lonely Hearts Club Band*
> *Yellow Submarine*
> "Revolver"
> "Please Me"
> "Help!"
> "Rubber Soul"

II. FAMOUS COMPOSITIONS

II.A. *4′33″* by John Cage

Remember when you were in the primary and you played the silence game? Close your eyes and think back. Imagine yourself sitting there, making no sound whatsoever. Was it really silent? Let's try it now. Let's sit for a few seconds and see if we can truly make silence. There. Was it completely silent? Did you hear any sounds? I did. I heard some cars going by outside. I heard the hum of the heating system. I heard some people talking out in the hallway. I even heard some birds chirping.

Is there really such a thing as silence? Today I'd like to tell you about a very special piece of music that explores the question of what silence really is and whether making silence is even possible. But here's the twist: at the end of my story, I want you to help me decide whether this piece of music is really music at all! Let's begin.

The piece of music I want to tell you about was written in 1952 by American experimental composer John Cage. It's called *4'33"*. If that seems like an unusual name, well, that's because it's a very unusual work. You see, Cage wrote *4'33"* for any instrument or combination of instruments. The catch is, he instructs the players not to play or make any sound for the duration of the piece's three movements. In the score, each movement contains only one marking, the word *tacet*, which is Latin for "be silent."

Can you imagine a piece of music that is made up of no sound? Neither could the audience at the premiere performance of *4'33"* in 1952. Expecting some fancy music at the fancy concert hall in Woodstock, New York, they watched the pianist walk onto the stage, sit, and, to mark the beginning of the piece, close the keyboard cover.

After a short time of doing nothing, the pianist then marked the end of the first movement by opening the keyboard cover again. He repeated this for two more movements for a total of four minutes and thirty-three seconds. You can imagine that the audience, expecting to hear the pianist play written sounds by the composer, felt a little cheated. Some probably even felt like the whole thing was a big joke.

But John Cage wasn't joking. He intended to challenge the very definition of music. He wrote his piece to question the nature of silence. According to John Cage, the "music" in the piece consists of the ambient sounds of the environment and not on organized sounds written by him and interpreted by the piano player. According to John Cage, *4'33"* was his most important work. It embodied his belief that "any sounds may constitute music," an idea he came upon by studying Zen Buddhism.

Cage got the idea for the piece when he went to an exhibition by his painter friend Robert Rauchenberg, who had painted a series of blank white paintings. Rauchenberg liked the idea that the different lighting in the gallery at different times of day and the movement of people's shadows across the blank white surface of the paintings would constitute the paintings themselves. John Cage was intrigued by this and wanted to do the equivalent in music.

Many people were angry when *4'33"* was premiered. They felt that John Cage was being cheeky. Not only was he questioning the nature of music, but he was also exploiting the social regimen of going to a concert. People felt that John Cage was taking advantage of the audience's high expectations. After all, where else, but

in a prestigious concert hall, expecting to hear music by a high-status composer and performer, would people sit and listen to four minutes and thirty-three seconds of complete silence? Audiences were sometimes upset or even angry, not realizing, of course, that they themselves were part of the music!

Despite the controversy, *4'33"* is a popular and enduring work. In December 2010, an international simultaneous performance of *4'33"* took place. Over 200 amateur and professional musicians and artists from all around the world, conducted live via video link, performed the piece by sitting in silence for four minutes and thirty-three seconds.

So, what do you think? Do you think a piece of music where the performer does nothing counts as music? Think about it. Imagine that the piece of music you want to write is a container with a beginning and an end and you can fill that container with any combination of sound and silence, which is basically what a composer does. Why can't you fill the container only with silence? Isn't that still music? Well, many musicians, artists, and philosophers continue to weigh in on the question of the nature of music.

Would you like to listen to a performance of *4'33"*? I know! Why don't we perform it ourselves? Or shall we play the silence game again? Let's see what sounds we can hear during the silence this time.

II.B. *CARNIVAL OF THE ANIMALS* BY CAMILLE SAINT-SAËNS

Note. This story works best accompanied by a recording of the music. Each movement is named after the animal it represents.]

I'm thinking about a composer who lived in France about 150 years ago named Camille Saint-Saëns (pronounced san-SONZ). Although Camille was a serious composer, he still loved a good joke. In fact, one of his

most famous pieces of music was written as a joke. It's called *Carnival of the Animals*. The students in Camille's music class requested him to write it. When they heard it, they thought it was very funny, and, as it turns out, so did many other people. It's one of Camille's most famous compositions. I'd like to share it with you.

Many different kinds of animals turn up in the carnival. You'll find swans, tortoises, roosters, elephants, donkeys, birds, a lion, some kangaroos, and even some pianists. Well, I suppose pianists are animals too! Also, Camille selected a very special orchestra for his *Carnival,* because he wanted the instruments to represent the different animals. Before we discuss the animals in the *Carnival,* let me tell you a little bit about Camille's orchestra.

An orchestra is made up of dozens of players all playing together to make whatever sound you can imagine. You would think having so many people playing all at the same time would be confusing, but, fortunately, a person called a conductor stands in front of the orchestra and leads them by gesturing with his or her hands and a waving a baton.

Usually, the instruments in an orchestra are grouped into four families, but to represent the animals in his *Carnival,* Camille uses only three of the families: the strings, the woodwinds, and the percussion.

The string family has instruments made of wood, with four strings that the player plays with a bow. You've probably seen a violin, viola, cello, or bass before. The woodwind instruments are basically long cylinders made of wood, metal, or plastic with holes in them. The player makes a sound by blowing into the instrument and covering certain holes with his or her fingers.

Clarinets, oboes, flutes, and piccolos are all members of the woodwind family. The percussion instruments are usually things you can touch, strike, or hit to make a sound. Xylophones, glockenspiels, drums, and pianos are all percussion instruments.

Does it seem funny that the piano would be considered a percussion instrument? Well, because the piano has lots of tiny hammers inside that strike the strings when the player presses a key, people consider it to be a percussion instrument. The piano is very important in the *Carnival,* as you'll see in a moment.

[*Note.* Here, you can begin playing the music.] The first animal to arrive in Camille's unusual carnival is the lion. The strings play a marching tune to show the lion strutting around his kingdom and the pianos roll and crash to render a frightening roar. Then the music goes quiet again as the lion sits to survey the land. But the animal lets out one more roar before proudly marching off.

Then come the hens and roosters. The violin and viola play spiky, jumpy music as the hens scratch, cluck, and squawk. The piano plays high trills when the rooster comes around trying to get attention from the hens. When the rooster comes into the picture, he's played by the clarinet, but it's hard to hear him over the hens' squawking and clucking.

Next come the donkeys. They chase each other around and around as the piano music rushes up and down the keyboard. Normally, donkeys are pretty slow animals but not in Camille's *Carnival.* The music goes up quickly and rushes back down again, almost as if the donkeys are racing. Finally two loud crashes on the piano tell us the donkeys are exhausted and have had enough.

The tortoises are next. Again the strings play their melody, but this time they play a slow, plodding dance. They slowly dance around until only the piano is left playing. The tortoises are tired from all that dancing.

After the tortoises leave, the piano starts playing a waltz tune that means the elephants have arrived. A waltz is a graceful dance that in Camille's time was very popular at parties. The double bass comes in to portray the elephant. The sound of the double bass is deep and gruff as it lumbers along. This elephant tries to dance, but it's too heavy and clumsy, so as the piano plays faster, the elephant just stomps around as best it can.

Now that the elephant has finished his dance, the kangaroos are announced by piano music that seems to hop and jump. It almost sounds as if kangaroos themselves are jumping on the keyboard as the music leaps all over the piano. Sometimes the piano plays very quietly as the kangaroos stand still.

Next up are the fish in the aquarium. If you listen carefully, you can hear in the music all the tiny fish with their colorful scales and funny faces. The flute and the string instruments play a gentle, gliding melody as the fish swim through the water. In the pianos, you can hear gentle rolling waves. And finally, glittering above on the surface of the water is the sun, portrayed by the glockenspiel.

Now Camille starts to get silly. The next group in the Carnival is the animals with long ears. You can hear a donkey hee-hawing in the violins as they play loud squeaky notes. Hear how the donkeys bray louder and faster and the violins start to squeak and squawk.

After the donkeys exit; springtime comes and the soft, sweet sound of a clarinet plays the cuckoo's song. The cuckoo sings two notes, one high and one low. Behind the clarinet cuckoo, you can hear the pianos playing the noises in the woods. Leaves seem to rustle and breezes brush through the trees.

The cuckoo ushers in a host of birds, played by the flute in high, fast melodies. Can you hear how the birds rush around and flap their wings up and down? The music sounds light and active, just like little birds on the wing. The piano plays their chirps and trills, while the violin plays the very air they hover in. Finally, the music goes higher and higher. Where are the birds going?

And now Camille has his little joke. Even though they aren't animals, here come the pianists to join the carnival. Unfortunately, they don't play very well. They're like beginners who sit and practice their exercises. You can hear them playing the same music over and over again, making the other animals feel bored. Are you getting bored yet? Do you hear that melody in the string instruments? They're telling the pianists to hurry up and stop playing. Finally the pianists stop.

Now after the pianists come the fossils. They are the bony skeletons of dinosaurs coming out in the night under the moonlight to dance a spooky dance. In the xylophones, you can hear the bones rattling along as they dance. The stars are out, and you can hear the tune "Twinkle, Twinkle, Little Star" played on the pianos. In the end, all of the other instruments join in the jolly dance.

At last, the most beautiful animal of all comes on the scene. You can hear slow and graceful music as the swan makes his entrance and glides across the serene river. In the background, the pianos play the rippling water. Now the cello plays suddenly loud and then soft as the swan glides nearer and flutters his wings. At the end, the swan drifts off into the distance, and all you can hear is the ripple of the water.

Now we have come to the finale, and all the animals in the orchestra come out for a grand parade. After some swooshing sounds played on the piano, the orchestra plays a parade song. After a few measures full of floating fish, the donkeys rush by, hooves clattering. Then the violins play the jagged, pointy music of the clucking hens and roosters. Next come the kangaroos hopping up and down on the pianos. All the animals come out in the finale in succession, and they all dance together for the grand finale of the *Carnival of the Animals*.

Would you like to listen to the whole piece on your own? Maybe you'd like to make a listening map of what's happening in the piece. Let me show you how.

II.C. *The Farewell Symphony* by Joseph Haydn

I'm delighted to tell you a story about one of the world's best-loved symphonies, *The Farewell Symphony* by Joseph Haydn. Our story begins in the summer of 1772 in the town of Eisenstadt, Austria, on Prince Esterhazy's lavish estate. Prince Esterhazy was a very wealthy nobleman with a passion for music. He employed his own orchestra consisting of twenty-two musicians and their director, Joseph Haydn.

Haydn's job was to write music for the prince, manage the musicians, and repair the instruments. The musicians' job was to keep the Prince and his guests entertained, and they were very busy, for Prince Nicholas demanded opera and ballet in the evenings, chamber music in the afternoons, and outdoor music for strolls in the garden. He had music for formal balls, dinner music to accompany particular meals, sacred music for his chapel, and even trumpets to herald the arrival of guests.

Haydn and the musicians were so busy that they never got to see their families. As the summer wore on, they began to get homesick and complain. They persuaded Haydn to go and ask the Prince if their spouses and children could come and join them. Haydn did so, but the Prince refused. After all, his palace only had 126 rooms! When you took into account his many guests, there was hardly enough room even for his servants' families.

When Haydn took the news back to the musicians, they were furious. But what could they do? Anyone who complained would be fired. In spite of their frustration, they all agreed to stick it out until the end of the summer. But summer ended, autumn came, and winter set in, and still the Prince didn't let the musicians go home.

The musicians came to Haydn once again, asking him to appeal to the Prince. This time Haydn was cautious. He went home and tried to think of a plan of how to communicate to the Prince the musicians' frustration. Finally it came to him. In less than two weeks, he wrote a brand-new symphony that would give the Prince the message. As he handed out copies of his new symphony he told the musicians his plan. They poured all of their emotions into rehearsing the new piece.

On the night of the performance, the musicians were already waiting on the stage for the Prince and his guests to arrive. The Prince listened carefully as they began playing. The first movement was fast, in an unusual key, with explosive chords, streams of quick repetitive notes, and lots of tension. The Prince thought the music sounded rather angry. Haydn felt that it expressed the musician's frustration at being kept so long away from their families.

The second movement was different, with light splashes of sound trickling from the strings. Sorrowful tunes passed from one instrument to the next, first to a violin and then to an oboe. The Prince felt how sad the music was. It expressed the musicians' sorrow over being separated from their families.

The third movement was a dance. It was light, and quick, but then the cellos and horns broke in with a clumsy, loud noise. It almost sounded like a mistake. But when it happened again, the Prince realized that the musicians were making fun of him in the music, since he was a terrible dancer. During the many balls he threw at the palace he was always stumbling and stomping on his partners' toes.

Finally, the fourth movement came and with it the clearest message of all. The music was mellifluous and magnificent. After the final, resounding chords, however, something special happened. A slow section began, during which, one by one, the instruments began dropping out, and as they did so, the musicians quietly stood up and left the stage. Gradually the music got softer as the instruments dropped out until only Haydn was left, playing a violin solo. When his solo ended, he too got up and left, leaving the stage empty.

The Prince got the musicians'' point. He said goodbye to the musicians and let them go home. This is why Haydn's Symphony no. 45 has the nickname "The Farewell Symphony." Shall we listen to the symphony, or shall we say farewell to each other for now and have another story on another day?

II.D. *The Heroic Symphony* by Ludwig van Beethoven

Today I want to tell you the story of a very special piece of music: *The Heroic Symphony* by Ludwig van Beethoven. Do you remember hearing about Beethoven? If you don't, I'll tell you a story about him on another day.

For now, our story starts in the late eighteenth century when Beethoven was living in the city of Vienna, then the center of art and music in Europe. He was making a nice living as a pianist. In fact, he was the best pianist in town, if not in all of Europe. Wealthy people paid Beethoven large sums of money to come to their homes and play for their guests. Beethoven wrote music that showcased his keyboard talents, and when he played, everyone cheered. Beethoven had everything: talent, fame, and money. But he also had a secret. No one was aware that Beethoven was slowly going deaf.

For Beethoven, losing his hearing meant an end to his music career. How could a pianist play music if he can't hear it? So he sought out many forms of treatment. Finally, he went to the town of Heiligenstadt to see a doctor. At that time, medicine wasn't as advanced as it was today, and the doctor in Heiligenstadt recommended many treatments, all of which Beethoven tried. He ate a special diet, exercised regularly, and rested his ears. Finally, the doctor concluded that his treatments were a failure. Beethoven was going deaf. His career as a pianist was over.

At first, Beethoven was saddened by this news. He contemplated suicide, writing a long farewell letter to his brothers. "Without performing, without my music, what reason is there to live?" he wrote. But it occurred to him that although his ears were failing, his imagination was strong and nothing could take that away from him. If he could imagine music, he could write it down. By the end of his stay in Heiligenstadt, Beethoven had decided to devote his life to composing. He felt that becoming a great composer would give his life meaning. Filled with hope, he returned to Vienna.

Back in Vienna, Beethoven searched for inspiration for his next composition. He wanted his music not just to entertain people but to exhilarate them, to make them think, and to touch their souls; so he sought a great heroic figure to write about. One day he read in the newspaper about a French war hero named Napoleon Bonaparte. Bonaparte helped to rid France of a cruel and unjust king. He created a government run by the people, and he promised religious education and freedom to all people, not just the wealthy ones. In Napoleon Bonaparte, Beethoven found his heroic figure.

Now that he had a subject for his symphony, Beethoven needed a melody that was as heroic and bold as Bonaparte. He had a hard time finding such a melody. One day, while out for a walk, he saw in a magazine a picture of Bonaparte astride a magnificent stallion: handsome, unafraid, and certain of victory. Beethoven thought of his own struggles against deafness and a magnificent melody galloped into his head. He ran home and started working on his new symphony.

For five long months Beethoven worked, blending his own life struggles into a four-movement symphony about the life of Napoleon Bonaparte. Finally, when he was finished, he played his Bonaparte Symphony on the piano for a close friend. The first movement of Beethoven's new symphony was full of the sounds of cannon blasts and battle calls, soldiers' laments, and horses galloping forward across battlefields. The second movement was a sad, slow funeral march, full of longing and anxiety, with the specter of Death hanging over it. The movement probably reflected Bonaparte's advance across the battlefield as well as Beethoven's inner suffering. The third movement was a dance of celebration in which the battle is ended and hope appears on the horizon.

But the fourth movement, the most difficult for Beethoven to write, was the symphony's crown jewel. Beethoven based the movement on the legend of Prometheus, who brought humankind the gift of fire. The way Beethoven saw it, Bonaparte was like a modern Prometheus, giving humankind the gift of liberty. Into this movement, Beethoven packed the full range of human emotions—love, anger, sorrow, joy. After Beethoven struck the final chords on the piano, his friend declared Beethoven's new symphony to be a masterpiece.

Beethoven spent the next couple of weeks making a second copy of his symphony to be sent to Napoleon as a gift. Just as he was putting it in the envelope he learned some terrible news. Napoleon Bonaparte had crowned himself Emperor of France. Can you imagine, a man who worked hard to give people freedom from tyrannical rulers becoming himself a tyrannical ruler?

In the eyes of Beethoven, and many people throughout Europe, crowning himself emperor meant that Bonaparte the freedom fighter had become Bonaparte the tyrant. Beethoven was so enraged that he grabbed his copy of the new symphony and ripped it to shreds. Can you imagine, destroying five months of work out of anger? His friend had to shield the second copy from Beethoven so that it wouldn't be destroyed.

Well, eventually Beethoven calmed down. He took the second copy of the symphony and scratched out the name Bonaparte until a hole appeared in the paper. Then he wrote "Eroica" below it in large letters. You see, Beethoven had decided that the symphony wasn't about Bonaparte. It was about himself, about humanity, about the heroism within us all.

The Heroic Symphony was first performed in 1804. No one knew then the story behind the work, but everyone was moved by it. Beethoven had accomplished what he'd set out to do: He exhilarated people, made them think, and touched their souls. From then on, Beethoven felt his life once again had meaning.

II.E. *Pictures at an Exhibition* by Modest Mussorgsky

In the 1870s, St. Petersburg in Russia was a thriving city, a major center of fashion and culture in Europe. Everyone living there felt a sense of hope and prosperity, especially the young artists and musicians, who looked to the future with a sense of excitement.

Three friends in particular concern our little story: Modest Mussorgsky, a composer, and his two friends, Vladimir Stasov, a writer, and Victor Harmann, an architect. The three great friends loved to get together on sunny mornings and spend the day working on their various projects. They belonged to a group of artists who were keen to make their mark in the world. Modest wanted to write great operas. Victor wanted to design fantastic decorative structures, like towers and gates. And Vladimir wanted to travel the world writing about all of Russia's great talents.

But sometimes life doesn't go as planned, and in 1873, tragedy struck the three friends. Victor died; his death was very sudden. It came just after he had finished a design for a building competition—a magnificent structure for the City Gate of Kiev. Victor had always wanted to see one of his designs built in stone. Sadly, this was not to be.

Modest was saddened by Victor's death. He expressed his sorrow in a letter to Vladimir. "Why should a dog, a horse, a rat, live on and creatures like Hartmann must die!" he wrote. For the next few weeks, he hid himself away from his friends, suffering the loss of his dear friend Victor. When he did go out in public, he was a completely different person. His face was swollen and red. His hands shook. He was irritable and mean. He even stopped writing music. Everyone was worried about him.

One day, Vladimir and some of Modest's other friends decided to organize an exhibition of their late friend Victor's art. They spent the winter gathering his work. By

February, they had over 400 paintings and drawings to show the world. It was to be a very special exhibition.

On the day of the opening, Vladimir went to Modest and invited him to come. Modest refused. Seeing Victor's art would be too painful. But Vladimir wouldn't take no for an answer. He had a reputation for being a pretty bossy person. All of his friends called him "The Great General." And, like a general, he practically ordered Modest to come.

When they got to the gallery, Vladimir reminded Modest that a special part of their friend Victor lives inside all of those he left behind. "Remember Victor," said Vladimir, "and the pain of his passing will ease." Modest was very sad to see Victor's art, so he asked Vladimir to let him go into the gallery alone.

When Modest entered the gallery, he was struck dumb. Hanging on the walls were all of his dear friend Victor's hopes and dreams. As he strolled through the gallery, each picture brought back sweet memories of their friendship. The first picture to greet Modest was one of a little gnome, all grumpy and sad, as he had been. One picture showed a gloomy old castle Victor had designed for an opera. There were some costume designs for a ballet. Another painting showed a park in Paris, where lovers strolled, birds flew about, and children played next to a swing. Modest was one of those children, and he remembered that day fondly.

Many portraits were part of the exhibition. A portrait of a wealthy man, Samuel Goldenberg, sat alongside a portrait of Schmuyl the old beggar. Some peasants that Modest and Victor had come across while out for a stroll were depicted as well. Victor had painted everything from a bright, sunny early morning market to dark candlelit catacombs. His whole life was hanging in the gallery. Even a character from Victor's favorite folktale was represented: Baba Yaga the witch, sitting in her hut built on chicken legs. One picture in particular struck Modest: the Great Gate of Kiev.

Modest was so impressed with the beauty and glory of Victor's design that he resolved to build it for him, only not out of stone, out of music.

Modest rushed home and went straight to his piano. He hadn't played for months, but suddenly, in thinking about Victor's art, he was full of ideas for music. He created musical versions of ten of Victor's portraits. With feverish, dancing sounds, he painted a sound portrait of the little gnome. Next came the ancient castle, and the beautiful park with its chirping birds and playing children. He painted the wealthy man Samuel Goldenberg, the beggar, the peasants, the bright marketplace, and the dismal catacombs, all with brushstrokes of music. Finally, in great crashing chords, he painted Victor's magnificent Great Gate of Kiev.

It took Modest many weeks of working at his piano to finally blend all of his musical pictures into one composition. To tie it all together, he added a picture of himself walking through the gallery, moving from one painting to the next. When the music was finished, he wrote the title across the front page: *Pictures at an Exhibition.* He immediately mailed his music to Vladimir, with the inscription: "To the Great General, in Memory of dear Victor. June 27, 1874."

In the years that followed, Modest enjoyed great success as a composer. He wrote operas and many famous piano pieces. All the while he kept his dear friend Victor alive inside him. Vladimir also went on to great success as an art critic. He traveled all over the world, writing articles that told people *about Pictures at an Exhibition.* He helped to ensure that the memory of Victor lives on in the music of his friend Modest Mussorgsky.

I wonder if you'd like to hear Victor's pictures now? Do you think Victor would be happy to know that 140 years later, some children in a Montessori class on the other side of the world are listening to this music and thinking about him? Do you think he might be thankful to his friend Modest Mussorgsky for bringing his pictures to us? I know I'm grateful. Let's have a listen.

II.F. *Rhapsody in Blue* by George Gershwin

George Gershwin was a popular songwriter of the early twentieth century who lived in New York City. Together with his brother Ira, he composed music for Broadway musicals. His career really took off in 1920 when he wrote a hit song called "Swanee." He wrote popular songs for nightclubs, movies, and Broadway shows. As talented and versatile as George was, however, he hadn't written much classical music.

You see, in George's time, people listened to jazz in nightclubs, where they would dance and have fun. On the other hand, people listened to classical music in concert halls, where they would sit quietly in the dark and listen. The two kinds of music couldn't have been more different. That is, until George came along. Imagine his shock and surprise when he saw an article in the paper one day proclaiming that he was going to be premiering a new classical concerto at a concert taking place in only five weeks. After all, George was not working on any concerto at all!

At first, George panicked. He went straight to his friend Paul Whiteman, the organizer of the concert, and told him that, not only had he never written a concerto, but that five weeks was not enough time to write one even if he could. His friend Paul encouraged him, however, and in the end, George was determined to give it a shot.

So he went home to try to work on his concerto, but no ideas came to him. He listened to concertos by many of the composers that came before him, people like Franz Liszt and Frederic Chopin, but nothing inspired him. He went on walks, bought brand new papers and fancy pens, went to the piano and tried to improvise something, but nothing came to him. He was completely stuck for an idea. Frustrated, he thought of calling his friend Paul and canceling the whole thing. But sometimes ideas lie in wait for us and then pop into our heads at the most interesting times in the most interesting places.

One day, George boarded a train for Boston, where he was going to start rehearsing a new musical. As he sat in his train seat, brooding over his concerto, the clickity-clack of the train wheels started to absorb his attention. Soon, he was moving his feet and tapping his fingers along with the rhythm. He looked out the window and let his mind wander. He thought about all of the music that he knew and loved. The rhythm of the train wheels reminded him of dancing the foxtrot at the Palais Royal in Harlem. He remembered as a child roller-skating past the Barron Wilkins Club in Harlem, where he sat on the curb and listened to the sound of ragtime pouring out of the windows onto the busy street.

After listening for a long time to the train wheels, George got an idea in his mind of how his entire concerto would go. He decided to mix all the music he loved, ragtime, blues, jazz, Klezmer, and foxtrot, into one big tapestry. His concerto, in George's own words, would be "a sort of musical kaleidoscope of America—of our vast melting pot, of our incomparable national pep, our blues, our metropolitan madness."

So, while in Boston, George worked on his concerto whenever and wherever he could. He worked in his hotel room, during rehearsal breaks, in the morning at breakfast, on the train to and from rehearsals, and late at night long after the theater had closed. George poured all of his energy into his concerto. After two weeks, with his concerto almost finished, he returned to New York and showed it to his friends. His friends thought it was brilliant, but for George, the piece wasn't quite finished. He felt it was missing something, some beautiful melody that would tie everything in this musical collage together.

One night, just after he got back to New York, George went to a party in a spacious penthouse on top of a tall skyscraper. At the party was a grand piano, which of course George couldn't resist sitting down and playing. As soon as he sat down and looked out from his vantage point at the glittering city lights, he realized how much he'd missed New York City, and a beautiful melody started flying from his imagination into the keys of the piano. He had found his beautiful melody, the centerpiece of his new concerto.

After another week, George completed his concerto. He played it for his brother Ira, who thought it was amazing. Now, all George needed was a name. He wanted to call it *American Rhapsody*, but Ira thought he could come up with something with a bit more panache. Ira had just been to a museum and viewed a painting by James McNeill Whistler called *Arrangement in Gray and Black* and thought it might be cool if George added some color to the name of his new piece. George immediately thought of *Rhapsody in Blue,* and the name stuck.

Finally, the night of the premiere of George's concerto arrived. George was surprised when he drove up to the theater to see a big crowd of people waiting outside to get in to hear the music. The concert was actually a showcase of "modern music" with all kinds of different pieces of music being played before George's concerto. And while that music was playing, the audience began to get bored and restless. They were expecting to hear "modern music," something new, something avant-garde, but the concert consisted of music one might hear in a regular nightclub. The audience started to shout and complain. Some even got up to leave.

Seeing this, George quickly rushed out on stage and sat at his piano to begin his concerto. When the audience heard the howl of the opening clarinet melody, with its screechy, bluesy tune, they stopped complaining and began to listen. Soon, the brass joined in, followed by warm, sultry strings.

George's mix of jazz and classical music astonished the audience. They loved watching him cross hands as he played fast melodies and thick chords on the piano. They reveled in the clickity-clack driving rhythms of the orchestra. George had wowed them with his musical melting pot. There was even a banjo to add to some of the excitement. The audience began to dance and sing along, something that would never happen at a classical concerto.

George showed great perseverance in creating his *Rhapsody in Blue,* and, in so doing, he created an American masterpiece. How about if we listen to the piece? I wonder if you'll be able to hear the bluesy and jazzy parts. Does it sound like America to you?

II.G *Danse Macabre* » by Camille Saint-Saëns

Paris, France, is a colorful, lively city. It's nicknamed "the City of Light," and it's no wonder. At night, the lights of the Eiffel Tower glitter over the rooftops, and the streets are bathed in a warm glow that spills out from cafes, restaurants, and art galleries.

Underneath the streets of Paris, however, is a vast underground cemetery—a long network of dark tunnels lined with, can you guess? Over six million human skulls and bones. Can you imagine what a spooky place that is? This eerie place was created in 1786, when bones from overcrowded French cemeteries were transferred there. Later, victims of the French Revolution were buried there. Today, the Paris Catacombs are a popular tourist destination. You and I can get tickets to go down and walk the hallways lined with spooky bones. Wouldn't that be interesting?

Well, many famous poets and writers of the nineteenth century ventured down into the catacombs for a bit of adventure. One of them was the French composer Camille Saint-Saëns, who found in the Catacombs inspiration for one of his most famous pieces of music. It's called the *Danse macabre* ("Macabre Dance"), and I'd like to tell you about it.

Saint-Saëns visited the Catacombs on an autumn night in 1872. While he was walking around down there in the darkness, the light from his candle must have flickered along the bones and made them appear to dance. His visit so inspired him with visions of skeletons rising out of their graves and dancing that he decided to write a spooky piece of music on that very subject.

One day shortly after, Saint-Saëns came across a poem by the French poet Henri Cazalis, who himself had visited the Catacombs. Mr. Cazalis's poem was about Maestro Death. Part of it goes:

> *Zig and zig and zig.*
> *Maestro Death keeps time.*
> *Tapping his heel on a tomb.*
> *Zig and zig and zag on his violin.*
> *At midnight he played a dancing tune.*

Determined to compose his spine-chilling song, Saint-Saëns visited Cazalis and asked him if he could set the poet's words to spooky music. Cazalis approved, and Saint-Saëns rushed home and wrote the song in just a few days.

Sometime later, Saint-Saëns brought his scary song to a dinner party hosted by Augusta Holmes, a famous singer. After dinner Saint-Saëns invited Augusta to sing his new song for all of her guests. She sang the song with great beauty and emotion. Saint-Saëns was angered by her performance. He wrote his song about skeletons rising from the grave, but Augusta had sung it like it was a romantic love song. Clearly, Saint-Saëns's intentions had not come through in his music.

That evening on the way home, Saint-Saëns felt discouraged. How could he get the audience to hear his intentions when listening to his *Dance macabre*. He decided to rewrite the music so that there would be no mistake about what he wanted. As soon as he got home he began rewriting his song into a full orchestral composition. Saint-Saëns worked on his new version of the *Danse macabre* for two years. He marked carefully in the score every musical effect he wanted. He indicated precisely how each note should be played. He even invented some notation symbols to indicate sounds that had never been heard before.

For example, instead of the violins drawing the bow across the strings like usual, Saint-Saëns instructed them to smack the strings with the wood part of their bows to make the loud clacking sounds of the rattling bones. He also indicated that the violins should tune their E strings a half step lower, to make the interval of a tritone, which in the Middle Ages was nicknamed "the devil's interval."

In his quest for spooky sounds, he mixed waltzes with funeral songs and experimented with different instruments, like the xylophone, which until the *Danse macabre* had never appeared in an orchestra. In fact, the xylophone was so rare an instrument, Saint-Saëns had to indicate in the score where one could be purchased.

More than 2,000 people attended the first performance of the *Danse macabre*. It was a spooky performance. The piece began with the twelve strokes of midnight ringing out on the harp. Then the first violin plays the haunting melody of Maestro Death. Then, one by one, skeletons began to rise from their graves and dance. The cellos played high straining melodies, the wood of the violin bows played the bones clacking, and the xylophones clicked as the skeletons danced along with Maestro Death's tune. Through a spooky gloom, the skipping skeletons glowed white, and Death began to play a funeral waltz.

With trombones blasting and cymbals crashing, the dancing, jumping skeletons started to fly around, swooshing and twirling. Then, sunlight appeared on the horizon as the oboe played the rooster's call. The timpani rumbled as Maestro Death ended the song and the violins clicked and clacked as the skeletons scampered away.

The performance was followed by complete silence. No one knew what to say. They were appalled by what they heard. Some people clapped, but many others shouted insults at the stage. They were outraged. They thought the piece was scandalous, nonsensical, and horrific. The critics harshly dismissed the *Danse macabre* in the press. Saint-Saëns didn't mind. The orchestra had played his *Danse macabre* exactly the way he wanted it. He had stayed true to his vision and finally brought his dancing skeletons to life. In the end, the *Danse macabre* became one of Saint-Saëns's most celebrated and popular works.

I wonder what it would sound like if skeletons could rise from their graves and start dancing at the stroke of midnight? Why don't we listen to the *Danse macabre* and find out?

II.H. The Four Seasons by Antonio Vivaldi

Even in the eighteenth century, the city of Venice was a popular tourist destination. People loved to visit the island city, where they could ride on a gondola through the narrow canals, feed the pigeons in lovely St. Mark's square, or go to a concert at one of the city's many cathedrals and concert halls. Venice was a city that was rich in music. The theaters were full of opera, the canals were replete with folk songs, and St. Mark's Basilica was filled to the brim with the sounds of trumpets and trombones.

One of the main attractions in the musical city was the Osppedale della Pietá orphanage, where orphaned and abandoned girls were given safe haven and taught music. Each week the girls of the Pietá performed a concert. Visitors gathered in the great hall and watched as the musicians appeared in the upper gallery behind an ornate iron grill that shielded them from view. When they played, the most beautiful music flowed down from their violins, violas, cellos, and filled the air above the visitors' heads. The Pietá orchestra was one of Italy's finest.

The girls of the Pietá rarely left the orphanage. Their only visitor was their teacher and music director, a priest named Antonio Vivaldi. The girls loved Vivaldi. They affectionately called him Padre Rossi, which means Father Redhead, because of his wild, flowing red hair.

Vivaldi was in charge of composing the girls' music, maintaining their instruments, and giving them lessons, for, in addition to being a composer, he was an accomplished violin player.

He used to sit with the girls sometimes, in lieu of rehearsing or giving lessons, and just tell them musical stories. Often, he sat with his violin and brought to life stories about valiant knights, evil sorceresses, and lovelorn maidens. He took the girls on imaginative trips to far off places, where they strolled through exotic cities, danced in silk gowns, and climbed high mountains.

Life at the orphanage was difficult, you see. None of the girls had parents, and many of them had physical disabilities and sicknesses. Vivaldi did everything he could to lift the girls' spirits.

But the chief governor of the Pietá was not so happy with Vivaldi's free-form, fanciful style. He believed that the girls ought to have a more formal musical education, with a focus on proper playing technique. He didn't think Vivaldi should waste their time telling stories. So, one day in 1718, the chief governor dismissed Vivaldi from his post. The girls were sad to see their friend and teacher gather up his things and leave the school.

Vivaldi went to Mantua, but he missed the girls terribly. He toured around Italy, playing violin for wealthy dukes and princes. He kept himself busy composing operas, concertos, and sonatas. He became an international success. Despite this, he missed Venice, and especially he missed his students, the girls at the Pietá.

Some years later, back at the Pietá, the governors got wind of Vivaldi's success. They came to regret dismissing him and got the idea to offer him his job back. Having the now famous Vivaldi as their music director would really draw in audiences, but since he had become an international celebrity, the Pietá could scarcely afford to hire him again. So instead, they sent Vivaldi a letter inviting him to continue to compose for the Pietá orchestra. Vivaldi accepted their offer and agreed to send the orphanage two new compositions a month.

The first of these new works arrived in a package with the word Spring written upon it. It was something of a musical poem. It is full of the sounds of birds singing, and of flowing and murmuring streams. Then a storm comes and the orchestra explodes with thunderclaps and lighting flashes. Once the storm passes, the birds return with their happy song. Then we find ourselves in a meadow, with the violins playing the sound of a herd of goats grazing peacefully and the violas representing their barking dog. The other strings render the rustling leaves and the swaying grasses. Finally there begins a peasant dance, as high on the mountaintops, a shepherd plays his pipes. A lilting song representing the scent of flowers flows out of the strings.

In the coming months three packages followed: Summer, Autumn, and Winter.

Together, these four pieces formed a larger work called *The Four Seasons*. When The *Four Seasons* was finally published, an explanatory sonnet accompanied each movement. Vivaldi wrote these sonnets after he'd written the music. Much to his delight, the governors of the orphanage invited Vivaldi back again and again to rehearse with the girls whenever he could find time in his schedule. By 1729, Vivaldi had supplied the orphanage with over 140 concertos. But among all those works, *The Four Seasons* remains a favorite.

I wonder if the music for *The Four Seasons* is so special because it expresses how much, with each passing season, Vivaldi missed the girls of the Pietá? Why don't we listen to *The Four Seasons* and you can tell me what you think?

III. MUSICAL INSTRUMENTS AND ENSEMBLES

III.A. The Western Symphony Orchestra, Part I: Sections and Instruments

[*Note:* This story is a bit long for one sitting. Break it up over multiple days.]

Sit back, relax, and listen to my story. I want to tell you about the symphony orchestra. The name orchestra, incidentally, comes from the Greek word *orkhestra,* which is the name of the area in front of the ancient Greek stage reserved for the chorus.

The first thing you might notice, when you listen to an orchestra, is how big it sounds. So many instruments playing so many different sounds, and yet they seem to come together so seamlessly. The fact is, dozens of players make up an orchestra. Can you imagine? A hundred or more people simultaneously making such amazing, magical music!

Although orchestral music sounds complicated, it might make things simpler to think of it as being only made up of four sections, or families: strings, woodwinds, brass, and percussion. Just like people's families, every member of every instrument family has a special part to play in the music, and no one instrument is more important than any other. Under the leadership of the conductor, each instrument takes and gives focus in order to interpret each composer's ideas.

Let me tell you about the personalities of the various instruments and their instrument families and how they work together to create a thrilling musical experience.

The String Section

The expressiveness of the orchestra comes from the string family. Strings provide the orchestra with a rich, deep body of sound. They can play light, happy, and lyrical melodies, or scary, dark melodies. They can be used to create all kinds of effects. All of the instruments in the string family look alike and they are played in the same way. Their strings can be plucked or made to vibrate with a bow. In some pieces of music, like in the *Danse macabre* by Camille Saint-Saëns, the strings make an interesting clack-clacking sound when the player smacks the wood of the bow on the strings.

The string section has five groups of players—the first and second violins, the violas, the cellos, and the double basses. The strings are so important, being the backbone of the orchestra, that they sit at the front of the stage during a performance, closest to the audience and surrounding the conductor. First violins, who usually carry the melody, sit on the left, with the second violins behind them. On the right the cellos and double basses sit, with the violas behind them. Harps are also considered part of the string section, though they look much different than the other strings. The harp is usually placed behind the violins. If a piano is included in the orchestra, it is placed behind the conductor, between him or her and the audience.

THE VIOLIN

One of the most versatile and expressive instruments in all of music, the violin was invented in around 1550 as a replacement for an earlier instrument called a *viol.* The violin player holds the instrument between the chin and left shoulder and makes a sound by plucking or drawing the horsehair strands of the bow across the violin's metal strings and using the fingers of the left hand to press on the strings to make notes. Violins are made of wood. Their beautiful shape is the model for the other stringed instruments (except the harp). Although it looks simple, a violin has more than seventy parts and a hollow body that serves to resonate and project its rich sound.

THE VIOLA

The viola has also been around since the 1550s. The viola is slightly larger than the violin. While the violin has a singing, bright tone, and carries the highest notes in the string section, the viola's size gives it a lower tone with a darker, more somber sound. Not many pieces of music are written that showcase the viola, but some of the most famous, such as *Harold in Italy* by Hector Berlioz, or the Concerto for Viola and Orchestra by Bela Bartok are wonderful examples of beautiful music featuring the viola.

THE CELLO

The cello, though larger than both the violin and the viola, is also one of the most expressive of all the instruments. Cellos used to be a lot bigger than they are now, but it was Antonio Stradaveri who, in 1770, set the cello at its current size. To play the cello, a player stands the instrument vertically between the knees so that the neck of the cello rests on (usually) the left shoulder. The player sits behind the instrument and draws a sound out by drawing his bow horizontally across the strings. In the late 1800s, a small adjustable pin or spike was invented that suspended the cello above the ground to give it more resonance. Before then, players just had to grip the cello with their knees. Imagine how strong your legs would have had to be to play the cello then!

THE DOUBLE BASS

The double bass is a huge instrument that didn't enter the orchestra until the late 1700s, around the time of the American Revolution. To play the double bass, the player has to sit behind it in a manner similar to the cello, only on a much higher stool. Often, double bass players have to stand during an entire performance. Modern orchestras have as many as eight double basses in order to provide a deep, rich bass sound.

Notes on the double bass are so low that in order to notate the actual pitches a composer wanted he would need a really long piece of paper. Because of this, composers write for the double bass an octave higher than the notes actually sound. The double bass is also featured in jazz and early rock 'n' roll bands, where they call it a "stand-up bass."

THE HARP

The harp is one of the oldest and most beautiful instruments in the orchestra. It looks a lot different and it plays a lot differently from the other instruments in the string family. The concert harp is six feet tall and has forty-seven strings that the player plucks or strums. The harp has the largest range of all the orchestral instruments except the piano. To play a harp, the player sits and uses the thumb and first three fingers of both hands.

The harp also has seven double-action pedals that enable the player to change the pitch of the strings. Even though the harp is one of the world's oldest instruments, it has only been a member of the orchestra for the past 150 years.

The Woodwind Section

The woodwind instruments sometimes carry the melody and sometimes blend with the strings to give warmth to the orchestra's overall sound. They have a misleading name, in a way, because some of them are made with metal, ivory, and even bone. But they all are played with "wind"—in other words, the player blows into the instrument to make the sound. Unlike the string family, whose instruments almost all look alike, members of the woodwind family come in all shapes and sizes.

This is as it should be, because the size and shape of a woodwind instrument helps to create its sound. Woodwinds also vary in how they are played. Flutes and piccolos have a hole that the player must blow across. Other woodwind instruments, the clarinet, the oboe, and the bassoon, use a reed, a narrow strip of cane that vibrates when a player blows air through it.

The woodwind section is located in the center of the orchestra, right in front of the conductor, because the tone of these instruments carries so well and can easily be heard above the other instruments.

THE FLUTE AND PICCOLO

The flute has been around since antiquity. The modern flute was invented by a man named Theobald Boehm in 1847. A flute is made up of a two-foot-long metal tube divided into three parts with holes bored into it. It has thirteen movable keys with pads on them, which the player depresses with the fingers to cover holes and make notes. Usually, the flute's bright, silvery voice can be heard playing the same notes as the first violins. The piccolo (the Italian word for "small") is just like a flute, only it's half as long and is made of wood and metal. The piccolo has the highest sound in the orchestra, and its sound rings out easily above the other instruments.

THE OBOE

The oboe was invented in France in the seventeenth century. It consists of a long tube made out of wood, which, like the flute, has holes bored into it. A network of keys allows the player to cover the holes and make notes. Unlike with the flute, the player blows air through the oboe's double reed to make sounds.

Oboe players spend hours making their own reeds. They have to get them just right in order to suit their particular playing styles. Because the double reed compels the player to force the air into the instrument at a very high pressure, the oboe has a very clear, focused tone. The tone of the oboe is so clear and consistent that all the rest of the instruments in the orchestra tunes to the oboe's A. The oboe's voice can have a plaintive or sad quality, but it can sometimes sound quite playful.

THE CLARINET

Like the oboe, the clarinet is played with a reed. The clarinet's reed is clipped to the mouthpiece and made out of cane, but it's a single reed, not a double reed. Also like the other woodwinds, the player makes notes on the clarinet by depressing its many keys. The clarinet is basically a long tube made of ebony or molded plastic with a base that flares into a bell shape. Clarinets have a smooth, mellow voice, capable of producing a wide range of notes, from warm, low notes to clear, pure upper notes.

Clarinets come in many varieties depending on the range of notes they cover. There are B-flat and E-flat clarinets, which cover medium to high notes, and a bass clarinet, which has a tube so long its neck is bent and the bell is curved upward, so as to be less awkward for the player to play. Clarinets aren't just played in the orchestra. You can also hear clarinets in jazz and marching bands.

THE SAXOPHONE

Another relatively young instrument, the saxophone was invented in 1846 by Adolphe Sax. He meant to create a hybrid between the clarinet and the oboe. It has a single-reed mouthpiece like the clarinet, but it's big and, well, brassier, as its body is made of brass. It has a long, flared bell, too, which makes it stand out among the woodwinds.

Saxophones come in different sizes too. Soprano saxophones play high, creamy notes; alto and tenor saxophones play in the middle range; and baritone saxophones play deep, crackling low tones. Saxophones were originally used in military marching bands, but eventually were adopted into the orchestra. They are most often associated with jazz music.

THE BASSOON AND CONTRABASSOON

The bassoon has the very important job of playing the bottom notes of the woodwind section, and it does its job very well. It has a huge body made of almost eight feet of wood tubing bent into a U shape, and it produces a deep, dark, rich tone. Because it plays at such a low pitch, the bassoon rarely gets a solo, but when it does get a solo, it can play smooth, long melodies that are very expressive.

Because the bassoon is so large, a bassoonist must hold it to one side, next to the knee. To support the weight of the instrument, the player has to use a seat strap, which hooks to the bottom of the bassoon. The bassoon also has a double reed, like the oboe, and, like all the woodwind instruments, it has a network of keys that enables the player to make notes while blowing.

As large as the bassoon is, it's not the largest instrument in the woodwind section. That distinction goes to the contrabassoon, which is made up of sixteen feet of wooden tubing. The contrabassoon plays very low, rattling notes. Since both instruments are so big and heavy, they require a lot of work from the musician.

The Brass Section

The power of the orchestra comes from the brass section. The instruments in this section are usually made of, well, you guessed it, brass. Their sound comes from the player blowing air into them, similar to the woodwinds. Unlike the woodwinds, however, the brass instruments have no reed.

To produce the brass instrument's loud, clear sound, the player must tense his or her lips, place them against a cup-shaped mouthpiece, and blow through them, making the lips vibrate just like the double reed in an oboe. The air in the brass instrument then vibrates and the tone varies depending on how tense the players lips are. During really long pieces of music, a player's lips can get quite tired. Often orchestras have an extra player called a "bumper" in the brass section to take over when the other brass players get tired.

Brass instruments are made up of a long metal tube with a bell at one end. Many brass instruments have valves that enable the player to alter the shape of the tube in order to vary the pitch. The tubes are coiled into different shapes to make them more portable. Their portability and loudness makes them ideal for marching bands. Usually, the orchestra has one or two trumpets, French horns, trombones, and tubas in the brass section, sometimes more. Because they have such a strong, blaring sound, the brass instruments sit at the back.

THE TRUMPET

If you lived in medieval times, you might have heard a lot of trumpets, especially if you were a member of a royal court. Those long instruments that are played from the balcony whenever the king enters the great hall are trumpets. Trumpets have been around for more than 3,500 years. They were even found in King Tut's tomb! It's no wonder, the trumpet has a loud, piercing, clear sound that has been used to send signals, frighten enemies in battle, and begin ceremonies. Trumpets are a staple instrument in jazz as well as orchestral music.

The trumpet, like the other brass instruments, is a long metal tube that flares into a bell at the end. The key to the trumpet's sound is its mouthpiece, which is small and shallow, allowing the player's air to shoot through the instrument. The bell of the trumpet also contributes to the sound, as it sends the sound forward, helping to produce a full tone.

To alter the "color" of the tone, the trumpet player can stick a mute in the bell of the trumpet. If you listen to a jazz band, you can sometimes hear a "wah-wah" sound coming from the trumpet soloist. That's the muted trumpet. The trumpet also has a tuning slide to alter the overall pitch of the instrument. Three valves on the top allow the player, by pressing them in different combinations, to play different notes.

After a while of playing, the trumpet starts to gurgle a bit. This happens because the player's breath condenses inside the tube, causing water droplets to form. To fix this, the player simply presses the water key, or "spit valve," which opens a hole in the tube and allows the water to drain out. That's why during long orchestral pieces, the woodwind players sometimes wear raincoats!

THE FRENCH HORN

French horns are also ancient instruments. Early human beings made them out of animal horns—hence the name "horn"—and blew into them to send signals during their hunts and to warn others of danger.

The French horn didn't appear as it looks today until the 1800s. Before then, they were just long tubes of metal coiled in a circle. Once the valves were added, the French horn took a permanent place in the orchestra. The French horn has a mellow, velvety sound that blends well with the other instruments of the orchestra. Composers use the French horn to bridge the sounds of the woodwind and brass. The voice of the horn can be brassy and loud or smooth and round.

The French horn is a difficult instrument to master. While holding the hefty instrument and adjusting i with the right hand, which is placed inside the bell of the instrument, the player uses the left hand to work the valves. The valves switch between the French horn's two sets of tubing: one tube is shorter for playing higher notes, and the other is longer for playing lower notes. The French horn also comes with two different mouthpieces for playing higher or lower notes.

THE TROMBONE

That funny instrument with the slide going in and out is a trombone. Trombones have been in the orchestra since the 1400s, when they were invented as a means to improve upon the trumpet. In those days, the trombone was smaller and was called a "sackbut." The word *sackbut* comes from the French *saquebute,* which was a medieval lance with a hooked end that was used to pull things. The curve of the trombone's slide reminded people of this medieval lance.

The slide allows the player to change the length of the trombone's tubing, thus providing a wide range of notes to play. A player must push and pull a slide while blowing into the mouthpiece to create the trombone's rich, low sound. Trombones fill in the middle harmony between the French horn and the tubas. They can make a funny sound called a *glissando,* which is sometimes used to produce the funny effect of someone smiling or frowning. Sometimes in cartoons, when something bad happens, the trombone makes *a bwa-bwa-bwa-bwaaa* sound. Most orchestras have three trombones, two tenor and one bass.

THE TUBA

The biggest member of the brass family, and the member with the lowest voice, is the tuba. Although it's big and makes deep notes, the tuba can play a wide range of notes very quickly and nimbly. Tubas were first used in military marching bands in the 1820s. The last to be invented, it's the youngest member of the brass section.

The tuba, like the bassoon and the double bass, is important to the orchestra because of its deep, low sound. The tuba is made up of a huge conical brass tube that bends around and around, beginning at the mouthpiece and culminating in its large, upward- or forward-facing bell.

When playing the tuba in an orchestra, the player rests the instrument on his or her lap and blows into the mouthpiece while pressing different notes on the valves. The highest-pitched tuba is called the euphonium. Euphonium comes from the Greek word which means "sweet-sounding."

The Percussion Section

The percussion section provides lots of colorful accents, rhythms, and effects in the orchestra. If you hear a thunderstorm, a lightning flash, or the steady march of a band coming down a New England street, as in Charles Ives's *New England Holidays Symphony,* you can thank the percussion instruments.

The greatest variety of instruments can be found in the percussion section. It' full of instruments that you can tap, shake, or bang on with sticks. You would think that such a wide range of instruments would require a whole bunch of players, but in reality, there are usually only one or two percussionists playing during a concert. One percussionist can play many different instruments because all percussion instruments rarely play at the same time.

The percussion section sits at the back of the orchestra, on either side of the brass, because the colorful sounds it creates can carry out over the rest of the orchestra. There are really only two types of instruments in the percussion section: pitched and nonpitched. Pitched instruments include the timpani, which are drums that can be tuned to play specific notes, and the xylophone, glockenspiel, or tubular bells, all of which can play melodies. Nonpitched instruments just make a sound, like the woodblock or a snare drum.

THE TIMPANI

The timpani (singular = timpano) are among the most fascinating instruments in the percussion section. Because they underline the chords that the rest of the orchestra is playing, they are extremely important members of the percussion family. The drumheads of timpani can be tightened and slackened by a foot pedal to produce specific notes. If the pitches of the timpani need to be adjusted during a performance, the player leans in close to the skin of drum while the rest of the orchestra is playing. Usually, orchestras have three or four timpani, each tuned to a different note.

To play the timpani, the player strikes the drumheads with a beater. The timpani came from European military marching bands of the seventeenth century. They were smaller then, but still too large to carry, and so they had to be slung across the back of a horse and played by a mounted band member.

THE BASS AND SNARE DRUMS

That boom-boom sound you hear in the orchestra combined with the rat-a-tat-tat come from the bass and snare drums. Together, they keep the beat during fast, galloping sections of music. They can also produce some nice effects, too. A player can make the sounds of distant thunder by making a soft drumroll on the bass drum. The bass drum is just a large cylinder with drumheads on both sides standing on a special stand. It produces a low, booming sound that bites through the rest of the orchestra and can provide a nice, strong downbeat.

The snare is also a cylinder with drumheads on both sides, but it's smaller. It sits on its stand with the one head facing upward. The top head on the underside has tight wires stretched across it to produce its rattling sound. Drummers use a wide variety of sticks to get different sounds out of these two drums. They play the drums with soft-headed beaters, sticks, and even wire brushes. Working together, the bass drum and the snare drum can play all sorts of cool rhythms.

THE XYLOPHONE, GLOCKENSPIEL, AND CELESTA

Nobody is quite sure whether the xylophone comes from Asia or Africa. In Java and Bali, gamelan ensembles use a similar instrument to the xylophone that is made up of long wooden bars resting on cloth. The earliest written record of a xylophone in use comes from Mali in West Africa. Because the xylophone is a versatile instrument that can play melodies and chords, and because it has a dry, crisp sound that cuts easily through the sound of the orchestra, it is one of the most important instruments in the percussion section.

The xylophone is made up of many individually tuned wooden bars laid out flat on a metal frame like a keyboard. The bars that correspond to the white keys are in front, and the black keys are in the back. Beneath each bar is a resonating tube that is tuned to the same pitch as the bar above it. When a bar is struck, the air vibrates in its resonating tube, projecting and sustaining the sound. The player strikes the bars with a hard or soft beater, depending on what sound is desired. A xylophone players can hold as many as four beaters at once—two in each hand—allowing them to play faster and to strike many bars at once, creating chords.

A glockenspiel is similar to a xylophone except that it's smaller and its bars are made of metal. The word glockenspiel comes from two German words, *Glocken,* meaning "bells," and *spiel,* meaning "play." The glockenspiel doesn't need resonators, because when the player strikes the bars with her hard rubber beaters, the crisp, silvery, bell-like sound carries easily over the other instruments in the orchestra. The sound of the glocken-spiel can be dampened by a mechanism the player controls with the foot.

In 1886, Auguste Mustel created the celesta. By the looks of it, he wanted to create a glockenspiel whose bars could be struck by a keyboard. The celesta looks like a tiny piano, but it has bars inside instead of strings, and, similar to a piano, felt-covered hammers strike the bars whenever a key is pressed. Each bar inside the celesta also has its own resonating box to amplify the sound. Some composers prefer the soft, delicate sound of the celesta to the glockenspiel, but often both are found in orchestras.

THE TUBULAR BELLS

If composers want to render the sound of church bells, they often turn to the tubular bells, which are large metal tubes of various lengths suspended in a frame. The eighteen bells are also laid out like a keyboard, with white notes in front and black notes in back. The player strikes the bells with a hammer-shaped beater to get a beautiful bell-like tone.

THE CYMBALS, GONG, AND TAM-TAM

The cymbals, gong, and tam-tam have been around since ancient times. All three of them are just metal disks of various sizes. The cymbals are basically two thin brass plates that the percussionist crashes together to make a bright, sparkling crash. Usually you can hear the cymbals at the ends of pieces of music or when things get most exciting. Cymbals can also be softly swept together to make a soft swishing sound, or held with one hand and struck with a soft stick. Sometimes, the percussionist mounts the cymbals to a stand and uses two sticks to play a roll, which creates a lovely, exciting sound.

The gong and tam-tam come to us from the Asia. Each is a metal disk suspended in a frame. The gong is made of copper and tin and is slightly smaller than the tam-tam. The player strikes both with a large beater whose head is wrapped in wool or felt. The gong makes a billowing *bong* sound when struck, and the tam-tam makes a "crash."

THE TRIANGLE

That little metal triangle that people use to get you to come to dinner? Well, it has also been around for a long time, but it didn't join the orchestra until the eighteenth century. A triangle is just a steel rod bent into the shape of a triangle with one corner open. With one hand, the player suspends the triangle from a string and with the

other he or she strikes the instrument with a little metal bar, the beater. The triangle has a shimmering, silvery sound that easily projects over the rest of the orchestra.

The loudness of a triangle depends on its size. Larger triangles sound louder than smaller triangles. The player can also make a roll by quickly moving the beater up and down in one corner. Finally, when the rest of the orchestra is hungry, the triangle player can summon them to dinner by moving the beater quickly all around the inside of the triangle. (Just kidding!) In actuality, the triangle player in an orchestra would never do that. He or she would consider such a sound to be unrefined.

Keyboard Instruments

These instruments feature—you guessed it—a keyboard. Although the organ, the piano, and the harpsichord are very important in the development of the orchestra, today they aren't officially part of the orchestra, although most orchestras have a piano. Composers often write music for the piano to strut its stuff with the orchestra in the background, a kind of piece called a concerto, and once in a while a composer will write an organ concerto, but the harpsichord has largely fallen out of use since it was a member ensembles 600 years ago. Back then, the harpsichord was used to underline the music harmonically and rhythmically. In fact, the whole ensemble was led by the keyboard player. Today, the harpsichord, organ, and piano are more favored as solo instruments.

THE ORGAN

The organ is made up of a rank of differently sized tubes attached to a keyboard. When the organist presses a key on the keyboard, valves release air into the pipes, which then emit a lovely sound. The organ was the first keyboard instrument. The Romans used organs in their coliseums during sporting events, much like they are used today!

The organ was probably invented by Ctesibius, an engineer who lived in ancient Egypt in the third century BC. Organs were reintroduced to Europe in the ninth century when rulers in Byzantium presented them to European kings as gifts. Early organs were driven by water, but the Byzantine rulers figured out how to use air. To generate airflow through the pipes, they employed children to jump up and down on the bellows while the organist was playing.

Eventually, the organ made its way from noble courts to European churches, where valves were used to push air through the pipes when a key is depressed. The pipes of an organ emit a sound based on length, with larger pipes making lower sounds. Narrow pipes make a louder, more focused sound. The pipes on an organ can be made to sound like almost any instrument in the orchestra. They can sound like flutes, trumpets, oboes, and so on. Modern organs have as many sounds as a modern synthesizer!

THE HARPSICHORD

The harpsichord is the next oldest keyboard instrument. References to the instrument appears in writings over 600 years old. The harpsichord is also operated by a keyboard but, instead of pipes, it is made of strings stretched across a long steel harp. When the player presses a key, the strings are plucked, like a harp, by a plectrum.

Because the harpsichord was light and portable, and it didn't require ranks of pipes to make its sound, it became a very popular instrument in the home. Up until the eighteenth century, the harpsichord was used as a solo instrument in the homes and also in concert. It was a leading member of the orchestra at that time, having been used to underline the harmony and keep all the other players together. After 1810, however, it fell out of use. The piano was stronger and better able to keep up with the larger orchestras.

THE PIANO

Except for modern electronic instruments, the youngest keyboard instrument is the piano. The earliest pianos were made in Italy by Bartolomeo Cristofori in 1698. Cristofori gave his new instrument an Italian name, which means "harpsichord with loud and soft." But since that was rather a mouthful, he shortened it to *pianoforte,* an Italian word meaning *soft-loud.* Eventually the *forte* was dropped, and the instrument became known simply as the "soft," or the *piano.*

The piano was so named because it was the first keyboard instrument that allowed the player to control the softness of a note by varying the pressure applied to the key. In the 1770s, the first pianos were being mass-produced and began appearing in well-off people's homes. The piano is made up of a series of strings stretched across a steel harp encased in wood with a keyboard attached. When a key is struck, soft, felt hammers rise up and strike a string, after which a damper comes down to immediately mute the string.

A piano also comes with three pedals. The pedal on the right removes the dampers from hitting the strings, so that the notes can ring out and sustain instead of being dampened right away. The leftmost pedal shifts the entire keyboard sideways, producing a softer sound. The middle pedal, called the sostenuto pedal, allows the player to select a group of notes to be sustained while dampening the remaining strings. A full-sized piano has eighty-eight keys and represents the full range of the orchestra. The power and fullness of the piano's sound depends on the size of the harp inside. Concert grand pianos can be up to nine feet long!

Because of its strong sound and large dynamic range, the piano replaced the harpsichord both in the orchestra and as the favorite solo instrument in concert halls and in people's homes.

The Conductor

The last, and probably most important, part of the orchestra I want to tell you about is not an instrument, but a person. He or she holds everything together by standing at the front of the orchestra and leading the whole ensemble through gestures from his baton. This is the conductor.

Conductors wear many hats. They are not only in charge of keeping time and keeping everyone together, but they are also in charge of balancing all the parts and interpreting the music, making it come across to the audience as the composer intended. After all, most of the music written for orchestras was written by people who are no longer around to tell us what they wanted.

The composer's markings, the lengths of the notes, the softness and loudness, and the emphasis of certain instruments are all open to various interpretations. In early baroque orchestras, orchestras didn't have a conductor. Instead, the job of leading the orchestra rested with the keyboard player.

Eventually, orchestras added a conductor who stood to the side beating a staff on the ground to keep time. The composer Carl Maria von Weber was the person who made the innovations that we still see in the orchestra today. He placed the conductor on a podium in front of the orchestra, rather than conducting from the keyboard and gave him the little white baton.

While the individual players in the orchestra read from their individual parts when playing, the conductor has the full score in front of him or her to be able to see what everyone's doing all at once.

Conductors don't have to know how to play every instrument, but they have to know how to read music for each instrument, and they have to be familiar enough with instrumental techniques to communicate and get the sound they want out of each player. A conductor must also have a thorough knowledge of the intentions of each composer, know how to read markings on a score, and understand how to cue the individual sections of the orchestra while also keeping in mind the structure of the whole piece.

In my next story about the symphony, I'll tell you all about how it got started, and about which composers helped it to develop. In the meantime, let's listen to some music! See you then.

LISTENING:

The Young Person's Guide to the Orchestra by Benjamin Britten
Peter and the Wolf by Sergei Prokofiev
Carnival of the Animals by Camille Saint-Saens

III.B. The Western Symphony Orchestra, Part II: History and Development

Last time, we heard about the instrument families that make up the orchestra. Now, I want to tell you about how the orchestra started and how it developed. I'll tell you about some of the composers who helped make it what it is today. Let's get started.

Human beings have always had music, and they have always played music together in groups. Now, you could say that the first orchestras consisted of groups of musicians that gathered for festivals, funerals, or holiday celebrations. From picture evidence, we can see that people as far back as the Assyrians, who lived in around the seventh century B.C., formed orchestras that consisted of portable harps, dulcimers, double-reed pipes, and a drum. In the eleventhth century A.D., families of instruments grouped by their range—that is, how high or low they could play—appeared.

It wasn't until the late sixteenth century that the true form of the modern orchestra began to take shape. In the fifteenth and sixteenth centuries in Italy, wealthy families employed groups of musicians to provide music for dancing and for the court. But it was in the early seventeenth century, with the emergence of the theater, in particular opera, that music was written for groups of players in combination, that orchestral music really got its start. Though opera started in Italy, it quickly spread throughout Europe, being particularly popular in Germany, France, and England.

The Baroque Period 1600–1750

The period of European music between 1600 and 1750 is called the baroque era. The art and architecture in the baroque era was really complicated. Buildings were lavishly decorated with carvings of flowers, statues, and exaggerated images of love and tragedy. All of this decoration was also reflected in the music, which, at that time, was only written for kings and queens, the nobility, and the church. Only aristocrats could listen to music. Few common people got to hear it.

In a city called Venice, there stood one of the most magnificent cathedrals: the famous St. Mark's Cathedral in Piazza San Marco. St. Mark's is a good example of how the architecture of the time affected the music. The cathedral is made up of beautiful gilded arches, framing colorful mosaic scenes and topped with elegant statues. The music written to be played in this cathedral had to be as awesome as the building itself. When composers wrote music for St. Mark's, they actually placed the musicians in the balconies near the altar and throughout the church to surround the audience with music.

People who heard the music were amazed. These were the beginnings of orchestral music, and Venice, Italy, was its first important center.

One of the most famous composers of baroque music was Antonio Vivaldi. He was a priest and a gifted violinist. He taught violin in Venice at a music school for young orphaned girls. Vivaldi combined instruments in way that was unheard of for his time. Since the girls could play different instruments, they could play any idea Vivaldi could dream up. The girls at the orphanage gave incredible concerts.

Vivaldi specialized in a form of music called a concerto, which is a piece of music that focuses on a solo instrument, with an additional small group of instruments playing in the background. In fact, the word *concerto* comes from the Italian word *concertare,* which means "to harmonize." The format for the concertos Vivaldi wrote for the girls at the orphanage became the standard format for concertos written everywhere. They contained three sections, or "movements," the first played fast, the second played slow, and the third played fast again. Vivaldi wrote almost 500 concertos for the girls to play. The most famous of these is his *Four Seasons.*

Another famous composer during the baroque period was Johann Sebastian Bach, although he didn't become famous until a hundred years after he died. In his lifetime, he was a brilliant organist in the German town of Leipzig. In his time, composers didn't become well known unless they traveled. Bach couldn't travel because he had twenty-one children to take care of. It wasn't until the 1800s, when another famous composer, Felix Mendelssohn, rediscovered his music that Bach became famous.

Though Bach himself wasn't famous for his compositions during his lifetime, several of his sons became famous composers. Bach, on the other hand, was renown as an organ player. People in the region of Thuringia where he lived used to flock to hear him play. Besides being a great organist, Bach was also a great teacher. He wrote a guidebook called *The Well-Tempered Clavier,* which became known for its beauty as a work of music and for being a showcase for how good a keyboard player Bach was.

The baroque symphony orchestra was quite small compared to orchestras today. It contained two flutes, two oboes, and two bassoons in the woodwind section; two horns and two trumpets in the brass; a timpano in the percussion section; twelve violins, six violas, two cellos, a double bass, and a harpsichord. The harpsichord player or the first violin player typically led the ensemble. In fact, while all the other instruments had their parts written out for them, the harpsichord player had to improvise his or her part, having only a bunch of chord symbols on his or hermusic.

Sometimes there would be a conductor standing off to the side waving a rod or banging the time on the ground with a long staff. One conductor, Jean Baptiste Lully, actually injured his foot once while conducting when he brought the staff down on his foot. His wound became infected with gangrene and eventually killed him!

The Classical Period 1770–1830

The classical period lasted from 1770 to 1830. In the baroque period, music was very complicated, full of quick notes, fast-moving scales, and lots of decorations and filigree. But in the classical period, composers wrote simpler music that was easier to play and that was accessible to teachers, shopkeepers, and craftspeople, not just kings and queens. Music of this time followed strict forms and focused on technique and musical theory. The music reflected the tastes and trends of a time in Europe known as the Age of Reason.

By the 1700s, music was not just written for royal courts and churches. Common people began to attend concerts, which meant that composers were able to work for rich people who wanted to patronize the arts, just like the church and the nobility had done during the baroque era.

One of the most famous composers of the classical era was Franz Joseph Haydn. He was an Austrian composer who wrote 104 symphonies, operas, religious works, and numerous concertos. His music was considered new and fresh during his time and laid the foundation for composers even a century after his death. He spent much of his career composing on the estate of the wealthy Hungarian prince Nicholas Esterhazy.

On the Esterhazy estate, Haydn was in charge not only writing the music for the Prince's parties, dinners, and even to accompany his walks in the garden, but Haydn was also in charge of maintaining the instruments and caring for the musicians. This is where he earned his nickname "Papa Joe."

Another famous composer during the classical era was Wolfgang Amadeus Mozart, who was a student of Haydn. Mozart had exceptional musical skills even when he was very young. He could play the violin very well by the time he was five and wrote his first opera by age six. He mastered the piano and could write orchestral and vocal music with great ease at a very young age.

Most composers made lots of sketches, perfecting their ideas with crossed out lines and making changes at the last minute, but Mozart could write from memory a work that he composed entirely in his head.

As a child, Mozart traveled all over Europe showcasing his musical skills, keeping up a touring schedule that would make today's rock bands jealous. His first tour lasted an entire three years. In fact, he spent half of his time between the ages of ten and fifteen on the road. He showed off in front of royalty and mastered the musical styles of the countries he visited, like England, France, Italy, and Austria.

The third important composer of the classical period was Ludwig van Beethoven. Beethoven was important because his early music embodied the "reasonable" thought and art of the classical era but toward the latter part of his life he started to break new ground; His symphonies and string quartets got longer, more emotional, and contained much of the exciting, bustling drama of the Romantic era to come.

Beethoven was a rude, eccentric, sloppy man who went completely deaf by the time his Ninth Symphony premiered. He insisted on conducting the Ninth Symphony, although he couldn't hear it. The musicians in the orchestra had to ignore him as he stood in the front waving his arms around. At the end of the piece, when the audience broke into enthusiastic applause, Beethoven had to be turned around so he could see them clapping.

Thanks to Haydn, Mozart, Beethoven, and others, the orchestra of the classical era grew to be much bigger than that of the baroque era. The classical era added two clarinets to the woodwinds, plus French horns in the brass. Also, the orchestra got twice as many strings as before this time. The harpsichord, having fallen out of fashion when the piano was perfected, was replaced by the piano.

Classical composers wrote many concertos to show off the range and dynamics of the piano, which was a new instrument at the time. Beethoven was the first to experiment with adding a choir to the orchestra, which at first many thought was vulgar. Over time, though, audiences came to accept large choirs as a part of the orchestra.

The Romantic Period 1805–1910

By the time the Romantic era came around, orchestral music had evolved quite a lot. In the baroque period it was full of complex decorations and full of notes. In the classical period it became simpler, more thoughtful, and more formal. Beginning with Beethoven, composers in the Romantic era used what they had learned from the baroque and classical periods and took music in an entirely new direction. They wrote music that had exciting passion and profound drama. They overwhelmed their listeners with music that resonated with deep emotion, writing long, sweeping pieces about love and heartbreak and magical fantasies about goblins, witches, and swans.

Audiences in the Romantic era were not just made up of nobility and churchgoers. They expand to include a wider and more diverse audience, and so composers and musicians started to become stars in the same way actors and rock musicians are famous today.

Some pianists, like Franz Liszt, actually had the front rows of their performances filled with swooning ladies who would scream, faint, or throw jewelry or flowers at them when they played. Of course, performers, Liszt in particular, welcomed this worship and would make their compositions ever more virtuosic to impress their adoring fans. In the baroque era, fancy music was written to echo the tastes of art and architecture, whereas during the Romantic era, fancy music was written to melt the hearts of swooning crowds!

One of the most important composers of the Romantic era was Richard Wagner. Wagner grew up in the theater, and by the time he was a teenager he decided to write theater of his own. His dream was to fuse theater, music, art, and drama into one ideal work that he called *Gesamtkunstwerk*, which is a fancy German word for "total, ideal, or universal work of art."

Wagner supervised every detail of his lengthy operas, from writing the lyrics and libretti, to designing the costumes and sets. He even had his own theater built to his exacting specifications in Bayreuth, Germany, so his operas could be performed. His *Ring Cycle*, consisting of four huge operas that take sixteen hours to perform back to back, is one of his most famous works. Wagner used huge orchestras, sometimes with up to 200 players, but because his theater was designed so well, the orchestra never drown out the singers' voices. Just like Wagner's *Ring Cycle*, which told the story of a greedy dwarf who steals gold from the Rhein River so he can rule the universe, romantic music often told imaginative stories.

One composer who excelled at telling imaginative stories was Pyotr Ilych Tchaikovsky. Some of Tchaikovsky's best pieces were written for the ballet: *The Nutcracker* and *Swan Lake*. *The Nutcracker* is often performed at Christmastime, because it's about a nutcracker who comes alive to enchant a young girl on Christmas morning.

Tchaikovsky, like most composers in the Romantic era, often conducted his own works, although he was prone to hallucinations and was a bit of a hypochondriac. This fact that almost ended his career as a conductor when during a performance he was gripped with the fear that his head was falling off! He conducted an entire piece holding onto his head with one hand while waving his baton with the other.

Another famous composer from the Romantic era was a big man with a big white beard called Johannes Brahms. When, as a young man, Brahms attended a performance of Beethoven's Ninth Symphony, he decided he wanted to create music of similar quality, otherwise there was no point. Do you know what? He did. Today his first symphony is regarded as such a fine achievement that critics refer to it as Beethoven's Tenth. Soon after Brahms's death, people referred to "the Three Great Bs—Bach, Beethoven, and Brahms. Despite being a musical genius, Brahms was often not a nice man. He once told a group of friends, "If there is anyone here I failed to insult, I apologize."

During the Romantic era, thanks to a composer and conductor named Carl Maria von Weber, the orchestra came to look like what it is today. Von Weber designed the seating arrangement of the orchestra, with the conductor standing in the front, with the violins to his left and the cellos and basses to his right. He also put the woodwinds in the center and the brass and percussion off in the back.

Von Weber was the first conductor to use a little white baton to direct the orchestra. Today, the baton is an essential tool for directing an orchestra. The baton allows the conductor to make subtle, graceful gestures when they're conducting subtle, graceful music. Conductors liken their batons to magic wands!

As the orchestra became larger and larger, Romantic composers continually sought out new elements to introduce into their music. One innovation they used was to introduce country and folk melodies and rhythms. Using folk music allowed composers like Chopin, Weber, Liszt, Smetana, and Mussorgsky, (to name only a few) to come up with sounds that were exotic for concert audiences.

During the 1900s, the beginning of the modern era, composers continued to use folk music to inform their music. But they went even further, expanding their music by incorporating folk from other cultures—particularly from the Far East—as well as jazz, blues, and new science and technologies of the twentieth century.

The Modern Era 1900—Present Day

Over the past 115 years, the orchestra has experienced many changes. Many composers turned to European painting and poetry for inspiration, others turned to cowboys, and mountain ranges.

Some composers integrated electronic media such as tape loops, films, and computers. Composers wove random happenings, such as ambient sounds and silence into the fabric of their music. By the end of the twentieth century, composers were doing all kinds of experiments. Karlheinz Stockhausen's *Helicopter String Quartet* featured four string players playing screechy music together while each was suspended in a different helicopter!

The modern era in music uses elements from every musical period that came before, as well as borrowing from popular music, like jazz, blues, and folk. It also using techniques that didn't exist before in order to arouse the intellect and spark debate about the nature of music itself. Composers even made innovations in the way music was written. Instead of using traditional notes on a staff, composers experimented with graphic notation, such as using colored shapes and squiggly lines to represent their musical ideas.

The composer who began the modern era was Claude Debussy. Debussy grew up in France and began composing music in the 1890s. He had many poet and artist friends and himself admired the poetry of Edgar Allen Poe, who wrote poems with strange, exotic imagery. He was also influenced by the misty, dreamy work of the Impressionist painters, like Monet and Renoir. Although Debussy himself denied it, many feel that Debussy's work is the musical equivalent of the Impressionist paintings.

Debussy was also affected by the gamelan music of Indonesia, which he heard while visiting the Paris Exhibition in 1889. Gamelan ensembles are groups of musicians that play together, much like an orchestra, but they make music using bells, drums, gongs, and beautiful xylophone-like instruments. In combining the images of his favorite poet, Impressionist paintings, and gamelan music, Debussy created his own musical language. He even invented a scale called the "whole-tone" scale. If you pull down and play every other tone bar from start to finish, you'll hear what Debussy's whole-tone scale sounds like.

Igor Stravinsky was a Russian composer who was massively important to music in the modern era. He made his name writing ballet music for Les Ballet Russes in Paris, where he amazed and often horrified people with the sounds he created. One of his ballets, *The Rite of Spring,* caused a riot in the theater when it was premiered in 1913. Halfway through the music the audience members on opposite sides of the aisle started to fight each other, the police had to be called in, and Stravinsky had to flee the theater. Debussy was in the audience during the premiere, trying to quiet people down so he could hear the remarkable music.

Another big influential composer in the modern era was Arnold Schoenberg. While Stravinsky's music contained

unexpected sounds in unusual keys, Schoenberg created a system of music that had no key whatsoever. This kind of music is sometimes called *atonal* (a term Schoeberg detested; he preferred "twelve-tone music"). Unlike tonal music, in which the most important note is the "home" note, or the tonic, atonal music is music in which no note is any more important than any other.

Atonal music has a way of sounding like all the notes are wrong. The notes clash and rarely create pleasant harmonies, giving the music an eerie, unsettled feeling. The order in which the notes are played is governed by strict mathematical rules that even some musicians find hard to understand. For instance, Schoenberg invented a rule that he had to use all twelve notes in the chromatic scale in one melody, and, what's more, no note could be repeated until he'd used all the other eleven notes! Schoenberg himself called his music "serialism" or "twelve-tone" composition.

During the modern era, American composers started to make their name. Aaron Copland, for example, made music that invoked the open prairie and the life of cowboys. He used jazz rhythms and open harmonies from French music to make music that was uniquely American. George Gershwin was a pop songwriter who also blended jazz and classical music. He helped bring nightclub music into the concert hall.

In the modern orchestra, anything goes. A modern orchestra has twice as many woodwinds, twice as many brass instruments, including trombones and tubas (some modern pieces even ask for saxophones!) plus all the percussion instruments imaginable. Keyboard instruments, like the piano, celesta, and organ, are regular features of the modern orchestra. The modern string section is huge, enhanced by harps and gigantic double basses. Not only that, but technology has also allowed modern composers to incorporate film, computers, tape machines, and other multimedia into the modern orchestra.

Thanks to its rich history, and thanks to the creativity of all of the composers that have come before, orchestras today have many wonderful options when deciding what to play. When we listen to an orchestral play, we can be thankful to all of the amazing players, conductors, instrument makers, and composers for giving us such amazing music to enjoy.

LISTENING

The Four Seasons by Antonino Vivaldi
The Well-Tempered Clavier by J.S. Bach
Symphony no. 101, "The Clock" by Franz Joseph Haydn
Eine kleine Nachtmuzik by Wolfgang Amadeus Mozart
Symphony no. 9 by Ludwig van Beethoven

Symphony no. 5 by Ludwig van Beethoven
"Ride of the Valkyries" from *Die Walküre* by Richard Wagner
Symphony no. 1 by Johannes Brahms
Nutcracker Suite by Pyotr Ilich Tchaikovsky
Arabesque no. 1 by Claude Debussy
The Rite of Spring by Igor Stravinsky
Variations for Orchestra by Arnold Schoenberg
"Rhapsody in Blue" by George Gershwin
Appalachian Spring by Aaron Copland

EPILOGUE

With that, you have come to the end of the beginning of your journey. You now have the confidence, skills, and knowledge to bring your children the gift of music.

Before you got to the last pages of this book, you may have thought music was a secret language inaccessible to all but a chosen few gifted, talented individuals. But now, you likely have adopted a new view: that music is accessible everyone, even you.

Hopefully by now you consider yourself to be an instrumental (pun intended) part of the peace-making dream mentioned in the preface of this book.

This book has no more chapters to offer you. But as you turn this final page, with any luck, you'll feel yourself entering a new chapter, one in which you live out the rest of your days regarding yourself as a competent, knowledgeable, skilled teacher of music. As long as you feel that way, this book doesn't truly end. For it is with *you* that the flowering of the dream of attaining world peace through making music in Montessori really begins.

Appendix A

Listening and Singing with Children (Including Developmental Characteristics)[1]

LISTENING

Whether it's rustling leaves, humming traffic, babbling books, or lilting music playing through speakers as they shop, adults tend to tune out sounds in their environment. Certainly, children must learn how to tune sounds out as well, but they also have to learn to refine their listening and practice focusing on particular sounds. In today's world, television, the Internet, and video games have chopped up the children's attention into ever-smaller and more easily digestible sound bites. Part of your objective is to help the children to extend the time during which they can listen with attention.

You can improve your children's listening skills by modeling good general listening habits. Any time a child comes up to ask us a question, for example, stop what you're doing, keep your hands still, and turn to face the child. Repeat back some of what the child says. Maintain eye contact. Reflect what the child says so he or she can tell that you're listening. When you listen to children in this way, they will follow suit when listening to each other.

Along with your good modeling, talk to the children about good listening and teach them the above behaviors. Perform lessons such as how to listen in a group, how to take turns listening, how to interrupt someone when you have something urgent to say ("Pardon me," I'm sorry to interrupt you," and the like).

To develop children's ability to focus on a single sound in the environment, occasionally ask for their attention, and gently tell them to stop and listen. Direct the children's focus first to one, and then to many individual sounds in the environment.

As for listening to music, here are the steps you can take the first time you listen to music with children:

1. Sit up straight and symmetrically in your chair, and insist that they do the same.

Sitting up allows them to focus and be comfortable. They might sit cross-legged on the floor with hands on their knees or in a chair with both feet on the floor and hands in their lap.

2. Introduce the name of the piece and who wrote or performed it, plus one or more interesting facts about the piece or its composer.

3. Give the children a point of interest before listening: *See if you hear the sound of a cuckoo clock at the end of this piece of music* or *see if you can tell which two instruments play the final part of the piece.* Select a point of interest that occurs as close to the end as possible. You can also ask analytical questions, such as why the "Surprise Symphony" got its title.

4. Focus your attention on the music. You enhance concentration in the children by setting an example of *how* to concentrate.

5. Avoid eye contact with the children when listening to music. If you establish eye contact with a child, that child's focus of attention will move to you and away from the music.

6. Make it clear that you will discuss the music with the children after listening to it. Knowing this will help them focus on listening while the piece plays.

7. After the listening, have a quick discussion. If the children have nothing to say about the piece, offer aid in the form of open questions, such as:

"Did you hear . . .?"
"How did the piece make you feel?"
"What did the piece make you think of?"

8. Children love repetition. After listening to a piece a certain number of times, it becomes a friend children can welcome it again and again. End any music listening session with a familiar piece.

9. When listening, give the children choices. They may listen, not listen but be quiet, or work quietly in

another part of the room, being careful not to do anything that distracts from the listening. If older children have heard the piece before, you can excuse them from listening.[2]

Remember, part of whether children respond to music is a function of your expectations and behavior. If you believe that music is wonderful and worth listening to, the children will tend to feel the same way. If you dislike a piece of music, don't show it. Act as though every type of music is worthy of your attention.

SINGING

Frequent daily singing proves to be the most tried-and-true method for optimizing children's singing skills. Daily singing increases a child's confidence in singing, provides enjoyment, and results in a repertoire of enjoyable songs. For a primary class, you give daily singing experiences by

- developing a repertoire of short songs with simple melodies for use in the daily classroom routine;
- collecting or composing short tone-calls you can use with individual children;
- identifying and working individually with children who have not yet found their singing voice; and
- giving children opportunities to listen to good singing voices.

Most elementary children will improve their singing naturally without any adult intervention if you make singing a part of the daily routine. Greet the children with simple songs, incorporate songs into your morning gathering, sing a song as a "blessing" before lunch, or dismiss children with a song. Use "Hello, My Friends" as a greeting for each child at the door, for instance, substituting the words "my friends" for the child's name. Sing "Come Let Us Gather" when summoning the children to a gathering. Instead of ringing the classroom bell, get the children's attention during the work period by gently singing "Hello, My Friends."

You can also improvise new lyrics to familiar melodies to suit the needs of a unique routine in your class. Sing, for example, "Now it's time to go outside, go outside, go outside" to the tune of "London Bridge." Switch the words in "Hello, My Friends" to "Goodbye, My Friends" when dismissing at the end of the day. Improvise new lyrics to "Yellow the Bracken" if you want to calm the children, lull them to sleep, or set a peaceful mood.

SINGING POSTURE AND BREATH

During group singing, establish good singing posture (back straight, chin parallel to the floor, chest open) and good breath control. To develop good posture, ask the children to imagine that they are marionette puppets with a string attached to their heads. A puppeteer lets go of the string and their bodies flop forward, slightly bouncing. When the puppeteer pulls on their strings, their bodies slowly straighten, their chests, shoulders, neck, head, and arms moving into place. When sitting, have the children imagine that the puppeteer pulls the string at the top of their heads so their back straightens and their trunk, neck, and head line up in a relaxed upright position.

Encourage children to take a slow intake of breath before each phrase begins. Children should breathe at the natural cadence points and not in the middle of a melodic phrase. To support their singing, they can imagine they are standing waist-deep in a pool of water, with each hand holding a beach ball submerged halfway into the water. The higher the melody rises, the deeper the children push the beach balls down into the water. When the melody goes lower, tell the children to allow the beach balls to float up again.

TONE-CALLS

Sing short, two- or three-note melodies called tone-calls to improve the children's singing. Children throughout the world use tone-calls when playing games, calling each other, and teasing. The most common tone-calls are made from *sol, mi,* and *la.*

Sing tone-calls to summon children in from the playground, take roll call, or on any occasion when you need to call a child's name, as in Figure A.1.

If you sing a tone-call and a child echoes you on a different pitch, call again, matching the child's pitch, as in Figure A.2.

Working with Individual Children

Even when children practice singing every day for several months, a child who has normal hearing may still have trouble matching pitches. Don't be discouraged. Accept this situation as normal and offer this child individual help.

It could be that the child simply is not listening carefully or he or she may be confusing singing with speaking. Help the child find his or her singing voice by telling the "Mr. Brown, Mr. Black" story from chapter 12. Alternatively, use your voice in a dramatic way

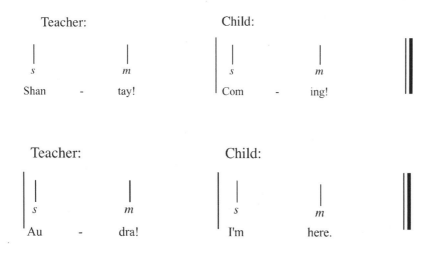

Figure A.1.

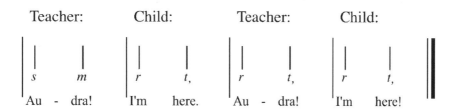

Figure A.2.

to portray different characters from read-aloud books or traditional tales such as "Goldilocks and the Three Bears" or "The Three Little Pigs." Try these other techniques:

- Imitate train whistles or sirens.
- Speak or sing short words or phrases, and ask the child to say whether you were speaking or singing.
- Invite the child to first speak and then to sing the first word of a tone-call. After the child sings it, start on his or her pitch, and sing the entire tone-call, asking the individual child to repeat after you.
- Use a pure, neutral syllable such as "loo" when focusing the child's attention on singing a particular melodic phrase.
- Make frequent use of the Kodály-Curwen hand signs.
- Perform short echo chants based on two- or three-note motives from known songs using the syllable "loo."
- Strengthen the child's tonal memory by singing mystery songs on "loo" and asking him or her to guess the name of the song. Sing part of the melody and ask what words go with those notes.

If you're a male teacher, the child will likely imitate your deep voice, which sounds an octave lower than his or her own. To help, sing a short tone-call in falsetto, and ask the child to imitate it. If he or she sings the wrong pitch, sing the tone-call again in falsetto, matching his or her pitch, gradually bringing the child to the correct pitch.

ASSISTANCE FOR OLDER CHILDREN

By the end of third grade, most children can sing songs with accurate pitch. Many children who still sing out of tune at this point have simply never developed good listening skills. When these children can differentiate between higher and lower pitches and perceive melodic contour, they will be able to reproduce pitches and melodies accurately.

To help children perceive melodic contour, simply ask them to draw the melodic contour in the air. (Some of the concept- and skill-building activities in chapter 12 will also help develop children's melodic perception and listening skills.)

Short vocal exercises also develop singing skills. They improve diction, tone production, and singing range. Practice them in the gathering or at times throughout the work cycle. Repeat the little exercises in Figure A.3 several times, moving up by half steps, making sure to breathe at the beginning of phrases and sing the entire phrase in one breath.

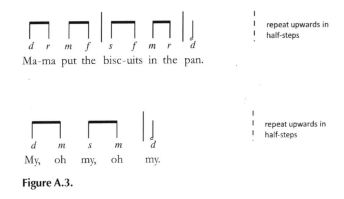

Ma-ma put the bisc-uits in the pan.

My, oh my, oh my.

Figure A.3.

REINFORCEMENT WITH INSTRUMENTS

The very first lessons in your Montessori albums call for the child to sing the pitch of a single bell after the teacher strikes the bell. Playing a note and asking the child to match it vocally improves coordination between the child's mind, ear, and vocal production system.

Rare is the individual child, however, who can hear a single pitch and sing it out of thin air. Locating a pitch among a spectrum of higher and lower pitches proves much easier. When the ear can *compare* pitches, the child can much more easily sing in tune; like finding a particular town on a map, the other notes in the melody become signposts and landmarks that orient the child to the target. For this reason, have the child sing a short motive of two or three notes rather than singing only one pitch in isolation. Once the child can sing an entire motive in tune, isolate the target pitch.

Accompanying children's singing with mallet instruments also improves vocal coordination. Enriching classroom folk songs with instruments that are in tune and that harmonize comfortably with a given melody helps fine-tune children's singing skills. Of course, this doesn't mean that children must sing accompanied at all times. Quite the contrary: provide young singers with many opportunities to sing a cappella so their minds can exercise the ability to hear and produce many notes on the harmonic spectrum without the help of an instrument.

MODELING

Children tend to sing a song in the manner you present it to them. They find it easiest to sing well and in tune when you model good, natural, beautiful singing. Take this with a grain of salt. You don't need to be a Luciano Pavarotti or Maria Callas to sing with your children. You should, however:

- sing in a natural, relaxed tone,
- radiate confidence,

- demonstrate good singing posture,
- sing in tune, and
- project enthusiasm.

Children enjoy much more fluid mastery of a song when you sing it correctly for them the first time. Before you introduce a song to your class, practice singing it a few times. Make sure you're singing at a comfortable pitch. You can even make a recording to help yourself learn the song.

If a song is too difficult for you to sing, but you really want to introduce it to your class, invite another adult or an older child to model it for the children. If the children have trouble finding or matching your pitch, have another child model the pitch.

Whatever you do, it's never a good idea to use a CD recording of the song as a model. CDs go through a professional production process, which means in many cases artificial sound processing effects have been applied to the singer's voice to enhance it, to keep it in tune, and to balance it with professionally produced instruments. Not only that, but attention must also be paid to the musical style and voice quality of the recording, as children will imitate the vocal affectations of the professional artist on the CD. Finally, using a CD as a model sends the wrong message, namely, that songs are sung best by professionals who sing for commercial purposes. In all cases, the best model for how to sing a song, aside from you, is *another, average, everyday human being.*

SUITABLE SONG MATERIALS

In chapter 9, you read in detail about why folk songs are the most suitable to sing with your children. All of the songs in chapter 14 fit those criteria. Also, appendix E lists some excellent folk-song collections.

Some qualities of a suitable song include:

- appropriate vocal range. Figure A.4 shows children's vocal ranges at specific ages.
- appropriate length: for young children, the songs should be relatively short;
- appropriate level of difficulty: refer to Kodály's sequence of elements in chapter 11 as a guide;
- appropriate text: songs about animals, songs that tell colorful stories, songs about topics that interest the child, songs that are historically authentic, and the like, but *not* didactic, instructional songs designed to "teach."

Even if you sing a suitable song, young singers require lots of repetition with songs and motives in order to grasp all the musical details. A short melody such as "Shoo

Ages 3 to 6

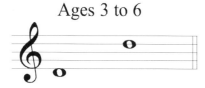

Ages 7 to 10

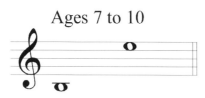

Ages 11 to 13

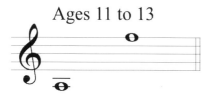

Figure A.4.

Roun'," for example, may require six to eight repetitions before the seven year olds in your group can retain and reproduce it with the words, melody, rhythm, and tonality intact.

CHILDREN'S DEVELOPMENTAL CHARACTERISTICS AND MUSIC

Bearing in mind the musical capabilities of the child at different stages of life will help you to pick the most appropriate song material for primary or elementary Montessori children (Irwin and Nelson, 1986). It will also help you when you put together musical performances with a mixed-age group of children. Appendix B contains suggestions for setting up mixed-age performances. The following traces the child's musical development from birth to age twelve. (Note that some children will be ahead of or behind this general sequence.)

Infancy to Age Three

- As babies, children begin to discover their vocal capabilities. They babble and make sounds. Gradually the sounds of their babbling rise and fall in pitch and increase in duration, becoming the precursor for singing (Campbell and Scott-Kassner, 2002).

- During the toddler years, the babbling takes on rhythmic significance. The child imitates the *contour* of melodies and phrases but not the discrete pitches.
- At two, the child babbles and sings short phrases on, for example, *sol* and *mi* or *mi* and *do* (intervals of a third).
- By age three, children develop repetitive rhythmic patterns in their spontaneous songs and start to increase their vocal range. They invent and enjoy spontaneous songs that have discreet pitches and recurring melodic patterns.
- At this point, children reproduce short nursery rhymes and childhood chants, and they associate them with simple movements.

Age Four

- At four, children begin to discover the difference between their speaking and singing voices. They sing in tune within a limited range of five pitches, and their vocalizations shift from the light, airy tone of the nursery to the boisterous, energetic singing of the playground.

Age Five

- At this age, children have a short attention span. They are frequently restless and need variety in activity and physical movement. They thrive on large, overt motions, such as walking and marching.
- Children's interests tend to be limited to their immediate experience. The best songs relate to the child's home and school experiences. Choose songs about animals, objects, occupations, and special occasions.
- Children can skip, jump, and hop. They have a natural interest in dramatic play.
- Five-year-olds like to mimic, mirror, and copy. They enjoy short repetitive songs that require physical movement.
- Children's kinesthetic and empirical knowledge precedes intellectual knowledge. They need concrete musical experiences as a foundation for conceptualizing musical concepts. Singing "Paige's Train" and moving fast or slow, for example, paves the way for the child's understanding of tempo.
- Many five-year-olds focus on only one aspect of a situation at a time. They have trouble comparing phrases or comparing and contrasting analytically various musical elements. They can step the beat *or* clap the rhythm, for example, but not both at the same time. What's more, they can focus only on one melody at a time. Children up to five years old have trouble singing part songs and rounds.

Age Six

- Children still learn best through singing, dancing, playing, and moving. They need concrete experience before they can conceptualize.
- Children need to see, hear, or touch objects to think about them accurately. Choose songs whose central objects or characters are present in the classroom in the form of storybooks, pictures, puppets, or props.
- Six-year-olds love stories with music. Sound stories, such as those found in chapter 16, and orchestral works like *Peter and the Wolf* or *The Sorcerer's Apprentice* appeal to them.
- Children at this age love make-believe and dramatic play. Choose songs in which children can pretend to be a "farmer" or a "bluebird."
- Six-year-olds also have difficulty singing in parts.

Age Seven

- Children still need concrete experiences in order to learn.
- Imagination, magic, and magical happenings become of interest to them.
- Seven-year-olds enjoy working with paper and pencil. They have an interest in musical notation.
- Children at this age like to classify objects and make lists.
- At home, these children might begin to express interest in taking private music lessons. Many children at this point begin taking piano or guitar.

Age Eight

- Now children can begin to distinguish between like and unlike musical phrases. They can classify and compare sounds.
- Children's fine motor skills improve dramatically. This is a good time to develop skills in writing standard musical symbols.
- Children at this age enjoy secret codes, mysteries, and puzzles as well as guessing game songs and songs in nonsense languages.
- Intellectual experience of musical relationships that involve durations, such as comparing note durations or lengths of musical sections, come naturally to eight-year-old children. They can relate concepts of meter and form.
- At this age, children like to talk and enjoy taking turns. They can spend time on individual performance, small-group performance, or performance that requires interaction between soloist and group.

- Eight-year-olds love humorous and nonsensical texts.
- At eight, children have an interest in history and the activities of their ancestors. Choose songs that dovetail with music of other cultures and that discuss or call to mind historical events.
- At eight and older, children are able to sing in parts.

Ages Nine and Ten

- These children enjoy learning through competition. They love rhythm-pattern identification and mystery songs.
- Nine and ten-year-olds have an acute awareness of self. At this point, solo-oriented activities can be awkward or embarrassing. They may appreciate the use of puppets as an aid when they demonstrate reluctance to sing alone.
- Children find motivation in playing musical instruments. Give these children ostinati and countermelodies on mallet instruments and tone bars when they perform folk songs or play singing games.
- The lives of musicians and composers interest nine and ten-year-olds.
- Although the need for concrete experience before intellectual understanding is diminishing, the use of *sol-fa* syllables, hand signs, physical movement, and manipulation of objects is still necessary at this age.
- At ten, children again have relatively short attention spans. Varied activities remain important.
- These children enjoy taking dictation. They like to hear melodic and rhythmic patterns and reproduce them on paper.

Ages Eleven and Twelve

- This age group tends to be highly competitive. They find activities involving team or individual competition exciting.
- Children at this stage like their musical experiences to relate to contemporary musical reality. They enjoy classroom activities that relate to music heard on the radio, on television, or on the Internet. They start to idolize pop stars and contemporary groups.
- Children either "love" or "hate" a subject. They might openly rebel against singing or playing classroom instruments unless the activities are part of a special group, club, or whole-class endeavor, such as a choral ensemble or a musical theater production. Children at this age have sophisticated needs and interests.
- Eleven and twelve-year-olds love questions like "What is the *largest* instrument?" or "Who was the *first* composer?" They find extreme comparisons like this highly motivating.

- Reasoning in the abstract comes easily to this age group. They love to explore the way things work. Activities centered around sound production, electronic music, the design and construction of musical instruments can be highly enjoyable to them.
- Children at this age have an interest in traditional camp songs. They love rich, authentic musical experiences such as part singing, choir, and folk dancing.

CHILDREN WITH SPECIAL NEEDS

Music has indisputable value for children with special learning needs. Many children who are unable to communicate verbally can express themselves through music (Irwin and Nelson, 1986). Here are some considerations for making music with children who have particular special needs:

- Children with vision impairment can participate in most musical activities and develop a deep understanding of the structure of music. They can develop singing, aural perception, instrumental, movement, and creative skills. To accelerate their learning, emphasize listening, including rote learning of songs and instrumental pieces. Assist them in musical movement.
- Children with extreme hearing loss can't participate fully in as many activities as those with vision impairment, but they can participate in some activities. They may never learn to sing accurately, but they can feel vibrations of nonpitched percussion instruments and respond to music with physical movement. They can also observe and imitate rhythm and dance movements made by others. With guidance, they can strum an autoharp or play melodies on pitched percussion instruments with your help or the help of another child.
- For children who are learning-disabled but whose sight, hearing, and movement capacity are neurotypical, success in music often motivates them to overcome difficulties in other subjects. Children with emotional management disorders, short attention spans, or physical body control issues that hamper their progress in other academic areas can often excel in music.
- Children with Down syndrome or other cognitive issues can develop skills in listening, moving, playing, and singing. They can participate in circle games and dances, following the lead of their fellow children and getting swept away in the fun of the game. They may need more time than other children to respond during echo songs or to follow certain movements. Praising every amount of progress children make and highlight their worthwhile contributions to classroom music-making stimulates their development.

NOTES

1. Techniques adapted from Irwin and Nelson (1986), and Campbell and Scott-Kassner (2002).
2. When you give these kinds of choices to the children, large-group listening lessons will not interrupt the work cycle.

Appendix B

How to Teach a Song[1]

Once you have selected appropriate song material, you can use either of two methods (or a combination of the two) for teaching the songs to children: rote and note.

ROTE METHOD

Teaching a song by rote—through oral and aural means—is one of the most effective ways to present a song. To teach a song by rote, you can (1) give the children at least three opportunities to listen to the complete song and then (2) present fragments of the song sequentially (oral) in short motives or phrases. The children listen (aural) and then echo those fragments. Teaching the song "Shoo Roun'" using this method unfolds like this:

1. After telling a quick story about the origins or history of the song, tell the children the song's name. Begin teaching the melody and words. Say something like: "Listen and pat your knees while I sing."[2] Sing the song all the way through, modeling how to pat the steady beat, while the children pat their knees and listen.
2. Ask a question about the characteristics of the song: "Can you hear how the melody rises and falls? Draw the melody in the air." Sing the song again as the children draw in air the melodic contour.
3. "What word is sung on the highest pitch of the song?" Sing the song again and get the children's answer.[3]
4. "Listen and sing after me."[4] Sing the first phrase of the song: "All around, shoo roun'." Have the children imitate.
5. Repeat the first phrase as necessary.
6. "Listen and then sing after me." Sing the second phrase: "We won't marry, shoo roun'." Children imitate.
7. Repeat the second phrase as necessary.

8. Continue through the song in this way, singing each short phrase and having the children imitate.
9. Now challenge the children to sing larger chunks of the song: "Let's sing the first *two* phrases, first me, then you." or "Let's sing the first half of the song. Listen and repeat."
10. When you're confident that the children know the song, say, "Now we're ready to sing the whole song. Let's sing it all together." Sing the song together with the children.
11. Finally, say, "Now you can sing the song without me. I'll get you started." Set the pitch and tempo (see below), and have the children sing.[5]

To teach by rote songs with complex structures, such as "King Kong Kitchie," which has multiple verses plus a chorus and refrain, teach the sections of the song separately in the following order:

1. The chorus. Use the above rote method to teach the chorus of the song: "Kai mo, kee mo, kai mo kee. Way down yonder in the hollow tree," etc.
2. The refrain. Teach the children the "response" part: "Whatever I sing, you answer with *King kong kitchie kitchie kai me oh.*"
3. The verses. Sing the verses yourself and have the children sing the response and the choruses. Do this for the first several performances until the children memorize the words.

Teach echo songs such as "Purple Light" by merely saying, "Repeat after me," and singing the song phrase by phrase, the children echoing your every phrase. Touching your ear signals the children to listen, and an open palmed "come with me" gesture tells them when to sing.

To teach call-and-response songs such as "Skin and Bones," "Hill and Gully Rider," "Just from the Kitchen," and "John Kanaka," in which the response is different from the call, say something like "Whatever I sing, you answer *Shoo li loo.*" Then sing the verses yourself until the children memorize the words.

Rote-teaching a long ballad with refrain, like "Sweet Betsy From Pike," can become tedious once the children know the melody of the verses. To keep the song fun, teach the refrain first, and then teach only the first verse by rote. Avoid teaching all of the words line by line, and simply perform the song frequently, singing the verses yourself. After a few performances, the children will learn the words to the verses.[6]

If you must teach the words to a long folk ballad line by line, teach each verse by speaking, not singing, the words and having the children echo you. Then sing the verses in their entirety.

You can also teach a song by rote using a whole-song approach. Here is how this approach unfolds in teaching, for example, "The Owl Sings."

1. Tell a story about the background of the song or the Yuma Indian culture to engender enthusiasm and establish context.
2. Ask the children to listen for two things that will appear before dawn comes.
3. Sing the song in its entirety.
4. Discuss how the music sets the mood. Ask the children what the "Oo" sound represents, for example, or a question like, "What might a Yuma Indian parent see and hear around him or her while rocking a baby to sleep?"
5. Sing the song again, and invite the children to flap their wings like an owl, or sit imitating the way owls move, or pretend to be mommy and daddy owls rocking their babies.
6. Sing the song a third time, inviting the children to sing along with you *in their heads*. Say, "Put the song in your head" or, "Sing in your imagination."
7. Now, invite the children to sing the song with you.
8. "I'll bet you can sing the song without me. I'll get you started." Give the starting pitch and tempo, and have the children sing the song by themselves.

A third approach, known as *immersion*, has the children listening to you sing the whole song to the extent that they individually require before joining in. You can introduce a song by simply singing the song and telling the children, "Join me when you know it." This method works well with short, repetitious songs that only have one verse. It's also useful for teaching the refrains of songs. If the children don't pick up the song the first time, simply repeat it until they join in.

Use a mixture of these rote techniques to create variety and make song learning effortless and enjoyable.

NOTE METHOD

Teaching a song by note involves the children reading from notation. Start by having the children read or perform the song's *rhythmic patterns* in sequence, gradually adding the melody sung on *sol-fa* syllables, until they can sing the song with you and on their own. Proceed as follows:

1. Establish context by telling a brief story about the song's background or by telling something interesting about the song.
2. Present the notated rhythm pattern[7] of the first phrase of the song. "Take a minute to practice. Silently chant and clap the familiar elements."
3. "Let's chant and clap as I point to the individual elements." Perform the rhythms with the children as you point to the elements: *ta, ta, ti-ti, ta.*
4. Repeat as necessary.
5. "Now sing with me." Sing the melody attached to the rhythm in *sol-fa*. If you've written the rhythm pattern in stick notation on a whiteboard, write the *sol-fa* letters below the rhythm stems. If you've used popsicle sticks, you can make little disks with the *sol-fa* syllables on them to place below each stick.
6. If the next phrase of the song is the same as the first phrase, proceed as follows: "Now, let's sing the next phrase. It begins on *mi."* Sing the next phrase with the children.
7. "Let's try singing these phrases with our hand signs." Sing the phrases together while showing hand signs and saying the *sol-fa* syllable names.
8. If the next phrase is different from the first, repeat steps 2 through 6 with the new pattern.
9. Now present the notated song in its entirety. "Let's clap and chant the rhythm of the whole song." Clap and chant the rhythm of the song with the children.
10. "Now let's slowly sing the melody with our *sol-fa* syllables and hand signs." Slowly sing and show hand signs together with the children.
11. Repeat as necessary.
12. "Let's read the words to this song in rhythm."
13. "Let's sing the song with the words."
14. "I'll bet you can sing the song without me. I'll get you started." Set the pitch and tempo (see below), and have the children sing.

Teaching Part Singing

After children have developed the skills to sing in tune, and their unison singing sounds unified and cohesive (which will happen quickly with daily practice), the next natural step is singing in parts. Children derive special pleasure and pride from the harmonies that result. The progression, in terms of difficulty, of part singing usually follows this sequence:

1. Children add a chant or an ostinato to a known song.
2. Children sing rounds and partner songs (*quodlibets,* whimsical combinations of familiar melodies or texts).
3. Children sing countermelodies.
4. Children sing parallel harmonies.

Children *after eight years of age* can successfully sing songs in two-part arrangements, such as melodies with drones and ostinati. Fourth-year children can perform canons (rounds), partner songs, and countermelodies in two independent groups. Reserve multiple ostinati, three-part canons, and two-part choral pieces for children in the fifth and sixth year. A good song to test your children's abilities to sing in parts is "Senuwa," in which one part sustains a note while the other part sings a more active melody. To support them, lead the singing, sustaining the note as the children sing the melody above.

WORKING WITH MULTIPLE AGES

A word of caution: children below third year have difficulty singing multiple parts and often lack the motor skills to perform complex dance movements. With a group of mixed-age children, then, some creative groupings can help overcome developmental barriers.

Wherever possible, when grouping your children for part singing, think of the first-years as one child. Group the first-years together to play a simple quarter-note rhythm part on an instrument, or have them sing with you. They can plug their ears and watch your lips, or they can be placed a small distance from the other children. Divide the third-years and older into groups of mixed ages so that at least one older child is leading the group. That way, the younger children in the group can tune out the other parts and focus on imitating the older child. For example, if you are singing "Ah, Poor Bird" with a lower elementary class, seat all of your first-years together, or seat them with you and have them sing the main melody. Distribute simple ostinati, countermelodies, or drone parts among mixed groups of second-years and third-years.

If you want to add instruments to your performance, give the first- and second-years the simplest part: the steady beat on a percussion instrument. A first-year playing the beat on a tambourine will feel powerful and important holding the entire group together. Distribute any other instruments, such as mallet instruments or ukuleles among the children third-year and above.

OSTINATI

Your children's first foray into singing in parts comes from adding a repeated vocal pattern, or ostinato, to accompany a melody. You can invent an effective ostinato by examining the melody of the song and writing a repeated melody that gels well harmonically with each measure of the song. Here are some guidelines:

1. Keep the ostinato between one and two measures in length.
2. In major-key songs, a two-note melody alternating between *sol,* and *do* always works well. In minor keys, alternate between *mi,* and *la.*
3. If the melody of the song is built from a pentatonic scale, *any* pentatonic ostinato sounds good.
4. Likewise, *any* pentatonic ostinato built on the tonic sounds good against a melody in a major or minor key. (For songs in major keys, use an ostinato built from the major pentatonic on 1 or the minor pentatonic on 6. For songs in minor keys, use an ostinato built from the minor pentatonic on 1 or the major pentatonic on 3.)
5. When writing an ostinato that's not pentatonic, intervals of a third or a sixth stacked against the melody sound best. Fourths, fifths, and octaves sound hollow, but passable. Seconds or sevenths only sound good when they resolve to thirds, fourths, or fifths on strong beats.
6. Write the ostinato outside the range of the melody, (but not beyond the children's singing range). In other words, if the melody moves in the middle range, write an ostinato that occupies the upper and lower ranges. If the melody moves in the high range, write a middle or low ostinato.
7. Strive for contrasting note durations. When the melody moves in long durations, the ostinato should be more active, employing shorter note durations and vice versa.

To see these guidelines in action, look at Figure B.1, which shows ostinati composed for the song "Ah, Poor Bird."

To teach a song with an ostinato, follow these steps:

1. Teach the song as a unison song—everyone sings the melody together.
2. When the children can sing the song very well independently, sing the ostinato yourself or play it on a melody instrument.

Ah, Poor Bird

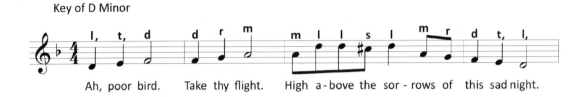

Key of D Minor

osinato 1: alternates between mi and la

ostinato 2: high range. Harmonizes with
main melody mostly in octaves and sixths.
Uncomfortable intervals resolve.

ostinato 3: Built (roughly) from F pentatonic

Figure B.1.

3. Invite a small group of children to sing the melody with you or along with the instrument.
4. After the children have several opportunities to sing the ostinato, let them try it independently. Feel free to add vocal or instrumental support.

At first, add only one ostinato to a melody. As the children's part singing skills develop, and as they get older, add two and even three ostinati. When adding multiple ostinati, keep in mind that the most effortless harmonic blends come from ostinati built from pentatonic scales.

CANONS, ROUNDS, AND PARTNER SONGS

The most fluid part singing experiences for elementary children come from singing canons and rounds. A canon is an imitative song in which one group begins singing the melody and, upon reaching a certain point (indicated by a number in the score and referred to as "at the canon"), is joined by another group singing the melody from the

beginning. To ensure maximum fulfillment, take the time to be sure that the children feel secure singing the song's melody as a larger group, and then in smaller groups. When the children know the melody and can sing it very well, follow these steps:

1. Start with a two-part round. Cue[8] the children to begin singing the song while *you* softly sing the second part of the canon. (The number 2 in the music indicates where the group must be when you start singing.)
2. Then, select a small group of children to sing *with you* at the canon.
3. Divide the class equally, so that two parts can maintain their independent parts while singing. Make sure at least one older child sings in each group.

If the children have trouble maintaining their part, try:

- seating all the children with the same part together;
- having the oldest children in the group sing the loudest;
- assigning a separate movement to each part, such as patting knees or snapping fingers to the steady bea; or

- having the younger children plug their ears and tap a foot to the beat as they sing, or follow your beat as you conduct in the air.

To sing a quodlibet (partner song), which combines two melodies from different folk songs, use the same procedure. Make sure that the children know both songs really well. Good melodies to combine for partner songs are "Lil' Liza Jane" with "Turn the Glasses Over," "London Bridge" with "Seagull, Seagull," and "Ah, Poor Bird" with "Chairs to Mend." Experiment with changing the lyrics to the songs to tell a story or make new songs. Also experiment with combining other songs to see which melodies go together best.

COUNTERMELODIES

You can add countermelodies, or *descants*, above a first and usually more familiar melody. Usually a countermelody sounds above the main melody, but it can also appear below the familiar melody. Countermelodies occur in quodlibets, such as the one that results from combining "Lil' Liza Jane" and "Turn the Glasses Over," or "Seagull, Seagull," and "London Bridge." Songs like "Banuwa" contain multiple countermelodies.

Compose countermelodies following the same guidelines as those for composing ostinati. The collection *46 Two-Part American Folk Songs* (Bacon, 1973) contains many examples of good, short songs with countermelodies.

To add a countermelody to a song, use the same procedures as in teaching a round:

1. Make sure the children are comfortable with the main melody.

2. Have them sing the main melody while you softly sing the countermelody.
3. Have a group of children sing the countermelody with you while the others sing the main melody.
4. Divide the class into two (or more) groups, one singing the main melody and the other singing the countermelody.

NOTES

1. Techniques adapted from Irwin and Nelson (1986), and Campbell and Scott-Kassner (2002).
2. In general, be sure that each time the children listen to you sing they have a task to do, such as patting the beat, drawing the melody in the air, listening for particular words, or, if you're in the Practice Stage of Kodály's unfolding elements curriculum (see chapter 11), listening for a particular melodic or rhythmic element.
3. It's good for the children to hear the entire song at least three times.
4. Instead of saying these words, you can simply touch your ear when you want the children to listen and make a "come with me" gesture with your open hand outstretched, when you want them to repeat after you.
5. As the children sing the song alone for the first time, you can help them along by singing short snippets of the song where you hear they're having trouble. You might, for example, just chime in singing one or two of the lyrics on pitch, as in, "*All around . . .,*" "*. . . got no lover. . .,*" etc.
6. Refrain from having children read from lyrics written on a whiteboard or piece of paper. The written words will steal their focus. As you sing the song's melody, effect the song's movements, and model good singing, you want the children's eyes and ears entirely focused on you and on the music.
7. You can present this rhythm using stick notation on a whiteboard or popsicle sticks on a rug.
8. For tips on cueing children during singing, see appendix C.

Appendix C

How to Lead a Song[1]

Speaking of "enlightened generalists," when you and your children make music together, you take on the role not only of music teacher but also of song leader and conductor. As song leader, you sound a starting pitch, establish a tempo and indicate exactly when the group should begin to sing. As conductor, you provide a visual or aural cue that represents the steady beat and tempo of the song.

SONG LEADER

Start the children singing by sounding the starting pitch and establishing the tempo by chanting words such as "ready sing" or "now begin." Figure C.1 on the next page gives an example.

Start a song in triple meter like in figure C.2.

Start a song with a pickup note (anacrusis) in a similar way, but make sure to say "ready sing" before the anacrusis, as in Figure C.3.

You may start a song by singing the tonic chord if you choose. This helps establish the "tonality" of the song. Sing *do mi sol mi do* on the any pitch you like, or starting from *do* in the key of the song. Chanting "one, two, ready sing" on the starting pitch, however, proves sufficient to orient the children, even if it doesn't establish the tonality of the song.

CONDUCTOR

Once you've started the song, keeping the children together and maintaining the tempo is a matter of establishing either visually, or aurally, the steady beat. Visually, you can keep the beat using conducting patterns. To conduct, hold your hand in a relaxed position, palm facing downward, and, from your elbow, mark the steady beat by waving your forearm in the patterns indicated in Figure C.4 for songs in duple and triple meters.

When conducting, allow your arm to fall with a pronounced bounce on beat 1 and a slightly less pronounced bounce on beats 2 and 3, so that the children see the accented and unaccented pulses.

You can also mark the steady beat with an aural cue instead of a visual one. Aural cues include patting on your knees, clapping, or playing the steady beat on a percussion instrument such as rhythm sticks or hand drum.

When conducting part-songs and canons, you will need to cue groups of children to begin. Set up the cue ahead of time (at least one or two measures) by making eye contact with one member of the group, preferably the oldest child. On the *beat before* the cue, give the group a signal: a simultaneous nod and, with the hand that isn't conducting or playing a percussion instrument, point to the group with an open-palmed invitation gesture or with an index finger, as in Figure C.5.

NOTE

1. Techniques adapted from Irwin and Nelson (1986) and Campbell and Carol Scott-Kassner (2002).

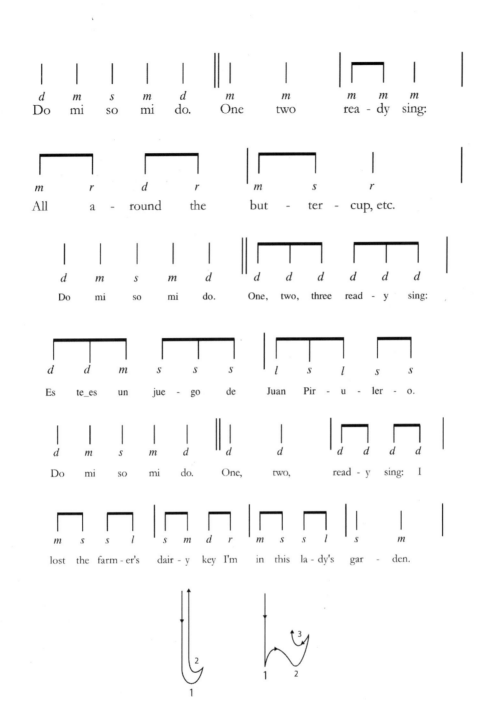

Figure C.1.

Figure C.2.

Figure C.3.

Figure C.4.

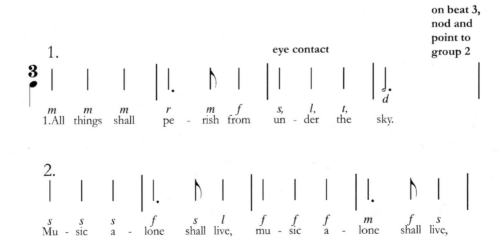

Figure C.5.

Appendix D

Music Grid Paper

Appendix E

Resource List

Table E.1. Historical/Philosophical Research Materials

Author	Title	ISBN (where available)
Bacon, D.	*Hold Fast to Dreams: Writings Inspired by Zoltan Kodály*	935432035
Barber, N., Barratt, M., Blackwood, A., and Kelly, E.	*The Kingfisher Young People's Book of Music*	
Bónis, F.	*Selected Writings of Zoltan Kodály*	851620213
Citron, S.	*The Musical from the Inside Out*	
Csikszentmihalyi, M.	*Flow: The Psychology of Optimal Experience*	
Dobzay, L.	*After Kodály: Reflections on Music Education*	9037074333
Eösze, L.	*Zoltan Kodály: His Life in Pictures and Documents*	9997785169
Herboly, Koscár	*Zoltan Kodály: Music Should Belong to Everyone: 120 Quotations from His Writings and Speeches*	9632045009
Houlahan, M. and Tacka P.	*Zoltan Kodály, A Guide to Research*	815328532
Lawyer, A.	*Maria Montessori and A Child's Total Development in Early Childhood*	
Montessori, M.	*Creative Development in the Child, Vol. I*	
Montessori, M.	*The Montessori Method*	
Montessori, M.	*To Educate the Human Potential*	
Montessori, Mario M.	*Cosmic Education*	
Zemke, L.	*The Kodály Concept: Its History, Philosophy, and Development*	09166508X

Table E.2. Musicianship

Bacon, D.	*185 Unison Pentatonic Exercises*	9995393301
Berkowitz, S., Fontrier, G., Kraft, L.	*A New Approach to Sight Singing*	
Bertalotti, A.	*Solfeggi Cantati*	
Cannel, W. and Marx, F.	*How to Play the Piano Despite Years of Lessons*	
Cser, L.	*Harmony and Musicianship with Solfege*	
Crowe, Edgar	*The Folk Song Sight Singing Series, Volumes I-VII (unison), and Volumes VIII-X (two-part)*	
Gorow, R.	*Hearing and Writing Music: Professional Training for Today's Musician*	
Hartyányi, J.	*An Ode for Music: 11 Analysis of Choral Compositions of Zoltan Kodály*	9632055017
Hegyi, E.	*Solfege According to the Kodály Concept, Vols. 1 & 2*	9630101181
Kodály, Zoltan	*333 Reading Exercises*	
	Pentatonic Music Vols. I–IV	
	Let Us Sing Correctly	
	Bicinia Hungarica Vols. I–IV	
	Fifteen Two-Part Exercises	
	77 Two-Part Exercises	

(Continued)

Table E.2.   (Continued)

66 Two-Part Exercises
55 Two-Part Exercises
44 Two-Part Exercises
33 Two-Part Exercises
22 Two-Part Exercises
Trinica: 29 Progressive Three-Part Songs
Epigrams: Nine Songs for One or Two Voices
24 Little Canons on the Black Keys

Table E.3.   Folk Song Collections

Boshkoff, R. and Sorenson, K.	*Multicultural Songs, Games, and Dances*	
Brocklehurst, B.	*The Sounds of Rounds and Canons*	
Choksy, L. and Brummit, D.	*120 Singing Games and Dances for Elementary Schools*	13635038001
Erdei, I. Knowles, F. and Bacon, D.	*My Singing Bird: 150 Folk Songs to Sing, Read, and Play*	935432108
Erdei, P. and Komlos, K.	*150 American Folk Songs to Sing, Read, and Play*	913932043
Johnson, R.	*Folk Songs North America Sings*	969183704
Harvey, B. and Cullen, S.	*Young Voices, World Songs*	
Heath, C.	*The Song Garden*	
Heath, C.	*The Song Garden Games and Activities Book*	
Jones, B. and Lomax Hawes, B.	*Step it Down: Games, Plays, Songs, and Stories from Teh Afro-American Heritage*	820309605
Locke, E.	*Sail Away: 155 American Folk Songs to Sing, Read, and Play*	
Lomax, A.	*The Folk Songs of North America*	
Mathias, S. and Kleven, E.	*Songs and Games for Young Musicians*	
Niles, J. J.	*The Ballad Book of John Jacob Niles*	
Orozco, J. and Kleven, E.	*"De Colores" and Other Latin-American Folk Songs for Children*	
Tapper, T.	*The Child's Own Book of Great Musicians (Series)*	
Trinka, Jill	*The Little Black Bull and Other Folk Songs, Singing Games, and Play Parties for Kids of All Ages, Vol. 4*	1-888895-41-1
Trinka, Jill	*John, the Rabbit and Other Folk Songs, Singing Games, and Play Parties for Kids of All Ages, Vol. 3*	
Trinka, Jill	*Bought Me a Cat and Other Folk Songs, Singing Games, and Play Parties for Kids of All Ages, Vol. 2*	
Trinka, Jill	*My Little Rooster and Other Folk Songs, Singing Games, and Play Parties for Kids of All Ages, Vol. 1*	
Waterhouse, C., Allen, L., Compton, E., and Hollins, N.	*How Can I Keep From Singing!: Songs and Musical Activities from around the World for 8–13 Year Olds*	
Work, J. W.	*American Negro Songs: 230 Folk Songs and Spirituals, Religious and Secular.*	

Table E.4.   Methodology

Choksy, L.	*The Kodály Method I and II*	
Choksy, L.	*The Kodály Method: Comprehensive Music Education from Infant to Adult*	135168992
Choksy, L.	*The Kodály Context: Creating an Environment for Musical Learning*	
Daniel, K.	*Kodály Approach*	
	Kodály in Kindergarten	
	Method Book I (1979)	
	Method Book II (1986)	0916656209
	Method Book III (1987)	0916656225
Daniel, K.	*Kodály Approach*	
	Method Book IV (2000)	
	Advanced Curriculum, Books V and VI (2002)	
	(self-published. Available by contacting kszaszi@earhlink.net)	

Table E.4.   (Continued)

Dobszay, L.	*The World of Sounds*
Duffy, M.	*Children of the Universe: Cosmic Education in the Elementary Classroom*
Eisen, A. and Robertson, L.	*An American Methodology*
Gillen, L. and Gillen, J.	*Yoga Calm for Children: Educating Heart, Mind, and Body*
Goodkin, D.	*Now's The Time: Teaching Jazz to All Ages*
Hickey, M.	*Music Outside the Lines: Ideas for Composing in K-12 Music Classrooms*
Irwin, P. and Nelson, J.	*The Teacher, The Child, and Music*
Kline, T. F.	*Classic Tunes & Tales: Ready-to-Use Music Listening Lessons & Activities for Grades K-8*
Montessori, M.	*The Advanced Montessori Method, Vols. I and II*
Rappaport, J.	*The Kodály Teaching Weave, Vol. I*
Epstein, M. and Rappaport, J.	*The Kodály Teaching Weave, Vol. II*
Feierabend, J.	*Conversational Solfege*
Herboly-Kocsár	*Teaching of Polyphony, Harmony, and Form in Elementary School* 9630157276
Houlahan, M. and Tacka, P.	*Sound Thinking: Developing Musical Literacy, Vols. I and II* 913932531
Sheehan Campbell, P. and Scott-Kassner, C.	*Music in Childhood: from Preschool through the Elementary Grades*
Storms, J.	*101 Music Games for Children*
Wheeler, L. and Raebeck, L.	*Orff and Kodály Adapted for the Elementary School*

Table E.5.   Music History

Abraham, C.	*Shostakovich: A Life*
Anderson, M. T.	*Strange Mr. Satie*
Bryant, J.	*Music for the End of Time*
Calenza, A. H.	*Camille Saint-Saëns's Danse Macabre*
	Gershwin's Rhapsody in Blue
	Pictures at an Exhibition
	The Farewell Symphony
	The Heroic Symphony
	Vivaldi's Four Seasons
Gerstein, M.	*What Charlie Heard*
Grout, D. and Palisca, J.	*A History of Western Music*
Hewitt, K. and Krull, K.	*Lives of the Musicians: Good TImes, Bad Times, and What the Neighbors Thought*
Kendall, C. W.	*Stories of Women Compsers for Young Musicians*
Kingman, D.	*American Music: A Panorama*
Larson, K.	*Where the Heart Beats: John Cage, Zen Buddhism, and the Inner Life of Artists*
Lesser, W.	*Music for Silenced Voices: Shostakovich and his Fifteen String Quartets*
Levine, R.	*The Story of the Orchestra*
Nichol, B.	*Beethoven Lives Upstairs*
Rachlin, A.	*Famous Children (Series)*
Rosenstiel, L.	*The Life and Works of Lili Boulanger*
Turner, B.	*Carnival of the Animals by Saint-Saëns*
Venezia, M.	*Getting to Know the World's Greatest Composers (Series)*

Table E.6.   Music Notation

Gardner, R.	*Music Notation: A Manual of Modern Practice*
Goetschius, P.	*Lessons in Music Form*
Gould, E.	*Behind Bars: The Definitive Guide to Music Notation*
Kelly, T. F.	*Capturing Music: The Story of Notation*
Martineau, J.	*The Elements of Music*
Stone, K.	*Music Notation in the Twentieth Century*

Table E.7. Web Resources

Site Title	URL
Mama Lisa's World	*http://www.mamalisa.com*
Libra Vox: Acoustical Liberation of Books in the Public Domain	www.libravox.org: https://librivox.org/stories-of-great-composers-for-children-by-thomas-tapper/
American Musicological Society: Music Books for Children	http://www.ams-net.org/childrens-lit/childrens-lit-CC.php
The British Kodály Academy	http://kodaly.org.uk
Youth Opera International	http://www.youthoperaintl.com
Kodály Center for Music Education at Holy Names University	http://kodaly.hnu.edu/song.cfm?id=592#analysis
Montessori Nuggets	http://montessorinuggets.blogspot.com
North American Montessori Teacher's Association	http://www.montessori-namta.org
Music Staff	http://www.musicstaff.com
Square Dancing 101	http://acme-corp.com/teamGuest/R/2_426/sd101/Square%20Dancing%20101.htm
Multicultural, Cross-cultural, and Intercultural Games and Activities	http://wilderdom.com/games/MulticulturalExperientialActivities.html
The British Library: Opie Collection of Children's Games and Songs	http://sounds.bl.uk/Oral-history/Opie-collection-of-children-s-games-and-songs-#_
Association Montessori Internationale	http://ami-global.org
Southern Oregon and Washington Kodály Educators	https://sites.google.com/site/swoketest4/
Montessori Teacher's Institute for Professional Studies	http://montessoriteachersinstitute.blogspot.com/search/label/Elementary%20Transcripts?&max-results=200
Smithsonian Folkways	http://www.folkways.si.edu
Montessori Special Needs	http://www.montessorispecialneeds.com/index/
Making Music in Montessori	www.makingmusicinmontessori.com
Organization of American Kodály Educators	https://www.oake.org/about-us/the-kodaly-concept/
The Kodály Institute at the Ferenc Liszt Academy of Music	http://kodaly.hu/zoltan_kodaly/kodaly_concept
The International Kodály Society	http://www.iks.hu/index.php/home1/the-kodaly-concept
The Kodály Inspired Classroom	http://www.kodalyinspiredclassroom.com
Rhythmically Yours Music Materials on Etsy	https://www.etsy.com/listing/470817632/rhythm-blocks?ref=shop_home
Lesson Planet	https://www.lessonplanet.com/lesson-plans/kodaly-method/all
Kodály Sequence of Concepts, courtesy of the Kodály Center for Music Education at Holy Names University	http://kodaly.hnu.edu/pdf/Sequence_of_Concepts.pdf
British Columbia Kodály Society of Canada	http://www.bcksc.ca/home
International Music Score Library Project	https://imslp.org

Appendix F

How to Match Scales and Chords

When you want to enrich folk songs by adding melodic accompaniments or ostinati on pitched percussion instruments, how do you determine which scales to use? How do you know which chords to use if you want to add an autoharp or a ukulele?

The easiest way is to find out the key of the song by looking at the key signature in the printed music. (See chapter 7, for a discussion of major and minor key signatures.)

If you have learned the song by rote, or if you're reading the song from stick notation and you don't know the key signature, follow these steps:

1. Place your major-scale strip in front of your tone-bar layout with the number 1 on any tone bar, and pull down the corresponding notes. The note on 1 is *do*.
2. Play the scale a few times to get it in your ear, and see if the range is comfortable for you to sing.
3. Use Table F.1 to work out what pentatonic scales to play on tone bars or bells, what bars to remove from mallet instruments, and what chords to play on the ukulele or autoharp.

As an example, suppose you're singing a song from stick notation and you want to establish a key. Place your major-scale strip with 1 on any note, say, B-flat. Consulting Table F.1 tells you three things:

- You can create ostinati or melodic accompaniments with the B-flat, C, D, F, and G tone bars or bells.
- You can create ostinati or melodic accompaniments on mallet instruments with the E-flat and A bars removed.
- Any combination of the chords B-flat major, C minor, D minor, E-flat major, F7, or G minor will sound great on ukulele or autoharp. Use your ear to determine which chords among the six available sound best at particular moments in the song.

MATCHING SCALES AND CHORDS TO A CHILD'S COMPOSED MELODY

Suppose a child has composed an original melody and wants to accompany it with ostinati, accompaniments, or chords. You can analyze the melody to find out on what scale the melody is built. This isn't as difficult as it seems.

If the child is composing from the tone bars using a major-scale strip, you can match the melody to a key by simply looking at where the child has placed 1, or *do*. If, for example, the child composes a melody using the major-scale strip with 1 in front of B-flat, you know that B-flat is *do*; therefore, the child is playing in B-flat major. You can then consult Table F.1.

What if the child isn't playing from a scale strip? What if he composed a melody on the tone bars with all of the tone bars pulled down, or on a classroom xylophone with no bars removed? For starters, see if the notes fit into a key by consulting Table F.2, which shows the note names in almost every key.

If the child's melody contains the notes E, F, B, and G, for instance, consulting Table F.2 reveals that those notes fit in the key of C. Melodic ostinati and accompaniments with C-major and A-minor pentatonic and chords in the key of C will sound great with this melody.

Bear in mind that some combinations of notes belong to more than one key. The notes A, C, D, E, and G, for example, belong in the keys of F, G, or C. In such a case, you could either pick one of the three keys or create ostinati and accompaniments from one, two, or all three of those keys. You could set up a C-pentatonic scale on the xylophone by removing the B and F bars, pulling out the G, A, B, D, and E tone bars. Next, you can choose progressions using the chords from the key of F on the ukulele.

Some combinations of notes don't easily fit into a key. A child may come up with a melody from the chromatic scale, for example, or from an exotic scale of his or her

Table F.1. Scale and Chord Pairings

Key	Pentatonic Scales to Use	Bars to Remove	Available Ukulele or Autoharp Chords*
C major/ a minor	C pentatonic: C,D,E,G,A a minor pentatonic: A,C,D,E,G	F,B	C, d*, e, F, G7, a** a, C, d, E7, F, G
G major / e minor	G pent.: G,A,B,D,E e minor pent.: E,G,A,B,D	C,F#	G, a, b, C, D7, e e, G, a, B7, C, D
D major/ b minor	D pent.: D,E,F#,A,B b minor pent.: B,D,E,F#,A	G,C#	D, e, f#, G, A7, b b, D, e, F#7, G, A
A major/ f# minor	A pent.: A,B,C#,E,F# f# minor pent.: F#,A,B,C#,E	D,G#	A, b, C#, D, E7, f# f#, A, b, C#7, D, E
E major / c# minor	E pent.: E,F#,G#,B,C# c# minor pent.: C#,E,F#,G#,B	A,D#	E, f#, g#, A, B7, c# c#, E#, f#, G#7,
B major / g# minor	B pent.: B,C#,D#,F#,G# g# minor pent.: G#,B,C#,D#,F#	E,A#	B, c#, d#, E, F#7, g# g#, B, c#, D#7, E, F#
F major / d minor	F pent.: F,G,A,C,D d minor pent.: D,F,G,A,C	Bb,E	F, g, a, Bb, C7, d d, F, g, A7, Bb, C
Bb major / g minor	Bb pent.: Bb,C,D,F,G g minor pent.: G,Bb,C,D,F	Eb,A	Bb, c, d, Eb, F7, g g, Bb, c, D7, Eb, F
Eb major / c minor	Eb pent.: Eb,F,G,Bb,C c minor pent.: C,Eb,F,G,Bb	Ab,D	Eb, f, g, Ab, Bb7, c c, Eb, f, G7, Ab, Bb
Ab major / f minor	Ab pent.: Ab,Bb,C,Eb,F f minor pent.: F,Ab,Bb,C,Eb	Db,G	Ab, bb, c, Db, Eb7, f f, Ab, bb, C7, Db, Eb
Db major / bb minor	Db pent.: Db,Eb,F,Ab,Bb bb minor pent.: Bb,Db,Eb,F,Ab	Gb,C	Db, eb, f, Gb, Ab7, bb bb, Db, eb, F7, Gb, Ab
Gb major/ eb minor	Gb pent.: Gb,Ab,Bb,Db,Eb eb minor pent.: Eb,Gb,Ab,Bb,Db	Cb,F	Gb, ab, bb, Cb, Db, eb eb, Gb, ab, Bb7, Cb, Db

* In this column, upper-case letters indicate major chords and lowercase letters indicate minor chords

** For simplicity's sake, I'm leaving out the seventh degree in major and the second degree in minor, which are both diminished chords. Dealing with diminished chords requires a level of theoretical knowledge that is beyond the scope of this book. If you're curious, appendix E lists some good books on music theory.

Table F.2. Note Names in Almost Every Key (Major and Natural Minor)

Scale Strip	1	2	3	4	5	6	7
C major	C	D	E	F	G	A	B
a minor	A	B	C	D	E	F	G
G major	G	A	B	C	D	E	F#
e minor	E	F#	G	A	B	C	D
D major	D	E	F#	G	A	B	C#
b minor	B	C#	D	E	F#	G	A
A major	A	B	C#	D	E	F#	G#
f# minor	F#	G#	A	B	C#	D	E
E major	E	F#	G#	A	B	C#	D#
c# minor	C#	D#	E	F#	G#	A	B
B major	B	C#	D#	E	F#	G#	A#
g# minor	G#	A#	B	C#	D#	E	F#
F# major	F#	G#	A#	B	C#	D#	E#
d# minor	D#	E#	F#	G#	A#	B	C#
F major	F	G	A	Bb	C	D	E
d minor	D	E	F	G	A	Bb	C
Bb major	Bb	C	D	Eb	F	G	A
g minor	G	A	Bb	C	D	Eb	F
Eb major	Eb	F	G	Ab	Bb	C	D
c minor	C	D	Eb	F	G	Ab	Bb
Ab major	Ab	Bb	C	Db	Eb	F	G
f minor	F	G	Ab	Bb	C	Db	Eb
Db major	Db	Eb	F	Gb	Ab	Bb	C
bb minor	Bb	C	Db	Eb	F	Gb	Ab
Gb major	Gb	Ab	Bb	C	Db	Eb	F
eb minor	Eb	F	Gb	Ab	Bb	C	Db

own invention. In this case, exercise caution. At the beginning of his or her musical journey, you want to set the child up for success. When the child composes music *with the intention of combining melodic and chordal instruments*, the more comfortable and pleasing the notes and chords sound with the melody, the more successful he or she feels.

At first, before the child has developed the refined taste to enjoy the nuances in the spectrum of comfortable and uncomfortable sounds, he or she will find lots of clashing notes discouraging. On the other hand, he or she will experience the most pleasure when choosing melodies and harmonies that blend beautifully together. The notes in pentatonic scales, for example, sound beautiful and harmonious in any combination. Remember that the Montessori balancing act between freedom within limits comes into play in music. The child will actually experience more creative freedom if given a set of boundaries. Enact some rule or get the child into the habit of selecting a "palette" by choosing either a major- or minor-scale strip and placing it in front of the tone bars *before* composing.

Say something like: *Music is communication. We can't communicate if we don't agree on what language we're using and what words are comfortable and not comfortable. If you want to compose music to be played together with others, just like in a conversation, everyone must establish an agreed-upon vocabulary. In music, this vocabulary takes the form of a scale—the series of tones from which you will build all the melodies and chords you use in your conversation.* You could also compare the scale to an artist's palette of colors: *Before embarking on a painting, an artist chooses a color palette. The musician's color palette is a scale.*

Don't worry that you'll be limiting the child's creative freedom. Setting healthy boundaries around explorations by restricting scale choices will actually free the child so that he or she won't get discouraged by clashing notes or mental gymnastics, making music effortless and within reach. The child will easily be able to combine instruments to create harmonious compositions and performances. Later, the resulting love for music will spur the child on to more in-depth studies.

This isn't to say that children in your class can't compose music that has clashing tones. The child may well insist that his "vocabulary" comprise an invented scale, the chromatic scale, or even a random selection of notes that don't fit into a key. Trying to steer the child in any other direction might discourage him or her.

In such a case, set guideposts for the child by writing down all of the notes in the melody and stacking them in alphabetical order, creating a scale. Then, have the child create ostinati and accompaniments using the notes in this new scale. Likewise, create chords from the notes in the new scale by playing two or more of them in different combinations simultaneously. As long as the young composer sticks to the notes in his or her scale, no matter how many instruments he or she writes for, the composition will have a sense of unity and cohesion, even though some notes may clash.

When it comes to adding chordal instruments, however, a melody based on an invented scale or the chromatic scale will be difficult to match with compatible ukulele or autoharp chords. In this case, I recommend using a piano instead. With a piano, the child can easily play chords made out of combinations of the notes in his or her melody by simply pressing down the keys.

MATCHING MELODY NOTES TO A CHILD'S CHORD PROGRESSION

Occasionally, a child will come up with a chord progression on a ukulele or an autoharp and want to know what melody notes can be used to go with the chords. In this situation, you can first find out if all of the chords in his or her progression fit nicely within one major or minor key and construct melodies from the available scales. To do this, pretend each chord in succession is the tonic—the I chord—and see if the other chords make sense according to Table F.1.

For example, say the child comes to you with the chords E minor, G major, and C major. Start by pretending that E minor is the tonic, and see whether the other chords make sense in that key. Checking Table F.1, we see that if the chord progression were in the key of E minor, G would be major and C would be major. That checks out! So the scale choices the child could use are G-major pentatonic or E-minor pentatonic. If, on the other hand, you pretend G is the tonic, then these chords also check out: G is major, E is minor, and C is major. With a tonic C, the chords don't quite match; although E is minor in the key of C, G is a seventh chord.

If the chords don't fit nicely into one key, then your job is a little more difficult. You won't be able to find one set of notes that the child can play that will match well with all of the chords. The child will have to use a different scale over each chord.

To do this, the child can pretend that for the duration of time each chord sounds its root note is the tonic, *do*. This means that if a child comes to you with the chord progression E-flat major, F# minor, and C major, then for all the time the E-flat major chord is sounded, the E-flat-major pentatonic and G-minor pentatonic scales will sound good. When the chord changes to F# minor, however, the child will have to switch to A major and F#-minor pentatonic.

This method is all right for composing, but the child will encounter more clashing notes and run into problems resolving uncomfortable notes into comfortable ones. This method will take time for the child to get used to and can be potentially discouraging.

Set the child up for success ahead of time. Have a basket of chord- progression cards available for use in composing. You can glean the chord progressions from popular songs, folk songs, or from Table F.1. Have some cards with only two chords on them and other cards that have up to four or five chords. This way, the child can effortlessly make music, undaunted by clashing dissonant notes, complicated music math, or the tables in this appendix.

Appendix G

Index of Songs

Table G.1. Songs Indexed by Tone Set and Range

Title	Tone Set		Range	Meter	Game	Page
		Two- and Three-Note				
Snail, Snail		m s	m3	2/4	line	
That's A Mighty Pretty Motion		d r m	M3	4/4	circle	
Pizza Pizza, Daddy-O		m s l	P4	2/4	circle	
Rain, Rain		m s l	P4	2/4	circle	
		Four-Note Major Pentatonic				
Bye, Bye, Baby		d r m s	P5	2/4	circle	
Let Us Chase The Squirrel		d r m s	P5	2/4	partner	
Shoorah		d r m s	P5	2/4	circle	
Skin & Bones	l,	d r m	P5	6/8		
Just From The Kitchen	s, l,	d r m	M6	2/4	circle	
King Kong Kitchie	s, l,	d r m s	P8	2/2		
Turn The Glasses Over	s, l,	d r m s l	M9	2/4	Circle	
Hill And Gully Rider	s, l,	d r m s l	M9	4/4		
		Five-Note Major Pentatonic				
Bluebird		d r m s l	M6	4/4	circle	
Bow Wow Wow		d r m s l	M6	4/4	circle	
Great Big House In New Orleans		d r m s l	M6	2/4	circle	
Paige's Train		d r m s l	M6	4/4	circle	
Riding On The Railway		d r m s l	M6	2/4	circle	
Rocky Mountain		d r m s l	M6	2/4		
Hello, My Friends	l,	d r m s	m7	4/4		
Purple Light	l,	d r m s	m7	2/4		
Song Of The Snowflakes	l,	d r m s	m7	2/4	circle	
Charlie Over The Ocean	s, l,	d r m	M6	6/8	circle	
Cotton Eye Joe	s, l,	d r m	M6	2/2		
Amasee	s, l,	d r m	M6	2/2	2 lines	
Shake Them 'Simmons Down	s, l,	d r m	M6	2/4	circle	
		Five-, Six-, and Seven-Note Major				
Sailor, Sailor		d r m f	P4	3/4	scatter	
Oats And Beans And Barley		d r m f s	P5	6/8	circle	
Grizzly Bear		t, d r m f s	m6	2/4	circle	
The Old Gray Cat	s, l, t, d m		M6	6/8	hiding	
My Aunt Came Back	s, t, d r m f		m7	4/4	circle	
Shoo Roun'	s, l, d m f		m7	2/4	circle	
Rock My Soul		t, d r m f s l	m7	4/4		
Green Grows The Willow Tree	s,	d r m f s	P8	2/4	scattered	

(Continued)

331

Table G.1. (Continued)

Title	Tone Set	Range	Meter	Game	Page
Little Johnny Brown	s, l, d r m f s	P8	2/4	circle	
Here Comes Sally	s, t, d r m f s	P8	2/4	circle	
Follow The Drinking Gourd	m, s, l, t, d r m	P8	4/4		
El Mar Estaba Serena	m, l, t, d, r, m, f	m9	3/4		
Seagull, Seagull	s, d r m f s l	M9	4/4		
Dona Nobis Pacem	s, t, d r m f s l	M9	3/4		
Six- and Seven-Note Major Pentatonic					
Lil' Liza Jane	d r m s l d'	P8	2/4		
The Farmer's Dairy Key	d r m s l d'	P8	2/4	double circle	
My Mama's Calling Me	d r m s l d'	P8	4/4	circle	
Tideo	d r m s l d'	P8	4/4	double circle	
Lead Through That Sugar And Tea	s, l, d r m s	P8	2/4	2 lines	
Hold My Mule	s, l, d r m s l	M9	2/4	double circle	
The Farmer In The Dell	s, d r m s l	M9	6/8	circle	
John Kanaka	s, d r m s l d'	> M9	2/4	double circle	
Minor or La-Pentatonic					
My Paddle (The Canoe Song)	m, l, d r m l	> M9	2/4		
The Owl Sings	l, d r m s l	P8	3/4		
El Mar Estaba Serena	m, s, l, t, d r m f	m9	3/4		
Eight-Note and Longer Major					
Senua de Dende	d r m f s l t d'	P8	4/4		
Si Si Si	d r m f s l t d'	P8	4/4		
Sweet Betsy From Pike	d r m f s l t d'	P8	6/8		
Come, Let Us Gather	s, l, t, d r m f s	P8	4/4		
Paw Paw Patch	s, t, d r m f s l	M9	2/4	2 lines	
Banuwa	f, s, d r m f s l t d' r' m' s'	> M9	4/4		

Table G.2. Songs Indexed by Rhythmic Element

Rhythmic Element	Title	Page
♩ ♫	Amasee	
	Banuwa	
	Bluebird, Bluebird	
	Bow Wow Wow	
	Bye, Bye, Baby	
	Come Let Us Gather	
	Cotton Eye Joe	
	Dona Nobis Pacem	
	Follow The Drinkin' Gourd	
	Great Big House In New Orleans	
	Green Grows The Willow Tree	
	Grizzly Bear	
	Hello, My Friends	
	Here Comes Sally	
	Hill And Gully Rider	
	Hold My Mule	
	John Kanaka	
	Just From The Kitchen	
	King Kong Kitchie	
	El Mar Estaba Serena	
	Lead Through That Sugar And Tea	
	Let Us Chase The Squirrel	
	Lil' Liza Jane	
	Little Johnny Brown	
	My Aunt Came Back	

Table G.2. (Continued)

Rhythmic Element	Title	Page
	My Mama's Calling Me	
	My Paddle (The Canoe Song)	
	The Owl Sings	
	Pizza, Pizza, Daddy-O	
	Paige's Train	
	Paw Paw Patch	
	Purple Light	
	Rain, Rain	
	Riding On The Railway	
	Rock My Soul	
	Rocky Mountain	
	Seagull, Seagull	
	Senua De Dende	
	Shake Them 'Simmons Down	
	Shoo Roun'	
	Shoorah	
	Si Si Si	
	Snail, Snail	
	Song Of The Snowflakes	
	Sweet Betsy From Pike	
	The Farmer's Dairy Key	
	That's A Mighty Pretty Motion	
	Tideo	
	Turn The Glasses Over	
	Bluebird	
	Bow Wow Wow	
	Come Let Us Gather	
	Follow The Drinkin' Gourd	
𝄾	Hello, My Friends	
	Hill And Gully Rider	
	My Aunt Came Back	
	My Paddle (The Canoe Song)	
	Purple Light	
	Riding On The Railway	
	Rocky Mountain	
	Seagull, Seagull	
	Senua de Dende	
	Si Si Si	
	Song Of The Snowflakes	
	Cotton Eye Joe	
	Rock My Soul	
▬	Seagull, Seagull	
	Paw Paw Patch	
	Tideo	
♬♬	Turn The Glasses Over	
	Charlie Over The Ocean	
	Oats And Beans And Barley	
♫	Pizza, Pizza, Daddy-O	
	Riding On The Railway	
	Skin & Bones	
	Sweet Betsy From Pike	
	Charlie Over The Ocean	
	The Farmer In The Dell	
♩ ♪	Oats And Beans And Barley	
	Skin & Bones	
	The Old Gray Cat	

(Continued)

Table G.2.   (Continued)

Rhythmic Element	Title	Page
♪ ♪	Follow The Drinkin' Gourd	
	Hill And Gully Rider	
	John Kanaka	
	Lead Through That Sugar And Tea	
	Lil' Liza Jane	
	My Momma's Calling Me	
	My Paddle (The Canoe Song)	
	Riding On The Railway	
	Seagull, Seagull	
	Senua de Dende	
	Shoo Roun'	
	Si Si Si	
	Banuwa	
♫ or ♫	Just From The Kitchen	
	Lead Through That Sugar And Tea	
	Let Us Chase The Squirrel	
	Lil' Liza Jane	
	My Mama's Calling Me	
	Sweet Betsy From Pike	
	Turn The Glasses Over	
	Banuwa	
	Charlie Over The Ocean	
♩.	The Farmer In The Dell	
	Follow The Drinkin' Gourd	
	Oats And Beans And Barley	
	Skin & Bones	
	The Old Gray Cat	
	The Farmer In The Dell	
𝄾.	Amasee	
♩. ♪ and ♪ ♩.	Dona Nobis Pacem	
	Follow The Drinkin' Gourd	
	Hello, My Friends	
	John Kanaka	
	King Kong Kitchie	
	El Mar Estaba Serena	
	Lil' Liza Jane	
	Riding On The Railway	
	The Owl Sings	
	Seagull, Seagull	
	Senua de Dende	
	Si Si Si	
	Song Of The Snowflakes	
	That's A Mighty Pretty Motion	
	Shoo Roun'	
	Green Grows The Willow Tree	
♪ ♪ or ♫	My Momma's Calling Me	
	Sweet Betsy From Pike	
	That's A Mighty Pretty Motion	
	Turn The Glasses Over	
	Shake Them 'Simmons Down	
♩.	Bye, Bye, Baby	
	Come Let Us Gather	
♩	Cotton Eye Joe	
	Dona Nobis Pacem	
	Hold My Mule	
	John Kanaka	
	King Kong Kitchie	

Table G.2. (Continued)

Rhythmic Element	Title	Page
	El Mar Estaba Serena	
	Let Us Chase The Squirrel	
	Lil' Liza Jane	
	Little Johnny Brown	
	The Owl Sings	
	Riding On The Railway	
	Rock My Soul	
	Sailor, Sailor	
	Seagull, Seagull	
	Si Si Si	
	That's A Mighty Pretty Motion	
	Come Let Us Gather	
	Sailor, Sailor	
𝅝	Dona Nobis Pacem	
𝅘𝅥 |	El Mar Estaba Serena	
𝅗𝅥.	The Owl Sings	
	Sailor, Sailor	
	Si Si Si	

Table G.3. Songs Indexed by Subject/Theme

Subject/Theme	Title	Page
Fruits, Plants, Nature	Follow The Drinkin' Gourd	
	Charlie Over The Ocean	
	Green Grows The Willow Tree	
	Grizzly Bear	
	El Mar Estaba Serena	
	Let Us Chase The Squirrel	
	Oats And Beans And Barley	
	Paw Paw Patch	
	Purple Light	
	Rain, Rain	
	Rocky Mountain	
	Shake Them 'Simmons Down	
	Song Of The Snowflakes	
Animals	Bluebird	
	Bow Wow Wow	
	Charlie Over The Ocean	
	Hill And Gully Rider	
	Hold My Mule	
	King Kong Kitchie	
	Let Us Chase The Squirrel	
	My Paddle (The Canoe Song)	
	Purple Light	
	The Old Gray Cat	
	The Owl Sings	
	Seagull, Seagull	
	Snail, Snail	

(Continued)

Table G.3.   (Continued)

Subject/Theme	Title	Page
Professions	The Farmer In The Dell	
	The Farmer's Dairy Key	
	Sailor, Sailor	
Vehicles	My Paddle (The Canoe Song)	
	Paige's Train	
	Riding On The Railway	
	Seagull, Seagull	
Characters/People	Cotton Eye Joe	
	Charlie Over The Ocean	
	Great Big House In New Orleans	
	Here Comes Sally	
	John Kanaka	
	Lil' Liza Jane	
	Little Johnny Brown	
	My Mama's Calling Me	
	Rock My Soul	
	Skin & Bones	
	Sweet Betsy From Pike	
Travel/Places	Follow The Drinkin' Gourd	
	John Kanaka	
	My Aunt Came Back	
	Purple Light	
	Riding On The Railway	
	Seagull, Seagull	
	Turn The Glasses Over	
Everyday Objects	Tideo	
	Turn The Glasses Over	
	Just From The Kitchen	
	The Farmer's Dairy Key	
	Lead Through That Sugar And Tea	
	Pizza, Pizza, Daddy-O	
Lullaby	Bye, Bye, Baby	
Greetings	Hello, My Friends	
Singing, Music	Come Let Us Gather	
African Language	Banuwa	
	Senua de Dende	
	Si Si Si	
Peace	Dona Nobis Pacem	
Names	Just From The Kitchen	
	Riding On The Railway	
Actions/Motions	Amasee	
	Here Comes Sally	
	Hold My Mule	
	Lead Through That Sugar And Tea	
	My Mama's Calling Me	
	Pizza, Pizza, Daddy-O	
	Shake Them 'Simmons Down	
	Shoo Roun'	
	Shoorah	
	That's A Mighty Pretty Motion	
	Tideo	

Table G.4. Songs Indexed by Cultural Origin

Origin	Title	Page
American	Bluebird	
	Bow Wow Wow	
	Bye, Bye Baby	
	Charlie Over The Ocean	
	Come Let Us Gather	
	The Farmer In The Dell	
	Great Big House In New Orleans	
	Grizzly Bear	
	Hello, My Friends	
	Here Comes Sally	
	John Kanaka	
American (cont.)	Just From The Kitchen	
	King Kong Kitchie	
	Lead Through That Sugar And Tea	
	Let Us Chase The Squirrel	
	Li'l Liza Jane	
	My Aunt Came Back	
	My Paddle (The Canoe Song)	
	Oats And Beans And Barley	
	The Old Gray Cat	
	Paige's Train	
	Paw Paw Patch	
	Purple Light	
	Rain, Rain	
	Riding On The Railway	
	Rocky Mountain	
	Sailor, Sailor	
	Shake Them 'Simmons Down	
	Skin & Bones	
	Snail, Snail	
	Sweet Betsy From Pike	
	Tideo	
Anglo-American/British	Turn The Glasses Over	
	Green Grows The Willow Tree	
	Seagull, Seagull	
African-American	Shoorah	
	Amasee	
	Cotton Eye Joe	
	The Farmer's Dairy Key	
	Follow The Drinking Gourd	
	Hold My Mule	
	Little Johnny Brown	
	My Mama's Calling Me	
	Pizza, Pizza Daddy-O	
	Rock My Soul	
	Shoo Roun'	
	That's A Mighty Pretty Motion	
African	Banuwa	
	Senua de Dende	
	Si Si Si	
European	Dona Nobis Pacem	
Carribean	Hill And Gully Rider	
Native-American	The Owl Sings	
	Song Of The Snowflakes	
Latin/South American	El Mar Estaba Serena	

Bibliography and Suggested Readings

Abraham, Cathy. "Smooth Transitions in Child Care," 2010. http://www.childcarelounge.com/articles/smooth-transitions.php.

Anderson, M. T. *Strange Mr. Satie*. New York: Viking, 2003.

Anderson Moore, Kristin, M. P. P. Zakia Redd, M. A. Mary Burkhauser, M. P. P. Kassim Mbwana, and M. A. Ashleigh Collins. "Children in Poverty: Trends, Consequences, and Policy Options." *Research Brief* (2009).

Bacon, Denise. *46 Two-Part American Folk Songs*. Olympia, WA: Kodály Center of America, 1973.

Barber, Nicky, Mark Barratt, Alan Blackwood, Elinor Kelly, and Chris de Souza. *The Kingfisher Young People's Book of Music*. New York: Kingfisher, 1996.

Batipps, Mylin. "The Science Behind Music." *The College of New Jersey Journal* (online) (2013). http://www.presstv.ir/detail/159672.html.

Berkowitz, Sol, Gabriel Fontrier, and Leo Kraft. *A New Approach to Sight Singing*. New York: W. W. Norton and Co., 1960.

Bolkovac, Edward, and Judith Johnston. *150 Rounds for Singing and Teaching*. Milwaukee, WI: Boosey and Hawkes, 1996.

Brumfield, Susan. *Making Music! Musicianship in the Children's Chorus*. Lubbock: Texas Tech University, 2008.

Brumfield, Susan, and D. Glaze. *Kodály Levels I and II: Course Materials*, 2006.

Bryant, Jen. *Music for the End of Time*. Grand Rapids, MI: Eerdmans Books for Young Readers, 2005.

Calenza, Anna Harwell. *Vivaldi's Four Seasons*. Watertown, MA: Charlesbridge, 2002.

Calenza, Anna Harwell. *Pictures at an Exhibition*. Watertown, MA: Charlesbridge, 2003.

Calenza, Anna Harwell. *The Farewell Symphony by Joseph Haydn*. Watertown, PA: Charlesbridge, 2004a.

Calenza, Anna Harwell. *The Heroic Symphony*. Watertown, MA: Charlesbridge, 2004b.

Calenza, Anna Harwell. *Gershwin's Rhapsody in Blue*. Watertown, MA: Charlesbridge, 2006.

Calenza, Anna Harwell. *Camille Saint-Saens's Danse Macabre*. Watertown, MA: Charlsebridge, 2013.

Campbell, Patricia Sheehan, and Carol Scott-Kassner. *Music in Childhood: From Preschool Through the Elementary Grades*. Belmont, CA: Wadsworth Group/Thompson Learning, 2002.

Cannel, Ward, and Fred Marx. *How to Play the Piano Despite Years of Lessons: What Music Is and How to Make It at Home*. Milwaukee, WI: Hal Leonard, 1981.

Choi, Ae-Na, Myeong Soo Lee, and Jung-Sook Lee. *Group Music Intervention Reduces Aggression and Improves Self-Esteem in Children with Highly Aggressive Behavior: A Pilot Controlled Trial*. National Center for Biotechnology Information, 2008. http://www.ncbi.nlm.nih.gov/pmc/articles/PMC2862931.

Choksy, Lois. *The Kodály Method: Comprehensive Music Education from Infant to Adult*. Upper Saddle River, NJ: Prentice-Hall, 1974.

Choksy, Lois, and David Brummitt. *120 Singing Games and Dances for Elementary Schools*. Englewood Cliffs, NJ: Prentice-Hall, 1987.

Citron, Stephen. *The Musical from the Inside Out*. Chicago, IL: Ivan R. Dee, 1991.

Colwell, Richard, and Peter Webster, eds. *MENC Handbook of Research on Music Learning: Volume 2: Applications*. New York: Oxford University Press, 2011.

Csikszentmihalyi, Mihaly. *Flow: The Psychology of Optimal Experience*. New York: HarperCollins Publishers, 1990.

Davies, Rie. "Making Music May Improve Young Children's Behavior." *Science Daily*, September 2013.

Duffy, Michael, and D'Neil Duffy. *Children of the Universe: Cosmic Education in the Elementary Classroom*. Hollidaysburg, PA: Parent Child Press, 2002.

Erdei, Peter, and Katalin Komlos. *150 American Folk Songs to Sing, Read and Play*. Milwaukee, WI: Boosey and Hawkes, 1974.Evarts, John. "The New Musical Notation: A Graphic Art?" *Leonard* 1, no. 4 (1968): 405–12.

Fey, Laurel. *Shostakovich: A Life*. New York: Oxford University Press, 2000.

Foran, Lucille M. "Listening to Music: Helping Children Regulate Their Emotions and Improve Learning in the Classroom." *Educational Horizons* 88, no. 1 (2009): 51–58.

Forrai, Katalin. *Music in Preschool*. Translated by Jean Sinor. Fitzgibbon, Australia: Clayfield School of Music, 1998.

Gerstein, Mordicai. *What Charlie Heard*. New York: Frances Foster Books, Farrar, Straus and Giroux, 2002.

Gillen, L., and J. Gillen. *Yoga Calm for Children: Educating Heart, Mind and Body*. Portland, OR: Three Pebble Press, 2007.

Goetschius, Percy. *Lessons in Music Form*. Boston, MA: Oliver Ditson Co., 1904.

Goodkin, Doug. *Now's the Time: Teaching Jazz to All Ages*. San Francisco, CA: Pentatonic Press, 2004.

Grout, Donald Jay, and Claude Palisca. *A History of Western Music*. New York: W. W. Norton and Co., Inc., 2001.

Hallman, Susan. "The Power of Music: Its Impact on the Intellectual, Social, and Personal Development of Young People," 2010. http://www.laphil.com/sites/default/files/media/pdfs/shared/education/yola/susan-hallam-music-development_research.pdf.

Hallman, Susan, John Price, and Georgia Katsarou. "The Effects of Background Music on Primary Children's Performance." *Educational Studies* 28, no. 2 (2010).

Harvey, Barb, and Sue Culen. *Young Voices, World Songs*. Minneapolis, MN: Seward Montessori School, 2008.

Hickey, M. *Music Outside the Lines: Ideas for Composing in K—12 Music Classrooms*. New York: Oxford University Press, 2012.

Holt, John. *How Children Fail*. New York: Dell Publishing Co., 1964.

Holt, John. *How Children Learn*. New York: Pitman Publishing Co., 1967.

Irwin, Phyllis, and Joy Nelson. *The Teacher, the Child, and Music*. Belmont, CA: Wadsworth Publishing Co., 1986.

Jones, Bessie, and Bess Lomax Hawes. *Step It Down: Games, Plays, Songs & Stories from the Afro-American Heritage*. Athens: University of Georgia Press, 1987.

Kendall, Catherine Wolff. *Stories of Women Composers for Young Musicians*. Evansville, IL: Toadwood Publishers, 1993.

Kingman, Daniel. *American Music: A Panorama*. Belmont, CA: Schirmer, a Division of Thomson Learning, Inc., 2003.

Kirschner, Sebastian, and Michael Tomasello. "Joint Music Making Promotes Prosocial Behavior in 4-Year-Old Children." *Evolution & Human Behavior* 31, no. 5 (2010): 354–64.

Kline, Tod F. *Classic Tunes & Tales: Ready-to-Use Music Listening Lessons & Activities for Grades K—8*. West Nyack, NY: Parker Publishing Co., 1997.

Kodály, Zoltan. *333 Reading Exercises*. Milwaukee, WI: Boosey and Hawkes, 1943.

Krull, Kathryn, and Kathleen Hewitt. *Lives of the Musicians: Good Times, Bad Times (and What the Neighbors Thought)*. New York: Houghton Mifflin Harcourt Publishing Co., 1993.

Larson, Kay. *Where the Heart Beats: John Cage, Zen Buddhism, and the Inner Life of Artists*. New York: Penguin Press, 2012.

Lawyer, Amie. *Maria Montessori and a Child's Total Development in Early Childhood*, Ph.D. diss., Chaminade University of Honolulu, Hawaii, 2004.

Lemouse, Mack. "Will Background Music Affect Your Concentration." 2015. http://www.healthguidance.org/entry/11767/1/Will-Background-Music-Improve-Your-Concentration.html.

Lesser, Wendy. *Music for Silenced Voices: Shostakovich and His Fifteen String Quartets*. New Haven, CT: Yale University Press, 2011.

Levine, Robert. *The Story of the Orchestra*. New York: Black Dog and Leventhal Publishers, Inc., 2001.

Lewis Brown, Laura. "What Music Should My Child Listen to?" *PBS Parents*, 2015. http://www.pbs.org/parents/education/music-arts/what-music-should-my-child-listen-to.

Locke, Eleanor G. *Sail Away: 155 American Folk Songs to Sing, Read and Play*. Milwaukee, WI: Boosey and Hawkes, 1981.

Marchak, Nicole. "The Grace of Music." *Grace and Courtesy: A Human Responsibility*. AMI/USA Conference (Oak Brook, IL, July 23–28, 1998), 1999.

Markham, Laura. "Why Kids Need Routines and Structure," 2013. http://www.ahaparenting.com/parenting-tools/family-life/structure-routines.

Martineau, Jason. *The Elements of Music*. New York: Walker Publishing Co., 2008.

McDonell, Janet. "Grace and Courtesy for the Primary Child: Theoretical Foundations." *Grace and Courtesy: A Human Responsibility*. AMI/USA Conference (Oak Brook, IL, July 23–28, 1998), 1999.

McKeever, J. *Introduction to Music Lecture*. Montessori Institute of Milwaukee, 2009a.

McKeever, J. *Lecture on Degrees of the Scale*. Milwaukee, WI: Montessori Institute of Milwaukee Training Lecture, 2009b.

Mishel, Lawrence, Josh Bivens, Elise Gould, and Heidi Shierholz. *The State of Working America*, 12th ed. Ithaca, NY: Cornell University Press, 2012.

Montessori, Maria. *The Advanced Montessori Method: Volume 1*. Oxford, England: Clio Press, 1991a.

Montessori, Maria. *The Advanced Montessori Method: Volume 2*. Oxford, England: Clio Press, 1991b.

Montessori, Maria. *To Educate the Human Potential*. Thiruvanmiyur, Chennai: Kalakshetra, 1991c.

Montessori, Maria. *Creative Development in the Child: Volume 1*. Thiruvanmiyur, Chennai, India: Kalakshetra Press, 1998.

Montessori, Maria. *The Montessori Method*. Mineola, NY: Dover, 2002.

Montessori, Mario M. "Man's Spiritual Expressions: Music and Language," 1956. http://montessorinuggets.blogspot.com/p/mans-spiritual-expressions-language-and.html.

Montessori, Mario M. *Cosmic Education*. Association Montessori Internationale, 1976.

Montessori, Renilde. "Grace—the Felicity of Being." *Grace and Courtesy: A Human Responsibility*. AMI/USA Conference (Oak Brook, IL, July 23–28, 1998), 1999.

Music Educators National Conference. *The School Music Program: A New Vision. The K—12 National Standards, PreK Standards, and What They Mean to Music Educators*. Reston, VA: Author, 1994.

Music Educators National Conference. *Performance Standards for Music Grades PreK—12*. Philadelphia, PA: R&L Education, 1996.

Music Educators National Conference. *Benchmark Student Performances in Music: Composing and Arranging.* Philadelphia, PA: R&L Education, 2002.

Nichol, Barbara. *Beethoven Lives Upstairs.* Chicago, IL: Harcourt, 1993.

Niles, John Jacob. *The Ballad Book of John Jacob Niles.* Lexington: University Press of Kentucky, 2000.

Over, Richard. *The Dictators: Hitler's Germany, Stalin's Russia.* New York: W. W. Norton and Co., 2004.

Parlakian, Rebecca, and Claire Lerner. "Beyond Twinkle, Twinkle: Using Music with Infants and Toddlers." *YC Young Children* 65, no. 2 (2010): 14–19. http:www.jstor.org/stable/42730563.

Pickens Tartt, Ruth. *Ring Games: Line Games and Play Party Songs of Alabama.* CD Liner Notes, 1959.

Pottish-Lewis, Phyllis. *The Elementary Child as a Member of Society: How Through Understanding and Implementation of Montessori Principles an Adult Can Manage an Elementary Classroom to Fully Aid the Child's Development.* Rochester, NY: AMI/USA, 2011a.

Pottish-Lewis, Phyllis. *Elementary Classroom Management: How to Implement Cosmic Education.* Rochester, NY: AMI/USA, 2011b.

Pottish-Lewis, Phyllis. "Music: Beethoven." *Association Montessori Internationale—Elementary Alumni Association Journal* (2012).

Pottish-Lewis, Phyllis. *The Artistry of a Montessori Teacher.* Rochester, NY: AMI/USA, 2014.

Prellwitz, Sarah. "10 Facts about Poverty in China." *Blog: The Borgen Project* (2015).

Rachlin, Anne. *Famous Children: Beethoven.* Hauppage, NY: Barron's Educational Services, Inc., 1965.

Read, Gardner. *Music Notation: A Manual of Modern Practice.* New York: Taplinger Publishing Co., Inc., 1979.

Rosenstiel, Léonie. *The Life and Works of Lili Boulanger.* Rutherford, NJ: Fairleigh Dickinson University Press, 1978.

Smith, Charles Edward. *Folk Music U.S.A.* CD Liner Notes, 1959.

Stamp, Jimmy. "5 1/2 Examples of Experimental Music Notation," 2013. http://www.smithsonianmag.com/arts-culture/5-12-examples-of-experimental-music-notation-92223646/.

Stephenson, Margaret E. *Lecture on the Construction of Man.* Montessori Institute of Milwaukee, 1991.

Stephenson, Margaret E. *The Core of the Elementary Classroom: "Help Me to Help Myself".* Rochester, NY: AMI/USA, 2002.

Storms, Jerry. *101 Music Games for Children: Fun and Learning with Rhythm and Song.* Alameda, CA: Hunter House Inc., 1981.

Tapper, Thomas. *The Child's Own Book of Great Musicians: Bach.* London, England: Theo. Presser Co., 1915a.

Tapper, Thomas. *The Child's Own Book of Great Musicians: Mozart.* London, England: Theo. Presser Co., 1915b.

Tapper, Thomas. *The Child's Own Book of Great Musicians: Schubert.* London, England: Theo. Presser Co., 1916.

Tapper, Thomas. *The Child's Own Book of Great Musicians: Beethoven.* London, England: Theo. Presser Co., 1917a.

Tapper, Thomas. *The Child's Own Book of Great Musicians: Haydn.* London, England: Theo. Presser Co., 1917b.

Tapper, Thomas. *The Child's Own Book of Great Musicians: Wagner.* London, England: Theo. Presser Co., 1918.

Tapper, Thomas. *The Child's Own Book of Great Musicians: Chopin.* London, England: Theo. Presser Co., 1919a.

Tapper, Thomas. *The Child's Own Book of Great Musicians: Grieg,* London, England: Theo. Presser Co., 1919b.

Tapper, Thomas. *The Child's Own Book of Great Musicians: Handel.* London, England: Theo. Presser Co., 1919c.

Tapper, Thomas. *The Child's Own Book of Great Musicians: Verdi.* London, England: Theo. Presser Co., 1919d.

Index

About the Author

Michael Johnson is a singer/songwriter/composer and an AMI-certified Montessori educator with ten years of experience teaching music to children and managing Montessori elementary classrooms. Originally from the San Francisco Bay Area, he holds an MA in Music Education from Portland State University in addition to a Montessori Elementary diploma, which he received from the Montessori Institute of Milwaukee. Michael is also certified in the Kodály method of teaching children music.

An avid performer, Michael has recorded seven albums and appeared on stages throughout the United States and the United Kingdom performing original pop music. In 2013, he performed with a small choir of children for 3,500 Montessori practitioners at the Montessori International Congress in Portland, Oregon. Michael leads music workshops for teachers around the world.

Michael has written a full-length musical, *Success!*, which made the third round of selections at the 2013 and 2015 National Music Theater Conference at the Eugene O'Neill Theater Center. Also a lifelong cartoonist, Michael has created a comic version of *Success!* that can be found at www.successcomic.com.

Making Music in Montessori is his first book.

To investigate more into Making Music in Montessori, see:

www.makingmusicinmontessori.com

To read about Michael's musical projects, please visit:

www.reclinerlandhq.com

www.parksandrecreationhq.com

AUTHOR CONTACT INFORMATION

Michael Johnson

mjmusiced@gmail.com